HOW TO
PROFIT
THROUGH
CATALOG
MARKETING
THIRD EDITION

KATIE MULDOON

NTC Business Books
NTC/Contemporary Publishing Group

Library of Congress Cataloging-in-Publication Data

Muldoon, Katie.
    How to profit through catalog marketing / Katie Muldoon.
       p.   cm.
    Includes bibliographical references and index.
    ISBN 0-8442-3572-5
      1. Mail-order business.   2. Direct marketing.
  3. Commercial catalogs.   I. Title.
  HF5466.M843   1995
  658.8′72—dc20   94-39785
                                    CIP

Published by NTC Business Books
A division of NTC/Contemporary Publishing Group, Inc.
4255 West Touhy Avenue, Lincolnwood (Chicago), Illinois 60646-1975 U.S.A.
International Standard Book Number: 0-8442-3572-5

19   18   17   16   15   14   13   12   11   10   9   8   7   6   5   4   3   2

**In Memory
of
Jesse Lieman**

*who captured pink clouds
and shared them*

CONTENTS

❖ ❖ ❖

In the 12 years since my first book on catalog marketing debuted, cataloging has taken on whole new dimensions. While the field is still populated by the type of entrepreneurs who helped make catalogs a viable, desired business, new entrants are rapidly creating new types of catalogs that widen the appeal of shopping by mail, and even electronic means, even further.

Old-timers, too, have added to the diversity of catalogs, producing "spin-offs" that use the power of segmented databases to give birth to catalogs that meet particular buying patterns of specific segments of the population.

Therefore, this book addresses both the needs of new enterprises as well those already in existence that, even though experienced, still wisely strive to refine and sharpen their businesses in order to realize continued growth and profitability.

To the best of my knowledge, there is no book that completely covers every aspect of catalog marketing, or direct marketing for that matter, as this one does. Having worked on the user side and the service side (working with well over 200 different companies over time), I understand firsthand how critical it is to know how each and every aspect of a direct mail business must work together. This book attempts to give you the information you need to understand the job you must do as it relates to every stage of successful cataloging.

Just as important, for those considering going into cataloging, it gives a detailed overview that can guide your decision as to whether or not catalog marketing is right for you.

There is no doubt that cataloging is exciting and very popular with Americans (as well as other countries) today. It's a national business that brings real joy to the lives of many people. But putting the fun of owning, operating, or working for a catalog aside, it is also a real business that this book treats realistically. Success does not happen overnight. It takes discipline and plenty of hard work. This is a fast-paced, constantly changing business and one you need to stay on top of to ensure initial and continued success. There will be times when the advice of catalog professionals, knowledgeable in their particular area, is of utmost importance. Having read this book, you will be in a position to understand the business, thus making better use of any professional help you deem appropriate.

Use the table of contents to guide you through the book. Most people find that reading the sections that interest them the most, as well as those with which they need help at the time, is the best way to approach this volume of information.

Please understand that this book has been constructed with a "middle ground" approach. Nothing in any business is absolute; view the information here as a guideline and never let it replace testing. Again and again, you will hear two frustrating phrases in our industry: "It depends" and "Test, test, and test again." Although they may sound like evasions, they are used by those with the most experience. Testing is one of the major advantages of direct marketing. It allows you to customize ideas for your particular audience. Experience has shown me time and again that what worked wonderfully for one cataloger was a lousy idea for another. You must find out what is best for your business by seeing its effect, carefully and in a controlled test atmosphere, on your market and positioning. You'll see numerous testing techniques throughout the text.

This book has been based on my real-life experiences—going on three decades' worth. But it could not have been written without the support and assistance of a great many friends and business associates. Most especially I would like to thank Bob Bunshaft of Pacific Arts Publishing for his expertise on credit card processing; Belinda Butti of DOTS for reviewing the production section; Ken Ellingsen of LWI Holdings, Inc. for his knowledge on overseas sourcing; Leila Griffith, freelance merchandiser, for reviewing the merchandise section; Andrea Hill for her knowledge of DRTU; Sandy Grossman of AB&C for reviewing the back-end chapter; Rick Kropski of Alden Press for his in-depth knowledge of mailing/tracking procedures; Iris Shokoff of Iris Shokoff Associates for reviewing the media section; and John Van Horn of Alden Press for reviewing the production section. A special thanks to Melinda Little of The Company of Women for lots of overall information and tons of support.

I would like to express my appreciation to those who have generously allowed specific sections of their catalogs, forms, and other related materials to be reproduced. These graphic depictions enrich the book and provide truly helpful information.

Those with whom I work most certainly deserve special acknowledgement, as helping with the production of the book was labor added to their regular workload. Thanks go to Robin Glat, who diligently checked every source for permission to reprint. Special appreciation is also due to Brigid Witkowski, who double-checked my typing, corrected most of the manuscripts, coordinated the examples with their titles, and handled a million other important details.

Thanks too to my editor, Anne Knudsen, who asked exactly the right questions, ensuring that readers will actually understand what it is I'm trying to say.

But it is to my husband, Jacob R. Baer, that I owe the greatest debt. He provided a great deal of information and math on the chapters devoted to back-end, analysis, and business plans. Plus, he was there for me every second, putting up with late nights, early mornings, and weekends devoted to writing this book.

CHAPTER ONE

❖ ❖ ❖

What Is Catalog Marketing?

Catalog marketing sounds simple enough. Many believe it's merely the selling of merchandise or services through a multi-page, printed medium called a catalog. But it's much more complicated and interesting than that. No longer is just putting pictures on paper. Today's catalogs tend to be positioned to niches—small segments of particular interests. So, first you must clearly understand whether or not your niche is both distinctive enough and, conversely, large enough to gain and hold a potential customer's attention. Next, you have to source unusual merchandise that offers both a sufficient margin for you and real value for today's cost-conscious consumer. Then you'll need to create highly motivational copy and designs that make your approach unique and incorporate enough proven techniques to ensure success.

To do all this, you'll need the kind of planning required for any growing business. That takes time, forethought, and the right team. Time is required to lay the financial, positioning, and people foundations.

Because catalog marketing is also direct marketing, it gives you the added benefit of being able to immediately determine, through analysis, exactly what you did right and what you did wrong—and take corrective action. To use this wonderful ability, you'll need to have systems in place to monitor every action you take, from what merchandise you run, to what lists you rent, to sales facilitators (generally incentives) you use. Every tactic will have an effect and you will, through careful tracking and analysis, know the real value of each.

As you can see, catalog marketing encompasses a whole range of activities and disciplines which, as a whole, create what has become a dynamic and greatly accepted method of shopping. Few people can resist flipping through the colorful pages of a well-done catalog and then using one of many quick and easy options to order from it. Figure 1-1 shows some of the steps of putting together a catalog.

The Catalog Shopping Boom

Mail order continues to grow as more and more households discover the ease and convenience of shopping at home. *Entrepreneur*'s December 1993 issue names mail order as

❖ FIGURE 1-1
Catalog Program Flow Chart

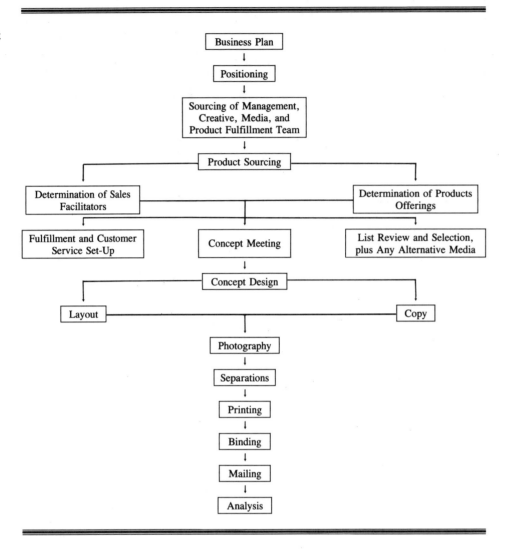

one of the "15 hottest businesses for 1994." Some of their reasons include the following statistics:

> According to the Direct Marketing Association, more than half the U.S. adult population ordered merchandise by mail or phone in 1993. And, according to the WEFA Group, an economic research and forecasting firm, catalog sales grew from $53.4 billion in 1993 to an estimated $57.4 billion in 1994. But the swell doesn't stop there: The WEFA Group estimates catalog sales will enjoy continued annual growth of nearly 6.6 percent, reaching $66.6 billion by 1996.[1]

This study also showed that employment in the catalog industry surpassed 330,000 persons in 1992, a growth of 10 percent overall since 1988. This number should increase to 365,000 (a growth of 10.6 percent) by 1996. Total employment in the U.S. economy generated by the catalog industry grew from 508,000 in 1988 to 566,000 in 1992, a growth of 11.4 percent over four years and is expected to continue its growth pattern, reaching 620,000 by 1996. Gross domestic product (GDP) linked to the catalog industry grew from $28.6 billion to $41.7 billion during the same period (1987–1992). In 1992, the catalog industry produced 0.7 percent of the nation's total GDP.

These are just a few of the reasons that new consumer and business-to-business catalogs are born practically every day. Catalog companies that were unknown a few years ago are now household names and have impressive profit centers. Well-known companies that were never involved in cataloging before have discovered this lucrative way of serving their customers, opening every avenue of potential purchase.

More entrants into the field naturally mean more competition. Again, according to facts compiled by the Direct Marketing Association (DMA), catalogs now account for 22 percent of the postal mail stream. But there are many contributing factors behind the growth trend which predict that catalog shopping will continue to expand.

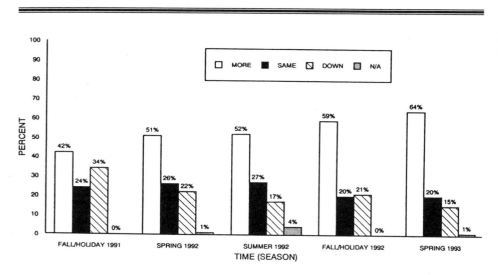

❖ FIGURE 1-2
Number of Catalogs Mailed during a One-Year Period

SOURCE: Direct Marketing Association. *DMA 1993/94 Statistical Fact Book.* DMA, 1994, 173.

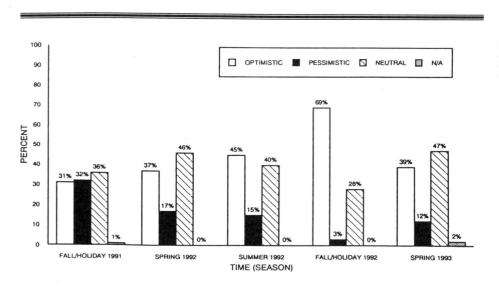

❖ FIGURE 1-3
Survey of Catalogers Outlooks over a One-Year Period

SOURCE: Direct Marketing Association. *DMA 1993/94 Statistical Fact Book.* DMA, 1994, 173.

❖ FIGURE 1-4
Percentage of Catalog Shipments Returned by Customers

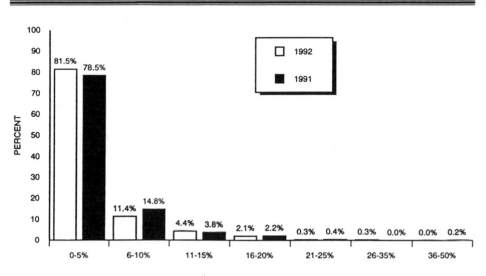

SOURCE: Direct Marketing Association. *DMA 1993/94 Statistical Fact Book.* DMA, 1994, 101.

Rising Customer Satisfaction

More than 88 percent of Americans opened, read, looked at, or set aside for later reading catalogs received in the mail.[2] Furthermore, catalogs are rated the most useful and interesting form of advertising mail. Over 53 percent of consumers find them useful, and another 30 percent find them interesting. And customer satisfaction, always high, has risen. In 1987, 90.4 percent of users were very satisfied with service from a mail order company; in 1989, that number grew to 93.4 percent.[3]

The reason for the numbers is the true dedication of catalogers. This dedication is based on good business sense, because acquiring a customer is a costly enterprise. Most catalogs do not make money with the first purchase, but rely on subsequent purchases from the same person, amortizing the expense of acquiring that customer over a lifetime of buying. As in any business, loyalty means increased sales as happy customers tend to buy more and more.

Virtually Unlimited Product Acceptance

Consumers truly like the benefits of buying by mail and have proven receptive to purchasing everything from automobiles to circus tents to homemade jellies and from high-ticket designer clothes to low-ticket knickknacks this way. Neiman-Marcus has added to its fame and garnered tremendously valuable press coverage from its tradition, started in 1960, of offering outrageous his-and-hers gifts in its Christmas catalog. These gifts have run the gamut from an $80,000 bubble boat built like a flying saucer to a customized painted portrait of a customer's cat for $9,000. The tenth annual his-and-hers gift was a new breed of cat, the California Spangled Cat, which sold for $1,400 until stock was depleted.

Catalogers, such as JS&A (now more famous for its infomercials than its catalog), showed how merchandise inventiveness was, and continues to be, the cornerstone of cataloging. Through its hallmark, trend-setting copy approach, JS&A developed and sold thousands of "Bone Fones," forerunners to today's Walkman. Omaha Steaks continues to sell prime filet mignon at an astonishing $33.30 a pound, and there is no doubt that its customers believe this quality product well worth it. And Lillian Vernon is famous for her personalized products, which offer everything from 80 personalized pencils for only $12.98 to your own set of customized marbles at just $9.98.

In the business world, catalogers offering business products selling for thousands of dollars no longer need to rely totally on their sales force, as the acceptance of catalog shopping has proven that price points have virtually no ceiling. For one, IBM has sold a Communications Controller for mainframes for $1.2 million from just one of its four different business catalogs! It is not unusual for IBM to sell products costing between $10,000 and $500,000 from its AS 400 and RISC catalogs.

Busier Working Women

Five out of six households today are managed by women, and 60 percent of women over the age of 16 earn paychecks.[4] In a poll of women conducted by Roper for Virginia Slims, 45 percent of respondents believed they had enough leisure time in 1975, but only 35 percent believed the same of their lives today. Studies also showed that women no longer shop for fun because they simply no longer have that kind of leisure time during regular shopping hours.[5]

This lack of time is reflected in both households where women live with a partner and those where women are the main wage earners. Income trends indicate that, during the 1980s, incomes for two-worker families nearly doubled, yet incomes for female-headed households income rose only a bit more than 50 percent.[6] Even though women generally make less than their husbands, they are unlikely to return to full-time homemaking because their added income allows the family to achieve middle-class status and the benefits associated with that status.

In households with partners, many women find themselves holding down two jobs—performing work outside the home and, often, still doing the same amount of housework traditionally expected of them.

It's no wonder that when women shop by mail, many of the items they select are convenience-oriented! As these women, who are the traditional shoppers, find their time split between caring for a family and working at a job that is either outside the home or operated from it, they have come to understand that their time is valuable, whether they choose to spend it working, enjoying their families, or treating themselves to leisure activities—an area of increasing importance to Americans in general. Hence, women have come to rely on and trust the increasingly popular, always-ready-when-you-are catalog. Not only are they able to shop from the comfort of their homes at any time of the day or night, but the fact that the merchandise has been preselected into basic "boutique-by-mail" categories makes selection easier.

In a properly merchandised catalog, products have been carefully chosen from thousands of possibilities, saving the customer the hassle of physically searching through store after store and department after department. For the woman whose day often consists of endless decision making, whether in an executive position or answering her child's constant questions (or both), preselected merchandise is a welcome change.

Catalogs also allow the customer to see merchandise as it will appear in her home, as it looks on women who fit her self-image, or as her husband or child might use it. Catalog copy often suggests ways in which she can use a product to better her life, ways she may never have had the time to discover on her own.

Because either she or one of her friends has ordered from a catalog before, she knows that merchandise is guaranteed and that, more often than not, customer service is surprisingly caring and prompt. Because she is an experienced shopper, she knows that catalogs often have bargains and prices that are competitive with retail. Most important, she knows that catalogers strive to maintain a level of quality that will encourage customers to keep purchasing from their catalogs because repeat purchase is the lifeline of catalog marketing.

It isn't only women who feel there is never enough time, because it doesn't just *seem* like there is less time to do the things you want, there *is* less time. Isaac Lagnado, principal of Tactical Retail Solutions, Inc., has research that shows that the average consumer has only five hours of shopping time available per week to purchase food, housewares, and apparel. Mr. Lagnado observes, "Time in the '90s is like money was in the '80s."[7]

Thus, consumers make good use of their valuable time and turn to the stores that are open whenever they need them, 24 hours a day, seven days a week—catalogs!

Double-Income Households

Earning power is on the rise. Contrary to what some have predicted, a Conference Board study reported ''households earning $100,000 or more a year will double by the year 2000, to 4.3 million. There also will be an 'explosive' rise in households earning $50,000 or more a year.''[8] This is largely due to the increase of women in the work force; the same study predicts that 78 percent of women will work outside the home by the turn of the century, as compared to 70 percent in 1990. There is additional security in double-income households; even if unemployment hits, one partner is still likely to be working.

Still, even high earners may not choose to purchase such major items as a home. Rather, as in past times of economic concern, consumers have turned to smaller luxuries, those generally provided by catalogs, and there is no reason to believe this practice will not continue.

Thus, the outlook for catalog sales will continue to grow because, due to time stress, this high-income group will need convenience and demand high quality.

Acceptance by Graying America

The desire to shop by mail is keeping up with another trend: the aging of our society. By the year 2000, 23 percent of households will be headed by 45 to 54-year-olds earning $75,000 or more. While this group will be in their peak earning years, they will also be saving for retirement and big health care costs. Many will be living alone, but married couples will still account for half of the households, equal to two-thirds of total consumer spending. Women will also be retiring, and interestingly enough, due to pensions not realized by previous generations, will have more money than in the past.

The DMA reports that, according to Simmons Market Research Bureau, 44 percent of Americans over the age of 65 (nearly 1.3 million people) shopped by mail or phone in 1991. *Modern Maturity* believes that the top reason older Americans shop from home is that they don't have to deal with crowds. Plus, they can find those unique hard-to-find products easily and simply without leaving the comfort and security of their homes.

Security and the safety of one's home could become even more important to all Americans, especially to those who feel that because they are older they may be more susceptible to crime. In Faith Popcorn's highly praised and well-read book, *The Popcorn Report*, she states that fear of crime (the ''Armored Cocoon'') will continue to motivate consumers to rely on mail order shopping. She says, ''Mail order sales topped $200 billion in 1990, up from $82.2 billion just ten years before. Phone chat lines, rent-a-cat services, the 'Video Fireplace,' new wider-cut sit-down jeans, were all telling indicators of trend entrenchment . . . all of which pointed to a rather cozy, comfy kind of hiding, an almost '50s sense of domesticity.''

The Computer Influence

The business computer is one of the main reasons direct marketing has become so successful and should be acknowledged for its effectiveness. Because of the computer, catalogers are able to decipher their customers' desires quickly and accurately. Promptly identifying and meeting customers needs can result in superior merchandising and increased customer loyalty through better customer service. Computerization also promotes more cost-effective mailings through timely analysis, improved cash flow due to fast and accurate determination of real inventory needs, and much more.

From the customer's perspective, this means that when they call to place an order, the order taker usually knows if the item is in stock, how long it will take to arrive at its destination, and, if not in stock, when it will be available. Further, it means that customers can be taken off or added to lists with a simple phone call. The number and types of catalogs a person receives are largely dependent on his or her buying behavior.

Computers are now an inexpensive essential, and software programs designed specifically for the operation of catalogs are available for large and small companies alike.

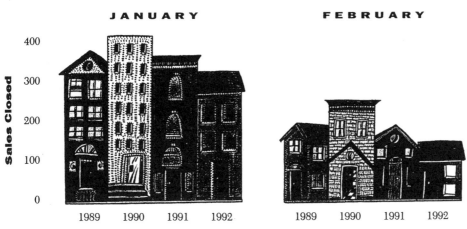

Source: Reprinted from the September 1993 issue produced by *Real Estate Today®* by permission of the National Association of Realtors®. Copyright 1993. All rights reserved.

❖ FIGURE 1-5

Comparison of January/February Home Sales, 1989–1992

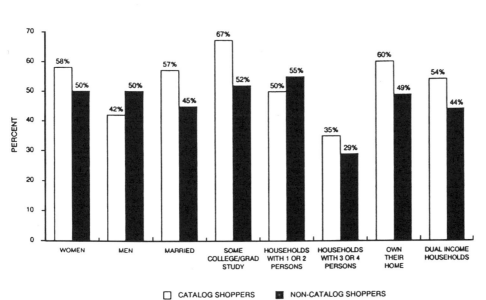

Source: Direct Marketing Association. *DMA 1993/94 Statistical Fact Book.* DMA, 1994.

❖ FIGURE 1-6

Demographics of Catalog Shoppers Versus Noncatalog Shoppers

Therefore, the only real concern is accurately projecting growth so the computer system you buy will adapt efficiently to your future needs.

In addition, thanks to desktop publishing, catalogs can be prepared faster and cheaper than ever before. The film from which printing plates are made has seen such advances in computer techniques that its cost has dropped, whereas its ability to refine and manipulate images has risen (see Chapter 7).

Credit Cards and Toll-free Numbers

Ordering by phone is more fun and easier than ever, as knowledgeable, friendly catalog representatives are instantly ready to respond to their customers' needs. Simply select the merchandise, get your credit card number ready, and pick up the phone. Not interested in talking with somebody? Just fill out the form (that way you'll have a record) and pop the order in the fax. Faxing your order, a combination of ordering by mail and phone, has found increasing acceptance . . . and almost always provides catalogers with a higher-than-average dollar order.

Toll-free 800 numbers have been around since 1968, and some catalogs report that by providing this response option, they have increased their sales by as much as 60 percent. Others question whether or not this cost truly generates added revenue. But most have chosen to offer the service if only to remain competitive. Even L. L. Bean, who reportedly tested the idea for years, finally came around to offering their customers this service in 1986. Very few catalogers do not provide toll-free numbers for ordering and service.

In past years, the toll-free option has been expanded to include free calls to customer service. While a natural benefit to the customer, catalogers' concerns are the cost of calls and the extra time their representatives must spend on them. Still, it is a trend, and careful training of customer service reps can provide both service for the customer and the right economics for the cataloger.

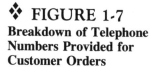
❖ **FIGURE 1-7**
Breakdown of Telephone Numbers Provided for Customer Orders

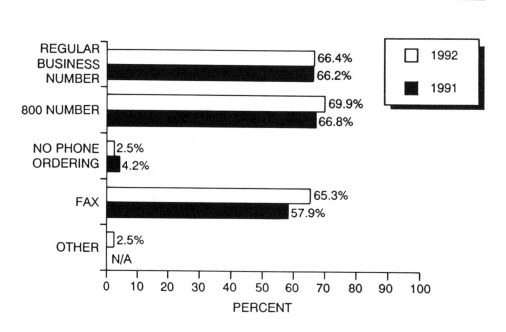

SOURCE: Direct Marketing Association. *DMA 1993/94 Statistical Fact Book*. DMA, 1994, 119.

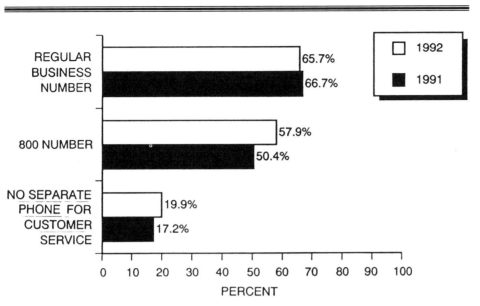

❖ FIGURE 1-8
Breakdown of Telephone Numbers Provided for Customer Service

SOURCE: Direct Marketing Association. *DMA 1993/94 Statistical Fact Book*. DMA, 1994, 119.

Though credit card usage has seen some roller coaster numbers in recent years, their use continues to grow, though using checks for catalog payments has escalated even more. House credit, or proprietary credit cards linked to the cataloger providing them, is one method many feel helps ensure customer loyalty.

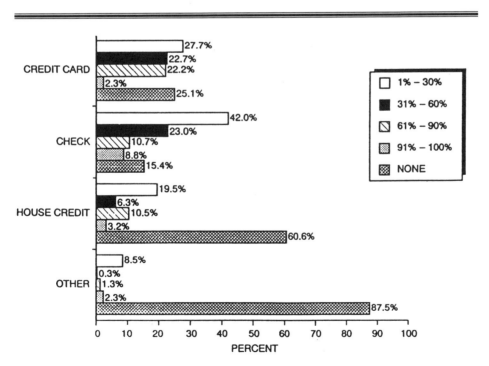

❖ FIGURE 1-9
Methods of Payment Most Commonly Used for Catalog Orders

SOURCE: Direct Marketing Association. *DMA 1993/94 Statistical Fact Book*. DMA, 1994, 91.

Instant Delivery

Two of the major drawbacks to ordering by catalog used to be the customer's need to have the product immediately and to touch or feel the product before purchasing. Through super-quick, often overnight, delivery, these two obstacles have been largely removed. Next-day or two-day delivery gets products where they're going in record time, and this in turn allows the customer to touch/feel the product. A simple call to the cataloger or United Parcel Service (UPS) means that, if the customer is dissatisfied, the article can be on its way back within three days. Sometimes consumers pay this cost, but if the error is the cataloger's, the company will absorb the expense. In some cases, the customer never pays to return an item!

Increasingly, the cost for this quick service is minimal—only about $5.00 over the cost of regular delivery. Some catalogers are even offering this premium delivery at no extra cost, so it is likely that others will follow.

Standards of Guaranteed Service

Once considered a marketing advantage, especially over the perception of lackluster retail service, satisfying the customer before *and* after the sale has become a primary goal of every catalog. Guarantees, such as Lands' End's "Guaranteed. Period." slogan, make the point loud and clear. If there is a problem, the cataloger will solve it quickly, professionally, and to the customer's benefit. Studies abound as to both the long-term and immediate benefits of a satisfied customer—the most important being loyalty and repeat purchasing.

How Catalogs Have Evolved

It all started in 1872, when Aaron Montgomery Ward issued his first catalog. Only one page, it answered what Ward perceived as a real need—more products at better prices than consumers could find in their own neighborhoods.

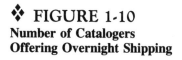

❖ FIGURE 1-10
**Number of Catalogers
Offering Overnight Shipping**

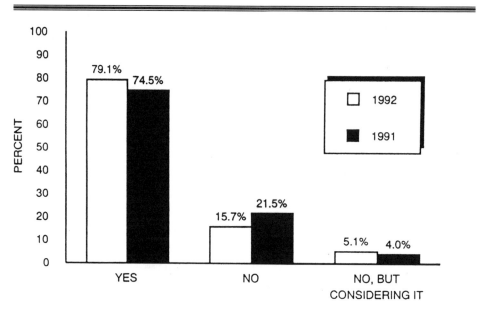

Source: Direct Marketing Association. *DMA 1993/94 Statistical Fact Book*. DMA, 1994.

In 1886, Richard Sears founded what most consider the granddaddy of catalogs: Sears, Roebuck and Company. By 1897, the company had a 700-page catalog of 6,000 products. By 1906, this fledgling company had developed sales in excess of $50 million. In 1991, Sears was the nation's third largest cataloger—up from sixth in 1990, after United Services Automobile Association and Time Warner.[9] Following the demise of its "Big Book," Sears' sales dropped to $1 billion in 1993.[10]

Sears and Ward were *the* "big-book" catalogs, which, in their heyday, offered everything from tires to lingerie. Both companies have ceased to mail under their own names, but are actively involved in joint ventures with such niche catalogers as Hanover Direct. The big-book catalog has become a thing of the past. Today's consumers tell us that due to demands on their time and attention spans, they prefer to shop via boutique-style catalogs. These catalogs, through merchandising and graphics, attempt to portray a lifestyle with which readers can identify.

Another old-timer in the industry and one of the first to understand the customer's need for market-driven products began with $400 in 1912. L. L. Bean started his company to sell the rubber boot he had invented, adding outdoor clothing and equipment to the line over the years. L. L. Bean had mail order sales of $848 million in 1994.

Spiegel, Inc., also an early starter, has made impressive maneuvers with its huge customer database of names by segmenting those names and creating specialized niche catalogs to serve them and bring new customers into the fold. It seems to be working. Spiegel had record-breaking revenues of $3.016 billion in 1994, a 28 percent increase over 1993.[11]

Catalogers increasingly have been pulling many titles, some complementary, some diverse, under one roof. This strategy is most often credited to Hanover Direct, which now includes such titles as Colonial Garden Kitchens, Domestications, Essence by Mail, Mature Wisdom, Gumps, and Undergear. The number of catalogs changes rapidly, but has been as high as 23 and, as of the end of 1994, had mail order sales of $768.8 million with a goal of $1 billion by 1996.

Catalogs are not limited to large corporations; many entrepreneurs still find lucrative niches for establishing new businesses. In 1984, Gun Denhardt and her husband Thomas began Hanna Andersson, a catalog specializing in Swedish-made clothing for children. Their first mailing, in 1983, was only 73,000; in 1992, this catalog mailed 12 million copies for gross sales of $40 million. In 1994, sales were $47.5 million.[12]

Nor is this growth limited to consumer catalogs. Businesses, too, are well served by the catalog industry. One prime business catalog example is Quill Corporation, started by Jack Miller in the back of his father's chicken store in 1956. Using only a simple postcard to advertise products at savings, Quill served 850,000 customers in 1992, offering them a host of office supply products through its mailing of 45 million catalogs and through sale flyers. A 37-year-old company, Quill had sales of slightly under $400 million in 1993.

Using untested methods, early catalogers directed sales efforts into relatively uncharted territory. Catalogs were few and far between, so there was little competition. The cost of printing, postage, and paper (the three most expensive items for a cataloger) was very low compared with today's prices. Being a pioneer is never easy, but most would agree that it took an entirely different set of skills than are needed by today's catalog marketer.

Newcomers appeared on the scene, saw what successful innovators like Roger Horchow (who is credited with starting the first "upscale, life-style" catalog) were doing, adapted their techniques to a slightly different market, and, without changing the basic strategy, succeeded as well. Soon there were catalogs to supply everyone's needs, from electronics to lingerie and computer software to tools. There was also competition and lots of it. The amazing part is that most catalogers were mailing to the same mail order–responsive customers.

But the competition has increased even more, with consumer attitudes changing dramatically in smaller and smaller time frames. So, more than ever, we are seeing the emergence of new types of catalogs teamed with new, more refined techniques. But almost all are based on those old, tried-and-true premises.

Different Kinds of Catalogs

Basically, catalogs are divided into two markets: consumer and business-to-business.

Consumer Catalogs

Consumer catalogs not only come in a wide variety of shapes and sizes, they increasingly come ready to serve a wide range of different purposes. The primary types of consumer catalog are unaffiliated, retail, manufacturer-supported, incentive, nonprofit, co-op, syndicated, international, and catalog showrooms.

Unaffiliated Catalogs.   The privately held entrepreneurial catalog was how catalogs as we know them started. Today, many of these privately held companies have gone public, but their premise remains pretty much the same. Their catalogs are stand-alone ventures whose main purpose is to sell goods by mail. If they have a store or stores, it is used as a complement to the catalog and/or as an outlet for unsold goods.

Some of the most famous names in our business make this an illustrious group, including Lillian Vernon and Lands' End, and there are hundreds of lesser-knowns. The actual number of stand-alone catalogs is difficult to determine because they are predominately privately held.

Retail Catalogs.   In the consumer arena, there are three different ways of looking at retail catalogs: traffic generation, independent profit centers, and a combination of both. Traffic generators are just what their name suggests—they are intended to generate traffic into the store, and associated costs are not directly charged against the sales generated by such a program. An independent direct mail profit center, on the other hand, must account for its marketing expenditures with sales that can be tracked directly to that program. Resulting in-store sales are most often not attributed to the direct mail program, since its main intent is to create sales outside the store.

Today, though, most catalogs in this group are hybrids that effectively combine direct mail solicitation and traffic generation to achieve the best of both worlds: a synergy which, through exciting photography and copy, drives the consumer into stores where he or she gains confidence in the products he or she may also wish to purchase through the catalog.

Interestingly enough, this synergy works differently for different stores. The Bombay Company, for instance, has found that its retail customers are more profitable than its catalog shoppers, so it uses its mailing pieces primarily for traffic generation. Conversely, The Body Shop has found its mail order customers financially more valuable than those who visit its stores.[13]

One retailer that does not doubt the value of its catalog is Williams-Sonoma. Sonoma's catalog sales for the third quarter ending October 31, 1994, increased 62 percent, whereas its retail sales rose only 17 percent.[14]

Manufacturer-Supported Catalogs.   Manufacturers are also entering the catalog business in increasing numbers. While many traditional catalogers manufacture some of their own goods, manufacturers historically have avoided selling directly to consumers for fear of reprisal from their standard sales outlets, namely retailers, distributors, and dealers. This view, however, has been changing rapidly.

Coach Leatherware, owned by Sara Lee since 1985, is one of the prime examples of a manufacturer selling goods to consumers by any method the consumer wishes. Coach, noted for its fine leather goods, has expanded to offer silk scarves and leather luggage.

Coach contributed an estimated $380 million to Sara Lee's estimated $17 billion in sales for the year ending June 30, 1995.

Besides selling to retailers in the traditional method, Coach also has its own stores and its own catalog. Although Coach maintains that retail is its first priority, representatives also state that catalogs have become the company's most profitable channel. For example, in 1995, Coach operated more than 90 full-price stores and 30 factory outlets and mailed 18 million catalogs per year to store customers and prospects. Two-thirds of those catalogs went to names from the company's house file. The mailings themselves were segmented— some for traffic generation, others for off-the-page sales.

Like other manufacturers who combine retail operations and catalogs, Coach has discovered the synergistic nature of these complementary selling methods. Customers who shop in the stores become comfortable with the product and may overcome any previous reluctance to shopping by mail. Those who read the catalog may view it as a preview to the products that await them in the stores.

Incentive Catalogs. Premium incentive catalogs offer consumers discounted merchandise (often famous brands) with proof of purchase of a particular product or by gaining points through frequent purchases of particular products. Consumer incentive catalogs were once best known as trading-stamp catalogs, which allowed stamps saved from product purchases from a wide variety of companies to be redeemed for merchandise. It is no news that the trading-stamp business has been negatively affected by changes in the economy and a host of other types of discount merchandise. Therefore, this business has been a significant decline. However, packaged goods companies, such as General Mills, still offer customers the opportunity to save on merchandise if they redeem coupons found on the goods they manufacture.

Two of the leaders in this field come from the tobacco industry, which has seen crippling legislation in recent years and needs strong reinforcement of its brands even more than most industries. Catalogs for RJ Reynolds's Joe Camel and Phillip Morris's Marlboro offer branded items, such as T-shirts, lighters, jackets, and so forth, for no or very little cost with redemption of points earned through purchases or proofs of purchase on packages.

Procter & Gamble and Colgate Palmolive, too, have dabbled in the catalog business, preparing catalogs of children's toys and gifts in catalogs that offered discounts on these items with an initial purchase.

Incentive catalogs are also being issued by service companies, such as AT&T and Citibank. Again using the point collection system, these companies offer loyal customers a variety of off-price products and services.

Nonprofit Catalogs. Nonprofit catalogs, produced by such well-respected nonprofit institutions as the Metropolitan Museum in New York City, also appear to be on the rise. While their main goals is generally to attain a profit, their secondary mission, sometimes just as important, is to provide education about their organization's goals. For example, The Museum Collection, founded in 1979, is a cooperative catalog venture consisting of over 40 museum participants; Winterthur Museum (Winterthur, Delaware) mailed 5.5 million pieces in 1990 for total sales of $8.5 million; and The Art Institute of Chicago sends pieces which it believes have an air of fun, unlike other serious museum catalogs.

Nonprofit catalogs are not limited to museums, but are as diverse in type and character as any other segment of business. They can be large ventures, like Save the Children, or adjuncts to regular fundraising, such as the Catalog for Disabled American Veterans. There are those backed by zoos (the San Diego Zoo is one), and those that are cause-related (Greenpeace).

Organizations with nonprofit status currently enjoy some privileges not realized by their for-profit brethren, such as reduced outgoing postage costs. However, legislation that could adversely affect this is underway. Over the last few years, there has been much discussion and concern among legislators over what is termed "revenue forgone." In essence, this is money the government pays the postal service for handling the costs of its nonprofit class mail and other nonprofit group mailings. Naturally, this causes nonprofit mailers great concern about how a proposed increase in postage will affect their businesses (see "Postage" in Chapter 7).

In a time of intensified competition, some believe that, even if postal costs are somewhat equalized between nonprofits and for-profits, the former will continue to have an edge by appealing to prospects' emotions as well as their needs. By choosing a nonprofit organization over a for-profit one, buyers may feel they are doing something for themselves and something for society as well. This "do good, feel good" aura has been slightly diluted of late by for-profit catalogers who have associated themselves with highly visible organizations that help the homeless, give medical aid, support the environment, and so on. These catalogs tend to give a percentage of their profits (most often 5 percent) to the affiliated nonprofit organizations, thus establishing the same emotional tie as nonprofit catalogers.

The other side of the coin is the need to meet strict Internal Revenue guidelines related to nonprofit ventures. One main area affected by these guidelines is merchandising. Products must reflect the mission statement of the organization. This explains why museums offer reproductions, zoos offer merchandise showcasing animals, and so forth. This is a double-edged sword, because it allows the catalogers to have unique merchandise but requires the time and cost of developing that higher-risk merchandise. However, in most cases, merchandise developed exclusively for an organization provides higher margins.

Co-op Catalogs. Co-op catalogs consist of combined "mini-catalogs" from a variety of companies, most often catalogers that already have independent catalog operations. The mini-catalogs are usually printed as individual sections (see Chapter 7), each containing representative products from a particular company. Orders may be directed to one combined phone line set up for the purpose or to the individual company number, or may be placed via an order form, which can be individual or combined. Frequently, a noncatalog company acts as the coordinator, charging a few or commission on sales for its services. The advantage to catalogers is shared production costs and the opportunity to reach new audiences that may be too expensive to address otherwise.

One place where you often see these catalogs is in seat pockets on airplanes. Today, some airlines offer the ability to order via phone right from the plane and pick up the item at the airport. According to *Catalog Age,* one such company, Sky Mall, has "a virtual monopoly in the air with almost all domestic carriers now offering it. Participants include such catalogers as Sundance and Hammacher Schlemmer. Customers/passengers can use the Air Fone (at the cataloger's expense) to place orders and request delivery upon arrival (10 percent do this) or delivery either to their hotel or home."

Syndicated Catalogs. Syndicated catalogs bear the name of a particular company, but they are usually not produced by that company, which also carries no inventory of the merchandise offered.

Basically, syndication allows a well-known name to lends its prestige to a catalog without actually running the catalog business. The syndicator, knowing that response is often higher to well-known and respected names, pays a commission to the company under whose name the catalog is mailed. The syndicator sources (or locates and coordinates) the merchandise, physically produces the catalog, and performs all the functions of operating a catalog business.

Oil companies were some of the first to use this merchandising technique. The combination of generous credit terms and prestigious oil company names made the programs highly successful. Soon entertainment–credit card companies used this merchandising effort to create a secondary profit source. Likewise, some manufacturing companies create a catalog consisting of their products alone. They then give or sell this catalog to retail stores that offer their products. This allows the stores, which are often quite small, to "share" the cost of what might otherwise be a cost-prohibitive selling vehicle. For instance, Catalyst's Cycling Guide, which offers a wide range of cycling activities including off-road cycling, racing, family riding, and bicycle touring, is customized by many different local retailers and seeks to promote in-store traffic. Dealers are recognized for their expertise. The catalog is mailed by cycling stores and space is provided for the store's name and location. Catalyst has an annual circulation of 694,500 and an average order of $80.[15]

International Catalogs. Reflecting the state of business as a whole, catalog marketing is turning to the promise of riches to be gained abroad. One example is Austed's, a catalog of golfing equipment, which recognized the sales potential inherent in Japan, a country with 13 million golf enthusiasts, and entered this market in 1990. L. L. Bean has taken its traditionally American look to Japan, as well, answering a Japanese desire for American-made leisure products. Spiegel, in an agreement with Otto-Sumisho, opened an Eddie Bauer retail stores and distributed a catalog in Japan in the autumn of 1994. Bauer also ventured into the German market with a catalog.

Viking Products, a business-to-business cataloger, mails more than a million catalogs to prospective British customers, according to the DMA. This venture, begun in 1990, yielded $50 million in revenue and has grown 30 percent per year since its initiation. Inmac, who has experienced worthwhile success in Japan, now mails in England as well. Further, it plans, through its new global networking division, to publish its catalog in five languages and distribute it to eight countries. Inmac reports that nearly 60 percent of its sales are international.

This fertile market is accustomed to direct marketing. The DMA reports the following statistics:

> According to Syndicat National de la Communication Directe, a French direct marketing association, 48 percent of advertising expenditures in France are reserved for direct marketing. In Germany, nearly 40 percent of advertising dollars go for direct marketing, says the German Direct Marketing Association. And, in the United Kingdom and Canada, direct marketing accounts, respectively, for 21 percent and 22 percent of advertising expenditures, according to the Direct Marketing Association United Kingdom, Ltd. and the Canadian Direct Marketing Association.

Others are discovering the potential of America's neighbor to the south. JC Penney has plans to launch a catalog/retail project in Mexico in the fall of 1994. *Catalog Age* reports:

> Penney's project will involve a drop of millions of copies of a Spanish-language catalog targeted to a broad audience. The book will be larger than the company's U.S. Christmas catalog but smaller than its big book. The mailing of the catalog will be timed to coincide with the opening of the company's first store in Monterrey, Mexico. It also plans to open three stores in Mexico City and one in Guadalajara by the end of 1996. Each store will have catalog ordering desks, and catalogs will also be sold in the stores.

And there's also America's northern neighbor. Canada is not a large market, but is traditionally more responsive than the American market. However, customs regulations have, in the past, made marketing there less than simple. Now going through a process of positive change, revision of these regulations should encourage marketers to move toward this mail order–responsive population. Lands' End, for instance, launched a direct response advertising campaign in September 1993, mailing 250,000 copies of its fall prospector catalog to Canadians.

Regal Greetings, the second largest mail order company in Canada, believes that Canada is a prime target. *Direct Marketing* quotes Tony Keenan, president of Regal Greetings, as saying:

> Some of the obstacles to be overcome by the Canadian catalog industry include the two languages, different rules and laws, the lack of lists, few mail-responsive space vehicles, a higher level of consumer skepticism, exchange rates and shipping costs. Any effort to break into the Canadian mail order market should include a Canadian warehouse operation, Canadian merchandising and marketing input, Canadian employees and use of Canadian services, agencies and list brokers.

This is true of any international market. You need to use the expertise available within that country; don't assume that a simple adaptation of what you already know will translate in tone as well as language.

Catalog Showrooms.   Noted for their *really* big-book approach, catalog showrooms have historically backed their many-page catalogs with stores of impressive square footage to let customers physically inspect the merchandise on display. Orders are usually taken by the staff after the customer has filled out one of the order forms located throughout the store. One sample is displayed; the merchandise for distribution is taken from backroom stock when the customer presents the completed order form.

Catalog showroom catalogs are primarily viewed as traffic generators which, due to their low prices and high perceived value, help get customers into the stores. But, lately, catalog showrooms have fallen on tough times. The largest, Service Merchandise, had sales of $3.4 billion in 1991 and net earnings of about $76 million. However, it now presents itself as less of a catalog showroom than a store with a catalog, although the catalog represents minimal sales. Consisting of 361 national stores, Service Merchandise also distributes more than 650 million publications to customers.[16] Its nearest competitor, Best Products, Inc., is operating under Chapter 11, filed in January 1991. Best saw its stores shrink from 225 to 160 in 1993, but it still plans to mail between 100 million and 150 million promotion packages per year.[17]

Business-to-Business Catalogs

In the rapidly growing business-to-business area, you'll find entries from such giants as IBM, Lotus, and AT&T to small companies serving almost every business need. Jack Miller, president of Quill Corporation, one of the largest suppliers of office products in the United States, says there are at least four reasons for the continued growth and success of business-to-business catalogs:

1. The constantly rising cost of sales calls
2. The difficulty of creating a "pull-through" demand in the business field
3. Constant, rapid changes in product technology
4. Profit-margin pressure at the manufacturer level

The diversity of catalog types is almost as large as that of consumer catalogs, and this is where you will find totally unique niches. There's everything from the conservative Daytimers, who sell business diaries, to New Pig, a catalog of waste absorption products which has a pig as its omnipresent mascot. Consumer catalogs, too, have editions devoted to the business market. Two prime examples are Calyx & Corolla, a flower catalog, and Harry & David, famous for their fruit and other food items. The corporate sales for these two companies continue to add impressive bottom-line profits to their businesses.

According to *Catalog Age*'s May 1993 issue, "business-to-business catalog sales gains for the first quarter range from 3 percent to 25 percent. Profit margins and customer retention rates have also improved . . . [Some catalogers] never even felt the effects of the recent recession."

Although business-to-business catalogs have many elements in common with their consumer brethren, they also have distinct needs. These are addressed in Chapter 17.

Consumers' Opinions

Companies in the catalog business have recently begun to turn more and more to focus groups to get a better understanding of what potential and current customers think about their endeavors. Focus groups can help define attitudes, expectations, and perceptions. Here are some observations made from a compilation of focus groups:

1. **Consumers trust catalogs.** Catalogs are eagerly anticipated, and many consumers immediately take their catalogs "right to the bathroom" for some quiet time, confirming what industry experts have always suspected.

2. **Catalogs are used as a form of fantasy.** Without a doubt, one of the reasons for the good feelings toward catalogs is that, as many focus group attendees have said, "catalogs are dreambooks." They present "things to look forward to." Some attendees have stated that catalogs allow them to take a step beyond their real world and be someone slightly different without any risk.

   Catalog order takers, they report, are not judgmental, unlike some retail store personnel. You can, from the privacy of your home, take a little risk on that red dress or expensive chocolate and no one will make you feel that you've made a foolish decision.

3. **Catalogs are just plain fun.** In this stress-intensive, uptight world, catalogs offer a respite—some simple, harmless fun that brings the instant pleasure of shopping and the enjoyably delayed (but not too delayed) pleasure of receiving the purchased item.

4. **Consumers compare prices.** Catalog buyers are savvy, and they want and know value. Prices are compared not just to retail, but also against any other relevant catalog they receive. Yet, unlike years before, catalogs are not necessarily considered expensive. True, customers feel some offer higher-priced items, but plenty also offer "bargains" and good prices.

5. **Catalogs act as educational tools.** Attendees say they "get ideas" and "learn things" from catalogs. Some examples they cite are what is in fashion and how to wear it, how to decorate their homes, what cookware is best for their type of cooking, and so on.

6. **Consumers continue to savor uniqueness.** This is why catalogs succeeded when they first started and it still do. Those who come to focus groups say catalogs contain items they don't see in stores.

7. **Consumers depend on variety.** Beyond uniqueness, another attribute frequently mentioned is a "more unusual selection."

8. **Consumers love the convenience.** This part has not changed; if anything, catalog shopping has become even more convenient. Many consumers simply don't like to go (store) shopping.

9. **Only one area is a negative hot spot with consumers—postage and handling.** Their concern is not so much the cost, as the fairness of the traditional postage and handling charge, which assesses charges based on the total dollar amount purchased but does not seem to take weight into account. A few catalogers address this issue by charging fees based on the individual weight of the items ordered, in combination with its shipping zone. But as this requires an additional step for the customer, most catalogers do not, at this time, endorse charging by weight and shipping zone.

Understanding the Mail Order Market

As with all other industries in the United States, the catalog business depends on the overall economy. However, one big advantage direct marketers have over almost everyone else is the ability to segment their market by geographic region and adapt mailing quantities accordingly. If one part of the country shows signs of ailing, mailings to that area can be decreased and increased to another part of the country that shows signs of vitality.

Likewise, parts of the country adversely affected by such natural disasters as floods, hurricanes, or earthquakes can be temporarily suppressed from your mailing list. The DMA publishes a list of zip codes that reflect areas that may be experiencing delivery hardships.

This ability to "move" your store to less economically depressed regions of the country is certainly helpful, but the key to success lies in your ability to accurately predict and analyze trends.

Potential Markets

To identify potential markets, you must be aware of what is happening around you. Read newspapers and periodicals that clearly state how consumer needs are changing. The clues are all there; the hard part is interpreting them.

Spotting a trend and acting on it is one of the reasons "boutique" catalogs were born. Catalogs today have continued to realize a specific need and answer it. Some relatively recent entries have addressed such specific segments as Hispanic heritage, gay lifestyles, a return to "new age" thinking, and even nonelectrical products for the Amish!

For instance, what type of merchandise does the consumer buy from catalogs? Apparel continues to lead, but not only has the competition increased, as the bar in Figure 1-11 indicates, the percentage of sales has decreased. Perhaps the trend to follow is in home furnishings and/or housewares, which showed a percentage increase for 1992.

❖ **FIGURE 1-11**
Types of Merchandise Bought from Catalogs, 1991–1992

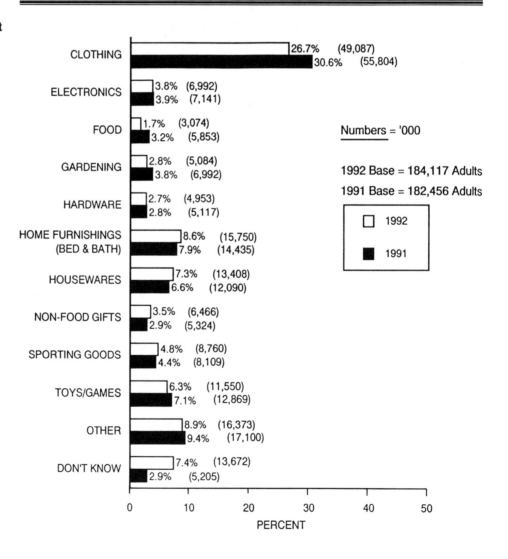

* Numbers in parentheses are given in thousands. Findings are compiled from a base of 184,117 adults in 1992 and a base of 182,456 adults in 1991.
SOURCE: Direct Marketing Association. *DMA 1993/94 Statistical Fact Book.* DMA, 1994, 88.

In addition to looking at general trends, understand just who shops from catalogs. A survey from *Research Alert* indicates that the typical catalog shopper is between 25 and 54 years old, with 25 percent in the 35 to 44 age group. Catalog shoppers earn more than their noncatalog counterparts and seek more convenience devices. They read more, eat at full-service restaurants, and attribute more importance to labels. Seventy percent of catalog shoppers are the primary grocery shopper in their households, compared to 58 percent of noncatalog shoppers.[18]

The fact that catalog shoppers make more money naturally makes them more likely to own the latest and more expensive products. But before deciding on any category for your initial catalog or a spin-off of an existing catalog, consider this question: How long will the demand last? Try to plan now for any adaptations you may need in merchandising should consumer attitudes change.

No formula can determine where the next opportunity in cataloging lies. Successful direct marketers have built their businesses by correctly assessing trends and needs. Corporations have entered direct marketing partly because of their ability to do this well. Success depends on the right combination of research and good instincts—and having the courage to act before the competition does!

Catalog Size

The size, shape, and product density of catalogs have changed over the years, and this trend, too, must be watched. The big books of yesterday (such as Sears Roebuck and Montgomery Ward) are virtually extinct. More targeted marketing naturally creates more focused sales vehicles. Therefore, it is natural and wise to ask, "How many pages should my catalog be?" and "What format should the catalog use?" The specifics of these questions are addressed in Chapters 7 and 8 but Figures 1-12 and 1-13 provide an interesting overview.

❖ **FIGURE 1-12**
Sizes Used for Primary Catalogs

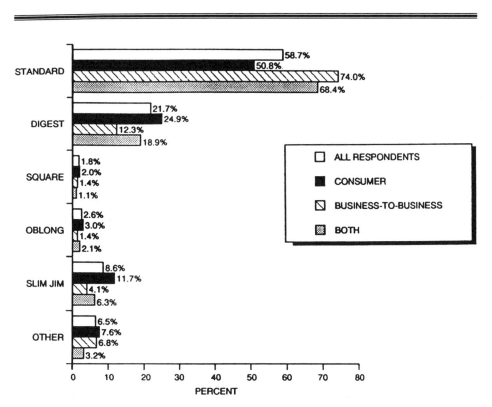

SOURCE: Direct Marketing Association. *DMA 1993/94 Statistical Fact Book.* DMA, 1994, 98.

❖ **FIGURE 1-13**
Average Number of Pages in Primary Catalogs

A greater proportion of respondents note having less than 24 pages in their primary catalog in 1992 vs. 1991.

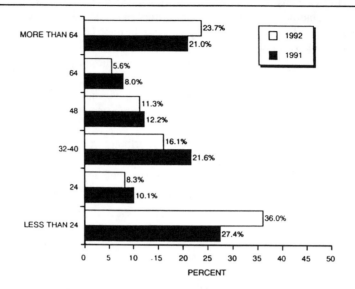

SOURCE: Direct Marketing Association. *DMA 1993/94 Statistical Fact Book*. DMA, 1994, 98.

Benefits of Going into Retail

As addressed previously in this chapter, specialty catalogs are spawning specialty retail stores. As department stores become less and less appealing to consumers, catalogers are taking advantage of newly emerging niches and expanding their sales options by opening carefully located stores.

A common method for determining the location of a potential store is to examine a catalog's sales results by geographic area. A clustering of results is a clear indicator that this location would support a store. Some companies that have used this method report that initially mail order sales can decrease by up to 50 percent, but regain their original level within three years while the stores flourish.

Interactive Shopping—An Emerging New Breed

Interactive, electronic catalogs are expected to add another mode of shopping to the consumers' already extensive mix within five to ten years. It has been estimated that anywhere from 15 to 50 percent of households with televisions will have interactive capabilities by the end of the 1990s and may spend up to 80 percent of their disposable income on products supplied by interactive services.[19]

Some forward-thinking companies have already experimented with catalogs on video and CD-ROM. Video-based catalogs were mostly produced by entrepreneurial companies and have virtually disappeared. Why? Customer acceptance of what was less-than-stimulating entertainment was not high enough to offset the cost of production, which could run from $6 to $10 per tape.

But that was the first of a long series of attempts at making interactive shopping both entertaining and motivational. Today, there are many signs that computers, televisions, and telephones will converge into one easy-to-use ordering tool. Alliances between such communication giants as Time Warner and US West, and Viacom and AT&T only confirm the direction interaction is now taking.

While all companies eagerly await the technology that will allow this hybrid, others experiment with the current forms of electronic communication—some with more success than others. Even with their failings, these current forms of interaction seem to be the hottest ways of reaching an increasingly sophisticated audience.

Computer-based Shopping

On-line Services. Prodigy, America On-Line, and CompuServe have long offered a limited number of customers the opportunity to shop nationally via their computer. Other more segmented services, such as WESTLAW, an on-line computer research service offering law-related publications and court decisions, and Bloomberg Ltd., an on-line financial information service, also provide the potential for niche advertising. (Don't assume that a segmented service like a financial information service is for finances only. Bloomberg showcases Brooks Brothers and Teleway, the parent company of 800-FLOWERS.) And there are even local services, such as Local Villages, that feature regional on-line services.

But the high hopes of these companies have been curtailed largely due to what many view as the inaccessibility of the computer information offered. Limited graphic capabilities force the offering to be text-based, a less-than-compelling method of presentation.

Prodigy remains the dominant player, with 2 million members and an estimated 41-percent market share as of spring 1993.[20] A joint venture of IBM and Sears Roebuck, this service has yet to make money. Begun in 1988, it is estimated that the company has accumulated losses of $800 million and reaches only 1 million homes, just 5 percent of the 20 million U.S. homes that have personal computers.[21]

Yet this form of shopping has many highly placed supporters. In *The Popcorn Report*, Faith Popcorn predicts the demise of traditional forms of shopping:

> In Orwell's classic *1984*, the state controlled the screen. In the year 2000, the consumer will control the screen. The computerized shopping screen.
>
> The home cocoon will be the site of the future shopping centers. All members of the family will be able to shop from one location. Instead of going to the store, the store will come to us, no matter how unusual the product or how frequently needed. On our screens, we'll be able to hear about the latest new products or styles, or order up our old favorites.

CD-ROM. CD-ROM catalogs, with their impressive graphic capabilities, seem to offer more promise than on-line services. For instance, Apple Computer, Redgate Communications, and EDS produced a multimedia, interactive disc filled with video, sound text, *and* pictures called En Passant. Lands' End, Tiffany & Company, L. L. Bean, and Patagonia are some of the participants in this electronic catalog of 18 companies' offerings. Naturally, the disc sells the participants' products, using full-motion video and audio, and incorporates entertainment in the form of complementary editorial. Mailed in December 1993 to 30,000 randomly selected prospects from the Apple Computer database, the disk does not have model capability. The on-disc order form is only for reference when calling in orders via the 800 number.

Maybe the greatest potential for this type of catalog lies in the business-to-business sector. Here, catalogs with thousands of products could provide their best customers with a CD-ROM disc containing every product offered.

One such company is Personal Electronic Catalog and Ordering System (PECOS) which has a brochure clearly stating its function: "Any company that processes large amounts of routine orders, order inquiries and purchase activity, or needs to communicate price and product information accurately and frequently with customers, will significantly benefit . . . (plus it will) minimize (a company's) variable operating costs of sales and associated labor related costs by streamlining the order entry process." This catalog has three major components: an electronic catalog (which views pages the same as one would with a paper catalog), a database search engine (which enables users to search a database of products on seller-defined parameters and select items for purchase), and an ordering system (which

❖ **EXAMPLE 1-1**
With the En Passant electronic catalog, users simply load the disk and double-click on the shopping bag icon to enjoy a new shopping experience.

builds purchase orders and allows them to be transmitted electronically to the cataloger). This system also has an "advertising" platform from which advertising co-op dollars can be generated.

One of the main benefits of CD-ROM to a cataloger is the ability to quickly update information, including ever-changing prices, allowing them to send customers new discs at less cost than a completely reprinted catalog. Customers, on the other hand, can have their computers instantly search out the item or items they desire, and order at the push of a button via their modem. There's no need to re-enter credit information, as these statistics are already programmed into the catalog's database.

Acceptance of this mode of delivery has yet to be determined. Vic Cherubini, president of E.P.I.C. Software Group, which makes interactive electronic catalogs, reports that the company's best results stem from a follow-up reminder in the form of a telephone call or postcard. At that point, usage of the electronic catalog can run as high as 60 percent.

Television-based Shopping

The biggest news of the 1980s was the advent of The Home Shopping Network. The oldest of what was once a large group of home shopping channels, The Home Shopping Network was born in Clearwater-Tampa in mid-1985. Featuring pitchpeople who are friendly but also intensely sales-oriented, this method moves products at previously unheard-of rates, reportedly as many as 8,000 units in 10 minutes at $20 each during top selling seasons. The Quality Value Convenience (QVC) channel reports taking orders for more than $19 million worth of merchandise on a single day in January of 1993.[22]

Chatting on the air with callers gives this relatively new method of shopping credibility and a chance to "touch" the customers. And Home Shopping makes the ordering process simple. With your first order, you receive a customer number; the use of this number combined with touch-tone ordering means you can enter your order in a matter of minutes without ever actually talking to an operator. The winning combination of personal attention, low prices, and easy access to desirable impulse items has definitely won many converts to this shopping mode. In 1992, close to 13 million American adults ordered merchandise via this method. However, finding a winning combination is not easy. Up to 18 companies once competed in this arena; today, there are only two major players.

❖ TABLE 1-1 Consumer Use of Television Home Shopping Programs

	Home Shopping Network (HSN)		Quality Value Convenience Channel (QVC)		Other	
	Number of Adults*	% of Total Adult Base	Number of Adults*	% of Total Adult Base	Number of Adults*	% of Total Adult Base
Watched in last three months	12,960	7.0	11,003	6.0	4,124	2.2
Times bought in last three months						
1	1,780	1.0	1,404	0.8	646	0.4
2–5	3,024	1.6	1,892	1.0	998	0.5
6 or more	817	0.4	1,319	0.7	213	0.1
Did not buy	7,340	4.0	6,388	3.5	2,271	1.2

* In thousands.

SOURCE: Direct Marketing Association. *DMA 1993/94 Statistical Fact Book.* DMA, 1994, p. 173.

Because the rewards can be so immense, shopping channels appear to be on the rise again. Wireless direct broadcast satellites now hang over our heads in more than one way. *Direct Marketing* reported:

> The 6,000-pound Hughes Electronics Corporation satellite is the first of two satellites which will hang in the sky during 1994 to provide U.S. and Canadian homes equipped with 18-inch dishes to receive more than 150 crystal clear channels. No more wires. And at a cost competitive with Cable-TV. They say consumers will pay about $35 per month, competitive with Cable TV. About 38 percent of U.S. homes no longer need to wait for cable to be laid to their front door.[23]

But this same article asks the key question: "But at an advertised cost of $900 per dish/decoder installation, will many more than the early adopters buy in?"

Alliances spring up almost every day. Just two of the powerhouse duos are Time Warner and Spiegel, and Apple Computer and Redgate Communications Corp. Retailers, such as Macy's, Saks Fifth Avenue, and Sharper Image, also look to this method of selling as an enhancement to their future.

One of the largest and most talked-about ventures is that of Time Warner. Originally slated for testing in Orlando, Florida in April 1994, 4,000 consumers will be able to test all of the new interactive technology, including video on demand, interactive shopping, games, and so forth. Exemplifying the volatility of this new medium, this project has been rescheduled regularly.

Beyond this, Time Warner and Spiegel have a joint venture called Catalog 1. Scheduled for primary testing in four markets, this shopping channel will target more upscale customers than those who traditionally use such shopping venues as The Home Shopping Network. On January 21, 1994, *Friday Report* indicated that Catalog 1 "will broadcast 84 hrs. a week but then expand to 24 hours a day of live and repeated programming. . . . catalogers selected to participate have distinctive strengths, including direct marketing expertise, superior customer service, quality merchandise, strong brand identity and 'instant recognition and trust.' "

Broadcast Television and Infomercials

Broadcast Television.   Television, in general, has always been appealing due to its ability to reach so many potential new customers. But high costs and low returns have made in unusable for most catalogers. As cable has grown and TV has splintered into bite-size pieces, some companies have found that these new niches match their audience's profiles. For instance, a seller of thermal underwear found success on a weather channel. Harry & David, during the 1993 holiday season successfully aired 30- and 60-second ads which sold specific products, such as their well-known "Tower of Treats"—boxes filled with a variety of foods, such as cookies, fruits, and candy.

And TV is not as expensive as most believe. You can produce a two-minute video (called a short form) for about $10,000 (and that assumes there is no existing footage). To construct a reliable media test that goes to regional and split markets, you'll need another $20,000.

A big benefit of TV is its speed. You can analyze the results three times a day and pull it within 72 hours, saving money on the air-time costs if the results do not meet your needs. Products need high mark-up to work on TV. One example: If a product costs $8, it should sell for $30.

Infomercial.   Most often taking the form of a talk show, this form of commercial usually has a ''natural'' setting where participants ''discuss'' the product in an interview format. According to the National Infomercial Marketing Association (NIMA), 1992 gross product sales generated by infomercials were $750 million, up from $350 million in1988. Sales are projected to reach $900 million in 1993. This doesn't include the $2 billion generated by the home shopping channels.

Once considered a slightly less than pure format, infomercials have come into their own. Bob DeLay states:

> For nearly a decade infomercials have been a ''fringe'' marketing channel, the domain of entrepreneurs and fast-buck artists alike. But in the last 18 months, advertisers and mainstream direct marketers have taken them seriously. In the 10 years from 1984, infomercial revenues have escalated from $5 million to nearly $1 billion.
>
> With growth also came increases in production costs—from an average of $30,000 to $250,000 for a half hour infomercial. Cost of media time has also ballooned—nearly 500 percent. And the barrage now adds to TV clutter with some 175 infomercials a week on broadcast stations and cable networks.[24]

While this is a concern, most advertisers find a way to overcome the clutter. A case in point is Saks Fifth Avenue, which sold $600,000 worth of its Real Clothes merchandise in May 1993.

This medium will continue to evolve into a truly educational, as well as entertaining, form of selling. As in other direct marketing offers, though, the product must be the star, surrounded by the positioning which gets it noticed and inspires purchases.

Without doubt, the much-discussed ''information superhighway'' provides potential. What has yet to be determined is whether consumers truly desire interaction, and what might be called invasiveness, from their TVs, or whether they prefer to use these devices in the traditional passive entertainment mode.

Small Business Success Stories

Entrepreneurs launched the catalog business—famous names, such as Sears, Ward, Horchow, and Vernon. Today, probably due to the fairly high entry cost for an individual, catalogs with lesser sales are decreasing in number. *Catalog Age* published a survey in December 1993 indicating that respondents with sales under $1 million are fewer than in previous years. Yet 97 percent of the respondents were privately held and 88 percent were independent.

So the good news is that those in the business are increasing their sales. To quote *Catalog Age*:

> The percentage reporting revenues under $1 million . . . has dropped from 39 percent last year to 34 percent this year, while the percentage of respondents that report revenues of $1 million to $9.9 million increased from 43 percent to 46 percent this year. Nearly 8 percent of respondents this year (vs. nearly 5 percent last year) report revenues of $10 million to $19.9 million and about the same percentage as last year (13 percent) report revenues of $20 million or more.[25]

Many entrepreneurs find that the rewards of owning and running a small business are plentiful. Here are some success stories.

Sweet Energy

Carole Ann and Tom Ziter are the owners of Sweet Energy catalog. A few months before Carole's 50th birthday, her husband started inserting notices of the event (without her knowledge) into all packages going to customers. Did these customers care? Carole received 2,000 extraordinary birthday cards and letters! Many contained notes detailing how much the catalog and the people behind it meant to their customers. One started like this, "For your birthday I wanted to give back to you something more precious than anything you can touch or see—which you give to your customers with each order you send out."

Sweet Energy has been in business for over 12 years, has gross sales of almost $2 million and, due to the composition of its work force, calls itself the "Home of the Working Mother." It sells apricots and other dried fruits, as well as nuts and chocolates. It has a fairly typical catalog but a less conventional overall program, which consists of loyalty builders such as a newsletter, dividend checks paid to customers, personalized letters enclosed with every order, and hand-addressed birthday cards.

Like many other entrepreneurs, Carole started the business as a hobby by running mail order ads in the back of home-oriented shelter magazines. As the hobby has grown into a million-dollar business, Carole notes that her company not only provides healthy foods to people across the country, but also gives seasonal employment and training to working mothers who want to spend some time at home and some time working. And she may be creating jobs in more ways than one would naturally think of—the local post office representatives said that 9 out of 10 pieces of mail are addressed to Sweet Energy.

Dakin Farm

Dakin Farm got its start in 1960 when Sam Cutting III, a fighter pilot in the Vermont Air National Guard, bought a farm that produced ham, bacon, poultry, and other meats. These were slowly smoked over smoldering corn cobs on the farm. Dakin now sells this tantalizing array of delicacies with aged cheeses and pure Vermont maple syrup. Back in 1960, when Dakin Farm was just a tiny mom-and-pop store open during the summer months, the business brought in only $10,000. Now it has grown to gross sales of over $1 million, and its two retail stores gross nearly as much.

Running a small business doesn't mean that you have fewer inventory problems than the bigger guys. Sam Cutting IV tells a story of frantically trying to find and smoke orders for 4,800 turkey breasts, a new product, when the projections had been for 300! With the help of a neighboring smoke house, the farm filled all the orders but lost money in the process.

Sam feels that there are five criteria to success:

1. Have a strong crossover between retail and mail order.
2. Have a product of exceptional quality and uniqueness, and make it convenient to use (Dakin's food products are simple to serve and give).
3. Adapt creatively to a changing marketplace.
4. Take good care of your established customers to be sure they remain loyal.
5. Be sure you are positioned to cut overhead when necessary and still run the business efficiently.

For Sam and his family, running a mail order catalog means that his father, who loves being a farmer, can work with high-quality agricultural products. For Sam, it means that he can run the catalog, be the businessman he wanted to be, and still live in a beautiful part of the country, surrounded by lakes and mountains.

Diebold Design

Peter Diebold of Diebold Designs considers himself an "exporter," because he exports his greeting cards to virtually every state but New Hampshire and Vermont even though he's based in New Hampshire. "What do you do when business is lousy regionally?" Peter asks. "You go into the 'export' business!" Peter's tiny company sells lots of cards not only because Peter is an exceptionally clever designer, but also because he has loyal customers who are thrilled that they can actually talk to the creator of the cards.

Diebold Designs is 14 years old, has eight mostly part-time workers, and is "too tiny" to talk about sales dollars. They rent about 20,000 to 30,000 names a year and also turn to magazine ads and general requests for names for mailing, such as those asking for a catalog by phone. Peter got started when a stockbroker asked him to design his company's Christmas card, and for years stockbrokers made up the majority of the business. But we all know what has happened to stockbrokers in the 1990s. So Peter has turned his attention to nautical themes and found a new equally successful niche. He feels the rewards are great because he's achieved his dream of a nonregional business that lets him be both a businessman and an artist in a location he loves.

The Company of Women

In 1988, Melinda Little started The Company of Women on what she would now term an absurdly small shoestring, and it has been a struggle to build it up to the million-dollar business it now is. But every minute (or almost every minute) has been worth it because Melinda was looking for a business that brought more than the normal rewards. By far, the largest percentage (81%) of dollars generated by the catalog benefit the Rockland Family Shelter, an agency serving victims of domestic violence and rape, as well as the homeless.

A model for nonprofit sustainability, the catalog hopes to become a growing source of unrestricted funds for the shelter, thereby enabling it to become less dependent on public funding. The belief is that this success will breed other similar successes. One side benefit is that the catalog acts as a market for women-owned businesses, as well. Because the shelter tends to assist mostly women and children, the merchandise in the catalog has evolved to products that celebrate womanhood. Women manufacturers have responded by creating exclusives to complement this theme. Items offered in the catalog include t-shirts, posters, and mugs.

A recent letter to Melinda shows why the trials and tribulations of running a catalog on "the world's tiniest budget" can be worth it. The letter, in part, reads: "I just wanted to take the time to commend all of you for your devotion to and concern for the never-ending struggle for women's rights and the right of all to live in a safe environment. I know that women all over the world applaud your efforts to bring some positive support to their lives . . . through a catalog of informative materials. . . . You may not think that a single catalog can make a difference in someone's life, but believe me, it does."

Historic Housefitters

Nancy and Dave Sposato both wanted career changes and were in the midst of renovating an old house when the bright idea came to them to start a catalog of quality hardware. From experience, they knew that expensive and inexpensive hardware was available, but they found no good-quality, reasonably priced hardware. A little research told them that home fix-up was on the rise, so it seemed a natural niche. Hence, Historic Housefitters, a catalog of "Quality Period Hardware and Fittings" was born in 1986.

Dave went from a position in which he was responsible for high-volume, corporate type purchasing to working primarily with craftspeople. He explains the differences as follows: "Our suppliers often have a very different attitude from what you might normally expect. Once, when asking the price for a wrought iron hook, I was told it was $10. 'But what if I buy 100?' I asked. 'Then it's $12 each' was the reply. Obviously craftspeople are not into the boredom of repetition!"

During the past year the business outgrew the Sposato's home and moved to commercial office and warehouse space. Customers have always been obtained through space ads (no list rentals); the catalog has grown from 20 black-and-white pages of all line drawings to 48 pages using color and black-and-white photography and drawings. Today, Historic

Housefitters has sales of $400,000 and three employees. Though still a small business, Nancy and Dave would never trade it. Dave speaks for them both when he says, "It gives us control over our own fate and a real reduction in the stress-level. Plus we're proud of our products and our service and our customers' loyalty to our business."

Wild Apple Graphics

Wild Apple Graphics was founded in 1989 by John and Laurie Chester, and its first catalog was produced in 1990. Although John and Laurie were bankers by trade, they had enough confidence and youth to believe that they could become art publishers. Plus, due to the fact they had just traveled around the world together for five months, they felt they could manage the challenge of working and living together.

Their first catalog consisted of inserts pasted one by one into die-cut folders, a painstakingly slow process. It was the rebellion of the babysitter (one of those enlisted for making the folders and inserts into catalogs) that convinced them to produce a more traditional publication.

Laurie says that even though they are a business-to-business cataloger, they try to incorporate the same principles that Lands' End uses. In a very short time, this little business has grown dramatically. Last year sales were under $1 million; this year they're projected to be $7.5 million!

As with other entrepreneurs, a catalog business lets the Chesters lead the kind of life they want, which in their case means working on a farm, getting to spend plenty of time with their children, their horses, and their llama.

When Direct Marketing Works

If you do the job right, catalogs can be both lucrative and rewarding. Study the how-tos carefully and find your own way of adapting them to create a better and more distinctive catalog. Get the right kind of professional help and start mailing. After all, how many other businesses offer you the entire U.S. market (or more) without your having to leave the town where you live? And how many other businesses offer you the opportunity to develop loyal customers who, through correspondence, practically become members of your corporate family?

The Lew Magram Catalog

Being aware of new trends and finding the special niche is not limited to new marketers. For instance, what do you do when the market you've dominated for more than 30 years is no longer pulling the response you need to keep your head above water? The Lew Magram catalog, faced with such a predicament, didn't just sit there. It took what some might call bold and risky, but ultimately rewarding, steps to transition itself from a high-fashion menswear catalog to one offering upscale, high-fashion women's apparel.

Lew Magram, Ltd. began in 1948 as a one-man business selling shirts out of a midtown New York City storefront. Mr. Magram's entrepreneurial spirit paid off. The storefront soon expanded into a highly successful retail store. According to Erv Magram, Lew's son and president of Lew Magram, Ltd., almost every show business star you could name in the mid-1950s owned a Lew Magram custom shirt.

In the mid-1960s, the first Lew Magram "Shirtmaker to the Stars" catalog was produced. As high-fashion menswear flourished in the mid-1970s, so did the catalog. Then, according to Erv, menswear became more traditional, and the market decreased dramatically. Not only did it become more difficult to merchandise the catalog, but the items themselves were no longer selling.

Caught in a Catch-22 situation, the Magrams took a bold step. Armed with their in-house "secret weapon"—Melaine, an experienced buyer and Erv's sister—the Magrams added five women's apparel items to the spring 1981 catalog. Not only were the items successful, but the move opened a floodgate of response from the men's list. Buying history had indicated that women were buying for men. These results showed that the men's list consisted of a mail-order buying household in which the wife had taught her husband to order by mail. Now, finding the opportunity to buy for herself, she did.

In 1982, the enthusiastically received women's apparel began to take precedence over menswear. This trend continued until it was decided that menswear, because it was not paying for its space in the catalog, should be dropped completely. Accordingly, the Lew Magram list has changed dramatically. Their buyers in 1994 were 98 percent female!

With its move from the original Shirtmaker to the Stars to the new "fashion specialists," the Lew Magram catalog is an example of an ingenious marketing strategy that turned a downward trend into a continuing success story.

Frederick's of Hollywood

In 1946, Mr. Frederick, who actually existed, launched a mail order lingerie business from a tiny one-deck loft on Fifth Avenue in New York City. In 1947, he moved to California and changed the name to Frederick's of Hollywood. He was the first real dream merchant selling fantasy fashions. Frederick is quoted as saying, "The cornerstone of our endeavor is the design of garments to render women even more sexually appealing than they normally are." This is, generally speaking, still the kind of motivational appeal that might help sell products. But the way this message is delivered in our current society has changed, affecting the enduring allure that Frederick had built into his fashion.

Noticing this changing trend was not easy, since throughout most of Frederick's history, its fashion seemed scandalous. Remember, back in 1946 only "bad girls" and Frederick's of Hollywood customers wore black undergarments. But there was no doubt that this positioning was starting to age. When now-president George Townson joined the company in 1985, the bottom line was in trouble due to outdated business assumptions, more sophisticated competition, and a host of other problems. From mid-1983 to mid-1985, the stock tumbled 73 percent, from $7.00 to $1.90 per share, and profits turned to a loss for the first time in Frederick's history.

The company first turned to research to better understand their new customers' attitudes. Here they learned that customers wanted Frederick's to be pretty and romantic, spicy and sensual, casual and sporty. One of the first steps toward this attitude was a change in the logo design and a move from catalog illustrations to real models. Frederick's further adapted to the new attitude by deleting some of the more overtly sexual items from its product offerings and redesigning its stores with marble and glass.

And the changes have worked. Mail order sales grew from $9 million in fiscal 1986 to $59 million in fiscal 1994. Operating profits in 1994 were over $2.4 million, and catalog distribution increased from 41 million in fiscal 1993 to 46 million in fiscal 1994.

❖ **EXAMPLE 1-2**
(a) The old Frederick's of Hollywood catalog was slightly risqué and used hand-drawn illustrations. **(b)** Today's catalog features photographs and a more refined overall presentation of merchandise.

❖ CHECKLIST

✔ Catalog marketing continues to grow in sales and acceptance.
✔ Be aware of *all* the steps needed for success.
✔ Use the consumer trends that increase catalog acceptance.
✔ Stay on top of and fully understand how trends affect your business.
✔ Be sensitive to how consumers view catalogs.
✔ Keep abreast of the latest trends in interactive shopping.
✔ Create your own success story.

End Notes

1. *Entrepreneur,* December 1993.
2. U.S. Postal Service. "Household Diary Survey," 1991.
3. DMA Library and Resource Center.
4. Grey Advertising. 1990 survey.
5. *Adweek's Marketing Week,* June 25, 1990.
6. *Research Alert,* September 7, 1990.
7. *Friday Report,* January 21, 1994.
8. *The Wall Street Journal,* October 13, 1993.
9. Fishman, Arnold. *1991 Guide to Mail Order Sales,* 1991.
10. *Catalog Age,* August 1994.
11. *The Bruce Report,* Feb. 28, 1995.
12. *Catalog Age,* Apr. 1, 1995.
13. *Direct,* July 1993.
14. Williams Sonoma Annual Report to Shareholders, Oct. 30, 1994.
15. *Catalog Age,* September 1993.
16. *Catalog Age,* October 1992.
17. *DM News,* June 14, 1993.
18. Census Bureau. In *Research Alert,* September 18, 1992.
19. *Cablevision,* September 20, 1993.
20. *Advertising Age,* April 5, 1993.
21. *Direct,* August 1, 1993.
22. *Target Marketing,* March 1994.
23. *Direct Marketing,* January 1994.
24. *The DeLay Letter,* February 7, 1994.
25. *Catalog Age,* December 1993.

CHAPTER TWO

Getting Started

The cart belongs behind the horse. Before considering what it takes to put together a successful catalog, you ought to know that no successful operation can start until you have harnessed four basic resources: the right positioning, money, physical space, and personnel.

How to Position Your Catalog

To make your catalog the strong selling vehicle it needs to be, you must make it clear to the potential buyer just what the catalog stands for. In other words, you must create a *brand* and support that brand with a clear, memorable image. You can probably think of many catalogs that have become brands unto themselves: Sharper Image, known for its electronic wizardry; Lands' End, which has made service and value its major thrust; and Victoria's Secret, which has transformed undergarments into the stuff of romantic dreams.

A brand's *image* is the face it presents to the world through many mechanisms, such as product, package, name, location, advertising, and so on. In turn, the world interprets the brand through many filters: experience, perceptions, preconceptions, value systems, and so forth. According to Young & Rubicam, a major direct marketing agency, this is a two-way process of input and output. Input is what we want consumers to think or feel; output is what they actually think or feel. These two perspectives are expressed in:

1. The brand-personality statement (also called the *positioning statement*), which sets the brand's goals

2. The brand-personality profile, which is the consumer's perception of the brand

These help the viewer's imagination determine if something is appropriate for him or her.

In the marketplace, meaningful product differentiation becomes increasingly difficult when product categories experience the following situations:

♦ Brand proliferation (many of the same product images competing for the same market)

♦ Little or no technological insulation (no edge in technological developments, such as one auto company providing airbags before others have the capability)

♦ Alternatives that are virtually indistinguishable to consumers on a physical or functional level

Therefore, the most important weapon marketing may have is a clear-cut positioning statement that results in an easy-to-understand personality with which consumers identify. Once the need for a brand's personality is understood, three alternative courses of action are possible:

1. **Maintain it.** This works for a healthy brand that targets its current users; however, it can be shortsighted.

2. **Modify it.** This, of course, recognizes the need or opportunity to appeal to a broader group of prospects.

3. **Change it.** In this case, you must be willing to lose current users in an effort to attract new users.

Writing a Positioning Statement

Take the time to sit down and write a definition of what your catalog stands for. This exercise will help you unearth and clearly define why your catalog is better than your competitor's. Make this statement available to everyone on your creative and marketing team to ensure that what you wish to convey to your customers is in synch with what your team is saying through copy and graphics.

Based on the annotated questions in Table 2-1, create your own positioning statement form and have each of your team members fill it out. You will be surprised at the differences when you review the completed forms. This will confirm the need for a central statement.

Combine what you consider the relevant data from each of the team's forms into one concise document. Use as many adjectives and adverbs as you can to describe exactly what makes your catalog unique. It is not uncommon for this form to act as the basis for the tagline for your catalog. And never underestimate the value of a well-written tagline. It helps your customers truly understand the positioning of your catalog.

The following examples should give you a better idea of what a completed form should look like. Although they are different, both are for companies involved in catalog marketing.

Example 1.   The first positioning statement is from Muldoon & Baer, Inc., a direct response consulting group.

1. **What is the product?**
   A direct response consulting and creative production service organization focused on the catalog segment of direct marketing.

2. **At whom is the product aimed?**
   Both large and small companies that (a) currently have a direct response program, (b) want to start a direct response program, or (c) are considering starting a direct response program.

1. **What is the product?**
   The product is the catalog, not the merchandise within that catalog. Therefore, you should say something like, "An upscale, consumer-based catalog of highly wearable, well-priced, contemporary garments developed for unisex use."

2. **At whom is the product aimed?**
   Describe the demographics and psychographics of your target audience.

3. **What is the consumer perception of the product area as it relates to this product?**
   What is the reputation of your type of product in the mail order and retail environments? What is the consumer's attitude?

4. **Who are the competitors?**
   Don't just list other catalogs here. Your competition comes from everywhere and definitely includes retail.

5. **What are the product's unique benefits (that is, how does the product differ from the competition)?**
   There is always something that makes your catalog different and better than its competitors. Merchandise, service, your company's years in business, your knowledge of the targeted segment—whatever it is, list it in as much detail as possible here.

6. **What is the unique selling proposition?**
   Take everything you have said until now and turn it into a sentence or two that summarizes those findings.

7. **What are the credibility factors?**
   It's not enough to say it, you need to prove it. Now that you know your unique selling proposition, how does your company back up this (or these) statement(s)?

8. **What factors in the sociological environment affect the product?**
   What's going on around you that will affect your catalog and its offerings? This is where knowing consumer trends in action and attitude becomes critical.

9. **What factors in the economic environment affect the product?**
   What is happening in the economic arena that affects your marketing? Have competitors become more price-oriented? Are potential customers distracted by events which negatively or positively affect their personal economics? Understand outside financial influences as they might affect you.

10. **Do any legal considerations affect the product?**
    Consider both the direct marketing industry and your particular business.

❖ **TABLE 2-1**
The Positioning Statement Form

3. **What is the consumer perception of the product area as it relates to this product?**
   Consulting firms are viewed as organizations run by people who can't get "real" jobs. Also, some prefer to work only with an in-house staff for several reasons:
   a. They believe they know more about their business than anyone else.
   b. They can't afford consultants or don't think they're worth the cost.
   c. They don't want to lose control over their business.
   d. They don't want to reveal proprietary information.

4. **Who are the competitors?**
   a. Other direct response consultants
   b. Both general and direct response creative shops
   c. In-house marketing/creative staffs

5. **What are the product's unique benefits (that is, how does the product differ from the competition)?**
   Muldoon & Baer provides expertise in all aspects of direct response marketing, from business/mailing plans and market research, to the creation and development of positioning through production, plus advice on fulfillment/customer service procedures and policies, backend analysis, and database design and usage.

6. **What is the unique selling proposition?**

   Muldoon & Baer offers unique expertise in all aspects of direct response marketing, from business/mailing plans and market research, to creative development and production supervision, to fulfillment recommendations/ review, backend analysis, and database design.

7. **What are the credibility factors?**

   a. Our current client list and case studies demonstrating success in the above-mentioned areas

   b. Industry recognition

8. **What factors in the sociological environment affect the product?**

   a. Limited client budgets

   b. A proliferation of direct marketing agency buy-outs and agency consolidations, resulting in concern about stability

   c. A growing number of nonusers exploring direct marketing

9. **Do any legal considerations affect the product?**

   For the industry:

   a. Invasion-of-privacy issues

   b. Postal requirements

   c. Industry self-regulation

   For Muldoon & Baer:

   a. Responsibility for advice

   b. Responsibility for confidentiality

   c. Responsibility for art materials

Example 2.   The second positioning statement (which contains an additional area, the economic climate) is for The Company of Women, a cataloger of products celebrating women.

1. **What is the product?**

   A socially aware catalog of products that will inspire and help women today take control of their lives and respond effectively to their changing roles in society.

2. **At whom is the product aimed?**

   Financially and socially secure females interested in combining their purchasing power with the aim of ending violence against women and supporting women-owned businesses.

3. **What is the consumer perception of the product areas as it relates to this product?**

   The catalog is a communication device, providing potentially desirous products plus a link with a worthwhile endeavor—helping other women.

4. **Who are the competitors?**

   a. Other worthwhile causes, such as public broadcasting, that use the sale of goods to raise funds

   b. Women's bookstores

   c. Nontraditional catalogs, such as Ladyslipper and National Women's History Project

   d. More traditional catalogs targeted primarily at women, such as Seasons and Casual Living

5. **What are the product's unique benefits (that is, how does the product differ from the competition?)**
   The purchase of these products benefits a worthwhile cause and allows the purchaser to buy for herself while helping others. The catalog also celebrates womanhood.

6. **What is the unique selling proposition?**
   Highly targeted, emotionally appealing, largely exclusive product line that provides customers with products that "advertise" their feelings while allowing them to support a worthwhile cause.

7. **What are the credibility factors?**
   a. The fact that The Company of Women is five years old
   b. A growing track record and customer base
   c. The credentials of the staff, directors, and consultants
   d. Audited financial statements and a business plan

8. **What factors in the sociological environment affect the product?**
   The prevalence of violence and discrimination against women. For example, many customers who placed orders during the Thomas/Hill confirmation hearings expressed an emotional connection between what they were seeing on TV and the work of The Company of Women.

9. **What factors in the economic environment affect the product?**
   a. The increase in the number of women working today and the related decrease in leisure time to spend shopping at retail outlets. Many of these women are working out of necessity, not desire.
   b. The increasing emphasis on value, thus making the emotional appeal of the product more important. Lower price points are also more important as well.
   c. The proliferation of catalogs. Positioning, therefore, must fully use the emotional appeal of the product's social agenda to sway purchasers from selecting similar products from competitors.
   d. The difficulty of raising working capital.

10. **Do any legal considerations affect the product?**
    a. Product liability issues may affect merchandising decisions.
    b. Invasion-of-privacy issues, postal requirements, and industry self-regulation may influence the company's marketing program.

A Few More Words on Positioning

Positioning isn't just what you say, it's how you say it. Today, consumers want entertainment with their sales pitch. Catalogs can no longer afford simply to show pictures of products and list pertinent information regarding that product. Consumers view catalogs as an escape, something that lets them take a few safe steps away from their normal lives.

Many catalogers have found effective ways of bringing fantasy into consumers' lives. J. Crew gives its clothing a special aura by using models and location settings that exude an "old money" feeling. Models are trim, young, freckled, and wholesome, and are frequently seen frolicking in settings that show they are leading the good life. The illusion gives readers a sense that if they purchase this clothing, they too will lead this kind of life.

❖ **EXAMPLE 2-1**

J. Crew catalogs feature models who are trim, young, and wholesome, photographed in settings that show them leading ''the good life.''

J. Peterman, who began with a catalog of unusual casual clothing, broke all the rules when he chose to use drawings of his products rather than the more traditional photographs. Most often featuring only one product per page, long copy sets the mood, convincing buyers that this clothing will makes their lives more adventurous and interesting.

❖ **EXAMPLE 2-2**

This page from a J. Peterman catalog shows the distinctive use of illustrations and text to highlight the unique style of clothing offered.

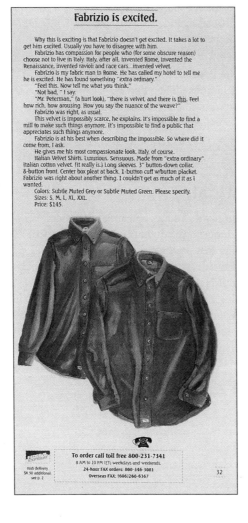

Home-oriented catalogs, which have proliferated in recent years, use fantasy to its fullest advantage with luscious settings that showcase the beauty of the products.

Another catalog famous for its fantasy element is Victoria's Secret, which takes basic undergarments and transforms them, through product design and appealing photography, into highly romantic desirables.

Almost any catalog, consumer or business-to-business, can create an atmosphere of pleasure that meets customers' needs. Bulb catalogs can show delectable gardens; business catalogs can show offices or work environments in which readers would love to see themselves. Achievable fantasy is a strong method of creating a catalog that is distinctive and clearly positions your catalog in a way the customer will remember.

How Much Money Will You Need?

The capital needed to start and run a catalog depends on how big you want your business to be and how long you are willing to wait for results. If you are content with achieving a million-dollar business in a few years' time, your investment can be less than that of someone who wants to have a multi-million-dollar business within, say, five years.

There are two ways to go about building a catalog business:

1. Renting proven mail order lists. This method is usually used in conjunction with a minimum of 100,000 nationally mailed catalogs.
2. Using ads and other means (not lists) to collect names of potential buyers. With this method, quantities printed are usually in the low tens of thousands.

List rental is generally the method of choice for one very good reason. Proven mail order lists that match your market niche are abundantly available (at least during your first growth spurt). The response to these lists is generally high enough to quickly supply the customers you need for a fast return on your investment because those who have already bought through mail order, if satisfied, tend to spend much more than prospects. So, lists provide more people who spend more money faster than accumulating names via print ads.

The advantage of using print ads to acquire names is that it is less of an investment because you won't need to print and mail as many catalogs. Most catalogers who choose this method use small circulation magazines that, like rental lists, overlap the niche of their merchandise mix and positioning. In the ads, they either sell products directly off the page or advertise their catalog for free or for a small fee. The advantage of this method is that it assumes similar thinking between this audience and the one to which you are marketing; hence, readers are likely to be interested in what you have to sell. The disadvantage is that niche-based magazines have smaller circulations and are unlikely to supply the volume of names needed to quickly build your customer list enough to supply the financial resources you need. Another result of having a small number of customer names is that mailings will be fairly small, meaning you will be unable to take advantage of the lower costs associated with volume discounts (in merchandise, printing, postage, and so on).

Using rental lists usually means you will break even by the third year (this is highly dependent on many factors, one of the most important being the margins, or how much to retain, on the merchandise you sell). Running ads to acquire names can take, on average, five to eight years to break even.

Since a five-to-eight year break-even isn't acceptable to most companies, the first method is preferred by new entries and, therefore, the one on which this book concentrates.

If your company already has its own list of customers, this can be a cost advantage (you won't have to pay list rental or magazine insertion fees), but must be approached cautiously. Your company's database may be useful in that it has something in common with your offer, but always remember that these names are not necessarily names of people who are inclined to buy by mail. And proven mail order–responsive customers almost always outperform compiled names (those names that simply have a common element). Test a portion of your company's mailing list, dividing that test into segments if they are available (for instance, one segment may include customers who have bought recently or who subscribe to something beyond basic products or services). Then move forward after you have results to back this decision (see Chapter 11).

Any way you look at it, selling by catalog is costly. Although the return on investment can be substantially higher than in other industries, catalogs require large time and financial commitments (see ''Economics'' in Chapter 15). The degree of commitment depends on the type of business you have or work for.

Corporate Businesses

For ventures that are part of a corporate diversification plan, the usual procedure is to establish a budget through the corporate development or new projects office. As with any potential investment, a business plan must be developed. This plan is reviewed in detail, with the profit potential considered alongside other demands on the corporate financial and personnel resources. Sometimes, corporations elect to purchase existing catalogs rather than develop one of their own.

Entrepreneurial Businesses

For the individual entrepreneur, the process is both easier and harder: Easier because the individual has already made a singular mental commitment to the project, and harder because one person usually does not have the large financial resources available to corporations. The entrepreneur should prepare a three- to five-year business plan and evaluate it as stringently as a corporation would. This plan should be revised every year and used as a planning as well as a money-raising document. If the project appears viable after analysis, from where does the money to finance it come?

◆ **Yourself.** You know your own resources. You may have no investment income or you may have large sums available from other successful business ventures. You must consider what you can afford to invest and the other possible investment opportunities you may need to forgo.

◆ **Friends and family.** Many major catalog companies were started with help from family and friends (one of the most famous being the Horchow Collection). They can often show you where your business plan or presentation is weak and how it can be improved. Even if they do not provide funds, friends and family can be a positive aid.

◆ **Venture capital firms.** Most venture capitalists require proof of a successful business track record. Some of the questions you might be asked are: Have you managed another business successfully? What has your track record been? Do you fully understand the business you are about to enter? What has your monetary commitment to this business been, or what will it be? If you haven't put money in, why should they? Venture capitalists seldom invest in a pure start-up—that is, an untested idea. They prefer to put development money into existing businesses that either have a history of success or show potential for it. If, in fact, they do invest, they will require a strong measure of control, in both active participation and stock shares. Many large banks have a venture capital or merchant banking department. Visit your bank; even if it has no such department, your banker can refer you to venture capital firms and other banks.

But be warned: There is very little venture capital available today, especially for what is generally considered a retail investment.

◆ **Suppliers.** Your prospective suppliers can help in two ways—with credit and with cash. The credit terms they give you can be used to reduce the "up front" cash required in your business plan. In addition, some suppliers have actually invested in new catalogs. But remember, you may become locked into using that supplier even when you no longer think he she is doing an adequate job.

◆ **Banks.** As a rule, banks will lend you money only when you have money (the exception is those that have venture capital or merchant banking departments, as previously mentioned). For start-up ventures, most banks will not, without guarantors or security, lend more than you have already raised as capital. Therefore, it is usually best to go to the bank for funds after you have other financing commitments.

If you cannot obtain a bank loan, investigate the programs of direct loans and bank guarantees managed by the U.S. Small Business Administration (SBA). Under its bank guarantee program, the government guarantees 75 percent to 90 percent of the loan, depending on the loan amount and terms, so many banks look favorably on SBA loans. For specific application requirements, see your banker or visit your local SBA office. Even if you do not need the SBA loan services, their specialists can assist you in writing a business plan and provide you with valuable information on opening your own business. Remember, SBA considers a retail or service business small even if it has annual sales of up to $3,500,000.

Read and/or subscribe to publications that focus on small business. These can be extremely helpful in pointing out the most current ways of finding financial and other aid. For instance, *Your Company,* an American Express publication, devoted the entire back page of their Winter 1994 issue to "Where Women Owners Can Go For Help." Turn to the Resources section at the back of this book for these and other sources of information.

What Physical Space and Equipment Will You Need?

By far, the largest amount of space needed is warehouse space. Offices are often in the same building as the warehouse.

One of the advantages of a catalog is that the catalog is the "store"; you don't need a fancy address or a location in a high-rent district to impress your customers. Your warehouse should be located in a low-rent, low-salary area, easily accessible to both full- and part-time workers. Many catalog operations are located in small towns, where the space is not expensive and part-time labor is plentiful. Good examples of such towns are Hanover, Pennsylvania, home of Hanover House and its many catalogs, and Dodgeville, Wisconsin, practically put on the map by Lands' End. But locate near major modes of transportation and shipping centers.

Remember to keep your warehouse's shipping and receiving areas separate to reduce pilferage (see Chapter 13). Also, for a small catalog, locating office space close to the warehouse allows some people to do two or more jobs at the start.

Another factor to bear in mind when selecting space is future growth. As your catalog business grows, you will need room to expand. Planning for this in advance will keep the cost of expansion to a minimum. If you have carefully shopped for space and the per-square-foot rate is reasonable, try to commit to more space than you initially need.

A viable alternative, particularly in the early state of catalog growth, is to have order entry, processing, and physical fulfillment (all or part of it) performed at an outside service center. Although the per-order costs may be higher, there will be no need for substantial capital investment. And you won't need to worry about the hiring problems generally associated with high seasons. Additionally, the time available for marketing and merchandising will be increased. If desired, these operations can be brought in-house later.

You must also plan for the future when considering equipment, but it is important to avoid overcommitting yourself. If you are using outside creative and fulfillment services, your needs will be minimal—basic office furniture and computers. One excellent alternative to buying computer and copying equipment is to consider leasing. If your business plan calls for quick expansion, don't buy computer hardware that will quickly be outdated.

For furniture, remember that you do not need to establish fancy quarters. Many small businesses wisely choose used furniture for many of their needs. But don't skimp to the point where you endanger health. Ergonomic furnishings that support your health and that of your employees with proper lighting, seating, and computer aids, such as wrist rests, should be considered in balance with what you can really afford.

Should you choose to do your order-taking and product fulfillment in-house, you will, of course, need considerably more equipment. Hints for methods of reducing these costs are covered in Chapter 13, but the following list of materials will get you started:

- Telephone system, including software (may include an automatic call director [ACD])
- Fax
- Order-entry and processing computer hardware and software
- High-speed modem for charge card processing
- Copier
- Bar code readers and writers (labelers)
- Platform dollies
- Pallet jack
- Fork lift
- Small shopping cart(s)
- Order-picking lift
- Racking for bulk storage
- Adjustable shelving/racking (preferably gravity feed) for picking area
- Conveyer
- Packing table(s)
- Tape-dispensing guns
- Automatic scales and shipping software (United Parcel Service, the U.S. Postal Service, Federal Express, and so on)
- Personal computer for data read is connected to the order entry computer
- Postage meter

Don't forget desks, chairs, files, and workstations.

What Are Your Personnel Needs?

The most important resource of any catalog business is its employees. As many established catalogers have found, talented, experienced catalog specialists are rare and increasingly expensive. You really have five options:

1. Use the services of an executive search firm (advertisements for such firms can be found in the direct marketing publications listed in the back of this book).
2. Run classified ads for experienced direct marketers.
3. Train an inexperienced person (preferably from within your own company if this start-up is part of a larger organization).
4. Turn to organizations (such as the New York City–based Direct Marketing Educational Foundation, part of the Direct Marketing Association) and colleges offering direct marketing courses for direct marketing newcomers.
5. Network through suppliers, family friends, and associations.

Table 2-2 shows the job functions for which outside consultants or services can be used in place of internal staff. Some find that using outside sources, while initially more expensive, reduces their overall financial commitment and brings instant expertise. Obviously, many functions can be performed by the owner or other personnel assigned to more than one job. The following sections show how an organization might be structured over time. The job descriptions are not all-inclusive, but are meant to give an idea of the types of functions performed. In a large operation, each job description might be a page or more in length.

❖ TABLE 2-2
Job Functions Chart

Job/Function	Outside Service Equivalent
Merchandise manager (Merchandising vice president) Buyer	Buying services
Creative director Copywriter Artist Production manager	Direct marketing agency or Freelance professionals
List manager	List broker/manager
Statistician (analyst)	Computer service bureau
Marketing manager (marketing vice president)	Direct marketing consultant Direct marketing agency
Envelope opener (order processor)	Fulfillment service
Telephone order taker Telephone manager	Telephone-answering service
Data-entry personnel Office manager (data processing manager) Picker/packer Receiving/shipping clerk Warehouse manager	Fulfillment service
Customer service personnel Customer service manager Operations vice president	Fulfillment service
Bookkeeper Accounting manager/vice president	Accountant Fulfillment/computer service bureau
Finance vice president Personnel manager/vice president	Outside accountant
Attorney	Outside attorney
Owner/president	
Secretary/receptionist/administrative assistant	

Merchandising

The *merchandise manager/vice president of merchandising* supervises and advises buyers, negotiates contracts with major vendors, makes the final selection of merchandise to be offered in conjunction with marketing, and determines merchandise pricing. He or she reports to the vice president of marketing or the owner/president. *Buyers* source merchandise, negotiate with vendors, arrange for backup merchandise, and set delivery terms, and so on. He or she reports to the merchandise manager.

Design

The *creative director* is responsible for the design and graphics image of the catalog. He or she works with the merchandise manager to determine items to be featured and may also supervise production while reporting to the marketing manager/marketing vice president. Reporting to the creative director are *copywriters,* who review merchandise and write copy for the catalog, and *artists,* who are responsible for layouts through preparation of photo separations.

Marketing and Production

The *marketing manager/marketing vice president* has overall responsibility for creating, producing, and marketing the catalog, and reports to the owner/president. The *production manager* is responsible for scheduling, purchasing, and coordinating outside services, such as photography, separations, printing, and lettershop. This person works in conjunction with the creative director and may report to him or her or to the marketing manager/ marketing vice president. A *list manager* projects mailing quantities on the basis of past results and available names, works with outside list brokers to select lists for testing and rollout, and either coordinates with an outside list manager or is in charge of internal list management. He or she reports to the marketing manager/marketing vice president. A *statistician,* or *analyst,* uses historical and current data to project catalog sales, customer attrition rates, and inventory needs. He or she also develops customer segmentation models and reports to the marketing manager/marketing vice president.

Office Services/Data Processing

The *operations vice president,* who reports directly to the owner/president, is responsible for order processing, data processing, fulfillment, customer service, maintenance, and security. The *office manager* or *data processing manager* reports to the administrative vice president or owner and is responsible for all order processing and data-entry staff and their functions. *Envelope openers and order processors* open and batch orders and may check for errors caused by improperly filled-out order forms, missing checks, and so on. *Data-entry personnel* enter order data into a computer or write orders on forms. Both data-entry personnel and order processors may be full- or part-time. The *telephone manager* is responsible for telephone order staff and script and order-form development. He or she also monitors calls. *Telephone order takers* take phone orders, fill in order forms, and may attempt to sell more merchandise. They report to the telephone manager.

Warehouse Operations

The *warehouse manager* reports to the operations vice president or owner and has overall responsibility for merchandise receipt and storage, order filling, and shipping. He or she is also in charge of pickers/packers and receiving/shipping. *Pickers/packers* pick merchandise from shelves in the warehouse and take it to the packing area, where it is packed for shipment. In small businesses, a picker and packer may be the same person. A *receiving clerk* checks incoming merchandise shipments for quantity and quality, verifies vendor invoice data, and forwards the data to data processing or accounting. A *shipping clerk* verifies the order against the shipping label, handles postal meters or manifests, and forwards data to data processing or accounting.

Customer Service

The *customer service manager,* who reports to the operations vice president or owner, supervises the customer service staff and is influential in establishing customer service policies. *Customer service personnel* handle customer requests, complaints, and inquiries received by phone and letter and thus must be pleasant and patient.

Finance

Like other vice presidents, the *finance vice president* reports to the owner/president. He or she is responsible for cash flow, profit-and-loss projections, financial analysis, and banking relationships, and may also be in charge of long-term planning. The *accounting manager* or *controller* is responsible for the accounting staff, accounts payable, accounts receivable, tax reports, and tax filings, and reports to the finance vice president. *Bookkeepers* are responsible for keeping account books and systematic records of transactions. He or she reports to the accounting manager or controller.

Personnel

The *personnel manager* or *vice president* is responsible for finding and training new personnel, salary recommendations and reviews, union relations, employee fringe benefits, and compliance with all federal and state laws relating to personnel and their training. He or she reports to the owner/president.

Legal Affairs

Legal affairs are usually handled by an outside service, except in large corporations. An *attorney* reviews contracts and advises the company on legalities of promotions, FTC regulations, and so forth. He or she may review catalog copy. If the attorney is in house, he or she reports to the owner/president.

Top Leadership

The buck stops with the *owner/president.* In addition to running the entire catalog company, this person must spend time and effort on long-term planning and reports to a parent corporation or investors.

Administrative Support

For a new catalog, the *secretary/receptionist/administrative assistant* can be one of the most important people. A number of catalogs have been started by husband-and-wife teams plus one administrative employee.

Your Overall Organization

With the aid of outside agencies and consultants, very small teams have efficiently performed many of the catalog functions listed here. All team members have, at times, served as order processors, buyers, pickers, packers, and more.

Be sure that, as you interview potential candidates, you comply with all the equal opportunity laws. For information on this subject, write to the Equal Employment Opportunity Commission in Washington D.C., and your state's equivalent organization.

Areas such as list maintenance, merge/purge, printing and photography, and separations are not included in this job title list because, for the vast majority of catalogs, this work is performed by outside services. Finding the suppliers you need is a relatively simple matter. Sources include the Yellow Pages, industry organizations, and trade publications.

Although there is no real rule of thumb, most start-up catalog operations find it advantageous to use as many outside services as possible in the beginning. This keeps financial commitments to a minimum and allows the owners to really learn the business a part at a time.

Initially, consider keeping only marketing and merchandising in house. Turn to experienced professionals for creative, telephone, and fulfillment services. These can be brought in house as the operation and your expertise grow.

If you choose to follow this plan, your operation might look something like the organization chart in Figure 2-1. As a start-up you probably can't, but keep this structure in mind as your company grows.

❖ FIGURE 2-1   **Personnel Organization Chart**

First three months:

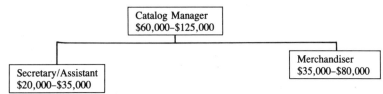

Assumes creative/production, fulfillment/customer service handled by outside source.

By the end of the first year, add:

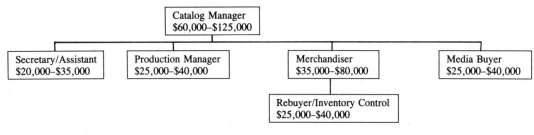

By the end of the third year, add:

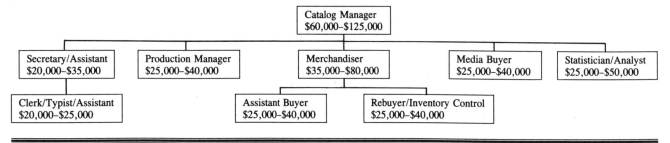

Where Can You Find More Information?

What you need to start a business would take a book unto itself covering every detail. *Brass Tacks Entrepreneur* by Jim Schell is published by Henry Holt and Company and gives an in-depth overview to being an entrepreneur.

Whether you are an independent entrepreneur or acting as one within a corporate structure, you need to be able to anticipate what is coming and think on your feet.

✔ Create an adaptable, strong positioning statement
✔ Assemble your resources skillfully

CHAPTER THREE

❖ ❖ ❖

Knowing the Competition and Your Customer

N ever expose yourself to becoming noncompetitive through lack of information about your competitors. Once you feel you have a grasp of the trends discussed in Chapter 1, you need to understand the competition. The first step in beating your competition is knowing what you're competing with. Too many companies do this in a haphazard way, getting on competitors' mailing lists and noting rather abstractedly any changes they have made in their tactics. This approach is basically useless, because it's hit or miss.

An Updated Competitive Grid

What you need is a regular, consistent method for obtaining and analyzing what your competitors are doing. Use a competitive grid (Tables 3-1A and 3-1B) to clearly outline exactly what your competitors offer their customers. Remember this grid is useful only if it is updated regularly. Try to keep this information in a database, allowing anyone who works on your catalog to update it as information is obtained. Entries should be coded so the manager of the competitive database knows who to talk to regarding each entry.

Market Research

Market research is a very effective method for finding out who your customer is. The information you obtain can show a different customer profile from the one suggested by a customers' buying patterns. It can help you honestly evaluate your service and help determine new product development direction. Even more important, when constructed correctly, it will give you important data about your noncustomers and your one-time buyers.

❖ **TABLE 3-1A**   Competitive Grid as of [date]

Names of Competitors	A	B	C	D	E	F	G	H
Business Overview								
Independent or parent (State catalog name as well as that of any parent)								
Net sales (Can be estimate)								
Percentage of business (Break out if part of larger/smaller company)								
Number of years in catalog business								
0- to 6-month customers								
6- to 12-month customers								
Universe of customers								
Demographics (List age, income, gender)								
Average retail per item								
Average units per order								
Buys per year per customer (How often does customer buy)								
Dollar amount of average order								
Name generation (Source)								
Mailing pattern (Frequency of contact)								
Circulation (# of times per year)								
Health of business (Capsulize known information)								
Overview of offer (Capsulize known information)								

❖ **TABLE 3-1A** Competitive Grid as of [date] (continued)

Names of Competitors	A	B	C	D	E	F	G	H
Rate of growth (Can be estimate)								
Service Overview								
Toll-free order # (Hours)								
FAX order # (Hours)								
Toll-free FAX # (Hours)								
Toll-free customer service # (Yes/no, hours)								
Gift wrap (Type and cost)								
Gift certificate (Cost)								
Express delivery (Time needed)								
Express delivery charges								
Proprietary charge card (Yes/no, cost)								
VIP/loyalty program (Yes/no, type, cost)								
On-line inventory (Yes/no)								
Letter from company (Yes/no, where?)								
Socially-conscious program (Explain, include privacy)								
Guarantee parameters (How long, limited, unlimited)								

❖ **TABLE 3.1B Competitive Grid Example for (Company Name) as of [date]**

Names of Competitors	Alpha City	Baby Knows Best	Cuddly & Cute	D	E	F	G	H
Business Overview								
Independent or parent	Independent	ABC Conglomerate	Direct Marketing Enterprises					
1993 Net Sales $000	$1,500*	$10,819*	$150,000					
1992 Net Sales $000	not available	not available	$125,000					
Percentage of business and/or 1993 sales estimate for individual catalog	100%	10%	$35,700					
Number/years in *catalog* business	4	10	8					
0- to 3-month customers	14,082	27,617	45,701					
4- to 6-month customers	58,394	30,588	113,294					
7- to 12-month customers	12,069	40,837	281,203					
One year as for year ending ( )	48,952 (3/31/94)	99,042 (7/31/94)	440,198 (7/31/94)					
Demo:	86% female, average of 35, HHI$50M, most attended college, infant through 12 year children	Mostly female, affluent, well-educated, 40 Medium Age, $55MHHI	Average age 25–45, $50M HHI, 77% female, families with young children					
Products offerings	Gifts, unusual toys, books, costumes, games	Quality clothing for infants and children, some toys and gifts	Colorful children's clothing: dresses, pants, shoes and more					
Average retail range per item	$12.95–$19.95	$9.98–$29.98	$20–$44					
	1.6	1.13	1.5					
A.O. $	$64	$80	$50					
Name generation	100% direct mail	100% direct mail	100% direct mail					
Mailing pattern	4X per year	Not available	20X per year					
Circulation per year	2 million	4 million	8 million					

❖ **TABLE 3-1B** **Competitive Grid Example for (Company Name)** as of [date] (continued)

Names of Competitors	Alpha City	Baby Knows Best	Cuddly & Cute	D	E	F	G	H
Health of business								
Overview of offer	Educationally-oriented, good mix of product in bland presentation	Classic, easy care, appliquéd or patterned clothes at "value" prices, not service-oriented or highly promotional	Aggressively go for order with multitude of sales facilitators leverage brand extremely professional effort					
Estimated or known rate of growth	48% (Oct. '93 to March '94 vs. Oct. '92 to March '93)	46% (year ending June 94 vs. year ending June 93)	146% (Feb. to July '94 vs. Feb. to July '93)					
Service Overview								
Toll-free order number	7AM to 12PM EST Mon–Fri, 8 AM–10PM EST, Sat–Sun	24 hours a day, 7 days a week	24 hours a day, 7 days a week					
Fax order number	No	24 hours a day, 7 days a week	24 hours a day, 7 days a week					
Toll-free fax	No	24 hours a day, 7 days a week	Not toll free					
Toll-free customer service number	8AM–11PM EST Mon–Fri, 8AM–8PM EST, Sat/Sun	No separate number	Yes, does not state time					
Gift wrap	Free with order of 2 or more items	Not offered	Boxes and cards for $3 per item					
Gift certificate	No	Not offered	Yes, in $5 increments					
Express delivery	No	Not offered	3 and 2 business days					
Express delivery charge	No	Not offered	2 day, $5.75 extra 3 day, $15.50 extra					

❖ **TABLE 3-1B   Competitive Grid Example for (Company Name) as of [date]** (continued)

Names of Competitors	Alpha City	Baby Knows Best	Cuddly & Cute	D	E	F	G	H
Stated standard delivery time	No	7–10 working days	Shipped in 24 hours, received 4–8 business days					
Proprietary charge card	No	No	Yes					
VIP/loyalty program	No	No	Yes, Member, benefits not stated					
On-line inventory	Yes	Yes	Yes					
Personal shopping service	No	No	Yes, toll paid					
Letter from company	Yes, page 2	Editorial intro on page 2	Editorial pages 2,3					
Socially-conscious program (include privacy)	Yes, environmental message	Yes ($5 for name duplication elimination)	Recycling programs, $5 for name duplication elimination					
Other services	Delivery outside USA promoted	Birthday Club	TDD service, Discounts on quantities					
Guarantee parameters	Unconditional	Unconditional	Unconditional					

* Estimate for how income derived (see attached Competitive List Growth).

Note: All examples are fictitious.

Types of Research and When to Use Them

There are two main types of research: quantitative and qualitative. Quantitative research is explicit; it deals with numbers, percentages, and other quantifiable data. The market research form is most commonly used for this type of research. Qualitative research is more esoteric, dealing with opinions and attitudes, but can be very useful if you know how to use it. Direct marketers often use focus groups to obtain qualitative data.

All research should go to four groups:

1. Customers (usually those who order repeatedly during a recent period, say three times or more within three to six months)
2. One-time customers (not true customers, they are often referred to as trial resisters)
3. Nonbuyers (those you have solicited who have chosen not to purchase)
4. Inactives (those who once purchased regularly, but have ceased to do so)

Market research should be planned in the same way that you plan the mailing of your catalog. It should be administered regularly and have a baseline of results with which to match all subsequent efforts. This means one part of the research plan should be dedicated to asking the same questions of different people from the same segment over time. Additional new research should be incorporated into the plan and given its own baseline so you can compare changing attitudes.

Market Research Forms

A market research form can be enclosed with a shipment as a bounceback to customers, be part of an order form, or be designed to answer specific questions about a particular segment of the market (such as inactive customers) and mailed bulk rate. Customers are generally willing to share their thoughts without an incentive (such as a bonus gift). However, if your targeted group is inactive customers or noncustomers, you might offer a discount coupon on future purchases in return for filing out the questionnaire. Some catalogers also find attaching a dollar bill to be highly motivational. In any case, a postage-paid return envelope is mandatory.

The market research form should immediately tell your customers you need their help to do a better job for them. You should explain that any information they divulge will remain confidential and be used only to improve service. All questions should be concise and to the point. Do not ask a question unless you know that you can act on the answer. Make your form specific and don't try to find out too many things at one time. For example, research questions for a catalog of entertainment products might read like the following:

1. To what degree do you participate in the following activities? (Rate each activity from 1 to 5, with 5 being the highest.)
   ____ a. Reading
      ____ books
      ____ magazines
   ____ b. Puzzles
      ____ jigsaw
      ____ crossword
      ____ other
   ____ c. Yard sports
      ____ darts
      ____ horseshoes
      ____ other
   ____ d. Religion
      ____ TV
      ____ radio
      ____ video

        ___ audio

        ___ written materials

___ e. Vacation planning

        ___ video

        ___ brochures

___ f. Home decorating

        ___ video

        ___ TV

        ___ magazines and books

___ g. Home fix-up

        ___ video

        ___ TV

        ___ magazines and books

___ h. Relaxation

        ___ audio

2. Do you own any of the following? If so, how many?
   - ___ a. Videocassette recorder
   - ___ b. Compact disc player
   - ___ c. Audiocassette player
   - ___ d. Laser disc player

3. Has any member of your family purchased music in the last three months? _____
   - a. If so, who? _____
   - b. For whom? _____
   - c. Where was it purchased? _____

4. Have you gone into an audio store in the last three months and left without making a purchase? _____

   If so, what was the principal reason?

   ___ Item was not in stock.

   ___ I was unable to locate the product I wanted.

   ___ I couldn't find anything I wanted to buy.

5. In the music area, what are your greatest areas of interest (on a scale of 1 to 5 with 1 being strong interest and 5 being no interest)?
   - ___ a. Big band
   - ___ b. Blues/jazz
   - ___ c. Children's
   - ___ d. Classical
   - ___ e. Country
   - ___ f. Easy listening
   - ___ g. Gospel
   - ___ h. Contemporary Christian
   - ___ i. Oldies
   - ___ j. Rock
   - ___ k. New Age (relaxation)
   - ___ l. Marching band
   - ___ m. Bluegrass
   - ___ n. International
   - ___ o. Reggae

6. Has any member of your family purchased books in the last three months? _____
   - a. If so, who? _____
   - b. For whom? _____
   - c. Where were they purchased? _____

7. Have you ordered any products from a catalog in the last three months? _____

   If so, from which categories?

   ___ books

   ___ electronics

    ___ children's
        ___ toys
        ___ clothing
    ___ music
    ___ video
    ___ hobbies. Please specify _____
    ___ sports-related
    ___ health-related
    ___ home furnishings
    ___ home-fix up

If no, rank the following categories as to your future (within the next six months) level of interest:

    ___ books
    ___ electronics
    ___ children's
        ___ toys
        ___ clothing
    ___ music
    ___ video
    ___ hobbies. Please specify _____
    ___ sports-related
    ___ health-related
    ___ home furnishings
    ___ home fix up

8. In the last three months, have you wanted to **purchase** a videocassette, audiocassette, electronic game, or another home entertainment software product, and not been able to find it in your local retail store?

   If so, would you consider buying it by mail? _____ Did you feel that the store should have carried it? _____

9. Please indicate your age by checking the appropriate box.

a. Under 18 ☐	e. 35–39 ☐	i. 55–59 ☐	
b. 18–24 ☐	f. 40–44 ☐	j. 60–64 ☐	
c. 25–29 ☐	g. 45–49 ☐	k. 65–69 ☐	
d. 30–34 ☐	h. 50–54 ☐	l. 70 or older ☐	

10. Please specify your marital status.

    a. Single ☐   d. Widowed ☐
    b. Married ☐   e. Divorced ☐
    c. Separated ☐

11. Are you

    a. Male ☐   b. Female ☐

12. If you have any children currently living with you, please list their ages and genders below.

	Age of Child	Male	Female
a. Child #1	_____	____	_____
b. Child #2	_____	____	_____
c. Child #3	_____	____	_____
d. Child #4	_____	____	_____

    e. No children are living at home ☐

13. Please check the box that best describes your level of education.

    a. Attended high school   ☐
    b. Completed high school   ☐
    c. Attended some college   ☐
    d. Completed college (4 years)   ☐
    e. Attended or completed graduate studies ☐

14. Are you currently employed outside the home?

    a. Full-time ☐   b. Part-time ☐   c. No ☐

15. Please check the box that best describes your total family income before taxes.

a.	Under $10,000 ☐	f.	$50,000–$59,999 ☐
b.	$10,000–$19,999 ☐	g.	$60,000–$69,999 ☐
c.	$20,000–$29,999 ☐	h.	$70,000–$79,999 ☐
d.	$30,000–$39,999 ☐	i.	$80,000–$89,999 ☐
e.	$40,000–$49,999 ☐	j.	$90,000–$99,999 ☐
		k.	$100,000 or more ☐

Remember, open-ended questions, while informative, are very difficult to compile into useful information if you are expecting hundreds of responses. Your best bet is to provide multiple-choice questions, which are also quicker and easier for respondents, thus increasing your response rate.

Such confidential information as the respondent's name, address, salary range, and so on, should be requested on the bottom of your form, preceded by a paragraph explaining that the customer need not complete this section. Experience has shown that most people will complete a market research form if they have the option of remaining anonymous. If they do fill out this personal section, allow for some inflation in the salary and deflation in the age.

Since geographic data are becoming more and more important, zip code information should be obtained. If you ask for the zip code only in the confidential area of the form you might not get it. Therefore, place the zip code request within the body of the form. Should the respondent choose to remain anonymous, you will still capture that all-important number.

Keep the form simple and as short as possible. Response is usually poor if a form is too long or too complicated. Make sure it looks professional, is visually pleasing, and is easy to read. Double-space between the lines and use slightly more space between questions. Number each question for ease of data entry.

❖ EXAMPLE 3-1

This form from The Company of Women illustrates the important information to be included when conducting consumer research.

Dear Customer,

Thank you for your recent order. Please take a few minutes to answer the following questions. We are always looking for ways to serve you better and to include items in our catalog that will serve your needs. All information is only for our use in producing a better catalog and will be kept in the strictest confidence.

1. Did you make your most recent purchase from The Company of Women for
   yourself ☐   as a gift ☐

   1a. If you purchased a gift, was it for:
       a family member ☐   a friend ☐   a co-worker ☐   other ☐

   1b. What item(s) did you purchase? (*Please list below*)

   _____

   _____

2. The following is a list of categories featured in our catalog. Would you like to see more, the same, or less of the following types of products in future catalogs?

	More	Same	Less
Security Products	☐	☐	☐
Feminist Products	☐	☐	☐
Helpful Books	☐	☐	☐
Gift Items	☐	☐	☐
Clothing (Tee shirts)	☐	☐	☐
Travel Products	☐	☐	☐
Local	☐	☐	☐
Business	☐	☐	☐
Distance	☐	☐	☐
Products for Infants–5 years	☐	☐	☐
Products for Girls (6–12)	☐	☐	☐
Products for Teen Girls (13–17)	☐	☐	☐

Cause-Related Products	☐	☐	☐
Fitness Products	☐	☐	☐
Home Office Products	☐	☐	☐
Relaxation Products	☐	☐	☐
Clothing Accessories	☐	☐	☐
Decorative Plaques	☐	☐	☐
Health Products	☐	☐	☐
Ethnic Products	☐	☐	☐
Other	☐	☐	☐

3. The following is a list of ways people spend their leisure time. Please circle the number that best represents the amount of leisure time you spend on each of the following activities. If an activity is not listed, please add it to the list.

	Most of My Time				Little or No Time
Reading	5	4	3	2	1
Sports/Activities	5	4	3	2	1
Fitness/Gym	5	4	3	2	1
Gardening	5	4	3	2	1
Cooking	5	4	3	2	1
TV/Movies	5	4	3	2	1
Travel	5	4	3	2	1
Spending Time with Family	5	4	3	2	1
Volunteer Work	5	4	3	2	1
Other _____	5	4	3	2	1

4. How do you spend your daytime hours? (*Please check*)
Working at home/parenting, etc.   ☐ *Skip to 6*
Working at home in a business   ☐ *Answer 5b*
Working at a job outside the home   ☐ *Answer 5a*

5a. Are you employed outside the home?
Full-time   ☐ *Answer 5b*
Part-time   ☐ *Answer 5b*

5b. What type of business do you work at?

_____

6. Which of the following categories best represents your age?
Under 25 ☐   25–34 ☐   35–39 ☐   40–49 ☐
50–59 ☐   60–65 ☐   66–74 ☐   Over 75 ☐

7. What is your gender?   Female ☐   Male ☐

8. Which of the following categories best represents your annual household income before taxes?
Less than $25,000   ☐ $25,000 but less than $50,000   ☐
$50,000 but less than $75,000   ☐ $75,000 or more   ☐

9. Would you like to see more products included in future catalogs that are representative of your field of work?   Yes ☐   No ☐

9a. If yes, in what areas? (*Please list*)

_____

10. In future catalogs, would you like to see products that celebrate women who achieved political notability?   Yes ☐   No ☐

11. In future catalogs, would you like to see products that celebrate women sports figures?
Yes ☐   No ☐

12. What magazines do you read? (*Please list*)

_____

13. What is the very best thing about The Company of Women?

_____

14. What is the worst thing about The Company of Women?

_____

COMMENTS: _____

_____

Thank you!

Sample Size.   You only need a small sample size for market research forms because the data you want is usually trend or attitude data. It is not necessary to have an exact number if 30 percent of the customers sampled are dissatisfied with your order fulfillment and delivery. For example, if 400 people responded to your questionnaire, and 120 were dissatisfied, the following statement would be valid with 95 percent confidence: The percentage of dissatisfied people is between 25.5 percent and 34.5 percent. Obviously, as the number of responses goes up, the limits narrow for the same degree of confidence. For 1,000 responses, the limits would be 27.1 percent and 32.8 percent.

The real sample size problem underlying market research is not with buyers who normally respond well to an appeal for information, but, the difficulty with nonbuyers who have no vested interest in improving your catalog. To obtain a useful number of nonbuyer responses, it is usually necessary to mail many more questionnaires to nonbuyers than you do to buyers.

If you wish to use rented names of other catalogs' customers who have not responded to your offer, you need to go through the same clearance as you would for any other offer (see Chapter 11). This information is advantageous because it allows you to profile attitudes and demographics of mail order–responsive individuals who do not buy from your catalog versus those who do.

Here is an example of how you might schedule market research forms over one year. This should be integrated with any other forms of research, such as focus groups. The amount of research depends almost entirely on your budget. Many catalogers use market research forms rather than focus groups to save costs. This quarterly mailing schedule is a typical example of timing.

Spring
   Subject: Products/lifestyle (could be separate)
   Sample: 1,000 multi-buyers from last 12 months

Summer
   Subject: Why prospects didn't buy
   Sample: 1,000 nonbuying requesters

Fall
   Subject: Customer service
   Sample: 1,000 buyers from last six months

Winter
   Subject: Why second purchase wasn't made
   Sample: 1,000 one-time buyers

Your sample size should be based on receiving 400 to 1,000 responses. Allow for seasonal lag times.

Focus Groups

For this type of research, individuals sit around a table and, guided by a facilitator with a script, discuss the merits of your catalog. The ideal structure for focus groups is to divide them into the previously mentioned four groups (customers, one-time customers, nonbuyers, and inactives) and make sure they are held in more than one city, the average being three cities. Sessions consisting of competitors' customers can also be constructed. Information obtained during these sessions is evaluated and written up in a report prepared by the facilitator. The sessions can also be viewed and/or taped. Sessions generally run from an hour to two hours per group. It can be extremely helpful to the creative and marketing team who cannot attend these sessions to review audio- or videotapes. This can provide better understanding of to whom they are marketing, including the group's likes and dislikes. If you choose to watch through a two-way mirror, you can receive invaluable input from customers and noncustomers alike. If you desire, you can submit questions to the facilitator during the actual session. This should be done discreetly and kept to a minimum, but it does allow you to react instantly to information as it is received.

Market research facilities can be found through references, at trade show exhibitions, or in the Yellow Pages. Often, your facilitator will give a recommendation based on his or her experience.

It is up to the facilitator, working in conjunction with the facility, to find and qualify the attendees. Always bring catalogs and gift certificates to the focus group. Attendees, after talking about your catalog for over an hour, are very receptive to purchase.

Cost, including the facilitator, the attendees (who are paid a small fee), the facility, and the report can run up to $10,000 per session. This does not include any costs associated with those who view the proceedings.

These sessions are best used for direction rather than absolute information. Presenting creative concepts, product mock-ups, and the like can help you refine a program you have already planned. Always remember that, although this input can help you adjust your game plan, it should not, due to the small number of attendees, be the actual basis for the plan.

✔ Collect and continually update competitive information.
✔ Use research regularly.

 ❖ CHECKLIST

CHAPTER FOUR
❖ ❖ ❖

Planning

Great catalogs don't happen in a vacuum. It takes the abilities of everyone on your team to ensure that you create and continually monitor as well as improve the strategy you need to stay on top.

Strategic Planning

Try to incorporate regular strategic planning sessions into your business (see Chapter 15 for a look at the overall business plan). Involving the top people in your organization, these sessions should generally be held off-site so attendees can give their undivided attention to the task at hand.

For your first session, you will probably need two days. The first day should be devoted to brainstorming. All ideas are useful, and you will need a good moderator who is impartial and truly understands your business to keep the conversation on target and the information flowing. The second day it is time to prioritize all the ideas from the previous day and weed out the impractical ones. Don't forget to assign team members to the projects generated from the ideas in these sessions, and establish realistic time frames for assigned project completion.

After you have had your first strategic planning session, try to schedule these meetings quarterly, or at least biannually. It will give you the opportunity to update yourself and your team as to your successes and what still needs to be accomplished. Plus, you will need to add new strategies and tactics that allow you to adapt to new developments, products, and competition.

A typical outline of the material you will need to cover at your first strategic planning meeting might look something like this:

I. Introduction
II. Major Topics
    A. Major company objectives
        1. sales
        2. image
        3. other
    B. How to achieve these objectives
        1. understand the market
        2. status of database
        3. being/staying competitive

        4. increase average order
        5. increase response
        6. increase order frequency
        7. other

C. Definition of "good" customers
        1. sales amount
        2. repeat purchase/loyalty
        3. referrals
        4. interactive
        5. other

D. Methodology for attracting first orders
        1. acquisition methods
        2. policies
        3. products/offers
        4. timing
        5. pricing
        6. tie-ins
        7. other

E. Methodology for converting one-time buyers to repeat purchasers
        1. acknowledgment of customer's place in purchase cycle
        2. products/offers
        3. timing
        4. pricing
        5. services
        6. other

F. How to create a distinctive brand personality
        1. graphics
        2. organization
        3. services
        4. products/offers
        5. "voice"
        6. interactive
        7. social considerations, ethics
        8. consistency
        9. authority
     10. other

G. How to watch, cut, and control costs
        1. catalog
        2. product
        3. operations
        4. overhead
        5. other

H. Making best use of employees
        1. resources
        2. empowerment
        3. training
        4. motivation
        5. communication
        6. company culture
        7. other

I. Leveraging product/merchandise
        1. margins
        2. frequency
        3. current mix
        4. future mix
        5. effect on creative strategy
        6. other

    J. How to use operations as a marketing tool
        1. customer service
        2. VIP clubs
        3. guarantee
        4. stock positions
        5. credit
        6. humanize relationship with customers
        7. departmental interfaces
        8. environmentally sensitive products and packaging
        9. other
    K. Analytical needs
        1. real needs versus desires
        2. costs
        3. impact/real value
        4. other
III. Summary of Session
    A. Identity projects to be addressed
    B. Assign projects to team members with completion dates

Ten Ingredients for Catalog Success

There are lots of things to consider in planning your catalog business, but your first question should be, "What do I need for success?" The following list provides ten succinct points, including obvious and not-so-obvious answers.

Obvious Points

1. **Money.** To start a consumer catalog business that's going to generate millions within a five-year time period, you will need at least $1 million. Not instantly and not all at one time, but you will need it. You'll have unavoidable expenses, such as lists, postage, and inventory. You can cut corners and budget to your heart's content, but if you want to grow your business to $5 million or more, plan on preparing a realistic business plan that shows just how much you'll need and when.

2. **Time.** Running a catalog business is not a hobby; nor is it something that the existing staff of an ongoing business can add to their already-full workloads. Doing something right takes planning and commitment, and that takes time. Allow enough of it.

3. **Distinctive positioning that cannot be copied easily.** Your product line doesn't have to be unique; it just has to look like it is. Take J. Crew, for example. What could be classified as ordinary T-shirts and coordinates is anything but ordinary because J. Crew makes its clothing special through its positioning. J. Crew is the poor man's (or woman's) Ralph Lauren, built on American values, such as wholesomeness and real value. It gets to the root of Americans' desires and needs. The models, copy, and photography locations build a fantasy of casual wealth that seems to say almost anyone can afford this.

    This positioning is different from The Gap's. As successful as it is, The Gap's advertising has been very trendy, its product line eminently copiable, and its value pricing attainable by other stores. Trendy advertising works for a time, but soon the heat cools down. On the other hand, Ralph Lauren, which appears to be J. Crew's inspiration, has an approach that seems to base its claim on a deep-seated American desire: the craving to look as though one was born to old money.

4. **Customer service.** It's hardly news that customer service is now critical to success. You can't just go through the motions, you must have down-to-earth, complete dedication. One of the things that has made Lands' End so successful is its commitment to service. Lands' End didn't build its reputation by simply training its employees to handle calls. It practices what it preaches, telling employees that people are special and that they should treat others the way they themselves are treated at Lands' End. So, when you call this catalog company, the representatives' ingrained response is to treat you like someone important.

5. **Analysis.** If you don't really understand what is happening with every aspect of your business, before you know it, you might not have a business. One of the larger direct marketers is reported to have ten full-time analysts. They don't guess or use seat-of-their-pants marketing techniques to get their points across to prospective and existing customers. They know what those customers want, when they want it, and how they want it. You need to do the same thing on your own scale.

   Is there such a thing as too much analysis? Sure. We've all seen doorstop reports that mean nothing because nobody bothers to read them. Determine the top five reports you want daily, the seven or eight you need weekly, up to 20 you need monthly. How many you need is largely dependent on the size of your business (see Chapter 14).

Not-So-Obvious Points

6. **Flexibility.** What's a great idea today may not be so great tomorrow. If you're flexible, you can build on what you've already established, adapt it for the times, and keep right on growing. If you're locked into one theme, one way of thinking, or one product line, you're probably doomed. Plan ahead by using positioning that can be adapted.

   The Sharper Image is a great example. Here is a business that was built on the motivations of the eighties: grab as many "toys" as you can now and the heck with tomorrow. But this, as we all know, is not the eighties. So, The Sharper Image has expanded its product offering well beyond electronics and toys and dramatically dropped its price points. It's not unusual to see spreads that boast items for $25—can you remember any $25 items in a Sharper Image catalog in the past decade? Recent earnings show this strategy has led to continuing improvements.

7. **Timeliness.** The Old Testament said that to everything there is a season. And that season is getting shorter and shorter. Andy Warhol hit it on the nose when he talked about everyone having 15 minutes of fame, but now you could be talking about product trends. Consumers' attention spans are getting shorter and shorter. They want new products, and they want them now. Keep your offering up-to-date, both in product and creative approach, without losing the basic appeal you attained through your distinctive positioning.

8. **Controlled growth.** There can be too much of a good thing. Collecting customers and not servicing them through product quality and availability is suicidal. But some have done it. Enthusiasm for a hot catalog has made some catalogers forget about the back-end of the business. How much is it costing to acquire customers? How many times are they reordering? What's your attrition rate? Not minding these areas spells disaster.

9. **Disposability of product.** This translates into frequency of purchase, which translates into the ability to leverage your customer. If he or she only needs your product every so often, you are bound to hit a ceiling in sales no matter how great your other attributes are. Build some disposability into your offering.

10. **Database construction and manipulation.** Contrary to what some folks have said, databases are not an old idea currently being rehashed. We simply didn't have the computer capability to target within a list the way we do now. Get to know everything you possibly can about your customer, then use it in a relevant and inoffensive manner. Mailing the same offering to everyone is bad business because not everyone responds the same way. Treat good customers like the gold they are, encourage the marginally good ones to respond better, and drop the dead ones. Come up with special events and incentives that aren't seen every day. Knowing more about your customer makes you smarter when it comes to prospecting, too.

Creating a Time Frame for Catalog Development and Production

First and foremost, you need to know when the different phases of developing and producing a catalog take place. Creative production is most often the primary area for scheduling. A good rule of thumb is to allow 100 days from merchandise selection to "in-mail" for a new catalog. This can be condensed to 30 days for catalogs that are produced regularly by a sufficiently large, experienced staff.

But there's a lot more to creating a catalog than just the glamorous aspect of layouts, copy, photography, printing, and so on. Table 4-1 gives you an idea of a typical schedule for a new 32- to 48-page catalog (obviously, it would take more time for more pages unless additional staff was available). (For a variety of production schedules, see Chapter 7.) This schedule does not assign staff, but assumes that the organization chart outlined in Figure 2-1 (page 44), plus outside resources as needed, would be used. As in most businesses, you will need to do many things at once. A great deal of catalog planning and creation specifics overlap. The areas where this occurs most frequently have been indicated, but even the functions that are not indicated will need to overlap if the catalog is to be completed in a reasonable amount of time. Furthermore, each catalog operation has its own methods, so this time line should be taken only as a guide.

❖ CHECKLIST

✔ Incorporate strategic planning sessions into your business plan.
✔ Allow enough time for every element.
✔ Learn the ten secrets to success and create more of your own!

❖ **TABLE 4-1**
Typical Time Line for Catalog Development

Function	Time Frame
1. Write a business plan. a. Overall program models b. Individual catalog profit-and-loss models c. Cash-flow projections d. Initial inventory costs e. Initial order curves f. Interfacing various models to facilitate "what if" studies g. Documentation for all assumptions made to obtain model	4–6 weeks
2. Plan, attend, and transcribe action statement from strategy meeting.	1–2 weeks (can be concurrent with #1)
3. Establish positioning of catalog in market and set up merchandise parameters.	1 week (can be concurrent with #1)
4. Attend trade shows and markets for merchandise ideas and sampling.	Ongoing
5. Sample merchandise; provide vendors with merchandise information forms (MIF).	1 week (following show/market attendance)
6. Review merchandise and make preliminary selection, allowing for additional product.	3 days (for process only, does not include follow-up time)
7. Follow up with vendors on terms, collection of merchandise information forms, etc.	Ongoing
8. Establish customer service policies.	1 week
9. Investigate fraud and credit card services.	1 week (concurrent with #8)
10. Research telephone order methods (inside versus outside service, which service).	2 weeks (concurrent with #8 and #9)
11. Research fulfillment software and services; install or subscribe.	6 months
12. Research and make *preliminary* decisions regarding mailing lists.	1 week
13. Review commercial monitoring services.	1 week (concurrent with #8, #9, and #10)
14. Determine if items are to be picked up from a previous catalog.	Concurrent with merchandise selection
15. Finalize merchandise selection and paginate.	1 week
16. Send out vendor contracts.	1 week
17. Establish telephone order instructions, policies, and methods.	1 week
18. Accept bids and award contracts, complete with purchase orders, for copy, layout, and computerized art (if using outside services).	1–2 weeks
19. Determine special offers, rebates, and sales incentives to be offered.	1 week
20. Begin creative process: Provide complete information on new and pick-up products to art director and copywriter.	1–2 weeks
21. Begin design and computer production of the order form.	1–2 weeks
22. Begin design and computer production of the cover.	1–2 weeks (concurrent with #21)
23. Send out and receive preliminary bids for photography, separations and printing; cut purchase order for printer.	1 week
24. Begin layouts and copy; review, revise, and complete	2–4 weeks
25. Select models, stylists, hair and makeup artists, locations, props, etc.	1 week (concurrent with #24)
26. Have photography and separations rebid based on layouts; cut purchase orders to selected vendors.	1 week (partially concurrent with #24)
27. Layouts and photo samples due at photo studio.	1 week prior to photography

28.	Art director, photographer, and stylists(s) meet to finalize backgrounds, lighting, etc.	2 days–1 week prior to shooting
29.	Review and make corrections to initial copy manuscripts.	1–2 weeks
30.	Incorporate copy into computer used for layouts.	2 days
31.	Photography takes place.	2 weeks (partially concurrent with #24)
32.	Reshoots are done (if needed).	1–2 days
33.	Send photos, sized to layout, to separator for low-res scans.	2 weeks (partially concurrent with #31)
34.	Incorporate low-res scans into computerized layouts.	1–2 weeks (partially concurrent with #31)
35.	Review random scans.	4–12 days after photography
36.	Proofread layouts with type in position.	1–2 days
37.	Make final corrections to layouts.	4–7 days
38.	Order mailings lists and assign codes.	2 days (concurrent with creative)
39.	Implement customer service policies.	1 week (concurrent with creative)
40.	Merge/purge mailing lists.	1 week (concurrent with creative)
41.	Delivery of merchandise due at warehouse.	1 month before catalog mails
42.	Release order form to printer.	1–3 weeks prior to printing
43.	Release computerized disk to separator.	3 weeks prior to printing
44.	Return merchandise samples to vendors.	1–2 weeks after completion of computerized art
45.	Review composed separation and make corrections.	1–2 weeks prior to release
46.	Review blueprint for order form prior to printing.	1 week before press date
47.	Film due at catalog printer.	1 week before press date
48.	Ship order form to catalog printer.	1 week before press date
49.	Review blueprint from catalog printer.	A few days before press date
50.	Mailing lists, tapes, and format due at printer.	4 weeks prior to mailing
51.	Follow up on the delivery of order forms to printer.	Several days before press date
52.	Follow up on the delivery of lists to lettershop.	1–2 weeks prior to mailing
53.	Press run.	2–3 days, depending on quantity produced
54.	Bindery.	2–3 days, depending on quantity produced
55.	Lettershop, labeling, or inkjetting.	Concurrent with bindery
56.	Mail.	3 days–4 weeks
57.	Obtain mailing confirmation forms (3602s) from the post office.	Day after catalog is mailed
58.	Interpret and analyze lists, merchandise, offers, etc.	3–4 weeks, then ongoing

CHAPTER FIVE

❖ ❖ ❖

Merchandise Development

Every item considered for your catalog should be scrutinized and judged by ten essential criteria. Before you assemble samples from vendors—even before you go into the market to source merchandise—fix all ten firmly in your mind.

A Product-Selection Checklist

1. **Quality.** Does the merchandise you have selected or plan to select reflect your catalog's image? Will respondents be happy with the quality of the purchased item? Since a consumer does not see or touch the merchandise before purchasing it, but relies solely on the presentation of the item in the catalog, it is essential that the merchandise live up to—or, preferably, exceed—expectations. Keeping a customer is even more important than getting one, and feeling cheated quickly turns a good customer into an unlikely prospect for your next catalog offering.

2. **Price.** Is the item in the correct price range for your targeted audience? Consider the budgetary constraints or affluence of the audience you have targeted, not whether you or your friend would be able to afford the item or find it too cheap. For a low-ticket catalog, this could be the opportunity to test your customer profile by offering a few high-ticket items. Conversely, a high-ticket catalog may increase response and attain a larger customer base by incorporating a few lower-ticket items.

3. **Availability.** Is the item made or stocked in the United States? If not, does the supplier guarantee its delivery in time for you to meet your customers' needs? Have you found a backup source for the same item? It is never wise to offer an item if there is any doubt about having sufficient inventory to meet a possible demand, even if that item has the potential to become a best-seller. Customers could ultimately be alienated by unfulfilled orders.

4. **Exclusivity.** Does any other catalog offer the same item? Can you negotiate a similar, but exclusive style, or color? As catalogs become more competitive, exclusivity encourages shoppers to purchase from a specific catalog over competitors that all have the same merchandise.

5. **Uniqueness.** An item may be carried by other mail order companies but not be readily available in the retail market. Uniqueness is the major principle on which the first mail order catalogs were founded. In recent years, this quality may have seemed less important, but this is not true. Despite some element of risk in offering a unique, untested item by catalog, being the first to capture the direct mail market and the demand for a thoroughly different item can reward you abundantly with increased sales.

6. **Vendor cooperation.** Will the vendor offer two- or three-to-one backup—that is, will he or she hold 200 or 300 on your order of 100? This keeps your initial inventory costs down while protecting you from running out of what could become a hot item. Is the vendor easy to reach and fast at supplying samples? Does the company have the manufacturing capabilities to gear up to demand? Will your orders be filled with the same speed as those of large catalogs or retail chains? Will the vendor assist you in determining an honest sales projection until you have a history of your own on which to rely? Have the company's items proven good sellers (for you or other catalogers) in the past?

7. **Photographic potential.** Will the item photograph accurately? Too flattering a photograph can increase return and create dissatisfied customers; a photograph to the product's disadvantage will reduce sales.

8. **Cross-saleability.** Will the product encourage sales of other items offered in the catalog? For instance, if you wish to offer a necklace, does the necklace have matching earrings? Natural combinations such as this can help raise your average dollar order and please customers.

9. **Mix factor.** Are you sampling (locating and getting) too many items of one classification and too few of another? During the selection stage, keep a running tally, by category, of the items you're sampling, so you'll know which areas need last-minute, sometimes frantic, sampling for that perfect item in a category that may be "light" at the time of pagination. This tally also helps eliminate one of the greatest merchandising evils—running a "so-so" product only because it's readily available. (Tally sheets and pagination are discussed in Chapter 6.)

10. **Profit potential.** Will the product provide the sales dollars necessary to pay for the allocated space (see Chapter 6)? Does it have a better than two-time mark-up? In other words, if it costs $10, can you sell it for more than $20? And will the product be one without high returns and breakage—two areas that can dramatically reduce initial profits?

A prime rule in selecting merchandise is don't take anything for granted. Joan Burden Litle, president of The Catalog Connection, tells this classic story:

"We always make sure to test functional products. We tested several dog beds to find the perfect one for the catalog. They all looked roughly the same, but what a difference when our ten-pound weakling actually got on them. One was filled with plastic chips that made squeaking noises when moved, plus it sank down when the dog got on. The noise could be very annoying in the middle of the night. The other stayed poofed up and the dog was not only comfortable but felt like a king. Guess which one we ran?!''

Where and How to Look for Merchandise

Looking for merchandise first requires knowing where to go. There are specific subject shows noted for high attendance and merchandise variety. Besides these, a variety of "revolving" trade shows turn up in different centers around the country at different times of the year. Of course, shows and showrooms are for wholesale buyers only.

Overseas manufacturing and/or sourcing, due to the low cost of goods, has been on the increase. However, due to the complications involved, most catalogers don't purchase from other countries until their companies are at least several years old. (See the "Overseas" section in this chapter.) This section concentrates on domestic purchasing.

Subject Shows

The *National China, Glass and Collectibles Show/Washington Gift Show* is really two shows run simultaneously. It features about 1,300 booths showcasing an international array of mostly china and glass, but also jewelry, silver, woodenware, paper goods, and much more. Located at the Convention Center in Washington, DC, the show takes place every January and July. For more information, you can contact George Little Management, Inc., 10 Bank St., White Plains, NY 10606-1933.

George Little Management, Inc. also sponsors the *Boston Gift Show,* which takes place in March and September at the Bayside Convention Center.

The *New York International Gift Show,* held at the Javits Center in New York City, is the largest gift show of all. In addition to the usual offerings, it contains a craft pavilion, an international section, and the very popular "Accent on Design," as well as sections on "Kids' Stuff" and "Museum Resources." The show is held in January and August, and for many buyers, the January show is the most important U.S. show of the entire year.

The *New York Home Textiles Show,* in April and October at the Javits Convention Center, is also managed by George Little Management. Buyers in the United States and Canada may contact the company for registration and admission information.

Billed as the largest trade show in the world, the *Consumer Electronics Show* boasts most than 1,400 companies exhibiting in nearly 800,000 square feet of space. Product categories include audio, car audio, video, computers and games, telecommunications, and personal electronics. Buyers are also invited to attend conferences, workshops, and special exhibitions. The electronics show is held twice a year—for three days in June (Chicago) and for four days in January (Las Vegas). For more information, you can contact Consumer Electronics Show, 2001 Pennsylvania Ave., N.W., 10th floor, Washington, DC 20006.

Beginning in 1994, the *Mega Show* combined the Premium Incentive show, the Travel Incentive Show (formerly called the MITE Show), and the International Selling and Marketing Expo into one huge show held for three days at the Javits Convention Center, New York City, during the first week of May. Attendees need to present a business card. There is free admission for those who preregister by mid-April; otherwise you pay $15 at the door. For more information, contact Miller-Freeman, Inc., 1515 Broadway, 34th floor, New York, NY 10036, or P.O. Box 939, New York, NY 10108-0939.

The *International Jewelry Trade Show,* the largest jewelry trade show in the country, boasts an international array of 1,600 exhibitors and takes place twice a year in New York City. The exhibition offers the buyer the newest jewelry-store products and services. Note: To attend, you must provide identification showing that you buy fine jewelry at wholesale and sell at retail. For more information, contact Blenheim Fashion Shows, One Executive Drive, Fort Lee, NJ 07024.

Other shows about which you may wish to obtain more information include the *Chicago Housewares Show* (January or February), the *Atlanta International Gift Show* (January and July), the *Los Angeles Gift Show* (January and July) or *San Francisco Gift Show,* (February and August) and the *High Point Furniture and Accessory Mart* in North Carolina (April and October). Check with each show to find out what credentials they require for admission. Some are very strict and won't allow anyone who doesn't have a business license. Others will admit prospective businesspeople if they have a letter of explanation from their attorney or accountant; some will take just a business card.

Merchandise Centers (by City)

Chicago, Illinois. The World Trade Center Chicago is "It." Two impressive buildings consisting of three separate centers house this hub of activity. Standing next to each other are the Merchandise Mart and the Apparel Center. Bring your compass; these two buildings have more than 1,200 showrooms. Billed as the "world's first and largest design center," the Merchandise Mart showcases high-design residential and contract furnishings, floor coverings, lighting, giftware, antiques, and decorative accessories. Both have permanent tenants. On the second floor of the Apparel Center is the Expo Center, which houses temporary exhibits. Besides the Expo Center, the Apparel Center—the host of fashion for men, women, brides, and children—also features a 525-room hotel and fine shops and restaurants. The Expo Center features a variety of exhibits, from gift shows to toy and doll shows. For further information, write the World Trade Center Chicago, 470 The Merchandise Mart, Chicago, IL 60654.

Dallas, Texas.   Touted as "the world's largest wholesale merchandise mart," more than 350,000 retailers from all 50 states and more than 30 foreign countries attend this market. The International Apparel Mart and International Menswear Mart showcase more than 14,000 apparel and accessory lines. If you want furniture, lighting, gifts, decorative accessories, tabletop accessories, gourmet foods, toys, or bed, bath, and linen goods, turn to the World Trade Center and Trade Mart, where you'll find 16,000 hard-goods lines. In addition to the many product choices available, the Dallas Market Center offers special programs to facilitate international business, including translation services, trade seminars, and more. For information, contact the Dallas Market Center, 2100 Stemmons Freeway, Dallas, TX 75207.

Los Angeles, California.   Contained in a one-million square-foot complex are 300 of "the country's most respected and recognized showrooms." You'll find 13 floors of furniture, gifts, linens, decorative and holiday items, collectibles, china, glassware, jewelry, and much more. There are seasonal events, such as the January Gift and Home Furnishing Show, and informative seminars, such as Bridal Business, Collectibles, and Floral Design, plus design seminars on fabric and wallcovers, designs for lifestyles, and the psychology of color/color trends. Write for a directory or information from L. A. Mart, 1933 S. Broadway, Los Angeles, CA 90007.

Atlanta, Georgia.   Atlanta also has many opportunities for sourcing merchandise. The Atlanta Merchandise Mart and Atlanta Gift Mart have more than 300 showrooms combined. The Merchandise Mart is filled with gifts, decorative products, furniture, carpets, lighting, gourmet items, and so forth. The Apparel Mart shows distinctive lines of apparel and accessories. For more information, write to Atlanta Merchandise Mart, 240 Peachtree St., Atlanta, GA 30303.

New York City.   The whole city of New York is a showroom! The following list is just a small sample of merchandise categories with the approximate locations or building addresses. Remember, the best way to find that extra-special best-seller could well be to knock on as-yet-undiscovered doors.

- ◆ **Women's clothing.** New York is noted as the fashion center of America, and Seventh Avenue and the surrounding garment district, with its thousands of showrooms, are deservedly famous. A few of the largest showrooms are at 1407, 1410, and 1411 Broadway, and 485 and 530 Seventh Avenue. (For women's clothing directories, refer to the industry publications listed in the "Resources" section of this book.)
- ◆ **Children's clothing.** Try 112 West 34th Street.
- ◆ **Toy center.** Go to 200 Fifth Avenue and 1107 Broadway (two buildings connected by a skybridge).
- ◆ **Fur district.** This is in the area between West 28th Street and West 30th Street, from Avenue of the Americas to Eighth Avenue.
- ◆ **Trimming district.** Between West 36th Street and West 37th Street, Avenue of the Americas and Seventh Avenue, this district is great for baubles and beads,

feathers and ribbons, and other distinctive accessories you can make into unique jewelry, belts, and so on.

♦ **Jewelry districts.** The main district is on West 47th Street between Fifth Avenue and Avenue of the Americas. Another section runs a block in either direction from the intersection of Canal Street and the Bowery (a street), located diagonally across from the Manhattan Bridge, near Chinatown.

♦ **Men's clothing.** Go to 1290 Avenue of the Americas and the Empire State Building, located at 350 Fifth Avenue. Also check the lower west Thirties, between Fifth Avenue and Avenue of the Americas.

♦ **Gifts and decorative accessories.** Try 225 Fifth Avenue and 41 Madison Avenue.

♦ **China, linen, and imports.** Walk along Fifth Avenue from 23rd Street to 34th Street.

Aside from these general areas, there is the Jacob K. Javits Convention Center, which holds expositions and trade shows, such as The International Kids Fashion Show, the Midyear Variety Merchandise Show, the Spring Home Textile Show, and many others. While at the shows, don't hesitate to talk to the distributors of name brands who may not be showing at a booth. These representatives frequent trade shows and can offer a variety of information on products and product ideas.

Secrets of Successful Buyers

Merchandising is the most critical element to catalog success. You must constantly offer fresh product, at good prices, while maintaining acceptably high margins. This means you need to know what it takes to be a superior buyer.

♦ **Be snoopy and persistent.** Ask vendors annoying questions like "What have you got under the display table?" (at a show); "What are you hiding in the back room?" (at the showroom); "What's new that no one else has yet?"; and "What's selling well for my competitors?" Note: Don't always believe the answer to this last question. Some vendors are scrupulously honest, and some have a regrettable tendency to exaggerate the potential of an item they want to sell you.

♦ **Take a good vendor to lunch.** Instead of always expecting vendors to treat you like a valuable asset, remember that you're dependent on them, too. And maybe the next time a really great item comes in, you'll be the one notified first.

♦ **Be fair.** Keep in mind that vendors are in business to make money, just as you are. Be tough, but also negotiate differences in a reasonable manner. You'll soon discover which vendors appreciate a fair share and which ones will try to take advantage of you. Get rid of the latter ones; there's rarely an item worth that price.

♦ **Find exclusives.** Talk to vendors about creating a product especially for you. Since many of them already have their own manufacturing facilities, you'll be surprised how willing they might be to make small adaptations to an existing product, thereby changing it into something that is unique to your operation. If you don't order in large quantities, it's unlikely that you will be able to maintain an exclusive, but it is possible that the vendor will be willing to grant a certain time period in which you alone can offer that product. And don't always accept the quantity the vendor says you need to order to create that exclusive item. Not only is this negotiable, but other vendors may have much less stringent requirements on minimum quantities.

♦ **Recycle.** Don't forget that what once was old can be new again. All things have life cycles. Items that were exciting years ago but went out of style might be ready for reintroduction. This is true for past best-sellers that have lost their steam, too. Regularly revisit your old best-sellers to see if they can be reactivated.

◆ **Enforce quality control before the fact.** Quality control isn't something you enforce only after receipt of the merchandise. It must be in effect from the very beginning. The direct marketer who offers an item that doesn't last will find that customers don't last either.

◆ **Don't be shy about stealing ideas from your competitors.** In essence, they've done the testing for you. If you see a particular item repeated frequently, if selling space has enlarged, or if an item has moved to a high-selling area of the catalog (such as the inside front cover), it's usually a safe bet that you're looking at a winner.

Send for the product and hope the manufacturer's name and location are on it. If not, take a picture (clipped from your competitor's catalog, of course) to one of your loyal vendors (the one you took to lunch last week) and see if he or she knows who manufactured it. The vendor will help not only out of kindness, but because it's good business. The more successful you are, the more you'll be likely to buy from him or her.

But don't get totally carried away—make sure that your catalog maintains its own integrity and individuality by using competitors' products sparingly. Read every magazine and newspaper you can get your hands on. Take note of mailorder ads that feature the same merchandise again and again. Many direct marketing firms never run an ad on an item until it's proven itself in a catalog.

Look for "What's New" columns, frequently on products discovered or offered by retail stores. Regional magazines and home sections in newspapers are great for this.

◆ **Be alert to when a product has run its course.** Following a competitor's lead by offering the same or similar merchandise or a vendor's recommendation, is an excellent strategy as long as you're quick enough to understand when an item has "had it."

◆ **Make friends with other catalogers (competitors or not) and compare notes.** One of the best things about the direct marketing industry is its openness. While this has been curtailed somewhat in latter years, catalogers still trade information. Even though their product lines may not be similar, an exchange of information can help catalogers pinpoint trends and become better merchants.

◆ **Shop retail stores.** Always keep a pen and pad at hand to jot down sources and relevant information. Be polite when the department manager asks you to leave. Direct marketing is serious competition for retail, you know.

◆ **Check the labels in your own clothes.** If you like it enough to buy it and wear it frequently, so might someone else. See what that particular manufacturer is currently offering. Sometimes you're your own best "market research."

◆ **Ask friends.** Have you seen an item a friend owns and loved it? Find out who made it or where it came from. Again, it could lead to newer and better things. Also, a friend's creativity sometimes can create a product that never existed before. Spotting seashells artistically arranged in a basket once helped create a best-seller with a bonus: The consumer really had no way of "guesstimating" the cost of finding all the shells and putting them into the basket. This provided an item that gave great markup, and, even more important, consumers felt the product was well worth the price because either they didn't live where shell collecting was possible or the "repackaged" product saved them the time it would have taken to collect the shells themselves. Even if they had collected them, they might not have had the idea of arranging them so attractively in the basket.

A product with a hard-to-identify price is called a "blind item" and is critical to success because it will almost always carry more margin.

♦ **Think creatively.** What an item is originally does not dictate what it has to remain. Long johns with flaps were children's pajamas. It took the clever people at Hanover Direct, many years ago, to turn them into practical loungewear for adults and a best-seller in their time.

♦ **Treat your time like the premium it is.** Schedule visits to shows with visits to showrooms located in the same city or area. Don't believe that you can do more than you can during the day; make sure you leave enough time at appointments to get the information you need from a vendor. And don't schedule appointments too close together; it's important to be on time. Sundays are exceptionally busy days for shows; be aware that you will not get the vendor's undivided attention. Use Sundays for mentally sorting out the booths you want to come back to later in the week.

♦ **Have lots of stamina.** You can always spot experienced buyers by their comfortable shoes and oversized, but not too big, tote bags. The buyer who brings home the best-sellers knows that footwork is the main ingredient of success. There is no such thing as a good show or a bad show, only a show that wasn't worked properly. Even those shows that at first appear to be dismal (where nothing obviously stands out as a fresh new item) can be the change to unearth a gem of a product. Walking the shows, inspecting every booth, whether or not it initially looks promising, is the way fresh new products and best-sellers are discovered. Many novice buyers don't realize that it's often not the established booths (the ones generally located on the lower floors) that hold the real gems. It's those tiny little companies on the top floors—inconvenient to all, but chock-full of products.

Try to make the time to walk a show twice, and go a different direction each time. The way to really see merchandise in a booth depends on the direction from which you approach—coming at a booth from a different direction can help you spot items you simply didn't see the first time.

There are many well-known buildings that hold a cornucopia of merchandise and are especially reliable for that last-minute item you need to fill out a spread. But it's the unknown buildings that often control the "finds." Allow some time in your busy schedule to pick a building you haven't been in before and start walking. Knock on unfamiliar doors. Ask questions. If a particular vendor doesn't have what you're looking for, he or she may know who does.

But, before you start what quite often turns into a very long and tiring day, eat a good breakfast. Trite as it sounds, it will be the fuel you need to keep going, because it's unlikely that you'll find the time to stop for lunch!

♦ **Be prepared to explain who you are.** Besides plenty of business cards, carry current catalogs and lists of trade credit references with you to leave with new vendors. You have to pass their scrutiny, and giving them a broader idea of what your catalog is all about can help them guide you to the right product.

♦ **Think U—unique and useful.** Think of what you yourself might need in your everyday life. Generally, you'll find that the two requirements for an unknown product are uniqueness and usefulness—something different that solves a unique need or desire. Not being able to easily clear cobwebs out of the corner of a room caused one buyer to take an ordinary feather duster and add an extended wand. This was the beginning of another best-seller.

♦ **Know your sales history.** Naturally, there is nothing as beneficial as having results with which to guide your selections. Regular analysis of individual products, product categories, price points and effects of seasonality should be provided to the merchandising department by those doing the analysis. This can come from the marketing department or may be done by the buying staff. Either way, no buyer should enter the market without full knowledge of what has sold well and needs to be increased in similar type, and what has sold poorly and needs to be avoided (see Chapter 14).

A Merchandising Success Story.   Marshall Marcovitz, president of The Chef's Catalog, discovered what to most people would seem to be an ordinary plastic bristle brush. Using a true merchant's ingenuity, Marshall changed the bristle stiffness and the color, creating five different brushes for five different uses. That plain brush, repackaged on vegetable-shaped cards complete with clever instructions, evolved into five use-specific brushes that clean celery, potatoes, mushrooms, and carrots while saving the nutrients. The fifth even desilks corn!

How to Select and Care for Samples

It is usually best to make your final product selection from merchandise samples: Photographs or manufacturer's sales sheets can be misleading as to color, size relationship to other products, quality, and so on. However, it is sometimes better to review a photo or advertising flier on a product before sampling it. Many manufacturers and their representatives are willing to let you sample their merchandise at no cost. Don't hesitate to ask for free samples. But not all samples are free, and excessive sampling can quickly add up to a considerable sum of money, especially when such costs as "in and out" freight, unpacking and repacking labor, and recording time are added for each sample.

Return unwanted samples as soon as possible. Keep the samples from the products you have selected to check against the actual inventory when it is received. This will help ensure that you are sending your customer the same product you reviewed and determined worthy of offering in your catalog.

Keep a Complete Sample Log

Unless otherwise specified, vendors expect free (called "memo") samples to be returned in the same condition in which they were sent. Free samples that are damaged or misplaced may no longer be free; you may have to pay for them. Therefore, once samples arrive, they should be kept in a secure area and treated like the valuable investments they are. Keep the outer cartons as well as any inside packaging, the warranties, instructions, and so on, and be prepared to return items promptly. Too often, samples are carelessly opened and, in general, poorly handled.

Keep a log of all incoming and outgoing samples. One method is to use the letter you sent requesting the samples as the form for your log (see Figure 5-1). Photocopy the letter before mailing it, alphabetize copies by vendor, and place the copies in a ring binder. If you prefer to do this on computer, simply adapt this same system to your database of suppliers. Be sure to keep the information up to date and make follow-up phone calls on merchandise that is not received promptly. Log the dates of the phone calls to use later to evaluate vendors' reliability.

Always Use a Merchandise Information Form

Merchandise Information Form (MIF) is initially sent to manufacturers or left with them at trade shows or in their showrooms for items you are strongly considering for upcoming catalogs. The information on the form is used to prequalify a vendor, but it has many other uses too: to make the final merchandise selection; to clarify prices or questions

---

ABC Catalog Company
123 Main Street
Anywhere, USA 00000
Telex or Fax #(000) 000-0000

To _____ Date _____
         (manufacturer/importer/distributor name)

Your product _____ is being considered for inclusion in our
catalog _____. Please furnish _____ samples at once
       (name, season, year)   (quantity)
for possible photography use.

Product description _____

Your style no. _____

Color _____ Size _____

Cost _____ Retail _____

It is understood that, if not used, the sample will be returned to you and, if used, will be paid for in accordance with the price and terms on the accompanying Merchandise Information Form.

Please follow these instructions:

   1. Label each sample with the vendor's name, style number, and cost.

   2. Mark the outside carton "SAMPLE" for _____ Catalog.
                                         (season)

Thank you for your cooperation, and we hope to have a profitable relationship.

– –

For catalog company use only.

    Date item received _____

    Date item returned _____

    Date item sent to photographer/agency _____

    Date item returned from photographer/agency _____

---

about a product during pagination; to check against the vendor contract; and, later, to supply needed information to artists and copywriters. The thoroughness and speed with which the form is filled out are good indicators of a vendor's business behavior.

But be aware, no one likes to fill out forms, so this is an area to which you should plan to devote plenty of time to follow-up.

Filling Out the Form.   Start by adapting Figure 5-2 to meet your individual needs, then preprint it (or incorporate it into your computer) with your logo. Here are step-by-step instructions on how to fill it out.

   1. Fill in Section A with the name, season, and year of the catalog in which you are considering offering the merchandise (this is much faster if programmed in a computer). Next, indicate the period for which you wish prices guaranteed (verified by the vendor in section D). Have the manufacturer or vendor fill out the rest of the form.

   2. Note that in section B the manufacturer of the item may not be the sales representative. Also note that the form specifically asks vendors whether they supply free samples. The information requested on samples will help keep track

❖ **FIGURE 5-2**
Merchandise Information
Form—Long Version

ABC CATALOG CO.   Our Catalog No. _____
123 Main Street   Promotional Period ___ to _____
Anywhere, USA 00000
(800) 000-0000

A. Your product, listed below, is being considered to be featured in _____
    _____ during the period from _____ to _____.
    In order to make our final decision and develop strong copy for your product, we must have
    COMPLETE and ACCURATE information. Please complete this form and return it IMMEDIATELY
    to the address shown above.

    Incomplete information will not be considered.

    Product/mftr no.: _____   Item Name: _____

B. MANUFACTURER   SALES AGENT

        Name _____   Name _____
        Address _____   Address _____
        City _____ State _____   City _____ State _____
        Tel ( ) _____ Zip _____   Tel ( ) _____ Zip _____
    Principal _____   Principal _____
    Our orders should be sent to Manufacturer _____
                                        Sales _____
                                        Other _____
                                                        (Specify)
    To trace shipments, contact _____
    Will you furnish us with free samples? _____
    If not, specify charge per unit $_____
    How do you handle returns? _____
    Prior approval required?   Yes _____   No _____
    Return to _____

C. PRICING INFORMATION

        Suggested retail price $_____
        Usual mail order retail $_____
        Range of actual national retail prices   From $_____
                                                  To $_____
        Wholesale cost (before discounts) $_____
        Catalog/advertising allowance _____% $_____
        Quantity/discount _____ pcs. _____% $_____
        Net wholesale cost $_____
        Payment terms (include any discount) $_____
        Our catalogs are active for six months from issue date.
        a. Will your item be available for this period?
                        [ ] Yes   [ ] No
        b. Will you maintain your price for this period?
                        [ ] Yes   [ ] No

        Lead time on reorders _____

D. SHIPPING INFORMATION

        F.O.B. point _____
        What freight allowance is made? _____
        Master Pack: Quantity: _____ Carton: _____ Dimensions: _____
    Length: _____ Width: _____ Height: _____ Carton weight: _____
    Individual product carton size (specify each dimension) _____
    Individual product shipping weight _____
    Is this carton shippable/mailable? _____
    If not, can you provide shippers? _____
    At what cost? $_____

E. PRODUCT DESCRIPTION

Product Country of Origin _____

Fabric Country of Origin (if different) _____

Is this product imported?   [ ] Yes   [ ] No

Colors available _____

How long has the item been on the market? _____

Dimensions of products L _____ W _____ H _____ Depth _____ Diameter _____

If electric, is it UL-approved? _____ Fiber content _____

Vat-dyed? _____ Sanforized? _____ Machine wash? _____

Hand wash? _____ No iron? _____

Fabric care recommended _____

Size equivalents P ( )   S ( )   M ( )   L ( )   XL ( )   XXL ( )

If European sizing, state U.S. equivalents _____

Description of item (also include descriptive advertising material and be as specific as possible):

_____

_____

_____

_____

If item or part of item is gold-plated, specify:

_____ Karat   _____ Gold   _____ Gold-plated   _____ Electroplated

F. DELIVERY AND AVAILABILITY

Shipping time required from receipt of our original order _____

Lead time required on reorders _____

Can you drop-ship to customers? _____ Additional charges _____

What is your normal on-hand supply? _____

Is this an item you will be continuing? _____

This item will be available from _____ to _____

If you can grant us exclusivity, state dates: From _____ to _____

Does the manufacturer carry liability insurance?   [ ] Yes   [ ] No

If so, is vendor's protection provided?   [ ] Yes   [ ] No

Limits of insurance carried: $_____

Carrier _____

G. PHOTOGRAPHIC ALLOWANCE

If two black-and-white photos are not available or suitable, will you allow a credit for photography?

$100.00 for black/white _____ $150.00 for color _____

Authorized signature _____

PLEASE SIGN SELLER'S WARRANTY

This merchandise conforms with all laws, federal and state, as to labeling, brands, and so on. We agree to indemnify against any claims arising from violation of trademark, patent, or similar law, or from damage or injury to person or property caused by a defect.

It is understood that the commitment made above and the terms and conditions on the back of this form constitute an agreement for the promotion period indicated.

Signature _____ Date _____

Title _____

SEND ABOVE DATA AND COMPLETED FORMS TO:

ABC Catalog Company
123 Main Street
Anywhere, USA 00000

ADVERTISING AIDS

Please return with completed forms any catalog sheets, descriptive materials, and so on that will enable our layout and copywriting staff to do a better job in presenting your product. You are most knowledgeable about your own merchandise, its special features, uses, and so on, and we solicit your suggestions and comments.

of sample costs. Knowing the return policy will eliminate such problems as vendors refusing to accept returned samples without an authorization number for items that will not be offered in the catalog.

3. Section C will give you valuable insight into the current retail and mail order price structure. It will also serve as written confirmation of advertising allowances.

4. Section D requests the costs of freighting the item to your warehouse. The weight and size of the carton must be known to allow for proper warehousing of products. By knowing the cost involved in using the vendor's reshipable cartons, you can determine whether it is more cost-efficient to purchase your own shipping cartons.

5. Section E requests the product information needed for copywriting. It also serves as written confirmation of the particular benefits of the product, which, most likely, have been verbally discussed.

6. Section F provides essential information on the timing of orders. It also addresses the need for vendors to carry liability insurance on their products.

7. The last section requests financial assistance to photograph the vendor's merchandise. Not all vendors will agree to this, but it doesn't hurt to ask, and the dollars go directly to your bottom line.

8. The warranty will help protect you from possible consumer lawsuits arising from a product sold in your catalog, but it is not meant as a substitute for a contract (discussed in the next section). See information regarding liability insurance in Chapter 16.

9. The last paragraph restates the need for any sales material the vendor might have relating to the product. As the copy says, no one knows a product better than the vendor. This paragraph also reinforces the fact that this is not just an information form, but an agreement.

You'll want to customize this form to your own needs. For instance, a food company would need special FDA requirements met, shelf life of the product, ingredients, seasonings, and so on. Environmental companies need to know if the product consists of recycled materials and uses harmful chemicals in the processing.

Condensing the Form.   Due to the difficulty of getting manufacturers and vendors to fill out the long-version MIF, some catalogers choose to create a smaller version and use it in the preliminary product selection. However, this does not replace the longer version, which contains elements critical to the final decision process. This shorter version, with further adaptations, can also act as the information needed by your creative team once the product has been chosen. For an example of how you might condense the information form, see Figure 5-3.

Using a Merchandise Criteria Form

Another tool for running a product objectively is a merchandise criteria form, such as the one shown in Figure 5-4. This can be used to help determine whether specific items should be offered on a per-product basis. Using the categories shown in the figure, fill in the value of the product in question on a scale of one to five (five being the most valuable). Multiple that value by the weight you have assigned to that particular attribute. For example, in the figure, profitability has a value of 25 percent. If the product under consideration rated a five in profitability, you would have 5×2.50 for a score of 12.5. Do this for each category and add up the scores for the product. Be sure to adjust the categories and their respective weights to reflect the needs of your catalog.

❖ FIGURE 5-3
Merchandise Information
Form—Condensed Version

ABC CATALOG CO.
123 Main Street
Anywhere, USA 00000
(800) 000-0000

Our Catalog No. _____
Promotional Period ___ to _____

A. CATALOG

Issue: _____ Time period: _____

B. PRODUCT DESCRIPTION

Item name: _____

Product/mftr. no.: _____

Article no.: _____

Retail price (be specific as to what is included, eg, set of 4, in the price): _____

New? _____ Exclusive? _____

Availability? _____

C. SELLING POINTS

1. Write a brief statement of what you believe is the *single most important selling benefit* of the product or service.

_____

_____

_____

_____

2. List additional benefits in order of importance.

_____

_____

_____

3. List product features; be as specific as possible in describing product.

_____

_____

_____

_____

_____

4. Specify size/dimensions of product.

Height: _____ Width: _____ Length: _____ Depth: _____ Diameter: _____

5. List colors and other options being offered.

_____

_____

_____

Additional comments/information:

_____

_____

_____

Signature _____ Date _____
Title _____ Company _____
Phone _____ Fax _____

❖ **FIGURE 5-4**
Example of a Merchandise Criteria Form

Product description: _____

Projected order size: _____

Targeted customers: _____

Must meet the following minimal guidelines:

a.   Shipping cost not to exceed _____% of sales price (fill in % that is right for your catalog).

b.   Appropriateness to targeted customers and prospects

	Weight (%)				Value				
Profitability	25	0	1	2	3	4	5	×	2.50
Cross-sell potential	15	0	1	2	3	4	5	×	1.50
Uniqueness	12.5	0	1	2	3	4	5	×	1.25
Quality (value/image)	12.5	0	1	2	3	4	5	×	1.25
Inventory requirements	10	0	1	2	3	4	5	×	1.00
Merchandise fit	10	0	1	2	3	4	5	×	1.00
Availability	5	0	1	2	3	4	5	×	0.50
Reorder potential	5	0	1	2	3	4	5	×	0.50
Photographic clarity	2.5	0	1	2	3	4	5	×	0.25
Space needed to show properly	2.5	0	1	2	3	4	5	×	0.25

0 = lowest, 5 = highest

Scores: 0–20   Unacceptable product
            21–30   Re-evaluate; other considerations
            31–40   Add to catalog
            41–50   Sure to be a winner!

Pointers for Working with Vendors

Vendor-Selection Checklist

The most important quality to look for in a vendor is the right product, and the vendor who has it may suddenly seem irresistible. But before you let your infatuation with a particular product overshadow your business sense, ask yourself the following questions.

1.   **What are the minimum-order requirements?** Stocking too much inventory of an unknown product can prove painfully inefficient. If your operation is a small one, can you negotiate an arrangement that will allow a minimal inventory investment? If you're new in the business, have you made it clear that you are sincerely committed to this venture and that adaptability now will help ensure bigger orders as you grow? Consider making this latter promise a formal commitment, since more vendors have heard many unfulfilled promises.

2.   **How willing is the vendor to return or exchange merchandise?** You can usually sense the way a vendor feels about the goods offered. Does he or she play up the quality of the goods and the fact that this quality is backed by the company? Your contract with the company will give you the right to return unsatisfactory goods. But it is much better to deal with a vendor about whose products you are confident, and with whom merchandise return will be only a remote possibility.

   Beyond unsatisfactory goods, you will sometimes invariably take more stock than you actually sell. Work with your vendor to determine upfront what you will be able to return, if not for immediately reimbursed funds, then for future credit.

3.   **Will the vendor offer backup?** Can you place a small initial order with a guarantee that two to three times that number will be available to you if you need it? Clothing manufacturers find it difficult to offer backup, as a particular style or fabric is often available to them for only a short period of time, but hard-goods suppliers are often able to provide this valuable service.

4. **Does the vendor offer advertising allowances?** Be sure to get base prices before you ask this question. Some manufacturers have been known to say yes after adding the advertising allowance to the base price. If you don't know the base price and are unfamiliar with the ethics of the company, you may think you're getting a good deal when you're not. Advertising allowances can run anywhere from 3 percent to 15 percent off the base price.

   Manufacturers sometimes require that the company's name be listed in the copy block for their product. Be certain of details before writing the copy; it is disappointing to lose a promised advertising allowance due to ignorance of the specific conditions under which it was promised. And weigh the value of the discount versus "advertising" the vendor's name to your competitors.

5. **Is the vendor willing to give you a photographic allowance?** Alternatively, can the vendor supply a color transparency of the product? Some manufacturers allow a credit of up to $150 per item to photograph their products for a catalog. It may seem like a small amount, but considering how many photos are needed for a catalog, even small amounts can add up to a significant sum. Other vendors offer an existing photograph of the selected product.

   It is often better to take the allowance rather than the actual photograph. Supplied photographs may not fit with the creative image of your catalog and are best used for products that would require extensive set-up if you were to do them yourself. This is especially true if the product requires an outdoor setting that does not match the season in which you are shooting the catalog. For instance, a basketball hoop for a swimming pool would be difficult to shoot for a catalog produced in winter in the Midwest. You may also wish to take a vendor's photo if the use of a model is required; vendors sometimes have excellent in-use photos that will help add to the product's sales.

   To be on the safe side, you may wish to ask for a duplicate transparency or make a copy (with the vendor's permission) for yourself. Be sure to return the original in good condition to show that you can be trusted to care for any future transparencies you may require. And understand any penalty you may incur if you are unable to return the original photograph.

Knowing Your Cost of Goods

Margins, the profit you retain on the sale of merchandise, will make or break your business. A few points difference can add or deduct hundreds of thousands of dollars and will definitely influence the speed with which you recover your investment.

As a rule of thumb, a general merchandise, middle-priced catalog will strive for an overall cost of goods, including the cost of the freight in, of 45 percent. This is more difficult than it sounds, because you must not only maintain margins for yourself, but balance this with fair, competitive pricing. One method of doing this is incorporating exclusives into your product line, be they "blind" items, as discussed earlier, or products you manufacture yourself.

Cost of goods is not the same as mark-up. Mark-up is the percentage an item is increased from its cost. A two-time mark-up of a product costing $10 would be $20. The same item's cost of goods is approached from the other direction, meaning it's 50 percent of the retail price. Margin is the difference between the cost of goods and the sale price.

Another term with which you should be familiar is *keystone*. This means "to double." So to keystone an item is to double its price.

Because margins affect the price points offered in a catalog, some catalogers choose to position their catalogs as offering "low, low" prices. This is generally at the sacrifice of profit per product, but users feel this can be made up in volume because customers will likely respond at a higher rate if they know they're getting a bargain. What margin you take depends on your positioning and the effect on your bottom line.

Of course, the higher your order volume per product, the lower your cost of goods should be, thus increasing your margins. This is an area you should regularly renegotiate with your suppliers.

The Cost of Freight In

This area is too often overlooked by those starting in the catalog business. This cost will depend on product weight, type of packing, quantity shipped, and so on, and can make or break the profitability of a particular product. Most catalogs put this expense into the overall cost of the product, as this helps ensure that all major costs associated with an individual product are used in determining its true profitability.

Freight to the customer is not part of this equation. This expenditure is generally covered through the shipping and handling charges passed onto the customer (see Chapter 13).

Contract Negotiations

Negotiating the price of merchandise and hammering out the terms of a contract require tact, diplomacy, common sense, and a real understanding of how a contract should be structured. Remember: (1) Get everything in writing, preferably in a form contract; and (2) make sure that all papers are signed by the vendor and in your hands before you place an order. The actual terms and conditions of purchase may vary, but the reverse side of the contract order should cover these major points:

1. **Price.** The order must be filled at prices not higher than those specified in your contract. Also, the vendor must hold on the price even if the quantity ordered eventually varies upward or downward. The price should include duties, commissions to representatives, excise taxes, and any other taxes.

2. **Quantity.** You should receive the quantity you ordered, not more or less. If the quantity received is greater than the quantity ordered, the vendor must agree to allow overages to be returned at its expense.

3. **Delivery.** Since timely delivery is critical in mail order, the vendor must make delivery within the time specified in your contract. A vendor who has delivery problems must inform you in writing of the last possible delivery date, at which point you have the right to reject the new delivery date, cancel your order, and hold the vendor accountable for any and all damages.

    One of the alternatives you may wish to consider is having the vendor/supplier ship the merchandise directly to the customer.

4. **Warranty.** In addition to all warranties that are expressed or implied by law, the vendor must promise that each item will
    ◆ be suitable for the use intended.
    ◆ be free from defects that could create a life-, health-, or property-threatening hazard.
    ◆ be suitable for use; manufactured; labeled and packed for shipment in accordance with all applicable federal, state, and municipal laws and regulations; and registered under these laws and regulations.
    ◆ not infringe on anyone else's right, trademarks, and proprietary rights in general.
    ◆ possess all performance qualities and characteristics claimed by the vendor or product advertisements. The contract must assure you that the vendor has filed continuing guarantees with the appropriate referral agencies under all applicable federal statues. The control should also guarantee that the product does not violate any federal, state, or local statute, rule, or regulations, and that you will be supplied with all current warranties for the merchandise you purchase.

5. **Defective or nonconforming merchandise.** Merchandise that isn't "as advertised" by the vendor should be returned for refund of the full purchase price, repaired or replaced by the vendor, or repaired at the vendor's expense. The vendor must pay for all costs incurred in packing, shipping, and transporting the merchandise in both directions.

6. **Indemnification and damages.** The vendor, not the cataloger, should be held responsible for any claims, lawsuits, damages, judgments, and expenses (including those of attorneys) that might arise in connection with a product sold through the catalog.

7. **Insurance.** Require the vendor to supply you with a current certificate of insurance that also insures you for any losses or damages for a five-year period following the delivery of merchandise.

8. **Termination for default.** You can, in writing, terminate the whole or any part of an order if the vendor fails to make delivery in the time specified, fails to perform in accordance with the contract, or become insolvent or the subject of proceedings under law.

9. **Underwriters Laboratory listings and other approvals.** When it is required by law, vendors must provide you with approvals and ratings of their merchandise from testing or rating institutions, at their own expense.

10. **Inspection and rejection.** You have the right to reject any merchandise that does not fit the specifications of your order. Shipping of unspecified merchandise is considered a breach of contract. You can either return the merchandise at the vendor's expense and risk for full credit of the order price, or require the vendor to replace the merchandise at no cost to you. You can also sue for damages on the rejected goods and cancel any unfulfilled part of an order.

Consult your attorney for the exact wording to be used in your contract. And, remember, a lawsuit is never a substitute for dealing with a reputable, honest supplier.

One additional point: The contract should be sent to the vendor prior to issuing purchase orders. Contracts cover terms such as price and, as previously pointed out, clarify details. Purchase orders address such details as quantities actually ordered and specific due dates. Try not to issue a purchase order (which commits you to purchase) until you have a contract that formalizes the understanding between you and the vendor.

Private Labeling: Benefits and Problems

As consumers have become more and more value conscious, retailers and catalogers alike have responded by lowering prices, often at the expense of their margins. One solution to overcoming this reduced margin problem is to manufacture your own products. JC Penney, for example, has 75 percent private-label merchandise. But it is obviously not the only one. Spiegel, in 1993, attributed its improved sales to an emphasis on value-pricing and more private-label merchandise. And, according to a study published in *Catalog Age* in December 1990, 30 percent of catalogers responding to the survey intended to begin private-label businesses.

For example, assume it costs $10 to manufacture a blouse. If the manufacturer sells the blouse to retailers or catalogers for $20 they, in turn, may sell it to consumers for $40 (assuming all parties are keystoning, or doubling the costs of goods) and realize a 100-percent gross margin. If, however, the cataloger becomes the manufacturer, thereby bypassing the middleman, the cataloger stands to realize a substantially greater gross margin of 300 percent.

Private labeling, though, is not without potential problems, as manufacturing your own products may mean a greater commitment of resources, including the staff time it takes to generate ideas and coordinate product development efforts, the larger minimum quantities that may be required, and the increased upfront costs that you'll have to shoulder directly. You must also take time to develop clear policies to ensure that you protect your design rights.

In evaluating your decision to begin a private-label business, don't forget to weigh the value of the brand names you may now be offering against what will undoubtedly be a lesser-known brand (yours). For instance, in 1990, Eddie Bauer launched a $1 million ad campaign to promote consumer awareness of their private label.

Another advantage of private labeling is that the product is yours exclusively. This can be especially beneficial if your catalog has a unique niche and if it's difficult to source products that fit this niche. The Company of Women, a catalog of products that make women feel good about themselves, develops over 25 percent of its own products. However, Melinda Little, the company's president, warns of the potential pitfalls:

> I've been amazed at the success that we, as a small cataloger, have had in the area of product development. The margins we've begun to realize as a result have helped our bottom line tremendously. Nevertheless, we have made some grievous errors in judgment that have cost us thousands of dollars that we could ill afford.

Overseas Sourcing

As mentioned in the section on domestic manufacturing, overseas product sourcing is generally not initiated during the first year of a catalog operation. The driving forces behind exploring the world for product are unique products, higher margins, and exclusivity. Of course, there are also negatives to this form of product sourcing. But let's look at the positives first.

Advantages.   Lower tooling costs mean you can have the mold (or pattern) for your product produced less expensively than in the United States. For instance, tooling that might cost $50,000 here could run only $20,000 in the Far East.

There are also fewer quantity requirements. You may have to commit for only several thousand pieces, as opposed to many thousands of pieces in the United States. Asia is especially lenient on this point, but this varies from manufacturer to manufacturer. Those that are used to dealing with large volume buyers, such as discount chain stores, are rarely receptive to producing a custom-tooled product in a quantity of only a couple of thousand.

Disadvantages.   Overseas manufacturers generally require an irrevocable letter of credit both for first orders and as an ongoing policy. And these manufacturers will not ship until they receive such a letter. This can translate into a large cash outlay before you actually receive the inventory. Cash is tied up for a minimum of 30 days (during shipping time). As part of this letter of credit (LC), consider having the manufacturer ship you 100 samples for final approval before you have him or her manufacture the entire quantity.

Time can also be a negative factor. Shipment is almost always by ship because air freight, except for very lightweight items, is cost prohibitive. As already mentioned, however, small items can be shipped by postal service speed post or companies such as DHL for arrival within four days.

Depending on the country, the exchange rate can be quite volatile. But it's possible to get prices guaranteed for up to a year at a fixed exchange rate and fixed cost if rates do not shift too wildly. (This depends on what you are able to negotiate.)

Quality control can be a serious problem also. One of the reasons you are going overseas, remember, is to save on the cost of goods so you can have higher margins. This profit can easily be lost if the quality is unacceptable. Quality assurance controls may not exist in the country where your manufacturer operates. You can overcome this problem by writing your own quality control procedures and ensuring there are checks and balances throughout the whole process.

One way to watch for quality control with foreign companies mirrors the primary method you use with domestic vendors—only work with those with proven reputations for top goods. Get references and check them out. Try to find references from sources other than the manufacturer themselves, such as freight forwarders, agents, and other catalogers (more on agents in the following sections). Your agent can check where the product is being manufactured. You'll want to check where else products are being sold; you don't want a competitor to be selling the same products. Reputable companies, if they send defective merchandise, *will* take it back. But, remember, almost everything is shipped by sea, so the time it takes to get your original order and send it back, and reship it to you could add up to close to a season—something no cataloger can afford. (So, again, only work with trustworthy sources and hire a well-qualified, equally reliable agent.)

Kenneth J. Ellingsen, president of merchandising at LWI Holdings, Inc., suggests that one of the reasons for poor quality control is the lack of understanding by the manufacturer as to how the product will be used and sold in the United States. He tells the story of how kitchen timers were being sourced in the Far East by one company. Product samples and packaging were all approved, and packing requirements (how many items to a case and how many cases to a master) were determined. However, the manufacturer, without informing the buyer, felt it could jam a few more products into each case, thereby saving costs on the boxes. The timers were meant to hang from blister packs on a store rack. When they arrived, the blister packs were crushed beyond use and all had to be repackaged. The problem was the foreign company had never seen racks with products hanging on them, so it had no concept of how this product was going to be displayed. Ken now spends, as he puts it, "considerable time with the agent, telling them where the product is being sold, who will be buying the product, why the quality specifications must be met and why it must be packed as designed." Ken also thinks it is important to have your agents visit your business once a year to work with them first-hand in the environment in which the product is being sold.

The Importance of an Agent.   One method of attempting to control the problems of overseas sourcing is to hire a knowledgeable, reputable agent. One of the duties of an agent is to inspect merchandise before it is shipped. A good agent is also on the spot as your product is being manufactured. He or she is essential for handling all of the documentation and paperwork required. Although the country customs office determines what taxes you need to pay on individual products, the freight forwarder handles all paperwork. This can vary dramatically. Leila Griffith, a catalog merchandiser based in Atlanta, who is familiar with overseas buying says, "Taxes are different on every item; for instance, items as similar as men's and women's gloves will be taxed at two different rates." Freight forwarders also follow up on your orders, making every attempt to see that you receive delivery when you expect it.

Finding an Agent or Freight Forwarder.   Agents represent you, help you in sourcing merchandise, and consolidate details for you. Freight forwarders facilitate the process after the merchandise has been sourced, seeing that products are correctly distributed. Your main sources are trade publications, the foreign trade commission and export boards, and the Yellow Pages. Almost all countries have foreign trade representatives in major cities; you can find them in the Yellow Pages. Note that councils and boards will give you a listing of freight forwarders and agents by name, but they will not make recommendations. Others have booths at the major trade shows; some even exhibit at direct marketing industry conferences. Agents may also be found through freight forwarders, who are good references for agents you consider. Be prepared to wait for information. Those at the booths will note your interests, then determine who should see your request. This takes some time, plus the time it will take for those companies to get back to you. One example: A request for information left with a booth in August 1993 was filled in March 1994. Ken Ellingsen lists the following as characteristics of a good agent:

1. Speaks fluent English, as well as the language of the country with which you are dealing

2. Has an export license

3. Has dealt with American-based companies before and can offer trade references

4. Has or had direct marketing clients and understands the ramifications of delays in shipping, as well as quality issues

5. Is well connected in the field of merchandise you are pursuing

6. Has negotiated exclusives with manufacturers in the past

7. Is a good negotiator, period.

Start-up with Overseas Vendors.   If you wish to source product overseas, you'll need to know where the shows are. Information on trade shows are generally found in trade publications at foreign trade councils, or export boards (additional sources are listed in this chapter and in Resources at back of book). Send for literature on the show and determine if it matches up with the type of product you are sourcing. Ken Ellingsen recommends an invaluable source, the *Directory of Associations,* a two-volume set found in any good business library. It lists virtually all trade associations in the world. Simply call the association that is relative to your product and ask for show literature.

Arrange to meet with an agent, who will be essential for more than just translation; he or she will also follow up on all the details entailed in the buying process, such as ordering inventory based on your forecast or samples. The agent must also handle the packaging, including instructions or written information that goes with your product(s). (You write the instructions in English, he or she prints and inserts them.) An agent works on commission, usually 5 percent to 12 percent of the cost of the merchandise.

The first phase of overseas sourcing is generally to find a source for products that are already manufactured but give you the previously listed benefits of unique product, cost, exclusivity, and, when possible, minimal inventory commitment.

The second phase may be to manufacture your own products. Once you have a reliable, well-versed agent, you can rely on him or her to find potential manufacturers. Your agent will need a mechanical drawing and prototype, which you must have done by a qualified engineer (or the equivalent) in the United States. If this is a patentable idea, get patents both in the United States and abroad. After your agent takes your prototype and drawing to the manufacturer he or she has located, samples can be made. Tooling will be undertaken when you are satisfied with the final product.

Differences Inherent in Different Countries' Practices.   Of the two major buying regions, where do you go first, Europe or Asia? Be aware that in Europe laws vary from country to country as to the country of origin. This means that you may be buying something you believe is manufactured in one country, but in reality it is manufactured somewhere else. One story is of a company determined to find a "German-craftsmanship" product. Believing that they had done so, representatives were less than pleasantly surprised to find the item on one of their trips to Taiwan. The German item, because it did not have to be marked with the country of origin, was sold in Germany but was actually manufactured in Taiwan. The cataloger naturally constructed a much better deal with the Taiwanese manufacturer than it had with its German "distributor."

Understand that conditions change quickly. China is currently besieged with inflation and raw material shortages. Taiwan has a high labor rate and a shortage of factory workers.

Most buyers agree that Europe is the fashion and decorating center, a mecca of ideas. But the Far East is where the manufacturing bargains are. As with most things, it is probably best to have a combination of both.

Backup Vendors

Once you've found the perfect product, negotiated an ideal contract, and established an excellent relationship with the supplier it would be nice if you could sit back, relax, and wait for orders to come in. Then, magically, each one would be filled. This is not necessarily the way it goes. One reason is that even the most trustworthy vendors can have problems.

One item placed in a catalog turned out to be an overnight best-seller. The vendor was reputable, personable, and always did everything in her power to keep to the letter of the contract. Unfortunately, the warehouse burned down. (Note: This is often given as a half-kidding, not-so-funny excuse, but in this case, it was an all-too-real disaster). The vendor frantically tried to have more goods manufactured quickly and delivered by air freight, but without luck. Orders kept pouring in, and there was no product to fill them. This was a painful lesson in how valuable a backup source can be.

As you are finding a source for a product, make note of other suppliers who carry or can manufacture the same products or ones similar to those you are likely to run in your catalog. Although it is impossible to find backup sources for every item, it is possible for many. It is up to you whether or not you tell a vendor that you plan to use him or her only as a backup source (using backups is a common occurrence, so vendors will not be surprised). Request all the other information you normally get from a prospective source, including how much inventory the vendor has available at any given time and the lead time for orders. Keep this information on record for emergencies, and you'll greatly increase your chances of never being caught without inventory on a best-seller.

In some cases, a backup vendor can also be your main vendor for a different product. However, to better control inventory and avoid the unnecessary cutting of additional purchase orders, use common sense in limiting the number of vendors with whom you regularly do business.

Drop-shipping

The term *drop-ship* is used when the product is actually shipped from the supplier's warehouse directly to the customer. Orders are sent from the cataloger to the supplier for filling.

There are several advantages to this method of handling merchandise:

◆ Because you do not take inventory on products that are drop-shipped, your inventory costs are reduced and you do not have overstock problems. If sales are weaker than projected, you need not worry about how to dispose of leftovers.

◆ Drop-shipping is more convenient to you on certain kinds of merchandise. Oversized or monogrammed items are ideal for drop-shipping, because they are extremely expensive items to send. Large furniture, which could take an enormous amount of warehouse space if stocked in significant numbers, is often shipped directly from the manufacturer to the customer.

◆ Monogrammed items can be personalized in a great many ways, most of which take a wide variety of equipment. When monogramming is left to the supplier, the cataloger is saved the expense of purchasing the necessary equipment.

Of course, there are disadvantages to almost everything, and drop-shipping is no exception:

◆ Drop-shipping can be very costly. The manufacturer often charges a dropship fee to cover the time spent filling the order and passes on the shipping charge. These charges are almost always more than they would be if the cataloger filled the order because he or she would likely realize cost efficiencies from the overall shipping operation. And these costs are often too high to pass on to the customer. Therefore, the additional amount is often added to the cost of goods, resulting in reduced sales. Alternatively, it can be absorbed by the cataloger, but this will probably result in decreased margins.

◆ Experienced catalogers may wish to undertake a package delivery analysis to accurately determine whether or not their drop-ship sources are truly more or less costly. Help for doing this can be obtained at no charge from your carrier representative.

◆ You lose time. Not only is there the additional step of sending the order to the drop-shipper (although this can be expedited via fax), but there's the time spent following up on individual orders. And the customer can get the order later than if you had stocked the item in your own efficient fulfillment center.

◆ You can't use bouncebacks. It is unusual for drop-shippers to include your advertising material in outside orders (and you want to be sure that they don't include any of theirs). Therefore, you lose the potential of a valuable profit center from your own offers and/or from offers which you charge others to insert. Even if the drop-shipper agrees to include the material, you can't, without regular monitoring, be certain the materials were actually inserted.

◆ You give away your merchandise sources. Since drop-shippers most often use their own cartons or shipping labels, smart competitors can order an item to discover its source.

♦ In all cases, evaluate what it would cost you to perform the fulfillment in-house against what it costs to have it done by individual vendors. Don't choose drop-shipping because it appears easier. Look carefully at the cost efficiencies involved, remember how valuable prompt service is to your customer, and determine the pluses and minuses for each possible drop-ship product.

♦ You lose control. Depending on the interface between your warehouse and your vendors, you may or may not be able to provide your customers with instant (on-line) inventory status. And, to a degree, you must take your vendor's word for when items were actually shipped.

❖ CHECKLIST

✔ Create and follow a product-selection checklist.
✔ Know where the trade shows and merchandise centers are.
✔ Learn and practice the secrets of successful buyers.
✔ Use your sales history to guide your sourcing and selection.
✔ Control the cost of sampling through discipline and accurate records.
✔ Enforce the use of merchandise information forms.
✔ Create and use a merchandise criteria form for borderline products.
✔ Create and use a vendor-selection checklist.
✔ Always monitor and control your cost of goods.
✔ Always monitor and control your cost of freight in.
✔ Do not work without a tight and beneficial (to you) vendor contract.
✔ Find and hoard backup vendors.
✔ Evolve to private labeling and overseas manufacturing to ensure profitable growth.
✔ Use drop-shipping sparingly.

CHAPTER SIX

Merchandise Selection

The final selection of merchandise is made in the course of planning what products actually go on the pages—a process commonly referred to as *pagination*. Some people prefer to select merchandise for one page at a time; most prefer to visualize the merchandise as it will look on two facing pages called a *spread*. Because the profit from a catalog is manipulated and controlled by what is offered on a page or spread basis, it's the bottom line—profit—that should determine which items you select from the samples you have gathered. This section tells how to paginate for maximum profitability.

Preparing for Pagination

The physical process involved in setting up for pagination begins with assembling all samples and proceeds as you organize these samples into likely pages or spreads.

At this point, you have already requested and assembled samples of at least three to five times the number of products you plan to run in the catalog (see Chapter 5) and kept a log, by manufacturer and item requested, of samples with the date and quantity received. Next, tag each item with the cost, anticipated selling price, advertising allowance, and any pertinent details, such as "Limited quantities available" or "Exclusive to us" (see Figure 6-1). Then, set up tables and shelves with the merchandise. Allow one large folding-type table per spread or two spreads, depending on the number of items you plan to offer per spread. You also may wish to reserve one table as a general workspace. These tables are in addition to those on which you now have the merchandise displayed, because the products must move from one table to another.

You may wish to push a few tables against the wall or a partition in order to hang clothing, wreaths, or wall decorations. Additionally, you will need wall surfaces on which you can pin photos of pick-ups (the physical products would be positioned on tables beneath the pinned photos).

To help you locate products quickly as you get ready to place them in their spreads, display as many similar products together as possible. For instance, if you have several kinds of wallets, put these together. This will also allow you to see all product choices per category at a glance.

As you paginate, you can begin to consolidate the remaining merchandise in less space, thus continuously freeing more tables for pagination. Don't actually remove rejects from the room. Put them under the tables or in their own special sections. You may find, as you progress, that what seemed like a reject actually fits well on a particular spread. But be careful about using a reject just because it's there. The most common legitimate reason

❖ **FIGURE 6-1**
Merchandise Identification Tag

Product Name _____

Style No. _____

Manufacturer _____

Cost _____ Selling Price _____

Advertising Allowance? _____ Photo Allowance? _____

Extra Shipping or Other Comments _____
_____

for reinstating an original "throwaway" is that it complements a strong product in such a way that it offers potential add-on sales.

You may also wish to have a rolling file cart filled with vendor sheets, filed alphabetically, on hand. The merchandise tags will have the most important information quickly at hand to help in your "run/no-run" decision. Because most pagination meetings are held in a warehouse or some large area, having additional information handy can save you running back and forth to your office.

Using a Theme

There are two main types of catalogs: (1) high-density, directory types, and (2) lower-density, theme catalogs. Generally speaking, the higher-density catalogs paginate by category, and the lower density catalogs paginate by theme. The idea behind a theme is to create a visually pleasing environment, often color-coordinated, into which the customer feels comfortable stepping. Themes also provide the opportunity to put similar items together, assisting customers by showing an attractive way to decorate their home or mix and match clothing.

❖ **EXAMPLE 6-1**
Domestications uses vivid blues and a complementary decorating scheme in an inviting manner so customers want to reproduce the look.

❖ **EXAMPLE 6-2**   J. Crew uses bright reds and a special occasion
to tie together previously unrelated items.

❖ **EXAMPLE 6-3**   The high-density approach of Ross Simons's catalog
displays products by category rather than theme.

Determining the Number of Items per Page

The product density per page should be driven by the revenue needed for each page in conjunction with the catalog's overall positioning. Probably the most common density for a general gift catalog is 5.5 photos per one $8\frac{1}{2}'' \times 11''$ page. But within those 5.5 photos, there can be significantly more stock keeping units (SKUs), because products may have color and/or size choices. Additionally, one photo may carry more than one product with its corresponding copy.

Generally speaking, when you first begin a catalog, you opt for as tight a product density as possible. Because no one can predict winners at the outset, this helps provide enough product choices to help assure profitability. As you get better at knowing what will sell, you can increase the space allocated to best-sellers. The sales from these products should allow you, if you deem it appropriate for your positioning, to lessen the density.

Williams-Sonoma, whose Catalog for Cooks has long been in a digest format, chose not to increase its product density when it increased the catalog to a more traditional $8\frac{1}{2}'' \times 11''$: Both versions feature approximately 4.5 products per page. The assumption here is that Williams-Sonoma has merchandising expertise to support this lower density and feels that the ability to use larger photos provides the sales increases needed to pay for the space allocated. All reports say that the new size format has been highly successful.

But don't assume light density is the only way to go. Some catalogs, especially those whose platform is value, will opt for high density, putting as many products on a page as possible. When using high density, the catalog usually is categorized rather than themed.

Checklist of Important Pagination Factors

- **Photographic potential.** Although photographic potential is one of the criteria for selecting an item in the first place, it is sometimes forgotten during pagination.

- **Color.** Your catalog should attract the potential customer visually. When selecting merchandise, remember to plan color themes within the catalog to hold customer attention and invite page turning. Consider the season when selecting both color and merchandise, and be sure colors complement each other.

- **Complexity factor.** Products that have a multitude of features can sometimes require a great deal of photographic and copy explanation. Carefully evaluate whether the space that must be allocated to properly explain the product will reap the necessary sales.

- **Position.** Historically, areas of pull in catalog sales are (in order of strength):
  1. front cover
  2. back cover
  3. inside front cover
  4. inside back cover
  5. center spread (where the catalog breaks)
  6. around the order form

  This, however, is not cut and dried. What products are run on these pages naturally will affect how strongly customers respond to the pages.

- **Cost of goods.** Products should have acceptable profit margins, and consideration should be given to cost-offsetting factors, such as advertising allowances and freight cost (especially if you are torn between two similar items).

- **Freight.** This is especially important if you're using a postage-and-handling chart. This chart does not allow for extra heavy and bulky items, the extra cost of which you must either absorb or pass on to the customer.

Paginating Areas of Pull

Inside Front Cover

Generally, pagination starts with pages 2 and 3, also called the IFC (inside front cover). These two important pages should set the stage for what is to come. The products, graphics, and copy must not only grab customers' attention, but also indicate the type of merchandise you offer and the price points at which it is available.

Since the IFC is one of the strongest selling areas of the catalog, be sure to include several items that have shown strong sales in the past or that instinct tells you will become strong sellers. Color is especially important here, because a consumer who loses interest at this point probably will not continue to look through the book.

Another alternative, generally used by more established catalogs, is putting a feature editorial in this area. This approach is better reserved for catalogers who have a history of best-sellers strong enough to pay for editorial space that does not generate direct sales. Companies such as Lands' End that have historically made extensive use of editorials also have established a brand name they reinforce with this type of editorial support. However, recently even Lands' End, with some notable exceptions, has devoted more space to selling and less to editorial.

Most catalogers feel that the IFC is a good place for a small letter from the people behind the company. It gives the reader an opportunity to understand why the catalog exists and why they might want to identify with this particular catalog. Keep the letter short, punchy, and timely. Don't use this space, which is scanned quickly, to tell your life story. Tell customers and potential buyers what's new at your company (say, faster shipment) and/or what new products or product categories are in this particular issue (don't forget to tell them the page[s] on which they can find these great new items).

If your catalog is 64 pages or more, you may also want to consider placing an index in this area. Time is precious and catalogs of greater length can, with the help of an index, assist customers in locating specific needs. Furthermore, customers who have scanned the catalog quickly can, by using this index, locate that product they passed over but now have decided to purchase.

❖ **EXAMPLE 6-4** Lands' End devotes pages 2 and 3 to telling the story behind its knitwear and includes an index for quick reference.

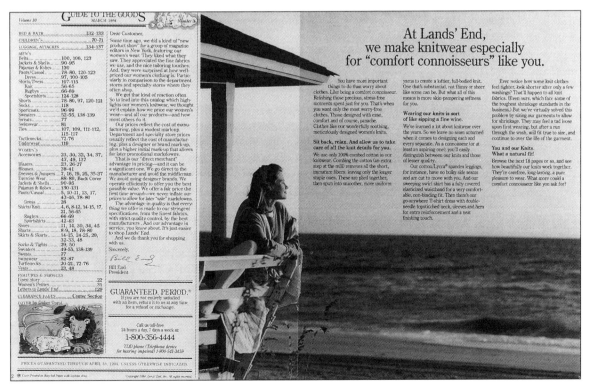

❖ **EXAMPLE 6-5**
Coming Home, a Lands' End catalog, showcases the people responsible for its products' features.

Meet the people who put the features in our Coming Home products.

If you've been on our mailing list since the beginning, we've now sent you anywhere from ten to thirteen Coming Home catalogs.

You've probably glanced at the cover of each one of them. Thought, "Gee, pretty cover." Then flipped through the pages, stopping to study a photo here or there. Maybe reading a little or a lot of what we've written. And then, you may have pulled out the order blank or gone to the phone to order one thing or another.

If so, you probably think of us as the "voice" you hear in the catalog. Or the operator you've talked to. Or maybe you think of us as people who take nice pictures of bedrooms.

What you may not think about is the army of people across the entire country, in fact, around the world, who actually make the products you buy from us.

People like Peggy Crews, a veteran of 27 years on the line in the hemming area of the Abbeville, Alabama plant that makes our sheets. (An amazing fact: it takes her one minute and eight one-hundredths of a second to do one of our hems.)

Or Craig Crider, product supervisor in the Seattle, Washington plant where our pillows and comforters are made. (Another amazing fact: counting a four-gram sample of goose down takes a full three hours.)

Or Ernestine Gregory, a shrinkage inspector at the Opelika, Alabama plant that finishes our sheets. Ernestine has worked there since 1947.

These are the people who make our products great. The ones who make sure that our sheets still fit after they're washed. That the colors in our sheet patterns actually match our solid sheets. That our blankets are properly napped. That the down in every single comforter and pillow we send out has exactly the fill power our specifications call for. In short: that every single detail is as near to perfect as possible.

To mark the second anniversary of our beginnings, we sent our three writers, Carol Briscoe, Karen Evans and Tom Moffett, as well as two of our favorite photographers, Keith Jay and Buck Miller, to plants across this country—in Portugal and Germany—to talk to the people who make all of this possible.

We invite you to meet them in this issue.

MARY NORDLOH
Editor

*Craig Crider,
Seattle, Washington*

Coming Home writers, Carol Briscoe and Tom Moffett, with William Dykes, Toni Cauble and Kent Whiddon in Abbeville, Alabama

*Charles Brackett,
▽ Dalton, Georgia*

*△ Dawn Bechard,
Seattle, Washington*

*△ Peggy Crews,
Abbeville, Alabama*

*△ José Silva Melo,
Guimarães, Portugal*

*△ Ernestine Gregory,
Opelika, Alabama*

About our January cover. The screen our model is "painting" was actually done by 73-year-old Peg Miller, a native of Chicago who now lives and works in Spring Green, Wisconsin. Although Peg has been painting all her life, she was only recently discovered.

PS Exuberant as it is, Peg's "Spring in the Country" is one of her more restrained pieces.

Index

Because we admire excellence in all areas of the textile world... we have assembled a collection of the finest Navajo textiles being woven today.

Our collection includes Two Gray Hills, Ganado, Vegetal Dye, Yei and Pictorial weavings, in sizes ranging from small tapestries to large rugs.

For a copy of our Navajo Weavings brochure, call our toll-free number.

2

The Order Form Area

The philosophy here is that customers will add items to the order as they fill out the order form. Impulse merchandise is often selected for the area around and on the order form. Some view this area as similar to a checkout counter at a supermarket. Notice how the counter invitingly shows such low-ticket items as chewing gum, razor blades, and magazines. Think about the impulse needs of your customer and offer products that naturally attract last-minute or add-on sales.

Don't make the mistake of using the order form as the catch-all for items for which you can't find a place in the body of the catalog. Make sure the order form has a theme, just like the other pages. For instance, Mauna Loa® Plantations continues a portion of its product offerings onto its order form while still including important ordering policies. Appleseed's order form features one highly usable, well-priced product, and offers it in a rainbow of colors.

❖ **EXAMPLE 6-6**   Mauna Loa® Plantations designs its order form
to coordinate with the products on the facing page.

❖ **EXAMPLE 6-7**
Appleseed's dickies come in
assorted colors, giving
customers an excellent
wardrobe basic to add to their
orders.

Other catalogers use this section strictly as a customer service area, promoting the assets they feel tell the customer how much their particular catalogs care. This is the place where customers look for information about your service policies, so no matter how you choose to use this space, include this information here (see Chapter 9).

❖ **EXAMPLE 6-8**
Orvis chooses to promote its special services with the personal touch by using its employees in its photographs.

❖ **EXAMPLE 6-9**
Ballard Designs sells what might be considered a risky product for mail order purchase: glass tops. The company diffuses customer concerns with well-thought-out information about safe packing with clear measurement instructions to ensure that customers get the right size when they order.

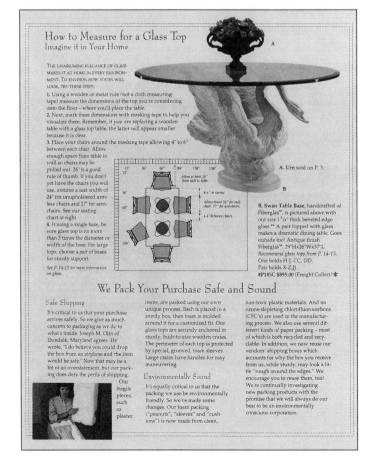

If your catalog has a high phone order rate, this page will stay in the catalog longer than if you have a high mail order rate. If this is the case, you may wish to treat the first page of the order form as just another page in the catalog and design it as a spread.

Inside Back Cover and Back Cover

The inside back cover should be a "grabber," too. Many people read a catalog from back to front. Realize the importance of the inside back cover, and use it both to make a statement and to increase sales through strong and inviting merchandise.

The back cover, all too often, is treated as a stepchild, even though it can be the second-best selling area of a catalog. In fact, the back cover could be the first impression your potential customer has of your catalog; no one guarantees the front cover will be seen first. Use this valuable area to promote enticing products that show value, uniqueness, and seasonal appeal. View the back cover as another window to your store. Show a tantalizing selection of related goods or promote one very strong product. Either way, make a statement about the content of your catalog that compels the viewer to enter with the full intention of buying. Make sure this area also has important call-to-action features, such as toll-free numbers and your guarantee.

❖ **EXAMPLE 6-10**
Boston Proper uses one dominant visual, but actually offers three complementary items for sale. Note the calls to action (a toll-free number and promise of quick delivery).

❖ **EXAMPLE 6-11**

Colorful Image's presentation reflects the season in which the catalog was mailed. By optimizing the space used, the company is able to offer a wide variety of different label designs and two products.

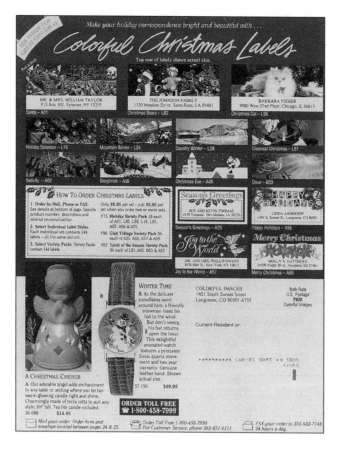

❖ **EXAMPLE 6-12**

Charles Keath, Ltd. gives readers a selection of product types and price points. The many strong call-to-action messages ask for orders.

The Front Cover

Because the front cover is a reflection of the merchandise shown inside, it is often set up last. That way, it will accurately set the pace for all the items to come.

There is much discussion about whether to sell from the cover. This ultimately depends on the image you wish to convey. But this space is valuable and should be used whenever possible. Should you opt for product display on the front and/or back cover, select the product to be shown for its photographic reproduction possibilities, its sales potential, and the image it projects. The appearance of the cover must be striking. A prospective customer who doesn't like the outside of the catalog will never open it.

❖ EXAMPLE 6-13
Brookstone's Hard-to-Find Tools cover boldly displays a product and notes the catalog page on which it is found.

❖ **EXAMPLE 6-14**
The cover of Time-Warner's Viewer's Edge showcases a variety of video titles, each supported by an impressively low price.

Helpful Hints for Pagination

As you continue the process of pagination, don't feel locked into any one item on a particular spread. Rearrange merchandise freely to meet your goals, both graphic and financial. (Financial goals are discussed later in this chapter under "Staying Objective during Pagination.")

Keeping Price Points on Target

You should develop tally sheets as products are selected. One sheet should segment products by category. Since merchandise selection can often be an emotional process, this will help determine whether there is an overabundance of certain product categories and whether others have unintentionally been overlooked. To prepare a tally sheet, break down your merchandise by category, as shown in Table 6-1.

Price range/points, which can be done simply as crosshatches on paper (Table 6-2), show the price balance that you should see in your product offering. The term *price point* means selling price. The establishment of the price per individual product and as an overall offering is critical to controlling profit. Another way to total price points is to tally the number of products you have in each price category—for example, $0–$10.00, $10.01–

$20.00, and so on (see Table 6-3). Price range comparisons use two condensed crosshatch charts to show that the products are not balanced (see Table 6-4). Customers are generally most receptive to the $40.00–$60.00 price range, and although you wish to offer many lower-ticket items to encourage a first purchase, too many could adversely affect your average dollar order.

❖ TABLE 6-1
Example of Merchandise Categories

Home Furnishings and Accessories

11 Furniture, bedspreads, decorative pillows, floor coverings
12 Table accessories—useful
13 Table accessories—decorative
14 Linens—bed and bath
15 Placemats, flatware, napkins
16 Entertaining, food service
17 Desk accessories
18 Frames, mirrors, wall accessories, clocks
19 Bed and bath, soaps, sachets

Indoor Leisure

20 Planters, plants, silk flowers
21 Food
22 Books
23 Hobbies, games, toys
24 Paper goods

Women's Accessories

30 Clothing
31 Belts, scarves
32 Handbags, small leather goods, umbrellas
33 Fine jewelry
34 Costume jewelry
35 Intimate clothing

Men's Accessories

40 Leisure clothing, sportswear, loungewear
41 Jewelry
42 Toiletries
43 Clothing—other than leisure

Travel Accessories

50 Luggage
51 Business accessories
52 Travel accessories—business and leisure
53 Wallets, small leather goods

Children's Wear

60 Clothing
61 Accessories—nontoy

Collectibles

70 Antiques
71 Limited editions

Outdoor Leisure

80 Sports equipment
81 Garden accessories
82 Pet accessories

Holiday Accessories

90 Stationery, gift tags
91 Tabletop
92 Hanging

Note: Numbers preceding subcategory listings are often used as the first digits of an SKU number for quick product category identification.

❖ **TABLE 6-2**
Price Range/Points

Price Range	Number of Items per Price Range*
$0–$10.00	||||| ||||| ||||| |||
$10.01–$20.00	||||| ||||| ||||| ||||| ||||| ||||| ||||| |||||
$20.01–$30.00	||||| ||||| ||||| ||||| |||||	
$30.01–$40.00	||||| ||||| ||||| ||||| ||
$40.01–$50.00	||||| ||||| ||||| |||
$50.01–$60.00	||||| |||
$60.01–$70.00	||||| ||||| ||
$70.01–$80.00	|||||	
$80.01–$90.00	||||
$90.01–$100.00	||
$100.01–$110.00		
$110.01–$125.00	|||||
$125.01–$150.00	||||
$150.01–$175.00	|||||	
$175.01–$200.00	|||
$200.01–$250.00	||
$250.01–$300.00		
$300.01–$500.00		
$500+		

* This column shows a lack of price-range targeting.

❖ **TABLE 6-3**
Price Point Tally Sheet

Price Range	Number of Items per Price Range
$0–$10.00	0
$10.01–$20.00	22
$20.01–$30.00	26
$30.01–$40.00	28
$40.01–$50.00	14
$50.01–$60.00	13
$60.01–$70.00	8
$70.01–$80.00	4
$80.01–$90.00	8
$90.01–$100.00	5
$100.01–$110.00	4
$110.01–$125.00	5
$125.01–$150.00	4
$150.01+	4

❖ **TABLE 6-4**
Price Range Comparisons

Approximate Optimal Ranges

Price Range	Number of Items per Range
Under $20.00	||||| ||||| |||||
$20.01–$40.00	||||| ||||| ||||| ||||| ||||| |||||	
$40.01–$60.00	||||| ||||| ||||| ||||| ||||| ||||| ||||| ||||| ||||
$60.01–$100.00	||||| ||||| ||||| ||||| ||||| ||||
$100.01+	||||| ||||| ||||| ||||| ||

Actual Ranges from Table

Price Range	Number of Items per Range
Under $20.00	||||| ||||| ||||| ||||| ||
$20.01–$40.00	||||| ||||| ||||| ||||| ||||| ||||| ||||| ||||| ||||| ||||| ||||
$40.01–$60.00	||||| ||||| ||||| ||||| ||||| ||
$60.01–$100.00	||||| ||||| ||||| ||||| |||||
$100.01+	||||| ||||| ||||| ||

Spread Record Sheets

Spread record sheets help keep you organized as you go along. For each spread, list the products to be shown (including the stockkeeping unit [SKU] number), the name of the manufacturer, the manufacturer's product number, and the description of the products—the color, size, cost, and selling price of each item—the advertising and photographic allowances (if any) and any information you consider essential for layout artists to display the items correctly. Identify the spread by name and by page numbers—for example, "Traditional All-American, pp. 10–11."

The form for spread record sheets can be prepared on a computer and information entered during the pagination process. It does not have to be perfect at the end of the pagination day, but should be updated with all information shortly thereafter. Table 6-5 shows an example of a typical spread record sheet.

Preparing the Artist and Copywriter

If at all possible, have the artist and copywriter present during pagination. This should be done the second day, after the marketing staff has determined exactly what goes on each page. Tables should still have the merchandise displayed; the marketing and creative team should follow the buyer through his or her description of each item. Use the spread record sheets as a guide and the place to record creative guidance information. For each product, this should include space allocation, props, and general input and guidance as to how the product should be shown. It is important for writers and artists to be present during the final phase of pagination so they will learn first-hand what makes a particular product unusual or desirable.

If it is impossible for your creative team to be at the pagination, be sure to supply the art department with Polaroids or photographic prints of the merchandise. Since you or someone on your staff will be the one taking these preliminary pictures (for layout purposes only), be sure to include easily recognizable items such as a pen, a ruler, or a person's hand, in each photo so the size of the item is readily apparent. Written measurements do not convey size nearly as effectively as a propped photo. If your product is small, you

❖ TABLE 6-5 Spread Record Sheet for Traditional All-American

SKU	Mftr.	Mftr's Product No.	Product	Color(s)	Sizes	Cost	Sell	Advert. Allow.	Photo Allow.	Props/ Comments
304-076	Able Products	49000	Two-pocket pant	Brown	6–18	$29	$65		$150	Show on model.
306-123	ABC Co.	72G44	Bow-tie blouse	Brown/ Blue Plaid	6–18	$14	$30	5%		#7,105 jacket in model's hand.
305-720	Jones	7105	Single-breasted jacket	Rust	6–18	$33	$72		$150	Show on model—top shot only.
301-533	Smyth	3425	Crew neck sweater	Blue	S, M, L	$23	$50		$150	Show on model.
302-783	Any Co.	613899	Scoop-neck dress	Blue	S, M, L	$27	$70	10%		Carries portfolio on pg. 4.
307-540	Roberts, Inc.	09486	Float dress	Gold	S, M, L	$25	$64	5%		Both models wear gold earrings #4618.
346-470	Smith	4618	Shell earrings	Gold	Pierced	$18	$40	10%		Show close-up on model's ear.

could even photocopy the actual product. This does not show color, but it gives a clear idea of size. You'd be surprised how well three-dimensional products photocopy.

Keep the merchandise information forms you or your vendors filled out previously in alphabetical order and readily available for reference. Any information added during pagination will be extremely useful to the copywriter and artist.

Have Fulfillment Operations Review the Pagination

It is also a good idea to have the head of your fulfillment operation review all products prior to the final selection. Ask him or her to stop by when all items are laid out on the tables, and go over each product together.

Operations should be alerting the buying staff regularly of any problems with quality control, breakage, or other such problems. However, asking operations to double-check the selected product helps ensure that you (1) do not run a repeat item that has current fulfillment problems, and (2) do not run a new product that the fulfillment people strongly feel will have shipping problems.

Staying Objective during Pagination

To merchandise by profit potential rather than emotion, you must keep several factors in mind during the pagination process:

1. Determine your overall sales goal.
2. Decide what response rate is realistic for your catalog.
3. Estimate what the number of products ordered per person will be.
4. Determine what the average dollar order must be to achieve the overall sales goal.

Know the Sales Goal

To determine your overall sales goal, you can work with a one-, two-, or three-year plan that shows what your direct marketing profit center must generate in dollars to be profitable during the chosen time span (see Chapter 15). For the purposes of judging a product's value, you can do this more simply—look at the initial, in-mail cost of a catalog and determine what you must generate in net dollars for the space that product occupies to cover that cost (see "Using Profit Potential to Evaluate Individual Products" later in this chapter).

Determine the Response Rate

If you are a first-timer with no history, you can start with the assumption that the higher the average unit price offered, the lower the response rate (this is not always true, but it gives you a starting point). For a general gift catalog with no customer base and no known name, use response figures ranging from .5 percent to 1.25 percent if the catalog's average unit price is $50 or more, or .75 percent to 2 percent if the catalog's average unit price is $50 or less. Responses may be higher, but these are realistic percentages. Higher percentage ranges can create overly optimistic expectations for an unknown catalog and can be emotionally and fiscally defeating.

Project the Number of Products per Order

Without a sales history or professional guidance, the number of products a customer will purchase per order is most difficult to determine. As a rule of thumb, higher-ticket general merchandise catalogs have fewer items per order; lower-ticket general merchandise catalogs have more.

Estimate the Average Dollar Order

A combination of the number of products per order and the average unit price, this figure, too, is difficult to determine without experience. A midprice general-merchandise catalog with an average unit price of $30 could expect around 1.5 units per order, or an average order of $45. The key to controlling profits is to observe how the addition or deletion of merchandise offered at different price points affects profitability (see Chapter 14).

Using Profit Potential to Evaluate Individual Products

Because individual response rates vary dramatically from product to product and are not predictable by novice (or even many experienced) catalogers, a good method for evaluating whether or not a product should be run is to quickly look at it strictly on the basis of profit potential during pagination. A rough estimate is made of the cost of the product's space and the dollars it will generate.

A way to do this is to divide the total in-mail cost of the catalog (including creative and production costs, lists, and postage, but not including overhead) by the number of pages. (For instance, a 32-page catalog costing $160,000 would have a per-page cost of $5,000). Then divide the number of photos per page (for this exercise, we're assuming there is one product per photo; in real life, you can adapt as needed). So, if this catalog has five photos per page, each photo would need to generate $1,000 in net sales, or $2,000 in gross sales if the catalog had only a two-time mark-up. Then, divide the net sales by the cost of the merchandise to determine the number of items that must be sold. Remember, this calculation is rough, since products seldom have equally allocated space. But it is a very important calculation, as it immediately removes any emotional attachment to a product and lets you make the "run/don't-run" decision based on facts that are as financially stable as possible at this stage of the process.

For example, let's assume that everyone loves a stunning crystal vase that costs $37.50 and sells for $75.00. Using the previous example, divide the net sales ($1,000) by the gross profit per item ($37.50) to determine the number of vases that must be sold: $1,000 ÷ $37.50 = 26.66, meaning that 27 vases must be sold for this item to break even. The next question that must be asked is, "Is this a realistic figure?" Many potential disasters have been avoided because it was immediately obvious that the number of units that needed to be sold was unrealistic. Chapter 14 contains a more detailed discussion of how to calculate response rates, average catalog orders, and space costs.

When to Repeat Items

Determining how many items to retain from one catalog to another depends in part on the mixture of products within your catalog. Obviously, a fashion catalog, which depends on the timeliness of its clothing styles, would be different from a catalog containing traditional home furniture. However, some guidelines hold true to all catalogs:

1. **Quality.** Has the manufacturer maintained quality? A decline in quality almost automatically means the product should be discontinued. After all, the quality of merchandise you offer directly reflects the quality of your company.

2. **Reliability.** How reliable has the manufacturer/vendor been? It is rarely worth continuing a relationship with a vendor whose late delivery has caused customer dissatisfaction. But problems must, of course, be evaluated individually. Is the vendor consistently problematic, or was there only one incident?

3. **Price.** Has the price gone up too much? If a price increase has become necessary due to increased cost of materials, is the higher price affordable? Or will the new retail price seriously discourage customers from buying? Also, has the vendor held to the price stated in the contract?

4. **The audience profile.** More conservative, less affluent customers tend to

prefer having their choices confirmed by seeing them several times before actually making the decision to buy. Affluent audiences, on the other hand, want to be "first on the block" to own a new item and will make the purchase the first time it appears. Knowing your audience's buying patterns is essential to determining how many repeat items you should offer.

A word of warning: Products have a faster "wear-out" than ever before, and this also affects some less affluent customers—those who strive to achieve a higher affluence rapidly. Do not become emotionally involved with your products, feeling that, given another chance, they will succeed. Unless they truly have not been shown to their best advantage, replace them with a new item. More often than not, new items will outsell marginal ones.

Handling Returns

If, for legal or ethical reasons, you cannot put all the merchandise back in stock, what can you do with it? Negotiate returns with vendors, especially for defective goods. Even though seasonality makes it unlikely that clothing manufacturers will take returns on goods, there have been exceptions where the vendor will take back the goods in exchange for a credit on future purchases. (Note: This is usually only true only on low-quantity returns.)

Items that are resalable can be offered at reduced prices within your catalog or in special flyers. If they are in the catalog, it is better to offer them in color rather than in black and white. Some find that items offered at reduced prices in black and white substantially hurt sales on the full-price items. But, when offered in color, reduced-price products have actually been known to increase response on full-price items.

Consider preparing a sale flyer for insertion as a bounceback or as a mailer to certain segments of your list. Track results of those who received the savings brochure against those who do not receive the brochure to make sure no deterioration is experienced overall. Naturally, don't create a sale brochure unless your volume and anticipated sales are sufficient to at least break even.

Another method of moving leftover goods is through bonus mystery gifts. Low-ticket items can make excellent bonus gifts, offered as "mystery" prizes when a certain dollar amount is purchased from the catalog.

Low-quantity items can usually be sold to employees, and if all else fails, there are always the jobbers, who will purchase the goods (including those that cannot be refurbished) for roughly 10 to 20 cents on the wholesale dollar.

 **CHECKLIST**

✔ Pre-organize pagination so time is used efficiently during the actual process.
✔ Be flexible during pagination.
✔ Refer to your checklist of pagination factors during the process.
✔ Select product for the sales effect it will bring to certain sections of the catalog (such as the back cover).
✔ Keep tally sheets of product categories and price points to be sure your merchandise plan is on target.
✔ Completely fill out spread record sheets for your marketing and creative departments.
✔ Keep the creative team involved from the start by offering them first-hand knowledge and complete information.
✔ Have operations make a final check of products during the last day of pagination.
✔ Be an objective merchandiser by using realistic sales goals as a barometer for including or excluding products.
✔ Understand when the risk of running a new item outweighs the value of running marginal repeat items.
✔ Reduce overstocks.

CHAPTER SEVEN

❖ ❖ ❖

Understanding Production

Production consists of many elements—mailing, printing, separations, photography, pagination—everything in the graphic process but the layout and copy. All of these elements must be carefully and realistically scheduled to ensure that the job turns out right and on time, as well as allowing for the interfaces necessary between the professionals involved in each aspect.

The Importance of Schedules

In order to achieve optimum results and cost effectiveness, catalogers allocate a certain block of time to each part of the creative/production process. Deadlines are determined by working backward from the date the catalog must be in the mail to arrive at the right time in prospective customers' homes. Because in-mail deadlines are extremely important in this seasonally dependent business, missing any deadline in the process means that time must be made up somewhere; this can cost money and jeopardize quality and desired delivery dates.

You need to determine a realistic schedule and stay on it. The amount of time needed for the creative and production work depends on the number of pages in the catalog, the number of photos to be taken, and who will be doing the work. First, find out how much time the printer and the lettershop will actually need to print, label, tie, bag, sort, and mail the catalogs. This can run from a few days to over a week, depending on the complexity of the job and the quantity involved. Then, working backward, allocate time for color separations or assemblies, photography, paste-up, typesetting, and so on.

A 72-page catalog with approximately 50 percent new products has been selected as a medium-range example. The time allocated per job area is shown in Table 7-1 to help you construct your own schedule.

❖ TABLE 7-1
Sample Production Schedule, including Dates and Time Allocated

Specifications: 72-page catalog plus order form, 360 products, film due at printer June 1. More time is given to first section to allow for format adaptations and smoothing of system. Dates indicate due date. Days indicate working days only. Schedule assumes use of external creative/production agency.

Pagination

| M | 2/15 | Final info to art team, organized in folders | |

Main Body of Book

Concept Work

Five spreads; photos will not be scanned in; space allocation will be shown

Tu	2/16	Client meeting to go over products	
Th	2/18	Finalize layout concept	2 days
Th	2/18	Initial copy to client	2 days
Tu	2/23	Revisions requested by client	2 days
W	2/24	Copy revised	1 day
F	2/26	Layout, with copy in position and spec'd for future writing to client	2 days
M	3/1	Client revisions to layout concept	1 day
Tu	3/2	Final layout concept to client; approved by client	1 day

Layout

Remainder of book (excluding cover, back cover, and order form), 30 spreads

W	3/3	Client input meeting	
Tu	3/9	Initial layouts for first 10 spreads	3 days
W	3/10	Revisions requested by client	1 day
F	3/12	Layouts revised	2 days
M	3/15	Second revisions requested	1 day
Tu	3/16	Layouts revised and approved	1 day
W	3/17	Client input meeting	
M	3/22	Initial layouts for next 10 spreads	3 days
Tu	3/23	Revisions requested by client	1 day
Th	3/25	Layouts revised	2 days
F	3/26	Second revisions requested	1 day
M	3/29	Layouts revised and approved	1 day
Tu	3/30	Client input meeting	
F	4/2	Initial layouts for next 10 spreads	3 days
M	4/5	Revisions requested by client	1 day
W	4/7	Layouts revised	2 days
Th	4/8	Second revisions requested	1 day
F	4/9	Layouts revised and approved	1 day

Copy

Remainder of book (excluding cover, back cover, and order form 35 spreads
Must be written to fit specifications. Partly written concurrent with layout.

Tu	3/2	Layout to writer	
F	3/5	Initial copy for first 5 spreads	3 days
Tu	3/9	Revisions requested by client	2 days
W	3/10	Copy revised	1 day
Th	3/11	Second revisions requested	1 day
M	3/15	Copy revised and approved	2 days
Tu	3/16	Layout to writer	
F	3/19	Initial copy for next 10 spreads	3 days
Tu	3/23	Revisions requested by client	2 days
Th	3/25	Copy revised	2 days
F	3/26	Second revisions requested	1 day
W	3/31	Copy revised and approved	3 days

M	3/29	Layout to writer	
Th	4/1	Initial copy for next 10 spreads	3 days
M	4/5	Revisions requested by client	2 days
W	4/7	Copy revised	2 days
Th	4/8	Second revisions requested	1 day
M	4/12	Copy revised and approved	3 days
Th	4/8	Layout to writer	
M	4/12	Initial copy for remaining 10 spreads	3 days
W	4/14	Revisions requested by client	2 days
F	4/16	Copy revised	2 days
M	4/19	Second revisions requested	1 day
Th	4/23	Copy revised and approved	3 days

Photography

Assumes use of two *concurrent* photographers; minimum of 10 shots per day; will need to increase at midpoint. At this time, assumes book can be divided equally. Schedule will need adaptation if photographers have individual specialties and book must be divided to fit them. Total of 35 spreads, 360 photos (assumes all new).

Tu	3/2	First 5 layouts (spreads) to photographer
Tu	3/16	Next 10 layouts (spreads) to photographer
M	3/29	Next 10 layouts (spreads) to photographer
Th	4/8	Next 10 layouts (spreads) to photographer
Th	4/22	Complete
W	4/28	Reshots

If illustrations are used, they are rendered concurrently with the photography. Model selection would also be incorporated into this schedule.

Photos and Copy into Computerized Layouts

Only deadline is indicated, not days, as copy would need to be fed regularly to artists.

W	3/16	First 5 spreads to client
F	3/19	Approved by client
M	4/5	Next 10 spreads to client
F	4/9	Approved by client
Th	4/15	Next 10 spreads to client
W	4/21	Approved by client
W	4/28	Final 10 spreads to client
M	5/3	Approved by client
M	5/3	Adaptations due to reshots to client
F	5/7	Approved by client

Professional Proofreading

F	3/19	First 5 spreads to proofreader	
W	3/24	From proofreader	3 days
F	3/26	Corrections incorporated into spreads	2 days
W	3/31	Reviewed and approved by client	3 days
F	4/9	Next 10 spreads to proofreader	
F	4/16	From proofreader	5 days
Tu	4/20	Corrections incorporated into spreads	4 days
F	4/23	Reviewed and approved by client	3 days
W	4/21	Next 10 spreads to proofreader	
W	4/28	From proofreader	5 days
F	4/30	Corrections incorporated into spreads	2 days
W	5/3	Reviewed and approved by client	3 days
M	5/3	Final 10 spreads to proofreader	
F	5/7	From proofreader	5 days
Tu	5/11	Corrected incorporated into spreads	2 days
M	5/17	Reviewed and approved by client	5 days

Marketing Review

Review all spreads for final adaptations.

F	5/21	Client/agency review	2 days
Tu	5/25	Corrections incorporated	2 days
W	5/26	Final approval	1 day
Th	5/27	Disc to separator	1 day

Separations

Th	5/27	Disc to separator	
M	6/14	First proof, randoms	15 days
W	6/23	Revise, color correct	7 days
W	6/30	Second proof, combined	7 days
Th	7/1	Final film to printer	1 day

Front and Back Cover

W	3/3	Client meeting to discuss concept	
W	3/17	Concept presentation	10 days
W	3/24	Revisions presented	5 days
W	3/31	Copy written	5 days
F	4/2	Copy incorporated into computer	2 days
F	4/9	Photo complete	5 days
M	4/12	Photo incorporated into computer	1 days
Tu	4/13	Presentation	1 day
F	4/16	Revisions complete	3 days

Order Form

Schedule concurrent with cover.

Internal Agency Staffing Assumptions

Artists: four full time, including art director (Art director will also oversee all photography.)
Copywriters: two full time
Photographers: two full-time studios
Proofreader: one freelance
Coordinators: two internal (one art, one copy); two external (one marketing, one detail)

❖ **FIGURE 7-1   Computerized Production Gantt Chart Shows Work Flow and Overlap**

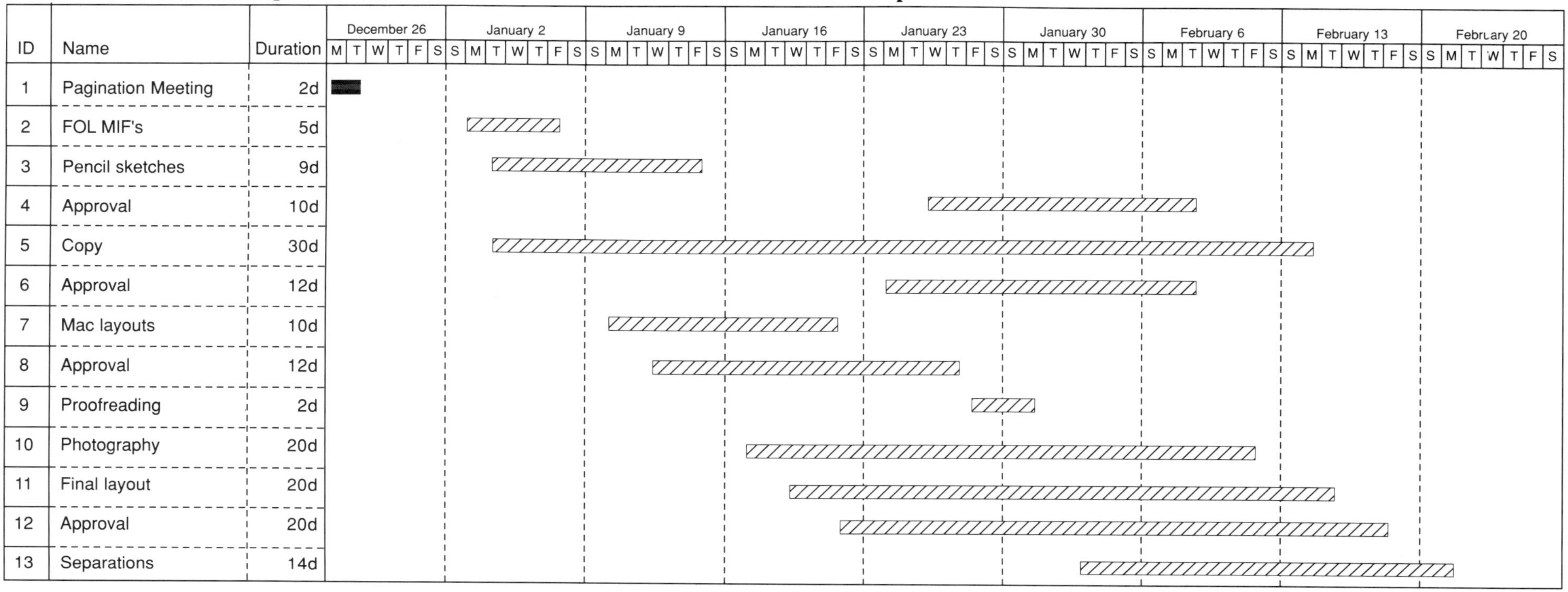

ID	Name	Duration
1	Pagination Meeting	2d
2	FOL MIF's	5d
3	Pencil sketches	9d
4	Approval	10d
5	Copy	30d
6	Approval	12d
7	Mac layouts	10d
8	Approval	12d
9	Proofreading	2d
10	Photography	20d
11	Final layout	20d
12	Approval	20d
13	Separations	14d

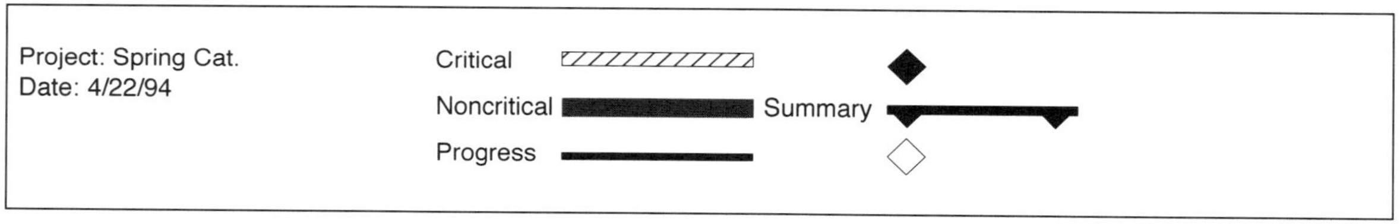

Critical

Noncritical

Progress

Summary

Project: Spring Cat.
Date: 4/22/94

ID	Name	Duration	Scheduled Start	Scheduled Finish	Resource Names
1	Pagination Meeting	2d	12/27/93 8:00am	12/28/93 5:00pm	Marketing Manager
2	FOL MIF's	5d	1/3/94 8:00am	1/7/94 5:00pm	Assistant
3	Pencil sketches	9d	1/4/94 8:00am	1/14/94 5:00pm	Artist
4	Approval	10d	1/26/94 8:00am	2/8/94 5:00pm	Marketing Manager
5	Copy	30d	1/4/94 8:00am	2/14/94 5:00pm	Copywriter
6	Approval	12d	1/24/94 8:00am	2/8/94 5:00pm	Marketing Manager
7	Mac layouts	10d	1/10/94 8:00am	1/21/94 5:00pm	Artist
8	Approval	12d	1/12/94 8:00am	1/27/94 5:00pm	Marketing Manager
9	Proofreading	2d	1/28/94 8:00am	1/31/94 5:00pm	Professional
10	Photography	20d	1/17/94 8:00am	2/11/94 5:00pm	Photographer
11	Final layout	20d	1/19/94 8:00am	2/15/94 5:00pm	Artist
12	Approval	20d	1/21/94 8:00am	2/17/94 5:00pm	Marketing Manager
13	Separations	14d	2/2/94 8:00am	2/21/94 5:00pm	Separator

Keep in mind the most expensive aspects of producing a catalog—the separations and printing—come toward the end of the production process. This, of course, is where time crunches usually develop. Being off schedule at this point can result in additional costs of 50 percent to 100 percent in overtime. If, for example, 100-percent overtime is incurred, separations quoted at $20,000 will cost $40,000. No one wants overtime. Suppliers dislike it because they must charge more for a job that, because of time limitations, is often not up to their standards of quality. The cataloger, however, is the biggest loser, paying more for less because of an inability to stay on schedule. Figure 7-1 shows a sample production chart created with Microsoft Project Gantt Production Chart, a software program that helps you organize each step in a job's progress, showing timeframes, due dates, and resources.

To ensure that your catalog will look good and be financially worthwhile, schedule carefully—then stay on schedule!

Understanding the Creative/Production/ Marketing Interface

A schedule is just words and numbers on paper if you don't understand exactly who does what when, and how the people responsible interact with each other. Having read about pagination, you now understand the process of product selection. But exactly what role does each player have and how does the creative process progress from the selection of merchandise to the printed piece? Let's take all the information we have learned, plus what we will be learning in this and the next chapter, and look at the process as a whole.

Note that the process outlined here is adaptable for use by an integral art team as well as an agency. Furthermore, in this outline, marketing and product managers are virtually one and the same, but could well be separate individuals, depending on the structure of the company.

1. Product Review and Pagination

Purpose:
  a. To determine exactly what products will be offered per catalog
  b. To allow all team members time to review products and achieve consensus

Process:

Day One
  a. All products (new or pick-up) under consideration should be displayed on large tables.
  b. Products should be ticketed with essential information, such as retail price.
  c. Merchandise managers should have prepared, prior to this meeting, condensed merchandise information forms (MIFs).
  d. Spread record sheets, detailing what items go on each page and how they should be shown, should be filled out as completely as possible (all products must be listed) and copies given to all creative team members. These sheets can be done on a computer or handwritten and entered into a computer at a later date.
  e. One key team member, with advice from others, determines exactly what goes on which spread.
  f. A pagination grid can be used to visually show the approximately space allocation of the entire catalog. For an example of a completed grid, see Figure 8-1 (page 194).

Day Two

    a. Creative review allows everyone to visualize and verbally sign off on the products agreed to.

    b. The coordinator determines what information is missing, and sets a deadline for when it must be received.

    c. The art team views the product, and the merchandise manager explains why each product is special (use the shorter MIF as a guide).

    d. The merchandise and marketing managers recommend features and space allocations to the creative team, noting the suggestions on the spread record sheets.

    e. Propping and any other relevant creative handling, such as how the model should be positioned, what type of table should be used for the item's background, what flowers might add color, and so on, are recommended by the creative team to the merchandise and marketing team and recorded on the spread record sheets.

Materials Needed:

    a. All information specific to the product to be offered (a condensed version of the MIF)

    b. Spread record sheets

    c. A table of merchandise categories and a histogram of price points (These should be used in conjunction with the analysis of these categories from previous catalogs.)

Attended by:

Function	Day
Merchandise managers	One/two
Artists	Two
Photographer	Two
Writers	Two
Fulfillment manager (to check for potential fulfillment problems and alert to past ones)	One
Coordinator of the project	One/two
Marketing manager	One/two

Time Allocated:

Two days

Follow-up Needed:

Function	Responsible Person
All MIF sheets and corresponding creative material, such as previously written copy or drawings of new products, should be put into individual folders by spread and made available to the artists and writers.	Coordinator
Histograms should be reviewed to determine if product mix should be altered.	Marketing manager

Time Allocated for Follow-Up:

Three to five working days

2. First Layout Review

Purpose:

To clarify the information obtained during the pagination meeting with regard to products to be run, features, and space allocation.

Process:

    a. Copies of rough pencil sketches (not necessarily to size) are presented to the relevant merchandise or marketing manager (and any others on the review checklist) for approval.

         ◆ Layouts should be presented in "waves," with three spreads (or six pages) being the preferred number to review at one time.

         ◆ Layouts should, if at all possible, be presented sequentially.

    b. Each reviewer indicates revisions requested in writing, and signs and dates the layouts.

         ◆ Complicated revisions should require the person requesting them to meet with the artist doing them.

    c. A deadline must be determined and enforced for the review process (this is most often done by the coordinator/traffic controller).

    d. Pencil revisions are not seen again in pencil format. Revisions will be reflected in the first computerized layouts.

Time Allocated:

    For pencils: maximum one day per six pages

    For approval: maximum two days per set of six pages

3. First Copy Review

Purpose:

To review copy for its accuracy and ability to sell in time to allow corrections before it is input into the computer. This is done concurrently with the pencil layout review.

Process:

    a. Copy is typed into a computer, allowing for space generally used by the same or a similar product in the past (this information should be available in the folders provided at the pagination meeting).

    b. Each reviewer indicates revisions in writing, and signs and dates the copy.

    c. Revisions are made on the copy disk before it is handed off to creative.

    d. Prior to or after each catalog is issued, a style guide (discussed later in this chapter) should be created or edited to reflect specific treatment of copy and layout. This guide should be circulated and agreed to by all team members.

Time Allocated:

    For copy: maximum one day per six pages

    For revisions: maximum one day per six pages

4. Second Layout Review (with copy in place)

Purpose:

To see and approve the combined copy, existing art, and plans for photography for the new products.

Process:

    a. Layouts will have any previous/pick-up art scanned by the computer in position as they will actually appear (low-resolution scans provided by separator) to the artist and are used to indicate position only (see ''Separations'' in this chapter). New products will be rendered in fairly tight pencils, including indications of how they will be shot and styled with props.

    b. If pencil revisions have been followed, there should be no need for rescanning at a future stage. Scans can be done at this stage.

    c. Copies are sent to all those involved in the review process and a professional proofreader.

    d. All requested changes are made in writing and dated.

Time Allocated:

    For layouts: maximum one day per six pages

    For approval: maximum two days per six pages

5. Photography Process

Purpose:

To expedite

    a. the effective shooting of photographs

    b. the approval of photos by art, product, and marketing managers

Process:

Prior to Actual Photography

    a. The artist reviews all layouts with the photographer, detailing position, lighting, and propping of the product.

    b. Photography and its associated materials are scheduled on a day-by-day basis (see ''Photography'' later this chapter).

    c. Distribute the schedule to catalog managers to alert them to when they will need to be in the set.

Actual Photography

    a. Determine the prop/model schedule (see ''Photography'' later in this chapter) based on backgrounds, product availability, and propping on a per-product basis.

    b. Catalog managers should be on the set for approval of their products.

    c. The art director provides full-time supervision.

Back-up Approval
    a. Photos are available for approval by catalog managers.

    b. Unless there is a major problem, these photos should not be reshot.

    c. Approved photography is released to the separator for low-resolution scans for ''in position'' placement by art team.

Time Allocated:
Preparation time: One to two days

Photography: Eight to 15 photos per day, depending on complexity

6. Final Layout Review

Purpose:
To approve all elements in position, including all previous corrections, prior to releasing layouts to the separator.

Process:
    a. Layouts, with all scans and layout/copy corrections, completed on a computer.

    b. Layouts are circulated and reviewed by catalog managers and everyone on the review list.

    c. Final written corrections (should be no more than 5 percent; ideal, none to 1 percent) are submitted and made.

    d. Final layouts are provided to catalog managers (and the review list) for record keeping only.

Time Allocated:
Review process: Full book in one day

Final editing: Full book in one day

7. Separations (film used to make plates for printing)

Purpose:
To review color, as well as all elements, for correctness

Process:
    a. Photos have been released to the separator for high-resolution scans (held at separator) and low-resolution scans (used by art team).

    b. Match prints (or other chosen proofing form) are reviewed and any corrections indicated by the production manager.

The floor chart in Figure 7-2 shows a simplified list of the functions involved in the creative/production process.

Pre-press Elements

Now that you understand scheduling, let's look at the individual elements that go into those functions sometimes referred to as *pre-press*. Certainly, these areas are also highly creative, but traditionally they fall into the production category.

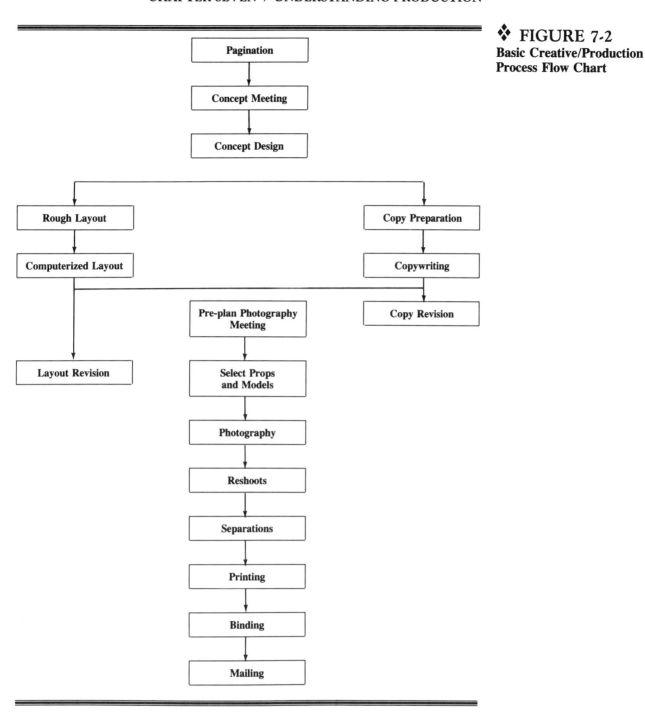

❖ FIGURE 7-2
Basic Creative/Production Process Flow Chart

Selecting Type

There are more than 10,000 typefaces available today—a bewildering number from which to choose. But the single most important criterion in selecting type is readability. You should be aware that the two main groups of typefaces (styles) that relate to catalogers' needs are serif and sans serif. Serifs are short cross-lines at the end of a main stroke. Sans (without) serif, as the name implies, has no serifs. Most books and newspapers are printed in serif type. Sans serif faces are often reserved for headlines or other such embellishments, and serif typefaces are used for the body copy; but both can be used creatively for either purpose. This book is printed in a popular serif face. Each typeface comes in a variety of point sizes, usually 6 to 118 point (see Table 7-2). A font is a full set of characters in a given point size of any style of typeface, such as Helvetica. There are variations within each style, such as light, bold, extra bold, italic, expanded, or condensed, which are basically just thinner, thicker, fatter, or longer versions of the same typeface.

❖ TABLE 7-2 Helvetica Type Sizes (6 to 72 points)

6 ABCDEFGHIJKLMNOPQRSTUVWXYZ

8 ABCDEFGHIJKLMNOPQRSTUVWXYZ

10 ABCDEFGHIJKLMNOPQRSTUVWXYZ

12 12ABCDEFGHIJKLMNOPQRSTUVWXYZ

14 ABCDEFGHIJKLMNOPQRSTUVWXYZ

18 ABCDEFGHIJKLMNOPQRSTUVWXYZ

24 ABCDEFGHIJKLMNOPQRSTUVWXYZ

30 ABCDEFGHIJKLMNOPQRSTUVWX

42 ABCDEFGHIJKLMNOPQR

48 ABCDEFGHIJKLMNOP

60 ABCDEFGHIJKLM

72 ABCDEFGHIJK

Determining Readability. The typeface reflects the personality of the catalog. A light, feminine typeface would be as inappropriate for an electronics catalog aimed at men as a bold, heavy typeface would be for a fashion catalog aimed at women. A more graphic, bolder type can be used in headlines for impact, but body copy should be simple and easy to read. A number of factors affect the readability of type.

♦ **Line width.** A line of copy that is too wide or too narrow (requiring too many word breaks) can make reading difficult. If it's too narrow, the breaks in the words will dominate the look and cause discomfort in reading.

♦ **Word and letter spacing.** Too much word or letter spacing can cause a sentence to look strung out. Too little can make sentences appear as one long word. Both can be discouraging to the reader.

♦ **Indenting and leading.** Indented paragraphs invite the reader to read on. Leading (pronounced *ledding*), the horizontal space inserted between lines of type, should be appropriate for the type size. Insufficient leading can make type appear "bunched."

♦ **Weight.** Consideration must be given to the effects of different printing processes on type. For example, because the gravure process screens all images on the plate, small point sizes and delicate, wispy fonts should be avoided to ensure clarity and definition when using this process.

When type prints on top of an image or drops out of the background (white type), either the type must be larger than normally selected or the artist must be asked to spread the type visually, making it appear larger. When surprinting, check to see that background colors have a density of *50 percent or less,* depending on the type size.

Doing a Character Count

The person who has selected the typeface and type size will divide the desired number of characters per line into the total number of characters in the original copy. (Each and every character of the typed copy is literally counted, as are the spaces between the words.) The total number of lines of copy is determined from this formula. At this point, the copy can either be cut (if it is too long) or lengthened (if it is too short). However, writing manual type specifications is fast becoming an exercise of the past. Copywriters almost exclusively use word processing and this means that writers can easily write to spec as the copy is created. Or, in the case of a copy-intensive format, the writer will lead the process, supplying the artist with copy to which he or she must adapt the layouts.

These days, if the layout is driven by graphics, the artist simply takes the copy, supplied on a compatible disc by the writer, and formats it to his or her creative specifications. If this copy must be cut or expanded, the artist will notify the writer, who will meet these needs by either supplying a new disc or dictating the changes to the artist. In either case, it is the artist who then makes the edits on computer.

The Typesetting Evolution

The typesetting industry has virtually been eliminated by electronic technology. Since type is now part of the desktop publishing process, considerations such as reproduction of type in printed form prior to separation have been largely eliminated. Since paste-ups, or mechanicals, are seldom used, computer printouts are used for approval of product position and copy only. These printouts, unlike their reproduction-quality predecessors, are not used in the final printed reproduction.

Previously, most typesetting was done by the phototypesetting method. There were many different types of machines, all of which operated like a personal computer. The typesetter sat at a keyboard in front of a display screen, typed the copy and format commands, then visually checked it; the computer produced typeset copy on reproducible-quality paper. As copy and typographic commands were read and analyzed by the computer, patterns of selected characters were called out of the memory section and imaged in the correct size and precise positions.

A key factor in typesetting was the reproduction quality of the printer that actually printed out the type. Laser printers usually had a 300-dot-per-inch (dpi) resolution. (The more dots per inch, the higher the density of the type and the better it reproduces.) However, whereas this was fine for creative use, production quality output required a unit that cost more and provided higher resolution, such as 480, 600, or even 1,200 dots per inch.

Graphics capabilities on more powerful personal computers and workstations now allow imaging and text-merging. In order to output halftone graphics, raster image processing (RIP) techniques have brought about typesetting procedures called image setting. The hardware, called an image setter, includes the RIP. The purpose of the RIP is to output a series of digital 0s and 1s in a format that permits the reproduction of line illustrations, halftones, screens, and logos. The final output is on coated paper, film, or even plain paper. In some cases, images can be output directly to a printing plate. The density of the digital information determines whether the output is draft (paper) or final (paper or plate).

Also note that most of these systems do more than just display words; they are actually automatic art boards. With the more sophisticated systems, you have WYSIWYG, or ''What You See Is What You Get.'' The copy is automatically composed in preselected typefaces and sizes, complete with correct spacing and some graphics, such as charts, so you can see on the screen exactly how it will look before it is actually printed.

There are many software packages available, but almost all of them have such features as magnification on specific areas, draft as well as final output, automatic column settings, the ability to work on two pages (usually $8\frac{1}{2}'' \times 11''$ verticals) at once, the flexibility of changing page area allocation, and so on. And they work on most microcomputers. Users of these graphic/type systems reported type savings from 30 percent to 80 percent, depending on volume, and a reduction of up to 50 percent of their art staff, which is one of the main reasons typesetting as an industry has virtually disappeared (see Chapter 8).

Style Guides

A style guide is a set of uniform rules for copy and layout to follow. It can save both time and frustration because its main purpose is to help ensure consistency throughout the catalog. This guide is especially beneficial if more than one artist and copywriter

❖ **TABLE 7-3**

Information to Include in a Style Guide

OVERALL

Organization
- ◆ How will the catalog be organized? By product category? By price point? By themes?
- ◆ How will it be formatted? Rules (lines)? Text?
- ◆ How will text be handled? Caps? Caps and lower case? Type size, font, weight? Color differentiation?
- ◆ How are the table of contents and index handled?
- ◆ Where are page numbers located? What is their type size, font, weight? Must they be on every page?

Ordering Information
- ◆ Where does it go? Will ordering information be on the front cover, as well as the order form? Specifically, where should it be located?
- ◆ What does it consist of?
- ◆ What, if anything, goes on every page, and what goes in a special area?
- ◆ What type size, font?

COVER

Elements
- ◆ What elements will always be required on the cover?
- ◆ How do these items need to be represented?

Logo/Company Name
- ◆ Where does it go?
- ◆ How big is it?
- ◆ What can and cannot be shown with it?
- ◆ What colors can be used?

Tagline
- ◆ Where does it go?
- ◆ What type font, size, weight?

Issue Date
- ◆ Where does it go?
- ◆ What type font, size, weight?

Special Offer(s)
- ◆ Will this ever occur?
- ◆ If so, should there be a consistent placement?
- ◆ What type font, size, weight? Use pictorial?

Product Reference
- ◆ If product is shown, will references be used?
- ◆ Is there a consistent placement/treatment? On the cover with the product or a separate listing on the back cover? Both?
- ◆ What type font, size, weight?

Strategic Theme
- ◆ How will the cover reflect the theme of the particular issue?

Price Listing
- ◆ Will there be a price listed for the catalog?
- ◆ Is there a consistent placement/treatment?
- ◆ What type font, size, weight?

GENERAL COPY

Capitalization/Punctuation
- ◆ Will the standard rules for grammar, capitalization, and punctuation for narrative copy be followed?

Abbreviations
- ◆ What will the rule be for using abbreviations?

Hyphens
- ◆ Will hyphens be used to finish a word that won't fit at the end of a sentence?

Numbers
- ◆ Should these be spelled out? Where? In body copy and/or charts? Captions? Call-outs?
- ◆ Which numbers does this apply to? Measurements? Years? Styles? Quantities?

Trademarks/Logos
- ◆ How and when should registration marks ® and/or trademarks ™ be used?
- ◆ Should vendor trademarks/logos appear on products?
- ◆ How shall all trademarks be used in conjunction with the catalog company's logo?

Type
- ◆ Type size, style, and face should be noted in parentheses near specific copy elements throughout the style guide.
- ◆ Where not specifically indicated, type elements may change for graphic effect (this should be kept to a minimum).
- ◆ Noncondensed, serif type is standard in body copy wherever possible for customer readability.

BODY COPY

Type
- ◆ Use specific font? Point size? Leading?
- ◆ What format (right justified, left justified, centered)?

Capitalization
- ◆ Should standard capitalization rules be followed?
- ◆ How should first letters of each word, including hyphenated words in item lead-ins, item lines, and charts, be treated? How should the first word in incomplete sentences in body copy be treated?
- ◆ If key letters are used, should they be capitalized?

Punctuation
- ◆ Should standard punctuation rules be followed?
- ◆ Should incomplete sentences have periods?
- ◆ Should a semicolon be used to separate series of similar elements in a list?
- ◆ Should exclamation points ever be used?
- ◆ Should hyphens and/or a series of periods be used between thoughts/incomplete sentences?
- ◆ Should the number of commas in one sentence be limited?
- ◆ Should series commas be used before "and"?

Elements of SKU Line
- ◆ What should the basic elements be?
- ◆ In what order should they be listed? Item lead-ins? Copy? Item Line? Price Line? Price only? Keying?
- ◆ How are any abbreviations handled?
- ◆ What type font, size, weight?
- ◆ How should capitalization/lower case be handled?
- ◆ For each SKU line, determine the type font, weight, color, for the SKU and price. What about the item listing? Cap head? Weight? How should items be ordered and placed in relationship to rest of body copy? How should hyphens be used and placed? Use dollar sign with price? Use consistent .99 price ending with decimal points? How should sets/groups be indicated in this line? Can abbreviations be used? If so, when?

Sale Prices
- ◆ What should the basic elements be?
- ◆ What font and size?
- ◆ Use color?

Guarantee

- Frequency of placement?
- How is heading treated? Color? Boxed or set off by italic or bold lead-in?
- Should icons be incorporated? What position do they have in relationship to the copy? Do they replace the copy?

Regular Body Copy

- Is the first sentence bold, cap and lower case, or simply handled the same as the rest of the paragraph?
- Indented? If indented, first paragraph only, or subsequent paragraphs only?
- Does ampersand ever replace "and"?
- Are numbers used as words or numerals? Does this differ per use?
- If photography contains more than one product, how should the items be identified?

Category Headers

- Bold? Italic?
- Logo-like treatment?
- Boxed?
- Caps and lower case?

Subheads/Category Lead-in Paragraphs

- Bold? Italic?
- Caps and lower case?
- Indented?

MISCELLANEOUS COPY

Bursts/Banners/Special Items (such as "New" and "Exclusive")

- Are words all cap or cap and lower case?
- Should punctuation be used? What punctuation?
- Should type be italic? Bold? Is type consistent with body copy and/or headers, or a separate design element?

Phone Numbers and Hours for Ordering, Fax, and Customer Service

- Frequency?
- Consistently placed? Where?
- Type font, size, weight? Color?

Call-outs

- Type size, leading, and font?
- If sentence, use end punctuation and initial cap? If not a sentence, should any end punctuation be used?
- Italic? Does type match body copy and/or headers?

Captions

- Type size, leading and font?
- Write as labels or short sentences?
- Capitalize first word? Use end punctuation?
- Place directly under photos or inside photos?

Footnotes (if needed)

- What type size, leading, and font? Use smaller type face than in body?
- Begin with any highlighted character such as an asterisk?
- Use end punctuation?
- Capitalize first word?

Special Editorial Elements

- Type size, leading, and font for head? For body?
- Use quotes and relevant punctuation?
- If endorsements are used, is city, state, and/or title abbreviated?
- Tinted backgrounds? Rules around area?

Cross-References

- Part of body copy? Separate line?
- Same type size and font as body copy?

Letter

- Will this be bound in or part of catalog?
- Who signs?
- Format? Type font, size, and weight?

Icons

- Specifically, how are they used?
- Size? Color(s)? Type font, size, weight?

work on your catalog and/or if you use freelancers. Remember to update your style guide after every catalog edition; you will be striving constantly to improve your catalog, and this will necessitate changes.

Use the outline shown in Table 7-3 as a starting place for creating your own style guide. Revise it with each catalog issue and be sure to cite specific examples for each category. Even though this is a living document that is adapted regularly, you should strive for consistency among catalog editions.

Proofreader's Marks

The accepted system for correcting typeset copy is with proofreader's marks. They are simple to learn and wonderfully efficient. Even more important, these marks are used universally and will be readily understood by your art team, the typesetter, or anyone involved in graphic arts (see Figure 7-3).

❖ **FIGURE 7-3**
Proofreader's Marks

MARK	MEANING OF MARK	MARK ON ROUGH DRAFT	CORRECTED COPY
⊕	Insert space	The art will be ready by noon.	The art will be ready by noon
⌐	Move copy to right	A Handbook of Policies & Procedures	A Handbook of Policies & Procedures
⌐	Move copy to left	A Handbook of Policies & Procedures	A Handbook of Policies & Procedures
⊐⊏	Center copy	A Handbook of Policies & Procedures	A Handbook of Policies & Procedures
⊏/⊐	Insert brackets	Mr. Robert Moss 1846-1937 lived a long and happy life.	Mr. Robert Moss [1846-1937] lived a long and happy life.
{/}	Insert parentheses	The United States of America USA is a great country.	The United States of America (USA) is a great country.
⌒	Close up space	The handbook coordinator will attend that meeting today.	The handbook coordinator will attend that meeting today.
run in	Run material in with material on line above	We hope to be going to Europe this year.	We hope to be going to Europe this year.
¶	Start new paragraph	. . . . The ten horrible days had passed. All were relieved. On the eleventh day, when everyone was. . . .	. . . . The ten horrible days had passed. All were relieved. On the eleventh day, when everyone was. . . .
no ¶	No paragraph	The decision was made to prepare handbooks for all programs. All participants were delighted with the decision.	The decision was made to prepare handbooks for all programs. All participants were delighted with the decision.
sp.	Spell the word out	The managers & supervisors were gathered for the meeting.	The managers and supervisors were gathered for the meeting.
⌐	Move copy up	We were all waiting for the book.	We were all waiting for the book.
⌐	Move copy down	I hope more information will be found.	I hope more information will be found.

Proofreader's Marks continued

MARK	MEANING OF MARK	MARK ON ROUGH DRAFT	CORRECTED COPY
∧	Insert word or letter	Close the ˬdoor when you leave.	Close the door when you leave.
⊙	Insert period	Send the manuscript to me⊙	Send the manuscript to me.
⸴	Insert comma	Later⸴ if you have time⸴ come to see me in my office.	Later, if you have time, come to see me in my office.
⊙	Insert colon	I have the following⦂coffee. sugar. and cream.	I have the following: coffee. sugar. and cream.
;	Insert semicolon	Stay calm⸴ do not panic.	Stay calm; do not panic.
?	Insert question mark	When will the new forms arrive?	When will the new forms arrive?
!	Insert exclamation mark	What a beautiful office!	What a beautiful office!
⸝	Insert apostrophe	Didnⸯt we have five reports when we left the meeting?	Didn't we have five reports when we left the meeting?
⸗	Insert hyphens	An up⸗to⸗date handbook is essential	An up-to-date handbook is essential.
⹂ ⹂	Insert quotation marks	Susan said. How long will the meeting take?	Susan said. "How long will the meeting take?"
⋇	Insert asterisk	Table 4-5.2 indicates the amounts spent for manuscripts last year.	Table 4-5.2 indicates the amounts spent for manuscripts last year.*
⸜	Delete	The speaker wore a green ~~and lace~~ tie.	The speaker wore a green tie.
ⓣⓡ or ∩	Words transposed	The conference was short too	The conference was too short.
stet	Retain material as it was originally stated. Let it stand	The speech was beautifully organized and delivered.	The speech was beautifully organized and delivered.
≡	Set underlined letter as capital	the time has come to develop a handbook.	The time has come to develop a handbook.
≣	Set entire word(s) in capitals	He will never do that again!	He will NEVER do that again!
ⓛⓒ or /	Set letter lowercase	Susan returned to College this year.	Susan returned to college this year.

Photography

The photographs in your catalog are your "store display." They are the only visual presentation of your merchandise that customers see before they make the decision to buy and before their orders arrive. Photographs are critical sales tools. So it is essential that your catalog photographs be tantalizing and realistic.

Evaluating and Selecting a Photographer

Selecting a photographer is, to a large extent, a matter of personal taste based on his or her photographic style, its relevancy to the positioning of your catalog, and how well you interact with him or her. Nowhere else in the creative process of cataloging does the saying "Beauty is in the eye of the beholder" hold truer. However, a few guidelines can help you stay objective during the process of choosing who will make your photographs.

♦ Check the photographer's samples. If he or she is a fashion photographer, be especially careful to note black-and-white clothing photographed in four-color. Can you see the individual folds of the black dress or the embroidery stitches of the white? Or is the clothing so poorly lit that details are lost? Or perhaps the photo is too "hot" (has been lit too heavily), resulting in a loss of detail.

♦ Does a photographer who specializes in still (nonfashion) photography add life to basically lifeless products? Is steam coming from the coffee in the cup? Are there bubbles in the cold liquid in the creamer? Is the monogram easily readable on monogrammed items?

♦ Talk with current mail order clients of the photographer you're considering. Is the photographer easy to work with? Does he or she stay on schedule and have mail order experience? Editorial fashion photographers may have exciting samples but too often they go for effect, forgetting the major purpose of mail order photography is to show the product clearly. Will the photographer work with you on reshoots, accepting the cost for some of them?

♦ Take a look at the studio. Does it seem large enough to allow work on your project concurrently with others, or will yours be put aside to shoot other products because of lack of space? Does the photographer do the shooting? Is it done by a knowledgeable assistant under the careful supervision of the photographer, or is the unsupervised work turned over to someone else once it is in the studio? Does the studio appear to be clean and organized? Sometimes the appearance of his or her work environment can be a good indicator of how well the photographer will keep to a schedule.

Keeping Photography Costs Down

Nothing is as frustrating as discovering too late that your photography costs are considerably over budget. Here are a few pointers on how to make sure this doesn't happen to you.

1. Get a written quote like the one shown in Figure 7-4 from the photographer and understand exactly what you are buying. Film and processing should be

❖ **EXAMPLE 7-1**
Sugar Hill's superb lighting shows an abundance of product detail.

included in the cost of each photograph or as a separate but definitive line item. Leaving film and processing as an open expense can encourage unnecessary Polaroids (most photographers shoot Polaroids before the final shooting) and unanticipated expenses in film use. Be certain there are no hidden charges. One photographer attempted to add a charge for studio rental and use of the telephone (for local calls) during the shooting! There may be an added expense for feeding models. Get an estimate of how much this will be. And don't allow the photographer to buy lunch for the whole photography staff at the same time! Props are additional, so get an estimate with a minus or plus 10 percent ceiling.

Other fees that may be incurred, and should be discussed before the fact, include the following:

◆ Pre-preparation meetings—the time the photographer spends with the art director going over propping, model selection, and so forth. This should be included in the photography cost, but be aware that some photographers will want to charge extra for this service.

◆ Travel days—don't assume that getting to and from a location or even the photographer's studio is free. Ask.

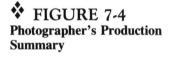

❖ FIGURE 7-4
Photographer's Production Summary

☐ *Estimate*
☐ *Invoice #*_____

► *To*

DATE
P.O. NUMBER
JOB NUMBER
A.D.
ART BUYER
CLIENT

Description

Rights Licensed

MEDIA USE:

PERIOD OF USE:

Fees			
PHOTOGRAPHY			
PRE-PRODUCTION			
TRAVEL	$	PER DAY	
WEATHER DELAYS	$	PER DAY	
POST PRODUCTION			

Production Charges & Expenses

CREW
STYLIST/HAIR/MAKE-UP
FILM, PROCESSING
PRINTS
INSURANCE
LOCATION/STUDIO
PROPS, WARDROBE
RENTALS
SETS/EXPENDABLES
SHIPPING & DELIVERY
CASTING
TRAVEL
MISCELLANEOUS

Post Production Expenses _____

TERMS: ESTIMATE: This estimate is valid for 30 days from the date of issue. Final billing will reflect actual, not estimated expenses, plus applicable taxes. Fees and expenses quoted in this estimate are for the original layout and job description only and for the uses specified. Additional usage fees upon request. Invoice: Payable upon receipt.
Late charge_____ % per month after 30 days.

PRODUCTION FEE
SUBTOTAL
SALES TAX %
TOTAL
ADVANCE

BILLED DIRECT:

TALENT

OTHER

TALENT FEES MAY NOT INCLUDE USAGES

BALANCE DUE

SIGNED BY (CLIENT IF ESTIMATE, PHOTOGRAPHER IF INVOICE)   DATE   *NON TAXABLE ITEMS

RIGHTS LICENSED ONLY UPON FULL PAYMENT OF THIS INVOICE AND SUBJECT TO TERMS AND CONDITIONS ON REVERSE.
PERMISSION IS GRANTED TO REPRODUCE IN WHOLE.
©1994 ADVERTISING PHOTOGRAPHERS OF AMERICA, NATIONAL

♦ Weather delays—it's not the photographer's fault if rain holds up the shooting, and he or she will most likely expect to be reimbursed for time lost.

2. Make sure all merchandise arrives on schedule. A written, hourly schedule (see Figures 7-5A and B) can then be made up for the photographer to follow. Backgrounds should be included in the timing to avoid unnecessary set changes. This system allows shooting to go like clockwork. But if one cog (item) is missing—for example, if merchandise does not arrive when expected— the whole system can come undone, resulting in extra expense.

3. Order duplicates, especially of breakable merchandise, to avoid frantic last-minute attempts to replace an item broken in shipment.

4. Have models try on clothing before the shooting day to be sure that garments fit perfectly. This will save a great deal of time and frustration at the studio.

❖ FIGURE 7-5A   Sample Shooting Schedule

Page #	Day/Date	Time Allocated	Product	Stylist	Prop	Model	Photographer	Product Manager and/or Art Director

❖ FIGURE 7-5B   Prop/Background Schedule

Day/Date Needed	Page #	Product with which Prop/ Background Goes	Prop	Background	Stylist Responsible	Product Manager

5. Go over the layouts in detail with the photographer, photographer's assistant, and/or stylist(s) from one day to a week before the shooting. Give as much input as possible. Should chemise dresses be shot with or without the belt, or both? Is there a special way to assemble an item that arrives in pieces? What is the right age for the child model using a particular product? (Determine at, or prior to, this meeting who will be hiring the models—you or the photographer).

6. Use tags or stickers to code all products to match the layouts so the photographer's assistant can set up the shots before you arrive.

7. Discuss usage prior to shooting and agree, in writing, to rights granted and period of use (see the form in Figure 7-6). Photos to be used only in a catalog may not be legally available for use in other promotions. Under the 1976 revisions to the copyright law, the photographer owns all the rights to use and reproduce the image from the moment it is shot, provided the notice provisions of the copyright law are followed. The photographer, in essence, leases the rights to the client for a fee. Be aware of what limitations, if any, the photographer has included in the estimate.

❖ **FIGURE 7-6**
Photograph Rights and Usage Form

ALL ASSIGNMENTS AND LICENSES ARE SUBJECT TO THE FOLLOWING AGREEMENT TERMS AND CONDITIONS

1. DEFINITIONS: This agreement is by and between _____ ("Photographer") and the commissioning party, ("Client", named on the face of this Agreement, including Client's representatives). Photographer's relationship with Client is that of an independent contractor. "Image" or "Image(s)" refers to the photographic or any other form of materials delivered by Photographer to Client. Photographer shall be considered the sole author of the Image(s). The Image(s) shall be the Photographer's interpretation, rather than a literal re-creation of any concepts or layouts provided the Photographer by Client or Client's representative. "Assignment" refers to the photography Assignment described on the face of this Agreement that Client is specifically commissioning Photographer to perform pursuant to this Agreement.

2. FEES, CHARGES AND EXPENSES: Client and Client's representatives are jointly and severally responsible for full payment of all fees, charges and expenses. The rights licensed, fees, charges and expenses listed on this Agreement only apply to the original Assignment description. Additional compensation is required for any subsequent changes, additions or variations requested by Client.

3. POSTPONEMENTS AND CANCELLATIONS: If Client postpones or cancels any scheduled assignment or "shoot date", in whole or in part, without first obtaining Photographer's written consent, Client shall pay Photographer 50% of Photographer's fees. If client postpones or cancels with less than 2 business days prior written notice to Photographer, Client shall pay 100% of Photographer's fees. Client shall in any event pay all expenses and charges incurred in connection with any postponed or canceled assignment or shoot date.

4. WEATHER DELAYS: Client will pay 100% of Photographer's daily weather delay fee (as set forth on the face of this Agreement) for any delays due to weather conditions or Acts of God, plus all charges and expenses incurred.

5. CLIENT APPROVAL: Client is responsible for having its authorized representative present during all "shooting" phases of the Assignment to approve Photographer's interpretation of the Assignment. If no representative is present, Photographer's interpretation shall be accepted. Client shall be bound by all approvals and job changes made by Client's representatives.

6. OVERTIME: In the event any Assignment extends beyond eight (8) consecutive hours in one day, Photographer will charge overtime for crew members and assistants at the rate of one and one half (1 1/2) times their hourly rate or fee.

7. RESHOOTS: Client will be required to pay 100% of Photographer's fee, charges and expenses for any reshoot requested by Client. If the Image(s) becomes lost or unusable by reason of defects, damage, equipment malfunction, processing, or other technical error prior to delivery of the Image(s) to the Client, Photographer will reshoot without additional fees, provided Client advances and pays all charges and expenses for the reshoot and pays all fees, charges and expenses for the initial Assignment.

8. INDEMNITY: Client shall indemnify, defend and hold Photographer and Photographer's representatives harmless from any and all claims, liabilities, damages, and expenses including actual attorney's fees and court costs arising from Client's use of the Image(s) or from Photographer's reliance on any representations, instructions, or materials provided or approved by the Client.

9. RIGHTS LICENSED: The right to reproduce or use any Image(s) in any manner is conditioned on Photographer's receipt of full payment and on use of copyright notice on all copies of the Image(s). Unless otherwise expressly stated on the front of this Agreement, the duration of any license is one-year from the date of Photographer's invoice and is for English language use in the United States of America only. All rights of every kind and nature in any and all media whether now known or hereafter developed, that are not expressly licensed or transferred in this Agreement are reserved by Photographer, including, without limitation, the right to use any Image in whole or in part in any form of derivative or collective works of any nature whatsoever. No license is valid unless signed by

Photographer. No rights licensed may be assigned or transferred in any manner without Photographer's prior written consent.

10. RETURN OF IMAGES: Client assumes all risk for all Image(s) delivered by Photographer to Client from the time of Client's receipt, to the time of the safe return receipt of the Image(s) to the possession and control of Photographer. If no return date appears on the front of this Agreement or on any related delivery memo, Client shall return all Image(s) in an undamaged, unaltered and unretouched condition within 30 days after first publication or use of the Image(s).

11. LOSS OR DAMAGE: IN CASE OF LOSS OR DAMAGE OF ANY ORIGINAL IMAGE(S), CLIENT AND PHOTOGRAPHER AGREE THAT THE REASONABLE VALUE OF EACH ORIGINAL IMAGE IS $1,500.00. Once original Image(s) are lost or damaged it is extremely difficult and impracticable to fix their exact individual value. Accordingly, Photographer and Client agree that the reasonable liquidated value of each original Image is $1,500.00. Client agrees to pay Photographer $1,500.00 for each lost or damaged original Image and Photographer agrees to limit Photographer's claim to that amount without regard to the actual value of the Image.

12. PAYMENT AND COLLECTION TERMS: Invoices from Photographer are payable upon receipt by Client. In any action to enforce the terms of this Agreement, the prevailing party shall be entitled to recover their actual attorney's fees, court costs and the maximum interest rate allowable by law. No lawsuits pertaining to any matter arising under or growing out of this Agreement shall be instituted in any other state other than the state of Photographer's principal place of business.

13. SALES, USE, OR TRANSIT TAX: Client is responsible for full payment of all applicable sales, use or similar taxes and for any subsequent assessment made by sales, use or other tax authorities in connection with the Assignment and/or the Image(s).

14. RELEASES: NO MODEL, PROPERTY OR OTHER RELEASE EXISTS FOR ANY IMAGE(S) UNLESS PHOTOGRAPHER SUBMITS A SEPARATE SIGNED RELEASE TO CLIENT.

15. ELECTRONIC DATA: Client shall not electronically or by any other means, methods or processes, whether now known or hereafter developed, in any manner use, scan, reproduce or copy any Image in whole or in part except as may be otherwise expressly stated on the front of this Agreement. Client shall not electronically or by any other means, methods or processes, whether now known or hereafter developed, in any manner retain, store, use or alter any Image in whole or in part, except as may be otherwise expressly stated on the front of this Agreement.

16. MODIFICATIONS, GOVERNING LAW AND MISCELLANEOUS: This Agreement sets forth the entire understanding and agreement between Photographer and Client regarding the Assignment and/or the Image(s). This Agreement supersedes any and all other prior representations and agreements regarding the Assignment and/or the Image(s), whether written or verbal. Neither Photographer nor Client shall be bound by any purchase order, term, condition, representation, warranty, or provision other than expressly stated in this Agreement. No waiver or modification may be made to any term or condition contained in this Agreement unless in writing and signed by Photographer. Waiver of any one provision of this Agreement shall not be deemed to be a waiver of any other provision of this Agreement. Any objections to the terms of this Agreement must be made in writing and delivered to Photographer within ten (10) days of the receipt of this Agreement by Client or Client's representative, or this Agreement shall be binding. No Images(s) however may be used in any manner without Photographer's prior written consent, and Client's holding, reproduction or use of any Image(s) in any manner constitutes Client's complete acceptance of this Agreement. The formation, interpretation, and performance of this Agreement shall be governed by the laws of the state of Photographer's principal place of business, excluding the conflict of laws rules in the state of Photographer's principal place of business. All paragraph captions are for reference only, and shall not be considered in construing this Agreement. This Agreement shall be construed in accordance with its terms and shall not be construed more favorable for or more strongly against Photographer or Client.

8. Delivery of merchandise and props to and from the studio or location isn't free or without risk. Get an estimate just as you would for props and understand, in advance, the terms of delivery. Figure 7-7 shows the terms set forth in the delivery form used by the Advertising Photographers of America.

Fashion versus Nonfashion Products

In mail order, still (nonclothing) items are often shot same-size—that is, the image you see in the photograph is exactly the same size as when printed. Fashion photos are generally shot random focus (with many different image sizes), using a 35mm camera, a Hasselblad, or a similar camera that shoots a $2\frac{1}{4}'' \times 2\frac{1}{4}''$ size. Since these cameras are lightweight and mobile, they allow more freedom of movement for the models and the photographer, resulting in better photos. The camera used for same-size photography is very large and hard to move. It is excellent for still photos, but too bulky to use when action or fluidity is required, as in fashion photography.

❖ FIGURE 7-7
Photographer's Delivery Memo

TO:		Date:
		P.O. #:
		Job #:
		A.D.:
		Buyer: #:
ATTN:		Client:

DELIVERY MEMO

The enclosed material, listed below, is submitted for examination only. Photographs may not be reproduced, copied, projected or publicly displayed without signed permission on Photographer's or Representative's Licensing Agreement. Use of this material as artist or photographer reference is specifically prohibited.

SET #	QUANTITY	FORMAT/DESCRIPTION/SUBJECT	ITEM VALUE

TERMS OF DELIVERY

COUNT. Please check count and acknowledge by signing and returning a copy of this memo to Photographer or Representative. Count shall be considered correct if copy is not received by return mail.

HOLDING FEES. After 14 days from receipt, a holding fee of $1.00 per item per day is payable until time of receipt by Photographer or Representative unless otherwise indicated above.

RETURN. This submission is conditioned on return of all items undamaged, unaltered and unretouched. Client (named above) assumes all risk for the items listed above from time of receipt by Client to time of receipt by Photographer or Representative. Please take special care in packing them for return. Do request a return receipt from your carrier.

LOSS OR DAMAGE. Reimbursement in case of loss or damage shall be determined by each item's reasonable value, which Client and Photographer agree is the amount(s) indicated above, plus the amount of any sales tax then due. At any time after the end of the agreed holding period, in the event of failure to return photographs, Photographer shall have the right to demand immediate payment in full of this amount.

MISCELLANEOUS. Objection to above terms must be made in writing within ten days. Any use of the photograph(s) listed above without written license will be considered willful infringement of copyright. Please read the back of this form before negotiating any use.

Accepted by: _____ Date _____

Location versus Studio Photography

Location photography can add excitement and intrigue to your catalog. It can also add expenses not associated with studio photography, such as the cost of lodgings, travel time for models, and food for the whole entourage. Also, if it rains, the hourly or daily rates for models, stylists, and photographers must still be paid. Location photography poses other problems as well. Lighting isn't controllable and sometimes can be detrimental to the appearance of the garments. If the sky is too overcast, clothing and photos in general can lose their brilliance. If it's too sunny, models get hot, makeup looks shiny, and everybody gets irritable. You may even end up photographing a fashion catalog for winter clothing—fur coats and all—in 99° weather! Try to look cool and fabulous wearing a fur coat on one of the sunniest, hottest days of the year, and you'll get some idea of how difficult location photography can be.

Yet, location photos can set a mood and establish credibility (if shot in a realistic and glamorous location) that cannot be duplicated in the studio. And sometimes arrangements can be made with airlines and hotels wherein these normal costs are waived in exchange for promotion within the catalog. Even under these conditions, extra expenses are generally incurred and location releases like the one in Figure 7-8 should be obtained. Be aware of all the costs involved and the potential problems of shooting on location, balance this against the image you wish to present, and make your decision.

Studio photography provides controllable lighting and weather conditions, two big pluses for catalogers. The cost, including props, is usually considerably lower than that of going on location. Yet studio photography can be boring. Here's where a good creative

❖ FIGURE 7-8
Sample Location Release Form

Date: _____

Studio Job #: _____

The owner/agent of the building/property located at:

_____

_____

hereby grants permission to photographer:

_____

to make photographs including any furnishings, signs, displays, etc. for the purpose of commercial sale or publication including advertising.

The photographer agrees to indemnify the owner/agent from and against any liability which may arise from the use of the building/property or photographs.

_____   _____
(Owner-Agent)   (Signature of Photographer)

_____   _____
(Address)   (Date)

_____
(Signature)

_____
(Date)

(Notes) _____

_____

_____

This form has been approved by
the Advertising Photographers of America, New York Chapter

team—your art director and the photographer—can make all the difference. Selecting the right backgrounds and props to create a memorable photograph, without overpowering the merchandise, is challenging but entirely possible. And don't forget, sometimes the solution is to keep the photographs wonderfully simple, allowing the design and graphic elements in the catalog to create an overall favorable impression.

❖ **EXAMPLE 7-2**
Two New York City–based catalogers use distinctly different approaches and create their own images. **(a)** Lew Magram adds dimension to studio shots with white-on-white forms as backdrops. **(b)** Lord & Taylor creates a rugged country atmosphere by shooting at an unnamed location.

New Photography Options

Even if you're in the production business, you've probably never heard of fixed-stop photography. But it is important because its use can save money, separation corrections, and even make-ready time at the press.

What is fixed-stop photography? Basically, it's contrast control. Instead of several bracketed exposures usually done manually by photographers, you get one mathematically calculated, optimum exposure—optimum because it greatly reduces color correction. One cataloger which, due to its product line, normally corrects 90 percent of scans, had to correct only 12 out of 65 when it cautiously changed from traditional to fixed-stop photography.

To understand how it works, a bit of background is necessary. Although desirable, it is unusual for an art director or production manager to arrange for the photographer and separator to talk to each other. And even then there are limitations to their communication since their work is very different.

You're made aware of these differences every time you look at a printed piece and wonder where the color went. You know something is missing, but you're not really sure whose fault it is. One of the problems is found in this simple fact: A color transparency can reproduce as much as twice the amount of density the offset press can put on paper.

In this case, density means light intensity, or the amount of light that actually strikes the surface being lit. And this can be measured by photographers. It's called an f/stop or EV-value, two phrases with which amateur photographers may be familiar. When you look at a photo, you see a variety of light and dark areas. In a typical photo, the difference in these highlights and shadows might be five f-stops—which is a problem because this is more than can be reproduced accurately on paper.

Separators measure light differently from the way photographers and printers do. They measure it by how much light can pass through a transparency. Printers measure light by how much it reflects off the page. This is why the printed piece too often doesn't look the way it did when you viewed it as a transparency.

In web offset printing, white paper (with no images) measures zero density. Conversely, the highest possible density is around 1.80 (depending on the type of press). For instance, a printed four-color image of a teapot from the lightest highlight to the deepest shadow would have an entire density range of 1.80. The problem is that the transparency from which this teapot was reproduced has a range of 2.80 (or more than five f/stops).

It sounds like something is missing—and it is. If you provide your separator with a transparency of higher than the 1.80 density the press can print, the information on that transparency will be condensed into a barely recognizable reproduction. The separator knows that the 2.80 transparency is not going to fit the 1.80 requirement of the press, so he or she must choose from three undesirable options: compress the highlight, compress the midtone, or compress the shadow. No matter which option is chosen, the color quality will be inferior.

The solution is to give the separator the right product to begin with. This can be done by controlling the density in the transparency and requires accurately metering highlight and shadow at the film plane. A responsive photographer will place light sources, diffusers, and fill cards judiciously and light the subject to fall within the 1.80 density range.

Since ordinary light meters don't measure density, the photographer will need to use either a TTL (through the lens) meter or a hand-held meter.

It is important to clarify that the four f/stop range, the secret to better reproduction, should apply only to the highlight areas and the shadow areas that should have detail. Supplying your separator and your printer with something they can accurately reproduce makes a lot of sense.

Some experts feel there is a downside to this. You will no longer see multiple bracketed exposures and pick one to match the other. With the fixed-stop system, you must trust that your photographer has correctly measured the light density and provided you with the one photo that will give you the best reproduction. As security, some photographers shoot two photos at the same exposure for backup.

Another benefit you may choose to take advantage of is the ability to gang-scan. Transparencies scanned using this method tend to show the same color correction throughout, a perfect situation for gang-scans.

Press OK's can go faster too. One cataloger reported that make-ready time to get the color up on a gravure run substantially decreased. She stated, ''I think I set a record for the shortest press OK while printing a 16-page catalog insert. One side had no corrections and the other side had only one. This was at a printer we've worked with previously, and prior to this the shortest press OK there was three to four hours.''

The best part to using fixed-stop photography can be the final outcome. Users report that you will have a quality product of which you can be proud.

Digital Photography

One of the hottest new subjects gaining popularity is digital photography. The main use of what is, in essence, electronic photography, is to create an image directly from the camera right into a computer—no prints, no processing. Some catalogers use this merely for positioning. By electronically ''shooting'' the product in the position and angle in which it will later be professionally photographed, the computer artist ensures that his or her layouts will be highly accurate. The big benefit to both the artist and the photographer is that this ''run-through'' allows the artist to be clear about how he or she expects the picture to be taken by the photographer. In addition, there is little rearranging of elements on the page once the photo has been shot, because it should fit exactly as planned (something that often does not happen when the artist is guessing how the product will fit before it is actually shot).

Photographers may, in some cases, eventually find themselves replaced. *Direct* magazine reports that Sony has a system that comes complete with video camera, digital processor, viewfinder, color monitor, remote control, and a software plug-in module. Its ''three-CCD'' is a charged-coupled device that converts light into electrons. Some systems calibrate the digital camera system so that all images captured under the same lighting conditions automatically assume the proper gray balance and tonal ranges. Technology will likely replace some of the lighting decisions previously made by the photographer and could make the photo process, at least for simple set-ups, easy for the same person who creates and produces the computerized layout to complete.

Location Photography and Freebies

Choosing a Location.   You may already know where you wish to shoot. Or, as is more common, you may have some idea but don't know the details of the location and how efficiently it might work when you actually need to get eight to ten shoots completed a day. One solution is to use location scouts. (Location-savvy photographers usually can recommend a good location scout.) In turn, a location scout, who should have plenty of experience on which to draw, can sometimes recommend which hotels will usually work with a photo shoot group. Location scouts charge about $350 per day plus expenses and can be found in the *Creative Black Book.*

Alternatively, you can rely on your photographer's experience regarding successful locations. This will save the cost of a location scout and the time in the schedule which you would have to allow for the scout to check out the location(s) prior to booking one. Although this activity is generally concurrent with other events in the schedule, using a location with which the photographer is familiar will also help things go more smoothly and faster once you arrive. Only hire a photographer who has done location shooting many times before.

Select a location that echoes the feeling your product line and catalog strive to evoke. Make sure the chosen location has enough alternatives for backgrounds; the last thing you want to do is bring extra props. Plan for the chance of inclement weather by knowing your options for shooting indoors. Every hour lost due to uncooperative weather costs you because the model and photographer's crew are still going to charge you for the time, whether they're working or not. It's always prudent to purchase location shoot insurance, usually available from your regular insurance company.

If you have a company travel agency, talk to them and see if they have any ideas for you. Even if they don't have experience with short-term group rates, they can at least provide you with some location ideas that tie in with the time of year you're trying to represent. They can also provide you with travel brochures that will give an idea of how certain locations look, as well as what hotels are available there.

Pay attention to other catalogs that are shot on location. Look through these catalogs carefully because the location where the catalog was shot, as well as where the crew stayed and what airlines they used, are usually listed in the catalog. When you see this kind of information, you can almost always be sure that discounts were negotiated. If those locations seem right for your catalog's positioning, find out if these companies will work with you.

When possible, try to stay in the United States for your shoot. Even though it may seem like fun, or a "free vacation" to go someplace more exotic, you'll find there are a lot more headaches attached to it.

Time of Year.   Since your photo shoot will probably take place about two months prior to mailing, the weather of your location shoot should be a deciding factor. For example, if you're planning on photographing a spring catalog in January for mailing in early March, you'll need to go somewhere warm to shoot. Unfortunately, this tends to be the high season, and you might not find the same discounts you would during the off season.

Beginning Your Search.   Discounts usually are dependent on the size, circulation, and distribution region of your catalog. Resorts, hotels, airlines, and such are more willing to talk to you if they know your company is going to give them significant and respectable exposure. Weather is also a major factor. Hotels that attract a college crowd don't need to give away free or discounted rooms during spring break. But they'd definitely be willing to negotiate in July. The following are some rules of thumb for location shopping:

1. Know your catalog's distribution region and quantity. Also, know your target market. Be prepared to answer questions regarding the days you're planning on traveling, the number of rooms you'll need, and your approximate flight schedules (for example, maybe only eight people will be staying for the whole shoot, and the models will be coming and going). Your answers to these questions will have a direct impact on the negotiations.

2. Start your calls early—it can take a long time to find the right people to help you.

3. Once you narrow down an area of interest (such as the Caribbean, Florida, or New England) you can begin calling hotels in that area. Ask to speak to the public relations or marketing department.

   You can also call the headquarters of some of the big hotel chains and tell their public relations departments you are putting together a location shoot and want to work out a reciprocal agreement. This way you're calling one source that covers many locations. For example, you may be interested in shooting in the Caribbean, and you know the Marriott chain has a lot of hotels throughout the Caribbean. The corporate headquarters might be able to tell you that Sam Lord's Castle in Barbados is often used for location shoots and there happen to be rooms available during that time of the year. Be flexible; it may be to your budget's advantage to end up shooting in Barbados when you originally thought you'd be heading to Aruba.

4. Call the major airlines and ask if they have group rates available. They may be able to set your group up on a package deal. Some airlines will give you discounted travel for a photo of their plane and/or logo and/or copy block somewhere in the catalog.

5. Before making that first call, have in mind some ideas of reciprocal arrangements with which you'd be comfortable. You can often offer something as little as a line of copy on page 2, saying, "Photographed at Sam Lord's Castle in Barbados" for free or discounted rooms. As always, see how much you can get for how little before you start offering a location picture with a full paragraph of copy and the hotel's logo. Decide what you're willing to include in your catalog and what you're not.

6. You'll also want to get an extra secured room or two near where you'll be shooting. This extra space will be needed for storing merchandise, as a changing room, and as a place for the hair and makeup person to work. Try to get these rooms thrown in for free. Understand that not every room will have an ocean view or other amenity; you are not there on vacation, so be willing to accept a lesser room location as part of your negotiations.

Shooting Abroad. If you're traveling internationally, make sure everyone, including the models, if applicable, have appropriate documentation, such as passports, in advance.

As part of your initial planning, check with customs. There is sometimes concern that if you are taking a lot of merchandise to a foreign country, the merchandise will be sold in that country. Ask customs what you'll need to do to prepare. One possibly is hiring a custom's broker. This person has the experience to safely and legally get your merchandise and equipment over and back. Be sure to hire someone who is very experienced and comes with plenty of recent references.

All merchandise being transported abroad needs to be clearly labeled. Create a detailed list of what's in each trunk. Include the item name, manufacturer name, content, origin of manufacturing, wholesale cost, and stock keeping unit (SKU) number. Put a copy of this list in the trunk and on the outside of it, and keep copies with you. Customs might ask to see this list before your departure. To prevent products from being sold illegally, they might also require you to damage each sample in some way, such as cutting the back of a garment, writing "sample" somewhere, and so on.

Other Important Issues. Airlines will most likely charge you extra for the photographer's equipment and merchandise trunks. Since this can be somewhat expensive, try to make special arrangements with the airlines for this fee and process prior to making a flight commitment.

Check with your location scout or hotel contact in advance to see if you'll need permits to shoot in different locations. Even if the hotel doesn't require it, the town might.

Always remember to send thank-you notes and catalog samples to everyone involved in this complicated process. They'll remember and be more willing to work with you again. For the same reason, be sure your photo crew remains respectful of the property on which they're shooting.

Many ad agencies that handle a lot of location shoots for their clients will have people who handle the arrangements. It is a full-time job and should be coordinated by an experienced person who can either make the necessary decisions or has ready access to the person(s) who will be making the decisions. It is also a good idea to have this person (often called a production coordinator) on the shoot. His or her job is to act as the troubleshooter, freeing the art director and photographer to concentrate on their work.

❖ **EXAMPLE 7-3**
Millers shows its riding clothes
in an appropriate setting:
car-free Mackinac Island.

Pointers for Selecting Models

Models reflect your catalog's image. Here are some points to keep in mind as you review
your choices:

♦ How old should the model be? Are you appealing to a young audience or a
more mature one? Customers not only identify with models but want someone
they would like to emulate. To be on the safe side, choose models who look
approximately ten years younger and at least 20 pounds lighter than your target
audience.

♦ How versatile is the model's expression? Sadly, some of the most attractive
models seem to have the same frozen smile locked in place all the time. Check
the potential model's portfolio carefully to find out if he or she can adapt to
the image of the product to be modeled. Be sure to see the models you wish to
use in a room together. The interaction between them on a set or location can
make or break a shoot.

♦ Sometimes a wholesome outdoor look is in order; sometimes a smoldering, yet
ladylike (or gentlemanly), look is required. But models should always look
happy about the products they're wearing. High-fashion models are allowed
distressingly sophisticated expressions (sometimes they look as if they are in
real pain), but mail order most often sells fun, status, and just plain enjoyment,
so if this is your positioning, the model's face should convey this.

♦ Is the model mobile or still and inexperienced? Since a customer will not
actually touch the garment until it arrives in the mail, the model must make the
product come alive and zoom off the pages and into the customer's life.
Fluidity of movement (or the lack of it) can make or break an item of clothing.

♦ How experienced is the model? Experience in front of a camera saves valuable
hours of shooting time. Unless your catalog has the kind of positioning that can
support a less-then-professional approach, don't be tempted to use your

lengths

Poplin swimwear we've prewashed to such an extent that fabric and color appear already much softened by sun and surf. In trunk, volley, and surfer lengths, each in your choice of our seven colors. Striped with twill tape—two stripes on surfer and volley, one on the trunks. We've clearly gone to great lengths here.

❖ **EXAMPLE 7-4**
J. Crew puts plenty of fun and action into its men's swimwear presentation and still manages to emphasize the product first.

❖ **EXAMPLE 7-5**
Norm Thompson knows that great shots have one common element: The model poses in such a way that the prospective customer can see every detail of the garment being sold.

good-looking next-door neighbor. Chances are he or she will freeze in front of the camera, cause the photographer to take many more rolls of film than anticipated, and, even then, give unsatisfactory results.

♦ Child models are a different story. In many cases, unprofessional children are as good as, and even better than, their professional counterparts. The inexperienced child model can bring a naturalness to modeling that some of the more experienced children unfortunately have lost.

Stricter laws apply to children than to their adult counterparts. For one thing, the child's parent or legal guardian must be on the set during the photo session. Work permits may be required, depending on the state, and some states forbid children from working during school hours. Additionally, the number of hours a child may work per day may be limited by state laws. Check the labor laws in your state, and don't assume that the hours a child works for you are the only hours he or she has worked that day. If the child was at another photo session prior to yours, you could be the one in violation.

In all cases, have models come for a ''go see'' before committing to them. The head shots sent to you by a modeling agency do not always reflect how a model looks today. One client selected a male model for his mustache. Imagine their surprise when he showed up on his ''go see'' sans mustache! The one in his photos was a fake. In another instance, a model who was supposed to be a size 8 showed up 20 pounds over her normal weight. She could never have fit into the clothes that were planned for her. Models are generally

❖ **EXAMPLE 7-6**

Eddie Bauer uses a mix of real people in its shots.

❖ **EXAMPLE 7-7**

The Company of Women highlights customers' satisfaction by using them as models.

booked through a modeling agency and billed directly to the client, but if you ask for assistance from your agency or photographer, you may incur a charge for their time.

Get a signed model release (like the one shown in Figure 7-9) for every model, professional or not, you use in your catalog. A model release, in essence, says that the person who posed in the photograph has no further interest in the use of the photograph. This allows you to use the photograph in a future catalog issue, in a space ad, or in any way you choose, without paying additional fees to the model (but don't forget to check usage rights with the photographer). Your photographer should have forms on hand for the models to sign. Be sure they are used and get a copy of each one. Should the photographer move to another location, or should you change photographers for some reason, you will have a copy of the signed release in your files.

❖ FIGURE 7-9
Sample Model Release and Consent Agreement

Date: _____

Studio Job #: _____

For the payment indicated, I consent to the use described below of the photographs made of me today by photographer:

_____

Description and Usage: _____

_____

I am providing modeling services as independent contractor.

Hours worked: _____   Payment: _____

_____   _____
(Model's Name)   (Photographer's signature)

_____   _____
(Address)   (Date)

_____
(   )
(Telephone)

_____ / _____ / _____
(Social Security #)

_____
(Model's signature)

_____
(Date)

IF MODEL IS A MINOR, PARENT OR GUARDIAN MUST SIGN BELOW

I am the parent or guardian of the minor whose name appears above. I consent to the above items on his/her behalf, and warrant that I have the authority to give such consent.

_____
(Parent's name)

_____
(Address)

_____
(Signature)

_____
(Date)

This form has been approved by
the Advertising Photographers of America, New York Chapter

Using a Stylist

There are several different types of stylists—food, hair, make-up, and general. All of them have one basic, very important function: to see that the product being shot is properly complemented via props or appearance of hair and make-up.

Food stylists are the artisans who physically prepare the food used to showcase a food-related product. They are the ones who actually shop for the ingredients to be used, then prepare the dishes for the shoot. The artful catalog food stylist must concoct a feast for the eyes that will not only photograph well, even under hot lights, but will complement the product with which it is shown, without overwhelming it.

Hair and make-up stylists can sometimes be one and the same, but more often than not are two different people. As their titles imply, these are the artists who make models appear perfect with painstakingly applied make-up and carefully controlled hair styling. As with the other types of stylists, their job is not over when they apply make-up and set/adjust the hair style. They must be on the set at all times, being alert to adjustments that need to be made as the photos are shot. It is up to them to be certain that untidy wisps of hair do not ruin that perfect shot!

General stylists usually specialize in different areas, such as hard goods (nonfashion) or fashion. Besides making sure that the props are placed correctly in the photograph, these stylists might also be responsible for procuring the props and backgrounds (this function can also be performed by the photographer's assistant). Another important aspect of their job is to contribute ideas on how photographs should be propped. A good stylist is highly imaginative, but also understands what props are meant to convey when shown with your products.

Stylists work on hourly, daily, or weekly rates, the same as photographers. Probably the best source for a knowledgeable stylist is your photographer. His or her experience with stylists can lead you to those who will fulfill your needs.

❖ **EXAMPLE 7-8**
Kitchen & Home takes a simple but very complementary approach with minimal use of props.

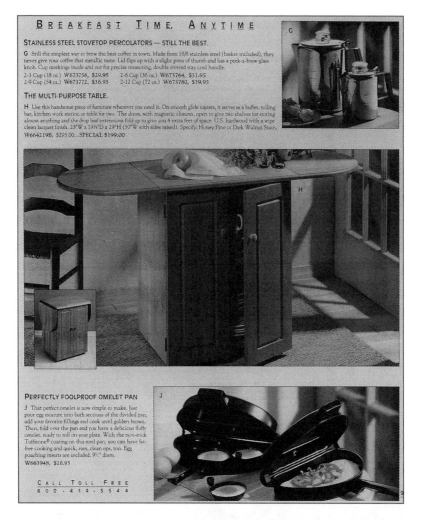

Retouching

Traditional retouching has largely fallen by the wayside. The major reason is the electronic abilities now inherent in the separation process. Want the garment to be another color, add polka dots, or take them away? This is easily accomplished by computer manipulation available during the separation process. Want to add a button or fix a stray hair? Again, electronics can come to the rescue. Perhaps a garment simply wouldn't iron properly and the wrinkles need to be ''ironed out.'' Or perhaps an item had to be held in position with a string, which now needs to be deleted from the photo. All of this is possible.

However, these adjustments are not free and you must be certain to determine which method, traditional or electronic retouching, will give you the best results for the cost.

If you choose traditional retouching, understand that it can be done directly on the transparency or on a color print (dye transfer). The first is preferable, although more difficult, because it does not take away from art's original quality. To retouch directly on the transparency, the artist must have a delicate hand and full understanding of the chemicals used for the corrections. If the retouching is not done properly, the scanner used in separations may not pick up the correction from the transparency, or it may pick up a *bloom*—a shiny or hot spot caused by retouching.

If you choose the electronic retouching, don't be tempted to use anything but a top-quality print of the transparency. Each successive step away from the original automatically means a reduction of quality, so don't compound this problem by opting for a less-than-perfect print. Here again, the artist can run into blooms. However, because the print is generally larger than the transparency, the retouched area is easier to see and easier to correct. The print must wrap around the cylinder used by a scanner (separator), so don't allow the print to be mounted on a board that's thicker than .006 inches.

Remember, before committing yourself to retouching, talk to both the separator and the retoucher. Define the problem clearly and rely strongly on their advice.

Attending the Photo Session

Your presence during the actual shooting, or the presence of a knowledgeable representative, is essential. No one knows the benefits of the merchandise or how it should be shown as well as you do. This is your final chance to make changes in the positioning of the product as shown in the layout. And, if there was any doubt in your mind as to how the product would look when photographed, this is the time to ask questions, while you can still make adjustments. But don't make changes willy-nilly. Being there also helps eliminate reshoots. Be alert to what is going on around you, and don't hesitate to speak up if you have questions about the way an item is being photographed. Watch the stylist or assistant as he or she sets up the shot, and understand the angle and the lighting that will be used. Review the Polaroids the photographer almost always shoots as a preparation before the actual photograph. Identifying a problem before the shooting is avoiding a problem. Always monitor the entire process.

A Real-Life Vignette.   Setting up the Stack 'n' Store Bins for a photograph for a toy catalog was a painstakingly long process. The client, who lived in another state, had chosen not to be at the photography session. Every bin had to be assembled, then correctly propped. To compound this, the photo was to include a child playing with a toy train in front of the bins. No one was more surprised than the agency in charge was to learn that the client was greatly upset when the photo arrived. The bins were not stacked correctly! The client had manufactured special wooden dowels with which to assemble the bins in a totally uncommon manner. Trying to explain the way the bins actually went together over the phone was impossible. What's more, all scheduled photography was complete, and there was little time to reshoot the photograph. The solution: The client took a photo showing how the bins should look. The agency used both the original photo and an insert of the client's photo to show that the bins could be used in a variety of ways. A potential problem was turned into a benefit—but the importance of the person who truly knows the product being present at the photography session was clearly demonstrated.

Making Changes—A Note of Caution

Deviating from props, backgrounds, and so forth you previously agreed to can change the cost from the estimate you approved. Make changes wisely, and ask if the changes will affect the cost before you arbitrarily make them. Don't be surprised if you are asked to sign a job-change confirmation (see Figure 7-10). This is for your protection as well as the photographer's. Reconstructing, weeks after the fact, exactly why changes were made is virtually impossible. Keeping track of revisions as they occur means you'll have an accurate record (not just sketchy memories) on which you can rely when invoices are presented.

❖ FIGURE 7-10
Job-Change Confirmation Form

TO:		Date:
		P.O. #:
		Job #:
		A.D.:
		Buyer: #:
		Client:

JOB CHANGE CONFIRMATION # _____ for Studio job/estimate # _____

This is to confirm costs resulting from the following changes, additions, or variations of the original job description and rights requested as agreed upon by the Art Director/Buyer and the Photographer or Representative.

DESCRIPTION   ADDITIONAL COSTS

1.

  A.D./Buyer initials: _____ Date: _____   Fees: _____
                                                                  Expenses: _____

2.

  A.D./Buyer initials: _____ Date: _____   Fees: _____
                                                                  Expenses: _____

3.

  A.D./Buyer initials: _____ Date: _____   Fees: _____
                                                                  Expenses: _____

                TOTAL ADDITIONAL FEES AND EXPENSES _____

These job changes will be incorporated into the licensing agreement, and are governed by the original terms and conditions except as noted above.

Art Director/Buyer signature: _____ Date: _____

Adding Impact with Illustrations

Although the first catalogs (such as Sears and Montogomery Ward) contained nothing but illustrations, the use of art to display products fell out of favor decades ago. Why? The commonly held belief is that photography not only shows the merchandise to its best advantage but also gives a sense of reality and a ''modern'' approach to the presentation.

But, as in all things, there are some notable exceptions to this theory. For example, J. Peterman, a successful clothing cataloger much talked-about in recent years, uses illustrations combined with engrossing copy to emphasize benefits and create an appealing aura. Vermont Country Store, which bills itself as the Voice of the Mountains®, has an old-time look and a ''general store'' merchandising approach. It combines photography and illustration for a down-to-earth feeling that works well with long product copy. Others, such as Disney, use the equity of their cartoon characters in conjunction with traditional photography.

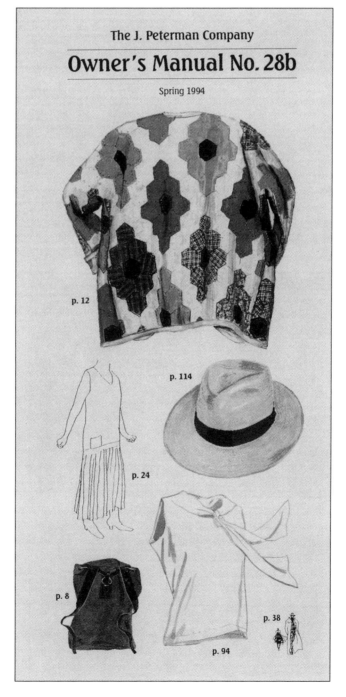

❖ EXAMPLE 7-9

J. Peterman uses illustrations like the one on this cover throughout his catalog.

❖ **EXAMPLE 7-10**   Historic Housefitters is one of the few catalogs that combines illustrations and photography.

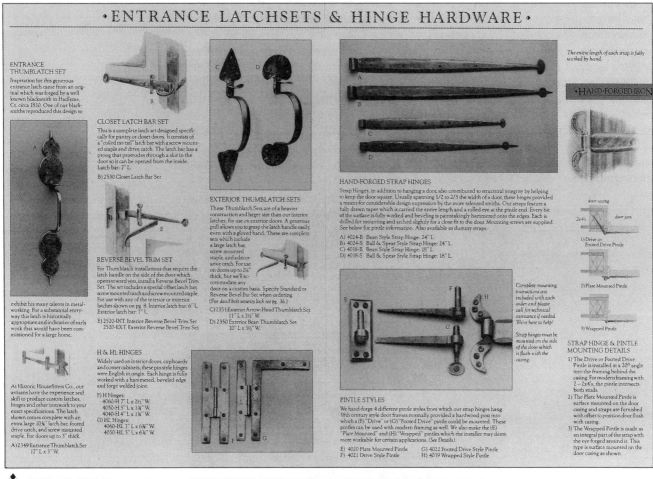

❖ **EXAMPLE 7-11**

Some catalogers, such as Norm Thompson's Departures, use photography inside and art illustration on the cover. Some even sell featured artwork in the form of note cards or posters.

Choosing to use illustrations is a matter of positioning and, once chosen, of monitoring results. Working with an illustrator is virtually the same as working with a photographer. Follow the same basic rules as far as budgets, schedules, rights, and so forth are concerned. There is one major difference, however. Generally speaking, illustrations take longer than photography and can't be visually conveyed prior to the final art as easily as photography. Remember, you're on the set during photography; it's unlikely that you'll be watching over the artists' shoulders as they draw. So be sure to see a sketch of the intended final art before long hours are put into the finished product. Artists will sometimes sketch several versions of the same "scene" (this is especially true for covers) at minimal extra charge. As with any supplier, the more you work together and openly communicate your feelings, the sooner you'll be able to "read each other's minds."

Electronic Publishing

As desktop publishing becomes the norm (see Figure 7-11), the line between creative and production is fading fast. Artists must be both designers and experts in preparing the Syquest disk (one brand of portable storage device in cartridge form that holds many megabytes of data) in the format needed by the separator. The process for creating the design on the computer is addressed in Chapter 8. However, it is equally important to understand some of the technical requirements of the computer process because your output must meet the separator's needs to ensure your film is representative of the version you saw and approved in the computerized layout stage.

The Process

In the past, layouts were simply layouts, copy was simply words on paper, and the only complicated part of the creative/production process was understanding exactly how separations were made. This is no longer true. Now it's all intricate, perplexing, frustrating, and even contradictory.

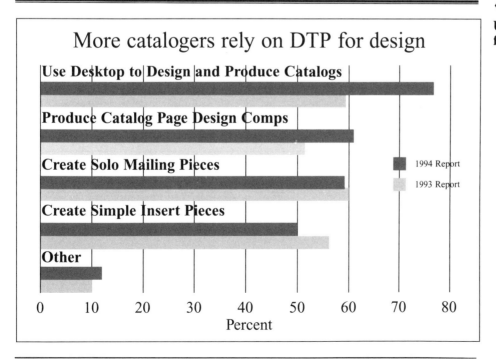

❖ FIGURE 7-11
Uses of Desktop Publishing for Catalog Design

Source: "The Catalog Report." *Catalog Age*, December 1993, 63.

Now, the artist must not only know how to design; he or she must also know how to prepare desktop publishing files (called CREF, for computer-ready electronic file) for successful output to film. You must avoid being caught in the web of blame associated with whether or not the files have been created to the separator's satisfaction and legitimate needs. If they haven't, this means overtime costs and missed press dates. It's at this stage that the artist says he or she did everything required and the separator says he or she didn't. What are you, a neophyte in the evolving business, to do?

To help reduce the chances of frustration during the transfer of files from the artist to the separator, think in the same terms as when you arrange for film to be created by the separator for the printer. Get both parties to agree to every detail and put it in writing. There is an excellent booklet, written by Ray Flatt of NEC, that can help you do this and better understand the needs of the desktop publishing process. It's called *CREF— Computer Ready Electronic Files* and available, free of charge, from Scitex Graphic Arts Users Association, Inc. (SGAUA), 305 Plus Park Boulevard, Nashville, TN 37217. The form shown in Figure 7-12 is reproduced from this booklet. Fill this, or something like it, out with your separator to clearly determine the parameters of the job. It's your separator's responsibility to see that such a form is filled out, but it will be your problem if something is misunderstood, so create one yourself if you have to.

❖ FIGURE 7-12
Separator's Job Form

The SGAUA CREF™ booklet also includes a handy checklist, adapted here and expanded with the help of the author.

1. Are all fonts (to be used in the job) on the disc that is being sent to the separator?

   The point here is to be clear. PostScript™ is generally more readily available at separators than TrueType™ fonts are. Both fonts have some of the same names, so there can easily be confusion. Run a test with your separator if you wish to use TrueType™ fonts. A complete listing of all fonts used to create the documents should accompany the disc for output. Don't assume because your artist has one typeface on his or her machine that the separator also carries it. And remember the legalities associated with software; it is illegal to copy the typeface and give it to the separator.

2. Have special text effects been done in a consistent manner, one which you and your separator have previously agreed on?

   For instance, outlines do not always reproduce as sharply as they seem to on the computer screen when drawn with Quark Express®, so Adobe Illustrator™ or Aldus Freehand™ is recommended.

3. Have all colors been defined correctly?
   - Process-defined colors should have Separation turned on (this is a checkbox within the software program).
   - A fifth color should be defined as spot color, and Separation should be turned off.
   - It is never wise to select color tints or shades from a color monitor. Pick up a printed guide and use this to make an accurate color choice.

4. Have borders or Scotch rules (double rules) been properly created? Are you sure your bitmapped graphic frames will reproduce properly?

   First, understand that *Vector-based* is a term that describes art in terms of a mathematical outline/fill, while *raster-based* means to describe it in terms of dots. Photoshop uses raster images; Illustrator and Freehand create vector images. Macintosh systems create layouts in both raster and vector art. The separator's RIP takes the Mac vector and raster art and converts all the files into one big raster-image file. When they are reinterpreted into dots, they can become choppy looking.

5. Are all images identified?
   - Every image should be identified unless you feel that you can clearly mark the exceptions only. Scanned line art should be marked ''LIVE'' on proofs. ''SILO'' should indicate those photos you wish to be silhouetted. Those for position only should be labeled ''FPO,'' meaning the art in place is not of reproducible quality but is there only for approval of the position in which it is shown.
   - Encapsulated PostScript (EPS) files must accompany the corresponding electronic file, include parent film from Aldus Freehand. Once placed in Quark Express document, the file name cannot be changed. An EPS file is an electronic pick-up consisting of artwork, created by a program such as FreeHand. This artwork is not photography, but art such as charts, bursts, and so on.

6. Does every file have a unique file name?

7. If you're sending a revised file, does it have a new name? Or is it marked REV 1, REV 2, or something similar?

8. Are you supplying 100 percent hard copy proofs?

   A hard copy, or printed proof, is very important for quality control. Be sure to include:
   - Print proofs with registration marks checked. This is not just for registration marks, but also to make sure there is a file name on the document; file names come up automatically when you print the registration marks.

◆ The proof should be titled, if necessary, to include marks.
◆ For black-and-white proofs, check color/gray scale and print colors as gray.
◆ The proof must be shipped with the electronic file.

9. Is the shipping media (the disk itself and its container) properly labeled?
◆ The electronic file media should have a title with your company's name and disk number.
◆ The shipping media container should be clearly marked with the publication/catalog's name, in-service date, and disk number. Remember, all Syquest disks look alike on the outside.

10. Have you collected and sent all job elements?
◆ A 100 percent hard copy proof.
◆ A hard copy of all electronic FPO elements—transparencies, reflective art, logos, and line art. Scanned FPO electronic files are not needed (these are your low-resolution, desktop scans).
◆ A computer-generated transmittal report or manual checklist form.
◆ A transmittal printout (directory list of your shipping media).
◆ A page layout file (your Quark Express or PageMaker document).
◆ Live TIFF (Tag Image File Format) files of the actual art placed in a document that is to be used to produce film (such as live black-and-white halftones).
◆ Live EPS files (of the actual art) placed in a document that is to be used to produce film.
◆ Parent files for any Freehand EPS files used in the document.
◆ Quark Express data and hyphenation if you are using Quark Express 3.0 or an older version (as most people are).

The SGAUA CREF booklet has a great deal of information that is essential for artists creating computer-ready electronic files. As Ray Flatt says, one of its major intents is to help the industry have "consistent, agreed-upon desktop habits." Since this would make all our lives less frustrating, it is advisable to send for the booklet and read it, even if you are not an artist. It will give you a better understanding of the process and act as a stimulant for your artist to go over any points that may not be imminently clear.

So far, the responsibility has been laid on the artist. But this is only part of it. The separator should, with your encouragement, take the lead in establishing *exactly* what is needed (this is where the form in Figure 7-12 comes in). Another critical point is when the computer disk arrives at the separator's. Someone must immediately open this file and determine if the specifications have been followed correctly. This must be done in a timely manner to allow for potential changes that may need to be made by the artist before the separations can proceed. Follow up a day after the disk is delivered and receive assurance that all is well.

Low-versus High-Resolution Scans

The images that represent your products as you see them on the computer screen can be produced in either high-resolution 300 (dots per inch) (DPI) or low-resolution 72 DPI. High resolution is the quality necessary for reproduction; low resolution is generally considered sufficient for positioning, similar to the way artists used to position photostats on mechanical art. But how do you actually get the images into the computer so you can see any resolution? They must first be scanned, and the quality of the scan is pretty much in direct relation to the cost of the scanner. A scanner simply "reads" the transparency, creating a digital pattern that the computer lets you see as a recognizable image.

Due to the cost of high-resolution scanners—anywhere from $15,000 to over $100,000, plus other necessary equipment—few art staffs actually own one. Therefore, the most common process is to send the photos to the separator for scanning. He or she will scan them to the size the artist has indicated and give the artist a disk containing low-resolution (most often called *low-res*) scans for position. The high-resolution scans, which are done at the same time as the low-resolution ones, stay with the separator for use in making the film that will eventually be sent to the printer.

Separations: The Step between Photography and Printing

Most consumer catalogs are printed in four colors. But how does one piece of film, the four-color photo, become the four distinct pieces of film necessary for printing? The step between the four-color photography and the actual printing of the catalog is called separation.

Four-color transparencies are mounted on the drum of a computerized imaging device called a scanner. A scanning head moves across the transparency, recording the amount of yellow, magenta, cyan (blue), and black. An output device records this color information as a screened image on film. The separator produces this piece of film for each of the four process colors. Yellow, cyan, magenta, and black are the four process colors used by printing presses for color reproduction. By making plates from the film, the printer can produce each of the four colors on press.

The scanner used in separations provides speed, economy, accuracy, and sharpness. Yet it has one major drawback: It separates exactly what it sees. If the color in the photographs is inaccurate, the color in the separation will be too. Although the scanner can be programmed to make adjustments in the four process colors, this changes the overall look and can affect areas you might prefer left alone.

Because of last-minute price changes inherent in the catalog business, it is most often wise to have type prepared on a separate piece of black film. This means that late-breaking changes in the black type can be made without affecting the other colors. If the type were incorporated into the other colors, revisions would affect four pieces of film, resulting in higher revision costs and even more time lost.

New introductions in the computerized imaging area are revolutionizing the industry every day. Today, electronic separating systems can retouch, redesign, change size, foreground, mask, color-correct, enlarge, reduce, distort shapes, clone, repeat, and much more. None of this is free, however, so familiarize yourself with what separators can do and what it will cost. Foremost, see that your separator has the best photography you can provide. No matter what wonders this new technology can perform, it's a basic fact that the better the quality of materials put on the scanner, the better and less expensive the end result.

Methods for Viewing Separations

The film itself is not the form in which you view the separations. To check separations, you can select from a variety of composed film proofing systems.

Color Keys.   Color keys are the least desirable and generally the least expensive proofing system. Each color is shown on a relatively thick acetate sheet, one on top of the other. One advantage is that color keys show exactly how much of each color will be printed. But because of the thickness of the acetate, colors may be somewhat distorted from the way they will actually print. Color keys are best left to those who have been reading separations for years and know how to compensate for the inadequacies of this form of proofing.

Chromalins, Match Prints, Transkeys, and Fuji Prints.   As you can see, this process has many names. All refer to a relatively inexpensive and often-used method. Colored powders, which represent the colors to be printed, are laminated to sensitized film. Even though the fill is composed of four different sheets, it is very thin and appears to be in one piece. One color lies on top of another as it will when printed, giving a relatively accurate indication of how the finished piece will print. But because the heavy paper stock to which the powders adhere is often whiter than the printing stock, the final printed piece may appear yellower (if the paper has a yellowish tint) or in some way different from the chromalin. *Trans keys* (also called *transfer keys*) are a similar method made by a different manufacturer. Some chromalins can now be adhered to the printing stock.

Progressive Proofs.   Progressive proofs (or "progs") are actual printed proofs of the film (separations) that show how the printed catalog will look when it goes to press.

Each progressive proof comes in a "set," which shows exactly how much ink there will be, per color, on separately proofed pages. This helps you check color accuracy. For instance, if you think the separator has not made the red heavy enough, you need only look at the sheet containing the red to determine if this is true.

But progs are printed on a sheetfed press, and you will most likely be printing on a web press. Since a sheetfed press prints more slowly than a web press, inks are trapped differently, resulting in a slightly different look from that of the web-printed piece. Also, the paper used to print the progressive proof should be the same as the stock you will use in printing. Too often a progressive proof is printed on a heavier, whiter stock, so the image produced in the proofing stage cannot possibly be duplicated on press.

Choosing the right proofing system depends on your budget, your separator's capabilities, and the requirements of the printer. Work closely with your suppliers, and be sure to let them know your needs and desires. Above all, don't be afraid to ask questions. Separations are one of the most confusing aspects of production. The more questions you ask, the more you'll learn and the better the overall job will be.

Steps in Viewing Separations

Because the separation process is fairly expensive, it is wise to understand the basics of the process so you will know what to view when.

Many production people opt to view the color part of the separations prior to seeing all of the elements in place. This means you have the opportunity to make color adjustments on the photos only, prior to type and any design elements being stripped into place. The advantage is that you do not make costly changes in the entire process when you change only the color photos, and, of course, you get to see the color photos a second time when they are in position.

Another potential cost-saver is to view Iris proofs before you view the composed film. Iris proofs (one name for several hands) are a sort of fancy printout directly from a computer, of better quality and higher resolution than most computer artists can supply, but not yet composed film. Again, the importance of seeing each step before it is composed is labor saving. Making changes before film is composed means the film does not have to be "taken apart" to make your changes, costing less time and money.

You can view separations in either reader's or printer's proofs. Reader's proofs show the separations with the pages numbered sequentially (the way customers will read them). Printer's proofs are in the form in which the printer needs to print them (in a signature). Printer's proofs are advantageous because they eliminate the extra step and cost of preparing two different sets of proofs (a reader's set for you and a printer's set for the printer), but they do not allow you to see pages side by side because they are in press imposition form. This makes it difficult to really understand how well spreads go together, so, unless you are very experienced in interpreting printer's proofs, it is usually wiser to view your separations in reader's proofs.

Buying Separations

It is often said that separations should be done by separators and printing done by printers. But some printing plants have excellent separation facilities. How will you know when to use the printer's separator and when to use an independent firm?

Get samples, price estimates, and recommendations from your printer's separation facility, just as you would from an outside separator. Also, bluntly ask the printing salesperson how the company's separations compare with those of outside sources. Some separation facilities located within printing plants are there for last-minute changes only, whereas others are regular suppliers.

Buying separations from your printer eliminates possible confusion over what the printer needs. Still, since not all printers have separation facilities that are as good as outside sources, you may choose to purchase your separations from one source and your printing from another. Ask your separator to talk with the printer's production manager. If necessary, have the production manager visit the separation plant. It is in their best interest (and yours) to know each other's equipment and how they can make the best use of it. Contrary to stories of animosity ("The color's not right because the separator's film was inferior"), true professionals work well together; they know it is the only way to get the best results.

Your separator and your printer should agree on the following:

1. Screen specifications
2. Screen angle
3. Density
4. Ink hues and order of color laydown
5. Form in which film is to be received
   - Negative or positive
   - Reader's or printer's proofs
   - Plate-ready intermediate
   - Progs, color keys, or chromalins/trans keys for color match
6. Press layout
7. Scheduling
8. Paper being used

Assemblies

Assemblies (the actual cutting and piecing together of the original same-size photos or transparencies of your product) are usually considerably cheaper than individual separations. However, due to the dropping cost of electronic separations, they are no longer in great use. Assemblies are best used for catalogs where color is not critical.

In this process, all transparencies are positioned exactly as they are to appear on a spread, then held in this position in an acetate sleeve. In a combination fashion and nonfashion catalog, any fashion photos that were shot in random focus are duped (duplicates to the correct size are made) and incorporated into the assemblies. The separator uses the assembly to separate one spread at a time, rather than one photo at a time. The advantage is possibly substantial savings over randomly separated photos. The disadvantage is the scanner will see the overall color, rather than treat each photo as a separate element. Some of the true color will invariably be lost, but some catalogers feel this disadvantage is negated by what can be a lower separation cost.

You may wish to investigate both random-focus and assembled separations. Be aware of the color discrepancies that can occur with assemblies and decide whether budget or truer color is more important. Remember, the consumer needs to know how the product looks, but common sense should tell you when exact color is essential (clothing or home decorations are two instances when color is an important consideration in the consumer's decision to buy).

Bluelines

Also be certain to request bluelines from your separator or printer. These "blue ink" photoprints made from stripped film will allow you to check for any errors in type. And, because they should be presented in the format in which your catalog will be printed, it will also give you a mock-up to check that all pages are in order and that the order form folds and inserts correctly.

A Look into the Future

In this quickly changing area of cataloging, the future could be a few weeks from now. But let's look at some current trends.

Increasingly, scanners are going digital, a method that breaks up a predetermined signal into a set series of numbers. When the digitized scanner tells the operator how much magenta, cyan, and so on, the film needs, it is not influenced by the limitations experienced using a normal scanning system.

Digitizing allows quick changes, such as photo cropping and airbrushing. Think of it as electronic magic markers, and you have an idea of the possibilities. Add a palette of about 16 million different colors and tremendous cost savings, and you've got both a happy creative director and a happy controller. Complete page make-ups of color subjects can now be made without the intermediate steps previously necessary. These advanced systems can separate color, make corrections, move colored areas from place to place, and screen almost anything you could ever want and probably more than you know what to do with. They can output the fully assembled film ready for platemaking. Several such systems are now available, the best known being Sci-Tex Response 300, and others are about to make their debut.

On one system, the operator uses an electronic wand to move, delete, and rearrange images and elements almost limitlessly. The image is seen on a screen like the one used with a computer. Background colors and image positions can be changed instantly, allowing the client to see exactly how the final product will look before it is made into film. Although it is still an expensive process, prices have come down, and many catalogers have found computerization to give immeasurable value in savings and error elimination. Color also will be consistent. Each color will be digitized using a computerized formula that allows no variations. Blue XYZ10 will be Blue XYZ10, no matter where it's separated.

In the near future, optical disks and/or CDs (compact disks) will be able to store four-color material at a reasonable cost. This means that storage and retrieval will be less expensive and will also permit both medium-priced ($250,000) and higher-priced ($1 million) color electronic pagination systems to process the material on either the optical disc or CD. Down the road, personal computers (PCs) will be able to write and retrieve material from these two disk systems, and new PC-based print systems will also be able to interface with them.

With the increasing use of satellite delivery systems, the cost for transmitting four-color graphics will decrease significantly. It is now feasible for color trade houses to transmit using satellite systems or optical-fiber technology that emits a stream of digits. This allows the transmission of graphics to any other trade house the transmitter chooses, no matter where it is located. Therefore, the originating trade house has the option of selecting either union or nonunion recipients—with all the obvious consequences.

Soon, soft proofing devices (video display terminals) will bring down the price of proofing even more because they will eliminate much of the hard-copy proofing currently being done. Using this technique, separators will be able to read the "footprint" of, for example, an offset press. The computer will accurately measure this distinctive footprint, noting such variables as dot gain, ink trapping, even the press-room environment, and instantly transmit the data back to the separator.

The way a press responds and how it lays down color will be known to the separator before any film is actually generated. Thus, film can be accurately prepared exactly as needed for the press on which it will print.

Paste-up, Mechanicals, and Finished Art

Due to desktop publishing, these terms are quickly becoming extinct in catalog production. If you choose desktop publishing or computerization for your catalog, you will not be dealing with paste-ups, mechanicals, or finished art as they have historically been used. However, since not everyone has made the move to computerization, it is worthwhile to spend a little time becoming familiar with the phrases you may come across during the production process.

This is especially true because a confusing aspect of the advertising business is that so many words are interchangeable. Paste-up, mechanical art, finished art, and "boards" all have the same meaning. For four-color work, that process (if you are not using desktop publishing) is the final assembly of position art ad type, all ready for the separator. The type and position-only photostats are posted to a stable surface, such as an illustration board, in the exact position in which they will appear when printed.

The photostats, often called "stats," are inexpensive, nonreproducible black-and-white photos. They are pasted on the boards to show the separator the position and cropping of the photos to be separated. Usually, the edges of the stats are wavy or "trapped" and FPO is written across the top of each stat. They let the filmmaker know that the stats are for position only and are not to be used as art. A tissue overlap attached to the mechanicals indicates any nonphoto areas to be colored, such as key letters or color borders; which photos are to be silhouetted (or outlined); type that is to be "knocked out" (white); and any other important information or instructions.

Although acetate overlays can be employed for such finishing touches as line/bar frames, this function is almost always delegated to the separator. Here, computerization creates cleaner, more accurate lines, faster and cheaper than humans can.

The Different Types of Printing

It may be a surprise that printers can do much more than just put ink on paper. Many offer separation services; most have the ability to make any last-minute changes in paste-ups that may be needed. Most printers can also bind in order forms, apply the address mailing labels, and oversee or provide a great variety of services designed to get your catalog into the mail efficiently.

Before beginning to design a catalog, you need to have a basic grasp of the capabilities of different printing methods and their effect on costs and creative work-up.

Because we hear so often of a new press that is said to outperform other presses, the choice of presses may seem unlimited. Yet all presses have some characteristics in common. All presses are either sheetfed (printing one sheet of paper at a time) or web (printing from a continuous roll of paper). All also print either single color or multicolor, requiring a completely separate printing unit for each color.

There are three basic types of printing:

1. **Letterpress.** A method based on relief (raised image) printing, this is seldom used in the catalog industry. It is usually employed for such items as stationery and cartons.

2. **Offset.** A method wherein the ink is transferred from a plate onto a rubber surface, then onto paper. This is the most common form of printing for catalogs. Offset has historically been best for runs of up to approximately one million impressions (depending on the number of pages and overall dimensions of the catalog). However, with new offset equipment, some presses are competitive even up to 10 million impressions. When you start printing one million or more 80-page (or more) counts, get quotes from both offset and gravure printers and compare.

3. **Gravure.** This is an extremely cost-effective method of printing four-color catalogs with runs of over one million impressions. Prints are from a surface etched with wells on a copper cylinder or wraparound plate.

Sheetfed versus Web Presses

Sheetfed presses feed one sheet of paper through the press at a time and print only one side at a time. Compared with web presses, sheetfed presses are slower, but, because they allow for more control over the movement of the paper as it goes through the press, printing quality can be superior. Web printers will argue that through updated technology, web presses not only hold their own, but can give even better quality than sheetfed. But it really depends on the expertise of the people operating the presses. Whether sheetfed presses print better is a moot point. Except for small runs (usually 50,000 or less, depending on the number of pages and dimensions of the catalog), sheetfed is rarely a cost-effective method of printing a catalog.

Web printing is not only faster, but, because the paper is in a roll rather than in sheets, printing efficiencies not available on sheetfed presses are provided. All catalog web presses have on-line folders that fold the printed material into signatures, all in one continuous, money-saving process. Since every piece of equipment has make-ready time (getting the color right each time the plates are changed), with a corresponding charge, the more functions one press can perform, the less expensive the total job.

Offset versus Gravure

In web offset printing, catalogs are printed on perfecting presses, which print two sides at one time. Standard offset presses can print four basic colors on top and four colors on the underside—commonly termed "four over four." For a special effect, such as a matte black finish or silver border, a press that can print five colors is needed.

A major difference between web offset and gravure is that web offset prints with a smooth surface and gravure prints from a surface etched with wells on a copper cylinder or wraparound plate. The copper cylinders used in gravure are more expensive than the metal plates used in web offset, but they are also more durable. This durability makes them excellent for long runs, because one doesn't need to change plates and do make-ready as often as on web offset. One way to determine whether a catalog has been printed gravure is to check for tiny dots in the printing. Although virtually invisible to the naked eye, the screened effect on the entire image is easy to spot with a magnifying glass, and you will see distinctive differences between the two forms of printing (see Figure 7-13).

Although gravure has many advantages, the high cost of the copper plates means that it is cost-efficient only for high runs—which translates into large-quantity mailings. In addition, there are many more offset than gravure printers. With more printers come more options, such as the dimensions of the catalog and competitive price quotations. Another difference between web offset and gravure is that whereas web offset prints with wet inks, gravure inks dry almost instantly, permitting each succeeding color to be printed over a dry color. Generally speaking, gravure nets more good impressions per hour than does web offset.

Think in Signatures

Paper starts through a web press as one long roll, usually 34″ to 38″ wide. After it has been printed, it goes through dryers, where heat sets the inks. It is then cut (or *slit*) and folded into smaller, more workable sizes, such as 8³/₈″ × 10⁷/₈″. Once it is folded, it becomes a *signature*. The size of the paper after cutting and its folded size determine the number of pages in the signature.

❖ FIGURE 7-13
Differences in Printing Processes

Letterpress
(ring of ink)

Gravure
(rough edges)

Offset
(sharp edges)

The standard number of pages from a web offset press is 16 (see Figure 7-14). (You can create a catalog that has a nonstandard page count, say 18, but this almost always calls for sheet-fed printing and is expensive.) Therefore, most catalogs consist of several 16-page signatures. Assuming that one image is being printed per unfolded sheet, commonly called *one-on,* two 16-page signatures make a 32-page catalog; three make a 48-page catalog; and so on. A 24-page catalog would usually be printed in one 16-page section and one 8-page section. One 16-page signature would be printed one-on and one 8-page signature two-on. For a total run of 100,000 catalogs, 100,000 impressions of one signature and 50,000 of the two 8-page duplicate signatures are printed. This is because printing two on (two images) produces two of the same signature per press impression.

Most offset catalogs are printed on 8-up press which deliver 32 pages either as one 32, two 16s, or seven 8s. The newest presses, such as the 8-up G25W or M3000, deliver 48 pages, generally as two 24s or seven 12s. Since you can combine these to create many different page counts, these are options you should investigate.

This may seem confusing at first. Select a reliable printer and rely on the printer's experience. Most printers gladly answer questions and welcome the chance to help you better understand how to get the most out of the services they offer.

Choose a Self-Cover or Separate Cover

A catalog can have a self-cover or a separate cover. The self-cover is less expensive because it is printed as part of the body signature.

A separate cover, as the name implies, is printed apart from the body of the catalog. An example of a separate-cover catalog is one that has two 16-page signature bodies with a 7-page cover, or a total of 36 "pages." One advantage of a separate cover is that a higher-priced, image-building paper can be used for the cover, and a lower-priced paper can be used in the body of the catalog.

Determining the Right Page Count

One of the most frequently asked questions is how many pages should be put in a catalog. Because you now have an understanding of how most presses work, you know that it is financially advantageous to work in signatures. However, you've also learned that you can divide signatures in two and that you can add a separate cover. And some printers have unique signatures and formats. But don't choose a format that cannot be duplicated

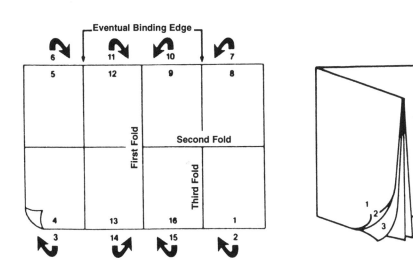

❖ FIGURE 7-14
**Sixteen-Page Imposition
Before and After Folding**

by any other printer, because if you find yourself unhappy with your present printer, where would you turn for a replacement?

The most important consideration when deciding on the number of pages to run is how many pages of strong merchandise you actually have. During pagination, there is a tendency to overmerchandise a catalog. Don't let this happen. Start with more pages than you need to meet your selections and cut to fit. Paginate your catalog, then sleep on your selections and delete marginal items the next day.

A successful cataloger quickly learns to run only the best merchandise on the correct number of pages for optimum press efficiencies. Never let press constraints force you to run additional pages for which you do not have salable merchandise.

Ensuring Quality Printing

How can you be sure that the printing will be what you expect?

1. Interview three to five reputable printers. Be sure to ask for recent samples and references from current clients.

2. If you are buying separations from a source other than the printer, make sure the separator, the printer, and your production coordinator meet. During this meeting, they should agree on the specifications the separator must meet to ensure that the printer can properly print the film. There are many horror stories of the printer blaming the separator and vice versa when something goes wrong on press. Such problems can be avoided if the two suppliers have the opportunity to discuss their needs and capabilities. Have them follow up by sending each other written specifications, with copies to you.

3. Don't buy based on price alone. There is a saying in the printing industry that you can't have price, quality, and service all at once. More often than not, this is true. If the price seems too good to be true, it probably is. What you'll save in printing dollars, you'll lose in quality and consumer sales. But don't go for the highest price either. Printing needs to be of adequate quality only. Leave award-winning printing to people who can afford it and publications that require it, such as corporate annual reports.

4. Go to press with your job and, if time permits, stay for the entire run. Be there to check every form as it comes off the press. Listen to the advice of your salesperson or the press foreman (who knows best what the press can do). Realize that some compromises may have to be made, but don't hesitate to tell the foreman if the color doesn't match your product. You know best what the product should look like. Once the job is running at full speed, monitor the work in progress. You don't want to discover, too late, that the latter part of the run was too red, water-spotted, or defective in some other way. There has been a court case in which a printer was held liable for a reduction in quality after the client had left. However, a ruling in your favor will not make up for lost sales.

Knowing Your Printer's Responsibilities—and Yours

Your printer is responsible for a print job that meets the quality standards of its samples and recommendations. Your responsibility is to stay on schedule, provide separations to the printer's specifications, provide the bindery information for the order form if purchased from a separate printer, and the mailing list tapes.

Remember, the schedule can mean the difference between a successful catalog and one that fails. If you follow the schedule from the printer for receipt of film, order forms (which you will probably purchase from a different printer), and mailing lists, it is the printer's responsibility to see that your catalog is in the mail by the agreed-on date. If you don't meet scheduled dates, delays in the receipt of your materials can result in much longer delays than the amount of time you are late. A good printer is probably a busy one with a tight schedule. If you are three days late with the film, don't assume you will be on press three days later than you anticipated. The printer may have someone who has stayed on schedule booked for those days and have to fit you in when possible. Sometimes this can be weeks later.

The printer should check the separations when they arrive and alert you to any potential problems immediately, not once you're on press. The printer should also provide paper that prints well. Even if you buy the paper directly from the mill, the printer should test it before actually going on press. If the paper appears to be a potential problem, replace it with stock the printer has on hand or get the mill to replace it. Once the presses are running, there will not be time to make this critical change.

It is common practice to have the printer mail the catalog, in which case the printer is responsible for preparing the catalogs properly for bulk third-class mailing.

Making Corrections on Press

To get good-quality reproduction, you must have good photographs, good separations, a good printer, and good paper. The best printer in the world can't make up for poor photographs, bad separations, or bad paper. Yet, some improvements can be made even during a press run.

First, let's discuss what to expect when you go on press. You will probably review forms as they come off press against your chromalins or press proofs. While you are making corrections, the press will be eating up paper. A certain amount of press approval time is built into the price quoted by the printer, but if you take too long, more paper may be used then was included in the quoted price. The result is a higher bill.

When making corrections, be aware of the way in which ink flows. Any color corrections directly affect all photographs "in-line," that is, in the same ink flow line. A correction to one item could adversely affect other photographs in the same flow line. So, for best results, be sure to provide the printer with quality separations and minimize the time spent approving press sheets. Some corrections can be, and often are, literally made at the last minute. Your press foreman will attempt to guide you, but use your best judgment, learn from experience, and try to provide even better separations the next time around.

Don't hesitate to employ the advice of those who have experience on press, such as your separator or production manager. But don't be tempted to take a whole crew along either. Too much direction from too many people will confuse the issue and lengthen your press time.

Getting the Right Paper

Paper is one of the most important, least-talked-about components of a successful mail order catalog. The way a catalog feels in a prospective customer's hands says much about your company. Remember, it's the customer's first and only physical contact with the company. Tests have shown that if the paper is of high quality, glossy, and heavy in weight, the customer perceives the catalog as offering top-quality, high-ticket products before even looking at the merchandise selection or prices. If the stock used is of a lower grade, light in weight, and coarse to the touch, a customer instantly assumes that the merchandise offered is lower-priced—not specifically of either high or low quality, but definitely budget-oriented. Therefore, your choice of paper stock should be taken as seriously as the selection of merchandise and lists.

Paper is divided into two basic types of finish: coated and uncoated. Within the uncoated there is antique, which is rough and bulky (mostly used for books); machine finish, very similar to antique but a little smoother; and wove offset, most often used in the catalog industry for order-form printing.

Coated paper is smoother and doesn't absorb ink to the degree that a noncoated paper does. Matte, which still doesn't appear glossy but, because of its coating pigments, holds color better than uncoated, is often used for commercial catalogs that don't require a slick look. The more coating pigments that are applied, the smoother and more ink-reception a paper becomes. These papers are often referred to as high-finish enamels. *Cast coating* refines this process even further, providing a mirrorlike surface. Although there are other finishes (such as vellum and embossed), these are not addressed here because they are seldom used by catalogers due to their expense.

Since paper can account for half of your printing costs, you must decide whether the benefits of offering the customer an immediate top-quality image will compensate for spending more on paper. How do you lean enough to make this essential decision? Printers can be helpful. They have a working knowledge of paper and a supply of paper at their printing facilities. They can make recommendations based on availability and price. Get samples of the paper along with prices, and keep the samples to check the paper after printing. Some printers have been known to switch paper on unsuspecting clients.

Paper salespeople are paper experts who represent a multitude of different paper mills, so they can offer you variety and experience. They will supply you with important information on basic weight, grade, and bulk. If you are buying a lot of paper (say 10,000 tons or more), get quotes and paper samples from them and compare. Even if you don't buy their paper, they know you can specify their paper to the printer, and that, when your business grows in size, you may purchase directly from them.

When paper is purchased directly from the paper manufacturer, the printer often charges a small (sometimes negotiable) paper-handling fee. Some printers have ink- and paper-testing facilities for checking paper supplied by clients. This can be essential to a smooth press run and represents optimal use of both time and supplies. The availability of paper changes, so be sure to check with both the printer and the paper company representative before you commit yourself. (See the "Paper Distributors" section in the Yellow Pages or ask your printer for contacts.)

Paper Characteristics for Good Print Quality

All of the following are important characteristics for good print quality:

- ◆ **Strength.** If the paper tears off or breaks as it travels through the press, it is useless.

- ◆ **Color.** Paper color directly affects the color of the merchandise portrayed. Paper with a yellowish cast makes a white product appear ivory. Type is most easily read against a soft white paper, and color reproduces best on neutral white paper.

- ◆ **Brightness.** Brightness is a function of paper shade (color) and whiteness. The brighter a paper is, the more the ink colors will stand out in contrast to the paper stock. If a catalog contains heavy, solid coverage on one side of a page, brightness need not be a prime consideration.

- ◆ **Opacity.** Opacity is a paper's ability to resist show-through. In general, the heavier or bulkier the paper, the more opaque it will be.

- ◆ **Smoothness and printability.** Smoothness refers to the evenness of a paper's surface. The smoother the surface, the greater the clarity of the printed image. As smoothness decreases, so does print clarity, especially in solids and halftones. Type is rarely affected.

- ◆ **Gloss.** Gloss is tied to smoothness and is a measurement (the amount of light reflected) of the amount of coating on the paper. Coated papers hold the ink on the surface, making the image clearer.

- ◆ **Affordability.** Remember, paper can be more than half the cost of your printing job!

Web offset paper is graded from premium (the highest quality) down to a No. 1, 2, 3, 4, or 5 (the lowest). There are a multitude of paper manufacturers, all using different names to describe their different paper grades. This can be confusing even to an experienced production person. Refer to Table 7-4 for a clarification of paper names.

❖ TABLE 7-4 Web Grades: Gloss Coated Papers

Mill	Premium #1	#1	#2	#3	Premium #4	Hi-Brite #4	Standard #4	#5
Blandin							Lithobrite	Lithoblade
Boise Cascade				Oxford Hi-Gloss		Dependoweb		Pubtext
Bowater								Carolina
Champion		Preference		Javelin Influence	Courtland	Sunweb ✿ Sunweb Recyld.	Briteweb	Textweb ✿ Textweb Recyld. Maineweb
Consolidated		Centura		Consoweb Brilliant	Consoweb Modern	Nova	Spyder	Consogloss Concycle ✿
Fraser								Fracote
Glatfelter				Old Forge ✿ EPA Enamel				
International				Miragloss	Miraweb	Liberty Hi-Brite	IB Web	Liberty Hudson
James River						Delta Brite	Surfa	Monterey
Mead		Signature	Mead Web	Northcote (F)	Northcote (RMP)	Escanaba		
Mohawk				50/10 Gloss ✿				
Papyrus / Newton Falls		Champlain ✿		St. Lawrence St. Lawrence ✿				
Niagara						Penstar	Pentair ✿ Pentair Recycle	Penagra
Northwest	Quintessence Quintessence Remarque ✿	Vintage	Northwest	(To be announced) ✿	Ranger			
Repap		Excellence	Lithoweb Plus	Multiweb	Spirit Hi-Brite	Midset	Predator Spirit R.E.C. Gloss ✿	Econoweb Publication Recycled ✿
Simpson		Solitaire	Shasta Tahoe Capistrano	Silverado Sonoma EverGreen ✿	Mesa		Nature ✿	
Warren		Lustro	Flokote	Warrenflo Somerset	Freedom			
Westvaco		Celesta	Sterling	Citation Velvo	Westmont Marva Deluxe American Eagle ✿			
Weyerhaeuser							Colonnade	Choctaw

SOURCE: JB Papers, New Jersey.
✿ Recycled

Recycled Paper

Catalogers are highly conscious of the fact that printed material is one of the contributors to land-fill problems and that, from time to time, catalogs are considered "tree killers." As with all businesses, direct marketers must weigh the cost of becoming environmentally friendly, because recycled paper can run as much as 10 percent more than that which has not been recycled.

For some catalogers, there really is no choice. Companies such as Patagonia and Seventh Generation base the heart of their positioning on their concern for the environment. For them to print on paper that was less than environmentally friendly could significantly undermine their image.

Certainly strides have been made in both cost reduction and quality improvement in recycled papers. In the past, they were both expensive and very poor in reproduction quality. And there have been other problems with recycled papers. *Folio,* in May 1993, reported:

> The challenge to the industry . . . remains to make a sheet that is not only lightweight, but also strong enough for the massive, high-speed pressruns. Recycled and virgin papers differ also in that recycled papers may contain somewhat more dirt specks. They also lose a point or two of brightness, although those who use recycled, such as Thomas W. Wolf of Rodale Press, say this loss is

virtually undetectable to the untrained eye. One last difference, though, may actually be beneficial . . . because recycled paper is more opaque than virgin, publishers may be able to go to a lower base weight, thereby saving on mailing costs.

Some direct marketers who have tested recycled against nonrecycled have found, alarmingly, that not only did it cost more, but, probably due to unclear reproduction, response went down. One excellent solution for the short term is to be sure that all of your correspondence (notes to customers, information in packages, and so on) is printed on recycled paper . . . and state that on the paper.

Recycled papers, though, are constantly improving, with some of the latest being virtually indistinguishable from virgin papers. Be alert as to what is changing in the recycled paper market regarding both price and quality, and plan to test it when the economics and positioning make sense for your catalog.

More Thoughts on Selecting Paper

A catalog should have sufficient weight or bulk to convey a feeling of substance to the customer. Because a small book, such as a digest, doesn't bend as easily as a larger one, the paper stock need not be as heavy. Tests should be conducted to determine the right appearance and weight needed to generate merchandise sales. For instance, tests for one high-ticket catalog have proven that catalogs printed on 60- or 70-pound paper produce better sales than those printed on 50-pound stock. Conversely, tests for a catalog of value-priced merchandise, printed on a higher-weight paper, showed that the extra cost for the better paper did not garner the response needed to pay for this expenditure. If your catalog has a good percentage of white space, you're probably better off using a free sheet or at least higher-grade groundwood. Paper tends to be classified as either a free sheet or a groundwood sheet. Although the processes that turn wood into paper always leave some wood-pulp fibers in the paper, free sheets have significantly fewer fibers than groundwood. With a free sheet, you'll not only receive better reproduction in ink-coverage areas, but the catalog in general will convey a cleaner, richer look than if it's printed on a stock containing groundwood. For catalogs with fairly solid coverage on the pages, look into lower-grade papers, but make sure they will still offer the desired reproduction quality. Another approach is to use a slightly lower grade and weight of paper for the body with a cover of better stock. The savings gained on the body paper can be applied to the additional cost of a separate cover.

As other costs, such as postage, have escalated over the years, paper is one of the major areas to which catalogers have turned to help them cut costs. However, paper costs are cyclical and *very much* subject to supply and demand. The bottom line is simple: Do not print on a higher-quality sheet than you can justify in increased response. The only way to know this for certain is to talk with experts and test different weights and grades.

The Price Quote

One of the most common problems with printing quotations is misunderstandings regarding specifications. Be sure that each printer receives the same specifications, in writing, and insist that price quotations be submitted in writing as well. Here's what your quote should contain:

1. **Trim size.** The finished size of a single page; width is always listed before height. Standard dimensions are:

Sheetfed Paper Formats	Web Offset Paper Formats
5½" × 8½"	5⅜" × 8⅜"
6" × 9"	8⅜" × 10⅞"
8½" × 11"	8½" × 11"
9" × 12"	17¾" × 26½" (maximum
11" × 17"	sheeted product deliverable
12½" × 19"	into web)

2. **Quantity.** The number of pieces to be printed, plus a cost per thousand for additional thousands over the original quantity.

3. **Number of pages.** Also indicate whether the catalog will have a self-cover or a separate cover.

4. **Paper.** The type of paper to be used, by brand name as well as weight.

5. **Copy prep or film assembly.** The cost for such preliminary presswork as revisional typesetting, paste-up, assemblies, or separations should be definitively outlined. If you are supplying the film, the quote should specify the form in which the film must be received by the printer.

6. **Proofs.** It is a good idea to have the printer pull a proof of supplied film before going on press, to make sure there are no problems. The quotation should indicate whether these proofs are included in the cost of printing the job.

7. **Color content.** This states how many colors are used in the job.

8. **Ink coverage.** This specifies the amount of ink coverage your job will involve.

9. **Binding.** The cost of gathering, trimming, and binding (generally saddle-stitching for catalogs) is included here.

10. **Mailing.** This includes the cost of applying labels, sorting, bagging, tying, and delivering to the post office. You are responsible for supplying the labels or tapes for ink jetting; the printer's lettershop puts the catalogs in the proper order for postal discounts.

11. **Freight on board (FOB).** This is the charge for shipping unmailed catalogs from a particular destination, usually used with a destination noted behind (such as FOB Dock), meaning the printer puts the catalogs on his or her dock and you must pay to ship from that dock to the final destination.

12. **Schedule.** You and the printer should agree on a definite mailing date and schedule.

13. **Terms of sale.** This is simply the method of payment.

All quotes should contain a written agreement or contract outlining the printer's responsibilities and yours. Read it carefully before you sign. Although you'll be telling the printer in what form (tape, Cheshire, or pressure-sensitive) mailing lists will be received, he or she will specify how packages must be marked. This will avoid confusion as to which code numbers belong with what lists. Confusion can occur because lists tend to look alike once they are removed from the carton in which they are sent. Although there should be codes both on the lists themselves and on the outer carton, these codes are often missing. Instructing brokers to code both helps eliminate confusion.

Making Use of Technology

We have seen dramatic changes take place in the last few years in two important areas of catalog marketing. Pre-press (the preparation of materials prior to printing) and post-press (the bindery part of the catalog-making process) have seen lightning strides using new technology. And, for the most part, this has been very good for those involved in production, largely because it has meant time and cost savings. Be in constant touch with your printer as to the evolving technologies available to make your catalog more cost-efficient and a stronger marketing vehicle. And supplement your knowledge by reading about these changes. Not every supplier will be able to afford to provide every new technology, but you still need to know what exists and whether your printer currently offers the technique.

Digital Platemaking

Totally filmless production is still more a matter of discussion than practice. But direct-to-cylinder work is happening. What this means is that color information about your catalog is never made into film; the computerized page files, including the high-resolution images, are converted to the printer's high-end pre-press system's digital format, from which press cylinders are etched. Currently, this process is only applicable for gravure printing.

Naturally, this eliminates some steps in the process, such as the physical stripping of film, and therefore results in savings. Fingerhut reports that their pre-press capacity has increased by almost half. But it also eliminates several checkpoints. "Going digital opens up a whole range of possibilities in screwing up gravure cylinders," warns Dan Krejca, R. R. Donnelley's product manager for catalog digital systems. With all the different digital production formats in use today, there is always a risk of data being garbled or lost during conversion. "The checks and balances in conventional production are bypassed in the digital world," Krejca says. "Catalogers have to be aware there is a serious risk of bad data getting through."[2]

Some feel that the quality of reproduction is better than through the more traditional production process. Fingerhut staff like the fact that they see proofs on the paper on which they actually print, rather than the laminated stock separators have traditionally used (chromalins, Fuji prints, and so on). Even with some concerns, there is no doubt that this process will move ahead and that the next wave will be for direct-to-plate offset printing. Eastman Kodak has developed a coating process that creates a tough, high-resolution offset printing plate that lasts. Unlike others that were limited to runs of 100,000, this plate can product 1 million impressions. However, it is an evolving technology and is still less than totally reliable. Other companies will undoubtedly follow with even better plates that can handle both direct-to-plate applications and long runs. As previously mentioned, this process, be it gravure or offset, is seldom used now, but look for it to increase in practice within the next few years.

Scent Strips

Scent strips were in their heyday in the 1980s with almost every magazine and many catalogs wafting a perfumed aroma. Printers incorporated a fragment scent, such as a perfume, into a portion (usually lightly sealed with a flap) of an envelope. Largely replacing the microencapsulation process of scratch-and-sniff, this method reportedly has a better image and retains the scent longer. However, some people found that they were allergic to the scents bound somewhat indiscriminately into their magazines and catalogs, so their use has decreased somewhat.

To solve this problem, some publications give their audience the opportunity to receive a version without the perfumed insert. And new technology allows fragrances and lotions to be packaged in smaller, sealed packets that can be affixed to the printed surface. Actual product samples like these have the following advantages: They put the product into the intended recipient's hands to try at her convenience, and they have been known to add up to 1.5 percent to overall catalog sales.

This technology can be eminently adaptable to a wide variety of uses, such as appetizing food aromas, sea breeze, floral arrangements, and so on. Certainly, always remember the cost versus the value, but stay alert to new techniques that might better your business.

Costs for manufacturing scent strips and packets can vary tremendously depending on the size, complexity, and cost of the fragrance or lotion you are using. Examples range from $1 per thousand to $25 per thousand, but even these costs would, of course, be affected by the quantity you desire. Check with your printer, he or she can give you the details or recommend a printer who handles this specific type of work.

Binding and Mailing

After your beautiful catalog is printed, you must get it in the mail. This is where a bindery (or lettershop) comes in. More often than not, the bindery is part of the printer's facilities. When it is not, catalogs must be shipped to the bindery and must arrive in the same condition in which they left the printer—flat and undamaged.

♦ Find out exactly how the lettershop wishes to receive the materials. This includes how the catalog is to be physically packed. For instance, should it be banded on skids or in cartons?

♦ Does the binder agree with all your specifications? If not, what is its preference? Consider having the printer talk directly to the binder, but be in on the conversation so you are aware of any expenses that may be incurred.

♦ Make sure every shipment includes a detailed packing slip and mark cartons legibly. For example:
Description: XYZ Catalog, Spring 1988
Source-Code Format: Code 123
Contents: 10,000 catalogs
Version: Cover A

The term *Version* indicates literally which version of a test this material belongs to. This example, ''Cover A,'' indicates there is a cover test of more than one cover.

If the printer is handling your lettershop, you naturally will need to ask the same questions, but will handle this through your printer's sales representative rather than talking directly with the lettershop and/or bindery.

Addressing

Addressing isn't very glamorous, but it certainly is essential. Without addresses, your catalog goes nowhere. If they're incorrectly created and/or affixed, delivery and response tracking will become major headaches. First, understand the different types of addressing available.

1. Cheshire or plain-paper labels are the least used and most old-fashioned. Made of thin paper, they are simply machine-glued to a specified surface, usually the back cover. They cannot be removed; hence any code contained on them cannot be transferred to the order form. And since coding of labels is essential for tracking list rentals (see Chapter 11), it is highly unlikely that you will use this type of label. Some plain-paper labels come with glue already on them, but since most lettershops are always on guard against labels falling off, they'll most likely only put more glue on them. And, since they cost more than plain-paper labels, this is not a good buy.

2. Pressure-sensitive or piggyback labels are initially attached to a waxy backing sheet. The self-adhesive label, complete with list code, is peeled off by the customer and attached to the order form. Why are they sometimes called piggyback labels? Because they can ''ride'' on top of the backing and can be put on the order form easily.

❖ EXAMPLE 7-12
Good Idea! catalog uses a label that must be removed and affixed to the order form to collect the list code.

3. Ink jetting is the most popular method of addressing catalogs. A magnetic tape is programmed with address information, as well as a list code and/or a pertinent message (see Chapter 11). Be aware that you must coordinate the space allocation and number of characters available for use with your printer before designing the back cover. Each printer has different but very specific requirements, and you must adhere to these or the message content could be drastically limited, thus reducing the impact. Some catalogs, through proper use of targeted messages, have experienced as much as a 50-percent increase in response.

Basic Bindery Information

Regardless of where it is physically located, the bindery's (lettershop's) responsibility is to sort, bag, and tie the catalogs to qualify for all possible postage deductions according to the rules and regulations of the post office. Your responsibility is to see that the bindery has the necessary information to do its job right. Be explicit on each of the following matters:

1. Mailing name/title.
2. Mailing date (or dates if it's a scheduled series) and any changes in the schedule.
3. Quantity to be mailed per mailing date.
4. Codes for each list and/or list segment.
5. Any changes in printed material. Is there more than one cover? Does a certain segment require an outer envelope or a different order form?
6. Total number of catalogs to be mailed. Are leftover catalogs to be mailed? If not, are they to be stored or sent to you or your agency by mail or truck? Nobody is happy if the lettershop mails surplus catalogs to do you a favor, leaving you with too few catalogs to fill such needs as inquiries from magazine ads.
7. Where and by what method catalogs are to be shipped.
8. What postage format to use. If indicia, who supplies the permit number, you or the lettershop?
9. Description, source-code format, and expected arrival date of mailing lists. Identify the contents on the outside of the package. Also, indicate the quantity contained within.
10. Type and position of address "label." (It's a good idea to include a dummy that indicates the exact position.)
11. When the postage check is due and to what postmaster the check should be written.

Remember, both your printer and your lettershop want everything to go smoothly. The more information they have before they receive your catalog, the better they can do

❖ **EXAMPLE 7-13**
Kemp & George catalog inkjets the address information and a special message, and even highlights the inkjetted code section with background pastels.

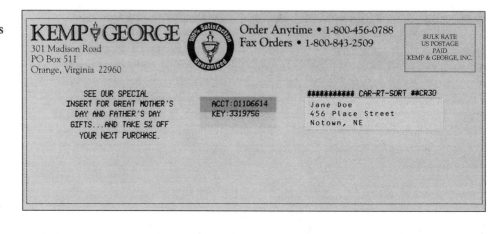

the job. When all the team members have the same information, teamwork can be one of the most important factors in a successful mailing.

Selective Binding and Personalization: A Big Marketing Tool

Selective (computer-controlled) binding is a technique used by some printers enabling custom-made catalogs to be created by binding on different covers or including different pages. It uses the same magnetic tape as does ink jetting. This customization enables the cataloger to develop catalogs on the basis of information about potential and current customers. The obvious advantage is the ability to test variations on a basic catalog with cost efficiency. Or to create catalogs that provide product-specific offerings to customer segments who have indicated a desire for this category of product.

Because all same-size catalogs, no matter what their differences, can be bound at the same time, postage discounts are maximized. Why? Because binding catalogs at the same time allows them to be sorted in zip code sequence, thus increasing their chances of qualifying for the lower postal charges (such as carrier-route and five-digit presort).

Electronic binding can also be employed to bind in postcards selectively. For instance, you may wish to bind in a tell-a-friend postcard to only the best-response segment of your house list. Or, a cataloger may want to bind in a postcard offering a special offer on a product similar to the one a customer recently purchased.

This same wizardry can also be applied to stickers. Tied into the same tape that drives the ink-jet imaging, these preprinted stickers can be applied to the front of the catalog to announce a particular offer or warn a certain segment of your list that, unless they order now, this could be their last catalog.

Though this selective binding has existed for some years now, it is too rarely used by catalogers. Rather, magazines have found it useful to have particular ads in one edition and not in another. One frequently mentioned example is that of Seagram's, which is a proponent of placing ads in only those issues where the individual reading the magazine is a potential purchaser.

However, ink-jet personalization is well used by catalogers. Adding a customer message to the back of the catalog is a simple and free add-on for those already ink jetting the recipient's name and address. Such messsages do have limitations in location and number of characters. Some printers can even ink jet the front or interior of the catalog . . . certainly added impact! Be sure to get the exact specifications from your printer before designing the mailing area of your catalog.

❖ **EXAMPLE 7-14**
Misco uses two different, highly targeted messages on its covers.

Nth Bag Sorting/Binding.   Sometimes called "the poor man's selective binding," this is merely sorting mailbags by nths (every other one, depending on the number of bags). This is far less expensive than selective binding and can still provide a most effective means of testing and/or segmenting offers.

Your Postal Receipt

Good lettershops automatically provide you with a copy of service form 3602 from the U.S. Postal Service. Two copies of this form are completed: one for you and one for the post office. This is your receipt for entry of mail into the postal system. It includes the following information:

1. **The date the catalog was taken to the post office.** Lettershops have been known to misrepresent actual mail dates, showing instead the date the client wants to see. The 3602 helps to prevent this from happening. But it is important to note that the 3602 shows the date the catalog goes into the post office. The date it leaves depends on the efficiency of the individual bulk-rate center and its current work load.

2. **The cost of postage.** Since you probably prepaid the postage to your lettershop, check the 3602s against the amount you paid. Sometimes the mailing quantity changes slightly, and there can be discrepancies or oversights on the part of the lettershop.

3. **The number of catalogs mailed.** Because spoilage can occur during label application, the number of catalogs mailed may differ from the one your lettershop provides. The lettershop is not trying to be devious; inaccuracies often occur quite honestly, so use the quantities on the 3602s, not those of the lettershop.

4. **The number of catalogs in each mail category.** This information will be most helpful in future analysis of response rates and average orders from carrier-route, five-digit-presort, and residual bulk third-class mailings. This can also be an additional check on postage costs.

Make it a point to get 3602s from your lettershop. They are a valuable receipt!

Postage

Almost all catalogs take advantage of the savings achieved by using bulk-rate third-class mail. To mail bulk-rate third-class, you need to secure a one-time permit. The cost is $75, and the permit number is yours as long as you use it at least once a year. (If you don't use it annually, the number may be reassigned by the post office and you will have to pay $75 for another permit.) In addition, there is a yearly presort fee of $75. The minimum for a bulk-rate third-class mailing is either 200 pounds or 50 pieces. These rates are lower for nonprofits (see Table 7-5).

For catalogers, the most common way to pay bulk-rate postage is by using indicia. (The other options are using a meter or precancelled stamps.) Indicia are defined by the post office as imprinted designations consisting of city, state, and a permit number used on mail pieces to denote payment of postage (see Figure 7-15). Indicia allow mailing only from the particular city, state, and post office shown. In order to use indicia, you must pay a one-time permit fee of $75—the same permit described for bulk rate and, similarly, the indicia number is permanent as long as the permit holder mails at least once in 12 months.

The city, state, and permit number may be omitted from the indicia if the permit holder has permits at two or more post offices and if the exact name of the company or individual holding the permit is shown in the permit imprint (see Figure 7-16). When this style of company permit is used, the mailing piece must bear a complete return address. The permit holder must maintain (and make available for inspection and audit on request of post office officials) records showing the post office at which any particular mailing was made, the date of mailing, the weight of a single piece, and the amount of postage paid. A sample piece from the mailing must also be available, and all records must be kept for a three-year period.

Since postage requirements can change overnight, stay informed by subscribing to such publications as the *Domestic Mail Manual* and *Postal Bulletin* (which can be ordered from the Superintendent of Documents, U.S. Printing Office, Washington, DC 20036).

	1994 Cost (cents)	Cost as of January 1, 1995 (cents)
Commercial bulk minimum piece rate		
Required	23.3	26.6
Five-digit	18.7	21.4
Carrier route	14.2	16.2
Walk sequence flats	13.7	15.7
Saturation	12.4	14.5
Pound rate*	60.0	68.7
Nonprofit bulk minimum piece rate		
Required	12.5	19.2
Five-digit	11.1	17.8
Carrier route	8.0	14.5
Walk sequence flats	7.8	14.3
Saturation	7.3	13.8
Pound rate*	34.1	55.2

❖ **TABLE 7-5**
Bulk Third-Class Postage Rates, 1994 versus 1995

* Plus piece rate adjustments.

BULK RATE
U.S. POSTAGE
PAID
Chicago, Il. 60607
Permit No. 1

❖ **FIGURE 7-15**
Sample Bulk-Rate Permit Label (Indicia)

BULK RATE
U.S. POSTAGE PAID
John Doe Company

❖ **FIGURE 7-16**
Universal Bulk-Rate Label (Indicia)

Preparing Mail for Optimal Postal Discounts

There are three important considerations when looking for your highest possible postage discount:

1. Do as much of the sorting as possible.
2. Understanding the post office's need to turn to automation for cost efficiencies and that automation affects how you should prepare the catalog for mailing.
3. The ability of the mailer to transport the mail deeply into the postal processing network, while optimizing postage and freight costs.

Presort Savings

If you presort your mailings, the post office will allow you a discount on the bulk third-class rate. Postal presorts are usually done by your computer house at the time of the merge/purge (see Chapter 11). The output list is sorted into zip code sequence and then run against a presort tape. Typically, charges are based on the number of names qualifying for the presort discount and include the mail-bag tags the post office requires.

Table 7-6 gives the approximate postage cost based on presorted mailings of 300,000, 500,000, and one million catalogs. Some typical charges are $2.50 per thousand names for carrier route–qualified names, $1.00 per thousand names for five-digit and residual (basic bulk) names.

Increasingly, printers offer services that can assist you in this area. Alden Press, for example, has a service called "VIP." This stands for Version Isolation Presort, and it works like this: The lists of the two (or more) titles are combined to determine the portion of each list that benefits from the combination. The result is three separate lists:

A only (for example, 35 percent of the list)

B only (for example, 35 percent of the list)

A/B combined (about 30 percent of combined totals over two million)

Only the combined list must be run selectively. This reduces costs, because you have minimized your manufacturing cost on a complicated bindery setup, and makes scheduling easier, because you can run faster on simpler machines.

❖ TABLE 7-6
Approximate 1995 Postal Costs Based on Presorted Flats*

250,000 Flats

Carrier route	17.00%	42,500	$0.162	$ 6,885
3 or 5 digit	78.00%	195,000	$0.214	$ 41,730
Residual	5.00%	12,500	$0.266	$ 3,325
			Average cost =	$ 0.208
			Total cost =	$ 51,940

500,000 Flats

Carrier route	29.00%	145,000	$0.162	$ 23,490
3 or 5 digit	70.00%	350,000	$0.214	$ 74,900
Residual	1.00%	5,000	$0.266	$ 1,330
			Average cost =	$ 0.199
			Total cost =	$ 99,720

1,000,000 Flats

Carrier route	54.90%	549,000	$0.162	$ 88,938
3 or 5 digit	44.90%	449,000	$0.214	$ 96,086
Residual	0.20%	2,000	$0.266	$ 532
			Average cost =	$ 0.186
			Total cost =	$185,556

* Flats under 3.3067 ounces without bar codes.

Destination Entry Savings

This is a post office program that offers greater control of the delivery process as well as savings in return for managing the transportation of mail to specific destination points within the postal system. There are three destination points:

BMC: Bulk mail center, one of the 21 locations in which bulk mail is sorted and routed to various areas of the country.

SCF: Sectional center facility, covers a range of zip codes as identified by the first three digits of the zip code.

Local delivery unit: A post office, usually a zip code.

National Change of Address

Another post office service, the National Change Of Address (NCOA) file will do everything that ZIP+4 does, including change the addresses of those who have moved and notified the post office within the last two years. This must be done by a licensed service bureau, again for a nominal fee. This should be done before every mailing, on both your list and the lists you rent, because the higher deliverability greatly offsets any cost.

Beyond the Basics

Palletization

Simply put, palletization means putting your mail—properly sorted, of course—on pallets rather than in mail sacks. The advantage? Faster, more accurate delivery, and delivery made in better shape. Sacked mail is cumbersome and, because of its soft sides, doesn't always protect precious catalogs as well as you'd like. With palletization, catalogs are stacked on stable pallet surfaces, which are easily loaded on and off trailers. Be aware, however, that there are tight restrictions on palletization of letter-size mail. The post office can advise you.

Dennis Meyer of Maxwell Graphics explains further:

Anyone authorized by the postal service can palletize mailings. The easier way to calculate how efficiently a mailing could be sent on pallets is to look at the geographic density of the addresses. The more addresses in one town or city, or in a five- or three-digit zip code grouping, the more likely the mailing can be palletized. A mailing that qualifies for the carrier-route rate should definitely be considered for palletization.

Also note that there are printers/mailers with advanced technology to presort the file for palletization while minimizing the manufacturing costs of this sophisticated process.

Co-Mailing

This process allows two catalogs of the same size to be mailed together to save postage. Catalogs need not be from the same company nor be of the same paper or even the same number of pages. By putting two different titles together, you realize the economies inherent in volume, which translates into lower postage costs. Furthermore, you will improve your delivery (because you are at a deeper sorting level) and have enabled better destination entry (at a deeper level in the postal system) because of the increased density (more pieces qualifying for drop-shipping discounts). For example, with co-mailing, some or more of your mailing may qualify for delivery to SCFs instead of BMCs. For co-mailing to work, the catalogs need to be the exact same size and have the same mechanical properties, such as where the address is ink jetted; trim specifications must also be identical.

The downside of this technique is that it can be a schedule coordination nightmare.

You and another catalog mailer must agree to the same mailing dates and coordinate the mechanical specifications of your catalogs. Although there are certainly savings, balance these savings with the time it takes to handle the details of the project and any potentially negative effect on adjusting your mailing schedule to meet that of your co-mailer.

Bar Coding

Since March 21, 1994, the U.S. Postal Service has required that letter-size mailers wishing to obtain automation discounts must use a zip + 4 + 2 bar code instead of a zip + 4 bar code.

Zip + Four

This is one of two techniques that helps ensure better deliverability. The post office will run your list against their zip + 4 file once. This computer program will correct incorrect or incomplete addresses; standardize the spelling of the city, state, and street address; add details that may be missing (such as full spellings of addresses); and add the zip + 4. After this one-time freebie, you should run your mailing list against this list through your computer service bureau, where it will cost you a nominal fee. The frequency depends on how many names are added to your list over what time period. Ask your service bureau's advice.

Zip + 4 allows bar coding, which saves you money. For instance, at the basic rate, the cost difference is 2.9 cents per piece. Software is available to convert the five-digit numbers on your list to nine digits and make the bar.

Zip + four + two

Although zip + 4 is still okay for flats (which is what most catalogs are), the U.S. Postal Service has, since March 21, 1994, required that mailers wishing to obtain automation discounts must use a zip + 4 + 2 bar code intend of a zip + 4 bar code. Commonly called the delivery point bar code (DPBC), this 11-digit sector segment is another way of doing postal sorting for further discounts. These additional two digits allow walk-sequence automation. This takes carrier route one step further in that it puts the mail in the sequence in which the carrier will be walking on his or her route. Those two extra digits are the two numerical numbers on your house. In its simplest case, for an address of 1002, the numbers would be the 02. This matter is of greater concern to other direct marketers than it is to catalogers because catalogers can only take advantage of this technology if they are mailing either a letter-size or digest-size catalog. But stay abreast of the advances in technology—you never know when changes might benefit catalogs.

Lettersize (Slim Jims) Versus Flat

Most catalogs are mailed as flats. The digest ($5^3/_8$″ × $8^3/_8$″) and Slimjim (6″ × $10^7/_8$″) catalogs—both are called letter-size—can qualify for letter-size rates. Either size must weigh no more than 3 ounces. Negotiations are being conducted to raise piece weight to the piece/pound breakpoint which is currently at 3.3067 oz.

The discount is given to letter-size vehicles because they can be processed by machine, thus saving labor. However, they cannot go through the necessary machine unless they are tabbed (glued shut with small tabs, one at each edge).

Some catalogers have been concerned that sealing a catalog will decrease response. Rick Kropski, manager of Corporate Postal Systems and Logistics for Alden Press, reports that ongoing tests they are conducting have shown this fear appears to be unfounded.

Response rates and average order size have been within normal ranges. Rick recommends that, as with any new technique, each catalog should test. Also, the tabbing process must be run cost-efficiently enough to justify its use, so be sure your printer has the correct equipment.

Add-a-Name

Consider adding names from a qualified pool of buyers to segments of your mailing that do not have enough names for presort qualification. This effectively enhances your presort quantities, again resulting in additional savings that will qualify for a lower level of presort. For example, if you add one mail piece to a segment that has only nine, you will have enough to move from a five-digit sort to a carrier-route level, for a net savings of 30.6 cents. This may sound like a little, but it adds up.

Rich Kropski from Alden points out that by using this system, you can also add hotline requesters (those last-minute names) at the last minute. Here, you get the best of both worlds—the latest names and more postal discounts. Alternately, if you have budgeted for a one-million name mailing, you might rent only 950,000. You fill out the balance needed from your pool of qualified buyers and add them strategically via add-a-name to assure the best postal rate and delivery.

Any time you qualify for lower discounts you also realize better sorting, which results in higher deliverability.

These techniques are complicated, even for those who have been in the business for years. Be sure to work with qualified experts, such as printers who specialize in catalog printing and mailing. They can advise you of the latest techniques that apply to your stage of the business.

Alternative Delivery

Very much what it sounds like, alternative delivery is a method of delivering an advertising vehicle through a means other than the post office. Delivery legally cannot place the advertising material in a postal box, so it is distributed directly to the doorstep of the home, sometimes in poly bags hung on residents' doorknobs or in delivery tubes. The two major players are Publishers Express (PubX) and Alternate Postal Delivery (APD). Publishers Express currently deliver to approximately 900 zip codes in more than 30 cities in the United States. This amounts to coverage of approximately ten million households, or roughly 10 percent of the total households in the country. The service is expected to continue to add more zips and cities. It delivers a minimum of one day per week; this day can vary, but it is constant for participants. Rates for inclusion are based on the weight of the catalog and allow for volume discounts. On average, the cost is 5 percent to 15 percent less than regular U.S. Postal Service delivery rates.

Participants have mixed feelings about the effectiveness of this method. Although it is generally less costly than using the post office, it has added administrative and transportation expenses. And, because the targeting is limited, the results are not always stellar. Like all areas in direct marketing, it is something that should be tested regularly. According to Publishers Express, "JC Penney began testing alternative delivery in 1989, and now uses Publishers Express to help deliver its catalogs in several Midwestern markets. Other catalogers, like L. L. Bean, have turned to alternative delivery companies like Publishers Express for special promotions and overruns."

Note that alternative delivery must be from the point of entry. The cost of getting it there is paid by the catalogers. Also, be aware that the heavier the catalog, the more favorable the cost comparison (alternative versus postal costs); the lighter the catalog, the less favorable the cost comparison.

Tracking Services

Due to concerns about delivery of the catalog once it enters the postal stream, some printers now offer services that help track the catalog's path as well as alert the post office of the importance of the catalog and its delivery. For instance, R. R. Donnelley & Sons has a tracking cycle called Operation Showcase. It goes like this:

♦ Six weeks prior to mail start-up, the publisher's R. R. Donnelley customer service representative submits an Operation Showcase request form.

♦ Four weeks prior to the in-home date, a five-digit runner with counts is provided to Operation Showcase either from Metromail, R. R. Donnelley's list services provider, or the customer's list processor.

♦ Operation Showcase sends letters and a copy of the cover to affected postal contacts prior to mailing outlining information they need to know to achieve desired in-home dates.

♦ As a follow-up, Showcase initiates phone calls to post offices with delivery counts of at least 1,000 pieces requesting confirmation that the mail is in place and will be delivered within the customer's delivery schedule.

♦ Showcase then issues daily and final delivery status reports. These reports are analyzed for delivery information and made available to the publisher, R. R. Donnelly's customer service and sales, and the U.S. Postal Service.

Alden Press has a similar service called OPTRAC™ which will do the following:

1. Draft a plan on postal drop-ship destination entry (the logistical plan of where mail will go before it's actually sent). Then follow up on the plan as it happens.
2. The report will identify the
   a. drop date
   b. trailer number
   c. destination
   d. quantity
   e. weight
   f. reservation date
   g. in-home date
3. Timely delivery of the report (given to the customer two times a week or as often as requested).

Alden also uses an in-home monitor service for diagnostic purposes so it can adjust its mailing programs around destinations that are and are not performing. This allows drop dates to be moved up for slow delivery areas, helping catalogers protect their investment.

The U.S. Postal Service also has a tracking service, called EX3C, that measures delivery performance within a desired in-home window target. There are 5,100 reporters ("seeds") in over 100 major city markets. This service should be used for a minimum of 500-million quantity mailing. Even though this is a USPS service, you will need to go through your printer, who must set up the necessary systems.

Because delivery is critical, always check with your printer to understand what systems are available to assist your catalog once it hits the mail stream.

❖ CHECKLIST

✔ Stay on schedule.
✔ Understand which type of printing best suits your catalog.
✔ Think in signatures.
✔ Live up to your responsibilities and make sure your printer does the same.
✔ Regularly re-evaluate your paper options.
✔ Use consistent information when obtaining quotes from different companies.
✔ Keep abreast of technology.
✔ Be sure your type is readable.
✔ Create a style guide.

✔ Plan every detail with your photographer.

✔ Get signed model and location releases.

✔ Negotiate for lesser costs if using locations.

✔ Investigate and evaluate new photography options.

✔ Know your rights to the photographs taken for your catalog.

✔ Select models in person and abide by applicable laws.

✔ Don't overlook the impact of illustrations.

✔ Take the time to educate yourself about electronic publishing.

✔ Work with qualified, highly recommended separators and stay up-to-date on available technologies.

✔ Put all specifications in writing.

✔ Understand that state-of-the-art binding and mailing capabilities are just as important as print quality when choosing a printer.

✔ Be clear in the information you give to the bindery.

✔ Get 3602 forms for every mailing.

✔ Get transportation and delivery reports in a timely manner.

End Notes

1. *Folio*, May 1993.
2. *Catalog Age*, February 1993.

CHAPTER EIGHT
❖ ❖ ❖

The Creative Process

Determine Your Company Image

Before you sit down with your designers, you must know your potential market and the image you wish to convey. Are you targeting an affluent market that's used to the better things in life? Then your design must reflect this life-style. Perhaps you want high-quality paper, contemporary graphics, and bold, colorful visuals. Or do your products appeal more to middle America, an older audience with less income, determined to buy only products that represent true value? Then, think "Norman Rockwell." Use lesser-quality paper, but not a low grade. Show the benefit of the merchandise and use clear photos with callouts (lines of copy describing the product features) that spell out the quality and value of the product. Here's where the positioning statement you have written (see Chapter 2) will help you be clear about your catalog's unique definition and how to convey it.

Catalog Design: Format and Layout

Once you understand the potential and limitations of catalog production, you are ready to let those creative juices flow. You want the best-looking, highest-quality catalog possible. But remember: You must account for every dollar you spend. Will those fancy rounded edges pay for themselves? Or will they look great, but fail to generate added sales?

The direct marketing catalog professionals you hire or have on staff also want a great-looking catalog. Their challenge is to create a visually commanding, articulate, and sales-oriented catalog for which there is no preset formula. A definitive idea of the targeted market and the budget are two important steps toward success. Understanding the creative language of artists is another.

Understanding Format

The word "format" when used in conjunction with the word "catalog" most often refers to its shape and size, although its overall general approach—including such elements as typeface, quality of paper, and, of course, design—can also be called its format. For instance, a mail order catalog can have a magazine-style format if it is the size of a magazine and its cover contains many of the elements often found on magazine covers.

Certainly, one of the most important design elements is the size of the catalog. Some people think that a smaller-size catalog will wind up on top of a pile of larger ones. Others prefer oversized catalogs, which they think will bury smaller catalogs. Unusual catalog

❖ **EXAMPLE 8-1**
For Self Care, bigger is better. This oversized (9⅞″ × 12″) catalog stands apart from more traditional-size catalogs.

sizes are sometimes chosen to stand out from the increasing number of similar publications, and printing capabilities have expanded to allow for new cost-effective formats without wasting paper. But don't choose a format that only one printer can produce; be sure to leave yourself options for price comparisons. And don't be novel at too high a cost; catalogs usually come in fairly standard sizes because the cost efficiencies of these sizes overwhelm the supposed gain of more distinctive, but much more expensive sizes. Odd-size catalogs can also mean different costs in postage. For instance, the letter-size format (minimum size 3.5″ W×5″ L; maximum size: 6⅛″ W×1½″ L; no more than a ¼″ thick) achieves significant savings (see Table 8–1).

Work with your printer, art staff, or creative agency to determine what size is best for your product line. Think in terms of production options that are economically viable and the importance of standing apart from the competition. Square, tall, oblong, side-stitched, 8⅜″ × 10⅞″ are just some of the choices. Choose the format that best suits your

❖ **TABLE 8-1**
Lettersize Postage Savings

	Flats*	Letters*
Basic	26.6 cents	22.6 cents
3/5 digit	21.4 cents	18.8 cents
Carrier route	16.2 cents	15 cents

* Weight not greater than 3.3067 ounces.

merchandise. If yours is a fashion catalog and has tall, long photos, you might opt for a tall, narrow format so the artist who lays out your catalog will have the right-size space to show the clothing off to its best advantage. In a square catalog, photos must be smaller and do not allow fashions to be shown at their best.

A 1994 survey in *Catalog Age* found the following catalog sizes to be the ones used most often in the industry:

Standard	58%
Digest	21%
Slimjim	7%
Oblong	1%
Other	13%

Choose your design concept carefully. It must be adaptable to potential changes in consumer buying habits. Too many elaborate design elements in your first catalog may lock you into a format that will not pay for itself. Begin with a simple concept. More complex adaptations can be tested in the future when the catalog has paid for itself and funds are available for experimentation. Don't be caught in the ego trap of designing a catalog that's great for showing off to country club friends but hasn't a chance of realizing a profit. Here are a few basic rules to remember.

1. Make sure the design represents your company.
2. Work with a professional direct marketing artist who knows the difference between award-winning and sales-generating graphics.
3. Select a design that will fit your budget; it can always be adapted to something more elaborate in the future.
4. Select a design that is adaptable to changing consumer needs.

63A,B A sheer white organza blouse and black chiffon palazzo pants pair up for a special evening out. Overlaid with lace across the front and around the sleeves, the peplumed, V-neck blouse with attached camisole is finished with gold-tone and rhinestone buttons, French cuffs, and a matching sash. The pants are lined and have an elastic waist. By Alex Evenings. Blouse in sizes S,M,L. Pants in 4-16. Both are polyester and from the USA. Catalog only.

63A. Blouse, 135.00.
63B. Pants, 85.00.

❖ **EXAMPLE 8-2**
Neiman Marcus uses a distinctive long and narrow format that makes its clothing look appealingly slenderizing.

Layouts

Layout is the rendering of pages to show the position and space allocation of photography and copy and to indicate the general feeling or "flow" of the catalog. During the layout stage, the cataloger should provide general input and make desired changes in the space allocation or copy to avoid later costs for photo resizing, resetting of type, and so forth (see Chapter 7).

Layouts, whether they are hand-drawn or computerized, may be four-color or black-and-white. At least two spreads should be in color, so you can better visualize the final product. The remainder of the layouts can be done in black and white with color indicators. Since it takes less time to produce a black-and-white layout when it is hand-drawn, and less-expensive equipment to produce one when computerized, using black-and-white layouts can be an important cost saver.

Basic Layout Types. Many catalog artists, especially since the advent of the computerized layout, work in a grid format. This can have many advantages, two of the most important being the consistency of the catalog's overall look and the ability to "drop" products in and out of a slot when replacing one item with another. Grid designs can look very much like a grid, or they can be adapted by allocating space differently for each product, giving the design more of a free-form feeling.

Grids for $8^{1}/_{2}" \times 11"$ catalogs tend to come in two- or three-column formats, with an occasional four-column design. Four-column designs, because they squeeze products and copy into a very narrow width, are not usually recommended.

❖ EXAMPLE 8-3
The Lighter Side puts a lot of products into its high-density, tight-grid format, thus offering readers a wide product choice in a minimal amount of space.

❖ **EXAMPLE 8-4**

Signals uses a three-column grid format but varies the design.

❖ **EXAMPLE 8-5**

Chef's Catalog's three-column grid format is not as obvious as some because products are not given equal space.

Alternately, artists can make dramatic use of a free-form design. Here elements do not fit into invisible squares but are designed unto themselves. This type of design can be quite beautiful, but it requires more skill and does not easily allow one item to replace another without redesigning the entire page. To anchor many individual elements, the artist will often have one large photo as the "centerpiece" of the free-form design. Sometimes this anchor appears in the middle of the page, effectively extending two pages into one continuous visual.

Knowing the Press Layout.   Before beginning the layout, it helps to understand how the ink will flow and where pages will be in relationship to each other on press. To select background colors compatible with the ink flow, the artist must see a signature from the printer. For example, it could be disastrous to make pages 5 and 6 red and pages 11 and 12 white. If page 5 were to be printed next to page 12, the ink from page 5 would flow onto page 12, producing a pinkish page instead of the desired white one.

Balancing color in layouts based on printing needs is an area too often overlooked by artists. Some compromises may have to be made in the position of merchandise, but proper layouts can minimize on-press problems.

Working with Artists in General.   Give your artists as much information as possible about the merchandise they are expected to portray. Include the following points for each product:

♦ The size of the item—so the product can be positioned and propped correctly.

♦ Unusual features—so the item can be shown "in use," if applicable, or alone for photographic effect.

♦ Previous sales history—to determine if the space allocated should be enlarged or decreased.

❖ **EXAMPLE 8-6**   Sugar Hill has one main visual in the center of the page to hold all the elements together. Note that the photo is positioned so no important product details are lost along the inside gutter.

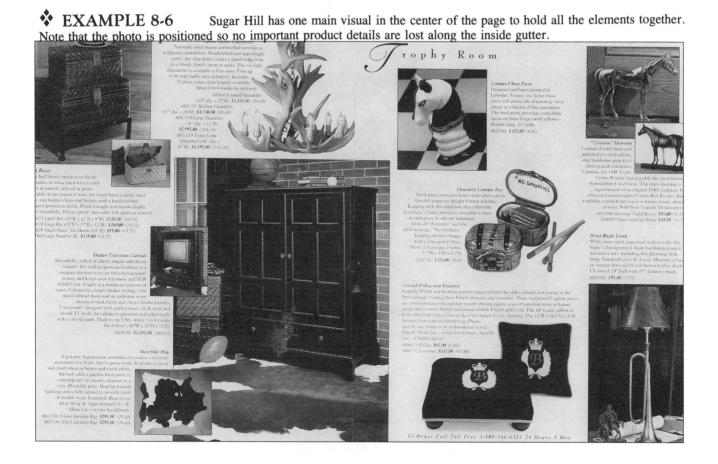

◆ The price of the item—if no previous sales history is available, this can allow the artists to give higher-priced items more dominance.

◆ Featured items in each spread—the reasons for selecting merchandise may not be known to the layout person. Let him or her know why some items might be more important than others.

All this information can be compiled in the spread record sheets discussed in Chapter 5, which can act as reference tools for each member of the creative and marketing team.

As the layouts progress, be sure to express both compliments and constructive criticism, but be specific. Make both your positive and negative feelings plainly understood. What don't you like? Do you have another catalog that may give the artist a better idea of what you want? Are the photographic areas too small? Does the fashion, as depicted, seem lifeless? Most artists welcome input and, if possible, will act on it. But be willing to listen to what they have to say as well. Let their experience help you create a professional catalog, one to which customers will eagerly respond—the first time or the fiftieth.

Working with Computer Artists.   There are undoubtedly many benefits to putting your catalog on computer. But there are some major differences from the way things were done when art was primarily a manual process. Before, the artist sketched some drawings in position on a board, and, after a few changes here and there, you trusted what you believed he or she had drawn and went on to the photography stage. After the photos were shot, black-and-white stats of the photos were put into position, type was set and laid in position, and you reviewed mechanicals, or paste-ups, that looked a lot like what you see on the first go-round with a computer.

The first pass from a computer almost always shows type and any pick-up photos in position. Sometimes, for the new photos, artists will simply indicate a space; a better way to do this is to insert drawings into that space to indicate how the items will be shot (not unlike the old method on hand-drawn layouts). So one major computerization advantage is that you have more complete layouts up-front and should have more time to refine them as the work progresses.

But, as the computerization of catalogs is still a relatively new medium, there is also a potential problem. Anybody with a Macintosh computer (Mac) can now attempt to present themselves as an artist. Unfortunately, it is not always true that learning to operate a computerized art program makes one an artist.

As Tom Burkholder, senior vice president of York Graphic Services, says, "The computer is only a tool." He uses this analogy: "If I decided to become a carpenter, I could readily purchase the hardware (lathe, saws, and so on), but even with the very best equipment, I'd be a poor excuse for a competent, well-trained professional who builds with wood. I would still lack the basic skills and talents to do the job."

How do you protect yourself from the computer charlatan who claims to be a competent computer artist? There are two approaches.

Approach 1. This approach works only if you are ready to make a commitment, because, in essence, it means that you take known artists (the kind that can draw with a paper and pen) and train them on a computer. This also usually translates into in-house creative, because the time and money commitment is simply not worth it if you are not working with one art team all the time.

Even if you provide the art staff with the highest caliber teacher, some artists will never become expert in computerized work. But you will have real artists with known talent working on your catalog. So how do you solve the problem that these great creatives are less than ideal with a computer? Use the creative artists to create and computer-savvy people to actually enter and manipulate work. Here's how it works:

1. The artist creates a rough layout, similar to the way he or she did in the past, but less polished.

2. You review the layout and indicate your recommended changes.

3. The Mac artist takes the creative and inputs it into the Mac. Any changes from here on are done by the Mac artist with the creative artist supervising every step.

4. Make sure the copywriter simply writes the copy. There is no need for writers to attempt to become typesetters and, in fact, this means that the computer artist will just have to undo any type commands the writer has attempted to incorporate into the copy. Writers are not designers, nor are they typesetters. Keep it simple and let the art people, with verbal input from the writer, get it into the Mac efficiently. Whether the copy is input before or after design depends on the project—what's the most critical, the copy or the design? Whichever is most critical should take the lead-off position.

Does this mean you're playing double because two people are doing the work of one? No. It means you're using the right people for what they do best. Accuracy, speed, *and* creativity will be the result.

Designing a rough before going to Mac art is a good idea for another basic reason: Most of us have not adapted to the idea that what first comes out of the Mac is not the finished product. It looks like a paste-up, therefore it is a paste-up (too many of us seem to think). This means there is little flexibility in the eye of those who first view it. Eliminate this problem, at least somewhat, by first creating what most people are more familiar with, the tissue (also called the rough layout). Then let the tissue act as a blueprint for the Mac artist.

Approach 2. Make the computer artist draw something without the aid of a computer. If you hire free-lancers, knowing the creative capability of someone who claims to be a Mac artist is like Russian roulette. Anybody can say they did a creative, but who knows whose input went into the final design. This has always been somewhat true, but is even more so now that one simply has to know how to use a computer art program. Get your potential free-lancer to resort to the old tried-and-true methods before you determine his or her value as a computer artist.

And, of course, there is much more to useful Mac art than just the design. You have to know that the person you are trusting to prepare your promotional material can put it into the format needed by the separator. Talk to the separator you plan to use and have him or her interview the potential computer artist. Separators know what they need, and they know what to ask the artist to make sure that he or she delivers it. Also ask the potential computer artist for references from separators with whom he or she interacted in the past. (See Chapter 7.)

To see the photos in position in a computerized layout, the artist must scan those photos into position. There are two main options:

Option One. Use a desktop scanner to produce a low-resolution scan for position only. Such scans are not reproducible and are only to show the separator and the rest of the creative team the proper size, cropping, and rotation for each image on a page. This is quick and usually takes the artist only minutes per photo (depending on the speed of the computer equipment). However, this adds up when you are talking about a catalog with 300 photos.

With this option, the artist scans the images, completes the electronic mechanical, and then sends a final laser proof and all the original artwork to the separator, who actually manufactures the job.

Option Two. Send the photos to your separator and have them scanned for reproduction, using the low-resolution image for position and the high-resolution image for reproduction when producing the final pages for film to be output and sent to a printer. With this option, the artist can, while placing these images, crop, size, position, and rotate them to fit your particular design. In essence, the artist actually assembles the page with a low-resolution image. The assembled pages can be returned to your separator who will automatically replace or swap the low-resolution image with the high-resolution, color-separated file.

The low-resolution version is very easy for the artist to work with because it does not bog down the system with a lot of memory restraints, thus allowing streamlined production work flow while designing. This saves you money because most separators charge additional for rotating images, which tends to slow down image processing. But be aware of some limitations concerned with this option:

1. Sizing of separator-supplied, low-resolution scans is limited to plus or minus 25 percent by most separators.

2. You must work from final selects, unlike low-resolution scanning which is for position only, so the extra time for making the final select must be factored into the schedule.

3. Depending on the separator, you may not be able to silhouette an image unless the separator does complicated masks.

Before making a decision, check on all three of these points to be sure you and your artist can live with the restraints. And be alert to the cost advantages of fast scanners. This means that in the not-too-distant future, the decreasing cost and increasing speed of scanners will allow scans so cheap and fast that you may choose to do them in-house or through your agency rather than through your separator.

A computer artist is much more than an artist these days; he or she must also be a technician and produce the final product in a form that fits the needs of the separator. So, just as you made sure that your separator and your printer were in sync before they began work, do the same with your artist and your separator. Their ability to work together is the key to making the production part of the computer process as painless as possible.

What Artists Should Know about Props and Backgrounds. Props are necessary to establish size relationships and reinforce the mood of the catalog. Even when written size specifications are provided, consumers still tend to order merchandise on the basis of a preconceived desired size. The use of props allows the potential buyer to know, at a glance, if the item is the desired size; this reduces returns.

❖ **EXAMPLE 8-7** Ballard Designs does an excellent job of showing an item as both a prop (in the bedding setting) and an item for sale (in a silhouette).

Avoid, if at all possible, using props that look as though they might be for sale in the catalog, although they aren't. Too many cases have been cited when these not-for-sale props are the very thing the customer wants, and you don't have them! This can be true of almost anything, so it isn't always avoidable, but watch for the chance to prop with salable items whenever possible. One cataloger used an antique tub as an impressive prop for bath accessories. Sure enough, two customers wanted it (and this was an expensive item). The cataloger owned the prop and not only willingly sold it to one of the callers, but also found another, similar one for the second customer.

Colorful backgrounds can put life into a catalog and emphasize a season. Red and green are naturals for the winter holidays; pastels for spring. But remember that a product will often take on some of the background color. Think twice before shooting a white vase on a red background. The red could give the vase a pinkish tint. Because consumers tend to buy what they see, you could have orders for a pink vase, when in reality you are offering the vase only in white.

Mood shots and overly propped photography don't belong in mail order. Customers should be able to see the merchandise clearly.

To avoid loss of time and misunderstanding, the display of the merchandise and the necessary propping should be clearly illustrated on the prop schedule (see Chapter 7). The layout artist should contact the photographer before actually beginning to choose props and backgrounds. Considerable expense and time can be avoided by using backgrounds and props available in the photographer's studio.

Finding props, arranging them during the photography sessions and seeing to their care is the responsibility of the stylists hired by the photographer (or you). If you pay for props, you have the right to own them (some catalogers simply donate them, depending on their value, to the studio), unless, of course, they are rented. If there are no stylists, you must make clear arrangements with the photographer as to who should handle this element.

Determining and Incorporating Cross-Sell.   Props provide an excellent opportunity for cross-sellings—referencing an item not necessarily sold on that page to another page or place on the spread. As all space allocated will be analyzed for its sales contribution, it makes sense to put a product for sale in space that might otherwise be occupied by a product you are not selling. The item used as a prop most probably does not warrant giving it two real selling spaces (with financial accountability for both), but, when used as a prop, it simply reinforces another product.

Walking the Reader through the Selling Images.   Through graphic illustration and subtly controlled layouts, the consumer can be encouraged subsconsciously to see every item on every page. Designs should flow effortlessly across a spread, with intermittent "hot" spots (created through the use of color or product space allocation) that grab the customer's attention. Getting the eye to move across the page can be accomplished with a variety of methods. One of the most common is a line drawn horizontally from the left to the right side of the page. A line of color in the middle of a page pulls the eye across the page and helps tie a free-floating product and copy together. Copy blocks should be placed as close as possible to the corresponding photos: Consumers are drawn to photos first and, if they cannot quickly find the right copy block, will leave the page in frustration.

Although designers can force consumers to "search" through a catalog page, studies indicate that the eye is happier if it flows from left to right in a "U" pattern. Scattered products and copy blocks will be rapidly scanned—and, often, rapidly discarded. And although readership does not necessarily equate with sales, it makes sense to assume that higher readership increases your chances of higher sales.

Also, note that most people tend to see the upper-right-hand side of a catalog first, which puts a heavier sales burden on this side of the spread. Give this extra consideration when designing *and* merchandising; you may wish to place your proven sellers on this side in order to help guarantee that you catch the prospect's attention and increase sales.

There is always a time and place for innovative layout, but consider combining innovation with proven techniques for optimal results.

❖ **EXAMPLE 8-8** Horchow Home Collection sells the props shown in its settings.

❖ **EXAMPLE 8-9** A bright green line tied to a red headline captures the reader's attention and draws the eye across the products on this spread from an Attitudes catalog.

❖ **EXAMPLE 8-10**   For this spread, Lands' End employs what some consider a typical "U" design.

Using Hot Spots to Grab Attention.   There is nothing better than a clean layout that clearly displays every product, but there are also techniques that enhance readership of certain products within that organized layout.

Crossovers.   This technique positions a photograph of a product across the page, creating a central focus around which all other photographs are situated. Two important points should be considered before this is done:

1. Be sure the photograph does not "cut" the item at the fold. This can obscure an important selling point.

2. Be certain your printer will be able to hold color and alignment accurately on these two facing pages. Remember, although they are facing in the final spread, they are probably not facing in the imposition (see Chapter 7).

Tinted backgrounds.   Tinted backgrounds, when used with a specific marketing purpose, can catch the reader's attention and almost guarantee that the featured product will be seen, thus helping ensure sales. But, unfortunately, this technique is often used indiscriminately, defeating its purpose. Have a specific reason for adding a pale tint of color behind certain products and their associated copy, and you will reap sales rewards. Some legitimate reasons are: special savings, consistent treatment of a particular type of grouping, and "attaching" two or more related elements (such as an inset photo with the main photo and its copy).

❖ **EXAMPLE 8-11** The Smithsonian catalog uses colorful bells in the center of the spread to draw the reader's eye across the page and successfully gets the prospect to see the corresponding photos.

❖ **EXAMPLE 8-12** Jackson & Perkins puts a pale beige tint behind colorful illustrations of flowers and their corresponding chart. This same tint ties in the special savings on Antique Roses.

Bullets.   Breaking important points out of the body copy can give potential customers the opportunity to understand the product's benefits at a glance. Try to limit the number of bullets used, since an excess just creates more copy and defeats the effect.

Use of color.   Colored type can shout information or be lost in a din of too much color. Like the other elements mentioned here, colored type should be used sparingly. Decide which message(s) you want the customer to see first, then apply color there. If everything is in color, nothing will be seen.

Insets.   When one photo inserts into another, it is called an inset. Most often used to illustrate a feature, design element, or alternate color that is not obvious from the main photo, insets are always smaller than the main photo. Keep them tied closely to the product they represent, either by putting them entirely within the photo or slightly outside, but still attached, to that feature photo.

Illustrations.   Research shows that illustrations are one of the first things the potential buyer will see. A well-done illustration not only captures attention, it explains details/ benefits in seconds, whereas copy might take minutes and still be confusing. Use illustrations to show hidden features and/or explain additional benefits.

❖ **EXAMPLE 8-13**

Improvements uses bullets and color to highlight features. Note the effective use of handwritten type in the copy block and two before-and-after examples.

❖ **EXAMPLE 8-14**

Barrie Pace Ltd. shows the vest for this jacket dress in an inset because the detail could not be seen clearly in the feature photo.

❖ **EXAMPLE 8-15**

A four-color illustration in Improvements shows how this less-than-glamorous-looking product is actually quite useful.

Using Type as a Graphic Element

Type, as discussed in Chapter 7, should always be readable and reflect the personality of the catalog. But it can be much more than that. Type can make a statement; it can make a product come alive; it can denote a change in feeling within a particular section of the catalog.

One cataloger, noted for its conservative products, announced that the reader had stepped into a different section of the catalog with big, bold, colorful letters, running the entire width of the page and displayed on a black background. This was distinctively different from what had gone before, which was soft and simple. Now the cataloger wanted to "wake up" the prospective buyer to the fact that the theme had gone from outdoor casual to big-city chic.

Another catalog uses hand-written messages within photos to add a homey touch to its important copy messages. Hammacher Schlemmer used big, colorful words such as "Pow!" and "Bang!" to make a selection of sound-driven products seem to emit noise right off the page.

Don't treat type as a static element. Constantly look for ways to make it reach out to your customers and prospects (never forgetting that it must always be readable). Follow these guidelines in making type decisions:

◆ Must act as a powerful graphic element.
◆ Be eminently readable.
◆ Walk the reader through the sales pitch.
◆ Fit the personality of the catalog and its audience.
◆ Never have too much leading between sentences.
◆ Never run wider than the eye reads.
◆ Almost never have a period after a headline.
◆ Almost never use smaller than 8 point.
◆ Almost never use sans serif in body copy.
◆ Almost never use knock-out type.
◆ Almost never use all caps in headings.

Allocating Space to Each Product

The space allocated to a particular product undoubtedly is related to the sales generated by that product (see Chapter 14). Therefore, it is important to understand how space should be allocated. Here are some pointers:

1. Allocation of space should not be based solely on the sales of one product. You must consider the sales of the entire page. How will increasing or decreasing the size of one item affect the other products? In a split test on space allocation, a major mailer discovered that increasing the space allocation of one clothing style by 50 percent increased its sales only 36 percent. But the reduction in space of other styles in the same spread resulted in less than the proportionate loss of sales. The result was that overall demand for merchandise in the spread rose considerably.

2. When everything is treated equally, nothing is really featured. The illusion of dominance can be created by visually increasing the space for one or two products. They do not take up any more space or dominate the spread, but appear to because the other products on that page have had their space allocations reduced minimally. This can have the effect of increasing overall sales without making one product pay for a large increase in its space allocation.

3. When one color of an assortment is dominant, that color generally outsells all other colors. If one color is to be featured, select the color that has the greatest sales potential. The one exception to this rule is when an unusually wide variety of colors is a major sales point; then showing the entire assortment is preferable.

4. When one product is to be featured, it should be one with broad appeal. If the product has a poor sales history, increasing the size will generally not benefit overall sales on the page. Unless a significant increase in sales has already been realized through an increase in space, giving a weak product even more space is of no benefit. In fact, it can have a negative sales effect.

Space Allocation Grid.   Determining what to put on what pages, how much space to allocate, and what placement particular items have on a page can be confusing at best and frustrating at worst. The spread record sheets used in Chapters 5 and 6 are undoubtedly helpful. But you will want to take this one step further, to a visual representation. Similar to what magazine publications use to help them determine how much space to give to editorial and advertising, a simple grid can work wonders in improving communication between merchandising and creative. Figure 8–1, from Improvements, shows how products are roughly allocated by the product team before hand-off to the art and copy team. This is done for every catalog and can be adapted by different artists.

This oversize sheet indicates two blank pages, representing spreads, side by side. Create page grids for every spread in the catalog. Within these grid blanks, space should be divided into grids and product names should be written in the spaces they will occupy. Because this is done for every spread, you can view the entire catalog at a glance. It will give you a feel for how the catalog will flow from page to page and will greatly aid artists when it comes to actually laying out each spread.

Don't forget to keep copy space in mind when allocating products. One photo can have many elements within it, one of the most dramatic examples being bedding. One beautiful photo of a "dressed" bed could have 15 to 20 stock keeping units (SKU) for each size sheet, pillowcase, comforter, bed ruffle, and so on!

Pacing.   Make sure that your design has enough changing interest from spread to spread that your audience keeps turning the pages. This is especially important as the number of pages in your catalog increases. Too often, one concept is decided on and simply repeated, with minor rearrangement, from spread to spread. This can be quite boring and should be avoided. Always keep the same feeling, through type usage and photography, but make the catalog move through section after section by using stimulating, shifting creative treatments.

The Front Cover

Simply put, if prospective buyers don't like the cover, they won't open your catalog. And if they don't open the catalog, they won't buy. In Chapter 6, we looked at whether it is advisable to sell off the cover, and in Chapter 7, cover art was discussed. But so much depends on the cover that it deserves even further consideration.

It is important to lay the groundwork for the cover by understanding how the rest of the catalog will be laid out. Because the cover must reflect the content of the catalog, it is most often designed after the rest of the publication has been laid out. It is very important to remember that the cover must be cohesive with the rest of the catalog; so although it must certainly be distinctive, it should not be thought of as an independent design.

First and foremost, the cover must reflect your company image. This, of course, can be done in many ways.

❖ FIGURE 8-1 Sample of a Grid Allocation Form

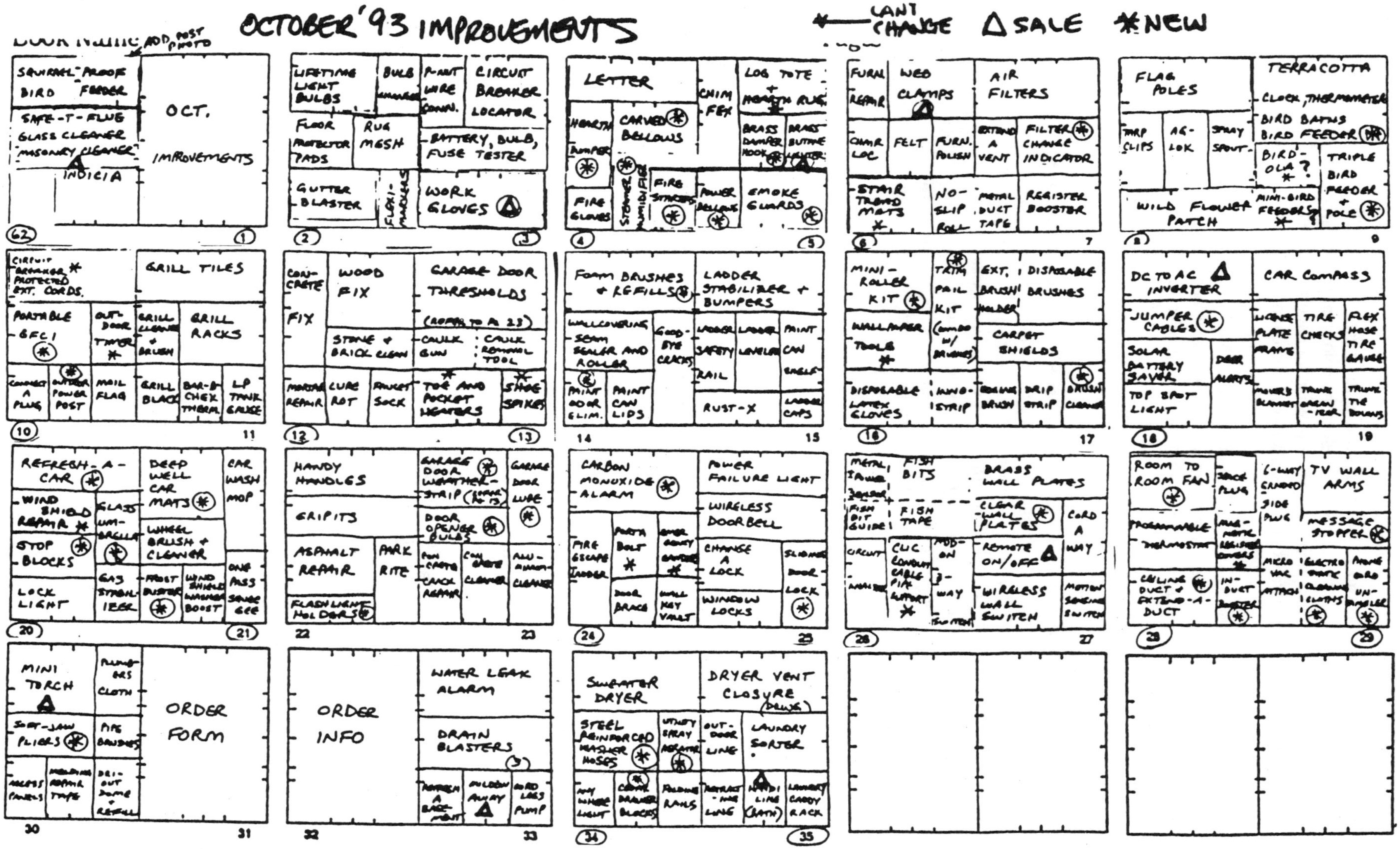

Essential Elements. You only have a few seconds to capture the attention of a potential reader and get him or her to open the catalog. So your message must be to the point, relevant, and outstandingly portrayed. What are the essential elements for creating this effect?

1. **Logo**. Make it immediately obvious who is behind this catalog. Don't design your logo so only you and the designer can read it. Put it in a dominant place.
2. **Tag Line**. Some catalogers do not feel this is critical, but many hours of research has shown that consumers want information. Use a tag line that states exactly what this catalog is about and what's in it for the potential customer. One good example written for Lotus said: "Up-to-the-Minute Selection of Hard-to-Find Products." This tag line makes three points: timeliness, carefully chosen items, and items you won't find just anywhere. It's also open-ended enough to allow for product expansions.
3. **Date**. Tell the customer the season for which this catalog is intended.
4. **Call to action**. Be it a product cross-reference, a toll-free number, or overnight delivery, make it useful.
5. **Restraint**. Don't try to sell everything at once!

The biggest mistake marketers and designers alike make is to try to put *everything* on the cover. Think in terms of three messages, including your logo and tag line. Three points of data are about all humans can handle in a few seconds, so don't frustrate them by trying to say so much that they ignore the entire message.

Basic Types of Covers. Though cover design is really unlimited, there tend to be some consistent approaches:

1. **Grid**. Many products, sometimes in combination with services, are presented in squares or other such geometric holding devices.
2. **Product as hero**. The product is featured, generally very close up.
3. **Product in use**. Very similar to the "product as hero" approach, but the item is shown as it is intended to be used.
4. **Life-style**. Graphic depiction of the overall theme of the catalog, such as a family having fun together.
5. **Editorial**. Magazine look, with an up-close photo over which is superimposed copy blocks indicating the new features in this issue.
6. **Philosophical**. Verbiage or graphics depict the catalog's reason for being.

Popcorn Factory (catalogs) show the diversity they have invested in what was once a simple food product. Dramatic photos on covers show ideal seasonality, yet make the statement that, with this catalog, popcorn is anything but ordinary.

J. Crew, like many other catalogs, relies on attractive people to get the first page turned. But J. Crew takes this technique one step further in using the appeal of a well-known model like Lauren Hutton, who has maintained her top model status for decades.

Sometimes simplicity and a consistent color will help reinforce your positioning. Tiffany & Co. does it right with a known (digest-size) format and famous turquoise color. The name of the company and the famous designer jewelry speak for themselves; anything more would detract from the appeal. One of the few consumer catalogers to use an envelope, Tiffany repeats the color identification with an overall turquoise envelope, die-cut to show the address. The envelope has no teaser copy, just the well-known Fifth Avenue address.

Although not too many catalogs do it, there is a time and place for selling off the cover. L.L. Bean, with its highly promotional Bean's Bargains, makes the savings message clear by showing a product, complete with its body copy and price, for sale on the cover. The company also employs another traditional means of getting attention—a banner in the lower left-hand corner of the page.

❖ **EXAMPLE 8-16**

Seasonality is strongly stated with the lavender, pink, and gold pastel cover punctuated by an unusual popcorn egg from Popcorn Factory.

SOURCE: Peter Kao, Greg Booth & Associates, Dallas, TX.

❖ **EXAMPLE 8-17**

J. Crew uses Lauren Hutton as a visual spokesperson on its cover.

A more traditional look is chosen by cataloger Lillian Vernon for its square-format catalog. But Vernon takes the traditional feel beyond the ordinary by adding a clever header to its logo ("Start the 1993 Holidays with Lillian Vernon") and by adding a metallic sticker proclaiming its deferred payment policy. Further, Vernon helps the potential buyer find the items featured on the cover with strategically placed, easy-to-read page references.

Photography is certainly not the only choice for a striking cover. Lands' End tends to interchange, sometimes using photography and sometimes illustrations. Its Coming Home cover tells the philosophy behind the company (a graphic approach used some years back by Lands' End proper). Through a majestic use of type combined with down-to-earth copy, the cover manages to be both upscale and homey.

❖ **EXAMPLE 8-18**

Tiffany uses an understated, totally elegant
design to get prospects to open its catalog.

SOURCE: Tiffany and Company, 1994.

❖ **EXAMPLE 8-19**

L.L. Bean's well-organized cover sells both a
product and the overall savings platform.

❖ **EXAMPLE 8-20**

Lillian Vernon's holiday cover is wonderfully traditional but
incorporates motivational aspects, such as the personalized
gift message tied with a bow.

❖ **EXAMPLE 8-21**

Lands' End's Coming Home cover plays up the
company's value position without using
photography.

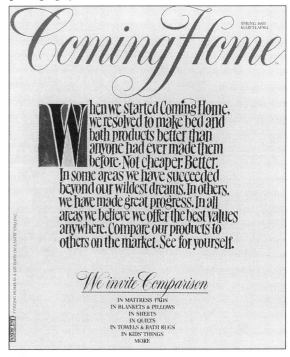

The Back Cover

Nobody guarantees the front cover will be the first thing prospects see. And even when the front cover is the first impression, some people estimate that at least 50 percent of the population reads back to front. Therefore, the back cover plays a mighty important role, too. The sad fact is that, too often, it is simply overlooked. Plan ahead for your back cover and make sure it also conveys your catalog's image. And, to some extent, think of how the back cover relates to the front cover. Although it is true that the front and back covers will seldom be seen side by side, they are most often seen right after each other, so have some commonality in their design.

Always consider showing at least one of the following on the back cover:

- ◆ Your toll-free or ordering number
- ◆ Your money-back guarantee
- ◆ Your best-selling "hot" new item
- ◆ Any special savings
- ◆ The credit cards you accept
- ◆ Endorsements from satisfied customers
- ◆ The number of years you've been in business (if it's an impressive number)
- ◆ The locations of your stores (if too many, just a blurb inviting customers to visit your stores
- ◆ Any special services you offer customers

One common approach is to sell three items: one best-seller, and two new items that from past history of similar items, show every indication of being best-sellers also. A variety of approaches to the back cover can be seen in the examples that follow.

Harry & David designates a floral gift a "Mother's Day Begonia," thus reminding readers of an important gift event. The company also promotes its fast delivery, special prices, store locations, and toll-free numbers.

❖ **EXAMPLE 8-22**
Harry & David uses a richly colored visual and strong copy to make sure this back cover has as much impact as the front cover.

❖ **EXAMPLE 8-23**

Jackson Trading Company fits six product offerings on its back cover.

❖ **EXAMPLE 8-24**

One approach, illustrated by White Flower Farm's catalog, is to feature one strong, representative product.

Knowing the back cover can be prime selling space, Jackson Trading Company fills every inch with product. The copy wraps around each product to help customers find the information they need to make a purchase. Inserted next to a product is an editorial promoting the cinematographer behind the videos being sold. A soft pastel background tint helps draw the eye without detracting from the product itself.

Finally, White Flower Farm designs a back cover that is almost as beautiful as its front cover. One dramatic photograph features an ''everything included'' border. The toll-free number displayed in a bright green background, beckons, and an ink-jet message gets the customer to turn the page.

Making Sure Your Copy Sells

A great-looking layout and effective design elements can help guide customers through your catalog, but it's the copywriter's job to clinch the sale. There's a lot more to motivational copy than just descriptions. The copywriter must inform, educate, and weave a spell that instills the desire and confirms the decision to purchase.

Judging the Importance of Copy versus Art

There is an age-old struggle between the writer and the artist as to who should take the lead when it comes to the creation of the catalog. The answer is really an obvious one once you've worked your way through the process a few hundred times. And that answer is, there is no pat answer.

Copy leads when the marketing and/or positioning is heavily reliant on information. One example of this might be the J. Peterman catalog, which uses a storytelling approach as the main thrust of its sell, supplementing the copy with line drawings presented in a simple format that most often uses one page to showcase each product. Another example would be for a highly technical product line, where the artist must consider space for specification and technical information before the piece can be laid out.

But the graphics should, more often than not, begin before the copy. For the most part, consumers rely on pictures rather than words for information and entertainment. And catalogs should entertain as well as sell. It is an error to simply show the product on the page, attach some simple explanatory copy and expect this offering to compete successfully with those that incorporate entertainment in each mailing.

The writer, in conjunction with the marketing team, should provide the explicit information needed by the artist to help ensure that this part of creative endeavor goes as smoothly as possible.

Get Organized

Before copy is begun, make sure your writers are organized and understand the format in which the copy should be written. Creative copy is wonderful, but organized creative copy is even better!

You already know about the two most important tools—the merchandise information form (MIF) and the style guide. If you're not up to creating an entire style guide, there is another solution. Devise a copy/layout/type formula (which originates with the writer); get everyone (the account executive, the client representative, the buyer, and so on) involved to add their thoughts about what the formula should contain; then stick to it. Here's an example:

1. Savings in headline all caps. Always "00% to 00% SAVINGS on," *not* "SAVE 00% on."
2. NEW! in headline all caps.
3. 4/$10.50–not set of.
4. Say (one pattern per set) when offering sets.
5. Heights, etc., in abbreviated caps (H).
6. Abbreviate quarts (qt.).
7. End paragraph with measurement.
8. All states, use PO abbreviation.
9. If size is important to product (for example 9" pie plates), put it in headline.
10. Watch use of quotes and make sure all quotes have beginning and ending marks.
11. If item is on sale, format is: Reg. $00.00 NOW $00.00.
12. When offering set of different-size items, it's: $23.00/set of three (or whatever number applies).
13. Measurements belong in this order: W × H × L
14. Diameter is Dia.
15. Subheads should be in upper and lower case.
16. An asterisk(*) denotes Exclusive. If a product is new and exclusive, always write "New Exclusive," not just "NEW." If it's just exclusive, use only *.
17. All prices (except regular or nonsale prices when used *with* a sale price) should be in bold.
18. SKUs should be large enough to read clearly especially if knock-out.
19. Products with patterns on the inside should not be propped unless the pattern can be clearly seen.
20. All cap type-spacing should show clear definition between words.
21. It is always The ABC Co., not Company.

22. If something is free, say it in the photo or in bold somewhere apart from the copy block.

This example has evolved; in other words, every issue of the catalog has been critiqued by everyone, and suggestions for improvement have been added periodically to the formula. So, after you've made up your formula, don't think that's the end of it. Just like the aforementioned style guide, you need to remember to go back and update it regularly.

How this critical information is obtained, and what it contains, is the heart of the creative process. Merchandisers need to provide writers and art directors with every bit of information they can lay their hands on to help sell the products the merchants have chosen to run. This means getting the cooperation of vendors in filling out MIFs. These come in many forms, both long and short, and can be used for different needs. The long form MIF is usually filled out before the product is actually selected and consists of space for the following elements:

1. Product under consideration
2. Vendor name, location, and phone number
3. Product specifications
   a. for selling
   b. for storage
   c. for shipping
4. Terms
   a. cost of goods
   b. advertising and/or photo allowances
   c. guarantees/warranties
   d. return policies

One other tool, the spread record sheet, is essential to seeing that your creative team has what they need to get the job done right the first time. (Note that you can delete the columns for such areas as cost and advertising allowance, shown in Chapter 6, for the creative team).These sheets are created during the pagination process and are intended to list each product as it will appear on a two-page spread.

Another reminder from Chapter 6: After the catalog is paginated, have the artist and the writer review all items with the merchant. At this time, notations as to how the items are to be propped can be inserted into the last column in the spread record sheets.

It sounds like a lot of work, but revisions caused by inadequate preparation are even more work, not to mention frustrating to every team member involved. So create your own forms and get it right at the beginning. And don't forget to allow time in the schedule for sufficient preparation.

The Process for Writing Effective Copy

Before the writer actually starts creating, there are some additional basic activities that must be completed:

1. Review the facts. Go over all the material that has been compiled by the merchandisers.
2. Unearth and understand the benefits. Materials supplied will be only the beginning of the writer's educational undertaking. To sell a product well, you must know it well. Good writers know when they don't have enough information to do a product justice, and they get on the phone and pull what's needed out of the merchandiser or manufacturer who does know.
3. Prioritize benefits and features. Now that tons of information have been obtained and digested, benefits must be placed in order with the most important first.
4. Determine the key selling benefit. *The* most critical part of the wiring process, this is the most important, convincing selling point.
   a. Keep it brief, pointed, and easy-to-understand.

    b. Review it for clarity and potential embellishment.

    c. Forget overused words, they have no effect on the potential buyer.

    d. This will serve as the basis for the headline.

5. Think in an inverted pyramid and follow the lead of the key selling benefit.

6. Write the SKU listing before the body copy to help determine fit and consistency with the lead-in/headline.

7. Write what you feel, then cut to fit. Keep the allocated space in mind but do not let it inhibit you when you first begin to create.

8. Then really edit for impact. It's easy to write long copy, but hard to write hard-hitting short copy.

9. Write benefits first, then features, per the list constructed from the merchandising materials.

Here are some pointers for writing effective catalog copy:

1. It's not what you write, but how you write it that makes a sale. Be scintillating and motivating. Remember, today's audience is often in a hurry. If your copy doesn't immediately grab and hold the customer's attention, the copy in other waiting catalogs will!

2. Be direct. Make sentences short and enthusiastic. Don't generalize. Get to the point. Unlike many space ads and most direct mail packages, you are working within a severely limited space. Learn to be a nitpicker, and you will get the sell across quicker.

3. State real benefits, not fluff. Benefits, substantiated by facts, sell products. As a noted copywriter once wrote: "Tell me quick and tell me true or else, my love, to heck with you. Less how this product came to be, more what the darn thing does for me."

   Think of customers asking themselves, "What can this item do for me?" and "What makes it unique?" "How will it improve the quality of my life?" If your copy is powerful enough to convince customers that they will be prettier, richer, healthier, and so on, you've practically ensured the sale.

4. Suggest ways of using the item that the consumer would perhaps never consider. For instance, a terry-cloth turban, normally used to protect hair while applying makeup, could convert into a shoulder carryall. When this idea was included in the copy, the surprise element ("What a great idea!"), coupled with the extra selling point, made the product a best-seller.

5. Encourage the potential customer to act in a specific manner. For example, "Buy one for a friend and one for yourself!"

6. Don't make the product sound too good. You will not only get returns but may lose a valuable customer.

7. Make your copy flow. It should have rhythm and sound pleasant to the ear.

8. Don't be too clever. By the time the reader deciphers your meaning, the momentum will be broken. Be creative, not elusive.

9. Read the copy without the photo. Does it demand attention, arouse interest, and call for action? If so, congratulations! You didn't use the picture as a crutch. Photos can add life to your words, but even the most vibrant photo can't make a product come alive. The copywriter must do that, and make the consumer want to own the product, too.

10. Don't forget to cross-sell. Does one product on the spread go well with another? Then state that in the copy!

11. Use captions, especially to describe the hidden features of a product and emphasize special details with callouts.

12. Let consumers know if a product is exclusive to your catalog.

13. Answer every question the customer is likely to ask. If you are not an expert on the product, ask questions and find out the answers. Otherwise, the

❖ **EXAMPLE 8-25**   Sharper Image shows how captions inserted into photos can quickly point up hidden benefits or features.

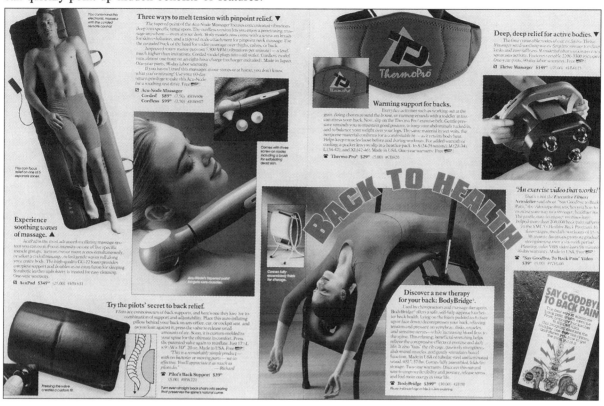

❖ **EXAMPLE 8-26**

Lands' End puts callouts to good use as they highlight the many pluses of their mesh shirt.

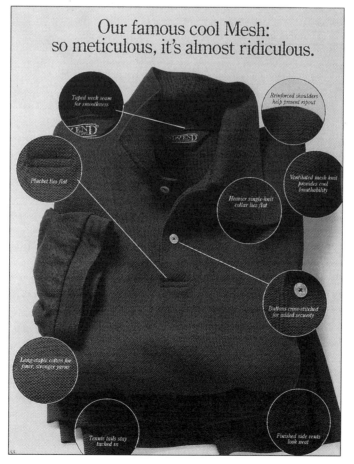

❖ **EXAMPLE 8-27**   Levenger's chatty copy puts readers at ease and pulls them into the catalog "family."

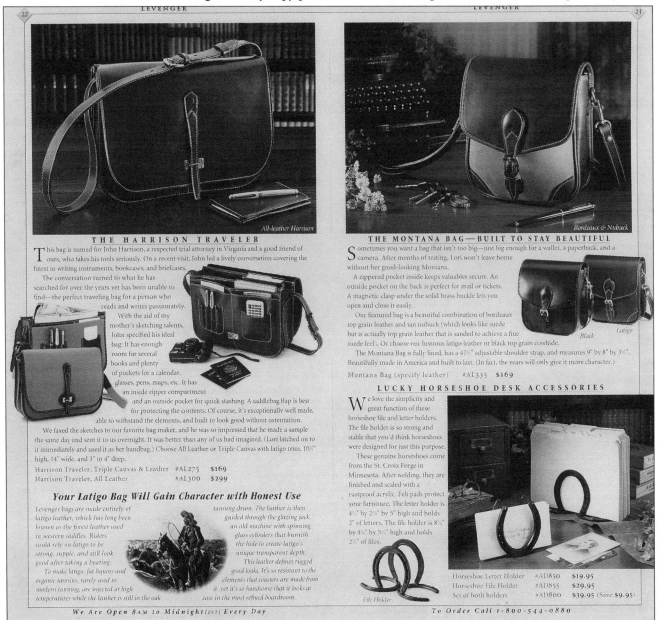

information necessary to convey the product's benefits will not be in the copy, and sales will be lost.

14. Get in the right seasonal mood. In Catalogland, if it's July, it must be Christmas! Even if you are still recovering from 100-degree temperatures on the Fourth of July, play Christmas music to help you get in the mood for tantalizing holiday copy. Make a file of advertisements that pertain to the season, holiday, or special event (wedding, graduation, and so on). By speaking the language of the season, you will increase sales.

15. Always turn to your MIF for help. Does the product have an interesting story behind it? Play it up and give the customer even more reason to buy.

16. Try a copy style that's unique to your catalog.

17. Read the copy out loud. If it doesn't sound phony or awkward, the customer should also be comfortable with it.

Points to Remember.
1. **Don't make the message too broad to understand; stay on target.**
2. **Don't make unsubstantiated claims. This is legally dangerous and will lose customers.**
3. **Don't overreact to competitors' positioning. Be aware of what your competition is doing, but don't let it totally drive your approach.**
4. **Don't use hackneyed words and phrases. Readers will skim right by what you are trying to say.**
5. **Don't fail to address your audience's needs.**

The Three Good Ps

Determining the exact copy approach to take depends on the three "good" Ps: personality, people, and product. (The three "bad" Ps in the catalog marketing business—or at least the most costly—are paper, printing, and postage.)

Know the personality of your catalog, the identity you want it to project. Just as Bloomingdale's invokes an image of refined elegance, your catalog should be readily categorized. Write your copy to reflect this personality.

Know the people to whom you are writing—their gender, age, income level, marital status, and life-style. What is important to them? What do they want from life—Love? Health? Success? Status? Financial security? The copywriter's job is to pinpoint customers' most prominent needs.

Joe Sacco, a well-known copywriter, states that "sensitivity to the needs, problems, moods, experiences, [and] language of others stands highest among human faculties. It is perhaps the most difficult state of awareness to achieve." He speaks of two copywriters, one of whom is me-oriented, the other who is not, and of how they approach selling a new product—a disposable insulin syringe featuring a new sharp needle.

The "me" copywriter has neither a desire to really get to know the product nor any curiosity about the person who is the customer. The quick and simple ways to express the benefits of the needle that come to mind are "hurts less" and "the gentle way."

The "not-me" copywriter, on the other hand, reads books on the subject of diabetes and observes that the word "sharp" pops up frequently in interviews with prospective customers. "No injection can be comfortable, but a sharper needle makes it easier." This copywriter determines the major product claim to be "sharpness" and the benefit, "unequaled injection ease," with which the customer can enthusiastically identify.

Exploring the outside world and discovering what is important to the person to whom you are writing isn't easy, but the success of your catalog is worth the effort. Think of this awareness as a photograph being developed in a darkroom. The more you learn about the person, the clearer and more focused the person becomes. But if you open the door too soon, the photograph will not develop. So, do your research. Talk to your merchandise buyers. They know the audience they are targeting. Study any market research available on your company's targeted or existing market. You'll soon discover a successful approach.

Finally, know your product. That's where the MIF can be useful. Properly filled out, it can save phone calls, money, time, and frustration. Even more important, it provides the vital information necessary to make the sale. Make sure the merchandise buyer fills in the form completely and sends you a copy. You should both keep the form on file for use when questions arise as to fabric content, size, color, and so forth. Master the three good Ps and your copy will make you, and your company's accountant, proud.

Making Every Headline a "Grabber"

A headline must immediately attract the customer's attention, convey a benefit, and offer an incentive to read on. Remember that self-interest is a strong motivator. Consider using such key words as "free," "new," and "exclusive." Whatever you do, don't be negative. Think positively, and so will your audience.

❖ **EXAMPLE 8-28**

For a holiday edition, Lands' End packs a lot of benefit into one headline.

Words like "bonus" or "free" get attention in headlines because they appeal to consumers' natural desire to save money. If you're offering a special value, state it clearly and boldly.

If an item is exclusive to your catalog, say so in the headline. Don't hide this important selling feature in the body copy. Better yet, display an easy-to-understand exclusive logo within the photo of the product or right next to the copy block. Not only will you call attention to the product, but you'll (1) look like a forerunner among the competition because you have products not available to other companies, and (2) satisfy a human need to have something not available to everyone else.

Copy is the most personal touch your catalog has with its customers. Make the lead-in easily identifiable with the product. Don't make lead-ins so clever or cute that the customer misses the point and has to hunt for the corresponding copy block. You could easily lose the reader's attention—and the sale.

Important Sales Tools

Sales tools such as endorsements and letters from the person behind the catalog are important incentives to buy that are too often simply dropped in at the last minute. However, you should plan the use of these tools with the same care you use to plan the rest of the catalog.

Endorsements/Testimonials.   Endorsements from satisfied customers can say more about a product than any amount of professional copy. Use them liberally and creatively. A standard method is to sprinkle them throughout the catalog, in which case they should be short and to the point. A potential customer should be able to get the message at a glance. They can also be used effectively as attention-getting headlines and even body copy.

❖ **EXAMPLE 8-29**
Page 3 of the Lands' End holiday issue taps a tendency for Americans to return to old-fashioned traditions.

❖ **EXAMPLE 8-30**   Brookstone knows how to make motivational statements with only a few words.

Quotes from famous people can also be used to establish credibility. One cataloger, a seller of outdoor wear, used endorsements from Olympic team members. Naturally, you need to keep the cost of this type of endorsement in relationship to the benefit in added sales.

Before running endorsements or testimonials, read about pertinent Federal Trade Commission regulations in Chapter 16.

The Catalog Letter.   One way to establish credibility for your catalog is to include a personal letter. In this manner, you can let customers know something about the people behind the catalog. Consider showing photos of the people who work at the catalog, of any retail stores you own, or, if attractive, the catalog facilities. People like identifying and/or connecting with someone they "know."

Explain how the catalog came to be, what makes it different, and what outstanding qualities—for instance, a special service—it may possess. If the catalog is an established one, give some history and accentuate the number of years it has been in business.

Use the letter to highlight particular products and trends within the catalog: "Customers tell us they've looked everywhere for a stepping stool that's lightweight, compact, and sturdy, to no avail. Well, we've found one. See page 17 for that wonderfully practical stool that meets all needs!"

The most common location for the owner's letter is either on page 2 or the front panel of the order form. Even if customers don't read every word—and they seldom do—they want to know a real person is behind the catalog. It helps to assure potential buyers that someone will receive their order and ensure their satisfaction.

Restate positive attributes like your money-back guarantee, quick delivery, easy toll-free number for ordering, and so forth. Without it, catalogs can seem cold and impersonal. Let customers know this catalog company cares. Just as you would automatically include a postscript on any well-written direct marketing letter, you should do so in your catalog letter. Use it for something special: a reminder of a particular gift-buying season or one of the pluses of your catalog.

❖ **EXAMPLE 8-31**
Gardener's Supply highlights a customer endorsement in its headline and in colored type next to the product.

But keep it short and to the point. Try setting all those essential elements in just a few paragraphs—the faster it *can* be read, the more likely it *will* be read.

If customers open your catalog, they have, in essence, let you into their homes. Your copy should convey the warm, friendly, yet never boring, attitude of a welcome guest who's there to enchant and inform. Don't let your customers down, and your catalog will always be welcome.

Body Copy: The Final Sale

The photo and the headline attract, and the price determines the seriousness of the intended purchase—but it's up to the copy to make the final sale. And copy should also reflect the "feeling" behind the company. It's the catalog owner's opportunity to talk to prospective and loyal customers. The tone of your copy can tell the person who will most likely never actually see your establishment a lot about the people from whom he or she has chosen to buy.

This latter point is well illustrated by a J. Peterman catalog. The copy weaves a spell around the product that takes it way beyond the ordinary. A typical product description goes like this:

America. In Poland or Paris or in Prague or Liverpool, they'd kill for a jacket like this. It's something they caught a glimpse of in every other American movie they

❖ **EXAMPLE 8-32**

J. Peterman sets the standard for long copy that casts a spell on readers.

ever saw. They saw it, but they never got even close to one. We, meanwhile, grew up with so many little things:

    hot rods, drive-in movies,
    non-electric guitars . . .

And the list goes on, evoking all the things Americans treasure. The pitch is for ''The American Baseball Jacket.''

But not all copy can, or should, be so fanciful. The Paragon, an old-timer in the business, shows us that old-fashioned, informative, friendly copy still does a good job of conveying an immediate benefit. Using another type of positioning, Gump's copy is unbeatable for creating just the right amount of ''snobbery'' and guaranteeing that you'll want to own something from Gump's more than ever before. More like poetry than copy, it is an excellent example of innovation that works.

Now let's take a look at two copy blocks written about exactly the same product. The first one reads:

CAPTIVATING BEDSIDE CARAFE SET is frosted pink glass with a swirl pattern. It has a tumbler top and matching coaster. 26-oz. capacity. 123-456 Pink Glass Carafe $10.00

How can this be improved?

THE COMPLETE CARAFE SET. It's 3 a.m. You're thirsty. But don't drag yourself out of bed! Simply reach over for our frosted rose glass carafe set complete with protective saucer and glass. A thoughtful touch for guest bedroom; an alternative holder for beverages at work. 123-456 26-oz. Carafe, Tumbler & Coaster Set $10.00.

❖ EXAMPLE 8-33
The Paragon explains the benefits of its product in just a few words.

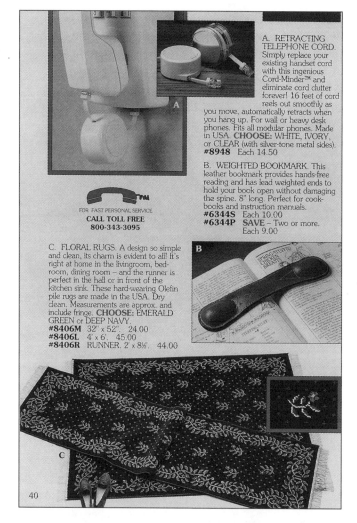

A. RETRACTING TELEPHONE CORD. Simply replace your existing handset cord with this ingenious Cord-Minder™ and eliminate cord clutter forever! 16 feet of cord reels out smoothly as you move, automatically retracts when you hang up. For wall or heavy desk phones. Fits all modular phones. Made in USA. **CHOOSE: WHITE, IVORY, or CLEAR** (with silver-tone metal sides).
#8948 Each 14.50

B. WEIGHTED BOOKMARK. This leather bookmark provides hands-free reading and has lead weighted ends to hold your book open without damaging the spine. 8" long. Perfect for cookbooks and instruction manuals.
#6344S Each 10.00
#6344P SAVE – Two or more. Each 9.00

FOR FAST PERSONAL SERVICE
CALL TOLL FREE
800-343-3095

C. FLORAL RUGS. A design so simple and clean, its charm is evident to all! It's right at home in the livingroom, bedroom, dining room – and the runner is perfect in the hall or in front of the kitchen sink. These hard-wearing Olefin pile rugs are made in the USA. Dry clean. Measurements are approx. and include fringe. **CHOOSE: EMERALD GREEN or DEEP NAVY.**
#8406M 32" x 52". 24.00
#8406L 4' x 6'. 45.00
#8406R RUNNER. 2' x 8½'. 44.00

40

In the second example, the writer immediately tells the customers that the set is ''complete''—it has everything they will need. She then goes on to create a scenario with which most people can easily identify. Furthermore, the color of the product isn't just pink, it's ''frosted rose.'' And it doesn't just come with a saucer, it comes with a ''protective saucer,'' meaning no water rings to ruin your bedside table. And the writer goes on to list other reasons for purchase. Even the SKU line has more sell in it, because it lists every product in the set.

An important point to remember is not to rewrite your copy to death. Many times, it's the first thought that's the purest, and continuous rewriting only distorts the original meaning. Learn to edit carefully, without refining to the point that the impact is lost. And let one writer be the dominant spokesperson. Copy (and layout) that suffers from conflicting input conveys this lack of direction to the customer. Give writers the value of your knowledge, a clear understanding of why revisions need to be made, then leave them alone. If the writer isn't right for you, get a new one, but ultimately, let the copy speak to your customer in one clear, concise, and appealing voice.

More Examples of How to Talk to Customers.   ''The best way to keep a grip on your sanity is to question everybody else's. Nobody has done this longer—and more poignantly—than our company's namesake. Latest in our collection of garments celebrating midlife dysfunction. 100% cotton white (shown) or heather tee [etc.].''

''On the road, though, you want something sleek and compact to hold your CDs in, and if it has a butter-smooth finish, all the better. Our embossed Marvelous Mark CD case holds 10 disks, and if that's not enough room to accommodate your collection, then order another. We've got lots.''

These are two examples of wildly individualistic catalog copy that speaks the language of the customer to whom the catalog is aimed. Here's another:

Want extra-stable footing in extra-slippery areas? We knew non-skid backing was a good idea when several different customers suggested it. They wanted Traffic Mat

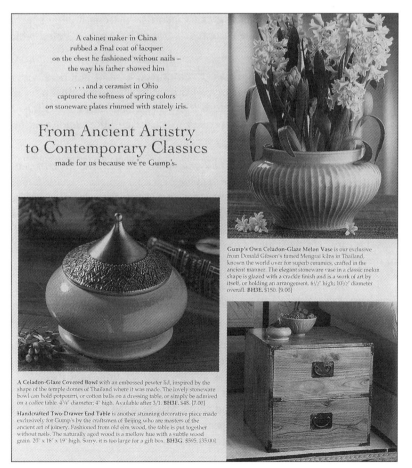

❖ **EXAMPLE 8-34**
Gump's copy has a poetic feel.

Durable Mat that would grip the floor even near the heaviest leaks. So we added black polyethylene to the back—and does this Mat ever stay put! You'll feel as sure-footed as a mountain goat. Baaa! (And you thought all we could do was oink!) Polyethylene barrier helps keep leaks off your floors, too.

This example has real punch because it not only uses all the standard copy rules for motivational writing; it speaks like the company it represents—fun, knowledgeable, customer-oriented. Let's try one more:

You want custom cuts? You got 'em! If you need PIG Mat in sizes other than those listed above, give us a Toll-Free call. In most cases, we'll tell you within the day when your order will be ready and give you the price. . . . You may not be used to that kind of service. But it's a way of life around the ol' Pig pen. Expect it and enjoy it!

If that copy block had been written in the style used by too many catalogs, it would probably have sounded something like this:

Custom Cuts Available. Call Our Customer Service Representative. Shipped in 24 Hours.

This copy is dry, without excitement or personality.

The first two copy blocks in this section are examples from the Doonesbury catalog, which is written to a highly targeted audience. The latter two copy blocks are from New Pig, a business-to-business catalog of leak and spill products. These two decidedly different catalogs have something in common, something that is absolutely critical in today's catalogs. They know how to create a language unique to their positioning and speak it in a way that today's customer not only understands but is also comfortable with. Both are direct, friendly, fun, and informative. They not only provide the customer with the knowledge he or she needs to make a buying decision, they also make the sales pitch conversational, something that is worth the time and effort it takes to read it.

Both are highly individualistic, based on the catalogers' positioning and knowledge of their customer. Not every catalog can support this strong a copy approach. So here is another, extremely well-written approach from The Apple Catalog which is somewhat more conservative:

Kensington NoteBook KeyPad—If you crunch a lot of numbers with your PowerBook, you'll find this keypad tremendously useful. Just plug it into the ADB port in the back of any Macintosh PowerBook and start calculating. Function keys reduce keystrokes and make it easier to exchange information with mainframe computers.[1]

It's not as funky as the other two examples, but the straight talk gets to the benefits in easy-to-understand, personable language.

Why has copy become more important than ever in the sales process? James A. Taylor, Ph.D., reported on shifts in consumer attitudes and behavior demographic tools to favor fidelity in the direct marketing dialogue during the DMA's 1993 Spring Conference in New Orleans. He made lots of interesting points, but a couple seem particularly applicable to the copy approach:

1. "The consumer expectation for directed correspondence is rising."
2. The "typical consumer has seen 500,000 TV commercials and millions of print ads."

Today's consumer is educated, savvy, skeptical, even cynical, and totally time-crunched. If your message doesn't get through in seconds, and talk in a way that the consumer understands, it simply won't be read, let alone absorbed.

As we mentioned previously in this chapter, always remember to read the copy without the picture; if it still sells, it's good copy. And read the copy out loud. If the words sound as if they are ones you would speak, then the copy is comfortable to the reader. Too much copy is stilted and just plain phony.

Know your demographics. Understand how your customers think and how they talk. Speak with one voice. Don't hire several copywriters and allow each of them to create their own way of speaking. It will sound disjointed, and the customer will be confused. Know who you are to your customer and make certain the voice of your catalog reinforces that positioning.

For instance, two catalogers were so intent on *really* understanding the essence of their catalog, they went beyond writing a positioning statement: They actually wrote a story of who the "person" in the catalog was. Just to clarify, this was not a profile of the audience, but a profile of the catalog. This document, which was written in essay form, elaborated on a day in the life of this catalog/person. One who really stood out was a female, mid-30s, suburban dweller, with a couple of kids, who played tennis every day. The profile went on to describe the types of clothes she wore, the entertainment and type of people she liked, and so forth. By the time the writer finished reading this essay, she knew exactly how to write the copy and make the catalog speak as the individual it should represent.

❖ CHECKLIST

✔ Choose a format that is both distinctive and flexible.

✔ Give artists and writers plenty of background information and input for best results.

✔ Understand the layout of the press before beginning design.

✔ Get props and backgrounds that complement, not detract or overwhelm.

✔ Use cross-sell for optimal merchandising.

✔ Incorporate eye flow into the design so the reader "walks" comfortably through each design element.

✔ Use "hot spots" for specific marketing functions; overuse diminishes their effectiveness.

✔ Make sure the copy is "attached" to its photo.

✔ Remember that type is a graphic element, not just words on paper.

✔ Plan the space allocation for the highest impact.

✔ Vary the pacing to keep readers turning the pages.

✔ Use the front cover as a window to your store.

✔ Treat the back cover with the same respect you give the front cover.

✔ Allow organizational and research time before starting to write copy.

✔ Individualize your copy.

✔ Concentrate on determining and effectively conveying the key selling benefit of each product.

✔ Make smart use of such sales tools as testimonials and the catalog letter.

End Notes

1. © Apple Computer Inc. 1993. All Rights Reserved. Used with permission.

CHAPTER NINE

❖ ❖ ❖

Generating Sales

In the catalog business, there are ways to increase sales, in both numbers and dollars per order. Some—like bouncebacks and toll-free numbers—are facilitating techniques that take advantage of opportunities inherent in selling by direct mail. Others—such as premiums, discounts, twofers, and sweepstakes—are outright incentives to buy. These types of techniques are on the increase. *Catalog Age* details the fact that there have been 105 percent more "special offers, discounts and other purchase incentives" over the last three years.[1]

Bouncebacks

Promotion materials called *bouncebacks,* included with your outgoing orders, are an excellent way to generate additional sales without incurring the cost of postage. A customer who is happy with a purchase is often in the mood to buy again, so be sure to provide the opportunity.

Some catalogers include extra order forms or catalogs from their current mailing with all outgoing orders. Others preplan an overrun of the order form and include only that. If you enclose a catalog, be sure to code it separately so you can determine if the extra cost is really paying off. Think, too, about the weight the catalog adds to your package. Does this additional weight add too much to the cost of shipping your product?

One way to almost guarantee that customers will notice your catalog and/or order form when they open the package is to have an attention-getting offer on the front of the catalog or order form. This can be in the form of savings or a "welcome" for new customers. Before going to press, check with your printer on the most cost-effective way to add a special savings message to a portion of your print run. Options include a self-adhesive sticker, a wrap, or a different cover.

If you are using a "close-out" type of offer, be absolutely certain that you have enough inventory. Remember, these are your most recent customers—ideal prospects for future offers—so don't take a chance on not being able to fill their orders by running items of which you have only a minimal inventory.

Whatever you decide to include in your outgoing packages, make sure the graphics are bright enough to attract attention. A strong offer, such as savings, a bonus gift, or a sweepstakes, works better than a standard product offer. Be sure to include a way for customers to respond. Never use a preprinted manufacturer's sales sheet designed for wholesale use. Industry newcomers are sometimes tempted to use this cost-saving shortcut, but it only confuses the customer and gives your competitors the name of your source.

Make sure the offer is an instant "grabber." Keep the price hurdle fairly low, under $40 if possible. You'll have customers' attention for only a few seconds, and you don't want price to put them off.

Some catalogers include actual samples of products that are often available for purchase. These free "bonus gifts" work best if they are product-related. For example, one catalog that sold silk clothing offered a free sample of a product that cleaned its silk product perfectly. Other such extras include perfume samples, seeds, recipes, and a host of how-to booklets, all useful items that help a cataloger stand out in a customer's mind and can create repeat business.

To determine if bouncebacks make sense for you, do a simple profit/loss statement. Generally, you need to have a fairly large quantity of packages going out over a relatively short time period to generate enough quantity for cost efficiencies in production.

The Many Types of Premiums

Defined as a price bonus or an award given as an inducement to purchase, premiums can be extraordinarily effective both in raising your average dollar order and in reactivating inactive customers. But, even if you think a premium is a good idea, always test it a control group first.

Begin by choosing a premium that reflects the merchandise you now offer. Also, make sure the premium is small and flat enough to fit into standard outgoing packages. Then decide what it should cost and what its perceived value is. As often as possible, the perceived value of a premium should be two to three times its cost.

Next, you must decide on the premium dollar requirement—the amount the customer has to spend in order to qualify for the premium. This is done by determining your current average dollar and the increase you realistically expect from offering a premium. For instance, if your average dollar order is currently $25, can you expect it to increase to $50, or would $40 or $35 be more realistic? In truth, a $10 increase is seldom accomplished in one step, and there is no set formula for establishing the percentage increase for which

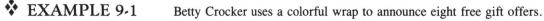

❖ EXAMPLE 9-1   Betty Crocker uses a colorful wrap to announce eight free gift offers.

Save $2.⁰⁰
when you order

There are lots of good reasons why thousands of gardeners order their seeds, bulbs, plants and gardening supplies from Burpee...highest quality products, top value, courteous service, and a guarantee you can depend on.

Now Burpee gives you one more good reason: a $2.00 savings when you order $10.00 or more by June 30, 1994.

Use this coupon to try out some of our exciting new flowers and vegetables—there are more than 140 new flower and vegetable seed and plant varieties plus other great garden products in the 1994 Burpee Garden Catalogue! Of course, there are hundreds of old favorites, too. You will find all the ingredients to start a home orchard, a berry patch or a flowering shrub border plus a broad range of garden supplies.

Just enclose the coupon below with your order, and deduct $2.00 from the total where indicated on your order form. We look forward to serving you in 1994 with the "best seeds that grow" and everything you need for your garden.

Save $2.00   BURPEE.
when you place an order of $10.00 or more from the 1994 Burpee Gardens Catalogue by June 30, 1994

Take a $2.00 discount on your Burpee catalogue order and enclose this coupon with your order form and payment. Mail it before June 30, 1994.

This discount coupon must accompany your order. Offer expires June 30, 1994. Not transferable. No reproductions accepted. Coupon has no cash value and may not be redeemed for cash or exchanged for products at retail stores. Offer void where prohibited, taxed or otherwise restricted.

Your signature

❖ **EXAMPLE 9-2**
Burpee Gardens uses an insert to test a two-dollar-off incentive.

to aim. Before you decide that a large difference between the premium dollar requirement and your current average is the method of boosting your sales order, check your sales history (if you have one). It is the best indicator of whether your audience is ready to spend substantially more than it has been, even if motivated by a premium.

Generally, it is more effective to increase the premium dollar requirement and product mix gradually. Let's assume that you decide to aim for a $55 average order. Find out the number of customers who already order $55 worth of merchandise. Multiply this number by the cost of the premium you wish to offer to determine the cost of the premium for your current $55 customers (assuming customers order consistently from one catalog to the next). Adjust for seasonal differences in response rates.

The next step is to look at the number of customer orders within specific price ranges: the number of $15.00 to $25.00 customers, $25.01 to $35.00 customers, and so on. (Table 9-1 illustrates statistically how premiums may increase the average order.) Then project the percentage of customers who are expected to increase their orders to meet your premium-offer requirement, and calculate the cost of the premium per category. (Note: Only a sales history will give you accurate increase percentages. Let common sense dictate assumed percentage increases. Obviously, the customers currently ordering in the price range closest to the premium dollar requirement will be more willing to spend the required amount and will convert at a higher percentage than those in the lower price ranges.) Add the cost of the premium for current and projected $55 customers to calculate the final projected cost of offering the premium. By comparing the final projected cost with the projected increase in profits per price category, you will have a good guide as to whether a premium is your answer to greater revenues.

If you are a first-time cataloger and rent lists, consider these other points:

◆ Does the list you intend to rent offer premiums now?

◆ If so, do those premiums have a higher perceived value than yours?

◆ Will the list owner allow you to rent the list if you are offering a premium? (Some won't).

◆ Even if you do attract the customer, effectively increasing your response, did the customer buy only because of the premium, and will he or she remain loyal?

❖ **TABLE 9-1**

Example of Increasing the Average Order through the Use of Premiums*

Average order	$45.00
Customer file	5,000

Before Premium

Price Range	Number of Customer Orders	Customers Accepting Premium (%)	Revenue Generated ($)	Expected Number of Premiums
$15.01–$25.00	650	6.25	13,000	41
$25.01–$35.00	900	12.50	27,000	113
$35.01–$45.00	950	25.00	38,000	238
$45.01–$55.00	1,100	50.00	55,000	550
$55.01–$65.00	800	100.00	48,000	800
$65.01–$75.00	400	100.00	28,000	400
$75.01–$85.00	200	100.00	16,000	200
			Total 225,000	2,341

Cost of premium	$2.00
Total premium cost	$4,682

With Premium

Price Range	Number of Customer Orders	Customers Accepting Premium (%)	Revenue Generated ($)
$15.01–$25.00	609	6.25	12,188
$25.01–$35.00	788	12.50	23,625
$35.01–$45.00	713	25.00	28,500
$45.01–$55.00	550	50.00	27,500
$55.01–$65.00	1,741	100.00	104,460
$65.01–$75.00	400	100.00	28,000
$75.01–$85.00	200	100.00	16,000
		Total	240,273

New revenue generated	$15,273
Less cost of premium	$4,682
Net new revenue	$10,591
New average order	$48.05

* Estimates are for illustration purposes only.

Premiums can also be an excellent way to remind old customers of how much they enjoyed ordering from your catalog and to reestablish old buying patterns (in which they bought from you).

Whether you are just starting out or have an established customer base, be sure to test your premium. If you offer it to everyone on your list, you won't know whether an increase in the average order and response is attributable to the premium or to an overall change in the buying habits of your customers. Construct a statistically valid test grid that offers different segments different choices. Such a grid might include headings such as the following:

Segments

0 to 12-month customers who have purchased more than once

0 to 12-month one-time customers

Rental lists

Tests

Free premium with order of certain dollar amount

Different free premium with order of certain dollar amount

Free postage and handling

Percentage off

Dollars off

It would be unusual and require a large database to do all of the tests listed here at one time. However, the headings give you an idea of your options.

Discounts That Get Consumers' Attention

Discounts give a specific percentage or dollar amount off the purchase price. They can be used to thank a new customer for requesting a catalog, to raise an average dollar order, to give people an incentive to order early, or for a wide variety of other purposes. One advantage to discounts is that you need not search for the perfect premium, invest in stocking it, and worry whether your customers will be receptive to it.

In deciding between dollars off or a percentage off, choose the one that appears to offer the best value. For instance, if your catalog has a $40 average order, which offer sounds like more to the customer—"10% off" or "$4 off?" The best way to determine this is to test both options, but if that is not possible, go with the one that appears to offer the highest reward.

Another alternative is to provide a tiered incentive. One excellent method, used by Victoria's Secret, is a tiered discount that provides higher discounts the more the customer orders.

Discount coupons also help track response to a traffic-generation program done in conjunction with a mail-order program, as the coupon, with its source code, is often returned to the store. Tracking these coupons has helped prove that direct marketing not only benefits the mail-order program but also substantially adds to retail sales.

Discount offers may be right for your catalog. Be sure to track the results carefully to determine the loyalty of customers acquired through this method, as well as the immediate benefits. For maximum effectiveness, tailor the discount program specifically to fit the image of your catalog and construct a test grid with headings like those shown in the section on premiums.

In some cases, discounts can be more than just a technique to lift response or increase average orders: they can also be the main focus of your catalog. Damark, for instance, makes its position clear in its tag line.

❖ **EXAMPLE 9-3**
Damark calls itself "The Greatest Deal Company."

Dollars-off coupons can also be a smart idea for welcoming new customers into the fold, as too many catalogers take their new customers for granted. And don't forget group discounts! Most catalogers receive requests for high multiples of products at a discount (for corporate gifts, schools, and institutions, depending on the product line), so why not make it clear that you are open to this type of selling? HearthSong, "a catalog for families," offers 10- to 20-percent discounts for schools, clubs, and organizations.

Twofers, Bundling, and Bonus Gifts

Three additional methods of gaining increased revenue are:

1. **Twofers**, where two of the same item are offered as a pair at a price that is less per piece than if you bought the two items individually (for example, $10.00 per set or $6.00 each).

2. **Bundling**, which refers to putting compatible items together at a discount. Each item is also offered separately.

3. **Bonus gifts**, or offering a specific bonus with the purchase of a particular product.

Offering a multiple of any item at a discounted price is such a tried-and-true method for increasing sales dollars that no catalog should ignore it. Such offers give the customer the incentive to buy and also help raise the average dollar order. And, in most cases, when offered the chance to buy two items at a slight discount over one item at a higher price, customers will opt for the "twofer."

Regardless of your merchandise mix, bundling several items generally helps get orders. Sometimes it's a natural grouping of items, such as bathroom accessories. Offer a bundling value that immediately conveys savings to a customer who purchases a tumbler, toothbrush holder, and soap dish. And tell your customers (for example, in the copy line listing the price) that they're saving money: "Save $5.00! Buy the set!" This has become an important and often-used technique in the catalog business.

To construct a bonus product offer tied to a specific product, take a look at leftover merchandise from previous catalogs. Perhaps an item that was a slow seller would be a natural tie-in with a new product in your forthcoming issue. For instance, suppose you are planning to offer a casserole as a new item, and the old, not-so-great seller is a ladle. Consider offering the casserole at your planned price and offer the ladle either as a free gift or at a greatly reduced price with the purchase of the casserole. Make sure, of course, that there is enough inventory. Books and manuals that relate to the main product being offered can also make great bonus gifts. Obviously, you will need to figure the cost of the bonus, including the cost of packing it with the main product during fulfillment; be sure this cost will be more than absorbed by the anticipated increase in response.

Test these types of offers on a minimal number of items before using a lot of them in each catalog. If you have a high-ticket catalog and are concerned about how customers will perceive such offers, stop worrying. Customers appreciate good value, no matter how high the price. But the way you present your savings offer should be determined by the overall image of your catalog. Present the bonus offer as a gift, specifically targeted to a time of year. Using the example of the casserole and ladle, point out that the ladle is a natural with the casserole, and also has many other holiday functions, such as dipping into the wassail or punch bowl.

And don't forget group discounts! Offering reduced prices to organizations that order in large quantities can provide a much higher-than-average order shipped to only one location.

Sweepstakes

Who can resist opening a catalog or package that promises riches, vacations, or dreams come true? Interestingly enough, focus groups have indicated that consumers have a high degree (91 percent) of trust in the honesty of such offers. Respondents buy, not because they think it's the only way to win, but because they're basically honest people who feel guilty entering the contest without buying. And they really want to enter the contest. Everyone likes the chance of getting something for nothing.

For catalogers, sweepstakes (often called *sweeps*) also initially pull more, but they decline in impact as the promotion is extended over several mailings, and in many cases, cease to pay for themselves. Additionally, some catalogers find that, although sweeps will work on a house list, they won't perform on rented lists. Yet, there is a silver lining to this cloud, because sweeps accomplish two major goals: getting the potential buyer to open the catalog and turn to the order form (which they will hopefully fill out). Another positive factor is that sweeps help the customer become familiar with the name of the catalog, which increases the chances of future receptivity. Be aware, though, that the long-term value of a sweeps-generated customer depends on traditional customer-keeping methods—quality of merchandise, speed of fulfillment, and caliber of customer service.

Sweeps can be cost-effective, especially if this cost is shared by a group of individual catalogs. And this brings up a little-known fact: Independent companies can arrange, prior to the sweeps offering, to divide the costs of the prizes. Another way of at least postponing the prize expense is to run the contest over a one- or two-year period, offering smaller, secondary prizes at timely intervals.

Some catalogers feel that sweepstakes are more cost-effective than premiums on a per-response basis. After all, if you're expecting 10,000 responses to a premium offer that costs $1, you definitely have to spend $10,000. But with a sweepstakes, you can amortize the cost over several promotions. With the fixed cost of a sweepstakes, you can expand your program without increasing your final cost.

Sweepstakes work best when the prize is relevant to the catalog. Here are some great examples: Safety Zone's big prize was a Volvo, the car most noted for safety; Tweeds, an apparel catalog targeted to the trendy, offers a chance to win a Jeep Cherokee; and the Disney Catalog showcases, naturally, a chance to win a trip to Disneyland.

If you decide to see what a sweepstakes can do for your response rate, be sure to do the obvious—test it against one or more controls and keep testing it. Track sweeps respondents against nonsweeps over a period to determine this method's long-term value. In general, sweepstakes offers tend to generate higher response when they are tied into a specific product or service offering. Look at the demographics of your audience, then tailor the prizes to its needs and desires. For instance, many marketers assume that respondents prefer a money prize, and surveys have backed this up. But, in reality, entrants want a money prize only if it's big money; they prefer a product to smaller cash awards. Interestingly enough, lotteries have helped add legitimacy to sweepstakes offers. Because they're highly publicized, customers see that people really do win, which encourages them to take a chance also.

One note of caution. Some established catalog businesses will not rent their lists to a catalog offering a sweepstakes. As you will learn in Chapter 13, you cannot use a name from a rented list unless you pay for it or unless that person becomes a product buyer from your catalog. However, when a person voluntarily sends his or her name in to a sweepstakes offer, that name becomes yours to use. Because this means that you might not need as many rental names, the original cataloger who was the source of the names might lose future rental profits.

If you decide that running a sweepstakes might be your ticket to increased sales, you'll need expert help. The legal considerations are outlined in Chapter 16, but professional help is strongly advised. Industry publications (listed in Appendix A) run ads of firms specializing in sweepstakes. The initial consultation is generally free, and the service fees are reasonable when you consider how complicated and legally dangerous sweepstakes can be for the novice.

Properly handled, sweepstakes do work. But be sure to proceed cautiously down the path to those riches.

Gift Wrap/Card Service and Confirmations

With more and more people relocating around the country, many customers prefer to have gifts send directly to the recipient. The offer of a gift wrap/card service can be a deciding factor when a customer is ready to order.

To ease into this service, start by offering a gift card only. Make sure your order form allows special areas for gift addresses and messages. Then simply transcribe the message from the order form to your gift cards, making sure the message is handwritten. Be sure to send the giver a confirmation that the gift has been sent. This is not only good service, but it will save you costly follow-up calls from customers.

Don't put a catalog bounceback in gift orders and be sure the packing slip does not state the price. Gift-givers do not wish the recipient to know how much a present cost.

After testing the economics and working out the fulfillment details of the card service, you may want to attempt gift wrapping. You can give free gift wrap with an order of any size or only when a specific dollar amount is ordered. Or you can charge a small amount for standard gift wrap and offer a range of prices for fancier wrappings. Talbots offers free gift packaging, complete with a gift box, paper, and ribbon. Neiman Marcus, on the other hand, offers three highly decorated boxes for $6.00, free with purchases of $500.00 or more. Before deciding which option is best for you, investigate the following:

◆ How much will the gift wrap or gift box cost? This, of course, depends on the size of the packages. Use the average box size for "ship-to" items as a guide. Not all ship-to items are gifts, but their average is more representative for gift wrap purposes than the average of all packages. However, for now, determine the average size of the packages sent most often.

◆ How much time does it take service personnel to wrap an item or insert an item into a pre-designed gift box? This, too, will vary according to size. Try several different sizes, and, for the time being, use the average to determine the dollar value of the time spent.

Once you decide to offer gift wrap, monitor the exact cost of the gift service, including confirmations and employee time, closely. Keep the wrap simple in the beginning and avoid such costly additions as monogrammed ribbon until you have a firm hold on the economics of offering this service. Gift wrapping has proven dangerously unprofitable for more than one catalog business. Many catalogers use pre-designed boxes with elastic ribbon rather than ribbon and separate wrapping.

Gift Certificates

Don't overlook this added sales revenue. Personalize your certificates and, at least in the beginning, offer them in specific dollar amounts. Treat them as you would any other stock-keeping unit (SKU) and promote them heavily during gift-giving seasons. For example, J. Crew positions its certificates as a gift certificate packet, complete with a message printed on the certificate and a copy of the catalog, all bundled in a "nifty presentation folder."

Toll-free Numbers: The Customer's Instant Touch with Your Catalog

Ordering

A major reason for the phenomenal success of mail order in recent years is consumers' lack of shopping time. The toll-free number places the means for shopping right at the customer's fingertips. It can be an essential element in the success of your mail order program and, with minor exceptions, should be offered.

When using a toll-free number, give it the display it needs for success by placing it on at least every other spread of your catalog. Provide, at a glance, the means to order

❖ **EXAMPLE 9-5**
Eddie Bauer has historically displayed its gift certificates in four-color illustrations on the back of its order forms.

a desired item. No one wants to search through a catalog to find the toll-free number. Also, be specific about the days of the week and the hours the toll-free service is available. If you offer 24-hour, seven-day service, say so with copy like, "Call Anytime."

Consider using a copy line that conveys a benefit of using the service, such as "For faster delivery, call toll free." You may wish to specify "Credit-card holders call 1-123-4567." As impossible as it may seem, some people don't realize they need a credit card to place an order by telephone. You can cut down on time, cost, and customer aggravation if you make this clear from the start.

Customer Service

A *Catalog Age* survey[2] revealed that, of the respondents to the survey:

Sixty-two percent offer 800 numbers for customer service.

Seventy-three percent of consumer catalogs offer toll-free ordering versus 64 percent from the previous year.

Forty-one percent offer fax lines for customer service.

Seventy-three percent offer fax ordering versus 65 percent from the previous year.

Toll-free service, whether for ordering or customer service, is a competitive edge more and more catalogers are finding it necessary to offer. When providing free calls to customer service, though, be sure to use a separate line so servicing the customer does not take lines and time away from order-taking. Further, be sure to carefully monitor service calls to ensure that good service is being offered within an acceptable time frame.

Several years back, my office was next to the customer service department of a catalog that was targeted to young women. I often overheard the customer representatives tactfully handling calls about dating and parental problems. It is not unusual for customers to turn to friendly reps for more than just advice on their order; be sure your telephone people are taught how to properly dissuade calls such as this and still maintain the customer's loyalty.

Two reference books on telemarketing you may find helpful are: *Encyclopedia of Telemarketing* by Richard Bencin, published by Prentice-Hall, and *Successful Telemarketing* by Bob Stone and John Wyman, published by NTC Business Books. You may also wish to consider the two-day seminar offered by the Direct Marketing Association: "Profitable and Effective Use of the Telephone, Inbound and Outbound."

In-House versus Outside Services

One of your most important decisions is whether to use an in-house or outside service. An in-house service is a costly investment, often requiring round-the-clock, seven-day-a-week personnel and enough incoming lines so customers don't get a busy signal.

Let's look at how costs might break out over a 24-hour period for a midsize catalog operation mailing about 3 to 4 million catalogs a year (See Table 9-2). Although it's true that no one can take better care of your customers than your own in-house personnel, compare these costs to charges assessed by outside service facilities. Then decide which method best suits both your pocketbook and your company's philosophy.

One concern about using an outside facility is inventory status and the ability to tell customers if an item is in stock. Most catalog companies do not wish a third party, the telephone answering company, to know their inventory data. Yet they also want their customers to know if an item is immediately available. A perfect example of this is Brownstone which, in early 1994, converted to a combination hardware and software setup that allows its computer to hook up with its outside telemarketer's system. This way, operators are informed of product availability without having to know inventory details. It also saves Brownstone money in customer calls and mailings that used to be necessary if an item was out of stock.

Toll-free numbers are more than just an answering service. Many catalogers offer an upsell and/or cross-sell program that allows the customer the option of purchasing additional products while placing an order. This can be very effective in increasing sales.

Time	Projected Order Volume	Projected Man Hours	Idle Hours	Total Hours	Approximate Staffing*	Cost ($)
7 A.M.–8 A.M.	15	0.75	0.19	0.94	2	17.50
8 A.M.–9 A.M.	45	2.25	0.56	2.81	4	35.00
9 A.M.–10 A.M.	60	3.00	0.75	3.75	5	43.75
10 A.M.–11 A.M.	50	2.50	0.63	3.13	5	43.75
11 A.M.–Noon	70	3.50	0.88	4.38	5	43.75
Noon–1 P.M.	80	4.00	1.00	5.00	6	52.50
1 P.M.–2 P.M.	80	4.00	1.00	5.00	6	52.50
2 P.M.–3 P.M.	65	3.25	0.81	4.06	5	43.75
3 P.M.–4 P.M.	55	2.75	0.69	3.44	4	35.00
4 P.M.–5 P.M.	50	2.50	0.63	3.13	4	35.00
5 P.M.–6 P.M.	40	2.00	0.50	2.50	3	26.25
6 P.M.–7 P.M.	20	1.00	0.25	1.25	3	26.25
7 P.M.–8 P.M.	25	1.25	0.31	1.56	3	26.25
8 P.M.–9 P.M.	35	1.75	0.44	2.19	3	26.25
9 P.M.–10 P.M.	30	1.50	0.38	1.88	3	26.25
10 P.M.–11 P.M.	15	0.75	0.19	0.94	2	17.50
8 P.M.–Midnight	10	0.50	0.13	0.63	1	8.75
Midnight–1 A.M.	5	0.25	0.06	0.31	1	8.75
1 A.M.–2 A.M.	5	0.25	0.06	0.31	1	8.75
2 A.M.–3 A.M.	5	0.25	0.06	0.31	1	8.75
3 A.M.–4 A.M.	5	0.25	0.06	0.31	1	8.75
4 A.M.–5 A.M.	5	0.25	0.06	0.31	1	8.75
5 A.M.–6 A.M.	5	0.25	0.06	0.31	1	8.75
6 A.M.–7 A.M.	5	0.25	0.06	0.31	1	8.75
Total	780			48.76		$621.25

Assumptions

1. Part-time employees are used.
2. Call time is three minutes.
3. Idle time factor is 25 percent.
4. Labor rate will vary with location.
5. Does not include nonorder calls.

Phone rate/minute	$0.15
Phone rate/hour	$9.00
Average labor rate	$7.00
Average labor rate, with fringes	$8.75

Cost per order
Labor	$621.25
Line charges	$351.00
Total per order	$1.25*

* See Chapter 15 for additional costs.

Many catalogers allow the 800-number customer to purchase an item available only on the day of the call at a discount from its normal cost. Furthermore, on-line access to inventory status, when teamed with your in-house 800-number order-taking, allows operators to instantly inform buyers of the delivery status of the items they have selected. Should a chosen product be unavailable, operators can be instructed to recommend alternatives, thus increasing the chances of keeping the sale and a satisfied customer.

Whether you use an outside service or an in-house department, the person who answers the toll-free service phone represents your company. His or her attitude and handling of the customer can make or break a relationship. If you have an in-house service, give frequent pep talks to those who have phone contact with customers. Consider offering bonuses or some other form of recognition for a job well done. Monitor calls, abiding by the laws that affect monitoring, to hear exactly how individual operators are performing. If you are using an outside service, place frequent test calls to make sure the service is performing its duties as well as you expect.

Outbound Telemarketing

Depending on the merchandise you offer, you may wish to investigate an outbound telemarketing service, sometimes also referred to as *out-WATS*. Due to its high cost in relation to most catalogers' average order, this is not frequently used but can be excellent in following up mailings for those catalogers offering high-ticket or service-oriented products. Therefore, this technique is more often employed by business-to-business catalogers. A potential customer may have planned to act on an offer but, for some reason, forgotten to do so. An outbound call that follows up on a mailing may be just the trigger needed to convince the potential buyer that he or she should give the catalog another look. If presented as a customer service, the call can actually enhance your company's image.

Reminding the customer that ordering is as easy as picking up the phone is important, too. Although not every outbound call will get a definite order, it can plant the seed for a future order. Inbound service, used in conjunction with an outbound program, allows easy accessibility. The customer can have the time to review your freshly presented offer (your outbound telemarketing people have courteously reminded him or her of the offer by phone) and then quickly (via inbound telemarketing) get back to you with an order. Such a combination has been known to increase sales for business mailers by an impressive 75 percent. Nevertheless, due to the small volume of outgoing calls anticipated by most catalogers, an outside service would be recommended, at least initially. Once response conversion data and corresponding additional sales dedicated to the outgoing program are known, in-house costs should be evaluated against the outside service. Outside services can assist you in writing the script the operators will use when calling customers. They can monitor calls for quality and customer attitudinal response, as well as actual orders taken. Of course, they will be the ones to actually place the calls and record any resulting sales, transferring order data to your fulfillment operation.

Conversely, you can use the downtime of your own in-house operators to place these scripted calls. Be sure to monitor their effectiveness on the customer for sales *and* the customer's favorable or unfavorable reactions to the attempts. We will talk more about this subject in Chapter 17.

Telemarketing is often under governmental scrutiny. Be sure to know the latest laws and regulations as they affect your use of this sales technique.

Overwraps That Add Selling Power

You may not be familiar with the term "overwrap," but you've probably seen instances of it—the extra cover of coarser offset paper attached to standard four-color glossy catalogs. More often than not, an overwrap announces something special about the catalog issue. One seafood catalog used a wrap to announce that recipients could place gift orders up to December 23. Fingerhut uses its wrap to inform recipients that unless they order they may not receive future catalogs.

When designed properly, overwraps can have the advantage of getting both prospective and existing customers' attention. They are usually less expensive than a cover change and can let you customize your message to certain segments of your list. This technique is especially useful for business-to-business catalogs, which often do not produce as many new catalogs per year as consumer catalogs.

Credit Cards—A Necessary Component

Credit cards are an essential part of your business. Consumers like them because they make ordering easier. You will find that, in most cases, credit-card orders have a higher average value than those paid by check (not to mention that credit cards are necessary for toll-free callers). Although many consumers hesitate to write a check for more than $20, they will charge well over that amount. Credit cards also add credibility. One small mail order firm quadrupled its sales after it started accepting credit-card payments.

❖ **EXAMPLE 9-6** Fingerhut wraps its regular catalog with a bonus gift offer that also reminds recipients that their catalog subscription is running out.

No catalog concern should be without Visa and MasterCard capabilities; Discover, American Express, and Diners Club are also recommended. The latter two cost more than the bank cards, but most catalogers feel that the higher average order they tend to generate is worth the extra cost.

An increasing number of companies are also offering in-house credit. For instance, Eddie Bauer suggests that customers "enjoy all the benefits of an Eddie Bauer FCNB Preferred Charge card." There is no annual fee, and this card is offered through First Consumers National Bank of Portland, Oregon. Private label, co-branded charge cards such as this can be negotiated through many banks.

The alternative to a co-branded credit card is a proprietary credit card, in which case the cataloger does not share the profits from the charge-card fees with the bank partner. But here, the cataloger also runs the risk of bad debt and fraud. Private label credit cards have the highest chance of success with companies that have a high-volume repeat purchase and are not too specialized. Of course, offering your own credit card can increase your chances of repeat purchases, as they help to instill loyalty.

To determine whether you should offer co-branded or proprietary cards, investigate the potential costs and profits of both, factoring in anticipated losses due to bad debt and fraud, before making your decision. Test the various name-brand credit cards in conjunction with your own if you decide to pursue this avenue to see which works best for you. (For how to handle credit-card charges for your catalog, see Chapter 12.)

Consider displaying drawings of the credit cards you offer, especially on the order form. Remember, a picture is worth a thousand words.

Actual and Pictorial Swatches and Samples

Swatches primarily appear only in solo mailings (the promotion received in an envelope that primarily sells only one product or product line). But with new technology, innovation is possible. And for catalogs with merchandise sales that would be greatly enhanced if the prospect could actually feel the product, swatches are an ideal answer. One of the objections to buying by mail has always been that the potential buyer cannot feel the product before purchasing it. With swatches and samples, this detriment is overcome. Current uses a poly bag to include samples of its greeting cards with its catalog (Example 9-7).

Swatches can also be made available to customers interested in certain products. For instance, Anticipations, which sells home decor products, states "Swatches on all upholstered furniture pieces are available upon request at no charge. Just call us Toll-Free . . ."

And don't forget pictorial swatches. These reproductions also help sell, because they clearly show the different colors and textures available. Use easy-to-understand names for the colors and put these names right on or next to the swatches.

Whichever type you are considering, understand the cost involved and test the response before making this technique a staple.

Endorsements and Testimonials

People want to hear what others think of a product and, although consumers have gotten more cautious about statements they perceive as advertising, they do tend to believe endorsements from real people and from institutions they trust. As discussed in Chapter

❖ **EXAMPLE 9-7**
Current includes actual samples in its polybagged catalog mailing.

8, incorporating positive comments from your customers into your catalog can have a positive influence on other customers' purchasing decisions.

You can even take it one step further, making your customers' endorsements a sought-after prize. For example, HearthSong promotes a "Parents' Choice Foundation Seal of Approval—Our Fifth Consecutive Year" on its cover. Other catalogs have created their own "review boards" consisting of a cross-section of people who are representative of the target audience. The task assigned to the board can be reviewing the product for quality, reading the copy for honesty, checking the efficiency of the delivery and service, and so forth. The board, which performs this review on a regular basis, then generates reports that can be published in the catalog.

Whatever form of endorsement you choose, be sure to let your satisfied customers and/or qualified entities (such as celebrities, experts, or users) speak to your customers for you.

Bonding Methods

Loyalty Programs

Programs constructed with the sole purpose of rewarding loyal customers have become common, thanks to the airlines' free mileage programs. Catalogers, too, understand the benefits of this technique. Neiman-Marcus, the upscale, Dallas-based department store, has long offered The InCircle® program that gives you one InCircle point for every dollar purchased on your Neiman-Marcus account during a calendar year. Sharper Image has a similar Frequent Buyers™ Program. It, too, rewards buyers with one point for each dollar spent in a calendar year: 1500 points earn a $75 certificate; 3,000 points earn a $200 certificate; 6,000 points earn a $500 certificate. Customers simply save their receipts. The cost of shipping and sales tax cannot be used nor can one product count for more than 1,400 points.

HearthSong takes a different approach with its Frequent Buyer club. In this case, customers pay an annual fee of $40 for which they receive a discount of 25 percent on all orders. Members are given a special (toll-free) ordering number and receive special product offerings and "early bird" specials.

Other Methods

Reward is not the only way to promote customer bonding. Recognition can have just as big an impact. A few years back, a children's clothing catalog decided to have a contest for its customers. They were looking for a child to use as a model on the cover and requested that catalog readers send in photos of their children if they would like their children to be considered as a cover model. Surprisingly, many readers also ordered merchandise so they could send photos of their child wearing the garments in which he or she might appear! The catalog received hundreds of photos of truly beautiful children, and the contest was successful for both the customers and the cataloger.

Other companies go the extra step of offering services relevant to their product line: Hanna Andersson, a children's clothing catalog, offers a newborn gift registry; Williams-Sonoma, a catalog for cooks, offers a bridal gift registry.

If your company has guiding principles or an overall mission, share them with your customers. W.M. Green features the beliefs behind its business practices on its catalog's back cover and tells the customer its people care. "Exceptional" is the key word in this company's five-point statement, which leads off with "Be exceptional direct marketers."

Mature Wisdom, a catalog devoted to the mature market, combines reward and recognition. Because this catalog is likely to have many grandparents among its customers, it wisely holds a "Kids Holiday Drawing" that awards $100 savings bonds to the subjects of randomly selected photos of grandchildren submitted by readers. Photos of winners are sprinkled throughout the catalog.

Companies like Lands' End and Sweet Energy make it a point to regularly feature photos of their employees and the lovely states in which these two companies are situated. Such photos help the customer feel part of a family by knowing the employees and feeling proud of their American connection. Sweet Energy even sends their customers dividend checks, which concretely reinforces Sweet Energy's belief that customers are a part of their company.

Other catalogers make it a point to touch base with their customers through mailings other than catalogs. One great idea is to send Thanksgiving and/or holiday cards, plus, if you have collected the relevant data, birthday cards. Most people will give you their birth date minus the year if you just ask. Don't include a solicitation as part of this type of mailing, but don't hesitate to follow up with one a couple of weeks later. If you test sending a card versus not sending one, you should see a higher response to the subsequent solicitation following the card mailing.

Find your own way of helping your customers to become a loyal part of your catalog family.

Promoting Exclusivity

If you have the only product of its type, this will most certainly help facilitate sales. Be sure to mention this in your copy and strongly consider designing a clear logo that indicates this product is exclusive to your catalog. Strive for exclusivity, as unique products have historically been the base of the catalog business, and products that are exclusive are usually also unique!

Socially Conscious Tie-ins

Catalogs that are under the umbrella of a social cause and/or give a portion of their profits to such causes are on the rise. The reasons are twofold: The majority of catalog companies are genuinely interested in the causes which they represent; and there is a halo effect to be gained by association with a worthwhile cause. Many catalogers believe the customer, given the choice between two catalogs with similar products, will choose the one that provides the added benefit of helping an organization with every purchase the customer makes.

One of the first companies to use this approach was Patagonia, which, since 1984, has been giving 10 percent of its pretax profits (the maximum allowed by law) to organizations that help preserve and restore the natural environment. The headline that announced this policy was great: "The first rule of intelligent tinkering is to save all the pieces." For Patagonia, a manufacturer of outdoor clothing and equipment, this tie-in makes absolute sense. It is further enhanced by the knowledge that the president of Patagonia has long been actively involved in environmental causes. Thus, this positioning shows the company cares about more than profits, and, due to its long-term dedication, the statement rings true.

Other catalogs with product mixes tied to the environment are also involved in charitable ventures. The Nature Company has sold trees, all the proceeds of which went to an international nonprofit organization dedicated to protecting endangered wildlife areas. This catalog also has a naturalists' hotline that gives more information about trees.

Smith & Hawken donates a portion of its corporate resources to nonprofit groups associated with the environment and has even given a $700,000 interest-free loan, to the Trust for Public Land, a group that preserves land for public use by buying it away from imminent development.

But the environment is hardly the only cause-related marketing used by catalogers. The Westbury Collection has given $25,000 or 5 percent of its sales, whichever is higher, to Second Harvest and heralds this on its cover: "Your purchase helps feed the hungry."

Godiva Chocolates offered "Benefit Balloting," by which the customer could choose from three charities, each of which gets a donation from the purchase (the customer paid for part of the donation). Plus the customer got to eat the chocolate.

Entire catalog businesses, not necessarily with nonprofit status, can exist for the sole or main purpose of supporting charitable works. The Company of Women is a catalog of products that make women feel good about being women; its main reason for being is to financially and emotionally support the Rockland County Shelter (in New York state) for abused women and children.

When considering whether or not you wish to be involved in this type of charitable endeavor, keep your positioning in mind. Don't be tempted to use donations merely as a marketing tool; the tie-in must ring true or the whole idea could backfire. So your commitment should be more than purely for effect. Really get involved, and be supportive with people and money. Then let your customers know of your involvement. And don't make a decision just on emotions. Understand in advance whether or not you can afford the commitment and whether it increases your responses.

Using Timely Messages

Unlike retail, which has the option of changing its merchandise display daily if it chooses, a catalog stays as it was printed for some time. But this does not mean that you cannot incorporate timely messages into that catalog.

Eddie Bauer addresses a common worry for catalogers: how to present a variety of products to span seasonal changes. Its solution is to tackle the problem head-on with an inside front page editorial that explains how, throughout the entire catalog, its fabric choices transcend seasons.

❖ **EXAMPLE 9-8**   Eddie Bauer devotes a full spread to an explanation of how its clothing transcends seasons and trends.

What Makes Sense Now

Clothes made to look like fall and feel like summer.

The kind of great, wear-anytime clothes that transcend seasons and trends. Because we've made everything lightweight. Mostly in cotton, with a few tailored pieces in fine, tropical wool. You'll also find lots of soft, buttery knits and washed twills. Now in sizes from 2 Petite to 18 Regular. So go ahead. Treat yourself to a terrific look now. You'll thank yourself for a long time to come.

All Week Long®

Every item we sell will give you complete satisfaction or you may return it for a full refund.

Prices in effect through January 31, 1995. Cover sweater, page 13. Vest shown above and opposite, page 9. All Week Long merchandise is not available in Eddie Bauer retail stores. ©1994 by Eddie Bauer Inc. All rights reserved.

2   3

When a San Francisco earthquake put Bullock's phones out of order, the company got back to customers with postcards, inserted between the second and third pages of the next catalog, stating how sorry Bullock's was that it could not handle their orders. The cataloger also gave all who received this catalog a discount to apologize for any inconvenience—a timely message that also showed Bullock's dedication to service.

Instant Gratification—A Major Motivator

Traditionally, one of the main obstacles to purchasing by mail has been the delayed time between ordering the product and actually receiving it. In recent years, this time frame has been shortened dramatically. Some business-to-business catalogers actually deliver the product within hours; you can call in the afternoon and receive it the next morning.

Because of this fast delivery and an increasing trust in ordering by mail, some marketers have taken to calling the holiday season "the fifth quarter." Many catalogers actively take orders up to two days before Christmas, guaranteeing delivery by Christmas Eve day. Other catalogers use a wrap, four pages that "wrap" the main catalog, to extend their selling seasons by announcing the day on which they can still promise delivery during this critical gift-giving season. Others use a sticker, usually just a few inches in diameter, affixed to an existing catalog and trumpeting the ability to deliver late into the season. For example, J. Crew alerts customers to its quick turnaround ability with this message on the cover: "Call by noon of the 24th and we'll still get it there." Details are spelled out on the order form.

To offer instant gratification, you must be sure that you have enough inventory in stock and can provide customers with on-line status as to the availability of the item they wish to purchase (more on this in Chapter 13). If you have the capability to deliver close to the time of need, don't be shy about promoting it on your front cover, back cover, and throughout the catalog. But be sure not to promise something you cannot provide, as unhappy customers do not make repeat buyers.

❖ **EXAMPLE 9-9**
J. Crew uses a timely message to ensure that customers know they can order up to the last minute before a holiday.

Personal Guarantee

One of the original stumbling blocks to purchasing via a catalog was the consumer's concern about the quality of the product and the reliability of the company. Although this has largely been overcome by the stellar service and insistence on quality offered by the vast majority of catalogers, the need to reinforce your policy for backing your products is still there. For example, Austad's well-displayed, specific guarantee from its sports and leisure catalog reads:

Guaranteed. We mean it.

We promise you'll be 100% satisfied with your purchase or you may return it for a full refund, credit, or exchange. This guarantee isn't for 30 or 60 days like some others; ours lasts throughout the product's lifetime with normal use. We will even take back customized products for exchange or credit toward your next purchase. Another promise: an Austad's exclusive symbol by apparel means it's generously cut for golf.

Prefer something shorter? Smith & Hawkins does an excellent job of conveying its message with these words:

All of our products are backed by our guarantee: If you are less than pleased with anything you order from this catalog, we will cheerfully accept it for an exchange or refund. No exceptions.

Sharper Image has a "No-Lemon Promise;" Lands' End is now famous for its "Guaranteed, Period." policy; and Early Winters shows it knows its outdoor audience with a "Belay Guarantee" reinforced by a climber hanging on a rock face and stating "When you're vertical on a rock face, a rope around your waist is a complete necessity. And you want that rope held by someone you trust. That's 'on belay.' "

But don't just put a lot of effort into writing and individualizing the guarantee; be sure to display it often and make it dominant. Consumers will look for a guarantee on the order form first, so be sure to include a version there. A common technique is to use your expanded guarantee verbiage here, and a condensed version throughout the catalog. This lets you be sure that your customer knows, in detail, what your guarantee stands for while reinforcing the message throughout.

If you enforce top quality control, don't worry that your customers will take advantage of a strong guarantee and send back too many returns. Consumers, more often than not, are quite honest and will only return something if there is really something wrong. Percentages for returns vary depending on the type of merchandise offered, your backorder position (how fast you are able to fill the orders), the cost of the product, and, as previously stated, how strict you are regarding quality control. An acceptable number of returns for a hard goods (not apparel) catalog is 4 percent, but catalogers strive for and achieve much lower numbers. Fashion catalogs, on the other hand, due to a tendency toward more back orders and size problems, can have returns as high as 25 percent. This subject is discussed in more detail in Chapter 13.

Whatever approach you choose, make sure it reflects the personality of your catalog. And be aware that if you do not specify the actual time limit of the guarantee, it becomes open-ended, which means you must honor it indefinitely.

Customer Service: Another Critical Component

Getting the customer is only half the battle; keeping customers is what really determines who stays in business and who does not. Telling customers—before they buy—the services your company offers illustrates just how well they will be treated and is essential. Talbots provides customers with such extra, sales-enhancing services as the Red Line Phone Service (which allows customers to be connected with a personal shopper via the company's Red Line phone, located in any of its stores) and offers a five-dollar Talbots' Gift Coupon to "help the environment" by alerting Talbots if you are receiving two or more of the same catalog. On another panel of the same order form, Talbots provides free gift wrap, their Red Door Express Service (two- or four-day delivery) and the option of using a Talbots charge. Talbots is so proud of its service that it even used this marketing advantage as the opening page in one of its issues.

❖ **EXAMPLE 9-10A**
(a and b) Red type highlights each of Talbots' customer service features. **(c)** A soft pastel background draws attention to "Simply Elegant" service benefits.

FREE GIFT PACKAGING.
Talbots complimentary gift packaging and ribbon are yours for the asking. And on orders being sent to another address, we'll even gift box your purchase for you and include a gift card with your own special message. Just let us know the recipient's name and address and we'll send the gift directly to them.

SHIPPING.
Your order will be prepared for shipment within 24 hours. If there is a delay, we will notify you in writing. Our standard method of shipping is via U.P.S., but we will ship by Parcel Post at your request if you have a Post Office Box or no street address. Please see below for our Red Door Express Service.

Alaska and Hawaii—We ship by Priority Mail at no additional charge.

Foreign Shipments—Shipments to foreign countries are sent airmail and charged **at cost plus** a $4 handling charge. We offer express service to most locations, although certain restrictions apply. All applicable duties and taxes will be paid by the customer. International orders must be paid in U.S. funds.

RED DOOR EXPRESS SERVICE.
Our Red Door Express Service offers you two- or four-day delivery anywhere in the continental U.S. via Federal Express ® delivery service. (Sorry, Federal Express ® does not deliver to APO/FPO addresses or P.O. Boxes.)

Two-Day Service — Guaranteed delivery within two business days of your order on in-stock items. $15 additional charge per address.

Four-Day Service — Delivery within four business days of your order on in-stock items. $5.50 additional charge per address.

RETURNS AND EXCHANGES.
If you are not satisfied with an item, please enclose the portion of your packing slip labeled "RETURN FORM" (noting the reason for return on the back) and apply the self-addressed return shipping label to the outside of the package. Please ship it prepaid and insured to: Talbots Customer Returns, 175 Kenneth Welch Drive, Lakeville, MA 02348. Or you may return it to any Talbots store. We will credit your original method of payment, excluding delivery charges.

GIFT CERTIFICATE. A 999415.
Let someone special choose just the right gift with the Talbots Gift Certificate. It arrives brightly wrapped along with our catalog. Available in $25, $50 or $100 denominations or in any other amount you choose. Just tell us the amount, the recipient's name and address and we'll do the rest.

TO PLACE YOUR ORDER, CALL US TOLL-FREE
1-800-8 TALBOTS
(1-800-882-5268)
24 HOURS A DAY, 7 DAYS A WEEK
OR USE OUR TOLL-FREE FAX NUMBER:
1-800-438-9443

FROM THE CONTINENTAL UNITED STATES (INCLUDING ALASKA), HAWAII, PUERTO RICO, THE U.S. VIRGIN ISLANDS AND CANADA.

TO PLACE YOUR ORDER FROM ALL FOREIGN COUNTRIES, EXCEPT CANADA, CALL (615) 558-6520. TO FAX YOUR ORDER (617) 740-1772. THESE ARE TOLL CALLS.

HAVE ANY CUSTOMER SERVICE QUESTIONS?
If you have any questions concerning your order, please call our Customer Service Specialists toll-free at **1-800-992-9010.** Our specialists are here Monday-Friday 7 a.m.-10 p.m., and Saturday, 8:30 a.m.-8 p.m. (EST).

SHOPPING'S EASIER WITH A TALBOTS CHARGE.
When you open a Talbots Charge account, you'll be among the first to learn about our special store and catalog promotions. To apply for a Talbots Charge card or **for inquiries about your Talbots Charge account** call toll-free **1-800-225-8204.** Our credit department is open Monday-Friday, 8:30 a.m.-12 midnight; Saturday, 9:30 a.m.- 12 midnight; Sunday, 10 a.m.-10 p.m. (EST).

USE OUR TELECOMMUNICATIONS DEVICE FOR THE DEAF.
We have a Telecommunications Device for the Deaf (TDD) to assist our customers who are hearing or speech impaired and have access to a TDD. Call toll-free **1-800-624-9179** anytime. If you need personal assistance, one of our Personal Shoppers will be on hand to assist you **24 hours a day, 7 days a week.** If ordering by mail, please include your TDD number on the order form.

❖ **EXAMPLE 9-10B**

HELP US HELP THE ENVIRONMENT AND RECEIVE A $5 GIFT COUPON.
At Talbots we're committed to doing what is right for our customer, as well as doing what is right for the environment. Please help us eliminate duplicate catalog mailings and we'll thank you by sending you a $5 Talbots Gift Coupon, good on your next purchase. Here's how it works: If you receive more than one copy **at a time** of the same Talbots, Talbots Intimates or Talbots Kids catalog, please send the back cover of each duplicate catalog, indicating which name and/or address is correct to: Talbots Environmental Committee, 175 Beal Street, Hingham, MA 02043.

RED LINE PHONE SERVICE.
When you're in any of our U.S. stores and can't find exactly what you're looking for, just pick up our Red Line phone to expand your shopping options. You'll be immediately connected with one of our Personal Shoppers, who will help you shop from our catalogs. Use your Talbots Charge or a major credit card and your selection will be prepared for shipment within 24 hours.

MAIL PREFERENCE SERVICE.
Occasionally we make customer names available to select firms offering merchandise that may be of interest to you. If you prefer not to receive these mailings, please copy your label exactly as it appears on this catalog and send it to: Talbots Mail Preference Service, 175 Beal Street, Hingham, MA 02043.

YOU'RE GETTING AWARD-WINNING CUSTOMER SERVICE WHEN YOU CALL TALBOTS.
Talbots is proud to announce that we have received the Direct Marketing Association's first-ever national "Award for Customer Service Excellence." The award is a direct result of our personalized service programs and strong commitment to our customer.

VISIT THESE TALBOTS STORES COAST TO COAST
ALABAMA Birmingham, Huntsville, Mobile, Montgomery **ARIZONA** Scottsdale, Tucson **ARKANSAS** Little Rock **CALIFORNIA** Bakersfield, Brea, Burlingame, Carmel, Costa Mesa, Fresno, La Jolla, Los Angeles, Mill Valley, Palo Alto, Palos Verdes, Pasadena, Pleasanton, Sacramento, San Diego, San Francisco, Santa Barbara, Santa Clara, Walnut Creek, Woodland Hills **COLORADO** Colorado Springs, Denver **CONNECTICUT** Avon, Essex, Glastonbury, Greenwich, Hamden, New Canaan, Ridgefield, Southbury, Stamford, Westport **DELAWARE** Newark, Wilmington **FLORIDA** Boca Raton, Gainesville, Jacksonville, Miami, Naples, Palm Beach, Pensacola, Plantation, Sarasota, Tallahassee, Tampa, Winter Park **GEORGIA** Atlanta, Augusta, Buckhead, Columbus, Macon, Roswell, Savannah, Vinings **IDAHO** Boise **ILLINOIS** Barrington, Bloomington, Champaign, Chicago, Lake Forest, Naperville, Northbrook, Oak Brook, Peoria, Rockford, Schaumburg, Springfield, Wheaton, Winnetka **INDIANA** Bloomington, Evansville, Ft. Wayne, Indianapolis, West Lafayette **IOWA** Bettendorf, Cedar Rapids, Clive **KANSAS** Overland Park, Topeka, Wichita **KENTUCKY** Lexington, Louisville **LOUISIANA** Baton Rouge, Lafayette, New Orleans, Shreveport **MAINE** South Portland **MARYLAND** Annapolis, Baltimore, Columbia, North Bethesda, Towson **MASSACHUSETTS** Acton, Boston, Burlington, Cambridge, Duxbury, Hingham, Holden, Lenox, Longmeadow, Marblehead, Newton, Northampton, Osterville, South Hamilton, Wellesley **MICHIGAN** Ann Arbor, Grand Rapids, Grosse Pointe, Livonia, Novi, Okemos, Portage, Troy **MINNESOTA** Edina, Minneapolis, Rochester, Roseville, St. Paul, Wayzata **MISSISSIPPI** Jackson **MISSOURI** Chesterfield, Kansas City, St. Louis, Springfield **NEBRASKA** Lincoln, Omaha **NEVADA** Las Vegas, Reno **NEW HAMPSHIRE** Bedford, Stratham **NEW JERSEY** Bridgewater, Edison, Haddonfield, Little Silver, Moorestown, Morristown, Paramus, Princeton, Ridgewood, Sea Girt, Short Hills, Sparta, Upper Montclair, Westfield **NEW MEXICO** Albuquerque, Santa Fe **NEW YORK** Albany, Binghamton, Chappaqua, Cold Spring Harbor, Dewitt, Fishkill, Garden City, Ithaca, Manhasset, New York City, Pittsford, Scarsdale, Stony Brook, Williamsville **NORTH CAROLINA** Asheville, Carrboro, Charlotte, Fayetteville, Greensboro, Raleigh, Wilmington, Winston-Salem **OHIO** Beachwood, Beavercreek, Boardman, Canton, Cincinnati, Cleveland, Columbus, Dayton, Fairlawn, Rocky River, Toledo, Worthington **OKLAHOMA** Oklahoma City, Tulsa **OREGON** Portland **PENNSYLVANIA** Bethlehem, Camp Hill, Chestnut Hill, Clarks Summit, Doylestown, Erie, Haverford, King of Prussia, Lancaster, Mt. Lebanon, Philadelphia, Pittsburgh, Sewickley, Springfield, State College, York **RHODE ISLAND** Cranston, Newport, Providence **SOUTH CAROLINA** Charleston, Columbia, Greenville, Hilton Head, Spartanburg **TENNESSEE** Chattanooga, Germantown, Knoxville, Memphis, Nashville **TEXAS** Arlington, Austin, Beaumont, Dallas, El Paso, Fort Worth, Houston, Lubbock, Midland, Plano, San Antonio **UTAH** Salt Lake City **VERMONT** South Burlington **VIRGINIA** Alexandria, Arlington, Charlottesville, McLean, Midlothian, Newport News, Reston, Richmond, Roanoke, Virginia Beach **WASHINGTON** Bellevue, Seattle, Spokane **WASHINGTON, D.C.** Connecticut Avenue, Georgetown, Wisconsin Avenue **WEST VIRGINIA** Charleston **WISCONSIN** Appleton, Madison, Whitefish Bay

TALBOTS PETITES STORES CALIFORNIA Costa Mesa, Palo Alto **CONNECTICUT** Avon, Hamden, Ridgefield **DELAWARE** Wilmington **FLORIDA** Tampa, Winter Park **GEORGIA** Buckhead, Roswell **ILLINOIS** Chicago, Oak Brook **INDIANA** Indianapolis **IOWA** Des Moines **KANSAS** Overland Park **KENTUCKY** Louisville **MARYLAND** Baltimore **MASSACHUSETTS** Cambridge **MICHIGAN** Grand Rapids, Troy **MINNESOTA** Edina **MISSISSIPPI** Jackson **MISSOURI** St. Louis **NEW JERSEY** Bridgewater **NEW YORK** Pittsford **NORTH CAROLINA** Charlotte, Raleigh, Winston-Salem **OHIO** Beachwood, Cincinnati, Dayton, Worthington **PENNSYLVANIA** King of Prussia **RHODE ISLAND** Newport **SOUTH CAROLINA** Charleston, Columbia **TENNESSEE** Knoxville, Nashville **TEXAS** Austin, Dallas, Fort Worth, Houston **VIRGINIA** Arlington, McLean, Richmond, Virginia Beach **WASHINGTON** Bellevue

TALBOTS KIDS STORES ARIZONA Scottsdale **CALIFORNIA** Santa Clara **CONNECTICUT** Westport **GEORGIA** Atlanta, Roswell **ILLINOIS** Oak Brook **INDIANA** Indianapolis **KANSAS** Overland Park **MARYLAND** Baltimore, Columbia **MASSACHUSETTS** Boston, Burlington **MICHIGAN** Troy **MINNESOTA** Edina **MISSOURI** St. Louis **NEW JERSEY** Bridgewater, Edison **NORTH CAROLINA** Charlotte, Raleigh **OHIO** Cincinnati **PENNSYLVANIA** King of Prussia, Mt. Lebanon **TENNESSEE** Germantown **TEXAS** Dallas **VIRGINIA** McLean **WASHINGTON** Bellevue

TALBOTS INTIMATES ILLINOIS Chicago **MASSACHUSETTS** Boston **MICHIGAN** Troy **MISSOURI** St. Louis **NEW JERSEY** Short Hills **NEW YORK** Pittsford **TEXAS** Austin

TALBOTS SURPLUS STORES CALIFORNIA San Leandro **ILLINOIS** Park Ridge **KENTUCKY** Lexington **MARYLAND** Towson **MASSACHUSETTS** Hingham **NEW YORK** Albany **OHIO** Cincinnati **VIRGINIA** Springfield **WISCONSIN** Milwaukee

TALBOTS CANADA STORES CALGARY, EDMONTON, MONTREAL, OTTAWA, TORONTO, VANCOUVER

OPENING THIS SPRING

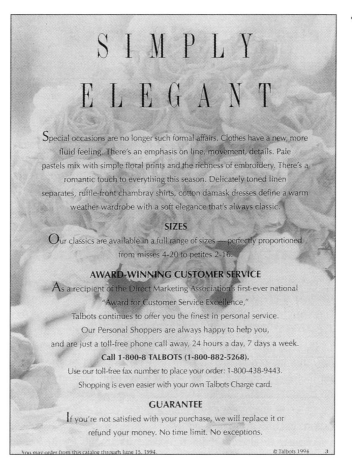

❖ **EXAMPLE 9-11**
Newport News's easy-to-understand approach makes readers feel that taking their measurements is easy and that they are profiting by using the measurement chart.

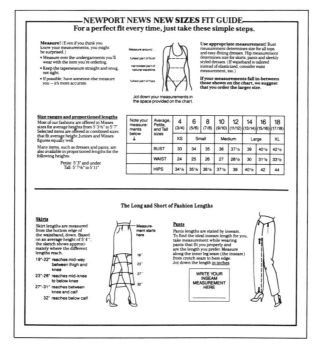

Leading catalogers, such as Lands' End, L.L. Bean, and a host of others, devote a great deal of their order-form space to ultraspecific size charts. This is an especially good idea because it helps customers order the size that's right for them (no irritating returns or dissatisfaction) and keeps return costs down for the cataloger, too. Newport News showcases a size chart that's easy to understand and helpful.

Tell-a-Friend Referrals

Some catalogers find that one of the best sources of new names comes from customers who list their friends and relatives as people who may wish to receive a catalog. Usually, "share-us-with-a-friend" space is allowed for one to three different names and addresses. Be careful to code these referrals in the order in which they are received. Some find that response decreases in correlation with the ranking of the names—that is, the names listed first are the best prospects, the last names listed may not even be worth mailing. Increasingly, postcard inserts are making it easier for customers to help you locate new prospects, and the referrer doesn't have to use the order form to give you those potentially valuable leads.

Inventive Promotional Groups

Whenever possible, incorporate promotional pluses that will make your catalog different in some way. For instance, Horchow once asked customers to test their buying skills. The copy read: "Just for fun, we'll give you the chance to play buyer and to pick the five items you think will be the big winners in this catalog." And what prize was offered for this tiny, but brilliantly, disguised combination of research and sales promotion? "We will announce both the customers with the best buying skills and the big five items in our October catalog." Just think of how many times potential winners had to flip through the catalog, seeing all those products again and again. Might they find something they didn't know they wanted to buy until the desire to win this contest caused them to really look at each and every product?

Another cataloger adapts this same technique for its younger audience by suggesting that their readers find a fictional character's pet frog, which has escaped from its box. This game is complicated by the fact that there are many frogs throughout the catalog and not all of them look like the special frog that is the heroine's pet. Those who solve the puzzle will be rewarded with a frog pen, free with any order.

❖ **EXAMPLE 9-12**

These bind-in postcards make it easy for customers to add their own or friends' names to Patagonia's mailing list.

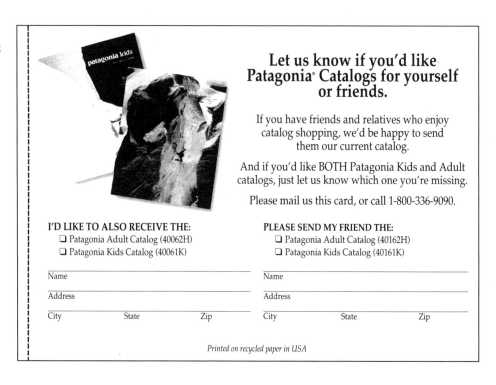

Let us know if you'd like Patagonia® Catalogs for yourself or friends.

If you have friends and relatives who enjoy catalog shopping, we'd be happy to send them our current catalog.

And if you'd like BOTH Patagonia Kids and Adult catalogs, just let us know which one you're missing.

Please mail us this card, or call 1-800-336-9090.

I'D LIKE TO ALSO RECEIVE THE:
❑ Patagonia Adult Catalog (40062H)
❑ Patagonia Kids Catalog (40061K)

Name _____

Address _____

City _____ State _____ Zip _____

PLEASE SEND MY FRIEND THE:
❑ Patagonia Adult Catalog (40162H)
❑ Patagonia Kids Catalog (40161K)

Name _____

Address _____

City _____ State _____ Zip _____

Printed on recycled paper in USA

Electronic Methods—An Evolving Opportunity

Phone Plus

Originally called Scan Phone, the name points up the fact that changing technology is responsible for many new methods of ordering. Developed by US Order and retailing for $199, this device is much more than a telephone: It incorporates a computer-like keyboard that allows customers to punch in their orders. A four-line viewing screen displays the numbers dialed. The first version of Scan Phone included a scanning wand with which the customer could swipe catalogs printed with bar codes. Catalogers who tested this item received lukewarm customer response. *Catalog Age* reported: " 'The Right Start received about 150 orders (in 1993) for sales totaling under $4,000,' says president Stan Fridstein. But, he says, that's not bad considering US Order only deployed 10,000 Scan Phones."[3]

Catalogers who wish to participate in the new Phone Plus version must pay a percentage of the sales made using the device to US Order.

Checks by Phone

A process that enables the consumer to pay by check for merchandise ordered by phone is still in its infancy. The customer's checking account number is first given to the cataloger, who, through a third-party processor, then submits a draft to the Federal Reserve System. The draft goes through within 24 hours of the phone order as if it were a regularly deposited check.

The process is easy for customers because they only need to read the numbers on the bottom of the check to the order taker. PhoneChek, a vendor of this service, after receiving a faxed copy of those numbers, identifies the customer's bank and creates a "check" in the customer's name. This check is processed like any other.

The advantage here, of course, is giving those who wish to pay by check the same ability to purchase by phone as those with credit cards now enjoy. PhoneChek charges $300 for the initial set-up. Thereafter, costs are $1 per check, regardless of the amount. The minimum is 100 checks per day or $100 per day.

The Order Form as a Sales Tool

Using Order Forms

As customers have become more comfortable with phoning in their orders, many catalogers have questioned whether order forms (and their cost) are really worth having. The answer is not a simple one. It partially depends on the age of your audience. More mature individuals are less likely to trust phone orders and want the security of an order form. Another consideration is whether your customer will be paying by check or credit card. Although, as previously mentioned, you now can send a check over the phone, it is still pretty difficult. If you have a very high phone rate and a younger audience, you may wish to test your need for an order form.

But remember many customers use the order form to collect their orders on paper before phoning them in. Plus, fax orders, which also require an order form, are gaining in popularity. So think twice about simply eliminating this sales tool. Test it carefully more than once, then make your decision.

Making Order Forms Work Harder

Put your order form to work; it must be much more than just a data-entry form that customers fill in. Tests have shown that creating an order form as a separate insert bound into the catalog is more effective than just using a page in the catalog itself as an order form. Although there is an extra cost associated with producing the order form independent of the catalog, for most catalogers, it more than pays for itself in increased sales.

Order forms can be one page or many and may serve a variety of purposes, such as selling merchandise directly from the form itself and/or clearly stating the catalog company's position on customer service, return policies, and other promotional advantages. When merchandise is offered, it tends to be either relatively low-priced impulse items or items offered at savings. Lillian Vernon uses every inch of order-form space to boldly state "FREE GIFT!" "50% SAVINGS!" and "FREE OFFER!"—phrases that guarantee you'll get the customer's attention. If you do sell merchandise, make sure the order form is not just a catch-all for the items you couldn't fit in the main body of the book. Give it a theme and treat this area with the same respect you do the rest of the catalog.

More and more, catalogers are leaning toward using this space purely for self-promotion. They display, in no uncertain terms, the customer services they believe set them apart from their competition. It's important to note that whether you choose to use your order form strictly for promotional messages or for selling merchandise, the items discussed in the following section should also appear.

The order form, because it stands out from the catalog, is a great place to make a last-minute sale, to reinforce the reasons readers should be buying from this particular catalog, and to get potential buyers involved to the point where they become buyers.

Creating the Order Form

Copy and layout must work hand in hand to keep the order form clean and simple without wasted space. Because designing an order form can be rather complicated, be sure to get a template from the printer before beginning your artwork. A *template* is literally a piece of paper or cardboard marked with the imposition for the particular size and folds of your order form. Keep the following guidelines in mind when creating your order form:

1. Leave plenty of room between lines so customers can write legibly. This will reduce incorrectly processed orders or calls to the customer for clarification.

2. Work with the data-entry people who will be using the form. Solicit their input and put it to use. Keep the information in the order in which your computer's data entry system reads.

❖ **EXAMPLE 9-13** Lillian Vernon does more than just offer its famous personalized products on the order form: The company enhances its sales potential with strong, repeated savings messages.

"We created our own line of Shoe Care Products because I want your Wissota Trader Shoes to last a lifetime!"

Bob Allen

It's always exciting to get letters from satisfied customers who are still wearing shoes from our factory that are 5, 10, 15 or more years old and still going strong.

Many of the letters are posted on bulletin boards for our employees to read. They take a special pride in knowing the shoes they work on can outwear and outperform most any shoe on the market today, foreign or domestic.

To get that kind of wear out of our shoes, proper care has to be taken. That's why we encourage the use of quality waxes, conditioners and oils such as our Executive Imperial® and Field & Stream® shoe care products.

Here are a few shoe care tips to help you get started.

Initial Shoe Care

After you try your new shoes on and make sure they fit, it's a good practice to apply a quality Carnauba wax to them. Even though our shoes are waxed and polished at the factory, the application can dry out.

Regular Shoe Care

When your shoes start to lose their shine, or if they've become dull or dirty, it's time to start your regular program of shoe care. Use our cleaner/conditioner and a soft cloth to remove dirt and restore oils. Let dry, then remove any residue with a horsehair brush. Apply Carnauba wax to restore the finish. If the surface is lightly scuffed, apply a shoe cream before the wax to restore the color.

It's important to think of quality footwear as an investment. You can enjoy your investment for many years to come with proper care.

Cedar Shoe Trees

Natural cedar wood absorbs moisture and leaves a pleasant, natural aroma. Adjustable. **U.S.A. (Men's sizes only - State Shoe Size on Order Form.)**
Stock # 9422

Special Price $19.00/pair

Executive Imperial® Shoe Care Kit
(For Leather Dress Shoes.)

- 2 Horsehair Shoe Brushes
- 2 Horsehair Applicator Brushes
- 2 Shoe Creams or 2 Carnauba Waxes (Black & Burgundy)
- 1 Leather Cleaner/Conditioner
- 1 Polishing Cloth
- 1 Shoe Horn
- 1 Leather Shoe Care Bag
- **Made in U.S.A.** (Horsehair brushes, imported)
  Stock # 9452 (with two shoe creams)
  Stock # 9453 (with two Carnauba waxes)

NOTE: See Shoe Care Refill items on next page.

Special Price $29.00 per kit

Field & Stream® Boot and Shoe Care Kit
(For Casuals, WALKABOUT® Walking Shoes, Sporting Boots.)

- 1 Boot & Shoe Oil
- 1 Mink Oil
- 1 Silicone Spray (Pump)
- 1 Leather Cleaner/Conditioner
- 1 Horsehair Applicator Brush
- 1 Cordura® Shoe Care Bag
- **Made in U.S.A.** (Horsehair brush, imported)
  Stock # 9459   **Special Price $19.00**

NOTE: See Shoe Care Refill items on next page.

❖ **EXAMPLE 9-14**
Wissota Trader uses its order form for add-on products to its basic shoe line.

❖ **EXAMPLE 9-15**
Ballard Designs proves that an order form can be a work of art. The attractive, two-color design includes an example of how to fill out the form.

428102

MAY WE SHIP TO AN ALTERNATE ADDRESS?

☐ This is a gift. Please deliver to the address below.
☐ I'm not home during the day; please deliver to address below.

Ship item(s) I have circled in the first column below to:

Name _____
Company (if applicable) _____
Address _____
City/State/Zip _____
Gift Message _____

PAYMENT METHOD:
☐ **Check or Money Order** enclosed. Make payable to Ballard Designs.
☐ **Charge.** *Credit cards are not debited until an item is shipped.*
  ☐ VISA (13 or 16 digits) ☐ American Express (15 digits)
  ☐ Discover (16 digits) ☐ Mastercard (16 digits)

Account Number _____
Expiration Date (required) _____
Cardholder's Billing Address (if different from ship-to address) _____
Signature (as printed on card) _____

Your order will be shipped to the above address unless you indicate otherwise. If the address above is a P.O. Box, please provide a street address! If the name or address is incorrect, print correct information below.

NAME _____
ADDRESS _____
CITY _____ STATE _____ ZIP _____
DAY PHONE ( ) _____ EVENING PHONE ( ) _____

TO ORDER BY CREDIT CARD, CALL (404) 351-5099
MON-FRI 7:30AM-11:00PM SAT 9:00AM-8:00PM SUN 11:00AM-7:00PM (EST)

Circle Items to Alternate Address	Page No.	Item Number	Color/Finish	Qty	Item Name	Glass Size	Thickness	Edge Type	Item Price	Shipping Charge	Total Item Charge
1	31	M418	Pewter	2	Neo Scroll Side Chair				298.00	17.00	630.00
2											
3											
4											
5											
6											
7											
8											

(Please Note: Glass tops are not returnable)

TO ORDER 24 HOURS A DAY,
COMPLETE THIS FORM & FAX TO: (404) 352-1660

ASK ABOUT AIR EXPRESS SERVICE

THANK YOU FOR YOUR ORDER!

SPRING 1994

Tear order blank along perforation to retain remainder of form for future reference.

Merchandise Total	
6% Sales Tax (Georgia Residents Only)	
Shipping Total	
Special Delivery Charge — Call for charges on freight collect, rush and outside USA.	
TOTAL	

3. Use screened areas to attract attention or guide the consumer to specific spaces, but use these screens in moderation. (Be sure that, if the order form is faxed, the screened information is still readable.) Too many tinted areas can make the order form confusing and be self-defeating. Consider using black and white or two colors at first; it's less expensive and easier to work with. Your order-form printer can screen black to achieve a gray-tinted area or use two colors, neither of which needs to be black, for more variety.

4. Be sure to request the customer's phone numbers in the applicable information area. If you have a problem with an order, you'll need to know where to get in touch with the customer, both day and night. Customers generally don't mind giving phone numbers if you specify why you need them.

5. If you rent your list, display the Mail Preference Service option. This lets customers know you are ready and willing to take their name off the lists you rent to others if they so desire (see Chapter 11).

6. List your toll-free or customer-paid phone and fax numbers boldly. Just because customers stop to read the order form doesn't mean they intend to use it; they may choose to call the phone service. And catalog shoppers have been conditioned to look on this form for ordering information, no matter which option they choose.

7. Keep your mailing list up to date by asking for a change of address. If space allows, you can leave an area for this information; if not, simply ask the customer to make appropriate corrections to the existing address.

8. Let the customers know that you can't deliver special carrier and overnight packages to a post office box. Specify that you need a street address or a rural route number. (Note: This does not apply to U.S. postal delivery.)

9. Include "Prices effective through (date)" so customers who retain the catalog will readily be aware of its age. This will also protect you against price increases. If you choose, you can add a line suggesting that customers call customer service to determine whether a product is still available after the expiration date of the catalog.

10. If you have fast delivery, state your company's turn-around time on a package; for example, "Orders filled within 48 hours of receipt." But don't exaggerate. It's worse to promise something you can't deliver than not to make a statement at all.

11. Do you ship outside the continental United States? Take a careful look at the cost. You may need to add a surcharge for items sent to Puerto Rico, Alaska, and Hawaii. And don't forget Canadian and foreign orders. Ask for payment in U.S. dollars only.

12. Plainly indicate "PLEASE PRINT." Some people need to be reminded to write their orders legibly. Valuable time can be saved in processing orders.

13. Make sure that the gift section is easy to coordinate; the address(es) to which individual items should be shipped must be identified clearly.

Use the following list to help ensure that your order form is complete. Both artists and writers can refer to this. An asterisk indicates that an item may not appear on all order forms, depending on catalog policy and the products offered.

◆ Company logo and address
◆ Credit-card number/charge-card logos (Visa, allow 13 to 16 spaces; MasterCard, 16 spaces; American Express, 15 spaces)
◆ Expiration date (allow 4 spaces)
◆ Signature line, with the words "required for charge orders" beneath the line itself
◆ Customer-service information, including hours
◆ Ordering instructions
◆ Sales-tax information

- Postage and handling information
- Special handling information*
- "Share us with a friend!" message
- Money-back guarantee
- Information about person ordering (name and area)
- "Ship-to" name, address, and area
- Screened "Thank you for your order" message
- Gift certificate*
- Gift section*
- Copyright*
- Price guarantee*
- Mail preference service
- Toll-free number, including ordering hours
- Association logos (such as Direct Marketing Association, local Better Business Bureaus, or relevant industry affiliations)*
- "Have you enclosed your check or credit-card information?" reminder
- "Items ordered together are not always shipped together. There is no additional charge for multiple deliveries."
- Method-of-payment information
- Cataloger letter*
- "Please have your credit card handy, since only credit-card orders can be taken by phone."
- Customer telephone numbers (day/night, home/office)
- Time period within which orders are shipped (if orders are shipped fast)*
- Address-correction copy line
- Bar code*
- Misprint disclaimer
- Source code (generally part of ink-jetted name/address)

In the ordering area:
- Page number
- Description
- Item number
- Size*
- Color*
- Monogramming information*
- Quantity
- Item or set price
- Total charge

Using an Envelope

Most catalogs use preformed envelopes as part of their order forms. An alternative to this is a flat order form, which must be folded down to envelope size, then glued or taped together to form a reply device that will contain a check or money order. Although flat order forms can be less expensive, they are generally inefficient because you must open them manually when you get them back. If you have automated mail opening, be sure the envelope format you select meets the machine's criteria. Also consider the extra time and effort for the customer in folding and securing the flat envelope as opposed to using a preformed envelope. Keep order forms small enough so that, when folded, they fit easily into the envelope provided.

Double Order Forms

To determine whether you should use a double order form, ask yourself five questions:

1. Will your catalog have a high pass-along rate?
2. Will it have a long life?
3. Can you afford the additional cost at this time?
4. Will it have a high incidence of gift giving?
5. Does it affect the overall weight of your catalog, which could adversely affect postage costs?

If your answer to questions 1 through 4 is yes, you should probably test the use of a double order form. However, if postage is adversely affected, test with and without the double order form to see if the additional sales outweigh the additional cost. A double order form should not be tested until a catalog is established. A note within the body of the catalog—"Order form missing? Simply call or write," plus a phone number, an address, and any other pertinent information—can eliminate the problem of a missing order form and help keep start-up expenses down.

❖ **EXAMPLE 9-16**
Betty Crocker knows its customers save coupons as part of their ordering process, resulting in a possible lag between orders, so it offers an extra order form for subsequent purchases.

Printing the Order Form

Order forms are printed on presses designed primarily for simple printing but complicated converting (folding, gluing, and so on). They print from one to four colors at a time, then actually make an envelope, apply glue, and perforate, all in one continuous line. In the past, catalog printers seldom had these capabilities; instead, they had to do each of the functions separately at far greater cost. This, like many things in the printing industry is changing, so check costs with your catalog printer as well as an order-form printer and compare. Remember to factor in the freight to get the order from from the order-form printer to the catalog printer.

With an order-form printer, the form is most often "gang" run, which means that several different order forms are run at one time. The result is even greater cost-efficiencies, but the order-form printer must have your artwork when it is due. Otherwise, the press will run without your order form, and it may be some time before there is another opening.

Be sure to approve a blueline of the order form before you go to press. This will assure you that it is being printed with the correct folds and imposition. If you supply the catalog printer with preformed envelopes or bind-ins, make sure the order-form printer puts the following information on the outside of each carton:

1. Customer and printer job number
2. Code number, if used
3. Printer name and date of mailing
4. Quantity

Be sure instructions to the catalog printer include a request to check bind-in quantities by code (if applicable) as soon as they arrive. Then, if discrepancies exist, there will be time to remedy the situation. Also, before ordering the bind-ins, check with your lettershop to determine the waste or spoilage factor, then order accordingly. Waste always occurs during insertion, so order extras. It's a small price to pay to ensure you have enough order forms to complete a mailing.

Inserting Order Forms

Don't assume that all order forms must be placed as the common central insertion. If a catalog consists of more than one 16-page signature, you may be able to insert the order form in a different location. Some catalogers who use separate covers choose to insert the front part of the order form between the front cover and second page; they then use this part of the insert as a highly visible placement for the letter from the president or special promotional copy. The back part (or data-entry section) of the order form then appears between the back cover and the last page of the signature. Others place the order form between two signatures—say, pages 16–17 and 32–33. The belief here is that this will cause the catalog to "fall" open in three different areas: the center and the two places in which the order form has been inserted. If the catalog automatically opens in more places, the assumption is there will be more sales on these pages.

However, most catalogers do insert the order form in the center of the catalog. Again, this is partially due to customer conditioning and a desire on the part of the cataloger to provide what is most comfortable for the customer.

As you will hear again and again, test the idea to see what works best for you.

The Postage-Paid Option

As we just stated, a major rule of cataloging is to make ordering as easy as possible for the potential customer. Therefore, providing a postage-paid envelope that eliminates the need for a stamp seems to make sense. Yet there are two major reasons why so many catalogers do not choose to prepay postage.

1. **Cost**. For prepaid (business-reply mail, or BRM) envelopes, the post office charges the normal first-class rate plus a 44-cent handling charge if you pay by

cash or have a postage-due account, or a 10-cent handling charge (plus first-class postage) if you have a business-reply account—for which you pay a $205 Advance Deposit accounting fee plus an $85 BRM permit fee. The cost runs from 42 to 76 cents each for prepaid envelopes, compared to no cost for postage when the customer supplies the stamp. In one test of postage-paid envelopes, orders increased, but the increase was not sufficient to cover the cost of postage.

There is a newer, less expensive service, but it requires more upfront work on your end. With this system, the cost is only a two-cent handling fee plus the cost of first-class postage. The requirements are as follows:

◆ Submission of a letter of request
◆ Fifty or more samples for review
◆ An established Advance Deposit account
◆ Zip + 4 printed on each piece
◆ Zip + 4 bar code and Facing Identification Mark (FIM) C printed on each piece (FIM C means pre–bar-coded business-reply mail)

2. **Nonorder mail**. A postage-paid envelope seems to encourage letters from lonely people, from consumers who see an opportunity to complain about everything in general, and from political activists who want to share their message. Such mail is not only annoying (cutting down on efficiency) but also comes right off the bottom line. The postage is prepaid even if the return envelope doesn't contain an order, and time is wasted in mail opening.

First-time catalogers are advised not to use postage-paid envelopes. As your catalog and mailing quantities grow, you can consider offering a postage-paid envelope to a small test segment. But before the test, check with the post office for current charges.

Using Color on Your Order Form

Without a doubt, color affects buying decisions. According to a survey conducted by *Better Homes and Gardens*, 94.2 percent of its readers stated that color generally influenced their buying decisions when ordering by mail. However, color also costs more, and because first-time catalogers may need to keep production expenses to a minimum, using four-color art on the order form may need to be postponed.

One solution is to select products that do not need color to help sales. For instance, a silver key chain is just as attractive when photographed in black and white as it is in color. Or, as many others have done, you can use only illustrations. Alternatively, forgo product sales entirely and use extra space to reinforce your catalog's image or positioning. For the data-entry section of the order form, black or one-color tints can be used to highlight special areas.

As your catalog becomes more established, four-color can be tested against black and white. Many catalogers use the outer part of the order form as simply another page in the catalog, designing it to look like one cohesive spread—which is one way to add two page to your catalog at minimal expense.

❖ CHECKLIST

✔ Test the value of putting a catalog or other offers in all outgoing packages.
✔ Understand how to use (and not use) premiums.
✔ Consider judiciously used discounts.
✔ Evaluate your merchandise for items that might sell off each other.
✔ Hire a specialist when offering a sweepstakes.
✔ Use an in-bound toll-free number for ordering.
✔ Determine if you will gain a competitive advantage with a toll-free for customer service
✔ Don't automatically assume that telephone services should initially be handled in-house.
✔ Watch your costs on gift wrapping.

✔ Extend the life of your catalog through overwraps.

✔ Collect and showcase endorsements and testimonials.

✔ Keep abreast of new electronic payment methods.

✔ Remember that rewarding customers through recognition can be as effective as monetary incentives.

✔ If at least 20 percent to 25 percent of your products are exclusive, state this boldly.

✔ Evaluate the benefits of socially conscious tie-ins.

✔ Keep all messages timely.

✔ Stay competitive in your delivery time.

✔ Personalize your guarantee.

✔ Understand that catalogs currently set the standards for customer service and yours must, too.

✔ Always give customers an opportunity to refer friends as potential new customers.

✔ Follow the order form checklist on page 240.

End Notes

1. *Catalog Age*, February 1994.
2. *Catalog Age*, December 1993.
3. *Catalog Age*, February 1994.

CHAPTER TEN
❖ ❖ ❖

The Mailing Plan

The purpose of a mailing plan is to lay out the quantity of catalogs you intend to mail, to whom, and in what time period. Think of it as a blueprint or game plan that helps you establish the basis for the number of customer and prospect contacts you plan to make for the year, as well as one of the bases for your financial plan.

What Quantity Should You Mail?

As in any business, higher quantities allow economies of scale; the costs for postage and printing, for instance, drop as the quantity increases. Team this with the fact that catalogers generally mail nationally, and you can see the advantages of mailing substantial quantities.

However, even though the cost per piece may be less, mailing more naturally costs more overall. So you must balance quantity price breaks with your ability to pay for larger mailings. On the reverse side of the coin, never mail less than 100,000 on a national basis. Anything smaller will provide such small response numbers per list used and per item sold, that the information gained will not be translatable to future mailings.

When planning quantity, don't forget to take postage presort discounts into account. Remember that mailing smaller quantities to test a mail date can cost you more in postage because you may not qualify for as many presorts if you test smaller mailings more often (see Table 10-1). Balance these costs against your need to know how well your catalog will perform on a per-month or seasonal basis.

❖ **TABLE 10-1**
Approximate Presort Postage Calculations*

	Carrier Route	Three-Five-Digit	Basic		
Rates	0.162	$0.214	$0.266		
	Carrier Route	Five-Digit (%)	Basic (%)	Total Cost ($)	Cost ($)/Piece
50,000	—	86.0	14.0	11,064	0.221
150,000	2.0	89.0	9.0	32,646	0.218
250,000	17.0	78.0	5.0	51,940	0.208
500,000	29.0	70.0	1.0	99,720	0.199
750,000	39.3	60.4	0.3	145,290	0.194
1,000,000	54.9	44.9	0.2	185,556	0.186

Based on Alden Press calculations and shipping weight <3.3067 ounces for flats (does not include bar coding or zip + 4 (U.S.P.S. rates as of January 1, 1995.)

Match Quantity with Seasonality

Almost all businesses experience seasonality. Consumer, gift-oriented catalogs, like retailers, do the most business in the fourth quarter of each year. Of late, some have even termed late November and the first three weeks of December the "fifth quarter" because it is so strong that it seems to deserve its own quarter!

The next best time of the year for catalogers has historically been the month of January. It has long been called "the me month" because this is the time when consumers turn to their own concerns. Following months of buying gifts for others and often confined to their homes due to inclement weather, these consumers use the bonus money (or money from gifts returned) to treat themselves.

Spring (the second quarter) also can be good if your catalog has outdoor-oriented items, but it almost always has less response than fall (the fourth quarter) and winter/spring (the first quarter). For almost all catalogers, summer is not a good time to mail, as consumers are away on vacation or distracted by longer daylight hours and good weather.

To offset weak seasons but still stay in contact with their customers, many choose to mail a smaller book containing only their best-selling items (or what they believe will be the best-sellers based on experience) to only their top rental lists and house (customer) file. It may also be necessary to mail during this period to collect new customers for the generally more profitable fourth-quarter mailings.

When setting up a mailing plan, remember that not everyone on your list should necessarily be mailed with the same frequency. Recency, frequency, and monetary (RFM) considerations (see Chapter 14) should be given to all house lists (lists of your customers), mailing more often to those who spend the most. The aggressive mailing plan shown in Figure 10-1 is for a catalog that is launched during the highest selling season. The first remail in November of Year 1 necessitates only a cover change; a new cover may be unnecessary if there is minimal duplication of names between the first two mailings. A catalog that is launched in the second-best selling season could use the Year 2 plan as its starting point. Mailings to the same customer segment in Year 2 must be no less than approximately six weeks apart (except for fashion and highly disposable product catalogs). All catalog versions for this year require cover changes. Mailings in Year 3 should be spaced similarly to those in Year 2 (the appearance of overlap in the schedule is due to the lack of segmentation definition). To see the financial results of this mailing plan, refer to Chapter 15.

The Best Time to Launch

In almost all cases, the fourth quarter provides more income, so this seems to be the right choice. But there are other factors to consider. If you launch in what is usually the busiest season, you will need to be absolutely certain that your inventory control and ordering systems are up to handling the volume of orders you may receive. This is very difficult to do with the first catalog, so many times it is advisable to launch in the first quarter of the year, giving yourself the benefit of the second-best selling season—and most of the year to get your systems and inventory management working smoothly before the big rush.

What Is a Remail?

One technique for amortizing the cost of a catalog over a longer selling period is the *remail*, meaning the same interior catalog with different front and back covers. Sometimes remails also change the first and last two interior spreads or some interior sections, adapting them to the seasonality and anticipated sales of the mailing. The belief here is that the customer will open the remail catalog, thinking it is a totally new version. Most consumers are well aware of this technique, but will still give the catalog a second look because of its new, seasonally relevant opening.

❖ FIGURE 10-1   Aggressive Mailing Plan

Year 1—Total Quantity, 750,000

	Jan.	Feb.	Mar.	Apr.	May	June	July	Aug.	Sept.	Oct.	Nov.	Dec.
In-mail	—	—	—	—	—	—	—	—	9/2	—	11/2	—
In-home	—	—	—	—	—	—	—	—	9/4–9/22	—	11/4–11/22	—
Quantity (thousands)	—	—	—	—	—	—	—	—	250	—	500*	—
Type	—	—	—	—	—	—	—	—	New	—	Remail	—
No. of pages	—	—	—	—	—	—	—	—	32	—	32	—
% new	—	—	—	—	—	—	—	—	100%	—	None	—
Segments	—	—	—	—	—	—	—	—	Rented	—	Rented	—
	—	—	—	—	—	—	—	—	—	—	House	—
	—	—	—	—	—	—	—	—	—	—	Multi	—

Year 2—Total Quantity, 2.1 million

	Jan.	Feb.	Mar.	Apr.	May	June	July	Aug.	Sept.	Oct.	Nov.	Dec.
In-mail	12/27	—	3/10	—	—	—	—	7/29	9/2	10/15	11/15	—
In-home	1/2–1/10	—	3/14–3/23	—	—	—	—	8/3–8/12	9/5–9/15	10/18–10/25	11/28–12/5	—
Quantity (thousands)	400	—	200	—	—	—	—	250	250	500	500	—
Type	New	—	Remail	—	—	—	—	New	Remail	New (partial)	Remail	—
No. of pages	32	—	32	—	—	—	—	48	48	48	48	—
% new	40%	—	Same	—	—	—	—	40%	Same	15%	Same	—
Segments	House, all	—	House segments	—	—	—	—	House, all	House, segments	House, all	House, segments	—
	Requesters	—	Requesters	—	—	—	—	Requesters	Requesters	Requesters	Requesters	—
	Rented	—	Rented	—	—	—	—	Rented	Rented	Rented	Rented	—
	—	—	Multi	—	—	—	—	—	Multi	—	Multi	—

Year 3—Total Quantity, 5.3 million

	Jan.	Feb.	Mar.	Apr.	May	June	July	Aug.	Sept.	Oct.	Nov.	Dec.
In-mail	12/27	2/2	3/2	4/2	5/15	—	7/2	8/2	9/2	10/2	11/2	11/27
In-home	1/2–1/10	2/7–2/15	3/7–3/15	4/7–4/15	5/20–5/27	—	7/7–7/15	8/7–8/15	9/7–9/15	10/7–10/15	11/7–11/15	12/2–12/10
Quantity (thousands)	750	500	300	400	300	—	250	400	400	500	750	750
Type	New	Remail	Remail	New	Remail	—	New	Remail	Remail	New	Remail	New
No. of pages	48	48	48	32	32	—	48	48	48	64	64	48
% New	35%	Same	Same	20%	Same	—	20%	Same	Same	40%	Same	50%
Segments	House, all	House, segment	House, segments	House, segments or all	House, segments	—	House, all	House, segments	House, segments	House, all	House, segments	House, segments or all
	Requesters	Requesters	Requesters	Requesters	Requesters	—	Requesters	Requesters	Requesters	Requesters	Requesters	Requesters
	—	Multi	Multi	—	Multi	—	—	Multi	Multi	—	Multi	Multi
	Rented	Rented	Rented	Rented	Rented	—	Rented	Rented	Rented	Rented	Rented	Rented

Total for 3 years = 8,150,000

* Only mail this heavy, this late in the season, if fulfillment has on-line inventory capability and high fulfillment commitment.

Re-mail has cover change only. (Re-mail may not be necessary if there is minimal duplication of names between mailings.)

Remails, in some cases, have been known to make enough money to pay for a loss on the first mailing. Because most catalogers attribute the cost of producing the catalog to the first mailing, remails are very inexpensive. The remail cost is based on postage and the incremental expense of printing a larger quantity once you are on press. Remails are most often sent only to customers and the multiple names from the merge/purge of rented lists (these are the names that appear on more than one rented list), which will be discussed in Chapter 11. Thus, there can be no rental name cost.

Be aware that there is some degradation in response every time a customer receives the same catalog. By monitoring this degradation, you can determine how many times it is profitable to contact your customer with the same catalog. All in all, remails can be a very efficient means of staying in touch and generating added sales.

A Less Aggressive Mailing Plan

You certainly do not have to build your business as quickly as the aggressive plan indicates. For the less aggressive plan shown in Figure 10-2, you would probably not use as many pages as in the first plan, so you would need less merchandising. This plan shows what it would be like to launch a catalog in what is usually the second-best selling season. Although the overall quantity for Year 1 is higher than in the more aggressive plan, the first quarter quantity is lower. As in the aggressive plan, mailings should occur approximately six weeks apart. None of the catalog versions in Year 1 have cover changes due to the small quantities in each mailing. Compare the quantities used in Year 2 of this plan with those in Year 3 of the more aggressive plan. In this plan, Year 2 remail versions all have cover changes.

Contact Strategy

There is more to saying in touch with your customers than just mailing them expensive catalogs. It is common knowledge that if you are not in the front of your customers' minds, the temptation to buy elsewhere may be too strong and you will lose their orders. So construct ways of staying in contact other than just mailing more solicitations.

Postcards, which are inexpensive and have high deliverability due to their first-class status, are one way that has found favor with many catalogers. Here you have the opportunity to leverage a catalog that is already in the customer's home with a special offer. Other catalogers make it a point to send customers birthday cards, anniversary cards, Thanksgiving cards, and Christmas cards. In-the-mail research also counts as part of your contact strategy.

❖ FIGURE 10-2   A Less Aggressive Mailing Plan

Year 1—Total Quantity, 950,000 (600,000 if program is launched in last quarter)

	Jan.	Feb.	Mar.	Apr.	May	June	July	Aug.	Sept.	Oct.	Nov.	Dec.
In-mail	12/27	—	3/10	—	—	—	—	—	9/2	—	11/1	—
In-home	1/2–1/10	—	3/14–3/23	—	—	—	—	—	9/5–9/15	—	11/4–11/14	—
Quantity (thousands)	200	—	150	—	—	—	—	—	200	—	400	—
Type	New	—	Remail	—	—	—	—	—	New	—	Remail	—
No. of pages	32	—	32	—	—	—	—	—	32	—	32	—
% new	100%	—	Same	—	—	—	—	—	40%	—	Same	—
Segments	House, all	—	House, all	—	—	—	—	—	House, all	—	House, all	—
	Requesters	—	Requesters	—	—	—	—	—	Requesters	—	Requesters	—
	Rented	—	Rented	—	—	—	—	—	Rented	—	Rented	—
	—	—	Multi	—	—	—	—	—	—	—	Multi	—

Year 2—Total Quantity, 2.5 million

	Jan.	Feb.	Mar.	Apr.	May	June	July	Aug.	Sept.	Oct.	Nov.	Dec.
In-mail	12/27	—	3/2	—	—	—	—	8/2	9/15	—	11/2	—
In-home	1/2–1/10	—	3/7–3/15	—	—	—	—	8/7–8/15	9/19–9/28	—	11/7–11/15	—
Quantity (thousands)	500	—	300	—	—	—	—	300	400	—	750	—
Type	New	—	Remail	—	—	—	—	New	Remail	—	Remail	—
No. of pages	32	—	32	—	—	—	—	32	32	—	32	—
% new	35%	—	Same	—	—	—	—	35%	Same	—	Same	—
Segments	House, all	—	House, segments	—	—	—	—	House, all	House, segments	—	House, all	—
	Requesters	—	Requesters	—	—	—	—	Requesters	Requesters	—	Requesters	—
	—	—	Multi	—	—	—	—	—	Multi	—	Multi	—
	Rented	—	Rented	—	—	—	—	Rented	Rented	—	Rented	—

Year 3—Total Quantity, 3.4 million

	Jan.	Feb.	Mar.	Apr.	May	June	July	Aug.	Sept.	Oct.	Nov.	Dec.
In-mail	12/27	—	3/2	—	5/15	—	7/2	8/15	—	10/2	11/2	11/27
In-home	1/2–1/10	—	3/7–3/15	—	5/20–5/27	—	7/7–7/15	8/18–9/2	—	10/7–10/15	11/7–11/15	12/2–12/10
Quantity (thousands)	750	—	300	—	200	—	250	400	—	500	500	500
Type	New	—	Remail	—	Remail	—	New	Remail	—	New	Remail	Remail
No. of pages	32	—	32	—	32	—	48	48	—	64	64	64
% new	35%	—	Same	—	Same	—	20%	Same	—	40%	Same	Same
Segments	House, all	—	House, segments	—	House, segments	—	House, all	House, segments	—	House, all	House, segments	House segments or all
	Requesters	—	Requesters	—	Requesters	—	Requesters	Requesters	—	Requesters	Requesters	Requesters
	—	—	Multi	—	Multi	—	—	Multi	—	—	Multi	Multi
	Rented	—	Rented	—	Rented	—	Rented	Rented	—	Rented	Rented	Rented

Total for 3 years = 6,850,000

Note: This plan shows what it might look like to begin in the second-best selling season. Therefore, quantity for the year is higher than Aggressive Mailing Plan, but first quarter is lower.

Mailings must be approximately no less than 6 weeks apart (except for fashion and other highly disposable product lines) to the same segment.

No cover changes due to small quantities.

❖ **EXAMPLE 10-1**
Betty Crocker offers customers
a chance to double their points
and get an added discount on
their already low-cost
merchandise.

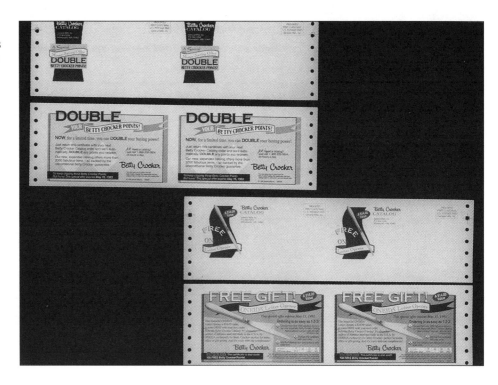

❖ **EXAMPLE 10-2**   Calyx and Corolla sends customers birthday cards containing the company's 800 number,
making it simple for them to order last-minute floral gifts. Eddie Bauer offers $5 off future purchases.

Contact strategies should plan out the different types of incentives you may wish to test throughout the year. Figure 10-3 shows an example of a contact strategy plan. (See more on incentives in Chapter 9).

❖ **FIGURE 10-3** **Sample Contact Strategy Plan**

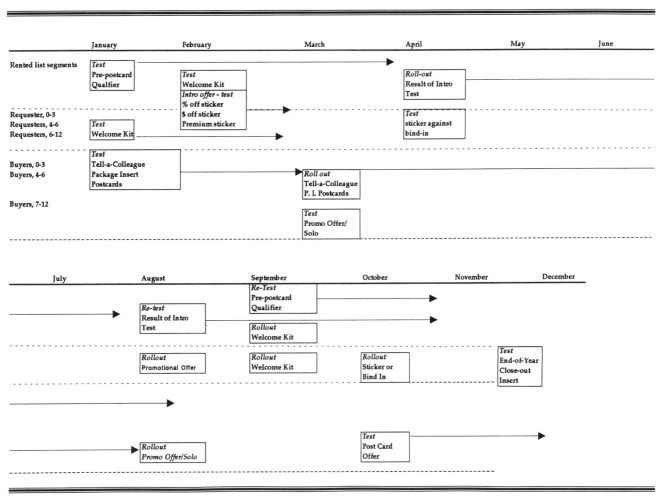

Reactivation Strategy

Once someone buys from your catalog, they'll stay with you forever, right? Wrong. Attrition rates can run as high as 50 percent. But, with work, this number can be reduced substantially.

To get sales from those who have not bought, first understand that there are really three types of customers and that they should not all be treated the same:

1. Requesters who have not purchased

2. One-time buyers, also called *trial resisters* (a packaged-goods term for someone who has bought from you once just to try you out and who is resistant to change)

3. Multibuyers who have not purchased recently (inactives)

This latter group is segmented according to RFM value and, if you have the capability, buying patterns (product category, product affinity, and so on). Programs should be developed for each of these three segments because, in many cases, they will not respond to the same stimuli.

Requesters

Requesters should be treated as the special people they are. Be sure they're sent a package that acknowledges their interest in your company and provides an incentive to purchase. Test this against a plain package without a message and a plain package without an incentive (a three-way test).

Then send a series of mailings to these customers. Whether each mailing needs a different message is something else you must test regularly, but many catalogers find that exactly what you say in each part of the series is important to converting requesters into buyers.

One-Time Buyers

You got the first order, but they failed to respond again. What did you do wrong? Again, treat this group differently. Send them a "welcome-to-our-family" kit that quickly and succinctly tells them what makes your company special (you can also test a mini-version of this at the requester stage). Test sending the kit in outgoing introductory packages versus in the mail right after the first order. Include an incentive, and, if possible, a concrete reminder to buy, such as an 800-number sticker or a premium.

An incentive is, more often than not, the most effective method of prompting another order. J. Crew's conversion testing includes wraps—letters saying "Thank you for the order" and explaining what J. Crew is all about. In all, single buyers receive a letter and three coupons to use over a six-month period. Offers are $10 off, free shipping and handling, and free express service. J. Crew also sends a customer-satisfaction questionnaire that, if returned, gives the respondent a coupon.

Inactives

Those who have purchased more than once but have ceased to purchase within a specified time frame should be a primary target for reactivation. View the reactivation process the way magazine companies view subscriptions. They use carefully planned appeals to sell a longer subscription well before the current one runs out. Each offer is determined by how long the reader's name has been on file.

Planned reactivation has the built-in benefit of purging your list of those who truly do not belong there. Past customers who are identified as steadfastly resistant should be moved off the list, rested, or deleted, depending on their potential value. Don't ignore an inactive customer just because he or she has been inactive for a while. Clean the list (see Chapter 11) and mail inactives an incentive; many catalogers find that the older the name, the better the customer's response to incentives.

The offer that works best will depend on your market and the product line you offer. Test a variety of methods, such as stickers versus cover changes, staggered bonus plans (a reward system by which you offer more savings as the customer spends more, this works well for furniture cataloger Yield House), and bind-ins. Some catalogers, such as After the Stork, a children's clothing catalog first offer $5 off to those who have not ordered for 18 months or more. Then they move to a last-chance sticker. In After the Stork's case, the stickers did not generate enough extra revenue to pay for the cost of the incentive. After the Stork also sends a clearance book to those customers who have been on the house list longer than two years.

Other catalogers use yes/no double-sided postcards as the third wave of their efforts, after they have tried the incentive and last-chance techniques. Simple in design, the postcard merely asks the customer, in a straightforward manner, to check "yes" or "no" to indicate whether or not he or she wishes to continue to receive the catalog. It is not intended to influence, only to get a true reaction. Its main purpose is to clean your list, but it has the added benefit of causing a lift on those who say yes as it appears they feel guilty about committing to more catalogs. The response to this postcard can be anywhere from 30 percent to 80 percent, depending on how loyal customers were to begin with. And, as you would expect, the range of those who say yes and those who say no is just as great. Again, it depends on the state of your list, how far back you are going, and to whom you are sending.

What do you do with those who do not respond? No one likes to delete or rest a name, so most catalogers keep mailing. But customers who say no mean it; several tests of these respondents proved they did not wish to purchase from the catalogs they refused. If you are really averse to deleting the names from your database, rest them for a few years, then clean them (NCOA) and try another test.

Planned reactivation is not always the answer. For example, it might be less effective for a children's list, because the age of the children dictates their (and their parents') buying behavior, and furniture catalogs, which need to rely more on list segmentation by buying patterns than on trying to prompt impulsive buying of a nonimpulse product. Also, if you determine that, even mailing very frequently, your customer segments pay out, you may not want to use reactivation. Exposures, a company that sells photographic frames and accessories finds that even though it mails its customers as frequently as 13 times per year—with more established customers getting 9 to 10—it does not need a reactivation program because all the issues make money.

Adapt these important techniques to your business; they can help ensure that you keep those all-important customers buying!

 ❖ CHECKLIST

✔ Always use a mailing plan.
✔ Allow for seasonality.
✔ Remember that quantities will affect your postage discounts.
✔ Whenever possible, amortize costs with remails.
✔ Prepare a formal contact strategy.
✔ Be ready to create a reactivation strategy so you can control attrition.

CHAPTER ELEVEN

Mailing Lists

Mailing-List Basics

The selection and rental of mailing lists—the names and addresses of prospective customers who have something in common—is the fastest and most economical method of both obtaining initial customers and building a base of customer names. The strategy you use to choose the names you rent can make or break your venture. The right names get orders, thus building your customer database: The wrong ones don't. Let's take a closer look at mailing lists and how you can put them to work for you.

Types of Lists Available

As already stated, a mailing list contains the names and addresses of prospects or customers who have something in common. These prospects fall into several categories.

1. Catalog mail order buyers. Those persons who have purchased goods from a catalog. Most often these are the best respondents.

2. Catalog requesters. Those who have requested a catalog but have not purchased from it. The request can be paid (the respondent paid a small fee, usually $1 to $2) or nonpaid (the catalog was free). Generally, paids will respond better than nonpaids.

3. Space-ad respondents. Those who have purchased a product through a magazine or newspaper advertisement but are not necessarily catalog customers.

4. Direct-response customers. Those who have purchased a product through the mail but not from a catalog or a space ad. These consumers can be good respondents, depending on how closely the products they bought match your product offering.

5. Subscribers. Those who have subscribed to a publication but are not necessarily mail-order product buyers. If their profile is extremely close to your targeted market, subscribers can be worth investigating.

6. Names derived from compiled lists, such as business and professional directories, telephone directories, and warranty registration lists. In the past, lists derived from such secondary sources were not highly effective. More recently, however, such lists have been distilled from large amounts of general data and sufficiently enhanced by demographic overlay information to make them occasionally effective for customer acquisition.

7. Fund-raising or political donors. Those who have responded to an appeal for contributions to a nonprofit organization. They are not necessarily open to purchase from a catalog but should be investigated as your catalog grows.

8. Electronic-media respondents. Purchasers of products sold via electronic solicitations, such as cable TV, are usually much more receptive to electronic offers than to catalog offers.

9. Sweepstakes "no's." Those who have entered a sweepstakes but said no to the product, service, or fund-raising offer are not a prime source for catalog mailings. (Sweepstakes "yes's" are part of the catalog's buyer file.)

10. Telephone-marketing respondents. Those who have responded positively to telephone solicitations. Worth testing, these respondents have good conversion rates for some mailers.

Data-Card Information for List Specifications

Mailing-list information is available on data cards or mailing-list cards. All information about a mailing list, no matter what the category, includes the number of consumers and their (three-line) home addresses or their (four-line) business addresses. Telephone numbers are sometimes available at an additional cost of about $20 per thousand, with most offered at $15 per thousand. In addition, the card contains many or all of the following facts about the composition of the mailing list:

◆ A gender breakdown.

◆ The source of the names (mail order, space ads, inserts, and so on).

◆ The average order size in dollars. Be wary of this one. Average order size may be "cummed," meaning that it represents the amount the person has spent

❖ **EXAMPLE 11-1**   Examples of mailing list cards from (a) Hanna Andersson and (b) Coldwater Creek show the information normally found on these cards.

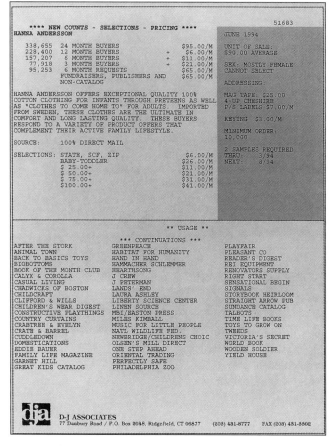

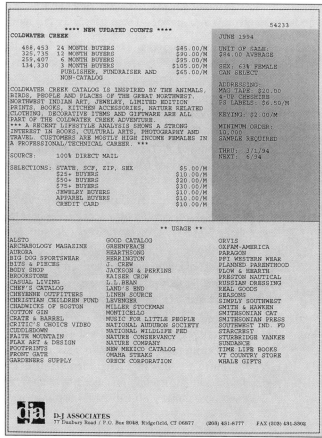

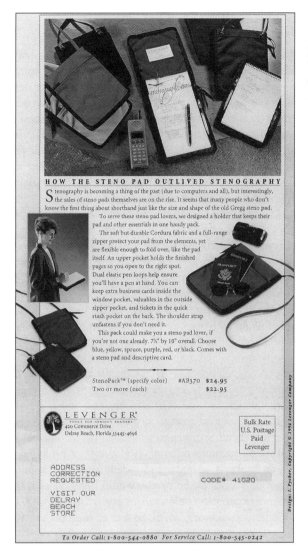

❖ **EXAMPLE 11-2**
Levenger source code labels have two tints—yellow and blue—to assist operators in directing customers to the numbers they need for coding.

with that catalog over a specific time period; it may be the average amount of the customer's last orders; or it may be the amount of the customer's last single purchase. Ask.

◆ Recency and number of names (the names on the list during certain time intervals, such as customers from the past three months, six months, and so on).

◆ The rental price per thousand, plus the cost per thousand for "selects," the segments, such as product category, chosen over and above the base list price. (Selects are discussed later in this chapter.)

◆ The minimum number of names that can be rented.

◆ Merchandise categories, when available.

◆ Type of addressing (Cheshire, magnetic tape, pressure sensitive).

◆ The state (sectional center facility (SCF—the first three digits of a five-digit zip), and zip code.

◆ Key-coding and tape charges.

◆ Information regarding the product line offered by the list owner.

◆ Demographics, if available.

◆ Foreign selects.

◆ The number of samples required.

◆ Usage

Just because a particular select is not listed on the data card doesn't mean it does not exist. Ask your broker.

List Brokers as Agents

The list broker acts as an agent in the mailing-list transaction and provides research services, professional judgment, and detailed recommendations on lists that may be profitable for you. A good list broker works with you to develop a marketing plan that includes both list testing and recommendations for subsequent "rollout" (continuation phases) based on initial test results. In addition, a broker should ensure that the names you ordered are delivered to the right location on the right date in the right format.

The broker must also present your catalog to the list owner for approval (owners have the right to refuse anyone). List owners clear the intended mailing date to see that competitive offers are not mailed at the same time. The broker bills you (the mailer) and transmits payment to the list owner/manager.

Commissions (usually 20 percent of the basic list price, which does not include selects) are paid to the brokerage firm by the list owner for the rental of the list, so there is no charge to the cataloger for the broker's services. Also be aware that brokers' commissions are negotiable if you are a larger mailer with millions of names and work primarily with one broker. Their services are one of the best values in the entire mail order supplier spectrum.

One of the greatest advantages a list broker has is daily contact with lists that work—valuable information for you, the client. Your broker may well recommend new lists or special categories that have recently performed well for other mailers with offerings similar to your own. The broker can, in most cases, also tell you which lists have been continued by certain catalogers. This is valuable information, because it tells you which lists your competitors have rented more than once. When receiving such information, be sure to clarify which lists are continuations and which are merely one-time tests.

It is to your advantage to give your broker as much information as possible (about your merchandise mix, past results, and so on) and enough time to put together an intelligent and useful recommendation. (Be sure your broker is not working with a competitor.) It is to a broker's advantage to recommend only lists that will give superior results. This is not only because he or she would like you as a long-term client, but also because a brokerage company only realizes profit through rollouts—seldom from small, initial tests.

When considering which broker to use, ask the following questions:

1. Does the broker's client roster include customers with products or markets similar to your own? Brokers tend to specialize in specific areas. Be sure to choose one with expertise in your market, not one who is trying to be all things to all people. But also make certain that your broker is not currently handling a competitor.

2. Is the broker currently recommended by other mailers or catalogers?

3. How did your initial mailing fare? Were the results reasonably good? If the broker made errors in list recommendations, and you have given him or her the results, has the broker taken obvious corrective action or has he or she continued to make the same or sadly similar recommendations?

4. As your program progresses, does your broker suggest new segmentation strategies and state-of-the-art demographic analysis?

Don't be dazzled by a personality. Ask your broker hard questions and expect to see bottom-line results.

The Highly Negotiable Rental Transaction

The basic list-rental transaction is for one time only, excluding remails (the mailing of virtually the same catalog to the multiple buyers obtained after a merge/purge of all the lists into one database). The rental names you and your broker select are taken from another mailer's "response" list or a compiled list. Usually a minimum number of names (5,000 to 10,000) must be rented from a response file. Compiled lists, depending on their size, require either a minimum or (if small) full rental. Response lists run from $45 to more than $100 per thousand; compiled lists cost about $40 to $45 per thousand. The selects often contained in response files can cost an additional $3 to over $40 per thousand each. (See the "List Selection and Usage" section later in this chapter.)

The list renter can be charged in two ways. *Gross payment* means a straight payment basis for the full quantity of names ordered. If you rent 5,000 names, you pay for 5,000 names, no matter how many are actually used. For instance, if you rent a list with a base cost of $60 per thousand and one select at $10 per thousand, the cost for 5,000 names would be $350. Gross payment is usually the only way you can rent names in the testing, or small-quantity, stage.

However, in the rollout stage, a big opportunity for price and quantity negotiation emerges, commonly known as a *net name* basis. The list owner is very often willing to offer some pricing flexibility in response to broker prodding. Negotiations are common in list rentals, so don't hesitate to employ them.

Net name payment makes a lot of sense because, when you rent a large quantity of names from several mailers, a certain percentage of names is inevitably duplicated among files. Duplication is determined during the computerized merge/purge process, which matches names against each other and finds the duplicates. Duplication can be quite large if you have targeted a small niche or been in the business a while. The owner of each selected rental file wants to be paid on the most lucrative basis possible but is usually willing to compromise for guaranteed payment for 85 percent or less of the names, regardless of whether the file is duplicated to a large extent among the files selected.

Under this arrangement, even if you mail only 75 percent of the names unduplicated, you still pay for 85 percent. On the other hand, if you mail 92 percent of the file, you have to pay for the full 92 percent. With this agreement, the owner's revenue is protected regardless of overlap, and you at least don't pay the full 100 percent for list quantities not used. Such an arrangement is generally negotiated for an order of 50,000 or more. Names you would not pay for include the usual intrafile dupes (duplicates within the individual rental files), DMA suppress file names (Mail Preference Service), and, in this case, names hitting against the house file (to the 85 percent or other preset limit).

You may well ask who decides which list owner gets paid and which doesn't. If the random allocation system is used during the merge/purge, payment is randomly allocated as well. However, because negotiations made prior to the merge/purge can make it financially beneficial for one list to receive more "hits," or duplicates, than another, some mailers use a hierarchy system during merge/purge. This places those rentals that have agreed to a net deal in a position where they will receive more hits than they would if they were "deduped" in a random allocation merge/purge.

Lately, however, the incidence of hits during merge/purge has risen, with many large mailers experiencing a net of only 40 percent to 70 percent. Some catalogers led the way in offering "net/net" names. In this case, the list owner agrees to charge only for the names actually netted after the merge/purge. This type of arrangement is negotiable for mailers renting larger quantities of names.

Net/net becomes even more important as mailers increasingly make use of computerized overlays, such as credit prescreens and geographic soliciting. In a computerized overlay, lists are overlayed with other data, such as geography or demographics, then filtered to "distill" the desired net combination. Paying for all the names needed to net a small, targeted amount has historically been prohibitive for many catalogers who could benefit from such enhanced lists. Be prepared to negotiate strongly and openly with the list owners/managers of databases that lend themselves to sophisticated manipulation. It is to everyone's advantage to pay for only what you use; the mailer wins because his or her cost is reduced, and the list owner wins with more frequent rentals.

As your catalog grows and you acquire customer names of your own, consider an alternative to renting: exchanging. The approach to an exchange of names varies from company to company. Competitors who may not rent to you will sometimes exchange. Generally, the more similar their market is to yours, the better the chance the list will perform well. But be aware of a potential limitation: Some established catalogers will allow further rentals only if you agree to exchange once you have names of your own. Usually, only one cost is involved: a brokerage fee of $8 to $10 per thousand for negotiating the exchange, processing it, and following through the order. (There is no broker's fee for selects either on an exchange or rental basis, and sometimes list owners exchange directly and avoid the base brokerage commission.) In addition, there is a computer-running fee of about $3 per thousand. Exchanges save mailers upfront dollar costs, thereby lowering the in-the-mail cost on a particular list.

List Selection and Usage

To develop the best possible list-rental strategy, a mail order marketer must first determine the customer profile. All rented lists should be selected for their suitability for testing against the existing or targeted customer profile.

Your Customer's Profile

For catalogers with an existing house list, constructing the customer profile means research, careful response analysis, and scrupulous maintenance of the customer list. The same essential facts shown on other list owners' data cards, such as education level, hobbies, buying habits, and income, must be gathered for the house list. This can be gathered through research (see Chapter 3) of your list and appending data to that same list. With data appending, your list is processed by a service bureau which runs it against outside lists, matching and adding information from those lists to yours. Your customer list must also include transaction histories (purchase and payment performance) and be segmented according to source, frequency of purchase, size of purchase, category of merchandise purchased, long-term value based on several buying seasons, recent purchases, and so on. This information should be collected as part of the fulfillment process (see Chapter 13). The more you know about the people who buy from you, the more successful you'll be in hunting for more like them. But keep in mind that the customer profile may change with each new catalog response analysis, so be sure to update your records.

Other Selection Factors

Both new and established catalogers need to ask themselves some critical questions before deciding which mailing lists to rent.

◆   What is the major thrust, image, or product of your catalog? What motivates customers to purchase? Is the catalog classic or high-tech? What makes it unique—quality, originality, or price? Is the merchandise geared to a particular life-style?

◆   What are the limitations on quantity, budget, mailing plan, and committed inventory? Have certain list categories been exhausted?

◆   What is the primary financial objective—immediate dollar return using minimum-risk lists (which may have smaller universes for potential rollout), or breakeven or slightly less return from higher-risk lists (which have huge universes and the potential for larger rollouts)?

Your answers to the first group of questions will help you determine the list type, in terms of life-style, best suited to your catalog's image. For example, if you sell medium-priced traditional home furnishings, you would be more likely to rent a list such as Williams-Sonoma's, which consists of buyers of gourmet cooking accessories that have relatively low price points, than a list such as The Sharper Image's, which consists of buyers of electronic items with higher price points.

Your answers to the second group of questions will help you identify your limitations. Budget, of course, is always a major consideration. But, especially for new catalogers, the size of the print run should be determined by your business plan, which is somewhat affected by the potentially profitable list quantities you can select, not the other way around.

Inventory should also influence this decision. If the merchandise you intend to stock is readily available, the size of your mailing need not be limited. However, if inventory is restricted, it might be wise to mail less or stagger your mailing to avoid running out of merchandise. As more product-category history becomes available, you can make inventory commitments with greater knowledge and comfortably increase mailings.

The primary financial objective, addressed in the third question, is obviously to make as much money as possible. Minimum-risk lists should always be tested first; you can expand into higher-risk lists later. Build a strong customer base, one that responds in hefty dollars, before testing marginal lists. Don't overlook long-term growth strategy, but make viable list selections so you are still around to complete your long-term strategy.

Plan your mailings on a per-category basis, testing several categories with the intent of rolling out (continuing) to more lists of the same type per category. This method adds structure to your thinking and testing, and gives you more than immediate results; it helps direct you to future list possibilities.

Selects—The Categories within a List

Another important consideration in list selection is the available *selects*, or descriptive categories by which the names in the list are grouped. The selects you choose can make or break your list program.

Merchandise Categories

Once you establish that a rental file contains names of people who have purchased goods similar to those you offer, you can sometimes zero in on purchasers of specific product categories, such as home furnishings, dining/entertainment, kitchen/pantry items, or decorative accessories. For the most part, this detailed product-selection option is available only from list owners with large universes. If the universe is large and a product category is not on the list card, ask your broker if one is in the process of being compiled.

Demographics

Most lists contain several demographic descriptors. They may all be crucial assessment factors, but only some of them may actually be available to you as selections. A rental-list profile often contains information breakdowns by gender, occupation, marital status, number of children, income ranges, education levels, and home ownership. The gender and age breakdowns are the ones most commonly available for rental. Beyond this selection, however, demographic information usually consists of aggregates or averages and is therefore of analytical value only (see Chapter 14).

Recency

The recency of a prospective customer's last mail-order purchase from a given company is a relatively good indicator of overall interest in mail-order offers. Recent customers are often active customers for the file's owner and for other mail-order companies as well. Almost all rental files contain ''hot line'' selections of customers who have purchased goods within the past zero to three months. But be cautious. Don't simply assume that a purchase was made in that time. The three- to six-month period depends on list updates and mailing times. Always clarify actual dates with your broker.

Frequency

The frequency select is often available as multibuyers, meaning those who have purchased more than once from a particular list. However, this information should be qualified by both time period and dollar amount spent. A customer who has made only a few purchases (none of them recent) over a three-year period could be presented as a frequent buyer or multibuyer. Frequency can be a valuable select, but only if you have a true understanding of what the list owner considers frequent.

Monetary Value

In list-rental terms, the monetary value refers to the dollar volume purchased by a selection of customers. Catalog lists are often available by average order amount. If your average order amount is, or is targeted to be, $50, it may not be profitable for you to rent a $20 select, since the majority of the list would show a purchase history below that of your target.

However, check the actual number of names within dollar selects. You may find the higher dollar qualifier has only a small percentage more than the lower dollar qualifier, making the higher dollar select (at its additional cost per thousand) not worth renting. Again, check to be sure that your understanding of average dollar order is the same as the list owner's and the manager's representing the list. Some average dollar orders represent the customer's last purchase; others are cumulative and represent a total buying history in dollars spent.

Geography

Most list owners offer state, zip, and SCF selects which allow you to rent their lists of specific states, zip codes, or SCFs. A motivating factor in choosing one of these selects is whether your merchandise appeals to customers in a certain region. The primary motivation, however, is to acquire more customers from the same zip code areas that have been successful in previous mailings.

Mail order customers are not spread evenly throughout all the zip code areas but tend to cluster in particular areas. Zip clustering computer programs, such as Acorn® and Prizm®, have proven useful in segmenting the national zip codes into groups. Therefore, if you can determine the particular characteristics of the zip codes in which your customers live, you could profitably select other areas that have these same characteristics.

Psychographics

Another method of obtaining prospects similar to your customer profile is called *psychographics*. The theory here is that people who have similar life-styles purchase merchandise in a similar pattern. The method is to run the house list against a rented database of names. This will help you determine your customer profile. Then, other names on the same database that fit the profile can be rented. You can take this even further than a general profile: You can identify buying patterns. If your house list, when run against a rented database, shows that 70 percent bought cameras within the last year, this might prove to be an excellent market for film or developing services, which you may choose to incorporate into your merchandise line. Be aware that catalogers have had mixed results using psychographic techniques. The value seems to vary for different catalogs. Innovative catalogers investigate this technique as their need for more names arises.

Source Media

Simply put, source media tell you from what source a list originated. Since you are prospecting by mail, you initially want to reach only those segments of a list owner's file that contain mail order–generated customers. Many companies have other sources for their customer names—such as lists of retail-store customers and gift recipients, sales leads, warranty-card registrations, and package-insert respondents—and they make these available for rental. In addition, customers can be acquired from other direct-response media, such as space advertising, telephone marketing, and direct-response television. The best match for a cataloger is the highest possible concentration of direct-mail–generated customers. If, for instance, you cannot specifically select out space-ad purchasers as opposed to direct-mail purchasers, the list card should specify the percentage that were direct-mail–generated.

Method of Payment

What method of payment was used by the majority of purchasers in a given rental file? Some owners offer selects based on the type of credit card used. This can be important, because some house-credit customers tend to respond less favorably than bank credit-card customers. Conversely, bank credit-card purchasers can prove to be a better select than those customers who paid by check, for the simple reason that credit-card customers often spend more.

Changes of Address

Changes of address (CHADs or COAs) can signify an upgrade in housing accommodations, an increase in income, or a promotion or transfer—and increased purchase of goods to go with these changes. The more recent they are, the better they tend to work.

Nth Name

When testing a list on a national basis, make use of the *nth name select*. This means that for a test of 10,000 names from a list universe or select of 200,000, you would receive every twentieth name. A true nth select gives you a valid cross section of the list tested.

However, in some instances, due to policy or computer-operator error, you may receive a list that is not a true nth select. Obtain a count by state or SCF from the computer service house for each rented list at the time of the merge/purge. Discrepancies will be evident. For example, an nth-name test may reveal zips no higher than 70000 (zips run from 00600 to 99999). In this case, the cataloger would lose in two ways: (1) Washington, California, and Texas, all high-response mail order states, would be missing, and (2) the test results would be somewhat invalid.

So insist that list orders specify true nth name selects. If, even after your best efforts, you discover that you did not receive an nth name select, try to negotiate a reduced list-rental charge for future testing. Do this only for lists whose response indicates they are worth the effort, even with proper nth name select.

Essential Self-Help Steps

Selecting the right lists for prospective mailing is a challenging task. Get all the help you can from your list broker, but do your own homework, too. On an ongoing basis, read the data cards that are mailed out by owners and managers. Your broker(s) can arrange for you to rent these lists. Standard Rate and Data Service, Inc. (3004 Glenview Road, Wilmette, IL 60091), publishes an extensive directory of lists, which provides new issues six times a year with semimonthly updates. Although thorough, this service can be overwhelming to the catalog newcomer. Purchase one to familiarize yourself with the types of lists available, then decide whether to subscribe. For full details, contact the vendor.

Beginning with your first mailing, meticulously record all list-rental activity and list selections tested. Systematically assign source codes to the customer-identification information used in the label key-coding step of the merge/purge (see "Merge/Purge" later in this chapter) and mail-preparation processes. An easy-to-read code, established when the initial response arrives, can be used for a list's entire purchase-performance history. By analyzing winning selections, you will be able to derive a marketing strategy for new audiences and categories with proven performance.

List prospecting will always be with you. Even experienced mailers have to compensate for a drop in customer activity or the attrition of their customer file. So establish your internal systems for list selection before your first drop in customer activity.

List Testing

List testing is an almost universally accepted convention. It allows a renter to mail a test quantity—say, 5,000, 10,000, or even 50,000 names—from another marketer's file to determine that file's suitability. Depending on the test results, the cataloger decides whether to go deeper into the file for more names (a rollout); he or she has no obligation to do so. Testing measures the performance of lists and/or list segments against each other to come up with a winning combination. Most often, a mailing consists of a combination of initial tests, rollouts, or previously tested lists, and the cataloger's own customer list.

Sample Size

One of the first questions you need to ask before testing a list is, "What quantity should we test per list?" The answer isn't, as some might think, "We'll just test the minimum requirement." Nor is it, "This list looks like it's a really close match to our market. Let's test a large number of names." Keep the following points in mind when you determine sample size:

- ◆ The higher the desired confidence level, the larger the necessary sample.
- ◆ The higher the expected test-response percentage (up to 50-percent response), the larger the sample necessary for the same confidence level.
- ◆ The wider the acceptable error limits on duplicating the test results, the smaller the necessary sample.

The sample size tested should be determined by a combination of these factors plus the potential universe to which you can roll out. Because the rollout may not perform as well as the test, statisticians have developed what is called a *confidence level*—meaning the level of confidence that the rollout will respond at the same rate as the test. A 90-percent confidence level means that 90 times out of 100, the rollout response will be within certain limits of the test response. Table 11-1 demonstrates this. As an extreme example, at a 99-percent confidence level, a 5-percent test response, and a $\pm.1$-percent error limit, a sample size of roughly 315,000 is needed. At the other extreme, at a 90-percent confidence level, a 1.5-percent test response, and a $\pm.5$-percent error limit, a sample size of 1,600 is adequate.

The tables are valid only if the sample size is smaller than one-twentieth, or 5 percent, of the total list size. If the test sample is greater than 5 percent of the total, you must use what is known as a finite population correction factor. This formula can be found in any standard statistical text.

Although the figures in Table 11-1 are intended as a guide, rollouts generally should not exceed three or four times the initial test quantity. In some cases, test panels are prearranged—the 5,000 or 10,000 names for the test are generated from the most recent mailings rather than from the overall list. This recency factor can create an artificial test response, which will lead to a statistically inaccurate rollout. One way to avoid this situation is to test odd numbers of names, such as 6,500 rather than the more standard 5,000. Ask your list broker to recommend list quantities that are most likely to have accurate results on rollout.

Error Error Limit (±)	Test Response							
	1.5% (.015)	2.0% (.02)	2.5% (.025)	3.0% (.03)	3.5% (.035)	4.0% (.04)	4.5% (.045)	5.0% (.05)
90% Confidence Level								
.001	39,891	53,038	65,959	78,745	91,396	103,910	116,292	128,537
.002	9,995	13,260	16,489	19,686	22,849	25,977	29,072	32,134
.003	4,442	5,893	7,329	8,749	10,155	11,546	12,921	14,282
.004	2,488	3,315	4,122	4,921	5,712	6,494	7,268	8,034
.005	1,599	2,122	2,638	3,150	3,656	4,156	4,652	5,141
95% Confidence Level								
.001	56,760	75,295	93,639	111,791	129,751	147,517	165,093	182,476
.002	14,190	18,824	23,410	27,948	32,438	36,879	41,273	45,619
.003	6,307	8,366	10,404	12,421	14,417	16,391	18,344	20,275
.004	3,547	4,706	5,852	6,987	8,109	9,220	10,318	11,405
.005	2,770	3,012	3,746	4,472	5,190	5,901	6,604	7,299
99% Confidence Level								
.001	97,967	129,960	161,621	192,951	223,950	254,615	284,952	314,955
.002	24,492	32,490	40,405	48,238	55,987	63,654	71,238	78,739
.003	10,885	14,440	17,958	21,439	24,883	28,291	31,661	34,995
.004	6,123	8,123	10,101	12,059	13,997	15,913	17,809	19,685
.005	3,919	5,198	6,465	7,718	8,958	10,184	11,398	12,598

Merge/Purge

Put simply, merge/purge is the purging of duplicate names by the computerized merging of all the list tapes you have rented. This process can save you thousands of dollars and your customers the annoyance of receiving multiples of the same catalog.

How Merge/Purge Works

1. Together with the list broker, you develop a list-rental schedule. The broker places the orders, with instructions for all tapes of rented names to be shipped to XYZ service bureau (this function is almost universally entrusted to a computer service bureau) by the predetermined date on which the merge/purge is to take place.

2. Each list owner's tapes arrive at the service bureau, where they are converted to a common format.

3. All "suppression tapes" are run against the duplicate-free tape. Suppressions include mailed segments of the house list, a house "bad debt" file (if one is maintained or subscribed to), unwanted zips, and the Direct Marketing Association (DMA) Mail Preference Service (MPS) tape. The DMA tape contains the names of approximately 3 million consumers in 1.7 million households, who have specifically asked that their names be deleted from direct-mail promotions. The monthly and quarterly files are updated against the U.S. Postal Service's National Change of Address program. Those requesting that they be on the list are added quarterly. This is a self-regulatory measure designed to offset any federal regulations against the use of mailing lists in general. Be sure that the service bureau you select uses the DMA MPS tape as a standard policy. It is extremely important that direct marketers help to enforce this self-regulation. Most service bureaus have cooperated with this effort by not charging for the service (see Chapter 12).

4. Eventually, through a systematic passage of tape against tape, a master tape, as duplicate-free as is currently possible, is constructed from the customer and

rented files. During the process, duplicate names are "knocked out." The names on the master tape are next sorted into zip code sequence. Then the number of names for each zip code can be counted to determine the zip codes that qualify, by density, for the U.S. Postal Service's (USPS's) presort levels (carrier route or five/three digit zip), which provide additional postal discounts. Those that qualify are arranged in presort sequence. The product is a tape or tapes, ready for printing on the label format selected for ink-jet or laser printing.

5. View what you have rented. A good service bureau will let you review samples (some even have on-line capability), which helps you verify you actually received what you paid for.

6. The service bureau should provide an easy-to-understand, detailed report, by list, of the duplication output counts (number of duplicated names by list). The broker follows up with each list owner, reports the results of the merge/purge, specifies the payment to be remitted according to prior arrangement, and participates in any post–merge/purge negotiations.

7. A good service bureau gets the job done on time. Getting the list to your lettershop late can be disastrous.

Purging Methods

The two main methods of duplicate elimination are fixed match code and mathematical equivalency algorithm. Each has its adherents, as well as its merits and problems. Both are complicated mathematical techniques. In simplified terms, the differences are as follows:

1. The *fixed match code* compares fixed elements of the computer-generated names and addresses as a means of identifying duplicates. This method does not identify duplicates as accurately as its counterpart.

2. The *mathematical equivalency algorithm* (sometimes called a *variable match code*) works similarly, but picks up more elements, weighing the value of more complex duplications. Today most service bureaus use algorithms, which allow levels to be set for different locations.

Duplicates or Multis

Since the performance of a list is based on the names it contains, the allocation of multibuyers (duplicates) is an important consideration. For the greatest accuracy, random allocation is the most-often-used method. First, duplicates in the house list should always have priority. After that, duplicates should be randomly allocated among the lists being purged. This will help ensure that each list retains its rightful proportion of multibuyers and that the response will be valid for each list. If, for example, the list that runs first receives the lion's share of multibuyers, the test results will be skewed in its favor.

Len Schenker, president of Anchor Computer, Inc., made some very good points in an article he wrote for *DM News*. Len advises:

Review with your merge/purge service what a duplicate is. As an example, if you're doing a consumer merge/purge, do you only want one to go to a household with the same last name? How about the junior/senior situation, one or two catalogs? How about multiple people at the same address, is that okay? Ask the company if there are differences in the way they identify duplicates between an urban area and a rural area. In rural areas, what might be identified as a duplicate, in a very small populated area, irrespective of address, may not be the same way that one should handle it if it was midtown Manhattan. . . . You should be able to select and key multibuyer segments within the job for check purposes and potential remailing.

It has become common practice to negotiate, upfront, the remaining of multibuyers. These names can be sent a second and even third solicitation at no extra rental fee if the mailing date, and the right to do so, are cleared prior to rental. Many catalogers use this technique to extend the holiday mailing season. A catalog is mailed with a scheduled remail of virtually the same catalog to house list and multis around mid-October—sometimes even mid-November.

Merge/Purge Costs and Savings

The cost of the merge/purge varies, depending on the computer service bureau. A typical cost would be $3 per thousand inputted names and $2 to $4.50 per thousand outputted names, depending on the form of output; tape or Cheshire labels cost less than pressure-sensitive labels. If we assume a mailing of 500,000 names and a duplicate rate of 15 percent, the input of approximately 588,000 names at $3 per thousand would cost $1,764. The output cost for the 500,000 names on tape, at $2 per thousand, would be $1,000. In some cases, there may be additional charges, depending on the number of lists tested. Zip-string creation may also cost extra.

In this example, you would save the in-the-mail cost of some 88,000 catalogs. A comparison of this amount with the cost of merge/purge shows why almost all catalogers use merge/purge. If the mailer is on a net name basis for list rentals, he or she could realize further savings of up to 15 percent on rental costs. In addition, a potential customer is not alienated by receiving a deluge of identical catalogs.

Zip Code Correction

If the response to a mailing is 2 percent or 3 percent, then 97 percent or 98 percent of prospective customers do not buy. One reason is that a certain number never receive catalogs because of incorrect zip codes. Today, most computer service bureaus will check for incorrect zip codes as part of their merge/purge operation, then match and correct the codes. In most cases, you pay only for the corrections, not the valid deliverable matches, so this procedure is cost-effective.

Although the numbers vary from list to list, assume that 5 percent to 35 percent of the addresses in a list do not have the correct zip/state combination. The catalog arrives at the wrong post office and is either forwarded to the correct one (unlikely) or not delivered. Considering the lost orders on a large mailing (the cost of each catalog thrown away), zip code correction clearly enhances results. (This is also discussed in the "National Change of Address System" section later in this chapter.)

Mail and Telephone Preference Service

A lot of people think they understand Mail Preference Service (MPS) and Telephone Preference Service (TPS) and are doing what they are supposed to do, but too often this is not the case. Remember that MPS and TPS are part of a database compiled by the Direct Marketing Association (DMA). It contains the name of individuals who do not wish to receive direct marketing solicitation by mail (MPS) or phone (TPS). Our industry runs these names against rented and house lists before mailing or calling. The major motivator for using these services is the possibility of governmental legislation that could be restrictive to list-rental needs.

Even if you do not rent names you need to use MPS. Running MPS past your house file gives you the opportunity to evaluate just what your definition of a customer is. For instance, if people who have said they don't want mail are on your house list, are you sure this is someone to whom you should be mailing? This is especially true if these names are older than 6 to 12 months.

It's true that nobody wants to give up names. But if customers have taken action to state their desire not to be on mailing lists, are you sure they have purchased from you recently enough to intentionally exclude you from this desire? Here is a chance for good customer service. If there is any possibility they don't want to be mailed, write and ask them. Position this correspondence so that your customers know you care about mailing responsibly. Then back it up with an offering within a few weeks. See if the halo effect increases sales. This way you'll do the right thing for the industry effort (and, ultimately, your business) and maybe immediately help your bottom line.

If you rent outside names, are you sure they have been run through MPS? Don't assume your service bureau is doing this. Ask and be sure.

There is absolutely no reason not to use MPS. Most service bureaus don't charge for the service. And, with the new data compression method being tested now, the time to run the tapes has gone literally from hours to minutes. If you have not heard about this new compression technique, you'll want to, so ask your service bureau.

Of course, there is much more than just running names against MPS. You must communicate this option clearly to your customers *and* prospects, both in writing and on the phone. Just how do you go about understanding and adhering to all that is being asked of you?

The DMA has a guide that tells about effective self-regulation called *Privacy: The Key Issue of the 90's*. This free publication has real examples you can use, so you don't have to spend a lot of time figuring out what your next steps should be. It will answer, in a clear, informative way, all the questions you have about MPS and TPS.

Another comprehensive brochure from the DMA is called *Opening the Door*. It's one thing for management to want to do the best job possible when it comes to MPS; it's another thing to make sure that employees are clear as to what they should do to make that happen. This attractively illustrated booklet is the educational tool that will help you ensure that the right training is in place.

Your List as a Profit Center

The primary reason for building a house list is to have a future market for your products. But the great sums of money you spend on list rental also create a potential profit center. As the owner of a valuable mail-order file, you retain control even if you decide to place your list on the rental market. You decide who rents your list, what portions to rent, and when to rent them. You have the final authority to approve or reject whomever you choose.

Renting Your House List

To offer your list as rental property, you should have at least 5,000 current (0- to 12-month buyers) names, and you should be implementing the following guidelines:

1. Continuously and actively build your customer base. The more names you have, the greater the potential for rollout and the more attractive your names are to possible renters. See Chapter 12 and be sure to code captured names by source.

2. From the very beginning, maintain segmentation data. Income from the rental of selects, such as recency, frequency, and monetary value, can substantially contribute to list-rental revenues.

3. Constantly work to obtain more information about your customers. The quest for life-style or demographic data should be never-ending. This information can be collected from customer surveys, telephone contact, customer-service input, fulfillment-package communications, and so on. Although your main reason for this effort should always be to benefit your catalog operation, the information gained will also help give your list an excellent market position and most certainly result in more rentals.

4. Keep your list in tip-top shape. Make frequent use of the USPS address-correction services and be sure that your order form encourages customers to note address changes. Incorporate this information into your files

immediately. Be sure to segment/delete names of customers who have opted for Mail Preference Service from any names you rent. Lists that are poorly maintained tend to generate poor responses, resulting in lower rollout income for their owners. Even more important, an improperly maintained list could translate into inferior sales for your own catalog.

Your List as a Source of Revenue

Renting your customer list can be a major source of revenue, especially if your list is well maintained and offers such selects as recency and dollar amount.

Some segments of your house list will be rented more often than others, and overall list-rental income will be a function of how well your list performs during testing by other mailers. An estimate of net annual rental income is $1 per name, but the figure can be considerably higher for a desirable list that is used regularly by many catalogs.

Assume a list rents for $80 per thousand names and has a $50-plus (average order) select at $10 per thousand additional, and a 0- to 6-month select at $5 per thousand additional. If both selects were taken, the gross revenue would be $95 per thousand names rented. Against this revenue, costs would include $24 in commissions for the broker and list manager (30 percent of the basic rate, which is $80 per thousand). Computer costs for a tape or Cheshire labels would be $2 to $3 per thousand, depending on the run. The cost of any labels would be passed on to the renter. Tape reels are sometimes provided at no charge, if they are returned, and the renter pays the freight charges. List maintenance and update costs are not considered here, because these functions would be performed even if the list were not available for rental. The renter ends up with net revenue of $68 per thousand (or $53 per thousand names if no selects are taken).

The annual net profit from list rental can be shown as an asset amount (the value of the list) on your balance sheet at the end of the year. Some catalogers also add the net yearly merchandise sales profit generated by their house list to their balance sheet as an asset. (The balance sheet should not be confused with the income profit-and-loss statements, on which these items always appear.)

Exchanging Lists

Another way to obtain revenue from the house list is through list exchanges. Some lists can be obtained only through exchange; others can be either exchanged or rented. Exchanges diminish list-rental income, but may be of more overall profit than rentals. For example, assume the same prices noted in the previous section for the house list ($68 per thousand net) and the list you obtain in the exchange, and a cost of exchange of $11 per thousand for the exchange. This means you are paying only $79 per thousand for a list that would have cost $95 per thousand to rent—a savings of $16 per thousand. This can change a marginal list into a profitable one.

Don't assume that every time you exchange lists you forgo rental income. Your list may not always be as desirable for rental as it is for exchange; by exchanging, you may be cutting your costs without losing rental revenue, as exchanging with some catalogers does not mean that you will lose rental income from others.

House-List Maintenance

List maintenance refers to the periodic updating and cleaning of the house list. Of increasing importance to catalogers is the fact that improperly maintained lists mean poor deliverability. If, as is usual, the catalog's own customers outperform those from rented lists, these valuable customers must not be lost because of this lack of maintenance.

At the time of receipt, any change-of-address notifications (for instance, postcards) received from customers should be input into your data files. The time period between updates usually depends on how often you mail. The more frequently you mail, the more frequently you should update your list.

Most house lists are maintained by computer service bureaus that own large mainframe computers. The best and least expensive method is to furnish your bureau with the order tapes generated by the in-house or data-entry service computers. The least desirable method is to send a printout or list of names, addresses, and order data, because it has to be entered by hand and checked for accuracy at considerable expense. Nowadays, most service bureaus can convert data from other formats to tape at a reasonable cost.

Usually, the computer service bureau also generates the tapes for those who are renting test or rollout segments of the customer file. The house list is set up to segment not only by nth name, but also by other selects the cataloger may offer, such as dollar and hot line. Again, the list's desirability for rental depends on how often it is updated and cleaned.

But before you put your list on the market, talk with representatives from a couple of knowledgeable list management companies. They can help you determine the potential worth of your list over a period of time. One disadvantage is that your customers will be receiving solicitations that may reduce their overall buying power. Whether this will adversely affect your catalog operation's bottom line is a decision only you can make through testing. If you have a large list, a smart move is to rent only a portion of it, then test the rented panel versus the unrented panel to see if sales are adversely affected. Some catalogers have discovered that list rental actually boosts sales from their customers. Should this not be the case for you, you always have the option of withdrawing your list from the marketplace.

Some catalogers today are also concerned about their customers' privacy and, for this reason, have withdrawn their lists from the market. Keep abreast of the ''winds of change'' when it comes to this potentially volatile subject, and understand the effect not renting your names will have on your overall business, not just the immediate financial aspect.

Your List Manager

If you decide to put your list on the market, you will need a list manager. You have two choices—internal or external management. Internal management uses staff time and budget allocations for such essentials as marketing, order processing and trafficking, and invoicing and collection. An in-house manager is completely familiar with the list and can devote his or her full attention to it. However, since good list promotion takes time, money, and expertise, in-house management is generally better left to large, established catalogers. Smaller companies usually do not have the experience or the time to do the job properly and, as a result, can lose valuable revenues.

Outside list-management firms specialize in marketing list properties to the direct-mail industry. Acting as the list owner's agent—for a typical commission of 10 percent of the rental fee—the outside manager prepares data cards for the list and promotes the list through direct-mail promotions, space ads, personal selling, trade shows, and more. Outside managers also handle all the processing functions, from coordinating mail-date clearances to collecting rental revenues. They work closely with list brokers to familiarize them (and their clients) with the merits of your list. If you think an outside list-management firm may be right for you, research the firms you consider, keeping the following points in mind:

♦ **Specialties**. Some firms specialize in certain areas. If a firm specializes, does it match your needs?

♦ **Performance**. How well has the firm promoted the lists it manages now? Ask to speak directly to some of its clients.

♦ **Size**. Consider how well the size of your business fits with the size of the firm's business. Will you be too small to get proper attention or too big for its staff to handle?

Decoys

Are you concerned that someone will unlawfully use your list more than once or mail it on an unauthorized date with an unapproved offer? To discourage and deter such practices, the direct-marketing industry uses a *decoy* (or *dummy*) system of *seed* (or *salt*) names. These names, which are purposely spelled in a unique manner (for example, Katie Muldoon might be shown as Catherine T. Muldune, with a similar change to the address), are planted in a mailing list. Should the recipient, who knows the approved rental details, receive an unauthorized mailing, the renter faces legal consequences and general censoring in the industry. Although not foolproof, this system discourages most attempts at misuse.

Increasingly, however, this system is running into problems. Multibuyers (the most responsive names which appear on a multitude of lists) are identified in a merge/purge, and because seeds are unique to each list, the multibuyers may be reused with relative impunity. Conversely, if the decoy name used isn't totally unique, it may inadvertently match a real name and accidentally get removed during the merge/purge. Obviously, with zip selects, the simple fact that only a geographic portion of your list is being rented can mean that the decoys you have on your list are not present in the zips selected. Database overlays can be a problem, too, as some public databases provide information on real households, but not always on your decoys.

The industry is aware that, as list enhancements and techniques become more sophisticated, so does the opportunity for misuse of the lists. New services, such as T. J. Litle Co. (Nashua, New Hampshire), use state-of-the-art systems to prevent unauthorized usage. Be aware that such companies exist and don't hesitate to investigate how their services can help protect one of your most valuable assets—your customer list.

Decoys have one other great advantage: They help you track catalog delivery as it moves across the country. Awaiting results is nerve-racking enough. With a system of decoys placed throughout the country, in urban, suburban, and rural areas, you will know when and where your catalog is delivered. This information helps both your results analysis and your peace of mind.

Taking Other Catalogers' Package Inserts

Another potential income generator is the rental fee for allowing others to put their solicitations in your outgoing packages. The solicitations, which must abide by the size you determine (see Chapter 12) can either be inserted loosely in the package or be contained in an envelope. If you put them in an envelope, it should contain a message indicating that your company endorses the offering inside.

The charge for package inserts ranges from $40 to $75 per mission and works under the same commission structure as the one used for renting your list. Your list manager will likely have, within his or her organization, a person who specializes in package inserts and will promote your insert program as part of your list-rental business.

List Usage Guidelines

The Direct Marketing Computer Association of New York City has attempted to present organized guidelines for the use of lists. Called *The Direct Marketing Association's Guidelines for List Practices*, it is available from the Ethics Department, Direct Marketing Association, Inc., 1101 17th Street NW, Suite 705, Washington, DC 20035-4704. This brochure is divided into three parts. The following guidelines are excerpted from this document.

General

1. All lists should be described accurately.
2. All advertising claims should be truthful.
3. All parties should agree to the lists' intended usage prior to usage of the lists.
4. All involved with list transactions should be responsible for the proper use of list data and should take appropriate measures to assure against unauthorized usage.

5. List rentals, unless otherwise agreed to, are for one-time usage.

6. Marketers should offer a means by which a consumer's name may be deleted or suppressed upon request.

7. Lists should consist only of those data that are appropriate for marketing purposes.

8. Direct marketers should be sensitive to the issue of consumer privacy.

9. Direct marketers should operate in accordance with all applicable laws, codes, and regulations.

Considerations for Mailing List Transactions

1. Clearly identify all parties in the transaction.
2. Understand what is being transferred.
3. Be clear as to what constitutes use.
4. Further, clarify the definition of "one-time use."
5. Know and agree to the method and basis of payment.
6. Set up what is to be received, where, and when.
7. Get and abide by approved mailing content and mailing date.
8. Understand such impacts on others as the potential prohibition of time periods for competitive mailings, use of MPS, seeding, and so on.

Suggestions for Advertising Acceptance

1. If the offer is unclear to you, it will be equally unclear to the recipient.
2. Make yourself the surrogate reader.
3. Decide what is in good or bad taste for your audience.
4. Know, via your broker, fraudulent addresses.
5. Be extremely careful of advertisements with no address which require the use of a toll-free number and charge card to order merchandise.
6. Be wary of payment for advertising with insufficient funds or account-closed check.
7. Use seeds or decoys to confirm the list was mailed the piece you approved.
8. When in doubt, ask for a sample of the merchandise.

As stated, this is only a partial listing; be smart and send for the original, which outlines the points in detail.

The National Change of Address System

As the in-the-mail costs of catalogs increase and many catalogers see a higher customer-acquisition cost, it becomes increasingly essential that catalogs are actually delivered. The post office has been under fire for some time for its suspected high undeliverability rate. The USPS presently records that 4.3 billion pieces of mail per year are undeliverable as addressed because the recipient has moved.

In an attempt to stop the rise of undeliverable mail and cut unnecessary costs for both the post office and mailers, the USPS has developed the National Change of Address System (NCOA). The service allows mailers to correct their address lists prior to mailing and consolidates all change-of-address information on one centralized computer database. This file is maintained in a zip + 4 format, updated monthly, plus a change-of-address file which is updated every two weeks. To participate, you must append zip + 4 coding to each address record as part of the NCOA process. Arthur D. Little Company (Boston) provided a study indicating that this procedure should correct at least 10 percent of the mail now handled. Not all service bureaus can provide this service, but there are many from which you can choose.

One of those selected, Direct Marketing Technology, spells out the advantages of this service in its newsletter:

Without NCOA

You would lose the cost-in-the-mail together with the cost of the mailing and the cost to key the correction.

If undeliverable as addressed, your mailing piece could be destroyed.

Your house files have more duplicates than are being identified.

With NCOA

Your net cost after NCOA processing may save thousands of dollars on your total mailing.

Improved deliverability—larger percentage of lists reaching targeted households.

Multis are identified before the merge/purge.

Also, according to Direct Marketing Technology, the processing sequence should take from one to five days and, depending on your mailing frequency, may not need to be used every time you mail.

As previously noted, lists and their selection are vital to a program's overall health. For an excellent, in-depth look at lists, C. Rose Harper's book, *Mailing List Strategies: A Guide to Direct Mail Success*, (McGraw-Hill), is highly recommended.

Database Marketing

A *database* is a collection of facts set up in a systematic manner and retrievable in many ways. A simple example might be a telephone directory: Here, the facts are the names, addresses, and telephone numbers of people in a specific area; the system is alphabetical. In another case, the telephone numbers might be for a government agency and the system set up by departments.

Types of Databases

Most catalogers today use databases. They have found that the more closely you can define your potential audience and maximize catalog delivery to those who fit the definition, the better the profits. This type of marketing is also cost-effective.

Database marketing has been made possible by the surge in availability and lower costs of computer systems. The ability to store, sort, and analyze large amounts of data exists today even with personal computers. In addition, using personal computers interactively with mainframe allows the cataloger virtually unlimited computing power. The types of analysis that can be performed, such as multivariate regression, can indicate the nature of profit-producing customers. This knowledge can be combined with other databases to efficiently find new customers.

Three types of databases are normally used in catalog marketing:

1. The in-house customer list, indicating not only names and addresses, but all the data on purchase patterns, sources, and so forth.
2. The output data of the analysis of prior mailings, such as list or house-file segment performance, geographic analysis, and so on.
3. Outside data banks, such as demographic overlays, life-style overlays, market-mapping programs, and ethnic data.

In its simplest form, the database program might be used to segment your house list by recency, purchase, or dollar unit of last order. Or, to set up an initial mailing of a new specialty catalog, you might segregate the names of all those who have purchased merchandise in particular categories. A more complex example is the matching or overlaying of your own database of names and addresses against a geographic/demographic census database. From this matching, you might obtain not only a demographic profile of your catalog customer, but also the geographic regions in which new customers are most likely to be found.

Market-research data can be added to your database to enhance its value. This could allow you to determine specific characteristics of the "best" customers and match them with compiled lists.

Database Technology

In order to better understand database usage, you should be familiar with a few basic terms. A *record* is a set of data describing specifics—an individual customer, item, transaction, or the like. For example, a customer's name and address may form one record. A *field* is one of the pieces of data in a record. For example, the name area in a customer record constitutes a field.

A database has a *multilevel architecture*. This is because the database needs to support three types of users: (1) the catalog company as a whole; (2) those who are using the database for answering questions or for analytical applications; and (3) the data-management system itself, including the machine that must retrieve, manipulate, and update the data.

These three levels are called *conceptual, external,* and *internal.* Each of these levels has a specific "user" associated with it. The *conceptual level* is associated with the organization as a whole (one user); the *external level* with the applications developers and those who need applications programming to answer their questions (for example, marketing managers); and the *internal level* with the data-management and data-entry groups (something catalogers need to look for when investigating databases or creating their own).

Types of Database Designs

There are three types of database designs in general use: *hierarchical, network,* and *relational. Semantic,* a fourth type (or perhaps a new subset of relational), is also slowly coming into being.

Hierarchical and Network Databases.   *Hierarchical* and *network databases* have limitations that specifically affect catalog business data, and therefore are not discussed at length here. These limitations include the following:

1. They can represent only linear relations, not many-to-many relations. For example, this would inhibit a cataloger from cross-referencing people in the database with multiple criteria such as purchases, geographic location, and so forth.
2. They have problems representing recursive relations. For example, a cataloger would have difficulty pulling the names of people who had previously purchased a particular item.

The Relational Database.   For the sake of a simplified description that is of use to catalogers, we might consider a *relational database* as having the appearance of a checkerboard, extended downward and to the right. The columns would have the fields, and the rows would be the records. No two rows would be the same (think of unique names in merge/purge operations). You can sort data any way you want. We could, for a very simple example, select any of the following:

1. All those with certain values in the third column.
2. All those with data entries on the red squares.

3. All those with a zip code of 10011 and a last purchase date within the last six months.

Among the advantages of relational databases to catalogers are higher degrees of

♦ **Data independence**. The ability to change the data or data representation without affecting the application programs. For example, adding large numbers of customer records is much easier with a relational database than with any other kind.

♦ **Extensibility**. The ease with which new application programs can be added.

This particular type of database might be used to generate the best customers to mail a spin-off catalog, or it might be used to determine which customers should not get particular mailings. This process needs to make use of the techniques discussed in Chapter 14.

As database usage becomes more sophisticated, those who fully understand its applications will undoubtedly have an advantage over those who do not. Keep up to date, read, and listen: The information is there to be learned—and improved on.

❖ CHECKLIST

✔ Know the types of lists available and their hierarchy when it comes to response.
✔ Learn to read a data card.
✔ Do research to find the right broker and provide him or her with enough information to guide you in your selections.
✔ Negotiate all list rentals.
✔ Compile and understand your customer's profile.
✔ Choose selects wisely.
✔ Be sure your sample size will allow you statistically valid roll-outs.
✔ Work with your service bureau to customize the merge/purge to your needs.
✔ Use MPS and TPS.
✔ Understand the overall business impact of renting your list.
✔ Work with your service bureau to avoid unauthorized use of your list.
✔ Use NCOA regularly on house and rented names.
✔ Collect information on your customers from the start in order to tap database marketing.

CHAPTER TWELVE
❖ ❖ ❖

Customer Acquisition

Whether you're a first-time cataloger or an old-timer, the acquisition of new customers must be a top priority. Like any other business, cataloging has an attrition of customers and to grow a business, these customers must be replaced with new ones. Obviously, you also need to have more people buying regularly (which satisfied customers do), so you want to keep adding new names to your customer files.

This chapter will show you some of the methods other than lists that you can use to attract new buyers. Mailing lists are still the number-one method used, but space ads and package inserts can also prove valuable. There are also new acquisition methods, such as on-line ordering direct from your computer as well as ads on the sides and/or back of your favorite cereal box (or some other packaged product).

Beyond Mailing Lists

Why are mailing lists the method most often used to acquire customers? The reason is quite simple: They almost always give the highest return. When you rent a mail order list of catalog buyers, you are soliciting someone who has already shown a propensity to purchase via the mail or phone. This is not necessarily true with, say, space advertisements, where the audience includes those who choose to buy by mail and those who don't. As you recall from the previous chapter, all individuals who actually order—from mailing lists or any other form you use to solicit an order—become yours and go onto either your customer list (if they have actually purchased something) or on your requester list (if they have requested a catalog but have not yet purchased).

Those entering direct marketing for the first time may wonder how they could ever need more names than appear on mailing lists. But there are five reasons why you can soon run out of names. First, catalog buyer lists have a high duplication factor, which results in fewer usable names. Second, only a certain portion of available lists meets the profile needed by your catalog. Third, many other catalogs use the same lists, resulting in increased competition. Fourth, some lists are available only on an exchange basis, whereby you exchange a predetermined quantity of your names for a predetermined quantity of another marketer's names. And fifth, some owners of large lists have taken their lists off the market, decreasing the overall pool of names available.

Catalog mailing lists are an essential part of your customer-acquisition program, but definitely are not the whole story. There are some other methods you should consider.

Space Ads

The main purpose of most space ads is to generate new customer names—customers who will purchase products from the catalogs you send them. In addition, they provide credibility and, of course, advertise your catalog as a brand of choice.

Calling for Media Kits

Your first major decision is where to run your ads. Investigate what publications are available by reading a Standard Rate and Data Service (SRDS) publication for Consumer Publications. You can purchase one directly from SRDS (offered as a subscription or by individual issue) by writing to SRDS, 3004 Glenview Road, Wilmette, IL 60091, Attn: Circ. Sales. You also can review one at your local library. Get copies of publications by sending for free media kits. Also, be sure to tell the magazines' representatives that you are a direct advertiser and expect direct-response rates. These are substantially less than general advertising rates. Generally speaking, direct ads will fall at the back of the magazine, but this is not always true, so check. The response is usually higher in the front of the book than in the back. As you become more experienced in magazine advertising, look into remnant rates. *Remnant rates* are the "leftover" spaces that have not been sold. One specialist in remnant space is Stephen L. Geller, Inc., Greenwich Office Park, Building Two, Greenwich, CT 06831-5115.

Reviewing the Magazines

Be sure to look through several issues of the magazine you are considering. Do lots of other direct-marketing companies advertise in this publication? Do those companies repeat their ads again and again? If there are no direct-marketing ads, don't be talked into running in the publication no matter what the magazine's representative says. What is the environment in which the ad will be appearing? How will this affect the creative presentation you will be making? For instance, if the environment is busy, you will want to keep your ad simple so it stands out.

Creating a Media Plan for Testing

As you did for your mailing lists, put together a media plan that tests different categories of magazines, such as food, fashion, shelter (home-type), and gardening. Select one or two magazines per category (depending on your budget), with the idea that if these magazines succeed you will have others in the same category to try in the future.

If your budget allows, also test different offers and/or approaches in the same magazine in the same month. Most magazines will offer A/B splits if the ad is of a certain size (one-third is usually the minimum size). *A/B splits* mean that every other issue will contain a different version. Make sure it is a true A/B split, not some other type of split, and that you are testing every other issue. There is almost always a charge over and above the cost of the ad insertion for an A/B split. Create a control ad (the one you believe has the best chance of succeeding; often the most traditional approach), then design an offer and creative approach that you believe has a chance of "beating the control." Be sure to have dominant source codes in each version so you can track the response. And make certain your telephone operators ask for and collect those codes. There is no point in testing if you do not collect the information necessary to understand the results.

Don't forget to test frequency of insertion. One time in a publication may not give you an accurate read of the results. Seasonality also can be very influential in results (the same as it is with your catalog mailing), so be sure to factor both frequency and seasonality into what you see in responses.

A media plan should also indicate expected response. This is a tricky point for those without experience (and even for those with it!). One way to approach the financial aspect is to determine, for product ads, how much you will need to generate to pay for the space. Although most catalogers do not actually make back their investment on the first order, this can be a gauge of whether you believe the publication's readers will be responsive enough. The true measure of success in space advertising is the responsiveness of the customer over time, and this is determined by lifetime value (discussed in Chapter 11).

After you have completed a media plan outline, like the one in Table 12-1, clarify your objectives by answering the following questions in writing:

- **What is the target market?** State the psychographic assumptions.
- **What is the print media budget?** State dollars allocated.
- **What is the media objective?** Indicate both overall and specific objectives.
- **What are the print media strategies?** State both overall and specific strategies, including unit, timing, frequency, costs, geography, position, and testing.
- **What is the media selection rationale?** Explain what criteria the media must meet to be selected.

Determining Your Budget

Although your media budget is highly individual, one rule of thumb is to use 1 percent of your gross sales. A direct marketing agency will generally research the publications, create the media plan, and place the space for you for a standard agency commission of 15 percent. This percentage becomes more negotiable the more space you place. Alternatively, you can hire a media specialist. These progressionals will do the same as the agency, but often have a set fee rather than charging a commission.

Running a Product versus Advertising the Catalog

Your second major decision is whether to run a product in the ad or just advertise your catalog. Some catalogers believe that customers who respond to an ad featuring a product are responding only to that product and will not convert to catalog buyers. Others believe that, by showing a product, you will not only help offset advertising costs but will also give the respondent a better indication of the kind of merchandise your catalog carries, resulting in a better catalog customer. Omaha Steaks, for instance, found that single-product space ads worked ten times better than catalog-only ads (although this is an exception). It believes one reason for this is because the company image—in this case, a supplier of juicy, mouthwatering steaks—is important.

In most cases, product ads will pull less initial response, but will convert a higher percentage. The product must be representative of your entire catalog line. It does no good to generate a high response for a particular product, but, because that product is unique to itself, not see the magazine respondent convert to a catalog respondent!

Color ads used to be considered prohibitively expensive by most marketers. However, as obtaining customers has become more difficult and "standing out from the crowd" more essential for attracting new customers, four-color ads have been increasingly used. For instance, Blair features a lot for the price in an off-the-page sales full-page ad, whereas Lands' End creates what appears to be a very effective black-and-white ad with a timely message about its quick delivery. Because the investment is greater for color, even more care must be given to monitoring the true value of a customer (discussed later in this chapter).

❖ **TABLE 12-1**
Media Plan Outline

Advertiser
  ◆ State the name of the company.
Product
  ◆ State the name of the product.
Geography
  ◆ State national or regional limitations.
Seasonality
  ◆ List any that applies.
Competition
  ◆ List primary and secondary competitors.
Creative tests (such as different art or copy approaches)
  ◆ Indicate splits, what tests are.
Results summary
  ◆ Indicate what results are expected and in what stage the program is (test, rollout).
Key marketing objective
  ◆ State the prime objective.
Target audience
  ◆ List key demographic assumptions.
  ◆ List key psychographic assumptions.
Print media budget
  ◆ Indicate dollars to be spent in this time frame.
Media objectives
  ◆ State the overall objective then amplify it with specifics.
Media recommendation
  ◆ State the time period this recommendation covers, then construct a grid such as the following:

Media Insertion Grid for Circulation and Cost

Circulation (thousands)	Issue on Stand Date and Closing	Net Cost	Net CPM	Unit (size and color of ad)

Total circulation _____
Total cost _____

Media Demographics Grid for each Publication and its Demographics

	Publication #1	Publication #2	Publication #3	Publication #4
Gender ◆ Female ◆ Male				
Median age				
Median household income				
% married				
% who attended/ graduated from college				

Source: Courtesy of Iris Shokoff Associates.

❖ **EXAMPLE 12-1**
Using product and price, Blair tailors this ad to its target audience of active but value-conscious *Modern Maturity* readers.

❖ **EXAMPLE 12-2**
Lands' End can use a simple, straightforward black-and-white ad because its message meets an established need.

Determining the Size of Your Ad

Small Single-Item Ad.   A single-item, small space ad can be a challenge, as you must fit enough information into the ad to do a good selling job. Because it's small, the ad may get lost or buried in the magazine and not be easily seen by potential customers. Also, the coupon, toll-free information, guarantee, and so on leave little space for a photograph and copy. For example, Omaha Steaks forgoes inserting a coupon in order to show the product at its best in minimal space. Although this ad seems to work for Omaha Steaks, don't automatically forgo the coupon. Most catalogers use one, and the only way to know how it will affect response to your ad is to test it.

It's difficult to choose just the right products, so you'll need multiple ads. A/B splits are preferable, as running ads back to back in issues (different months) has a seasonality effect, and you won't really know if it was the product that affected the results or the month in which it ran. No matter what, be sure the product is keyed to the audience of your selected publication(s).

Choosing the perfect product can be difficult. One experienced direct marketer, who makes a comfortable living by selling products through space advertisements, reports that he is pleased if two out of ten products perform well. And this is after years of experience. One way to hedge your bet is by making sure the product run in the ad has been a consistent best-seller in the catalog. And remember, when running a product, you should always give your audience the chance to simply request a catalog.

Large Single-Item Ad.   The single-item, larger space ad (a half page to a full page) affords the cataloger an opportunity to incorporate more ''sell'' into the ad and reinforce the company's image. It also often receives a better position within the publication. But it costs more, so be sure the product is a terrific seller, the offer is unmatched, and/or the publications selected provide outstanding results.

Probably the most common size in this category is the one-third, either horizontal or vertical (which looks like one long column). This size, as previously stated, usually allows A/B split testing, makes a fairly dominant statement, and is relatively affordable.

❖ **EXAMPLE 12-3**
Cambridge Soundworks employs a one-third square to sell a product and advertise its catalog.

Weatherproof Music.
Factory-Direct Prices.

The smooth, natural sound of speakers by Henry Kloss (founder of AR, KLH & Advent) can now be enjoyed outdoors: on the patio, by the pool, even on boats. *The Outdoor* is a compact, water-resistant speaker with accurate, wide-range sound. It comes in two versions: one free standing (shown above, $279 pr.); one for in-wall mounting ($329 pr.). Both versions are very well made, with stainless steel hardware and gold-plated connecting terminals. Use them in white, or paint them any color. Because we sell factory-direct, with no expensive middlemen, these speakers cost far less than they would in stores. Call for a free catalog and find out why *Audio* says we may have "the best value in the world."

For a free catalog, or to order, call
1-800-FOR-HIFI (1-800-367-4434)
Suite 204, 154 California Street
Newton, MA 02158 Fax 617-332-9229

CAMBRIDGE SOUNDWORKS

The country's largest factory-direct stereo company.

❖ **EXAMPLE 12-4**
Omaha Steaks makes an introductory offer to acquaint potential buyers with the unique aspects of its steaks. Note Dept. code.

Multiproduct Ad.   A well-done multiproduct ad can give consumers a better feel for the kind and variety of merchandise your catalog offers and can give your company a credible image because several products are offered. The multiproduct ad doesn't rely as heavily on the selection of a just-right product, but it is extremely hard to design in an attractive, attention-getting, and understandable manner.

Catalog-Only Ad.   Another alternative, in large or small space, is simply to showcase your catalog for free or a price. This approach is used a lot by experienced catalogers because it enhances their brand and provides them with more responses than offering a product will—and the more mature the catalog, the more difficult it is to find new names.

Product/Catalog Ad.   The product/catalog request combination allows consumers the option of buying the product or sending for a catalog with more product choices. The potential customer feels more comfortable buying from a magazine advertiser that has the financial stability necessary to produce a catalog. The catalog and product shown together can graphically attract the customer's interest more strongly than can a single-product or catalog-only ad, and can give readers the feeling this is a "real" company, not an individual with only one product to sell. The sales of the product help cover the cost of the ad.

Some Basic Rules for Space Ad Design

If you think you have only a short time to gain and hold the attention of the prospect with a catalog, think again. It is even shorter with an ad, so keep your message simple and direct. Do not try to tell a long-winded story in a small amount of space. A very few, extraordinarily talented writers can write a long copy, full-page ad, but this should be left to those who specialize in this format. For the most part, think three points: the headline, the main visual, and the closing sell (usually your toll-free number).

If it can fit in the size you have chosen, always include a coupon and your toll-free number. Most space advertisers also advise putting your address somewhere in the body of the ad, not just in the coupon area. Keep the coupon clean and simple. Try writing on it yourself, and be careful about putting a tint or color behind it. If you use a tint, keep it pale and easy to write on. A company once ran a coupon that was black with white type—try to write on that!

Make your source code dominant, easy to read and spot, so when the customer calls, your phone operator can quickly point out where the code is in the ad.

As with any other kind of direct-mail writing, use a benefit head, one that directs the reader to take action. Make sure the visual will reproduce well in black and white and in color on a paper stock over which you will have no control. And keep the type a readable size and typeface.

Generally speaking, the magic price points are fairly low, say $19.95 or $29.95. There are exceptions to this, but remember you're asking the reader to overcome a price hurdle—don't make it too high.

Catalog Collections

Another method of acquiring new customer names is through the catalog collections offered by some publications. *Spin,* for example, charges $1,650 for a one-time, $1/12$-page insertion. Or you can buy a $1/24$th size for just $850. Both prices come down with more frequent insertions.

❖ **EXAMPLE 12-5**   Spin's catalog collection showcases a variety of different catalogs at a low cost.

Alternatively, there are companies that present their catalog collections in catalog format and mail them to mail order–responsive lists. All you need to do is send the publication a photograph or product shot and a brief description of your catalog (some will also require a copy or two of the catalog). The cost of insertion in publication-type collections is less than if you run the ad alone, and you realize the added impact afforded by a section devoted entirely to catalogs. Each publication has its own method of presentation and handling catalog inquiries.

When asked how responsive readers are to catalog collections, publications invariably produce impressive statistics. But remember the response statistics quoted are a summation of all the advertisers listed in a particular issue or for a specific time period. Ethically speaking, publications should not reveal the number of responses generated by individual catalogs, nor do they have access to the percentage of catalog requesters who convert to customers. However, catalog collections can be a cost-efficient method of obtaining new names, and acceptable percentages of respondents can convert to customers.

In the catalog-type collections, the cost of insertion is most often based on your responses. For instance, The Best Catalogs in the World™ charges 50 cents for each consumer name it generates for your catalog.

When dealing with any catalog collection service, be sure to find out how quickly you will receive your names. The Best Catalogs in the World, as with most such companies, provides ''names and addresses of the consumers who have selected and paid for your catalog on a weekly basis.'' Only you should have the right to these names; they are not to be used by the advertiser or any other participant in the program. Be sure this is part of your contract.

In most cases, you can tell the advertiser how you want to receive the names: pressure-sensitive labels, magnetic tape, or floppy disk. There is generally a small fee for this service. As with any contract, read the details so you know before you advertise exactly what to expect and what the costs will be.

❖ **EXAMPLE 12-6**
Shop at Home has an impressive array of catalog participants in this 60-page version.

A Catalog Collection Survey

To determine just how effective catalog collections were, Muldoon & Baer once conducted an "in-house" survey for an article printed in *DM News*. The information obtained gave valuable insight into why the value of any mode of customer acquisition is highly dependent on how well the order (in this case, a catalog) is fulfilled.

On September 15, the agency ordered 95 catalogs from "Selections," a catalog section featured in *The New Yorker*. The total cost of the 95 catalogs was $183.35. More than two months passed, and only 60 catalogs were received. The majority (35) of catalogs were sent by first-class mail and were posted anywhere from October 17 to November 10 with the vast majority mailed in the week of October 21–28. This meant it took an average of six weeks for receipt. Three mailers used United Parcel Service (UPS) rather than bulk or first-class mail, thus getting extra attention.

Mission Orchards sent a catalog in a UPS box (cost, $1.40), along with six delicious pears, effectively giving each requester a catalog and a taste sampler for the $5.00 charge. Mission Orchards also inkjetted the label on the box with this message: "Your Free Sample & Request Catalog." The back cover carried this message: "Here is the catalog you requested. Savings coupon inside. We look forward to serving you." The latter copy achieved three important things: It made prospects feel welcomed, it told them they'd save money, and it suggested the cataloger would deliver what it promised.

In general, sending a catalog by UPS seems like an idea that gives a distinctive edge, but it could be problematic if the customer is not lucky enough to have a doorman or a friendly neighbor to take delivery of the catalog (although UPS will often just leave packages on doorsteps).

Of the 35 catalogs sent first class, 26 had envelopes, but only three mailers made any mention, by letter or notification on the outside of the envelope, that this was a new customer or that the material had been requested.

In the bulk-rate pile, consisting of 25 mailers, four catalogers used an announcement on the envelope and/or a letter. David Kay was a good example of how to do this attractively. He used bright green type, very visibly positioned in the lower left-hand corner of a white outer envelope, to announce "YOUR NEW CATALOGUE! Over 275 unique and useful products for all people who enjoy creating a world of beauty at home." This is good teaser copy—and a reminder that this catalog was requested and should therefore be of ongoing interest to the recipient.

Only nine mailers, including Spiegel, used discounts as incentives for potential customers. Many times, the mailer assumed that the dollar coupons enclosed with the catalog constituted the refund promised when the catalog was originally requested. If this is true of your offer, it is important to make a point of saying so.

Only two sweepstakes were used, but one gave an excellent example of how well a sweeps, with a little thought, can tie in with the catalog. The Cockpit (which cost $2.00) ran a Top Gun Sweepstakes, in which winners had the chance to get "top gun" treatment at Paramount Studios, a "top gun" leather flight jacket, classic aviator sunglasses, and so on.

As of a little less than a month before Christmas, only 63 percent of the catalogs requested had been received—even though it was over two months since a check was sent to *The New Yorker*. But the magazine cannot be blamed. As is standard for most publications and a lot of catalogers, it batches names on a once-a-week basis, forwards labels (60 percent of catalogs received actually carried *New Yorker* labels) to catalogers weekly until two weeks after the expiration date of the program, and batches any stray orders whenever it has enough worth forwarding.

There are really two observations to be made here. First, these catalogers took too long to get their catalogs into the hands of those who sent off their required fee. Getting the catalog into the prospect's home fast is essential. Statistics repeatedly show lost sales in direct proportion to slow delivery time. Second, of the 60 catalogs received, only 20 had anything interesting enough to write about, let alone buy from. And the really frightening part is that these catalogs fought for their prospects' time and money, not only with all the other catalogs requested, but also with established catalogers who had already proven they could deliver the goods.

Remember, a catalog is only as special as the customer thinks it is, so don't assume the potential customer will remember sending for the catalog and will love it upon arrival. Instead, make your catalog the one that stands out and gets the order.

Keeping these things in mind, both newcomers and experienced catalogers should test catalog collections as a customer-acquisition method. Telephone the publications that best fit the profile of your customers or your target market to determine if they now offer, or plan to offer, a catalog collection service.

Charging for Your Catalog

How much you charge for your catalog has traditionally had a lot to do with how well it will convert. Historically, free catalogs have had higher response rates but less conversion, but this seems to be changing as conversion on paid catalogs appears to be dropping. However, if you choose to charge for your catalog the options must fit your positioning. The most common charge is $1 to $2, but some very glossy catalogs with a great number of pages (usually several hundred) charge up to $10.00.

Increasingly, catalogers are refunding the cost of the catalog with a coupon customers can use toward their first purchase. Here's some data you might find helpful:

♦ Eleven percent of catalogers claim 25-percent conversion on paid catalogs, down from 21 percent claiming conversion on paid catalogs in 1993.

♦ Ten percent claim the same conversion on free catalogs, down from 13 percent in 1993.[1]

Package Inserts

Package inserts are most often small flyers (usually only a few pages long and around $5\frac{1}{2}'' \times 8\frac{1}{2}''$ in folded size) that are physically inserted into packages containing products going to customers. The most appealing feature of inserts is that they require no postage. They are also inexpensive to create and produce. But along with these pluses come some minuses.

Advantages

Although most catalogers have in-house insert programs, the following discussion addresses rental programs available from other catalog houses. These programs allow you to put your promotions into their outgoing packages for a fee (and subject to their approval).

Because package inserts go into packages containing newly ordered merchandise, you're reaching someone who has not only purchased by mail but also purchased recently. And the package contains merchandise the recipient desires, giving the insert the implied endorsement of the shipper. If the merchandise received meets expectations, the customer will be pleased and receptive to other mail order offers.

The cost of insertion is low, running from $45 to $60 per thousand, exclusive of the cost of producing the insert. Some think the more inserts per package, the greater the possibility the recipient will read them. Others think too many inserts mean too much competition. In reality, it isn't the number of inserts that matters as much as it is the strength of your offer. And more and more mailers are finding this a good avenue to pursue, especially if their tracking and analysis systems are in good working order.

Disadvantages

Inserts are placed in outgoing packages as orders are received and are processed by a mail order company over which you have no control. Therefore, you must rely on the projected number of outgoing packages supplied to you by that company. Of course, these projections are based on anticipated sales and can be different from actual sales—meaning the real number inserted may not be the number anticipated.

Additionally, you must trust that the insertions were not misplaced or lost and are actually going into the packages as promised. To a degree, a second problem can be circumvented by working with only the most reputable mail order companies and following up on the status of the inserts. Another smart approach is to work with list brokers who specialize in inserts; they have the contracts to ensure that your program is being implemented. And they can advise you on the most reliable insert programs.

Actual response can vary significantly (depending on the offer and presentation), but package inserts almost always produce fewer immediate sales than do offers mailed to lists with similar demographics.

Because the inserts do not physically go into the package until the order is received and processed, it may take longer than you anticipate for the insert to actually go out. Even then, you must allow time for the package to be delivered to the recipient's home and action to be taken on the offer.

Another disadvantage is that the inserts cannot be specified for such selects as average dollar order, sex, and zip code.

Weight and size restrictions imposed on your sales promotion for economic reasons by the company into whose packages the promotion is inserted can limit the presentation of your offer. This is not a major problem, but be sure to determine exactly what these specifications are before proceeding with development and production.

Some Basic Rules for Package Insert Design

The time it takes for those who spot the insert to decide to read it is barely seconds, so here is where you need your strongest offer yet! Again, the answer is simplicity and directness. A low price point, a close-out price, a limited time offer, a free catalog subscription—these are the types of offers that get noticed and acted on.

Do not try to jam every product you have into minimal space. Use a theme, as you would in your catalog, to pull items together. And abide by the rules outlined under "Space Ads."

❖ **EXAMPLE 12-7**
Omaha Steaks uses a gourmet gift certificate worth $20 to attract potential buyers' attention.

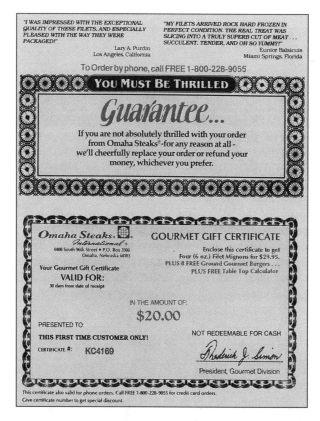

❖ EXAMPLE 12-8
Current puts an endorsement
message on the envelope
containing its package insert.

Co-ops

This method allows noncompetitors to combine the benefits of an in-mail offer with the cost savings of shared postage. The same promotional inserts that go out with orders can be combined with promotions from other direct marketers. These can be inserted into a carrier envelope and mailed to prospective customers. But, since many co-op offers are savings-oriented, you share space with cents-off coupons and similarly distracting offers. Furthermore, you don't choose the mailing date; the co-op does. Co-op packages are also subject to the same weight and size restrictions as package inserts. If co-ops work for you, the potential audience is extensive.

Co-op Catalogs

Co-op catalogs are a combination of well-known catalogs combined into one. Each cataloger presents its best products in a limited number of pages. Each individual catalog has its own order form, but sometimes there is one common toll-free number. The Sky Mail catalog often found in the backs of airline seats is one example.

The typical target audience (this changes depending on who the initiator of the co-op is) consists of male frequent business travelers, age 35 to 45, who find themselves repeatedly stuck in cities or hotel rooms in which they have already investigated all possible forms of entertainment. A captive audience, whether on a plane or in a hotel room, is receptive to new things to do—one of which might well be thumbing through a catalog. The success of participants in these co-op ventures depends on the products offered. For example, electronics appear to greatly outpull apparel.

Co-op Card Decks

Made up of loose or bound-in cards the size of a postcard, co-op card decks allow noncompetitors to share postal and production costs. The targeted market shares a common life-style or occupation and more often than not decks are mailed to a business address. The postage-paid format allows for quick and simple response, but the postcard format (usually 3″ × 5″) limits copy and art.

Their bulkiness alone helps guarantee the decks will stand out from the rest of the mail—a big plus, as it helps ensure they will at least be opened. These days, however,

❖ **EXAMPLE 12-9**
Business-to-business catalogers often use card decks for leads and off-the-page sales.

it's not unusual to receive several intimidatingly large packs per week. One glance tells the customer that sorting through them is going to take valuable time. If he or she has the time, the next step can often be sending for more literature, which in turn takes more time to read. The speed with which this material is sent and the efficiency with which the cataloger follows up on the prospect largely determines just how successful a card pack will be for the advertiser.

If the offer is for a product, such as a book, there's a good chance the advertiser has an instant sale. But, this can have a downside. Booksellers using this medium report a high response, but often too much bad debt and product return for it to be cost-effective.

Some innovative catalogers made good use of card packs by inserting a mini, four-color, multipage catalog. Initial tests were charged at the same rate as the standard postcard insert. Responses were excellent, and acquisition costs were at an acceptable rate. In general, advertisers have been pleased with the results of card packs, but lament the fact that the "card-pack glut" has cut response and productivity. Use this medium to truly pinpoint your target market for optimum effectiveness.

Statement Stuffers

Since statement stuffers are mailed with bills or statements regularly sent to consumers by department stores, charge-card organizations, oil companies, and so on, there is no postage expense. However, they share the same weight and size limitations common to package inserts and co-ops. Rental costs run from $45 to $50 per thousand.

Statement stuffers are available for general audiences as well as more tightly targeted markets. The offer arrives in an envelope showing the billing company's name, usually such an impressive one as MasterCard, BankAmericard, a well-known publication, or a service company, such as a local utility. Because they are mailed first class, stuffers have a more predictable date of arrival than promotions mailed via bulk rate.

Since some statement stuffers tie into the credit offered by the host company, customers have the prominently displayed option of buying now and paying later.

❖ **EXAMPLE 12-10**
Berlitz puts this four-panel insert into American Airline Frequent Flyer statements and features the ''host's'' name at the top. Notice the bonus offer of free miles with a purchase.

Tell-a-Friend Responses

Without a doubt, some of your best prospects are friends of current customers. Oftentimes, referrals from existing customers prove to have a response second only to your customer base. So be sure to give customers every opportunity to provide their friends with your catalog. Include tell-a-friend information on your order form or packing slip, or test separate postage-paid postcards in outgoing packages or in your catalog. Be sure to provide space for several listings and code each listing with a separate code. Many catalogers have found that the first reference is best; the second, second best; and the third, possibly not valuable at all. Do not treat these referrals as one big pot of names; remember the first name that comes to the customer's mind is probably the one who is more likely to want and order from your catalog.

❖ **EXAMPLE 12-11**
J. Crew collects ''tell-a-friend'' names on its order form and codes each name separately.

We'll send free catalogs
to you or your friends
1 800 782-8244

1. Name _____
   NAAA
   Address _____
   City/State/Zip _____

2. Name _____
   NAAB
   Address _____
   City/State/Zip _____

Publicity

Don't overlook the value of ''free'' publicity. Send copies of your catalog or photos of particularly outstanding products along with a press release to publications that may have an interest in your product mix. If the publication should choose to write about your company, the results can be amazing. One cataloger received coverage in more than 25 of the media including *US* magazine, *CBS News,* and the *Chicago Tribune* by simply sending the catalog plus a black-and-white glossy of a truly unique product (and suggested editorial copy) to a variety of publications. Publicity breeds publicity, and even those magazines that didn't receive the initial material soon called for information. The result was a surge of orders—and extraordinarily inexpensive new customers.

This type of publicity can be especially valuable for a new catalog, since the catalog in effect receives an editorial recommendation from the publication in which it appears. But it's just as valuable for such experienced players as Edmond Scientific, which reports an approximate 5:1 return on the $1,000 per month it costs the company to send out press kits.

Tips for Using Public Relations Successfully

Planning

♦ Make sure the goals and objectives of your public relations program mesh with those of your company. Put them in writing.

◆ Determine the target market. Keep information up to date.
◆ Releases must be noteworthy. Don't be the person who cried "Wolf."
◆ Understand the media you're targeting.
◆ Analyze your results.
◆ Look at what your competition is doing.
◆ Stand out. You need more than a piece of paper.

Preparing the Press Release

◆ Put the contact name(s) at the top with a phone number(s) along with "For Immediate Release" or "Embargoed for (date)."
◆ Begin with a headline that clearly summarizes the release and catches the reader's attention immediately. Try for unique positioning or use a hot product.
◆ Include a dateline with the place or even the exact date of the announcement. Treat media people with respect; they like to know they received the story on the day of its announcement.
◆ Write the most important part of the release in the lead paragraph. Use the exact wording you wish to see in print; it may be picked up as is.
◆ Follow up with additional background information.
◆ Close with a boilerplate, such as the company's history.
◆ Convey the company's goals and philosophy throughout.
◆ Target the release to the specific media being addressed.
◆ Include a brief cover letter when necessary.
◆ Include the 800 number for your catalog in the line that tells interested parties who to contact.

Follow-up

◆ Call the editors within one week.
◆ Find out if the publication is interested in the story and in what way. Provide editors with everything they need.
◆ Follow up regularly, but don't be a pest; lay off after three calls. Use your instincts.

Other Less Obvious Approaches

Innovative direct marketers have been exploring new approaches to customer acquisition. For the most part, these efforts have not proved to be as effective as the more traditional methods of space advertising and insert programs. However, since direct marketing's big advantage is the ability to test a new idea and know how effective it is, you should be aware of alternative sales vehicles.

Take-Ones

Take-ones allow you to reach large numbers of prospective customers at a low cost. Display racks, set up in such high-traffic locations as supermarkets, are often part of community bulletin boards, which help draw attention to the take-ones. Promotion pieces are usually similar in size and design to those used in insert programs, and a number of different companies' pieces are often displayed together—another attention-getter. Rates are on a per-store basis and range from $3 to $7 per month per store, depending on the length of distribution time and the number of stores selected. Take-ones are available on a city, neighborhood, or individual-store basis. The cost per thousand is low, and the potential audience high.

❖ **EXAMPLE 12-12**
Freestanding inserts (FSIs) reach a broad audience and tend to work best for low-price, high-value offers, such as this one from Artistic Greetings.

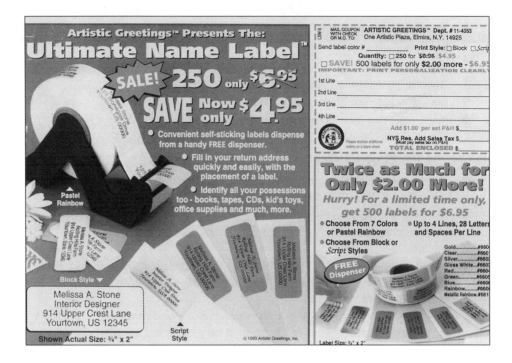

Freestanding Inserts

Distributed through Sunday newspapers across the country, freestanding inserts (FSIs) are the four-color fliers that contain cents-off coupons and mail order ads. Direct marketers can purchase remnant space at a special low rate—substantially less than that offered to national advertisers. The minimum is usually 1 million circulation, and although you can specify particular markets, there is no guarantee you will receive them. Likewise, since available space consists of "leftovers," circulation may vary somewhat. For a test of 1 million, the actual test quantity could be 800,000, 1 million, or any close variance. The cost per thousand (CPM) is $7 to $8, depending on the size and the circulation tested. You must supply the artwork.

Testing this method of customer acquisition is inexpensive and provides a potential market of many millions. Some catalogers choose to offer products, but others offer only their catalog. In either case, you must consider the middle-income demographics of this type of vehicle before deciding whether it is right for your catalog.

On-Pack Offers

Some companies use the existing equities they have on hand to accumulate customer names. General Mills has, for many years, offered its catalog on over 200 of its food products for 50 cents. At other times, it will offer products on the back or side panel of a food product's box.

Some companies are also open to allowing others to advertise on their medium. Arrangements such as this between a cataloger and a packaged-goods company must be individually negotiated.

Alliances

The joining of two companies to benefit both is another method of gathering new customers. Mystic Color Lab offered free processing to those who ordered a certain dollar amount from different catalogers. Calyx & Corolla sold flowers at a discounted rate to those who purchased a certain dollar amount from a Bloomingdale's catalog. Both catalog ventures garnered new names for both participants. Although the terms and conditions vary from offer to offer, only your creativity limits your potential for joint venture alliances.

Electronic Media

New methods of shopping, such as network and cable TV, on-line shopping, and more, are gaining popularity, mostly due to the success and visibility of home shopping channels and infomercials. Not only can you sell products off this medium, it can, due to strong visual excitement, also have a halo effect, increasing sales of your products through other media.

Long-time catalogers Harry and David have tested the waters by offering their famous "Tower of Treats" during the holiday gift-giving season. Other catalogers, such as Lands' End and L. L. Bean, have run ads offering a free catalog.

Reinforcing the message is critical in this medium, and commercials should, as Harry and David did, constantly reinforce the need for customers to order now and flash the toll-free number with which they can order. Advertisers should also be prepared to offer several credit cards for payment.

For an electronic media program, hire someone who knows this business backward and forward to put together a media plan, including projected response, before you embark on this exciting but complicated avenue.

DR TV. This medium works best, according to Andrea Hill of Anthill Marketing, when the target audience is women from 35 to 50 or men from 25 to 40. A 60-second spot is generally used for lead generations, and merchandise is offered to qualify the customer and defray the cost of the advertising. The cost to create the commercials runs from $20,000 up, and the minimum budget to place the spot in several test markets is usually around $100,000, although you can test just a few for as little as $20,000. The good news is that you can pull the spot quickly (time is cancelable within 48 hours) if it is unsuccessful, limiting your dollar exposure. The bad news is that many of the prime areas for testing sell out quickly. And, because you are paying less than full rate (anywhere from 30 percent to 80 percent less than general advertisers), you can be preempted by those who are paying full rate. You must work with a qualified broker who understands this medium and has access to time.

Realize that not every call will be an order; many will be for additional information, so have materials ready to send quickly. Be sure to use an inbound telemarketing firm that can handle the peaks and valleys inherent in this medium. An agency running remnant spots once wound up on a new primetime program! This involved great placement, but an overwhelming response that necessitated going back on press to print more catalogs.

Infomercials. Infomercials are really just another form of DR TV. In this case, they are lengthy commercials, often in a talk-show format. A 30-minute infomercial runs between $150,000 and $400,000. Most experts in this field strongly suggest using a celebrity to help attract the attention of the "channel surfers." Everything that has been learned from DR TV should be applied here: frequent repetition of the toll-free number to call for ordering, finding the right telemarketing firm, and the ability to quickly read your results.

On-line Shopping. The biggies currently are America On Line (AOL), Prodigy, and Compuserve. All offer on-line product availability though interactive shopping centers. If your product is the type that fits the profile of the regular computer user, this can be a good avenue for you. However, if your product requires top graphics, these systems have a problem because they still cannot deliver compelling graphics (although this is likely to change in the not-too-distant future). Remember, too, that the graphics quality depends on the monitor being used by the viewer.

Compuserve's Minimum Participation Plan is $10,000 per year. This allows 100 products with descriptions (changing products frequently is a key to success), 500 products without descriptions, and a $5,000 credit for advertising in *Compuserve Magazine*. In addition, there is a charge of 2 percent on all sales transactions tracked through order-entry software.

Prodigy has a rate base of 2 million members. They have a five-screen standard advertising unit (SAU) of $27,500 per month; the creative production fee is an additional $10,900. Regional buys can be made at substantially less cost, and there are a host of optional enhancements available at extra fees.

Allow time to produce an on-line computer "catalog"; it can take approximately four weeks and, like all of the newer forms of marketing, requires the talents of an experienced system user.

Responding to the Catalog-Request Offer

There is more to responding to a catalog request than simply throwing a catalog in the mail. You must construct a testing grid that allows you to understand the effect of certain offers and the effect of the amount of time between when customers request the catalog and when they actually receive it. You must test the effect of sending your catalog third-class bulk rate versus first class, a vast difference in cost and, depending on how many catalog requests you receive per day, a vast difference in time. Since you need 200 catalogs to qualify for bulk rate, this can be a problem if you are holding catalogs until you reach that number.

Timeliness

Getting the catalog to customers within their needed time frame can be critical. Be sure to monitor the effect of the catalog arriving within a few days versus a few weeks.

Appearance

Should your catalog come in an envelope announcing that this is a catalog the customer has requested? Envelopes add expense but can raise response. One alternative is adding a simple sticker with a message such as "Here is the catalog you requested." Be sure you do not take your prospective buyers' frame of mind for granted. Understand the value of alerting them as to the value of the catalog instead of simply putting it in the mail.

Evaluating Customer Acquisition

Most customers shop with a catalog for only a certain time period, and, during this time period, they spend a certain amount of money. How long they stay with the company and how much they spend determines their value as customers. Buying habits can differ dramatically depending on the source from which the customer is acquired.

It is important to evaluate the profitability of different media over a length of time. Too many catalogers tend to look only at the immediate value of a customer and not the long-term or lifetime value. (*Lifetime value* is how much the customer is going to spend over the period of time that he or she is your customer. This is discussed in Chapter 11.) This is understandable in a start-up venture, where immediate recouping of funds can be critical, but it is inexcusable for catalogers who intend to stay in business for a long time. You should keep meticulous records of customers' buying habits by acquisition source to be able to evaluate the value of your customers. For each media source, you need to consider the following:

1. How many years have these customers continued to purchase?
2. How many times did you mail them catalogs?
3. How much did each mailing cost?
4. What was their rate of response?

5. How much did they spend?

6. How much did you actually make (deducting cost of goods, and so on)?

7. What is their real worth as customers?

One cataloger discovered that lists showed the best immediate return, but space advertisements generated the best customers—those who continued to buy and spend. This cataloger cut back on list rentals and expanded the space-ad program. A superior customer evolved—one who spent more over a longer period.

❖ **CHECKLIST**

✔ Consider alternatives to list-rental methods of customer acquisition as your catalog matures.

✔ Carefully review the magazines in which you are considering inserting ads.

✔ Always create a complete media plan.

✔ Understand the financial ramifications of offering a product versus a catalog-request-only ad.

✔ Choose the size of the ad per publication based on your budget and your response expectations.

✔ Follow the rules for ad design.

✔ Investigate catalog collections early in your customer acquisition plan.

✔ Test charging for your catalog versus offering it free.

✔ Test package inserts, but first know what to expect.

✔ Understand the different types of co-ops and ease into them slowly.

✔ Never forget to use tell-a-friend information.

✔ Put publicity to work for you from the start.

✔ Always be on the lookout for less obvious ways you can profitably acquire new names.

✔ Consult experts when investing in media.

✔ Keep abreast of the emerging electronic technology that's right for your catalog's name acquisition program.

✔ Give a great deal of thought and planning to how your catalog looks when customers receive it and the time in which they receive it.

✔ Always code and track every response and understand its true value to your overall program.

End Notes

1. *Catalog Age*, December 1993.

CHAPTER THIRTEEN

The Back End

After the catalog has been merchandised, designed, printed, and put in the mail, the fun part starts—the orders come in! The physical fulfillment of these orders and any customer service that accompanies them is of utmost importance to your customers. Once they place their order, they want to know it will be handled efficiently and in a friendly, professional manner.

Commonly called the "back end," the operational part of a catalog covers the order intake (including data entry), physical fulfillment, inventory control, and customer service. Getting orders in and out in a timely fashion requires planning and a good back-up team.

The key to a successful back end is documentation, planning, controls, and measurement. Procedures should be designed to provide rapid and maximum service within your budget.

Customers who receive their orders promptly and in good condition order again and again. Statistics show that 20 percent more orders are received from customers whose initial orders are filled promptly. Those who wait and wonder often become quietly dissatisfied and just stop ordering.

Each catalog back-end operation has certain peculiar qualities. Very few are still manual; most, even the smallest start-up ventures, are or should be computerized. This chapter explains the functions involved for a company just starting out, as well as for one with approximately $20 million in sales. Higher sales would mean more equipment and more procedures, but the basic steps described would remain the same.

Seven Key Steps to Effective Order Intake

Figure 13-1 shows order intake, the processing of orders from mail arrival to database creation. Telephone orders are processed similarly. (See Figure 13-3 and Chapter 17.)

1. Pick up or receive mail from the post office.
2. Count pieces and log mail.
3. Open and extract orders, checking them for a complete name and address before discarding the envelope.
4. Sort mail by five categories:
   a. Orders
      ◆ Check/cash
      ◆ Credit card

    b. White mail (contents unclear or untrackable)

    c. Customer service

        ◆ Order or address change

        ◆ Backorder notice responses

        ◆ Responses to notices issued

    d. Payments

        Short payments or billing payments

    e. Other

5. Count and batch mail by sorted type:

    a. Create batch tickets with a reject or adjustment column on ticket and log the batch.

    b. The batch numbers should contain

        ◆ the date

        ◆ the sequential number of the batch

        ◆ the batch type; use two alphas such as

            PO (paid order)

            CO (credit-card order)

            CS (customer service)

            MP (money payment)

    c. Total pieces in batches should equal total mail received.

6. Log batches and counts in the log book.

7. For check or cash batches, set a maximum of between 25 and 50 per batch. If you use a computer system,

    a. Scan for omissions of essential data, such as

        ◆ name

        ◆ address

        ◆ source

        ◆ item numbers

        ◆ quantity

    b. Note the check amount on the order.

    c. If orders are flagged or pulled for any reason, including suspected fraud, you must adjust the batch ticket.

    d. Make an adding machine tape of the total dollar value of the checks (the computer system will add up the actual order values).

    e. Rejected orders go to customer service for special handling.

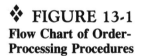

❖ FIGURE 13-1
Flow Chart of Order-Processing Procedures

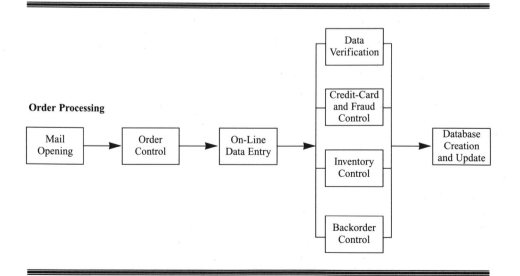

Order Control

Order control is the process that ensures that the manual operations in order intake are self-consistent and that batch totals and check totals are equal.

In a small company, the same person who handles the initial sorting may also handle order control. Figure 13-2 outlines the order-control process, which basically ensures that all batch totals match the order-form totals and that both are correct.

Manual opening, sorting, removal of contents, and counting can be tedious, time-consuming work. If you have 2,000 or more incoming pieces of mail per day, seriously consider automating. However, be aware that automation will most likely affect the design of your order form. Make sure that the design of your order form allows for easy opening and extraction, without destroying any vital printed information on the order form itself.

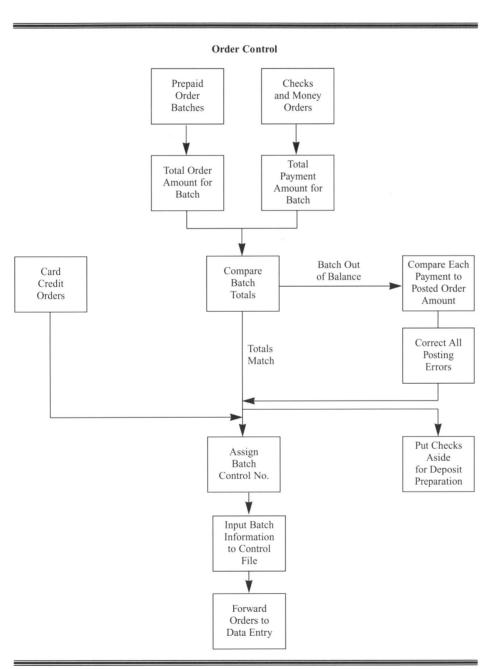

❖ FIGURE 13-2
Flow Chart of Order-Control Procedures

From Data Entry to Fulfillment

Now the order must actually be entered into the fulfillment system. During order entry, certain information must be validated:

1. Does the item description match the stockkeeping unit (SKU) number?
2. Is the price correct?
3. Have shipping and handling charges, as well as appropriate taxes, been added?
4. Is there a source, key code, or customer account number?
5. Are the city and state correct for the zip code?
6. For credit-card orders, is the number complete and the card current? What is the name of the issuing bank?
7. Has the customer provided daytime and nighttime phone numbers?
8. Does the customer wish his or her name removed from outside list rentals— Mail Preference Service (MPS)?
9. Does the order have a history of bad debt? (How to set up a system to handle this is covered later in this chapter.)
10. Are there customer-service flags on the account?

Next, two questions need to be answered: (1) Is the payment correct for the merchandise ordered; and (2) is the merchandise in stock or on backorder? The computer will automatically update whether the payment is correct. It will also show whether inventory is available by reserving each in-stock item and by updating the backorder file for out-of-stock items.

In addition, the following data should be input:

1. The date of the order
2. The customer name, including his or her title:
   a. None, Mrs., Mr., or Ms.
   b. Professional titles, such as Dr., Prof., or Rev.
   c. Military titles, such as Sgt. or Lt.
3. The customer address
4. Ship-to address information
5. The order number (Most automated systems will assign and display a unique number for each order as the orders are entered. This number should be manually posted to the source document to facilitate document retrieval.)
6. Type of payment and amount
7. Order type (mail, phone, or fax)

Guidelines for Data-Entry Productivity

Accurate data entry is of critical importance to the cataloger. Yet employee productivity should not be forgotten. After all, "time is money," and an efficiently run center makes everyone—employees and employers alike—happier. The following list for data-entry productivity is applicable to catalog operations of any size, from small start-up to established giant.

- Is the information to be entered presented to the operator in an orderly manner? Are the data on the order form in the same order as they are to be entered? Is enough space allowed on the order form for customers to fill in information legibly? Is the customer specifically asked to print?
- Do such common elements as the date the order was received automatically appear in other records once they've been entered?
- Is the operator's work station laid out so work can be processed in an organized manner?

♦ Are the equipment and programming cost-efficient? Or, by trying to save money, are you actually reducing employee productivity?

♦ Do you keep accurate records of time spent versus work performed?

Productivity and the quality of surroundings and equipment should never be taken for granted, but monitored and carefully controlled from the outset.

Letting the Computer System Work for You

In computerized operations, remember that you want the system to do the work. The concept managerially is to deal with the exceptions rather than every single order. Let the system find and highlight the exceptions so you can process the volume of clean orders more rapidly. These should be the majority if your printed order form and procedures were properly designed.

Here are some examples of what you should look for when unearthing exceptions:

1. **Incomplete orders**. Orders missing such critical fields as
   ♦ name
   ♦ deliverable address (house number, street, city, state, and zip code)
   ♦ item number (style, color, and size)
   ♦ missing payments
   ♦ missing quantities (on cash/check orders, divide money or item total by item price; on credit-card orders with no totals, default to one)

2. **Foreign orders**. If the order is not paid in U.S. dollars, if there is no Canadian credit-card account, or if the order is incomplete, processing problems result.

3. **Short paid orders**. Never edit for which category was shorted— merchandise, postage and handling or taxes. Only edit for the amount short (systems do it automatically).

Credit-Card Transactions

By some estimates, an average of 70 percent of direct-marketing orders are placed on credit cards. Credit cards provide convenient buying power to the consumer and faster payment to the merchant (in this case, the cataloger). The process is quite simple, but needs to be understood for the cataloger to take full advantage of this method of payment.

Bank Credit Cards

First, you need to understand some common terms used in the process. *Processor* refers to the company that actually handles the transaction (either the acquirer or a company acting on behalf of the acquirer). *Acquirer* refers to a financial institution, usually a bank. *Issuer* refers to the bank that has actually issued the credit card to the user.

The process works like this:

1. A consumer places a credit-card order by phone, mail, or fax.

2. The cataloger/merchant receives the order and first processes an authorization request through its credit-card processor which forwards the request to the card-issuing bank.

3. The bank (issuer) verifies the validity of the card, checks the funds available in the cardholder's account and sends back an approval or a decline response.

4. Assuming the order is approved, the cataloger processes and ships the order.

5. The cataloger then deposits the transaction through its processor, which credits its account for the amount of the deposit less any fees (usually within 24 hours).

6. The processor next sends a settlement message to the credit-card network which checks the validity of the transaction and settles it, by debiting the issuer and crediting the processor.

7. Finally, the issuer posts the transaction amount to the cardholder's account and bills the cardholder to collect payment.

To understand how this process works for nonbank credit cards, see the next section in this chapter.

Who Does the Processing?

Bank Cards.   In the bank-card world, there are a number of players. One is the acquirer, meaning the financial institution, usually a bank, which is a member of the Visa or MasterCard Association. The institution is responsible for acquiring transactions at the point of sale and entering them into the system for payment. Acquirers frequently use third-party processors to do this for them.

The issuer is also a financial institution who is a member of either the MasterCard or Visa Association (or both) and who issues credit cards directly to the consumer. The issuer is responsible for managing cardholder accounts, customer service, and receivables and billings.

Nonbank Credit Cards.   American Express (AMEX), Optima, Diners' Club, Carte Blanche, and Discover make up the lion's share of those cards that are not bank cards. The process is basically the same; the difference is that the cataloger settles directly with the credit-card company rather than with a processor. With AMEX or Discover, a third-party processor can get an authorization on a merchant's behalf, but the processor cannot settle. This means that its job is to convey the order to the credit-card company, which in turn must settle directly with the merchant.

Some direct marketers deal directly with AMEX, both for authorization and for settlement.

Third-Party Processors.   Third-party processors are service bureaus that specialize in credit-card processing. They are important in cataloging because they are dedicated to direct marketing, constructing their systems and services around the distinct needs of our industry. Furthermore, because of their great volume (you become one of a group of many catalogers), you will likely get lower-than-average rates (transaction fees). And third-party processors will probably provide better chargeback management than you could as an individual company. Chargebacks are transactions disputed by either the cardholder or the issuer, so it is important to keep your chargeback processing and its associated costs as low as possible. This is another area in which knowledgeable third-party processors can assist you.

There is a lot more to third-party processors than just processing transactions. Because they understand the direct-marketing business, many of their clients turn to them to help solve problems, such as noncredit-card–related fraud, the set-up of installment billing programs, and a network for referrals to other direct-marketing services.

Direct-marketing–savvy companies, such as Litle & Company (Salem, New Hampshire) and Direct Marketing Guarantee Trust (DMGT; Nashua, New Hampshire) should be two of the service bureaus you contact when you set up your credit-card processing program or if you are investigating ways to improve how you now perform the processing.

The Cost of Credit-Card Processing

Discount rate is a generic term that describes the amount your sales will be "discounted" in order to pay for the use of the credit-card company's services. A nonbank will charge you your sales minus its discount rate, which is some percent of sales. With a bank card, the discount rate really encompasses three areas:

1. The interchange rate, or what the card-issuing bank gets for floating the funds
2. Fees and assessment, which are retained by MasterCard and Visa
3. What your processor charges you

You may be charged a percentage of sales (which covers everything) or you may be charged on a per-transaction basis with interchange fees and assessments being passed through. This is a highly competitive area, so negotiate.

In addition, if you use a third-party processor, the processor will charge conveyance fees (the cost of bringing a transaction from one place to another).

The Best Way to Process Your Credit-Card Transactions

Although transactions can still be processed manually, virtually all catalogers do it electronically. The investment is minimal, only around $300 for a point-of-sale (POS) terminal, and the time savings is well worth it.

There are two main options for connecting to your bank electronically:

1. **On-line**. This means you can process authorizations as you receive them.
2. **Batch.** Here you take all the orders received over a period of time (say, one day), then batch them to your processor for authorization. You then receive a file of responses for all of the authorizations, at which time you create your deposit or settlement file, consisting of all the approved orders. This is sent back to the processor to create your deposit.

In both cases, you will receive responses.

You can transmit electronically via a computer-to-computer link, whether mainframe, mini, or personal, or from a POS terminal, where you just type in the card number, order amount, and expiration date and get an authorization. When you shut down the terminal at the end of the day it automatically batches orders.

Chargebacks

A *chargeback* is a transaction disputed by either the cardholder or issuer. It is returned to the acquirer and ultimately the merchant. Certain rights and protections are afforded to all the players. It is a complicated process, requiring the services of a processor that can protect your rights as a merchant by reversing chargebacks on your behalf whenever possible. Even if you are experienced, don't assume you know all your rights and the protection you need. Banks tend not to be as experienced in direct marketing as are third-party processors specializing in the industry. These processors have systems built specifically for direct marketing's needs.

Basic Kinds of Chargebacks. The biggest type of chargeback is the unauthorized purchase. "I didn't buy this," the consumer says on receiving his or her bill, and promptly contacts the bank. The bank then creates a chargeback and sends it back to your bank, which makes a deduction from your account or starts the paperwork to resolve it.

The second most common chargeback is issuer-related. These are chargebacks that the issuing bank sends back due to processing problems, such as the wrong account number. Banks don't resolve these problems, they simply move to a chargeback automatically. Here again, it is a good idea to have a processor that understands how this works and doesn't let the bank get away with the chargeback.

Here are a couple of ways you can help reduce chargebacks:

1. Don't bill until you have actually shipped the merchandise.
2. Issue refunds as quickly as you receive cancellations or returns.

Credit-Card Fraud

Fraud in cataloging is not as big an issue as one might think, but it is an emotional one. In reality, it represents maybe 0.15 percent of total sales, depending on the merchandise offered.

A catalog company can take several measures to protect itself. One is to be alert to certain signals that a phone order may not be legitimate:

1. Does the caller seem nervous or hesitant? Does he or she have difficulty in answering specific questions? In a caring manner, ask for the person's home and office phone numbers. For example, "So that we may have no problems in delivering your order, could we please have the telephone numbers where you can be reached, both day and night?"

2. Is the caller having difficulty repeating specifics? If so, ask a question, "I'm sorry, but I'm not sure I got your zip code (or the spelling of your last name) right. Could you please repeat it for me?" If the person hesitates, you may be looking at possible fraud.

3. Does the caller appear to be rushing the order? Persons attempting fraud will try to get the order completed quickly, for fear the operator will ask a question they can't answer.

4. Is the caller a child? This may be a legitimate order, but placed without the knowledge of a parent. Be sure to get a phone number. Then, at a later time, call back to verify the order.

5. Does the caller sound intoxicated or under the influence of drugs? Catalog businesses that sell easily pawned items, such as electronics and gold jewelry, should be especially alert to these callers.

Be sure to always get both the billing address and the day and evening phone numbers so you can act on some of these suggestions.

Train your operators to note unusual calls. While an address verification service (AVS) attempts to determine if the card matches the bill-to address, you may wish to take additional action. Such calls can be handled in a number of ways:

1. If the order is to be sent to a third party (a name and address different from that of the person ordering), call the person who has supposedly ordered the product. You can pretend you are calling to verify a zip code or color choice. For instance, "Mrs. Jones, this is Mary Smith at ABC Catalog Company. We just wanted to let you know that your order for the footstool will be shipped to you within four days." Whether or not the person placed the order, he or she will appreciate the call. And remember that according to FTC regulations, those who receive merchandise they have not ordered are under no obligation to return it.

2. If the order is charged, ask the bank to confirm that the name and address on file are the same as the ones on your order. If they are, process the order.

If the order is charged to MasterCard or Visa, either collect the name of the issuing bank on the order form or during the phone order or ask your bank for the name of the customer's issuing bank. The first six numbers of the credit card (called the "bin number" or "bank identification number") are the code of the issuing bank. Alternatively, call the issuing bank and ask to check the cardholder's address against the address you have.

If an order is refused because a customer has exceeded his or her credit limits, don't assume he or she is trying to commit fraud. Hold the order for a few days and try again. The customer may not know the limit has been exceeded, or a payment may be on the way. If the order is refused a second time, use a modified form letter to contact the customer. Some telephone ordering systems allow the operators to authorize credit-card charges while the customer is still on the phone. If credit is refused in this case, make sure operators are instructed to ask for another credit card diplomatically. For example, "I'm so sorry, but it appears this credit-card company has not yet received your last payment. Is there another one you can use, so we can process your order without delay?"

No matter how careful you and your staff are, some attempts at fraud will succeed. Keep updated, complete records of all transactions. Some merge/purge service companies have a fraud file to which you can contribute names. In exchange, you can use the complete file to suppress bad names from your mailing.

In addition, you can use AVS, which checks the bill-to address. Visa will soon be requiring that this be done prior to processing if you want to get the best rates. It works like this: When you go to authorize a transaction, you need to include the customer's address for comparison against the bank card's database to see if it is a legitimate address. If there is a problem, the bank has codes that tell why; these codes will enable you to decide if you wish to process the order.

Different cards have different services designed to combat mail order fraud:

1. AMEX has a service called Consumer ID (CID), which is the four-digit number on the AMEX/Optima card. Ask for this number; if the person making the charge cannot provide it, this could be fraud.

2. Address Information Management System (AIMS) is MasterCard's new program that checks ship-to addresses.

The credit-card companies are focusing on preventing fraud or chargebacks. An example of this is Visa's requirement that as of April 1995, you must use AVS to get the best interchange rates and you must put your customer-service number in the merchant's city field on the cardholder's bank-card statement. Then, when customers get their statements they can immediately see the customer-service number to call if they have a problem with a particular charge.

Ideally, your computerized fulfillment system will have a good inventory control module to measure and allocate stock to your orders. In today's systems you must decide if you want a system that allocates stock once the order is entered, but prior to credit-card authorization and to release from out-of-pattern holds, or if you prefer to wait for authorization and complete approval. In the first scenario, the system might have to allocate inventory and then, if a credit-card authorization is declined, deallocate the same stock. If you delay allocation of stock until orders are fully authorized or approved, larger orders or credit-card orders may suddenly not have stock available because it would have been allocated on a first-come/first-served basis. These are confusing, but very critical, paths that should be carefully considered.

For more information on fraud, send for the Direct Marketing Association's brochure, written by Litle & Company, titled *Executive Guide/Fraud Detection and Loss Prevention in Credit Card Transactions*.

A Special Case for Start-ups

A *merchant account* is the cataloger's service account to which customers' charges are deposited. Getting a merchant account can be a real problem for start-ups. Processors see each applicant as an unsecured open line of credit. If a merchant goes out of business, the bank is stuck. And it's even tougher to get a nonbank card than it is to get a bank card, because nonbank cards want the merchant to have Visa and/or MasterCard before they give the new merchant their card.

Before you apply for a merchant account, Bob Bunshaft of Pacific Arts Publishing recommends that you have as many of the following as possible:

1. A description of your business structure
2. The background of your principals, as well as an explanation of their ability to run this type of business
3. Complete information about your products and/or services
4. A detailed marketing plan, preferably backed with market research
5. Samples of marketing promotion materials or mock-ups
6. A pro forma profit-and-loss statement (P&L) for at least two years

7. Bank and trade references
8. Comprehensive financial statements

Credit Cards as a Source for New Revenue

Catalogers should not think of credit cards only as a means of collecting payment. They are also a means of generating revenue. By developing marketing plans that encourage more purchases or larger orders through installment, continuity, and deferred billing, catalogers can increase their revenues. Giving a consumer the choice of spreading out payments, combined with the perception that there is no interest, can often see a 20 percent to 25 percent, or greater, increase in response to a particular product or product line.

MasterCard and Visa have their own regulations on how you can implement one of these programs. Check with them or a third-party processor experienced in this area, before initiating such a program.

Transactions by Check

Even though the convenience of credit-card buying has been a major contributing factor to mail order growth, many people still prefer to pay by check. The percentage paying by check depends largely on the average dollar order of the catalog. Higher-ticket catalogs tend to have a higher percentage of credit-card sales.

Checks have advantages in that they cost you no credit-card service fee. The disadvantage is that they can bounce sky high. And, unless your bank is extraordinarily fast at clearing checks, you probably will have shipped the merchandise before the check has cleared. (Remember, prompt order fulfillment is one of the major ways of keeping that valuable customer!)

The good news is that most customers are honest. The majority of bad checks bounce because customers erroneously believe there is enough money in their accounts. Simply redeposit the check; more often than not, it will clear. The bad news is that some dishonest people have discovered mail order can be lucrative for them, too. Here are some basic pointers:

1. New accounts are dangerous. Ninety percent of "hot" checks are drawn on accounts less than a year old, so watch out for low-numbered checks. The consecutive numbers in the far right-hand corner of the check (just like the ones you record in your personal checkbook) usually start at 101. Obviously, a low-numbered check isn't always a sign of fraud, so consider other factors as well. If the order is for a high dollar amount and/or is being shipped to another address, wait until the check clears to fill it.
2. Take into consideration the appearance of the handwriting on the check (and the order form itself). Unless you've been in the mail order business for some time, this may seem a strange statement. Yet, in the same way a good buyer knows that an item will sell and an artist senses the graphics needed for a particular catalog, so can the person who processes orders pick out a bad check. The detection really is an art and the signal of a potential problem cannot be put in writing, but one concern might be a check that is sloppy in appearance. If the person responsible for checking feels something is wrong with a check, even if none of the "alerts" applies, let the check clear before sending the order.
3. Be aware of checks without a preprinted name and address. This service is offered free or at minimal charge by banks to checking-account holders.

The authorities are aware that fraud is a major problem for catalogers and have taken steps to identify and arrest the culprits. If you experience excessive loss due to fraud, contact your local U.S. Postal Service (USPS) representative or the U.S. Secret Service. Bad checks come by mail, and they become hard evidence later if you have to prosecute. Receipt of fraudulently ordered goods can lead to prosecution, too, so keep law enforcement agencies involved.

In addition, be sure to address the following to guard against fraud:

1. Identify out-of-pattern check orders, including
   a. Higher-than-average order volume from checks
   b. Large orders with "ship to" addresses asking for express delivery
   c. Large check orders with no telephone number
2. Verify credit-card orders that are out of pattern
   a. In value
   b. In number of items
   c. In value and "ship to" address
3. Beware large, high-value phone orders
   a. To a "ship to" address
   b. For seldom-ordered high-ticket items

Physical Fulfillment

Now that the "in" part of order processing has been completed, it's time to begin the "out" part. This includes picking, packing, and shipping of ordered merchandise; an intelligently equipped and arranged warehouse; the physical package; and shipping the choices, combined with the intricacies of postage and handling. Figure 13-3 shows how fulfillment functions.

Pick, Pack, and Ship

Pick, pack, and ship is the physical movement of merchandise from its warehouse location "out-the-door." Here's one example of how it works. Some fulfillment operations pick each order individually, but it is more efficient to batch orders for picking. This can be a simple procedure and a computer system will follow these easy steps:

1. Select all orders that are not being held for a particular reason, such as incomplete information.
2. Sort the orders by type and number of line items:
   a. Drop-ship orders
   b. Express (next-day and second-day) shipments
   c. Single-line (one-product) orders (computer-sort these by warehouse location)
   d. Multiline (multiproduct) orders (further sort these by the warehouse location of the first item)
3. Group all orders into batches of 20 each.
4. Assign a batch number and a sequence number. For example, 1-10 is batch 1, order 10. If the "sold to" or "ship to" is different than the person ordering, issue a confirmation order (see Figure 13-4).
5. Create a label file (one entry per item ordered).
6. Sort the label file by batch number and warehouse location.
7. Print the shipping orders on your picking/packing slips.

❖ FIGURE 13-3
**Flow Chart Showing
Fulfillment Functions**

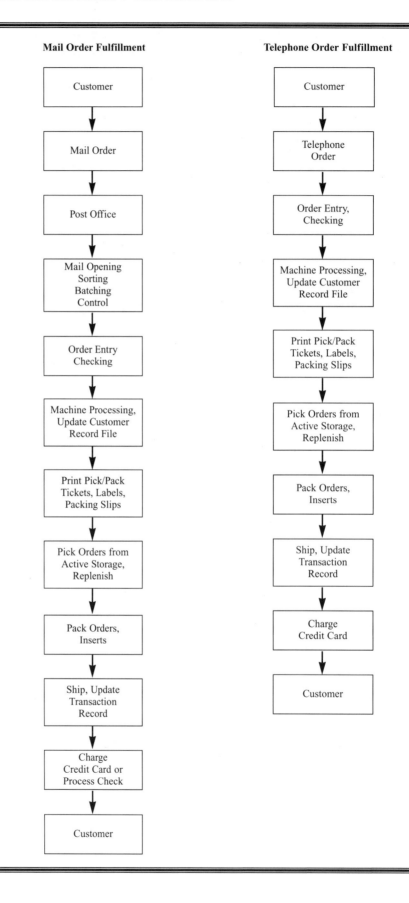

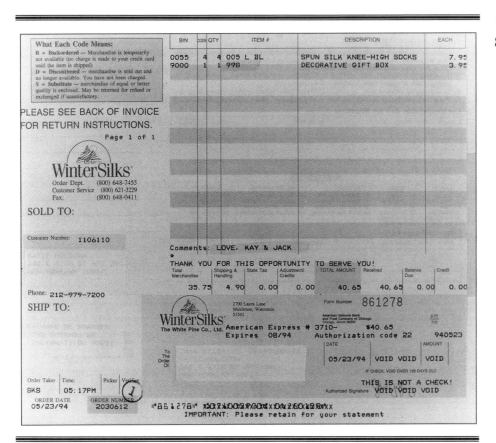

❖ **FIGURE 13-4**
Sample Confirmation Order

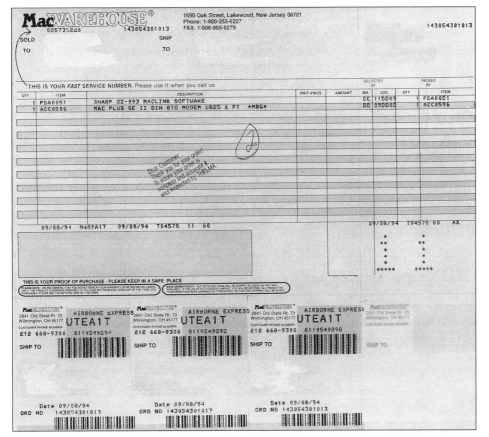

❖ **EXAMPLE 13-1**
MacWarehouse's picking and packing slips show the mailing labels.

Pick.

1. Take the first batch of picking labels to the appropriate warehouse location.
2. Pull the item indicated on the first picking label from the shelf on which it is located and attach the pressure-sensitive label, which, in some cases, is part of the picking ticket. (Note: Not everyone uses labels.)
3. Place the item, with its label, in the correct tray, which is on a cart.
4. Repeat the preceding steps until the entire batch has been picked.
5. Move the cart to the packing tables and unload.

Note: Some companies with high volume use stationary pickers as opposed to this method where pickers are mobile.

Pack.

1. Remove all the items for the first order from the tray.
2. Place the items on the packing table.
3. Match them to the corresponding shipping document.
4. Check the order for accuracy as each item is wrapped and packed.
5. Apply the shipping label to each carton. Enclose the packing slip and bounceback material.
6. Post the number of cartons and the packer's initials on the verification slip. The number of cartons can be preprinted on the computer.

Ship.

1. Each carton is weighed by the computer.
2. Put the package aside for postal or carrier pickup.
3. The computer-printed bar code on the label is read by the bar code reader and provides the date, weight, and shipping verification. If this is a charge-card transaction, the computer releases the order to be billed.

Note: Pickers should proof what they pick against the batch picking ticket based on the specified picking location code, item number, and item description. This is the first of two standard quality control checks in the process.

Hardware and Software Systems

Today, catalogers use fulfillment systems with a number of elements. Among them are bar code readers/writers, automatic telephone call directors (ACDs), automatic weighing scales, manifest printers, and warehouse location systems, all tied into their computer.

Computers for current fulfillment systems range from personal computers (PCs) to mainframes. Catalogers, ranging from the smallest using a PC to the largest on tandem mainframes, have grown to rely on computers not only for customer data analysis, but as the core of running their business. The order entry and transaction processing for today's catalog are virtually all computerized, as is a great deal of the physical-fulfillment process.

Here are some steps in fulfillment as they affect and are affected by the computer and its ancillary systems for an up-to-date catalog operation.

1. Merchandise is ordered by the cataloger from a vendor by means of a purchase order that is sent to the vendor by electronic file transfer. The file also contains the format of the bar coded labels to be affixed to the shipment.
2. On arrival and inspection, the bar coded labels are read into the computer which then updates the inventory status of the item, assigns it a (possibly bar coded) warehouse location, and releases the vendor's invoice for payment.
3. Mail orders are received and entered into the computer.

4. Phone calls are routed to the operators by the ACD, which also maintains statistics such as average ring time, abandons, and so on. Note that the trend is to computer-telephone integration, using the ACD to store and generate information so that, for example, the operator who answers the call will see on the screen the length of time the customer has waited in the queue. Additionally, with automatic number identification (ANI), the operator—although not disclosing it—can see on the screen the name and address of the customer calling. This allows the operator to verify the data that already exists on his or her screen, saving reentering time and reducing the risk of error.

5. Through the computer inventory lookup keyed to the SKU, both mail and (more important) phone customers can be told the inventory status of each item as it is entered.

6. The computer can transmit a tape to a third-party charge processor for authorizations or directly to charge-card issuers, such as Visa.

7. On authorization, the computer can print the pick/pack/ship information in the warehouse. And it can, prior to printing the ship information, select the least-cost shipping method based on cataloger-supplied weight and value data.

8. The pick data contains the warehouse location of each SKU, and the package label has the correct bar code for the shipping method based on the shipment weight (based on SKU and pack data already in the computer).

9. Orders requiring special handling for overnight delivery may be segregated by the computer.

10. As the outgoing package moves past the bar code reader, the shipment verification is read into the computer. The charge card is then debited, inventory is decremented, (you may move more items from bulk to pick areas), and the customer file is updated. This data are now available for customer service and the transaction becomes part of the customer record.

The Right Equipment for Your Company's Size.   Prepackaged software exists in profusion for fulfillment purposes. The systems range from programs for one station to those that handle hundreds of operators. A good guide to the available software is "Guide To Catalog Management Software" by Ernest Schell, published by Industry Publications International, Inc., Jenkentown, PA.

This publication is updated regularly and covers (in three volumes) PC-, mini-, and mainframe-based packages.

Setting Up the Warehouse

Every warehouse must be tailored to meet the requirements of the individual catalog operation. Even catalogs that have been in business for years periodically change the set-up to meet new needs or accommodate new equipment. See the floor plan in Figure 13-5 as an example. Here's a list of considerations for an efficiently run and well-organized midsize operation:

♦ Keep working aisles wide enough to allow easy movement of people and picking carts.

♦ Start-ups should probably locate materials by size and weight, keeping smaller items closest to the packing stations. For established catalogers with a sales history, it makes more sense to keep high-volume products closest to the packing stations. In both cases, keep items within a picking area in numerical sequence. A blackboard or poster can be kept at the end of each aisle to indicate the SKU numbers in that aisle (similar to the way a library marks book locations). Because many warehouses use part-time help, taping a picture of an item from the catalog to the corresponding bin or shelf can be helpful, especially if one shelf contains two items that look similar.

♦ Label all picking bins with bold magic marker or bar-coded labels.

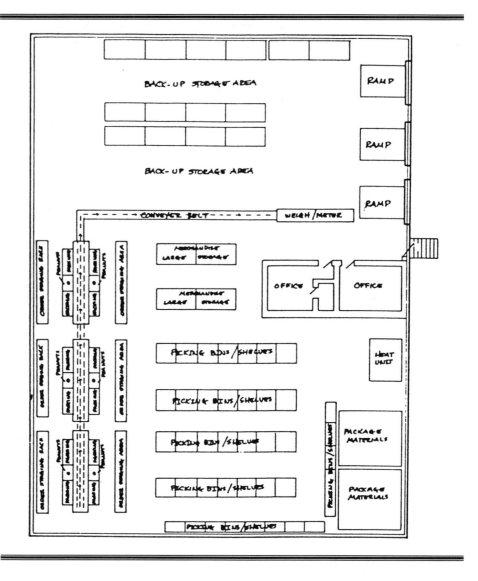

- ◆ Keep heavy prepacked items on the pallets on which they come. Store them in a separate area.

- ◆ Keep easily pilfered items on the highest tiers and away from doors or in a gated security area. Don't hesitate to let employees know that you will prosecute anyone who is caught stealing. Keep trash cans away from areas containing items that can be stolen easily, and don't let trash be collected near the warehouse area.

- ◆ Use rubber mats on concrete floors in the greatest activity areas or where employees must stand for long periods (especially packing tables and metering areas). They'll more than pay for themselves by reducing employee fatigue and increasing working time.

- ◆ Keep a section of the warehouse for stock backup, apart from the everyday pick/pack flow. Use a grid system to locate merchandise quickly. The floor in the backup storage area is visually divided into numbered sections. The computer system indicates the location of the merchandise. Be sure to keep this up to date as merchandise is moved. The computer will indicate items that must be moved from bulk storage to pick locations.

No matter what warehouse design you choose, don't be locked into it. Experiment and adjust to your changing needs.

The Right Way to Receive Merchandise

Every cataloger must find the right merchandise-receiving system. Here's a list of points to consider:

◆ Retain the original photographic sample to check against the merchandise as it arrives.

◆ Consider prepacking merchandise as it is received. Items most likely to be shipped in their own cartons can be totally packed or ordered prepacked from the vendor. Other items can at least be wrapped in foam. This will save time during pick/pack operations and protect products from damage while they're on the shelves.

◆ Instruct vendors to label outside packages with the item number, total unit quantity, and your purchase-order (PO) number. Your PO number should also appear on invoices and packing slips, whether the order is complete or partial, to reduce paperwork for both your staff and your accountant.

◆ Many catalogers, as part of their purchase order, furnish their vendors with bar-coded labels for incoming cartons.

◆ Instruct vendors to assign only one SKU-number item per master carton. This may not be possible at the beginning when you are ordering small quantities, but ask vendors to do this whenever feasible.

◆ For security reasons, don't leave cartons on the loading dock. Count them immediately. Shortages or damages must be noted on the freight bill at the time of delivery to expedite a claim settlement.

◆ Photograph merchandise cartons on the truck and loading dock for damage claims.

◆ Check all merchandise against the vendor's packing slip. Numerous errors occur in packing and the accompanying paperwork. Merchandise should be counted, statistically inspected, and posted to a receiving report (see Figure 13-6), which should then be compared with the purchase order by someone

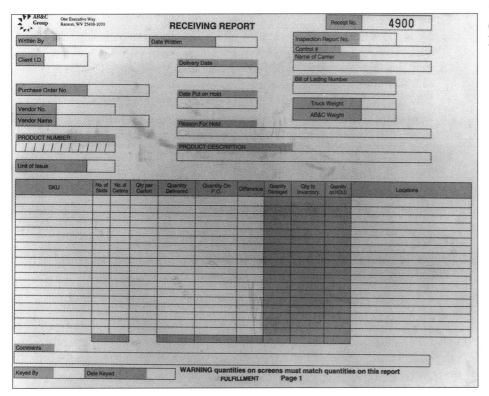

❖ **FIGURE 13-6**
Computerized Receiving Report

other than the receiving person. A receiving person who has a purchase order in hand is easily convinced that what should have been received is what has been received—and too often, this is not true.

♦ Keep a manual or computerized receiving log. Include the date, carrier, PO number (bill-of-lading number), shipper, number of cartons received, and the initials of the person who received them. This will help resolve disputes later.

♦ Some catalogs use bar code labeling for receiving, storage, warehouse movement, and shipping verification.

The Packing Station

1. The most sensible packing table for general merchandise is six feet wide, three feet deep, and 30 inches high—giving enough room to hold orders, supplies, and equipment. It should be fitted with a superstructure to hold shipping cartons. Do not provide chairs or stools; packers who stand tend to be more productive than those who sit.

2. Try not to use more than 5 to 12 carton or bag (soft pack) sizes. If more sizes are necessary, keep low-volume sizes farthest from the packing station. Avoid the use of UPS oversized cartons. (United Parcel's maximum size is a total of 130 inches in length and girth combined with a maximum length of 108 inches per package. Measure the five "surface" sides—the four sides of one end and the length of the package—and add them up.) Also, no single package should weigh more than UPS's 150-pound interstate maximum. But note that there is a large rate jump between 70 pounds and 71 pounds.

3. Pack high-value or easily pilfered items at a separate packing station, preferably one with added security.

4. Almost always insert a bounceback (catalog, order form, flier, and so on) in outgoing packages, but watch how this insertion affects the weight to be sure it generates enough income to compensate for any extra shipping costs.

5. Include how-to-return information (see "Customer Service" later in this chapter).

6. Be sure that someone other than the picker doublechecks outgoing orders before sealing packages. Check that product(s) match the order and that sales material, return instructions, notice of partial shipment, and so on, are all included.

7. Regularly check your scale for accuracy, especially if it's electronic. United Parcel and USPS provide valuable services, but there's no reason to overpay them. This is particularly true for third-class and priority-mail weight limits.

8. Keep an amiable relationship with carrier and postal personnel. It's to your benefit to develop a smooth relationship with the individual responsible for seeing that packages are picked up on time and delivered in good order.

9. Although UPS is supposed to do the loading of parcels on outbound trailers, mutual cooperation is to everyone's advantage.

10. When arranging parcels for pickup, position heavier items to the front, to be loaded first. This means they will wind up on the bottom, allowing lighter items to rest on top.

Keep Up with Electronic Options.   Newer techniques use bar code package labeling. This is read as the package moves on the conveyor belt. The computer calculates the weight and cost of various shipping methods and the package value and assigns the package to the selected form of shipping.

Additionally, for large catalogers, presort (USPS) or zone shipping (UPS) techniques are made easier through automated package sorting. Shipment verification is then given to the processing computer which updates the customer and order files. If the shipment is a charge-card order, the charge is then processed.

Image-Conscious Packaging

When a package arrives in a customer's home, the catalog's image comes with it. Compare it to a store: If the clothing is hanging straight on the racks, the aisles are clean, and the store looks generally inviting, you'll probably want to shop there again. The same is true of a mail order package. Here are some pointers on how to project a good image:

◆ Keep it neat and tidy-looking. This is the most significant physical contact your customer is likely to have with your company.

◆ Keep the label centered; avoid a torn or crinkled look.

◆ Use packing materials that are adequate to protect the item, but don't overdo it. Too much packing is not cost-efficient and can be annoying to the customer. To ensure that the packing material will do the job, send test packages to friends in various parts of the country. Breakable items generally should be wrapped in securely taped, white foam sheets, then put in the outer carton, which is filled with plastic pellets or chips. Avoid using shredded newspapers; they often leave the consumer's hands blackened by ink, which could come off on the product. Guess who will get the soiled item as a return?

   Environmental concerns must be taken into consideration when choosing packing materials. There has been a lot of negative press given to plastic pellets, and pellets that are biodegradable, though more expensive, are available. One cataloger uses shredded computer paper, thus saving the cost of having the paper taken away (this is a large company with lots of computer paper!). Before just jumping into an environmentally concerned solution such as this, understand all its implications. The computer paper is heavier than pellets (''peanuts'') and can affect the cost of outgoing packages. Determine what fits your company's image, then investigate the ever-changing options.

◆ Use plain paper labels and apply them with cellophane tape. Pressure-sensitive labels increase cost, can fall off, and, if preprinted separately, require additional labor to match with packing slips.

◆ Don't cut down cartons. This reduces the structural strength and can result in excessive damage and high returns.

◆ Whenever possible, put small items inside large items or tape them to the inside top flap of the box. Be sure the packing slip clearly indicates the number of items in the package to ensure that the customer does not throw the merchandise away with the packing material.

◆ The computer-generated packing slip should, when relevant, state that, ''This is a partial shipment. Other item(s) will be arriving in a separate shipment.'' Also, multiple-carton shipments should boldly indicate ''1 of 2,'' ''2 of 2,'' and so on, in case a shipment is separated in transit. Both procedures will save a great deal of customer-service time.

◆ Check with vendors to see if items can be purchased individually boxed in reshippable cartons. Many times, paying the manufacturer for the incremental cost is cheaper than packing the item yourself. But be sure the manufacturer's name is not on the outside of the carton; there is no need to give away your sources or confuse your customers.

◆ Carefully evaluate the benefits of soft-sided envelopes versus corrugated cartons. Savings can be considerable with the use of lined envelopes (or the Tyvek puncture-proof and waterproof version), because of the lighter weight and consequently lower shipping charges—and you can save on warehouse space and packing time. But although envelopes can be ideal for such items as hosiery, cartons almost always protect merchandise better and give the customer a more favorable impression of the catalog company. If you are using priority mail, the priority mail service will provide the envelopes and boxes.

Shipping Options

You can pack and ship from your own fulfillment center or have your vendors drop-ship. Why, in general, do catalogers do most of their own packing and shipping? What does it really cost? How do you charge for postage and handling? Read on.

United Parcel versus the Post Office.   The common belief is that UPS is the most usual way to deliver orders. But a highly economical alternative is the "pound rate" the USPS offers for bulk third-class mail. This may be the best method for similar size, "machinable" packages weighing under one pound.

For instance, a 12-ounce item can be sent anywhere (there's no cost difference based on zone, as with UPS) for only 64¢. Bulk-rate third class is computed at 68.7¢ per pound plus $.124 per piece for all non-presorted packages mailed at one time. Packages weighing 3.3067 ounces or less are charged the minimum per-piece rate, which is $.266. Conversely, UPS rates are based on the next highest pound. For instance, a half-pound package would have to be sent at the pound rate.

Individual parcels need not be exactly the same weight to qualify for bulk-rate third class, but at least 200 pieces—or a minimum total weight of 50 pounds per sack—are required at any given time. If, for example, you have 100 packages of 2 ounces each and 100 packages of 3 ounces each, all would be mailed at the minimum rate of $.266 each. Note, however, that all these packages must be metered with the correct postage, be sorted in zip code sequences, and comply with bag/tie requirements.

Schedule a meeting with your USPS customer-service representative, even if you are a small mailer, to determine whether this potentially cost-saving service is right for your company. The meeting costs nothing. Also, obtain a copy of the *USPS Domestic Mail Manual* (even before you meet with your representative). It clearly outlines all the rules and regulations regarding third-class mail. No mail order company should be without a copy of this publication.

Keep up to date by subscribing to postal manual supplements. If you decide the economics of the USPS service are too good to pass up and that your fulfillment center will have no problem conforming to its regulations and requirements, consider a few other points:

♦ How much longer will it take the package to arrive if it is sent via bulk rate rather than by UPS? Is the time difference substantial enough to cause customer dissatisfaction? Large shippers using this method have experienced delays of only two to three days over UPS, but this can vary depending on volume, location, and destination.

♦ How valuable are the products you plan to send? Third-class shipments cannot be insured (UPS packages are insured) or traced. Avoid shipping high-value merchandise via USPS.

♦ Are the additional services UPS currently offers worth the extra cost to you? For instance, if you inadvertently send a package to the wrong address, UPS will try, for a charge, to deliver the package to the right address and will inform you of the correction. It also has an "urgent inquiry" service, which is just what it sounds like. Call for delivery information, and UPS will try to get back to you with the answer in less than an hour. Its Merchandise Exchange program lets customers contact UPS directly for a pickup of merchandise with which they are dissatisfied. For a small fee, UPS arranges with the cataloger to deliver the new item in exchange for the old in one tidy process (this works for exchanges only).

Mailers who use a combination of UPS and USPS have had no significant problems with delivery of unsigned-for packages. But monitor USPS deliveries carefully. If customers receiving packages by this method are ordering less, it could be a sign they are unhappy with the time it takes for delivery. Have customer-service calls increased on the USPS parcels? This could be another sign that a problem exists. Always balance cost savings with customer satisfaction.

Overnight and Two-Day Delivery.   Those of us with first-hand experience of customer attitudes are not surprised to learn that customers tend to assume they will receive the product they ordered sooner than they usually do. Many catalogers have decided to address customers' expectations by giving the option of superquick delivery. Their suspicions that customers are willing and able to pay for "almost instant gratification" are turning out to be well founded. Bill Nicolai, formerly of the outdoor/recreation gear catalog Early Winters, was one of the first to offer overnight delivery. He reported that the average order was four times higher than slower deliveries.

No matter what your company's size, negotiate with the overnight-service company. Don't expect to pay the standard charge; rates are determined by a variety of factors, including weight and volume.

There's another advantage for the direct marketer who offers guaranteed superquick delivery: an extended selling season. So far, this appears to be especially true for major holidays, such as Christmas. Catalogers offering overnight delivery can watch sales still going strong up to several days before Christmas.

Erv Magram, president of the women's clothing catalog Lew Magram, cautiously tested an overnight delivery against a control panel that did not offer this premium service. The overnight service was very successful. But remember, there's more to implementing such a service than just contacting your friendly air courier. Orders must be processed correctly and quickly! Systems-processing adaptations may be needed to ensure the order is smoothly processed internally.

One unforeseen problem some current users have is that response is much greater than anticipated—with figures as much as 15 percent to 20 percent higher than the standard response, you get some idea of the potential hazards. If your warehouse isn't set up to handle this welcome, but potentially dangerous, deluge of "overnight" customers, your customer-service department may find itself working overtime—and you'll have a lot of disappointed, resentful customers who may quickly cease to be customers.

The effect of overnight delivery on inventory.   In recent years, the ready availability of overnight delivery has extended the fall/holiday selling season. Coupled with consumer confidence in the catalog industry, quicker delivery has led to what many refer to as the "fifth quarter." This is the period starting early in December and, in many cases, extending to December 23 or 24. As a result, the stream of orders during this period is accelerated, and many order curves show a steep rise. Thus, an SKU that has been a good-but-not-great seller may suddenly show a large increase in sales. The need for inventory sharply increases for certain items. If historical data is in place showing how the same or similar items performed in past fifth quarters, increased inventory needs may be projectable, at least for a category if not for each item.

If no data is in place it may be wiser for the cataloger not to risk a high overall inventory position. This may mean disappointing the consumer on particular items, but well-trained operators can minimize the problem. Anecdotal evidence suggests this approach is used by many catalogs that prefer to suggest alternate items rather than getting caught with high unsold inventories. This approach would also hold true for those categories/items where prior history does not indicate a realized demand.

Determining Shipping and Handling Charges.   Despite the common belief that most consumers object to paying shipping and handling, some tests have shown that, when given a choice, the consumer will pick a lower price plus shipping and handling costs over a higher price without shipping and handling. Some consumers understand that the cataloger spends money to send a product, and that their own time and the cost of gasoline, parking, babysitters, and so on, add up to more than they are paying in shipping and handling charges. Other consumers consider this a real "hot button," so carefully evaluate your real costs against "what the traffic will bear."

Getting at the Real Costs.   In general, there are four basic options for determining shipping costs. These have been outlined by Stanley J. Fenvessey in *DM News*:

1. **Manual metering.** This is the classic weighing and metering system that employs a scale and a postage meter. The meter tape is applied to the package. New electronic scales are available to simplify postage calculations.

2. **Metering by handheld scanner.** For this method, the zip code and package identification number must be printed as a bar code on the shipping label. The bar code is then read by a handheld wand or laser scanner. A microcomputer connected to both the scanner and the scale calculates and prepares a manifest. Employees can be trained to operate the bar-code wand in 30 minutes, and accuracy is reported to be 99.7 percent.

3. **Predetermined package weight.** Here, the weight of each item and its shipping container is predetermined and entered into a computer database. At the time of shipment, the computer is notified of the shipment by either scanning or keying the order number. The computer, using the precalculated postage, prepares a manifest listing.

4. **In motion.** This is the most sophisticated method and is quickly becoming the standard. A label similar to those used for handheld scanning is prepared. A fixed scanner reads the bar code as the package rolls across a scale that is part of the conveyor system. The scanner reads the data, weighs the package, determines the shipping cost, and prepares the manifest while the package is in motion, without the need for an operator.

Using a manifest system.   The word "manifest" has been mentioned several times. What does it mean, and what are its advantages? A *manifest system* allows a company to ship products without a label showing the actual cost of shipping. (The normal meter used for UPS charges generates a label showing actual costs.) The manifest system allows the company to pass on its real costs, without alienating customers. If, for example, the shipping cost is $3.50 and the customer has paid $5.75 for shipping and handling, the customer could feel cheated—temporarily forgetting the cataloger's costs for labor and shipping materials. This potential problem can be circumvented by keeping a manifest or log of daily UPS charges. Figure 13-7 shows a computerized shipping manifest. If you are not using the manifest system, simply keep a daily log of the information shown in the figure.

Ways of charging.   The three most common ways of charging customers for postage and handling are the following:

1. Nothing is charged (the cost is absorbed by the company or in the selling price of the item).

2. The cost of postage and handling is shown after the retail price of each item in the catalog.

3. A postage-and-handling chart is provided on the order form.

L. L. Bean used to charge no shipping and handling, but virtually no cataloger can now afford to offer this service to their customers. The Sharper Image displays the charge in brackets after the retail price; and all Hanover House catalogs use a chart. And some catalogers, like Spiegel, charge by weight.

Not charging for shipping and handling must be financially evaluated by individual companies. Can the cataloger afford to absorb the cost or increase the retail price of the merchandise to cover this expense?

The disadvantage of listing the shipping charge after the item is that a customer can subconsciously be discouraged from buying a product. What's more, if the customer has decided to purchase many products, this method of allocating separate shipping and handling charges for each product can add up to many dollars and may even persuade the customer to order less.

❖ **FIGURE 13-7** **Computerized Manifest System**

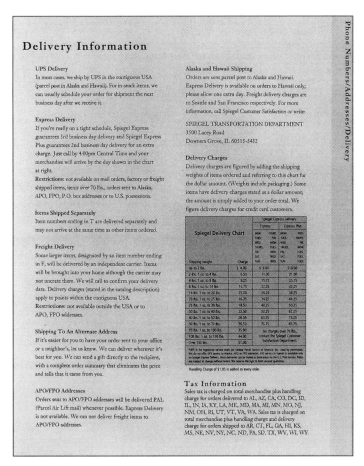

Source: Gerry King & Associates. Reprinted with permission.

❖ **EXAMPLE 13-2**
Spiegel bases its shipping and handling charges on the weight of the merchandise.

A shipping and handling chart is less likely to deter a customer from buying, because he or she sees it after deciding to buy. Figure 13-8 shows shipping and handling charges used successfully by a sampling of catalogers. To determine the best chart for your merchandise mix, follow the steps outlined in the next section. You will also need to segment merchandise by the price-point categories listed in the figure. Then, see if the average fulfillment cost per price-point category is adequately covered by the chart.

View your shipping charges as a totally separate area. Historically, it has been an accepted and smart practice for postage and handling to become a profit center in itself. This, however, has become much more difficult as customers have become more sensitive to shipping charges and the costs have increased for catalogers. Test different pricing structures to find one with which both you and your customers will be comfortable. And regularly recheck actual costs versus charges.

Estimating what to charge.   The weight of every product in the carton and packing material in which it is to be sent must be taken into consideration when determining what to charge for shipping and handling. Many people initially use the UPS charge for Zone 8 (the farthest you can send the product, unless you are receiving orders from Alaska, Puerto Rico, Hawaii, or Canada) to make sure the shipping cost is covered for all zones. These figures are estimates only, but they will help you decide what to charge.

Adjust your figures later, after you know which zone constitutes the average shipping point. For cartons and soft-side envelopes, figuring the cost of each piece is relatively easy. Only through experience will you learn how much packing material to allocate per package. Watch costs of shipments outside the continental United States carefully. Most likely, you will need to ask customers to pay a set surcharge.

Determine how long it takes warehouse personnel to put the product in stock, locate it in response to orders, pack the box, and load it on the UPS truck. Multiply this time by the packer's rate (include the dollars you allocated for overhead, insurance, and so on). The hourly rate varies, but let's assume the allocated rate is $8 per hour. The formula is:

Hours × Hourly rate = Labor cost

($1/12$ hour × $8/hour = $.67).

To determine the total cost of shipping and handling for UPS mailings, the following items are added together:

Labor cost	$0.67
Materials	0.50
UPS	3.51
Allocated overhead	0.50
Total	$5.18

A similar formula applies to costs of shipping by USPS.

❖FIGURE 13-8
Sample Shipping and Handling Prices Chart

If order totals:	Please add:
Up to $20.00	$4.25
$20.01 to $30.00	$5.25
$30.01 to $40.00	$6.50
$40.01 to $50.00	$7.50
over $50.00	$10.00

Add $3.25 for each additional order.

Fulfillment Start-up Guidelines

Here's what you'll need to start a fulfillment operation:

- Telephone requirements
- Postal requirements
- Packaging requirements
- Banking requirements
- Refund checks
- Item information
- Vendor information
- Forecasting/mail plan
- Stationery requirements
- Promotion specials
- Packing instructions
- Purchase-order information
- Pick document notes
- Kit listing by item (products comprised of multiple items)
- Narrative item information sheet
- Telemarketing/customer service and warehouse presentation
- Sample pick document
- Report distribution
- Data-processing set-up information

Fulfillment Productivity Guidelines

Several areas important to data-entry productivity, such as up-to-date equipment and well-organized surroundings, can also effectively increase fulfillment productivity. But some other guidelines also apply:

- Establish definite standards by which to evaluate employees—for example, a certain number of pieces (to be sorted or picked) per hour.
- Keep a weekly record (maintained by the employee or by a supervisor) of the work done by each employee.
- Reward employees who exceed the set standards with monetary or nonmonetary incentives (buy them flowers or lunch, give them a day off, award a trophy or merchandise certificate, or the like).
- Follow up on a regular basis, making sure the program is working for both the catalog company and its employees. These guidelines can also be applied to increase the productivity of office personnel.

In-house or Outside Fulfillment

Many catalogers choose not to maintain an internal fulfillment operation. Instead, they contract with outside vendors to accept telephone orders, perform physical fulfillment, or both. There are many configurations available, such as outsourcing everything except customer service. In general, external fulfillment is used by small to medium-size companies or companies who are starting a new venture—whether as start-up, a new division, or a new marketing/distribution channel. The majority of outside sources are well qualified and in effect are transparent to your customer.

Both internal fulfillment and outsourcing have advantages and disadvantages:

Cost.

   Internal Requires capital costs for equipment and location. Employees are a substantial payroll factor and training can be costly in both time and money.

External Uses a fee for service that can be equated to a cost per order, so there are minimal initial start-up costs. There is usually a start-up fee charged by the fulfillment service which is over and above the fee for service.

Control.

Internal Direct control that you monitor daily, made possible by close proximity, often in the same building.

External Third-party employees who, although dedicated, are not directly monitored by you and may not have as much enthusiasm and loyalty as those you employ yourself.

Generally speaking, using an outside fulfillment center is an excellent way for a cataloger to keep initial financial exposure to a minimum. Building a warehouse and staffing it with experienced, well-trained personnel can be a frighteningly high expense for an unproven venture. Many catalogers initially use outside resources for this service, moving parts of the function in-house as the catalog proves itself financially sound.

The first area to move in-house is almost always order taking: many believe this customer contact cannot be duplicated by a third party. Some companies, as previously mentioned, divide the services offered by a fulfillment house, putting the phone contact area in-house immediately and the physical product fulfillment with a service.

Numerous issues and options will affect the decision, and they will be different for each catalog. The inexperienced cataloger would do well to obtain qualified aid in assessing the relative merits of the choices available.

Determining the Cost of Fulfillment

Now that you have an overview of the process it would be wise to understand how the costs in that process break out. This will also be useful in determining whether to use an outside service or internalize the function.

Fulfillment costs fall into two categories: direct and indirect. Direct costs include

- Labor and systems
- Order processing, keying, picking, packing, manifesting, stocking, and receiving

Indirect costs are

- Freight (UPS, USPS, FedEx, and so on)
- Telephone line charges
- Packing materials
- Forms

Items often omitted from or not considered in the complete cost of fulfillment, might include

- Credit-card rates (transaction fees and authorizations)
- Bank charges
- Bad debt (write and collection efforts)
- Credit-card chargebacks
- Insurance
- Warehouse, equipment, and their maintenance
- Physical inventories
- Liquidation and write-off/markdown of excess stock and unusable returned merchandise

♦ Postage for FTC/backorder and other notices

Basically, the guidelines historically offered for an ongoing catalog are as follows:

1. Gross fulfillment costs will equate to between 14 percent and 18 percent of net catalog sales (this can be up to 21 percent for a start-up).

2. Net fulfillment costs (gross minus the postage-and-handling revenue) will equate to between 7 percent and 10 percent of the new catalog sales (this can be up to 12 percent for a start-up).

These figures will equate to between $4 and $7 for direct costs for an average catalog order. These figures are based on the following typical parameters:

Parameter	Value
Telephone (800-number) orders	70% to 80%
Mail orders	30% to 20%
Credit-card payments	75% to 85%
Line items per order	1.5% to 2%
Phone-order call time	3 to 4 minutes
Nonorder call volume	
(directly impacted by back order ratio)	10% to 20%
Shipments per order	1.1 to 1.3
Average shipment weight	3 to 4 lbs.

The typical indirect costs of fulfillment will almost equal the direct costs (about $4 to $7 per order):

Parameter	Value
Phone-line charge	About $0.11 to $0.19 per minute based on volume
Freight charges (average 2 to 4 lbs.)	Per parcel will cost between $3.16 and $5.14 for basic ground delivery services.
Packaging materials	Per parcel with dunnage and the shipping carton will be between $0.75 and $1.50.

When calculating labor costs, don't forget the expense of hiring and training. Remember training extends beyond new hires. If you call the telephone-room staff together for a 20-minute meeting and there are 10 in the meeting, that is 200 person-minutes you have invested in ongoing training. Brief daily meetings are great for morale and to check on the type of issues being encountered by staff.

These expense figures include a factor of operating expenses, not just for labor. Volume is the driving force.

Inventory Control

Determining how much of a particular item to stock is one of the greatest challenges direct marketers face. A cataloger must balance the cost of too much inventory against the possibility of losing customers due to sold-out merchandise. For catalogs with a sales history, past response lays the groundwork for inventory estimates, but for first-timers, it's strictly guesswork.

Forecasting

Everyone has different estimating methods. One start-up cataloger used the unorthodox method of ordering exactly the number of items, given the space allocated for the product, that he needed to make a small profit. His method worked (once), but he is one of the luckiest individuals ever to walk the face of the earth. His method is not recommended. Of those that are, let's take the easiest first.

Premailing Forecasting.   Sales history is a great starting point, but don't forget to consider other determining factors:

◆ **Seasonality**. Is the item great for cold weather, but not suitable year-round? Gift items are strongest in the fall, but are surpassed in sales by ''me-oriented'' products in January.

◆ **Recent sales trends**. Has the item shown a downward sales trend?

◆ **Placement**. Did the product move to a more or less prominent sales position within the catalog?

Even if a product is new, a similarity to past sellers gives it an estimating edge over a totally new product. Use the criteria in the preceding list to estimate for similar products.

For new products, you must use common sense and any sales information you can garner from vendors and other catalogers. A look at profit and sales projections for the catalog can also help. First, project the average order and response rate of the catalog. Multiply these two figures to determine your gross sales. Next, determine the in-mail cost of your catalog and the cost of merchandise. Now look at your sales projections. Do they seem reasonable, given promotion costs? It is helpful to divide your promotion costs by the number of pages in the catalog. This will show the gross sales needed to pay for each page. Next, divide the per-page number by the number of items on that page to get a rough estimate of gross dollars required to pay for a particular item. (This is not to be confused with square-inch analysis, which is discussed in Chapter 14.) On the basis of your rough estimate, you can make necessary adjustments to items that may be over- or underprojected. (See ''order curves'' in Chapter 15.)

❖ **EXAMPLE 13-3**   Spiegel uses a bind-in to pretest merchandise and assist in forecasting.

BE FIRST WITH THE FASHION AND SAVE 20%

We're sending you this preview copy of our fall Together! Catalog to help us predict the best-selling styles. To thank you for ordering early, we'll give you a 20% discount!

Call toll free or mail or fax the special order form on the other side by JULY 8, 1994 to receive your discount. You won't be charged until your order is filled, as soon as we receive the merchandise on OCTOBER 14, 1994.

BE FIRST WITH THE FASHION AND SAVE 20%

Order early from this preview copy of Together! and save 20%.

Look for your special discount offer inside the front cover.

SHOP TODAY TO BE FIRST WITH THE FASHION AND THE SAVINGS!

Postmailing Forecasting. Here's your chance to make up for any inventory-commitment errors. You can begin to plot a response curve, which will give you a more accurate assessment of your inventory needs.

Let's assume a 500,000 mailing, a 2-percent response expectation, and an average-order-size expectation of $70. That's 10,000 orders, equaling $700,000 in gross sales, that can be projected over a 13-week period as shown in Table 13-1. (The percentages in the table, of course, are only examples and are based on historical curves used by the direct-marketing industry. Each catalog responds differently.)

If orders continue to come in at the rate shown in Table 13-2, the response will be considerably higher than the 10,000 originally projected, and inventory will need to be adjusted (see Chapter 15 for additional information on order curves). The formula used to calculate the anticipated total demand in Table 13-2 is:

Cumulative orders ÷ by % anticipated completed sales = Anticipated demand.

For example, for week 1,

650 ÷ .06 (6% expressed as a decimal) = 10,833.

Inventory needs per item are generally projected by the computer using the same curve as for total orders. A better method is to generate demand curves by category. Projections should be updated to keep up with product demand.

When to Order

Another consideration is how long it actually takes to place orders and receive merchandise. To determine when to place an order, you first need to know the following information:

1. The number of units in stock
2. The number of units currently on order
3. The anticipated total number of units that will be sold (per Table 13-2)
4. The anticipated amount of time that will elapse between order placement and order receipt

Week	% Sales Completion
1	6
2	18
3	27
4	35
5	55
6	69
7	76
8	79
9	84
10	88
11	92
12	96
13	100

❖ TABLE 13-1
Example of Weekly Sales Projection (assumes another catalog has not been mailed during this time period)

Week	Cumulative Orders	Anticipated Completion of Sales (%)	Anticipated Total Demand
1	650	6	10,833
2	2,150	18	11,944
3	3,500	27	12,963
4	4,750	35	13,571

❖ TABLE 13-2
Example of Anticipated Demand Based on Cumulative Orders and Anticipated Percent Completion of Sales

Using the same formula employed in Table 13-2, project the demand week by week. For instance, assuming that 250 pieces are in stock and actual sales are 95 units by week 3:

95 ÷ .27 = Anticipated total demand of 352 pieces.

To determine the week you can expect merchandise to be depleted, divide the in-stock quantity—in this case, 250 pieces—by the anticipated demand, 352:

250 − 352 = .71 (71%).

According to Table 13-1, merchandise would be completely gone during the seventh week.

Now determine how much time is needed between placing the order and actual receipt. Factor in this time, allowing a few days leeway. Also, remember to update projections weekly. Even your own historical charts change with such buyer influences as the weather and economic trends.

One step beyond practicing overall sales is to determine the sales for a particular item. Here you need exception reporting which is a report of your top sellers. The same techniques apply but, in this case, the report will show you the stock remaining on individual items and how long this stock will last.

How Much to Buy

To determine the quantity you need to buy, answer the following questions:

1. How much storage room is available?
2. How much can you afford to spend, both initially and after taking cash flow into consideration?
3. How much insurance coverage do you have?
4. What arrangements have you made with the vendor regarding ordering quantity and product availability?
5. What is the cost in employee time and paperwork to cut multiple orders?

Each case must be considered individually, but always remember that the long-term cost of losing a customer due to product unavailability can mean much more to a bottom line than minimum overbuying.

Backorders: The Cataloger's Curse

It is impossible for every item to be in stock all the time. Figure 13-9 includes information on how backorders "flow" through the system. Basically, at the first stage after order entry, this chart breaks into three sections:

1. Merchandise is available and shipped.
2. Merchandise is in a backorder situation. As soon as new merchandise is received, it is released to inventory and orders are filled.
3. Merchandise is not expected to be available at any time in the future. The order cannot be filled.

❖ FIGURE 13-9   **Flow Chart Showing the Steps in Controlling Backorders**

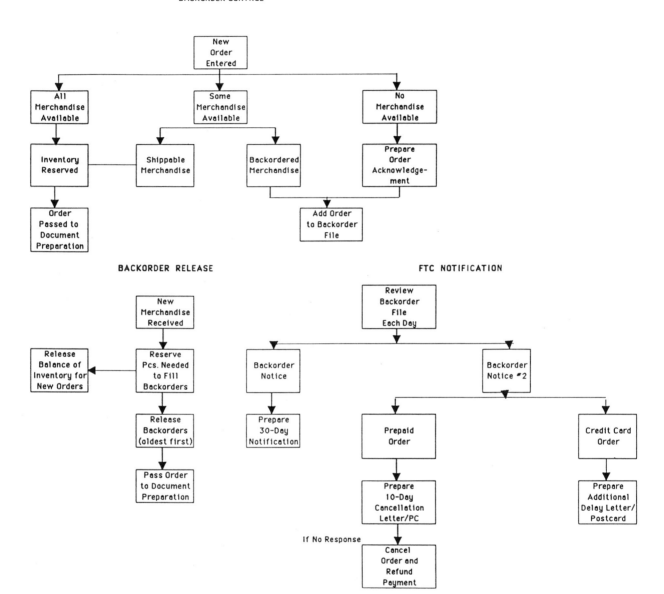

If the merchandise is not expected to be available, inform the customer by letter and refund the customer's money immediately. If merchandise is in a backorder situation, read on.

Adhering to Federal Regulations.   The Federal Trade Commission (FTC) takes its job seriously and so should you. Ignorance of the rules and regulations will not be an acceptable excuse if you inadvertently break them. Penalties can run as high as $10,000 per infraction, so read Chapter 16 and remember two major points:

1. If an item will not be available for delivery within 30 days and this has not been noted in the catalog, a first-delay letter with a free return communication device must be sent to the consumer who has ordered it—within 30 days of the order. This letter (or postcard) must include a postage-paid, preaddressed postcard or envelope with which the consumer can cancel the order (see Figure 13-10). Alternatively, the communication could provide customers with a toll-free number with which to respond.

2. A second-delay letter or postcard must be sent within the second 30-day period after the order. If the customer fails to respond within 14 days, the order must be canceled and a refund (if the payment was by check) must be processed (See Figure 13-11)

Each company should modify the basic form letters shown in Figure 13-10 and 13-11 to reflect its own personality. For example, Current, Inc., uses a double postcard in the company image.

❖ FIGURE 13-10   **Sample First-Delay Letter**

ABC Catalog Company
123 Main Street
Anywhere, U.S.A. 00000   Date
(000) 000-0000

Customer's Name   Order Number
Address

Dear Customer:

Thank you for your order for_____.

Due to unforeseen circumstances, shipment of your order will be delayed_____days. Please be assured that we will not deposit your check (or process your credit-card payment) until shipment can be made.

Thank you for your understanding and patience.

Sincerely,

P.S. We have included our latest catalog in the hope that we may continue to serve you in the convenience of your own home.
_____

If you wish to cancel your order, please check the appropriate boxes and return this letter to us in the enclosed postage-paid envelope:

_____Sorry, I can't wait. Please cancel my order and:

   [ ] Send me my check or a refund.

   [ ] Hold my payment as a credit toward my next order.

IF I WISH TO WAIT, I UNDERSTAND THAT I NEED NOT RETURN THIS FORM and that my order will be sent as soon as possible (maximum of 30 days).

Date _____   Signature _____

❖ FIGURE 13-11   **Sample Second-Delay Letter**

ABC Catalog Company
123 Main Street
Anywhere, U.S.A. 00000   Date
(000) 000-0000

Customer's Name   Order Number
Address

Dear Customer:

We are sorry to inform you that your order for_____
has been unavoidably delayed for longer than our original 30-day delay.

We estimate shipment time to be between _____and _____.
Please forgive us for this disappointing development.

We wish to continue to serve you and hope you understand that we are doing everything possible to speed your order. If you have paid by check and we do not hear from you within 30 days, a prompt refund will be sent. If you requested we charge your order, be assured that no charge will be made.

Thank you for your understanding and patience.

Sincerely,

_____

Please check all the appropriate boxes and return this letter in the enclosed postage-paid envelope.

   [ ] I am willing to wait—please don't cancel my order.

   [ ] I paid by check—please send me my refund.

   [ ] I paid by credit card—simply cancel my order.

   [ ] I paid by check, but wish the amount credited to my next order.

Date _____   Signature _____

❖ **EXAMPLE 13-4** Current uses double postcards in the company image for **(a)** first-delay and **(b)** second-delay notification.

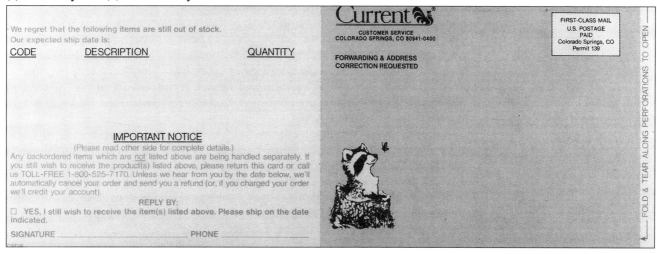

The importance of abiding by the FTC 30- and 60-day rules cannot be stressed strongly enough. Follow FTC regulations to the letter to keep out of trouble and have the added benefit of improved customer relations.

Effect on Repeat Purchases. Whenever possible, backorders should be avoided because they have a significantly negative effect on the likelihood of reorders from the customer base. Some studies have shown that the two most negative indicators causing repeat purchases were:

1. The number of times the customer was on backorder.
2. The total time of the combined backorders.

Backorders are also a problem because they cause partial shipments, leading to multiple shipments, which result in unnecessary costs—costs that will reduce profits.

Customer Service

Leonard Schlesinger and James L. Heskett, professors at Harvard Business School, wrote in a *Harvard Business Review* article that only 14 percent of customers stop shopping at a particular place because of the quality of the goods, but "more than two-thirds defect because they find service people indifferent or unhelpful." Service can even pay off after a mistake has been made. Schlesinger and Heskett report that 95 percent of unhappy customers will repurchase if the problem is promptly resolved.[1] Take too long, and the number drops to 70 percent.

A poor service attitude doesn't just cause a loss of customers; it causes a loss of money to the company in terms of employee turnover and training. The same Harvard study found that, for one company, "disruptions in work relationships and the transactional costs of getting employees on and off the payroll raised the total costs of employee turnover to 1.5 times an employee's annual salary." Furthermore, the analysis concluded that from an investment of 50 percent of an employee's salary in activities to eliminate turnover, the company "could reap a one-year payback."

Customers are the lifeblood of your catalog. Although they may be expensive to obtain, they constitute the heart of your profit. If they decide to order from a competitor, their loyalties may shift forever. Take care of your customers as you would your most prized possession.

Handling Complaints and Inquiries

Each customer complaint or inquiry should be acted on promptly. Make one person responsible for the first reading of every letter received to decide to whom it should be forwarded for proper action. Phone inquiries tend to make up the bulk of contacts in a catalog that promotes customer service. Stanley J. Fenvessy estimated there is a 30-percent to 40-percent increase in customer-service contact with a toll-free number. Although contact with your customer can encourage loyalty, this must be weighed against the high cost of this service. As in all aspects of direct mail, test to be sure. Most customer-service inquiries break down into five categories:

1. A need for more information on a particular product
2. The status of an order
3. Cancellations and changes
4. Returns
5. Refunds and credits

A Computerized System

For customer-service representatives to act promptly, they must, of course, have access to up-to-date information. Even small companies should investigate the benefits of computerized customer-service records. Microcomputers can handle a surprising amount of information, and computerization can make a big difference in the speed and accuracy with which you handle customer inquiries.

Another advantage of a computerized system is that it virtually eliminates the cold, impersonal printed letter often sent in response to a customer's problem. Although form letters can be a necessity, those that answer customers' complaints with the appropriate box checked are unfriendly and convey a lack of interest in the customer's problem. With a computer, you can capture every detail of a customer's order and recall it as needed. Then, when Mrs. Smith calls to find out where her order is, you can immediately tell her the exact date the order was received, filled, and shipped and the shipment method used. Depending on the shipping method, tracking systems will even give you the name of the person signing for the order. If she writes in instead of calling, either the computer can generate a letter addressing her problem, or you can personalize the form letter by adding the specific information from the computer file.

Informed Customer-Service Representatives

Customer-service people can do their job well only if they have the right answers when customers call. Put your representatives in a room that contains a sample of every product in your catalog. Then, if a question or problem arises regarding a product, service staff will have easy access to the product. Arrange a time with the staff to explain the products' intricacies or details that may be important to customers.

Be sure to capture every detail of a customer complaint or correspondence for each and every occurrence. Keeping good customer-service records will alert you to customers who have made more than one complaint in a short period of time. This may call for a personal letter to let the customer know you are monitoring the problems and will act on them immediately. Or, if a customer constantly returns items or repeatedly claims nondelivery, strongly consider deleting his or her name from your mailing list. Most people are honest, but some take advantage of the fact that a catalog may be operating from a distance.

Figures 13-12, 13-13, and 13-14 provide the information you need for several types of customer-service letters. Use them as content guides only, and revise them to meet your company's needs and add a more personal touch.

❖ **FIGURE 13-12**
Sample Incorrect Information or Payment Letter

ABC Catalog Company
123 Main Street
Anywhere, U.S.A. 00000   Date
(000) 000-0000

Customer's Name   Otder Number
Address

Dear Customer:

Thank you for your recent order for _____. However, we are unable to process your order for the reason(s) checked below:

[   ] Payment not enclosed

[   ] Order not enclosed

[   ] Incorrect amount of money enclosed

      $_____ enclosed
      $_____ correct amount
      $_____ amount due

[   ] Did not specify size

[   ] Did not specify color

[   ] Invalid credit card

    Please verify your credit card number. Charge cannot be validated with number as shown. Please write corrected number on the line below.
    Correct Credit Card Number: _____

[   ] Expiration date on credit card is needed before we can process your order.
    Expiration Date _____

[   ] Card is declined. Please contact your credit-card company if clarification is necessary, or submit an alternative credit card.

[   ] Other

Please make the necessary corrections and return this letter in the enclosed envelope. Thank you for your order. We look forward to serving you again.

Sincerely,

❖FIGURE 13-13
Sample Out-of-Stock
Refund Letter

ABC Catalog Company
123 Main Street
Anywhere, U.S.A. 00000   Date
(000) 000-0000

Customer's Name   Order Number
Address

Dear Customer:

Thank you for your order of our item _____. Unfortunately,
we no longer have that item available.

[   ] A refund check in the amount of $_____ is enclosed.

[   ] Be assured that the credit-card charges you authorized will _not_ appear on your
next statement.

Thank you for shopping with us. We hope we may have the opportunity to serve you in
the future. We have included our most recent catalog so that, should you desire, you
may make an alternative selection from the convenience of your home.

Sincerely,

❖FIGURE 13-14
Sample Refund Letter to
Dissatisfied Customers

ABC Catalog Company
123 Main Street
Anywhere, U.S.A. 00000   Date
(000) 000-0000

Customer's Name   Order Number
Address

Dear Customer:

Thank you for promptly returning the _____. We are sorry
you were not satisfied.

[   ] A refund check in the amount of $_____ is enclosed.

[   ] A credit-card refund voucher in the amount of $_____ is enclosed.

Please feel free to make an alternative selection from our latest catalog, which we are
sending along for your convenience.

Thank you for shopping with us, and we hope to serve you again in the near future.

Sincerely,

Don't be complacent about service. Hire a professional who is knowledgeable about
customer service to assess your company. Providing good service does not necessarily
mean hiring more people. It means making the most efficient use of the people involved
in customer contact.

Here are some pointers for consideration:

1. Eliminate management layers. Stay close to your customers.
2. Stay in touch regularly, whether that means listening to customers or
presenting them with relevant offers.

3. Be a role model. Service representatives will mimic your feelings about customers.

4. Be specific about how to improve service. Direction must be clear, and representatives must truly understand what each course of action is to be.

5. Recognize particular skills as they relate to customer service. Not everybody does everything well. Try to match people's skills to their jobs.

6. Invest time in training. It will be rewarding to customers and company alike, as you see decreased turnover.

7. Invest in technological support.

8. Openly show your support for service people and what they do.

9. Offer meaningful incentives.

10. Delegate some authority to service people.

Voice Response

Voice response (most commonly called VRU for voice response unit) generally is used most effectively for frequent callers who know what they want. Interactive voice response (IVR) and VRU are fairly interchangeable terms, but technically VRU routes calls and IVR is interactive. A noncatalog example of this service is when a customer needs to obtain information about his or her checking-account balance. There's no real reason to talk to a customer representative just to get the balance or even to pay bills. The VRU eases customers quickly to the right menu of information and allows them to punch in the correct number for the service they want. Other uses might be registering for classes or requesting literature.

However, it isn't quite as simple when it is taken further and customers are asked to use VRU to order merchandise. This is more difficult because, even with the catalog in front of them, it's possible they may want more information about particular items. Home Shopping Network (HSN), one of the consumer shopping channels, makes VRU work because, for one thing, the customer has the necessary information right in front of him or her on the TV screen. It also works because HSN has a lot of frequent buyers who, as in the checking-account example, know exactly what they want. Furthermore, they are accustomed to simply punching in their customer number to access HSN's database.

To implement any type of voice response, you must make sure your phone system has sufficient capacity and the correct data interfaces. It's a simple process if you want customers to make simple choices, such as just punching one, two, three, four. But if you want your customers to be able to enter a checking account number and have a lot of other options, VRU must be linked to multiple transaction systems and may also need to incorporate security functions. For instance, these security measures could require that customers provide their social security number with their account number, with the account number acting as a cross-reference. (In most cases, deposit and credit-card accounts are served by different systems.)

One big advantage of VRU is that you could, if you chose, eliminate the potential confusion of having two different 800 numbers for ordering and customer service. Rather, you could have customers call a central number and then prompt them with different numbers, operationally assigning a higher priority to ordering versus asking about an order. Isaac Frydman, a technical expert and partner in Almskog & Frydman Communications of New York City reports that it is important not to have too many prompts because users won't remember all of them as they progress through the list. Ideally, there should be no more than 4 or 5, a maximum of 6. The more frequent the caller, the more complex you can make the menus.

Some catalogers believe the business-to-business environment can make better use of VRU than consumer-based businesses, largely because the caller is frequently a repeat customer who simply enters a customer number. If the order is uncomplicated enough, you could go as far as actually having them enter the order. Voice Forms, a preset form, prompts the caller with such questions as "Number of items?" and "Regular delivery or express?" Building a script that looks like an order form is pretty basic, as is writing a script for checking order status. For instance, Sealand, a freight container company, has voice response that lets callers check on the status of freight in five different languages. Another version of this system might assign different 800 numbers for different languages. Weight Watchers, using ANI, makes meeting times and locations closest to their customers easily accessible by phone. Alternatively, the customer can enter a zip code and get location information.

Payback depends on cost but it is not uncommon to find that in certain industries, such as consumer financial services, upward of 70 percent of calls can be handled exclusively by VRU and never get to an operator. For a system with four or six lines, you could spend as little as $8,000 to $10,000. For 80 to 100 lines and up, the cost could be $500,000 plus host interfaces (such as links to amount data and/or your ACD).

Also because not everyone has a touch-tone phone (in some parts of the country, 25 percent of the population doesn't have touch tone) and not everyone will get the answer they desire, some customers will still go to an operator. And you should know that another technology is quickly advancing: speech recognition. With this, you can literally tell the phone your selection. This currently works best with discrete commands, such as ''one,'' ''two,'' and so on, because the software finds it more difficult to interpret a continuous string of words, such as a zip code. This option does show promise, with some users reporting higher than 80 percent accuracy, depending on application.

What consumers think of voice response.   Liz Kislik, a customer-service and phone-operations expert and president of Liz Kislik Associates (Valley Stream, New York) calls attention to the fact that acceptability of VRU is not total in the consumer arena. Some consumers are scared off by this technology, actually feel resentful, and have a ''Don't-you-want-to-talk-to-me?'' syndrome. One of the secrets is understanding when to use VRU for consumers. For instance, it's probably not a good idea if you want to foster a bonding relationship with a customer, because VRU doesn't provide that ''warm, fuzzy'' feeling you (and your customers) might desire. It does work, though, for those customers who advocate control and privacy. Ms. Kislik suggests that you evaluate whether your customer is an ATM-type person or the type who would prefer to use a bank teller. This will give you a good clue as to your audience's potential acceptance of VRU.

To a degree, you will have to accept that you will lose the opportunity to personalize communications, but you can still customize them somewhat. For instance, the customer can listen to different pieces of recorded messages. But it's just not possible to truly personalize without personnel because only people can react according to the immediate need of the person on the other end of the line.

Also be sure you know just how much benefit or damage using VRU does to your customer relationship. One way to do this is to make sure the caller ends up with a live representative. This will give you the chance to evaluate and/or probe for perceptions. Without this person on your end of the conversation, you can only take empirical information and extrapolate it.

If you choose to use VRU in your consumer program, what should the content of the message be? In general, always aim to strengthen the relationship. This is especially important with new callers. For these first-time people, you might make it a point to provide information about your company or to talk about special opportunities available only because this person has called (say, sales items or seasonally relevant happenings). No matter what, it's critical to provide straightforward instruction on how to get through the menu successfully. Don't be hokey or use a voice-over approach. Don't read the script like it is ad copy either; this is boring and will make it easier for consumers to tune out your message, just as they would background noise from a radio station.

How do you know if you have a good process in place? Some companies have the type of system that cuts into the recording when an operator becomes available. Interestingly enough, some customers will actually complain and ask to be given back to the recorded message so they can hear the whole thing. Without doubt, this indicates you may be onto something!

When using prompts (commands), what should the voice sound like? Here there are different schools of thought. Since consumers generally prefer to talk to a person rather than a machine, the ''voice'' should sound as much like a person as possible. And this should be a regular person, someone like one of your employees, not a radio announcer. This doesn't however, mean that you should use an employee to record the message, because they are simply not trained in such techniques as voice modulation, diction, and so on. Use a professional. Turn to the vendors who provide equipment or service; they usually have access to "talent."

Handling Returns Efficiently

Generally speaking, returns are an insignificant problem in cataloging, ranging from 1 percent (occasionally even less) to a high of 20 percent (higher percentages have been known to happen, but they are totally unacceptable). The percentage of returns is directly related to the type of merchandise offered. The higher percentages occur mostly in the clothing industry, where incorrect size or fit leads to exchanges.

Returns do occur, however, so no matter how large or small your catalog company, be certain to include explicit instructions outlining how to return enclosed merchandise in all outgoing packages. This does not increase returns, as might be expected, and substantially cuts down on customer-service calls.

The How-to-Return Form.   An easy-to-understand how-to-return form accomplishes several goals at once:

1. It makes it quick and easy for customers to solve a problem with merchandise.
2. For customers who do not have a problem, it reconfirms the company's willingness to stand by its guarantee to service any complaint they may have.
3. It helps keep the cost of customer service down.

If buyers can readily understand the form provided, it will save them time and eliminate the aggravation they fear may result from a direct confrontation on the phone. Instead, they can simply fill out the form, return the merchandise, and wait for the company to resolve the problem.

Depending on the size and economics of your company, how-to-return information can be displayed on the back of a computer-generated packing slip or merely photocopied and inserted in the package. Regardless of the format, no package should leave the fulfillment center without a form.

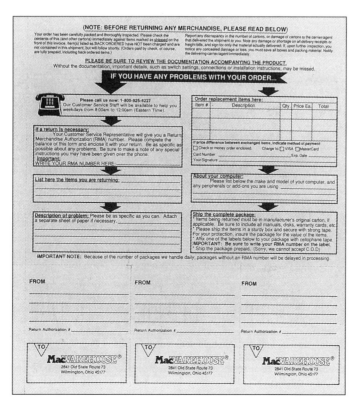

❖ **EXAMPLE 13-5**
MacWarehouse's how-to-return form (printed on the back of its packing slip) is very clear in its instructions. To expedite a return, it even includes perforated return labels at the bottom of the form.

Acknowledging Returns. When you do receive returned merchandise, a communication like the one shown in Figure 13-15 should be sent out. This lets your customer know that his or her return has been received and encourages new orders.

Some catalogers offer innovative services, such as free pickup or a return label, to make returns virtually painless for their customers.

Establishing Customer-Service Policies

Every cataloger needs to determine the best customer-service policies for his or her catalog. Here are some general guidelines to help get you started in writing your own policy:

- ◆ Whenever possible, process and send all orders within one week. The reorder rate for customers who receive orders promptly is more than 20 percent higher than for those who receive less efficient fulfillment. Also, customers who must wait too long for orders lose interest, too often resulting in returned merchandise.

- ◆ Submit credit charges for payment only after the shipment has been made.

- ◆ No merchandise substitutions are allowed by law unless clearly explained within your catalog. Customers often keep the substituted item only because it is too much of a hassle to return it. However, the next time they order by mail, they may choose to order from a competitor who didn't substitute merchandise.

- ◆ When some items are backordered, shipments should include a note indicating that the package contains a partial order.

❖**FIGURE 13-15**
Sample Acknowledgment of Returned Merchandise

STURBRIDGE YANKEE WORKSHOP,INC.
the Nation's Center for Traditional American Reproductions
90 Blueberry Road • Portland, Maine 04102-1989 • Telephone 207-774-9045

August 20, 1994

Dear Customer:

We are sorry that your order did not arrive to your satisfaction, and we have processed your request.

We have issued an immediate credit to your credit card account in the amount of $29.95 Please allow 1-2 billing cycles for this amount to be reflected in your credit card statement. If you have requested replacement merchandise, your credit card will be re-billed when we ship your new order.

We look forward to servicing your future home furnishing and gift needs.

Thank-you,

Customer Service

CUSTOMER-NO ORDER-NO
06974612   .H4660000.0064

♦ The customer should pay return postage unless the shipment is damaged or incorrect, in which case you pay.

♦ Do not make replacements or exchanges until the original item has been returned.

♦ Shipments should be made to those underpaying by up to $5.00* by check. The underpaid amount is billed with the shipment. Credit-card orders are adjusted and billed the correct amount.

♦ For underpayments of $5.00* or more, shipments should be held and the customer notified.

♦ "No collect calls" should be displayed on your order form; however, collect calls should be accepted.

♦ Credit-card overpayments should be submitted to the credit-card company in the correct amount.

♦ For check overpayments of $5.01* or more, a refund should be sent to the customer. For overpayments under $5.01,* a credit memo that the customer can apply to the next order or sign and return for a refund can be sent with the shipment. Be sure to explain exactly what the credit is for.

♦ Refunds for out-of-stock items that are not expected to be available should be issued within four days. If a customer claims nondelivery for items with a total value of $25.00* or less, reship the items—file a tracer, and keep open charge (do not credit the customer's charge) on the customer's account until the tracer results are known. Claims for items with a total value of more than $25.01* should be handled individually.

♦ If a customer claims to have returned an item but you have not received it, a new item or refund should be sent only if the customer agrees to file a tracer naming you as beneficiary.

* All dollar amounts in this checklist must be determined individually on the basis of your catalog's average dollar order, margin of profit, and processing costs.

True-Life Vignette.   To service a customer properly, you must first clearly understand his or her request. An example of what can happen if customer-service representatives misunderstand the complainant's wishes occurred at a major, well-known catalog company.

A male customer, on receipt of the slacks he ordered, found them too short. So, he pinned up the pants and enclosed a note saying that the amount by which he had pinned up the pants showed the additional length he needed. The customer-service people, however, misunderstood the instructions and shortened the pants to where they were pinned. The man, now slightly frustrated, sent the erroneously shortened pants back and included a pair of his own pants. His note indicates that the old pants he was sending were the length he wanted in the new ones. The customer-service people promptly shortened the customer's own pants and sent both pairs back to him!

Here's a case where customer-service people truly believed they were servicing the customer above and beyond the call of duty. In truth, they were guilty of not following the customer's instructions—twice! So, be sure your people take the time to read customers' requests carefully and really understand them.

Keeping Control

To run an efficient organization of any size, you need to establish a workable system of control reports. Daily reports show the status of work in progress and identify daily problems. Weekly reports evaluate the productivity and efficiency of a particular area. Monthly or work-cycle reports make use of all the previous information to highlight problem areas and spot trends.

Data Capture

Whether manually or via a computerized system, you should try to capture the following information:

- ◆ Date received
- ◆ Method of ordering
  Mail, phone, fax, or electronic (Faxed orders are growing in volume and data transmission will grow in the future.)
- ◆ Payment method
  American Express, MasterCard, Visa, Discover, check, cash, bill-me, and so on (with credit cards, get card number and expiration date)
- ◆ Source code
- ◆ Order number assigned
- ◆ Name of sold-to
- ◆ Address of sold-to
- ◆ Name of ship-to
- ◆ Address of ship-to
- ◆ Date keyed
- ◆ Items ordered
  Quantity of each item
  Date each item was shipped
- ◆ Total payment amount
  Postage and handling amount/value on orders
  Tax amount on order
  Merchandise amount on order
- ◆ Date and quantity of items returned
- ◆ Date and amount of refunds (for FTC compliance and to counter chargebacks)
- ◆ Date and type of notices issued

This information is not only essential for complete fulfillment, it is also the essence of your marketing and merchandising databases. Remember you will want to build your merchandising database for future forecasting and analysis. You will want to know the demand, price points, costs and net profitability of each and every item.

During the processing of your orders, you will want to capture other additional pieces of information essential to successful fulfillment processing and cost evaluations, including:

- ◆ Credit-card authorizations or declines by order number and customer.
- ◆ Weight, cost, and method of shipment for each parcel shipped on every order
- ◆ Manifest number, if appropriate, on every parcel shipped (required by UPS, FedEx, and so on) for any claims or adjustment
- ◆ Dates of cancellations
- ◆ Details of cancellations
- ◆ Identification of the individuals who
  keyed,
  picked,
  packed,
  inspected, or
  performed other work on an order
- ◆ Record of data or receipt of telephone calls/communications received from consumers
- ◆ Record of bad checks or fraudulent experience with a consumer

This is a lot of data, and it all lends itself to computerization and automation of one degree or another.

Types of Reports

Your first step is to decide which areas to address within your own company. Some suggestions are

1. Order counts
2. Inventory levels by item
3. Unit costs
4. Productivity levels
5. Number of customer complaints by type

A *mailroom report*, for instance, shows the quantity of mail received, how much mail still awaits attention, and how many hours per person were spent performing tasks. Monthly reports should be issued to check one month against another.

A *data-entry-report* follows the mail report in content. It includes a breakdown of work by type of data processed, the number of orders processed, the number of orders rejected, and the reason they were rejected.

Inventory-control reports shows the quantity of out-of-stock products by item, the date an item went out of stock, the anticipated arrival date of new merchandise, and the date orders were placed. Reports should also include total inventory levels by category.

Quality control requires physical inspection of merchandise at regular intervals. Reports (which should be read by merchandise buyers, too) should state how many units of a particular item were checked, the percentage of good versus bad quality by manufacturer, and the time spent.

Returns-control reports keeps track of product returns caused by delivery problems or customer dissatisfaction, including the number of customer-returned packages that were opened and the number that came back unopened. Weekly reports help speed up discovery of defective or unacceptable products and/or delivery problems.

A *customer-service report* includes a breakdown of complaints by type; source (customer, government agency, and so on) and seriousness of complaint; required research; simple form answer; and so on. You should also have a report that breaks down returns by vendor, so you can take action to eliminate problems with specific vendors. Weekly customer-service reports are essential. Customers are a cataloger's most valuable commodity, and trends must be spotted as soon as possible.

Reports more than pay for the time spent preparing them by helping a cataloger run his or her organization knowledgeably. No successful business can be without them: Structure yours to fit the individual needs and personalities they will serve. Keep all reports simple, to the point, and on time—a report received too late for timely action is worthless.

❖ CHECKLIST

✔ Understand the steps involved in order processing.
✔ Be sure all needed information is validated.
✔ Learn the terms necessary to understand credit-card processing.
✔ Look into direct-marketing–savvy third-party processors.
✔ Be clear on what you are charged for offering credit cards.
✔ Invest in a POS terminal.
✔ Learn how to reduce chargebacks and fraud.
✔ Understand that start-ups need to prepare thoroughly for credit-card application.
✔ Learn the major areas of concern to look for when accepting checks.
✔ Understand each step in the pick, pack, and ship process.
✔ Use a computer for the fulfillment process.
✔ Tailor your warehouse to your specific needs.
✔ Construct an efficient, effective merchandise-receiving system.
✔ Keep up with electronic options.
✔ Make sure your package reflects your company's image.
✔ Don't assume all packages must be shipped via UPS.
✔ Investigate overnight and two-day delivery, including the effects on your inventory.

✔ Always use a manifest system.

✔ Determine your cost of shipping, then decide how you will charge this cost to your customers.

✔ Use every bit of information to determine your inventory needs as accurately as possible.

✔ Take a variety of factors into consideration when determining when to order and how much to buy.

✔ Adhere to FTC rules.

✔ Understand that backorders will negatively affect customer's future buying decisions.

✔ Offer stellar customer service with the aid of computers.

✔ Check the point for how to use your customer-service people efficiently.

✔ Weigh the pluses and minuses of VRU.

✔ Handle returns efficiently, watching the percentage returned carefully, enclosing a how-to-return form, and using a return acknowledgment.

✔ Establish and enforce customer-service policies.

✔ Carefully collect data for building your database.

✔ Get regular reports that let you control your business.

✔ Determine whether to use in-house or out-sourced fulfillment.

✔ Know exactly what your fulfillment costs are.

End Notes

1. Schlesinger, L., and Heskett, J. L. "The Service-Driven Service Company." *Harvard Business Review*, September/October 1991.

CHAPTER FOURTEEN
❖ ❖ ❖

Catalog Analysis

The key to catalog success is continuing analysis, no matter how small or large the program. This is the only way to monitor the progress of your business, determine its weak and strong points, and improve or maintain profits. It is central to keeping customers.

In years past, many established catalogers had arrangements with service bureaus to use large mainframes to do the computer runs for their analysis. Today, most analysis is done on personal computers (PCs) in a marketing department or by the catalog entrepreneur. Even large-scale transactional data from fulfillment computers can be downloaded for use on a PC. For most catalogs, more advanced analytical techniques are still provided by third parties specializing in database analysis or data enhancement. The largest catalogs maintain staffs of statisticians with on-line access to minicomputers and mainframes to perform these tasks. Discussions of more detailed methods and some of the mathematical techniques involved are presented at the end of this chapter. Most of the analyses discussed in this chapter can be handled easily on a microcomputer, even by those unfamiliar with catalog analysis.

List Analysis to Ensure Profitability

List analysis enables you to evaluate the profitability of a list and each segment of it, whether it is a house list or a rented one. This is the only way you can determine which list or list segment to mail more strongly and which to discontinue mailing. For each list, determine: (1) the total number of catalogs mailed; (2) the total number of orders received; and (3) the dollar amount of sales generated. If you are mailing more than one subset of a list, such as 0- to 6-month buyers and 7- to 12-month buyers, remember to treat them as separate lists for initial analysis.

To determine the response-rate percentage for each list, divide the number of orders for each list by the number of catalogs mailed to it, then multiply by 100:

Response % = (Number of orders ÷ Number of catalogs mailed) × 100.

Next, determine the average order. Divide the total dollar value of the orders from the list by the number of orders from it:

Average order = Total dollars ÷ Number of orders.

Catalogers have developed a formula that combines the preceding two measurements into a third criterion, the amount of sales in dollars per thousand catalogs mailed. This criterion facilitates the comparison of many lists with different average orders and response rates. Divide the total sales dollars by the number of thousands of catalogs mailed. For example, if 10,500 were mailed and the sales were $32,400, you would divide the sales by 10.5. (You can also use dollars per catalog mailed.) Putting this example into an equation format, you would have

$32,400 \div 10.5 = \$3,085$ per thousand ($/M) or $3.09 per catalog ($/catalog).

The calculations can be done on a computer or on paper, but the computer makes it easier. Set up an electronic spreadsheet, as shown in Figure 14–1. The formulas used are shown in Figure 14-2.

Allocating Unknown Orders

Unknown or untrackable orders can result either from errors in data entry or the customer's failure to have the order form or catalog with him or her when calling in an order. Most likely, unknowns will result from the failure of telephone personnel to capture the list code when taking the order or the respondent's failure to use coded order forms or labels. Some catalogers refer to these situations as "white mail" (even though most are phone orders).

If orders from unknown sources are a high percentage of the total, the validity of the analysis and the accuracy of the rollout potential are impaired. To improve validity, methods have been developed to allocate these unknowns to the various lists used.

One method of distributing unknowns is simply to allocate them to each list in the ratio of known list orders to total orders (for example, if a list has 10 percent of the known orders, it will receive 10 percent of the unknown). The same technique is used to allocate sales dollars.

❖ FIGURE 14-1
Basic list analysis format

A	A	B	C	D	E	F	G	H
1								
2								
3								
4								
5								
6		List						Dollars
7	List	Name	Quantity	No. of	Total	Percent	Average	per Thousand
8	Code	& Selects	Mailed	Orders	Dollars	Response	Order	Mailed
9								
10	123		10,365	183	$33,264	1.77%	$181.77	$3,209
11	234		7,909	122	$25,083	1.54%	$205.60	$3,171
12	345		5,967	113	$17,201	1.89%	$152.22	$2,883
13	456		22,455	416	$63,239	1.85%	$152.02	$2,816
14	567		30,997	502	$70,293	1.62%	$140.03	$2,268
15	678		18,223	298	$39,887	1.64%	$133.85	$2,189
16	789		15,811	222	$38,871	1.40%	$175.09	$2,458

❖ FIGURE 14-2
Basic list analysis format showing formulas needed

A	A	B	C	D	E	F	G	H
1								
2								
3								
4								
5								
6		List						Dollars
7	List	Name	Quantity	No. of	Total	Percent	Average	per Thousand
8	Code	& Selects	Mailed	Orders	Dollars	Response	Order	Mailed
9								
10	123		10,365	183	33264	+D10/C10	+E10/D10	+E10/(C10/1,000)
11	234		7,909	122	25083	+D11/C11	+E11/D11	+E11/(C11/1,000)
12	345		5,967	113	17201	+D12/C12	+E12/D12	+E12/(C12/1,000)
13	456		22,455	416	63239	+D13/C13	+E13/D13	+E13/(C13/1,000)
14	567		30,997	502	70293	+D14/C14	+E14/D14	+E14/(C14/1,000)
15	678		18,223	298	39887	+D15/C15	+E15/D15	+E15/(C15/1,000)
16	789		15,811	222	38871	+D16/C16	+E16/D16	+E16/(C16/1,000)

First, subtract the total unknown orders (or sales) from the total number of orders (or sales). Then, divide the total number of orders (and the total dollars) by the known orders (dollars). This will give the unknown factors for orders,

Total orders from all lists ÷ (Total orders from all lists − Unknown orders) = Order factor,

and total dollars,

Total dollar sales ÷ (Total dollar sales − Unknown sales) = Dollar factor.

Referring to Figure 14-3, let's assume a catalog received 2,184 orders with 328 unknowns, and that total sales were $341,664, of which $53,826 was from orders where the list is unknown. (Since the phone orders are credit-card charges, the average order is generally higher than orders received by mail.) The order factor would be

$2,184 ÷ 1,856 = 1.1767.$

The dollar factor would be

$\$341,664 ÷ \$287,838 = 1.187.$

By multiplying the known orders and dollars by these factors, we obtain the allocated orders and dollars (Figure 14-3). Figure 14-4 indicates the formulas needed for the analysis.

❖ FIGURE 14-3 **Basic list analysis format with allocation of unknown sales sources**

	A	B	C	D	E	F	G	H	I	J	K	L	M
									Allocated		Allocated		Allocated Dollars
		List				Raw	Raw	Raw Dollars					
	List Code	Name & Selects	Quantity Mailed	No. of Orders	Total Dollars	Percent Response	Average Order	per Thousand Mailed	No. of Orders	Total Dollars	Percent Response	Average Order	per Thousand Mailed
								Order factor = 1.177					
								Dollar factor = 1.187					
10	123		10,365	183	$33,264	1.77%	$181.77	$3,209	215	$39,484	2.08%	$183.36	$3,809
11	234		7,909	122	$25,083	1.54%	$205.60	$3,171	144	$29,774	1.82%	$207.39	$3,765
12	345		5,967	113	$17,201	1.89%	$152.22	$2,883	133	$20,418	2.23%	$153.55	$3,422
13	456		22,455	416	$63,239	1.85%	$152.02	$2,816	490	$75,065	2.18%	$153.34	$3,343
14	567		30,997	502	$70,293	1.62%	$140.03	$2,268	591	$83,438	1.91%	$141.25	$2,692
15	678		18,223	298	$39,887	1.64%	$133.85	$2,189	351	$47,346	1.92%	$135.02	$2,598
16	789		15,811	222	$38,871	1.40%	$175.09	$2,458	261	$46,140	1.65%	$176.62	$2,918
17	Unknowns			328	$53,826								
19	Totals			2,184	$341,664				2,184	$341,664			

❖ FIGURE 14-4 **Basic list analysis format with allocation of unknown sales sources showing formulas needed**

	A	B	C	D	E	F	G	H	I	J	K	L	M
									Allocated		Allocated		Allocated Dollars
		List				Raw	Raw	Raw Dollars					
	List Code	Name & Selects	Quantity Mailed	No. of Orders	Total Dollars	Percent Response	Average Order	per Thousand Mailed	No. of Orders	Total Dollars	Percent Response	Average Order	per Thousand Mailed
								Order factor = +D19/(D19−D17)					
								Dollar factor = +E19/(E19−E17)					
10	123		10,365	183	$33,264	+D10/C10	+E10/D10	+E10/(C10/1,000)	(D10*J$2)	(E10*J$3)	(I10/C10)	(J10/I10)	+J10/(C10/1,000)
11	234		7,909	122	$25,083	+D11/C11	+E11/D11	+E11/(C11/1,000)	(D11*J$2)	(E11*J$3)	(I11/C11)	(J11/I11)	+J11/(C11/1,000)
12	345		5,967	113	$17,201	+D12/C12	+E12/D12	+E12/(C12/1,000)	(D12*J$2)	(E12*J$3)	(I12/C12)	(J12/I12)	+J12/(C12/1,000)
13	456		22,455	416	$63,239	+D13/C13	+E13/D13	+E13/(C13/1,000)	(D13*J$2)	(E13*J$3)	(I13/C13)	(J13/I13)	+J13/(C13/1,000)
14	567		30,997	502	$70,293	+D14/C14	+E14/D14	+E14/(C14/1,000)	(D14*J$2)	(E14*J$3)	(I14/C14)	(J14/I14)	+J14/(C14/1,000)
15	678		18,223	298	$39,887	+D15/C15	+E15/D15	+E15/(C15/1,000)	(D15*J$2)	(E15*J$3)	(I15/C15)	(J15/I15)	+J15/(C15/1,000)
16	789		15,811	222	$38,871	+D16/C16	+E16/D16	+E16/(C16/1,000)	(D16*J$2)	(E16*J$3)	(I16/C16)	(J16/I16)	+J16/(C16/1,000)
17	Unknowns			328	$53,826								
19	Totals			2,184	$341,664				2,184	$341,664			

Further effort is needed to make the analysis more useful. Other factors that should be added to the spreadsheet are:

1. The number of names mailed versus the number ordered. The loss of names in the merge/purge results in a higher actual cost per name mailed.
2. The actual cost of rented lists. Some lists that are marginally profitable as rentals can be mailed profitably as exchanges.
3. The gross merchandise margin for each list, or at least the average gross merchandise margin.
4. The actual cost in the mail.

These factors will let you calculate each list's contribution. Contribution is used rather than profit, because internal overhead and administrative costs must also be taken into account. Figure 14-5 shows the spreadsheet with these factors added; Figure 14-6 shows the formulas used.

The analysis can be done in a simple spreadsheet format on a PC by downloading or reentering the data from the fulfillment computer. It also might be done by a service bureau as part of the house file update or even on a sheet of paper. But it should be done. It enables a cataloger to decide whether a list should be dropped, retested, or rolled out. It also allows a cataloger to determine which types of lists and selects work best.

Zip Analysis

As larger quantities are mailed, another inexpensive and effective analytical tool, Zip penetration analysis, becomes available. This compares the response rates for each zip mailed and ranks them. It can be done for rental names and the resulting zip code list used to specify the names to be rented in the future or the names to be omitted from the rentals. Usually this analysis is done by a service bureau which can then provide a zip tape to the rental-list owners. One caveat should be noted: Only those zip codes where a sufficient quantity is mailed in should be considered in the analysis. In most cases, 100 is sufficient but fewer than 50 should not be used.

Square-Inch and Page/Spread Analysis

Square-inch analysis provides a guide to merchants and marketers for future products, categories, and price points. It points the way to increased sales and profits by increasing "good" products and eliminating "poor" ones.

Square-inch analysis indicates the profit or loss for each product. The basic format used (see Figure 14-7) is also used in page/spread analysis, so to simplify matters, we'll look at them together. First, let's make some assumptions:

1. The total cost of the catalog in the mail is $600,000.
2. The fulfillment charge for shipping and handling equals the fulfillment costs.

Product-Space Allocation

The number of square inches per product is obtained by simply measuring the space occupied by the product and its copy. Work with a ruler that shows tenths of an inch or a measurement template and use some judgment. If the photo is an easily measured rectangle, the result is obvious. But what if it's a silhouetted product? Measure the space that seems to be devoted to that product. Don't worry if you're off a fraction of an inch; it won't affect the result.

❖ FIGURE 14-5 Basic list analysis format through contribution

	A	B	C	D	E	F	G	H	I	J	K	L	M	N	O	P	Q	R
	List Code	List Name & Selects	Quantity Ordered	Quantity Mailed	Total List Cost	Raw No. of Orders	Raw Total Dollars	Orders Including Unknowns	Dollars Including Unknowns	Percent Response	Average Order	Sales Dollars per Thousand Mailed	Gross Margin	Margin Dollars Available	Actual List Cost per Name	Cost in Mail	Total Contribution	Contribution per Piece
1																		
2									Order factor = 1.177									
3									Dollar factor = 1.187									
4									Cost per piece = $0.597									
5																		
6																		
7																		
8																		
9																		
10	123	Exchange	14,846	10,365	$148	183	$33,264	215	$39,484	2.08%	$183.36	$3,809	50.00%	419,742	$0.014	$0.611	$13,406	$1.29
11	234	Exchange	9,187	7,909	$92	122	$25,083	144	$29,774	1.82%	$207.39	$3,765	51.00%	$15,185	$0.012	$0.609	$10,371	$1.31
12	345	Exchange	10,777	5,967	$108	113	$17,201	133	$20,418	2.23%	$153.55	$3,422	50.00%	$10,209	$0.018	$0.615	$6,539	$1.10
13	456	Exchange	30,000	22,455	$300	416	$63,239	490	$75,065	2.18%	$153.34	$3,343	49.00%	$36,782	$0.013	$0.610	$23,076	$1.03
14	567	Exchange	26,490	30,997	$265	502	$70,293	591	$83,438	1.91%	$141.25	$2,692	50.00%	$41,719	$0.009	$0.606	$22,949	$0.74
15	678	Exchange	25,500	18,223	$255	298	$39,887	351	$47,346	1.92%	$135.02	$2,598	50.00%	$23,673	$0.014	$0.611	$12,539	$0.69
16	789	Rental	20,398	15,811	$2,040	222	$38,871	261	$46,140	1.65%	$176.62	$2,918	51.00%	$23,531	$0.129	$0.726	$12,052	$0.76
17	Unknowns					328	$53,826											
18																		
19	Totals				$2,040	2,184	$341,664	2,184	$341,664									

❖ FIGURE 14-6 List analysis format through contribution showing formulas needed

	A	B	C	D	E	F	G	H	I	J	K	L	M	N	O	P	Q	R
	List Code	List Name & Selects	Quantity Ordered	Quantity Mailed	Total List Cost	Raw No. of Orders	Raw Total Dollars	Orders Including Unknowns	Dollars Including Unknowns	Percent Response	Average Order	Sales Dollars per Thousand Mailed	Gross Margin	Margin Dollars Available	Actual List Cost per Name	Cost in Mail	Total Contribution	Contribution per Piece
1																		
2									Order factor = 1.177									
3									Dollar factor = 1.187									
4									Cost per piece = $0.597									
5																		
6																		
7																		
8																		
9																		
10	123	Exchange	14,846	10,365	$148	183	$33,264	(F10*!S2)	(G10*!S3)	(H10/D10)	(I10/H10)	+I10/D10/1000	50.00%	(M10*/I10)	(E10/D10)	(O10+O$4)	(N10−(P10*D10))	(Q10/D10)
11	234	Exchange	9,187	7,909	$92	122	$25,083	(F11*!S2)	(G11*!S3)	(H11/D11)	(I11/H11)	+I11/D11/1000	51.00%	(M11*/I11)	(E11/D11)	(O11+O$4)	(N11−(P11*D11))	(Q11/D11)
12	345	Exchange	10,777	5,967	$108	113	$17,201	(F12*!S2)	(G12*!S3)	(H12/D12)	(I12/H12)	+I12/D12/1000	50.00%	(M12*/I12)	(E12/D12)	(O12+O$4)	(N12−(P12*D12))	(Q12/D12)
13	456	Exchange	30,000	22,455	$300	416	$63,239	(F13*!S2)	(G13*!S3)	(H13/D13)	(I13/H13)	+I13/D13/1000	49.00%	(M13*/I13)	(E13/D13)	(O13+O$4)	(N13−(P13*D13))	(Q13/D13)
14	567	Exchange	26,490	30,997	$265	502	$70,293	(F14*!S2)	(G14*!S3)	(H14/D14)	(I14/H14)	+I14/D14/1000	50.00%	(M14*/I14)	(E14/D14)	(O14+O$4)	(N14−(P14*D14))	(Q14/D14)
15	678	Exchange	25,500	18,223	$255	298	$39,887	(F15*!S2)	(G15*!S3)	(H15/D15)	(I15/H15)	+I15/D15/1000	50.00%	(M15*/I15)	(E15/D15)	(O15+O$4)	(N15−(P15*D15))	(Q15/D15)
16	789	Rental	20,398	15,811	$2,040	222	$38,871	(F16*!S2)	(G16*!S3)	(H16/D16)	(I16/H16)	+I16/D16/1000	51.00%	(M16*/I16)	(E16/D16)	(O16+O$4)	(N16−(P16*D16))	(Q16/D16)
17	Unknowns					328	$53,826											
18																		
19	Totals					2,184	$341,664	2,184	$341,664									
	1 2 3	4	5 6 7	8 9 10	11 12 13	14 15 16	17 18	19 20										

❖ FIGURE 14-7
**Product Contribution based
on Square-Inch Analysis**

A	A	B	C	D	E	F	G	H	I	J
1										
2										
3										
4					Catalog cost per square inch = $200.54					
5								Space		
6							Gross	Including	Cost of	
7	Item	Page	Category	Units	Sales	% Margin	Profit	White Space	Space	Contribution
8	1123	2	Patio	8,106	$38,294	53.01	$20,300	34.3	$6,879	$13,422
9	1234	2	Lawn	1,554	$2,592	51.12	$1,325	22	$4,412	($3,087)
10	1345	2	Kids	1,319	$21,028	52.43	$11,025	4.5	$902	$10,123
11	1456	2	Patio	4,253	$16,573	51.41	$8,521	7	$1,404	$7,117
12	1567	3	Patio	596	$6,774	52.20	$3,536	13	$2,607	$929
13	1678	3	Kids	526	$4,484	53.19	$2,385	13.8	$2,767	($382)
14										
15										

Allocating White Space

Because photos and copy don't completely cover a spread, some white space is left after all the measurements are added. For example, if your catalog is $8\frac{1}{2}'' \times 11''$, each page is 93.5 square inches, and each spread is 187 square inches. Calculating to one decimal place is more than adequate for estimates. If all the space allocations on a spread add up to 160.8 square inches, 26.2 square inches of white space remain.

If your catalog's front cover has been designed to show an image rather than to sell particular merchandise, it still has a cost. That space and cost is, by many catalogers, allocated over the whole catalog. To determine this space allocation per page, divide the total number of square inches on the cover by the number of pages in the catalog (less the cover). For a 32-page catalog (31 pages and image cover), the formula would be

93.5 square inches ÷ 31 pages = 3.0 square inches per page, or 6.0 square inches per spread.

The 6.0 square inches per spread are added to the 187 square inches for each hypothetical spread, giving a total of 193 square inches for the spread. If the cover is used to sell a product or products, most catalogers believe it should be treated like any other selling page and its space should not be allocated to the other pages. However, some catalogers feel that the cover, even if it is selling a product, helps contribute to the sales of all products within the catalog and allocate accordingly. It's your choice.

The White Space Formula.   To allocate the cost assessment of the white space between products, a common factor is derived for the spread (usually different for each spread) by dividing the total space by the product space:

Total space ÷ Product space = Factor (193 ÷ 160.8 = 1.2).

In the example, each product's allocated space is equal to 1.2 times its measured space. A product that has 10 square inches of measured space actually has 12 square inches of allocated space.

The Cost of Space

The next consideration is space cost. First, you must know the total in-mail cost of the catalog, including postage. Divide the total cost by the number of spreads, pages, and square inches in the catalog to determine the cost per spread, cost per page, and cost per square inch. For example, assume the in-mail cost to be $600,000. For an $8\frac{1}{2}'' \times 11''$, 32-page catalog, the cost per spread is $37,500 ($600,000 ÷ 16); the cost per page is $18,750 ($600,000 ÷ 32); and the cost per square inch is $200.54 ($600,000 ÷ 2,992). On the basis of the cost per square inch and the margin of each product, profit or loss contribution can then be determined (see Figure 14-7). In this example, we divide the cost by the 32 pages rather than 31. By allocating the cover space, we have automatically allocated the cost of the cover. This will give us the profit/loss contribution. But it is also useful to compare effectiveness of space usage. A product may show strong sales but occupy a very large space, such as a full page. How do its sales and contribution compare to those of other products occupying much less space? This is obtained by indexing the product sales versus the space occupied and is shown in Figure 14-8. Here, each product's percentage of sales or contribution is divided by its percentage of allocated space. This gives an index where 1 is the average.

Category Analysis

Knowing the profit and loss for each product in a catalog is not enough. The items should be listed by categories and an analysis performed for each merchandise category (see Table 6-2). This is done because merchandise tends to be sourced by category rather than by individual item. Buyers can be directed to increase or decrease particular categories on the basis of each category's profits.

Category analysis is somewhat easier if you have already done the square-inch analysis for items. Simply add up the space cost of all the items within a category and compare the result to the total sales from that category (Figure 14-9). To compare categories and their effectiveness in space usage, set up a chart as in Figure 14-10.

In this figure, the indices above 1 would indicate better-than-average sales. Very low indices, such as .25, are candidates for elimination. In the range of 0.8 to 1.2, moving the product, increasing the space used, or substituting a new photograph may increase sales. Indices above 1.25 indicate products that might be featured in the next edition. In this case, category D should be decreased or eliminated and categories F and G increased.

Price-Range Analysis

Similar calculations should be performed by using price ranges of merchandise as the type of categories. Add up all the space costs for items in each price range, and their net sales. Price ranges could be set as under $10, $10.01 to $20.00, $20.01 to $30.00, and so on. Set up a similar chart to analyze the results. In this case, the performance index is the ratio of net-sales percentage (in a particular price range) to space-cost percentage (for that same price range).

❖ FIGURE 14-8   Product Contribution based on Square-Inch Analysis

A	A	B	C	D	E	F	G	H	I	J	K	L
1												
2												
3												
4							Catalog cost per square inch = $200.54					
5								Space				
6							Gross	Including	Cost of	Percent	Percent	
7	Item	Page	Category	Units	Sales	% Margin	Profit	White Space	Space	of Sales	of Space	Index
8	1123	2	Patio	957	$38,294	53.01	$20,300	34.3	$6,879	4.41%	1.15%	3.85
9	1234	2	Lawn	79	$2,592	51.12	$1,325	22	$4,412	0.30%	0.74%	0.41
10	1345	2	Kids	751	$21,028	52.43	$11,025	4.5	$902	2.42%	0.15%	16.12
11	1456	2	Patio	921	$16,573	51.41	$8,521	7	$1,404	1.91%	0.23%	8.17
12	1567	3	Patio	154	$6,774	52.20	$3,536	13	$2,607	0.78%	0.43%	1.80
13	1678	3	Kids	82	$4,484	53.19	$2,385	13.8	$2,767	0.52%	0.46%	1.12
14												
15												
16												
17												
18												
19		Totals			$867,522				2,992			

❖ **FIGURE 14-9**
Category Contribution based on Square-Inch Analysis

Catalog cost per square inch = $200.54

	Item	Page	Category	Units	Sales	% Margin	Gross Profit	Space Including White Space	Cost of Space	Contribution
8	1123	2	Tabletop	957	$38,294	53.01%	$20,300	34.3	$6,879	$13,422
9	2243	2	Tabletop	65	$2,592	51.12%	$1,325	22	$4,412	($3,087)
10	2256	2	Tabletop	526	$21,028	52.43%	$11,025	4.5	$902	$10,123
11	1456	2	Tabletop	404	$16,573	51.41%	$8,521	7	$1,404	$7,117
12	1567	3	Tabletop	212	$6,774	52.20%	$3,536	13	$2,607	$929
13	1765	3	Tabletop	112	$4,484	53.19%	$2,385	13.8	$2,767	($382)
14	1196	4	Tabletop	339	$18,625	50.00%	$9,313	44.6	$8,942	$370
15	2316	4	Tabletop	72	$29,457	50.92%	$14,999	28.6	$5,735	$9,264
16	2329	4	Tabletop	50	$1,994	50.51%	$1,007	5.9	$1,173	($166)
17	1529	5	Tabletop	395	$16,175	50.21%	$8,122	9.1	$1,825	$6,297
18	1640	5	Tabletop	398	$12,748	48.00%	$6,119	16.9	$3,389	$2,730
19	1838	5	Tabletop	130	$5,211	50.64%	$2,638	17.9	$3,598	($959)
20	1269	6	Tabletop	230	$3,449	48.80%	$1,683	58.0	$11,625	($9,941)
26	Totals			3,889	$177,405		$90,975	275.5	$55,258	$35,716

❖ **FIGURE 14-10**
Category Comparison Chart

Catalog cost per square inch = $200.54

	Category	Name	Sales	Gross Profit	Space (Sq. In.)	Cost of Space	Contribution	Percent Space Cost	Percent Sales	Sales Index
8	A		$382,942	$203,005	1,073.3	$215,240	($12,235)	35.87%	34.73%	.097
9	B		$259,236	$132,527	644.5	$129,248	$3,279	21.54%	23.51%	1.09
10	C		$210,283	$110,254	499.0	$100,069	$10,185	16.68%	19.07%	1.14
11	D		$102,555	$52,303	513.0	$102,877	($50,574)	17.14%	9.30%	0.54
12	E		$67,740	$35,361	150.0	$30,081	$5,280	5.01%	6.14%	1.23
13	F		$44,840	$23,850	70.5	$14,138	$9,712	2.36%	4.07%	1.73
14	G		$35,132	$19,582	42.0	$8,423	$11,159	1.40%	3.19%	2.27
17	Totals		$1,102,728	$576,882	2,992	$600,076	($23,194)			

Some catalogers find a simple histogram useful for price-range analysis once they decide on the desirable mix of price ranges (see Figure 14-11). For first-time catalogers, this histogram is the only way of analyzing price ranges (or categories) prior to mailing.

By combining price ranges into more useful segments, you obtain the two histograms in Figure 14-12. One shows the actual range and the other the preferred range.

Using the price-range histogram can alert you to errors in your pricing strategy. In Figure 14-11, the cataloger has not determined the market and is attempting to appeal to both high- and low-end buyers. Additionally, orders for just one very low-priced item are seldom profitable due to high fulfillment costs.

Price Range	Number of Items Per Category
$0.00–$10.00	++++ ++++ ++++
$10.01–$20.00	++++ ++++ ++++ ++++ ++++ ++++ ++++ ||||
$20.01–$30.00	++++ ++++ ++++ ||||
$30.01–$40.00	++++ ++++
$40.01–$50.00	++++
$50.01–$60.00	|||
$60.01–$70.00	++++
$70.01–$80.00	++++
$80.01–$90.00	||
$90.01–$100.00		
$100.01–$110.00	|||
$110.01–$125.00	|||
$125.01–$150.00	||||
$150.01–$175.00	++++
$175.01–$200.00	||
$200.01–$250.00	|||
$250.01–$300.00		
$300.01–$500.00		
$500+		

❖ **FIGURE 14-11**
Price-Range Histogram Showing Lack of Price-Range Targeting

	Price Points as They Should Be (Approximately)
Under $20.00	++++ ++++ |||
$20.01–$40.00	++++ ++++ ++++ ++++ ++++	
$40.01–$60.00	++++ ++++ ++++ ++++ ++++ ++++ ++++ ++++ ++++	
$60.01–$100.00	++++ ++++ ++++ ++++ ++++ ||
$100+	++++ ++++ ++++

	Price Points as in Figure 14-11
Under $20.00	++++ ++++ ++++ ++++ ++++ ++++ ++++ ++++ ++++ ++++ ||||
$20.01–$40.00	++++ ++++ ++++ ++++ ++++ ||||
$40.01–$60.00	++++ |||
$60.01–$100.00	++++ ++++ |||
$100+	++++ ++++ ++++ ++++ |||

❖ **FIGURE 14-12**
Ideal and Actual Price-Point Histograms

Knowing Your Customers

Lifetime Value of Customers

The lifetime value of a customer to a catalog has been defined as the present value of net future cash flows from that customer (that is, how profitable a customer is going to be in the future and what that is worth or discounted to in today's dollars). Thus, determining lifetime value refers to net present value analysis as it applies to catalog customers. One important factor of this lifetime value is that it provides a measure by which we can establish the allowable cost of prospecting for new customers.

Catalog customers cease to buy at some point. This may be because of boredom with the catalog presentation or the merchandise, shifting loyalties, lack of service, or many other factors. In order to maintain profits, it is necessary to replace lost customers with a number of new customers at least equal to those lost. The question arises, "How much can be spent to acquire each of these customers?"

If we know the lifetime value of customers obtained through a particular method (space ads, rental-list mailings, and so on) we can determine, at least in gross, what we can afford to spend to obtain new customers. For example, suppose we know that customers derived from magazine advertisement A have a lifetime value of $10.00. We might decide that our allowable cost per customer obtained through magazine A is $4.00 each. In effect, we are saying that we are willing to spend 40 percent of a customer's lifetime value to obtain him or her.

Although a detailed calculation is beyond the scope of this book, we can show a simplified typical lifetime-value calculation for a customer group. Let us assume the following:

1. We are interested in calculating the lifetime value for customers obtained through mailing to a particular list or group of lists.
2. The catalog is mailed four times a year (for this example, we assume every three months).
3. We have obtained the following data from our customer files (for a similarly obtained segment):
   a. The average time as a customer is three years.
   b. Over this three-year period, we will net $105.00 per customer.
4. For simplicity, the $105.00 is equally divided among the 12 mailings, and the discount rate is 12 percent per year.

We now wish to know how much we can afford to spend to obtain a similar group of customers. Using a spreadsheet (almost all have formulas to calculate present value), we perform the calculation as follows:

Sum of net future cash flows	$105.00
Number of mailings (intervals)	12
Contribution/mailing	$8.75
Discount rate = 12%/year or per period	3.00%
Lifetime value = net present value	$87.10

If we had decided we would spend up to 40 percent of this sum to acquire the customer, we could afford a cost per customer of $34.94. Subtracting this from $87.10, we would then have a lifetime value (after acquisition cost) of $52.26. Carrying this a step further, if a rental list performs at 2 percent, then

$.02 \times$ Number mailed $\times \$34.84 =$ Number mailed $\times$ Allowable cost in mail,

or

Allowable cost in mail $= \$.70$.

This calculation does not take into account any net proceeds from the original acquisition method. If, in the example shown here, each customer who ordered made a purchase netting the cataloger $4.00, the equation would be

$.02 \times$ Number mailed $\times (\$34.84 + \$4.00) =$ Number mailed $\times$ Allowable cost in mail,

or

Allowable cost in mail $= \$.78$.

Obviously, for a catalog in a growth phase you would be willing to spend a higher percentage of the lifetime value of a customer than you would for a catalog with a large, mature house file. In many cases, loss would be acceptable.

In some organizations, due to corporate policies and experience such as profitable customer-acquisition methods, the calculation may be split. For those cases, the net cost or profit of the acquisition of the customer is not included, and only the future behavior of the customer is considered.

House-File Profiles and Analysis

A next logical analytical step is to consider the house file, its behavior, and in what ways a "good" customer differs from a "poor" customer or a nonbuyer.

Obtaining Data about Customers. A number of methods for finding out about customers are:

1. **Overlay.** Data from an outside source are run against the house file, and a report is generated about the composition of the file showing data-element matches or a profile. A profile provides a picture of the customer base or the individual segments therein. This can be used to make changes in the program. For example, if you found an extremely high median income in your multibuyer base as compared to single buyers, this would be a clue to why growth had leveled off. Further investigation (such as market research) might show that perception of high prices in the single buyers caused a lack of conversion to multibuyers. Adding some less expensive merchandise might attract a broader customer base.

2. **Appending.** The same sort of data used for an overlay are actually attached to the individual file records. Individuals characteristics, such as age, are determined. A large number of data sources exist for both overlays and appending. In some cases, in order to obtain the most "desirable" data, multiple sources must be used. *Desirable* is defined (in order of value) as:
   ◆ Individual data
   ◆ Data aggregated on a block level
   ◆ Carrier-route or census-tract/block data
   ◆ Zip code data
   Zip code data are, in general, the least desirable, because of the lack of homogeneity of most zip codes with large populations.

3. **Transactional data.** Data that have been collected in individual customer files are analyzed to determine customer value and purchasing patterns. Such data could include the standard recency/frequency/monetary (RFM), product or category purchases, and, as is now becoming more prevalent, cross-product or "product affinity" purchases (for example, customers who purchased a camera would most likely be interested in purchasing film).

4. **Market research.** The cataloger attempts not only to obtain demographic data (for buyers and nonbuyers alike), but also to determine customers' perception of the elements important to catalog purchases and how well these elements have been implemented.

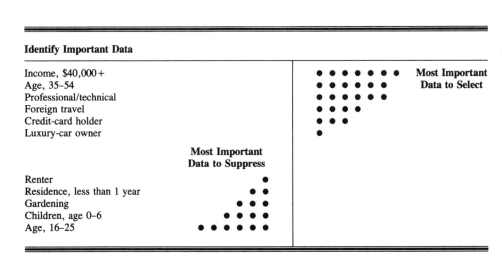

❖ **FIGURE 14-13**
InfoBase Data Profile Analysis

Identify Important Data

Income, $40,000+
Age, 35–54
Professional/technical
Foreign travel
Credit-card holder
Luxury-car owner

Most Important Data to Select

Most Important Data to Suppress

Renter
Residence, less than 1 year
Gardening
Children, age 0–6
Age, 16–25

The methods outlined in this chapter were selected to give you a basic understanding of catalog-analysis techniques. But there are many possible variations on these methods, such as the following:

♦ Category sales can be analyzed as a function of lists.

♦ Retailers can track exclusive-to-catalog versus common-to-store merchandise separately.

♦ Rate of response, customer-conversion rates, and customer value versus cost of acquisition can and should be tracked over time for different customer-acquisition methods.

♦ Mail order data can be used for retail-store site selection.

♦ Merge/purge results can be used to predict mailing response.

♦ Customer profiles can be developed on the basis of actual distribution rather than customer averages.

More Advanced Methods

Recency, Frequency, and Monetary Scoring and Segmentation

At some point in any catalog's growth, attention must be given to some form of scoring. Scoring and segmentation allow you to predict mailing results for the house file with some degree of accuracy. This, in turn, can be used to better target those names most likely to respond and even to cut off the mailing names least likely to respond. All of us have heard of the 80/20 rule; that is, 80 percent of the house file sales come from 20 percent of the customers. Most catalogs follow this rule in some form. But which 20 percent? Who are they? Scoring (by various methods) lets you determine the likely ranking of the individuals concerned and identify those most apt to purchase.

The RFM parameters define a type of scoring that is frequently used for ranking and segmentation. This relies on the general truth of the following statements:

1. The more recently someone has purchased, the higher the probability he or she will purchase again. For example, a 0-3-month buyer versus a 7-12-month buyer.

2. The more frequently someone has purchased, the higher the probability he or she will purchase again. For example, a three-time multibuyer versus a one-time buyer.

3. The more money someone has spent, the higher the probability he or she will purchase again. For example, a two-time buyer who has spent $250 versus a two-time buyer who has spent $35.

The simplified formula used would be:

$$Score = a*R + b*F + c*M,$$

where a, b, and c are weighting factors derived (usually) from regression.

For typical file sizes, this work is generally done by a consultant or service bureau. Larger catalogs with staff statisticians may perform the analysis internally. Because of its wide use, RFM is now considered a commodity by most service bureaus and is priced to be within the budget of any cataloger.

Once the file is scored it can be segmented into ranked deciles (or other divisions) and decisions made as to cut-off points for mailings, and so on. Other segmentation schemes might be used to determine the average score for customers obtained through various media, age groups, or other variables of interest.

Note that there are major *caveats* in all scoring. For instance, if there have been significant fulfillment/customer-service problems, they will, in the absence of relationship-repair measures, severely degrade the response regardless of ranking or scoring. Also, the absence of new merchandise from catalog to catalog can degrade house-file performance.

Regression Analysis

In its simplest form, regression analysis is used to determine the relationship between two variables, like height and weight. If the height versus weight of a randomly selected group of people were plotted on a graph, most of the points would appear to cluster along an imaginary straight line. A regression analysis gives the equation of this line and indicates how well it fits (matches) the data.

For catalogs, we might use the number of orders received and the time since mailing (or since the first order was received) to predict total results of the mailing. This is more complicated, since a straight line would not represent the most accurate equation. As seen in the curves in Chapter 15, this function might have a complex shape. We would write $y = f(x)$, where y is the number of orders received at some given time, and x is that time. Again, we would use regression to determine the final form of the equation (curve) and how well it fits. If it fits well, the equation can be used to predict order quantities at some future time in the mailing. However, as more data (orders) are received, the regression should be updated to refine predictions. Note that seasonality, particularly in the fourth quarter, will affect the shape of the curve. Also, increased frequency of mailing will shorten the order curve in many cases.

Another use might be to determine those variables or interactions of variables of most importance to customers' buying decisions. The equation might have the functional form $y = f(x_0, x_1, x_2, \ldots, x_n)$, with the x's representing variables and their interactions. Let y equal the probability that the customer orders. The x's might be characteristics of the catalog's customers, such as income, age, zip code, and so on.

Alternatively, you could set up a regression equation and systematically remove one or more variables at a time from the equation. The changes in the analysis results caused by the deletions would identify the important factors, as well as the important interactions between variables. You would then attempt to maximize your mailings to the type of person with the needed characteristics. For example, one analysis of a cataloger's customer file determined that the most important variables were:

- The number of times mailed
- The number of times on backorder (negative factor)
- The length of time on backorder (negative factor)

There are a number of variations on regression, such as logistic regression, that are covered in the texts described in the next section.

Other Analyses and Mathematical Methods

In any well-run catalog business today, a wealth of useful data is compiled. Mathematical techniques can help identify the most important data and define relationships between the variables. Often, these factors are not evident merely by compiling the data, but can be represented only by complicated mathematical functional relationships. Although these specialized methods require a high level of mathematical knowledge, you should at least have an understanding of their potential applications for analyzing catalog data.

Depending on the goals of your analysis and the form of your data, you might use a number of techniques. A good introduction to these methods can be found in *The New Direct Marketing* by David Shepard Associates (Homewood, IL: Business One Irwin). If you are mathematically inclined, detailed descriptions of the various methods can be found in such books as *Multivariate Analysis* by Dillon and Goldstein (New York: John Wiley & Sons, Inc., 1984).

Among the mathematical methods most used by catalogers today are various forms of regression analysis, Chi Automatic Interaction Detector (CHAID), neural networks, and fractal analysis. A certain amount of debate is ongoing among analytical practitioners as to which methods are most effective in increasing profits and reducing costs. Each of the methods seems to have advantages in particular situations. Seek advice from other catalogers before you implement any large advanced programs.

Using Analysis

The desired result of any analysis is an improvement in the bottom line of your catalog. A perfect analysis would result in totally individualized catalogs, received on the date specified for each person. From a list of 5,000 names, you might mail only 200 catalogs, and all the recipients would purchase exactly the expected merchandise, giving a 100-percent response rate and an extremely high average order. This scenario is highly unlikely, but you can't ignore analysis and leave the catalogs' growth to luck either. There is, however, a middle ground in which the results of the analysis far outweigh the costs.

After the analysis, use the results to compare the projected profit-and-loss (P&L) statement prepared before the implementation of your catalog to the actual P&L (see Chapter 15). Continue to compare P&Ls for each succeeding catalog. A P&L should be evaluated as one of a series, not in isolation. This will allow you to better understand the causes of increased profits or losses. For example, are losses due to some rental lists being mailed too often? Are your suppliers getting too high-priced? Or is it simply that sales are down? Maybe it's time for a new creative approach or a change of merchandise mix. A good cataloger constantly analyzes results and overall economics. You must use analysis, but no amount of analysis is helpful unless you use the results to improve the return on your next catalog.

❖ **CHECKLIST**

✔ Immediately collect the necessary data for sufficient analysis.

✔ Use list analysis to determine which lists and list segments to return to.

✔ Remember to allocate unknown orders during list analysis.

✔ Use zip analysis to understand geographic penetration.

✔ Let square inch analysis guide you in how much space to allocate per product, product category, and price point.

✔ Don't forget to allocate white space when using square-inch analysis.

✔ Determine the lifetime value of your customers by source in order to decide how best to invest your acquisition dollars.

✔ Keep abreast of the best way to obtain data about your customers.

✔ Use recency, frequency, and monetary analysis to segment your best customers for unique treatment.

✔ Investigate how to use regression analysis to refine predictions.

✔ Use analysis as an ongoing discipline.

CHAPTER FIFTEEN
❖ ❖ ❖

The Business Plan

To build a solid business, you need a business plan. The most important aspect of this plan is, of course, the financial one, although descriptive material helps to define and detail your business's charter and mission, especially at the onset. Always remember the financials are not a static set of numbers; rather, they are organic, changing as the course of your business and results change.

By setting up a business plan, evaluating it as circumstances change, and carefully monitoring the actual business results and comparing them to the plan, you can make needed changes in a timely fashion. Changes in key indicators will alert you to the need for remedial action—whether positive, such as increasing mailing quantities, or negative, such as reducing the cost of goods. These indicators include such items as average order, house-file-segment responses, rental-list responses, and so on. At the same time as you take corrective action, you should update and review the plan again.

Most people still write their business plans from scratch, but there are now excellent software programs that force you to answer the questions necessary to start and operate a business. To date, none of these are specifically for the catalog business, but they can be adapted relatively easily. These plans will not construct the financial aspect of your business, but they will help you determine your major needs in such areas as promotion, merchandising, and distribution.

The Overview

The first step in preparing a business plan is to write the verbal overview, outlining the rationale and economic reasons for your prospective catalog business. Having all the characteristics in the lists that follow is desirable, but seldom does every condition exist in a start-up venture. Obviously, the more the better.

Your overview should cover the following points:

1. **Reason for existence.**
   - ◆ The product line has attributes that can be better explained or shown in a catalog than in a store (for example, clothing styles that look better on a model than on a rack).
   - ◆ No other catalog is adequately serving this particular consumer need at this time.
   - ◆ The target market is large enough to be profitable.

   ◆ The market is relatively easy to reach.
   ◆ The product line has the potential for diversification.
   ◆ The product line is not seriously affected by seasonality.

2. Finances.
   ◆ Enough capital is available to sustain the venture over a reasonable start-up period (up to three years).
   ◆ The product line will provide a satisfactory return on investment.
   ◆ Sales will not be greatly affected by the loss of any one supplier.
   ◆ The anticipated margins will be higher than the norm.
   ◆ Frequency of purchase will be higher than the norm.
   ◆ The necessary facilities (warehouse, office space, and so on) are available at a reasonable cost.

3. Management.
   ◆ Key people have previous mail order experience.
   ◆ Key people also have previous experience running a business.
   ◆ Management is knowledgeable about strategy and long-range planning.

The plan itself can be quite extensive—or not—depending on your needs. For larger corporations and entrepreneurs requiring financing, an outline might look like this:

I. Executive Summary
    A. Background
    B. Concept
    C. Business Objectives
    D. Management
    E. Direct-Marketing Environment
    F. Marketing Strategy
    G. Trademark Equity
    H. Multichannel Opportunities
    I. Interchannel Consideration/Constraints
    J. Finance
    K. Conclusion

II. The Company
    A. Tax Considerations, Corporate Structure, and Location
    B. Products and Services
    C. Price Structure
    D. Customers
    E. Distribution
    F. Management

III. Objectives
    A. Primary Objectives
    B. Driving Forces
    C. Rationale
    D. Financial Objectives
    E. Position for Growth

IV. Management and Organization
    A. Organizational Philosophy
    B. Year-One Allocation of Responsibilities
    C. Additions/Changes for Year Two
    D. Organization Charts
    E. Responsibilities
    F. People/Talent Required
    G. Government Regulations
    H. Work Action Timeline

V. Marketing Plan and Sales Strategy
    A. Comprehensive Plan
    B. Product Strategy
    C. Marketing Positioning

Economics

The financial section of the business plan can be set up on a personal computer (PC). Programs such as Lotus 1-2-3 and Excel make profit-and-loss statements (P&Ls), cash-flow reports, and so on relatively accessible.

To determine the economics of your proposed catalog operation, you need to project profit and loss and cash flow. But before you do that, you need (1) cost estimates for the catalog, (2) operating expenses for the company, (3) inventory costs and turnover, and (4) sales and profit-margin figures. We will consider these one at a time.

Cost Estimates

Make cost estimates as accurate as possible by getting actual quotes from prospective suppliers. Be sure to ask suppliers for their payment terms, which will affect your cash flow. Table 15-1 is a checklist of items for which you should get cost estimates.

Operating Expenses

Catalogs do not exist in a vacuum. A company structure supports them, and the costs associated with this structure must be considered. Even if you are using existing space for your office, direct overhead costs must be allocated to the catalog. Potential cost areas are identified in Table 15-2

Operational Costs

When estimating your operational costs, be sure to cover the following items:

1. Administrative costs, such as salaries, space, office furniture, and personal computers.
2. Consulting services.

Computer and database costs
Concepts
Consultants
Cost of goods (inventory)
Database set-up and maintenance costs
Design/layouts through disk (assuming computer-generated)
Dupes
Freight (for products and order forms)
Fulfillment costs
House-file update
Illustrations
Inserting
Lettershop
List rentals
Location fees
Mailing labels or ink-jet tape
Merge/purge
Miscellaneous expenses (long-distance phone calls, messengers, air express, photocopies, taxis, and so on)
Models
Order forms
Paper
Photography (includes assistants, film and processing, and stylists)
Postage
Printing
Props/rentals
Reshoots
Retouching
Revisions (on any creative/production work)
Separations
Shipping costs, including overnight
Style (hair/make-up)
Stylist (fashion)
Stylist (food)
Stylist (stills)
Van rental

❖ TABLE 15-1
Checklist of Items for Catalog Cost Estimates

❖ **TABLE 15-2**
Checklist of Operating Expenses

Attorney/accountant fees
Corporate taxes
Equipment for office and warehouse (cost of purchase or lease)
Insurance
Miscellaneous (eg, dues and subscriptions, maintenance, and depreciation)
Office supplies
Rent
Salaries, fringe benefits, and employee-related taxes
Telephone costs
Travel and entertainment
Utilities

3. Credit-card charges. MasterCard/Visa, American Express/Diners Club, and Discover charges vary, depending on your average order and your banking relationship. Some fulfillment, phone, or credit-card processing services offer low discount rates for credit cards. These should be explored by new catalogers or established ones dissatisfied with their rates.

   To determine these costs, assume that a certain percentage of orders will be paid by credit card (as opposed to checks). Although the percentage varies from one catalog to another, the higher the average order, the stronger the tendency for credit-card use. For now, assume the following:
   ◆ Credit-card orders will be 50 percent of all orders.
   ◆ Two-thirds of credit-card orders will be paid by MasterCard or Visa. The discount rate will be a function of your average order, the order volume, and the chargeback ratio. Assume a discount rate of 3 percent for each.
   ◆ The remaining third of these orders will be paid with travel and entertainment cards, such as American Express. Here, use a higher discount rate of 4 percent to 5 percent.

4. Telephone-order costs. Many catalogers use telephone-answering service bureaus or full-service fulfillment centers to take telephone orders. This is recommended for new catalogers because of the high start-up costs and time demands of in-house service. Let's assume a telephone cost of $2.50 per order.

5. Fulfillment costs. The costs presented in the spreadsheet are based on outside fulfillment and include the telephone/mail receipt, order entry and processing, physical fulfillment, receipt of merchandise, storage, and so on (see Chapter 13).

Inventory Costs

No cataloger wants to run out of merchandise or be left with unsold merchandise that (unless you have an outlet or retail establishment) must be liquidated at a fraction of its cost. In an ideal world, the cataloger purchases exactly the correct amounts of products for the catalog, with enough stock to fill the last order and backorder. This, of course, doesn't happen. However, the closer you come to the ideal, the better your bottom line.

When to order is a function of predicted need for merchandise and the lead time from your order to the receipt of the merchandise. *How much* to order is a function of purchase cost, warehouse costs, and order demand. These will vary for each catalog and vendor and must be calculated by the cataloger for each situation. (For how to minimize inventory problems, see Chapter 12.) The cash flow illustration shows how inventory costs might look over a certain time period and under certain conditions. The actual numbers, of course, depend on the merchandise mix and the payment structure negotiated with vendors.

A rule of thumb used by some catalogers is that 50 percent of the inventory should be on hand the first month the catalog is in the mail, 30 percent the second month, and

20 percent the third month. However, due to customer demand for quicker delivery and the increased use of 800 numbers and credit cards, some catalogers now have as much as 90 percent inventory on hand when their catalogs mail.

An established cataloger controls inventory through a system that combines order backup, vendors who understand historical catalog sales curves and let him or her order accordingly, plus an analysis that predicts well ahead of time whether an item will be oversold (all this combined with overall customer-service concerns).

Projecting Total Orders.   The percentage of completion (number of orders received in a certain time) can be used to project the number of orders for an item. Historical order curves are modified by the current order curve to get the complete percentage. Then, the quantity of an item to be sold is determined by using the following formula:

$$\text{Total orders expected} = \frac{\text{Number sold to date}}{\text{Percentage of completion expressed as decimal)}.}$$

In reality, inventory control is complicated by such factors as minimum purchase requirements, large-order discounts, and delivery times. The cataloger must sometimes choose between overstocking and unhappy customers.

Order curves.   Order curves are lines that show the number of orders as a function of time. Time is calculated from the receipt of the first order because of the difference in the in-mail and the in-home receipt of the catalog dates.

Historically, an order curve of 13 weeks gave the completion percentages shown in Table 15-3. Curve for a slightly longer time period is shown graphically in Figure 15-1. However, there are considerable variations from this curve. For some catalogs, the order curve is completed in four weeks and never reaches more than 70 percent of the otherwise expected orders (see Figure 15-2). One of the influencing factors is mailing frequency—the more frequently you mail, the more likely it is you will shorten your curve. Frequent mailings literally bump into each other, and many catalogers report that customers are most receptive to the most recent mailing.

Another influence is the number of items offered and the number of those items that appear to be new. This, combined with some price points that do not have a high hurdle, allows the customer the luxury of purchasing now (often the new, lower-ticket items) and over time (often the higher-priced items, sometimes repeat items).

As catalogers mail closer and closer to the time of need, this too affects the length of the curve. Therefore, a catalog mailed in late November to catch the height of the gift-giving season, will naturally experience a shorter curve than one mailed a month earlier.

For the curve shown in Figure 15-1, the equation would be

$$\log(y) = a_1 + a_2 (\log x) + a_3 (\log x)^2.$$

Week	Percentage
1	6
2	18
3	27
4	35
5	55
6	69
7	76
8	80
9	84
10	88
11	92
12	96
13	100

❖ **TABLE 15-3**
Example of Completion for an Historical Order Curve

❖ **FIGURE 15-1**
Traditional Order Curve

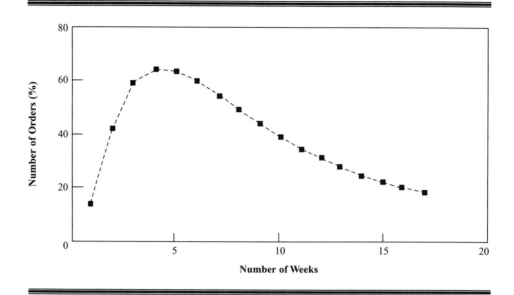

❖ **FIGURE 15-2**
Short-Cycle Order Curve

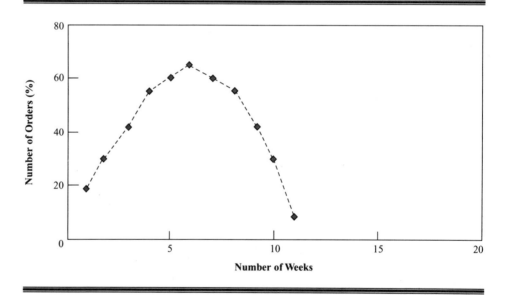

In this equation, x is the number of days since the first order, y is the number orders on the xth day. The values of coefficients a_1, a_2, and a_3 are generated by the computer using a regression program that fits the catalog order data to the best curve so future order projections can be made. As more data points are available, the error factor in the equation decreases. Another useful equation for obtaining the total orders for a catalog or a product is

$$y = a_1 + a_2 (\varrho^x).$$

In this equation, y is the number of total orders received by day or week x; a_2 is negative and rho is between 0 and 1. As x increases, the second term goes to 0, and a_1 gives the total orders. The shape of the curve is shown in Figure 15-3.

Affordable computer programs, such as SAS or SPSS, allow you to determine the curves and give you not only the coefficients and order predictions but also the probable

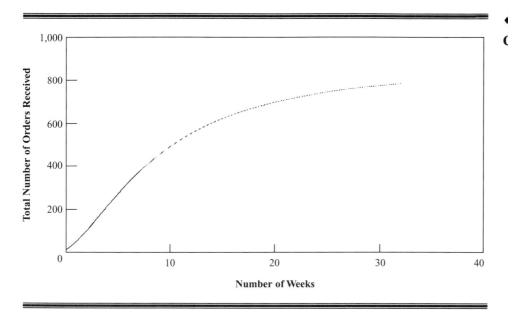

❖ **FIGURE 15-3**
Cumulative Order Curve

error limits on the results. With such a program, results can be updated daily or at least weekly to provide the data needed for inventory control.

Gross and Net Sales

As you develop P&L projections and cash flows, most expense items can be determined quite accurately. But sales projections must be estimated. For established catalogs, response rates and average order sizes from previous editions can be used as a basis for estimating gross sales, including seasonal variations.

Unless they are pretested offshoots of established operations, new or proposed catalogs do not have this advantage. Their sales projections must be based on estimates.

Projecting Gross Sales.   Gross-sales projections include the number of catalogs to be mailed, the response rate, and the average order.

Number of catalogs mailed.   Catalogs should never be mailed simply to bring the mailing to some preset total. The number mailed should be based on the number of perceived profitable names available. You may set up a projection based on a certain mailing quantity, but this should be updated continually as the number of available names becomes more apparent.

Response rates and average orders.   Estimates of response rates and average orders are subject to such influences as politics, weather, macroeconomics, and mail delivery. Again, the estimates should be updated on the basis of such information as published sales trends, conversations with other catalogers, or changes in the economy. The accuracy of these projections depends on many factors—political, environmental, seasonal, and so on—the influence of which may not be felt until the actual results of a mailing are known.

Calculating Net Sales.   The gross-sales figure is simply the total dollar amount of goods ordered; in other words, the sum total of all the orders received through the catalog. To arrive at a net-sales figure, you must make certain deductions from the gross-sales amount. These deductions are not uniform throughout the industry, and the form was used in this section are not meant to be all-inclusive or arbitrary, but simply to serve as guides.

From gross sales, make the following deductions:

1. Cancellations of orders and/or unable to ships.
2. Returned-merchandise costs. This amount depends on whether merchandise can be refurbished and resold from stock or sold through an owned retail outlet, or must be disposed of through a liquidator at a substantial loss. For fashion catalogs, the cost of returned merchandise can be a significant figure. Returns must be kept to a minimum to ensure profitability (see Chapter 6).

The formula for calculating net sales is simple:

Gross sales − adjustments (cancellations, returned merchandise) = Net sales.

For example,

Total Revenues	$352,550
Returns @ 10%	−35,255
Cancellations @ 5%	−17,628
Net sales	$299,667

Cash Flow

Records and Projections.   Even when a catalog operation is profitable, it may have peak periods of negative cash flow. A simple explanation for this is that catalog production and inventory costs must often be paid before the money starts coming in from orders. To help prevent poor cash-flow management, catalogers must keep up-to-date cash-flow records and projections.

In many cases, cash flows are calculated weekly as a combination of detailed sales and expense projections. In addition, when you get receipts from more than one catalog, you must do individual cash flows for each catalog, as well as an overall cash flow, to determine your total cash needs and surpluses.

Cash-flow projections should be as detailed as possible, and the assumptions should be included in the financial notes to the projections. A number of ''what-if'' studies should be done to determine cash needs and surpluses under a variety of circumstances, responses, and so on.

The Effect of Credit.   To minimize cash requirements and increase return on investment, you should always search out advantageous credit terms. Although this is easier to accomplish for established catalogers or large corporations, everyone should attempt to negotiate credit in two important areas: catalog production and merchandise inventory.

Depending on bank references, many manufacturers will give credit even on initial orders. This will not be true in all cases, but with each credit received or delivery deferred—which is also a form of credit—your cash flow improves.

Similarly, you should attempt to obtain credit from catalog production suppliers, printers, separators, typographers, and photographers. Many give credit under the right circumstances. Explore this with them openly, then be sure to meet the terms to which you have agreed. The more reliable you are with promised payments, the better your chances of increased credit for future catalogs.

The industry newcomer will find it hard to obtain credit on list rentals. However, with excellent references, it is sometimes possible. For an established catalog, the majority of list rentals will be on credit. Since list rentals are a significant factor in catalog costs, start working on credit with your list broker as soon as possible.

Unfortunately, there is one area where no credit can be obtained: Postage must be paid at the time of mailing.

Profit and Loss

The profit-and-loss statement summarizes the operating results, other income (such as list rentals or profits on shipping and handling), and other costs (such as interest on inventory financing). These financial data are the end result that indicates whether your catalog is successful.

Return on Investment. This figure, called ROI, is defined as the annual profit divided by the equity investment in the company. The result is expressed as a percentage. Although catalog companies usually have a relatively low pretax return on sales—generally around 5 percent to 12 percent—the return on investment is generally a very good one, sometimes as high as 35 percent or more. In some cases, companies with catalogs and retail distribution report this as "Return on Identifiable Assets," allowing the breakout of the catalog program without the high retail space costs.

Other Economic Factors

Your economic calculations and projections need to include several other categories of expenses. Postage is a place where you can significantly reduce costs (see Chapter 7). Merge/purge of lists is another, and zip code correction is part of merge/purge savings (see Chapter 11). The rental and exchange of your mailing list are opportunities to increase revenues (see Mailing Lists, Chapter 11). Finally, taxes and salaries have to be accounted for in figuring profit.

Taxes. Three types of taxes concern catalogers:

1. Employee-related taxes, such as Social Security and withholding tax.
2. Taxes on the overall income of the business.
3. Sales taxes on the merchandise sold through the catalog.

The first two should be discussed with your accountant or attorney before the actual start of business operations. You should also consult Chapter 16.

State and local sales taxes are currently of concern to catalogers, because they may be changing. The U.S. Supreme Court has ruled that if your only contact with a state is through the mails, advertisements, and/or common carriers (such as UPS), you do not have to collect taxes for that state. If, however, you have a "business presence" in a state, you must collect sales taxes for that state.

As state governments find the need to raise more money, they are attempting to create new definitions of a business presence to increase the sales taxes they collect. Because underpayment now can be quite costly in the future, all catalogers, whether new or established, should periodically consult their tax attorney to be sure they are in compliance with the complex and ever-changing sales-tax laws.

Salaries. Knowing the who, when, and how much of staffing is key for any business. The only difference between other businesses and direct marketing is a serious lack of experienced help. Because this is a relatively new—but booming—industry you may need to pay more than you expect for an experienced professional.

Salaries, of course, vary by area of the country and size of the company (to name just two key factors), so this is meant primarily to help you prepare a business plan. Although the figures in the following examples show a broad range, you will most likely be able to adapt them for your region and size.

Time frames also depend on the overall aggressiveness of the program. The scenario described here assumes that most creative, telemarketing, and fulfillment will be done by outside services. Job functions will be notably different if the telemarketing of fulfillment functions are done in-house.

For the first three months, a start-up company will probably need the following personnel (the salaries noted are industry ranges for small to medium-sized companies, and do not include any additional compensation such as bonuses, stock options, and so forth):

Manager	$60,000–$125,000
Secretary/assistant	$20,000–$30,000
Merchandiser	$35,000–$80,000

By the end of the first year, it will need to add

Rebuyer/inventory control	$20,000–$35,000
Production manager	$25,000–$45,000
Media buyer	$25,000–$40,000

By the middle of the second year, it may add

Fulfillment manager/coordinator	$30,000–$45,000
Controller	$45,000–$55,000

By the third year, the following people may be included:

Assistant buyer	$25,000–$40,000
Statistician/analyst	$25,000–$50,000
Clerk/typist/assistant	$20,000–$25,000

A business with aspirations of growing quite large (say, $2 million to $2.5 million within five years) might need a much more extensive organization. Figures 15-4 and 15-5 show the positions you will likely need to fill and also offer an example for those who wish to build a large company over a longer time period.

❖ **FIGURE 15-4   Generic Organization Chart, First Year**

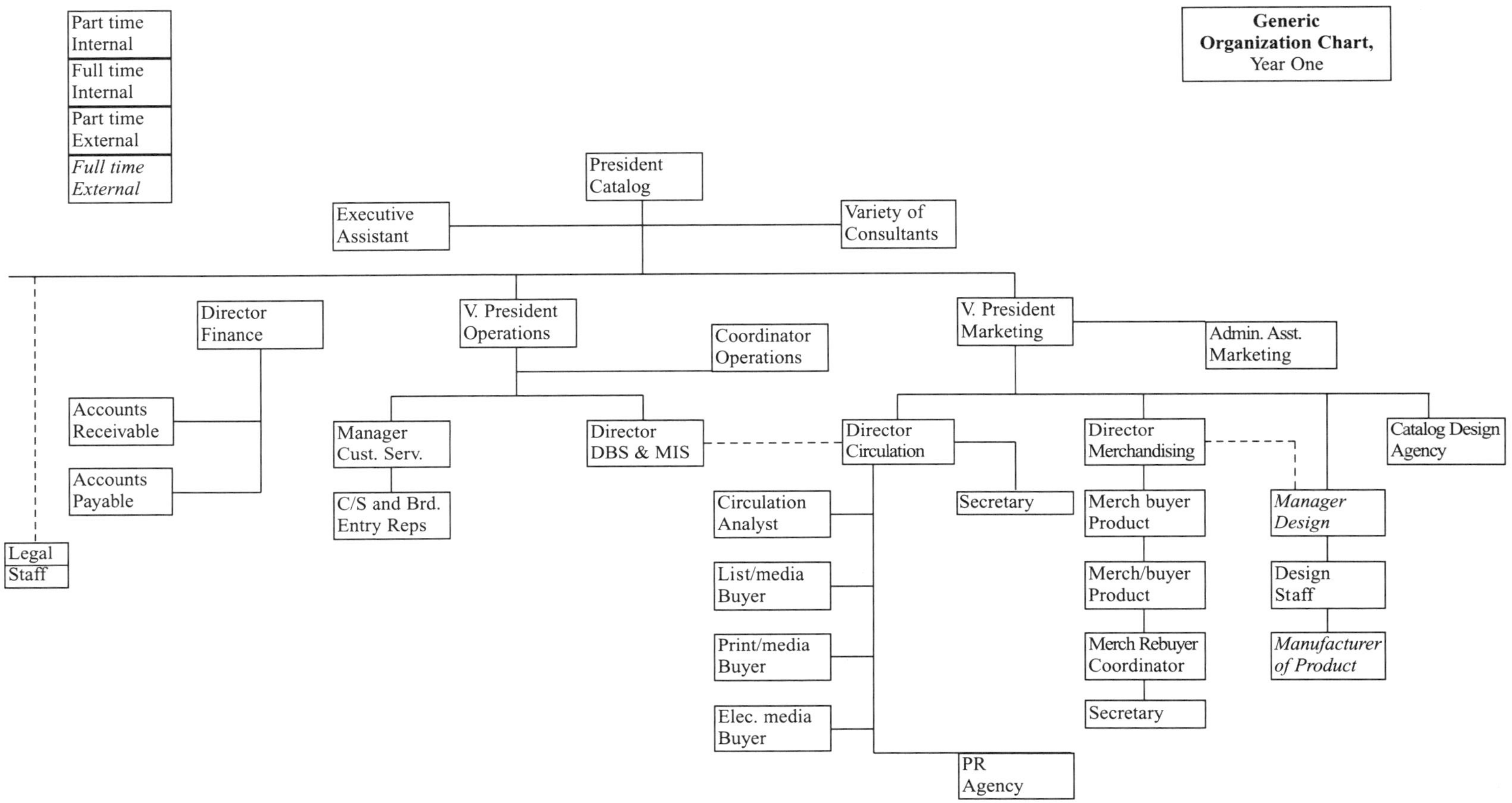

Generic Organization Chart, Year One

❖ **FIGURE 15-5   Generic Organization Chart, Second Year**

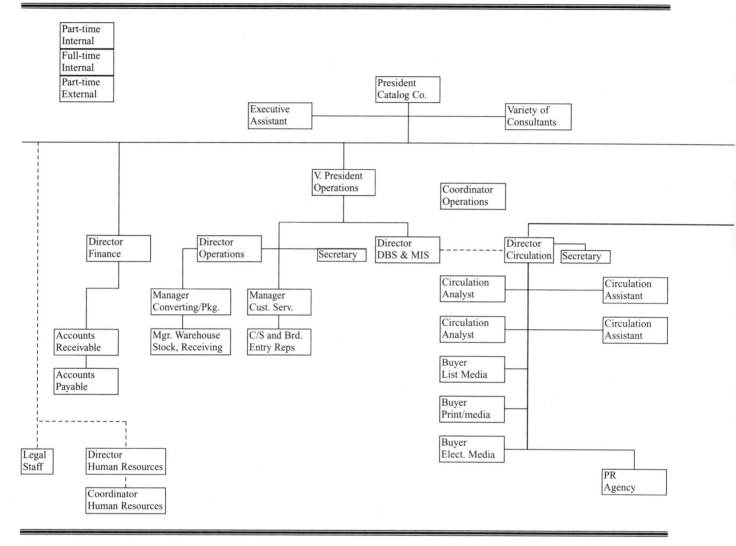

Example of a Simple Financial Set

A number of the discussions in this chapter are illustrated by a series of financial reports/ projections in the form of financial statements. The examples in this section have been developed to demonstrate how to set up reports and projections. Although the numbers used are internally consistent, they are *only examples and are meant only as a guide.* Each cataloger's financial profile is different, depending on the individual characteristics of the catalog and other factors, such as location. The generic examples presented here are for a moderately high-ticket, general gift catalog.

Mail Plan

The mail plan in Figure 15-6 is based on 32 pages, approximately $8\frac{1}{2}" \times 10\frac{7}{8}"$. The initial test quantity is 200,000. This would likely be divided among approximately 40 lists to obtain data on the performance of both individual lists and list categories. Consider the sample size in Table 11.1 (page 267) and a list that has a 2.0 percent response on a mailing of 6,250 names. This will be reproducible with 95 percent confidence in a future mailing as $2.0\% \pm .347\%$.

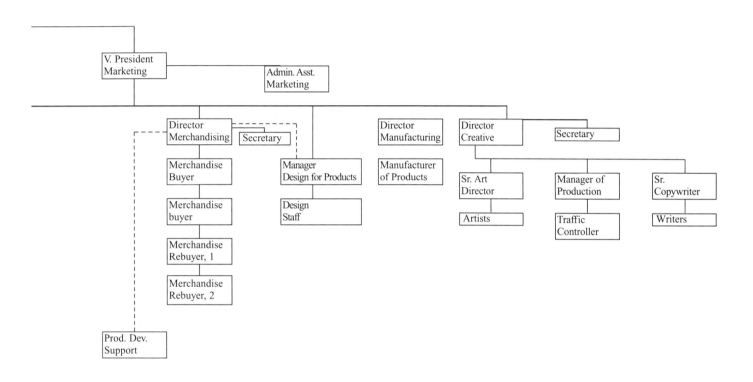

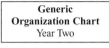

The mail plan is based on two mailings of catalogs with completely new (full) creative each and a remail where four pages have new creative. In reality, there would be some pick-up and the "all new" issues would show some savings from the figures given.

Plan Parameters

The plan parameters (see Figure 15-7) give two columns of response data. The initial data are for the first mailing of each segment. The annual increments show the effect of learning which lists and merchandise perform best as well as what creative approaches are most effective. The increases are added in equal increments over the year.

Date	Quantity	Type	Number of Pages
January	200,000	Full	32
March	150,000	Remail	32
September	200,000	Full	32
November	400,000	Remail	32

❖ FIGURE 15-6
Catalog Mail Plan

◆ **FIGURE 15-7**
Plan Parameters

Revenue

	Initial	Annual Increments
Buyer response rate	5.00%	25.00%
Buyer average order	$85.00	15.00%
Inquiry response rate	3.00%	20.00%
Inquiry average order	$75.00	10.00%
Rental name response rate	2.00%	15.00%
Rental name average order	$70.00	10.00%
Multibuyer (rental) response rate	2.50%	15.00%
Multibuyer (rental) average order	$80.00	10.00%
Buyer file attrition per year	33.33%	
Request names per catalog	3,000	
Shipping and handling revenue/order	$6.00	

Merchandise

Cost of goods (including freight in)	45.00%	
Replacements/refunds	10.00%	
Cancellations—not available to ship	5.00%	

Marketing

Pre-press cost per page	$3,100	
Page change (Remail)	4	
Printing cost per thousand	$225	
Postage	See Calculation	

Operations

Number of catalogs	4, 5, 8	
Administration	See Calculation	
External fulfillment cost per order	$14.52	

	% of Orders	Costs
Charge-card discounts and processing	80.00%	2.50%
Bad debt/checks	20.00%	2.00%

Attrition is taken at 33.3 percent per year for the buyer file and names are dropped in equal amounts at each mailing. For the time period covered, this is a conservative approach. Its use over longer time periods requires the use of analysis to determine which names should be dropped from the mailings.

Pre-press costs include:

◆ Design, layout, and copy through disk/cartridge
◆ Photography (no model costs)
◆ Separations

Printing is based on 32 pages, a self cover, on 60# (#3 grade) paper with a bound-in order form.

The plan assumes that 80 percent of the orders will be paid by credit card and 20 percent by checks. For the average order used and reasonable chargebacks, the discount rate should be at or below 2.5 percent for credit cards. The bad debt from checks is estimated at 2 percent of the 20 percent check usage.

The fulfillment cost of $14.52 per order is based on external fulfillment. The $14.52 figure is based on the average of a number of estimates by various vendors and includes pass-throughs such as UPS, and so on.

Postage Calculations

The calculation in Figure 15-8 assumes that the catalog is a "flat" (not letter size), and weighs less than the maximum per piece (only 3.3067 ounces). Presort ratios are approximate. Rates are based on current (1995) rates.

Administrative Costs

A detailed method of calculating full administrative costs is given in figure 15-9. For ease of calculation in the Profit/Loss and Cash Flow statements, administrative costs are shown as 10% of the net sales.

Profit/Loss Calculation

The number of rental names needed for each mailing in Figure 15-10 is the anticipated mailing quantity less inquiries, buyers, and rental multis from the last mailing that are being remailed. The multis are calculated as 20 percent of the prior mailings rental file. The list cost calculation is based on a 25 percent overbuy factor (if 100,000 names are needed, 125,000 are rented). Net sales are shown as revenues less returns and cancellations (not available to ship). Not shown are possible deductions for markdowns, royalties, or promotional costs. Shipping and handling revenue is taken at an average of $6 per order.

❖ **FIGURE 15-8**
Approximate Postage*

Quantity		Percent	Cost/Piece ($)	Total Cost ($)	Average Cost ($)
150,000	Carrier route	2.00%	$0.162	$ 486	$0.210
	5/3-digit	89.00%	$0.214	$28,569	
	Basic	9.00%	$0.266	$ 3,591	
200,000	Carrier route	17.00%	$0.162	$ 5,508	$0.208
	5/3-digit	78.00%	$0.214	$33,384	
	Basic	5.00%	$0.266	$ 2,660	
400,000	Carrier route	25.50%	$0.162	$16,524	$0.202
	5/3-digit	72.00%	$0.214	$61,632	
	Basic	2.50%	$0.266	$ 2,660	

* Based on minimum weight, not bar-coded. Approximate presort is based on Alden Press.

❖ **FIGURE 15-9**
Approximate Administrative Costs

Staff Salaries	Starts Month	Base	Fringe @ 27%	Total	Actual Year 1
Manager	−3	$60,000	$16,200	$76,200	$76,200
Secretary/Assistant	−3	20,000	5,400	25,400	25,400
Merchandiser	−3	35,000	9,450	44,450	44,450
Rebuyer/inventory	11	25,000	6,750	31,750	2,646
Production manager	11	25,000	6,750	31,750	2,646
Analyst	11	30,000	8,100	38,100	3,175
Fulfillment manager	18	35,000	9,450	44,450	0
Controller	18	45,000	12,150	57,150	0

Services

Legal and accounting					$10,000

Equipment

Furniture, computers at $6,000 per person					$36,000

Space

	Initial Group	Month 11 Hires	
Space @300 square feet per person and $1.50 per square feet per month	$16,200	$1,350	$17,550
	First-year total administration		**$218,067**

❖ FIGURE 15-10   First-Year Profit/Loss Calculation

	January	February	March	April	May
Type of mailing	Full		Remail		
Number of pages	32		32		
Quantity mailed	200,000		150,000		
File Sizes					
Buyers			3,358		
Inquirers	3,000		3,000		
Prospects/rentals	197,000		104,242		
Multis			39,400		
Total File	200,000		150,000		
Response Rates					
Buyers			5.00%		
Inquirers	3.00%		3.15%		
Prospects/rentals	2.00%		2.08%		
Multis			2.50%		
Average Rate	2.02%		2.27%		
Number of Orders					
Buyers			168		
Inquirers	90		95		
Prospects/rentals	3,940		2,163		
Multis	0		985		
Total Orders	4,030		3,410		
Average Order					
Buyers			$85.00		
Inquirers	$75.00		$76.88		
Prospects/rentals	$70.00		$71.75		
Multis			$80.00		
Overall A.O.	$70.11		$74.93		
Revenues					
Buyers	$0		$14,273		
Inquirers	$6,750		$7,265		
Prospects/rentals	$275,800		$155,196		
Multis	$0		$78,800		
Total Revenues	$282,550		$255,534		
Returns @ 10%	$28,255		$25,553		
Cancellations @ 5%	$14,128		$12,777		
Net Sales	$240,168		$217,204		
Cost of goods @ 45%	$108,075		$97,742		
Gross Margin	$132,092		$119,462		
Marketing Costs					
Pre-press (creative seps)	$99,200		$12,400		
Lists	$36,938		$19,545		
Printing/mailing	$45,000		$33,750		
Postage	$41,552		$32,646		
Total Marketing Cost	$222,690		$98,341		
Contribution	($90,597)		$21,121		
Operating Costs					
Administration	$24,017		$21,720		
Consulting	$10,000		$10,000		
Fulfillment cost $14.52	$58,531		$49,532		
Credit card charges	$5,651		$5,111		
Bad debt/checks	$1,130		$1,022		
Total Operating Cost	$99,329		$87,386		
Shipping and handling revenue $6.00	$24,180		$20,463		
Net Profit/Loss	($165,746)		($45,802)		
Cumulative P/L	($165,746)		($211,548)		

June	July	August	September	October	November	December
			Full		Remail	
			32		32	
			200,000		400,000	
			6,321		10,090	
			3,000		3,000	
			169,831		352,943	
			20,848		33,966	
			200,000		400,000	
			5.31%		5.64%	
			3.31%		3.47%	
			2.15%		2.23%	
			2.59%		2.69%	
			2.32%		2.37%	
			336		570	
			99		104	
			3,656		7,883	
			541		914	
			4,632		9,471	
			$88.19		$91.49	
			$78.80		$80.77	
			$73.54		$75.38	
			$82.00		$84.05	
			$75.71		$77.25	
			$29,614		$52,111	
			$7,819		$8,415	
			268,886		$594,250	
			44,342		$76,825	
			$350,660		$731,600	
			$35,066		$73,160	
			$17,533		$36,580	
			$298,061		$621,860	
			$134,127		$279,837	
			$163,934		$342,023	
			$99,200		$12,400	
			$31,843		$66,177	
			$45,000		$90,000	
			41,552		$80,816	
			$217,595		$249,393	
			($53,662)		$92,630	
			$29,806		$62,186	
			$10,000		$10,000	
			$67,273		$137,554	
			$7,013		$14,632	
			$1,403		$2,926	
			$115,495		$227,298	
			$27,792		$56,826	
			($141,365)		($77,842)	
			($352,913)		($430,756)	

Cash Flow Calculations

Cash flow calculations in Figure 15-11 are based on the following:

- ◆ Revenues are taken over three months as 50 percent in the month of mailing, 35 percent in the next month, and 15 percent in the third month. Shipping and handling revenue follows the same pattern.
- ◆ Goods are 100 percent in stock at the time of mailing and are paid for 30 days later.
- ◆ Pre-press is paid for 30 days after mailing.
- ◆ Printing and mailing are paid for 60 days after mailing.
- ◆ Lists are paid for 30 days after mailing.
- ◆ Fulfillment costs, credit-card discount and processing costs, and bad debt are charged as a percentage of revenue at the time the revenue is recognized.
- ◆ Administrative costs are averaged over 12 months.
- ◆ Consulting costs are a monthly average.
- ◆ Start-up costs are estimated at $100,000 and include three months of staff costs.
- ◆ All terms will vary with the nature of the catalog. A new mailer should expect to pay for much of the costs prior to mailing. As the catalog achieves some degree of success or if the cataloger has independent credit, better terms such as those shown may be obtained.

Depreciation, amortization, capital costs, interest, and taxes are not considered.

 **CHECKLIST**

✔ Write a verbal overview, making it as complete as possible.
✔ Gather cost estimates, including operating expenses, for the economics of the business plan.
✔ Determine sales and profit-margin figures, inventory costs, and turnover.
✔ Project total orders and create order curves.
✔ Project gross sales.
✔ Calculate net sales.
✔ Don't forget deductions.
✔ Allow for the ebb and flow of cash flow.
✔ Include the effect of credit on cash flow.
✔ Calculate the return on investment.
✔ Be aware of and include factors such as taxes on profitability.

❖ FIGURE 15-11 Cash Flow

	Credit Terms (from mail date)	Start-up	January	February	March	April	May	June	July	August	September	October	November	December	January
Cash at Start			($100,000)	($56,846)	($246,207)	($217,808)	($298,605)	($319,865)	($334,676)	($349,487)	($364,297)	($295,579)	($488,002)	($329,318)	($519,291)
Revenues																
Net sales			$120,084	$84,059	$144,627	$76,021	$32,581	$0	$0	$0	$149,031	$104,321	$355,639	$217,651	$93,279
Shipping revenue			$12,091	$8,463	$13,859	$7,162	$3,069	$0	$0	$0	$13,896	$9,727	$32,582	$19,889	$8,524
Total Revenues			$132,175	$92,522	$158,486	$83,183	$35,650	$0	$0	$0	$162,927	$114,049	$388,221	$237,540	$101,803
Expenses																
COG's 100% in stock at mail date	30 days		$0	$108,075	$0	$97,742	$0	$0	$0	$0	$0	$134,127	$0	$279,837	$0
Creative/separations	30 days		$0	$99,200	$0	$12,400	$0	$0	$0	$0	$0	$99,200	$0	$12,400	$0
Printing and mailing	60 days		$0	$0	$45,000	$0	$33,750	$0	$0	$0	$0	$0	$45,000	$0	$90,000
Lists including computer	30 days		$0	$36,938	$0	$19,545	$0	$0	$0	$0	$0	$31,843	$0	$66,177	$0
Postage			$41,552	$0	$32,646	$0	$0	$0	$0	$0	$41,552	$0	$80,816	$0	$0
Fulfillment costs	Follows revenue		$29,268	$20,486	$33,546	$17,336	$7,430	$0	$0	$0	$33,637	$23,546	$78,868	$48,144	$20,663
Credit-card costs	Follows revenue		$2,826	$1,978	$3,403	$1,789	$767	$0	$0	$0	$3,507	$2,455	$8,368	$5,121	$2,195
Bad debt	Follows revenue		$565	$396	$681	$358	$153	$0	$0	$0	$702	$491	$1,673	$1,024	$439
Administration	Monthly		$11,477	$11,477	$11,477	$11,477	$11,477	$11,477	$11,477	$11,477	$11,477	$11,477	$11,477	$11,477	$11,477
Consulting	Monthly		$3,333	$3,333	$3,333	$3,333	$3,333	$3,333	$3,333	$3,333	$3,333	$3,333	$3,333	$3,333	$3,333
Total Expenses		$100,000	$89,021	$281,883	$30,086	$163,981	$56,911	$14,811	$14,811	$14,811	$94,208	$306,472	$229,536	$427,514	$113,267
Cash at End		($100,000)	($56,846)	($246,207)	($217,808)	($298,605)	($319,865)	($334,676)	($349,487)	($364,297)	($295,579)	($488,002)	($329,318)	($519,291)	($530,775)

❖ FIGURE 15-12 Three-Year Summary

	Orders	Sales	P/L	% of Sales
Year-1	21,543	$1,377,293	($430,756)	-31.28%
Year-2	65,781	$4,870,090	($68,589)	-1.41%
Year-3	162,464	$15,760,801	$2,435,744	15.45%
	249,788	$22,008,184	$1,936,399	

Additional sources of income:
a. List exchanges and rentals are not considered

CHAPTER SIXTEEN

Legalities

Common Sense, Laws, and Regulations

Federal and state laws and regulations that affect the mail order business were not created to put direct marketers out of business or to inhibit the responsible newcomer. Most of them are based on common sense, truth, and fairness in advertising. This chapter gives you an overview of these rules. Get a copy of the actual regulations that seem to affect you and read them; this is as important as any of the merchandising or financial research you need to do. Take any questions you have to your attorney.

Supreme Court Affirmation of Direct-Marketing Rights

Setting an important precedent for the direct-marketing industry (with ramifications across all legal fronts), the Supreme Court has affirmed that the First Amendment's guarantee of free speech also applies to unsolicited direct-mail advertisements. That decision, rendered in 1983 in *Bogler vs. Young's Drug Products Corp.*, held that the First Amendment protects not only a speaker's right to communicate but also a listener's right to hear. This decision firmly cloaks direct mail with the same constitutional guarantees as other forms of general advertising.

Federal Trade Commission Regulations

The Federal Trade Commission (FTC) is a silent partner in your operation. It has a clear set of rules that you must follow to the letter. A full section is devoted to these requirements later in this chapter.

Postal Regulations

The U.S. Postal Service (USPS) is very important to you. It has rules and requirements regarding package dimensions, mail classifications, rates, and so on. It also has rules designed to protect both you and your customers. The *Mail Order Consumer Protection Amendments* were signed into law to give the USPS additional authority to combat false representation perpetrated through the mail. The succinct "Mailer's Guide to the Federal Fraud Statutes Affecting Direct Mail," published by the Direct Marketing Association

(DMA), takes a comprehensive look at the civil and criminal mail-fraud statutes. In layman's terms, the guide provides a basic understanding of the *civil* statutes, focusing on lotteries and false-representation schemes and the *criminal* mail-fraud statute. It provides the cataloger with an improved understanding of USPS laws governing direct mail. Pay close attention to all the requirements for mail order marketers.

Don't forget that direct marketers are important to the U.S. Postal Service as well. They are regarded as a gold mine by the Postmaster General's office, because they basically "pay the freight" for third-class mail and contribute about $500 million annually toward the institutional costs of the postal system. But you must follow the rules and the USPS will undoubtedly see that you do. The following publications will keep you up to date on all USPS requirements and any changes that are made:

◆ *Memo to Mailers.* Public and Employee Communications Department, U.S. Postal Service, Washington, DC 20260-3100. Monthly. Free to firms generating large quantities of mail.

◆ *Postal Bulletin.* Superintendent of Documents, U.S. Government Printing Office, Washington, DC 20036. Weekly.

◆ *Postal World.* JPL Publications, 128 C Street, NW. Washington, DC 20001. Biweekly.

◆ *USPS Domestic Mail Manual.* Superintendent of Documents, U.S. Government Printing Office, Washington, DC 20036.

Industry Self-Regulation

Strong industry self-regulation has served the mail order trade well in the long run. The Direct Marketing Association has promulgated its free publication "Guidelines for Ethical Business Practice," consisting of 43 articles covering all aspects of the mail order business that interface directly with the consumer. You can easily live by them, and, if you incorporate them into your company philosophy and operations, you will cover two fronts at the same time—customer relations and regulatory reality.

The Privacy Issue

The privacy issue looms large in the 1990s as major strides continue to be made in the computerization of society. In the area of general deregulation and digitized communications, Congress judged existing legislation inadequate for safeguarding access to a wide variety of information/communications about individuals without their prior consent or outside the realm of legal redress. In 1986, Congress enacted the Electronic Communications Privacy Act to close this gap as it relates to data communications. In the late 1980s, the Internal Revenue muddied the waters by attempting to compare its databases against commercial mailing lists to identify nonfiling deadbeats. Not surprisingly, this attempt engendered a negative backlash both from direct marketers who were enraged at the inappropriate use of their customer lists, and from Congress. Congress promptly introduced the Computer Matching and Privacy Protection Act of 1987. A more recent privacy action is the so-called "Bork Law," which prohibits the disclosure of video rental records.

These are just some of the installments in a saga whose recent history is of importance to catalogers and direct marketers in general. In the past 15 years, guaranteeing or safeguarding the individual's privacy has been a high-profile issue around which federal and state legislatures and consumer advocates have rallied. This preoccupation has extended to the subject of mailing lists, which have been viewed as a conduit through which personal information is transferred from one mailer to another.

As an outgrowth of the Privacy Act of 1974, the Privacy Protection Study Commission (PPSC) was created. One of its tasks was to determine whether mail order marketers should be required to remove from their mailing lists the names of any individuals who specifically requested that removal. When the commission made its recommendations, it stopped short of advocating that the proposal be made law, only because it felt adequate self-regulatory measures were in place within the direct-marketing industry. The DMA had already created the Mail Preference Service (MPS), designed to allow consumers' names to be deleted from large numbers of mailing lists. By contacting the association, consumers can have their names suppressed on a computer tape that is then circulated among the major mailing-list service bureaus, to be used in merge/purge runs against companies' mailing lists. More recently the DMA added the Telephone Preference Service (TPS), which allows for the removal of names from telephone solicitation calling lists. As of October, 1994, there were about 3.2 million individuals on the MPS list and more than 565,000 on the TPS list. The DMA also publishes "A Direct Marketer's Self-Regulatory Guide to the Use of Information."

An even better solution for both consumers and regulators is a practice begun at the time of the PPSC investigation. Many mail order companies offer their customers the option of having their names removed from the mailing lists they make available for rental or exchange. Some companies place the name removal-option copy on the order form with other mailing and order instructions. Others insert a flier within the catalog or mailing piece. Still others insert the notice in the package containing the ordered product. Such self-regulation preempts the need for federal legislation.

States are increasingly restricting the commercial availability of "public" mailing lists, such as those of utility customers and motor vehicle registrants. Be aware of these restrictions. (The DMA and the industry press monitor developments at the state level and can keep you informed.) Current and future restrictions can be managed, if all catalogers allow customers to delete their names from lists if that is their preference. In fact, the vast majority of companies that give their customers this option have found that only a small percentage of customers actually ask to have their names deleted.

Sales and Use Taxes

Sales taxes are inescapable. Consumers are used to paying them when they make retail purchases and expect to pay them when they order via the mail. The basis on which they are collected in the mail order business is easy to understand. In the case of *National Bellas Hess vs Illinois Department of Revenue,* the Supreme Court held that if the only contact an out-of-state cataloger had with a state was through the use of common carriers and the U.S. mail, such contact was not sufficient to establish the cataloger as a business presence (nexus) within that state. Therefore, under the commerce and due process clauses of the U.S. Constitution, the state could not force the cataloger to collect sales taxes from its residents.

Do you have a business presence in a given state beyond the use of a common carrier of the USPS to communicate and transact purchases? Does your company have a retail store, outlet, warehouse, sales office, redemption center, or similar continuous presence in a state where, regardless of activities related to the mail order business, it enjoys the advantages of municipal services. If so, this may constitute a *nexus.* (The basic premise of nexus is at the core of questions pertaining to mail order companies' liability to collect and remit sales and use taxes on a state-by-state basis.) Your company may be liable for collecting taxes and reporting income to each state involved. If you think you may be liable to pay state taxes, consult your legal counsel regarding what state agency you need to register with. This concept is defined as *sufficient nexus* by the U.S. Supreme Court, which has handed down several decisions in cases brought by varying state tax commissions against direct marketers and other businesses dealing with interstate commerce.

The most recent applicable decision is *Quill vs North Dakota* (May 1992). In this case, Quill had leased computer software programs to North Dakota customers, allowing them to order directly from Quill's computer. The Supreme Court held that, under the Commerce Clause of the Constitution, states may not require out-of-state marketers to collect sales taxes when they have no physical presence in the taxing state. The Court also held that Congress could pass laws that would require mail order marketers to collect sales taxes.

Many, if not all, states are now trying to find ground for jurisdictional nexus over direct-mail marketers. One reason for their increased fervor is the need to meet budget demands by finding new sources of revenue. Some catalogers believe they are also trying to protect local merchants.

No other issue is hotter for direct marketers—the states are zealous and organized in their attempts to force direct marketers to collect sales and use taxes, and, on the federal level, legislation is pending to authorize all states to require out-of-state marketers to collect and remit the states' use taxes. It seems the mail order tax issue is high on the agenda of every state tax administrator, legislator, governor, and federal representative. The reasons are quite clear: For several years, the federal government has been reducing contributions to state budgets. Several aggressive state legislators see direct marketers as a prime target and have been resourceful in launching a two-fold campaign to strip them of the protection afforded under the Bellas Hess and Quill decisions.

The arguments or rationale used by state legislators would turn the industry's own refinements against it. The tax seekers would redefine nexus by defining "presence" differently—by the use of an 800 number, national media, out-of-state banks, and the use of freestanding kiosks.

Of additional interest is the formation of the Multistate Tax Commission (MTC) comprised of 29 states that initiated the "Bellas Hess project" in 1986. A three-stage program by the MTC began with letters sent to hundreds of direct marketers offering amnesty from "past-due" tax obligations, but requiring the registration and collection of taxes in the 29 member states. There were few takers. The critical element of both the mailers' defense and the MTC objectives is the existing definition of *nexus* as defined by the existing Bellas Hess and Quill Supreme Court rulings. The MTC hopes to systematically chip away at it.

On the federal level, the issue looms larger with every session of Congress. There are industry defenses, such as heavy lobbying and organizations, to defeat all the administrative and economic consequences such tax obligations and compliance procedures would surely bring. On February 3, 1994, a use tax bill was introduced by Senator Dale Bumpers (D-AR). This bill would have allowed the states to tax mail order sales. This concept is allowable under the Quill decision which said, in part, that Congress could regulate interstate commerce. By setting minimum sales and a single rate per state for collection, the sponsors hoped to overcome the industry's stand on the complexity of taxing jurisdictions and the economic hardship of collection. This bill was defeated, as was a similar bill reintroduced by Bumpers in January, 1995.

Keep informed on this area and consult legal counsel specifically to determine your current liabilities, potential liabilities, and possible past liabilities. If your catalog company has a presence in a state or customer contact beyond the mail, seek legal counsel on whether to register your company and collect sales and use taxes. If you don't collect taxes, the state(s) may later impose this obligation and you may wind up with staggering penalties and past liability suits as well. The time to investigate is now.

Here are some practical tips on collecting and reporting for the states in which you are liable for tax collection:

♦ Get a copy of each state's tax table from the state tax commission. The tables will state the tax rates for cities, counties, and so on.

♦ Ask your customers to remit the appropriate sales tax on your order form (for example, "New York Residents Add Applicable Sales Tax," or "Residents of Illinois and New York, Add Local Taxes") and provide a space on the form for them to write in the amount.

♦ Although it is bothersome, you must reimburse a resident of a county with a lesser tax rate for overpayment of taxes. It is illegal to collect the highest tax rate on all orders from a given state. Avoid the problem by charging the correct amount.

♦ File quarterly and yearly state sales-tax reports for each applicable state. To avoid penalties, observe all state collection and reporting deadlines closely.

♦ Keep adequate records of collection and reporting for as long as each state requires. This can be quite a few years. Check with each state tax commission to determine its requirements. Failure to do so opens the door for state auditors to construct their own estimate of your liability.

♦ Use computer programs, such as Veritax, to compute amounts due.

Tax rates are subject to frequent change. For instance, some states require a tax on "handling" as well as on merchandise. Keep informed of changes in the states with which you are concerned. If you undercollect, you may have to pay the increase from profits.

The Federal Trade Commission

The FTC has issued significant Trade Regulation Rules (TRR), as well as guidelines and advisory opinions, that affect mail order operations. The directives in the following list are particularly important to catalogers, and you should be familiar with their contents from the moment of your operation's start-up.

◆ Mail or Telephone Order Merchandise (30-Day) Rule
◆ Rules applying to "Country of Origin in Mail-Order Advertising"
◆ Guides Against Deceptive Advertising of Guarantees
◆ Magnuson-Moss Warranty Act
◆ Guides concerning the use of endorsements and testimonials in Advertising
◆ Guides against deceptive pricing
◆ Guides on the Use of the Words "Free" and "New"

Copies of these regulations can be obtained from the Federal Trade Commission, Office of Public Information, 6th and Pennsylvania Avenues, NW, Washington, DC 20580.

All FTC regulations are included in the U.S. Code of Federal Regulations, Title 16, Commercial Practices, Chapters 1 and 2 (January 1993), published by the Office of the Federal Register, National Archives and Records Services, General Services Administration, and sold by the U.S. Government Printing Office, Washington, DC 20036. These volumes are reissued annually. Interpretations, summaries, and, in many instances, the full text of the regulations are found in *Do's and Don'ts in Advertising Copy,* available from the Council of Better Business Bureaus, 1150 17th Street, NW, Washington, DC 20036.

Be sure to get copies of the regulations and read them; better yet, read them with the assistance of an attorney. A summary of the regulations (minus as much "legalese" as possible) follows.

The Mail or Telephone Order Merchandise Rule

The Mail Order Merchandise Rule (16 CFR Part 435) more commonly called the 30-Day Rule, was issued in 1976 to deal with the problem of late or undelivered mail order merchandise. The rule outlines specific time requirements and notification procedures for the fulfillment of mail orders. Effective March 1, 1994, the rule has been amended to include telephone orders.

In essence, the Mail or Telephone Order Merchandise Rule states that unless there is a reasonable basis to believe that goods will be shipped within 30 days of receipt of a properly completed order, an advertiser must include a clear and conspicuous notice of the time in which shipment is expected to be made. In other words, if you know you won't be shipping until more than 30 days after an order is received, say so somewhere in the catalog. If no statement is included in the catalog, the merchandise must be shipped within 30 days.

Option Notices.   If there is a shipping delay, the 30-Day Rule requires you to notify your customers of the delay and inform them of their options. The first *option notice* must be sent before the promised shipping date or within 30 days after the order is received. It must plainly indicate the revised shipping date (of 30 days or less), and it must provide customers with the option to consent to the delay or to cancel the order and get a refund. The notice must also inform customers that nonresponse to this first notice implies their consent to a delay of 30 days or less.

If you are unable to ship the merchandise on or before the revised shipping date, you must send a *renewed option notice* that informs customers of their right to consent to a further delay or to cancel the order and receive a prompt refund. The notice must also state that if they do not agree in writing to this delay, their order will be canceled. Unless you receive your customer's express written consent to the second delay before the first delay period ends, you must cancel the order and provide a full refund.

You do not have to send a renewed option notice to customers who consent to an indefinite delay in response to the first notice. However, these customers retain their right to cancel the order anytime before shipment (a point that must be stated in the original notice).

Option notices may be sent by mail and should include a means for customers to respond with their preference, such as a prepaid business reply card or envelope. The FTC allows for the use of an 800 number to cancel orders. However, if there is ever a significant problem or an FTC audit of your system of delay handling, your 800-number order-canceling system must meet the FTC's standards of adequacy: The 800-number system could readily and consistently be used to cancel an order, and you provide adequate, competent staff to take cancellations and keep the records to back them up. It is not advisable to rely solely on an 800-number system for order cancellations. Failure to have records or other documented proof establishing the use of systems and procedures may give rise to a (refutable) presumption of noncompliance.

It is important to note that the seller does not have an absolute 30 days to send the first option notice. The rule is that the notice must be sent "within a reasonable time after the seller first becomes aware of its inability to ship within the applicable time. . . ." This may be as soon as a day after the order is received if, for example, the seller was notified of a long delivery delay on an expected merchandise shipment.

There have been a number of substantial FTC actions against direct marketers for violation of the 30-Day Rule. The most notable of these cases involved the JS&A Company based in Northbrook, Illinois, and headed by Joseph Sugarman. The company markets consumer and business electronic products, such as calculators, telephones, computers, and a host of advanced electronic products, via print space ads and infomercials. The company was noted for its lengthy selling copy and trendsetting advertising layouts. It was also well known for its rapid growth to multimillion-dollar sales status in a few short years. But a series of concurrent problems starting with a computer breakdown in the winter of 1979 disabled the company, affecting order fulfillment and backorder computer records. Reports indicated that only a fraction of the several thousand orders that were being processed were affected, but the FTC made an investigation.

The pivotal problem in the FTC's eyes was the wording of the delay notice, which was in the spirit of the regulation but which the FTC viewed as a violation. After protracted court battles that have received extraordinary industrywide coverage and were played out in Congress, the courts, and the consumer press, the case was settled. Joe Sugarman agreed to pay $115,000 in civil penalties, and his legal fees cost well in excess of $500,000.

The JS&A case was a bellwether the industry took very much to heart. The company was not a borderline or fraudulent operation; it was an eminently respectable firm, with excellent intentions, that fell prey to technical mistakes. This can happen easily, so be sure to follow the 30-Day Rule to the letter.

The FTC has prepared a summary, "Business Guide to the 30-Day Mail Order Rule," designed to answer questions mail order sellers have regarding the rule's requirements. The guide explains your responsibilities under the rule, provides sample option notices, and answers the most frequently asked questions about compliance with the rule. Copies are available both through the FTC Office of Public Information and from the Direct Marketing Association (Government Affairs Office), 1101 17th Street, NW, Suite 900, Washington, DC 20036.

Are You Affected? The 30-Day Rule probably affects your company. Its provisions affect all mail order firms, publishers, companies that offer premiums, and retail businesses that receive orders for merchandise to be shipped. It applies to orders generated through catalogs direct-mail packages, telephone marketing space advertising in magazines and newspapers, and TV and radio. If you are selling subscriptions, it applies to the fulfillment of the first issue. And if you are marketing a "continuity plan" product, you have your very own FTC-TRR on "negative option" programs. Purveyors of seeds and growing plants are also exempt. The FTC has explicitly stated that the rule applies to both consumer and business-to-business transactions.

When you analyze it, the rule is reasonable. Be sure to monitor your fulfillment operation carefully and systematically. The occasional mistake is not a problem, but your day-to-day system of operation must be absolutely sound.

Country-of-Origin Disclosures

In 1985, after lengthy industry struggles, changes to the textile and wool acts were enacted requiring that mail order catalogs and mail order promotional materials disclose in their descriptions of each textile and wool product whether the product was made in the United States, imported, or both. Accordingly, the Federal Trade Commission issued a TRR requiring disclosure of "Country of Origin in Mail Order Advertising." It is important to remember that this law applies not only to clothing but to all products that contain fabric in any part.

Guarantees and Warranties

Mail order companies have not been singled out for specific FTC coaching on the subject of guarantees and warranties in advertising. The industry is lumped in with all marketers and are subject to the FTC's "Guides Against Deceptive Advertising of Guarantees" and the requirement of the Magnuson-Moss Warranty Act.

One reason is that the actual number of customer returns of orders (that have been properly filled) is very low. With women's ready-to-wear, the rate can reach 25 percent but that is the highest category and is due to the fact that garment sizing varies significantly and fit is often the issue. So, when you state a company policy of "Satisfaction Guaranteed, or Your Money Back," not many people actually take you up on it. But for those who do, you must fulfill the promise.

Guarantees.   From a regulatory point of view, there are seven FTC guides on the subject of advertising guarantees, and they cover the following areas:

1. "Guarantees in General" requires clear and conspicuous disclosure of the nature and extent of the guarantee, the manner in which the guarantor will perform, and the identity of the guarantor.
2. "Pro-rata Adjustment of Guarantees" covers where guarantees are used.
3. "Satisfaction or Your Money Back" representations require that any conditions or limitations on refund guarantees be stated clearly. If a guarantee does not specify a time limit, the company must take back the merchandise no matter when. To avoid having to take back customer-damaged goods, the guarantor must specify "return in original condition." But remember, customer service is important and returns are few, so make the guarantee as much to the customer's benefit as economically possible.
4. "Lifetime Guarantees" defines "lifetime" as the customer's lifetime, unless clearly stated otherwise.
5. "Savings Guarantees" covers such statements as "Guaranteed lowest prices in town" or "Guaranteed to save you 50%." If you use or are considering using such claims or benefits, read the "Guides Against Deceptive Advertising of Guarantees."
6. "Guarantees Under Which the Guarantor Does Not or Cannot Perform" deals with the catchall category implied by the title.
7. "Guarantee as a Misrepresentation" specifies that a guarantee is not to be used or phrased to infer material facts. If it is, be prepared to assume legal responsibility for the truth of the representation.

These guidelines are shot, to the point, and simple to understand; they should not present a compliance problem.

Warranties.   The FTC issued a series of rules and interpretations to guide marketers, including mail order marketers, in the area of warranties. These rules apply only to written warranties covering consumer products. No one is required to give a written warranty, and there is no minimum requirement for the duration of a warranty.

However, if a product is warranted in writing by the manufacturer, the mail order marketer must make this warranty available to the customer before the sale. The marketer can print either the full text of the warranty or a notice that it may be obtained free on written request. The notice can be placed in one of three places in the catalog: on the same page as the merchandise copy; on the page facing the merchandise copy; or in a clearly referenced information section, such as the ordering-information section of the catalog. Requests for warranty information (you won't have many) should, of course, be filled promptly.

Endorsements and Testimonials

Many direct marketers have found testimonials and endorsements to be valuable marketing tools. Often, they add to the credibility of a marketer who is unfamiliar to prospective customers. Endorsements by experts, celebrities, or organizations are common, as are testimonials from satisfied customers or users of a product.

According to the FTC, endorsements encompass all advertising messages (verbal statements, demonstrations, pictures, signatures, seals, logos, and so on) consumers are likely to believe reflects the opinions, beliefs, findings, or experience of a party other than the mail order company. An expert is someone whose knowledge of the product or service, because of a particular experience or education, is superior to that generally acquired by ordinary individuals.

The FTC has issued four "Guides Concerning the Use of Endorsements and Testimonials in Advertising." They are straightforward and easy to understand and follow:

1. "General Considerations" covers three basic principles that are applicable to all endorsements and testimonials (which are considered identical to endorsements). They must be the endorser's honest views. They must not be distorted, reworded, or presented out of context. An endorser who is presented as a user of the product must be a *bona fide* user for as long as the message appears.

2. "Consumer Endorsements" specifies that if the consumer in the ad had a certain experience using a product, then all consumers should be able to get the same performance even under variable conditions. If the individual presented as an actual consumer, any photos must be of him or her, not a model or an actor paid to represent the endorser (unless the ad acknowledges this). Avoid the problem by not using models in place of real spokespersons.

3. "Expert Endorsements—Endorsements by Organizations" handles much more detailed endorsements involving testing procedures and collective judgment. Don't use either until you've thoroughly read the guide's requirements.

4. "Disclosures of Material Connections" states that if endorsers are paid, the ad must say so, unless they are celebrities or experts. (Generally, endorsers are not offered payment and do not ask for it.) An ad must also recognize any material connection between the endorser and the advertiser. However, the credibility of such ads is greatly reduced, so avoid them if possible.

Consult your attorney if you plan to use testimonials or endorsements. Contracts for testimonials are more or less standard, but celebrity and expert endorsers often require negotiated contracts.

Deceptive Pricing

The FTC has issued five "Guides Against Deceptive Pricing," intended to serve as "practical aids to the conduct of fair and legitimate merchandising." Although not aimed at direct marketers specifically, these guides affect structures often used by direct marketers, such as the two-for-one sale; buy one, get one free; one-cent sale; limited offers; wholesale prices; factory prices; list prices; manufacturers' suggested retail prices; and the use of "regularly," "usually," and "formerly." Pricing in general is covered, so be sure to get a copy of the guides.

1. "Former Price Comparisons." This covers the sale price compared with the former price of an item. You must have legitimately offered the product at the former price for the bargain offer to be valid. Increasing the original price with the express purpose of offering a large reduction later is regarded as a deceptive practice. Even if there were no sales of the same item at the former price, the bargain price is still valid. Beware of reducing an item's price insignificantly (for example, from $10 to $9.99) to mislead the customer when the former price is not mentioned in the sale copy.

2. "Retail-Price Comparisons: Comparable Value." As the guide explains, if you claim to be selling at below-retail prices in a certain geographic area, be reasonably certain that the higher price you quote is not appreciably more than the price at which the article is being sold in the area. Also, your merchandise must be of the same grade and quality as the merchandise with which you are comparing prices. If possible, clip and save the ad that shows the same or similar product offered at a higher price.

3. "Advertising Prices That Have Been Established or Suggested by Manufacturers or Other Nonretail Distributors." Few products are sold at manufacturers' suggested retail prices. This guide states that only if a number of stores are carrying the product at the retail price can you represent a mail order price as significantly lower than the manufacturer's suggested price. Ask the product supplier whether there are such stores in the area and check local retailers yourself.

4. "Bargain Offers Based upon the Purchase of Other Merchandise." "Buy one, get one free," "two-for-one sale," and "50 percent off" are all legitimate offers that often perform well in mail order. However, you can't increase the price of the first item or decrease the quality or quantity of either item in order to make the offer profitable. It must be a legitimate saving to the customer, as this guide makes clear.

5. "Miscellaneous Price Comparisons." This covers the catchall area that variations from the price strategies mentioned in guides one through four are controlled by the same principles. For example, a "limited offer" must indeed be limited in duration. A reduced price for seconds or irregulars cannot be compared with higher prices elsewhere for perfect merchandise.

These guides, like those mentioned earlier, are easy to understand and follow. They assure customers of genuine and truthful sales.

Free and New Merchandise

The FTC is unambiguous about the conditions under which direct-mail marketing may use the terms "free" and "new" in describing merchandise.

Free. Offering an item free of charge with the purchase of another item is a powerful incentive to mail order customers. Customers assume they are paying nothing for the free article and no more than the regular price for the other. The FTC makes the same assumption.

All the terms, conditions, and obligations on which the receipt and retention of the free item depend should appear in close proximity to the description of the offer of free merchandise or service. An asterisk near the word free is not regarded as sufficient. If, however, you don't want to give all the information on the cover of your catalog (as one example), you can use the term "free offer" on the cover and direct the customer to the page inside the catalog where details can be found, as long as you don't identify the item on the cover.

However, don't let these limitations stop you from making a free offer. Mail order customers are curious and adventurous by nature and can't resist turning "to page 10 for details." Once a prospect or customer gets inside the catalog, you are at least a third of the way to getting an order. This is one FTC requirement that can work directly in your favor.

Another reasonable FTC requirement concerns the use of the introductory offer that incorporates a free offer. In this case, you must discontinue the offer after a limited time, then begin selling the qualifying product or service separately at the same price at which it was promoted with the free offer. Free trial offers are acceptable if they clearly imply payment after the expiration period, and if all other terms are spelled out clearly within the promotion of catalog.

In addition, the mailing piece must contain all the terms of the offer, since this is the advertiser's contract with the customer. However, if your ad is a space ad accompanied by a coupon, the coupon can refer to terms in the ad, but the terms must be in a prominent place and appear in easily readable type.

New.   The FTC has issued several advisory opinions regarding the use of the word "new." Its position is that "it would be inclined to question use of any claim that a product is 'new' for a period of time longer than six months." Also, "a marketing program which lasts for more than six months and covers less than 15 percent of the population would not disqualify an eventually widely marketed product from being called 'new.' " According to the FTC, "new" means "recently discovered, invented, or developed," not new to a marketing area. Bear this definition in mind when using the word "new," and be circumspect.

Dry Testing

A practice very seldom used by catalogers, *dry testing* is the mail order method of promoting a product by mail before it has been manufactured or purchased as inventory. It sounds dangerous, and it is. Its only advantage is that it allows responses to the offer to dictate whether the proposed product should, in fact, be issued or made available. It is a legal practice, yet the FTC is monitoring its use and has issued an advisory opinion, which includes the following requirements for a dry test:

- ◆ The promotion must clearly state that sale of the product is only planned.
- ◆ The copy must indicate that an expression of interest or placement of an order does not necessarily mean the consumer will get the item.
- ◆ If plans to sell the product are dropped, notice must be given to prospective customers within four months of the first solicitation's mailing.
- ◆ Consumers must be given the opportunity to cancel, and no substitutions of other products can be made.

Credit Regulations

The FTC administers the maze of consumer credit regulations for mail order marketers, including the following:

- ◆ The Truth in Lending Act and Regulation Z (which concerns consumer credit selling) issued under that act

◆ The Fair Credit Billing Act
◆ The Equal Credit Opportunity Act (implemented by Regulation B and of direct application to most mail order marketers)
◆ The Fair Credit Reporting Act
◆ The Fair Debt Collection Practices Act

In 1985, a new "FTC Credit Practices Trade Regulation Rule" took effect. Taken together, the regulation in this area is extensive. If you plan to offer your own house credit, consult your attorney first. All these regulations are quite detailed and lengthy.

The Fair Credit Reporting Act deals with the use of books called "Credit Guides," which contain consumers' credit ratings, and the prescreening of prospective direct-mail customers for creditworthiness. Get a copy of the regulation if you are contemplating using either of these services. The act also contains many specific requirements for extending house credit directly.

The "Credit Practices" TRR provisions that are most important to direct marketers affect all consumer credit contracts in the areas of "confessions of judgment" and "waivers of exemption" clauses, which are now illegal. In other words, consumers may not be required to sign away their rights. For this TRR, the FTC has prepared a manual for businesses to provide assistance in compliance. For a copy, write or visit the FTC Office of Public Information.

The Fair Debt Collection Practices Act applies only to debt collection agencies that are trained by companies to collect their debts. Mail order firms employing such agencies should be familiar with the operating restrictions and guidelines imposed on them. Debt collectors may not (among other restrictions)

◆ use any false, deceptive, or misleading representation or means in connection with the collection of any debt, or
◆ "engage in group conduct . . . which is to harass, oppress, or abuse any person."

However, collection agencies do not have an exclusive license to collect bad debts. Many direct marketers administer their collection efforts internally. It makes a great deal of sense to set up an in-house system for credit-checking and preliminary dunning by letter and telephone. Bad debt is a bottom-line negative on all mail order promotions. It can range from as low as 1 percent to 2 percent to as high as 15 percent to 20 percent.

Sweepstakes

Many direct marketers have found that a sweepstakes can be effective in boosting mail order response (see Chapter 6). A close look will show that publishers use them extensively to solicit subscriptions and renewals. Fund-raisers have also used them effectively, as have many catalogers.

Although the FTC has not issued a specific regulation or guide on conducting a sweepstakes, the subject is of ongoing interest. Many states have specific laws governing sweepstakes, ranging from complete bans to requirements for posting bonds. These laws are often complex. It is also important to know that the USPS prohibits lotteries by mail. A lottery consists of three elements: chance, consideration (usually meaning some form of payment), and prize. Filling out an order, affixing a stamp, and rubbing a "magic spot" are not yet regarded as consideration, but many states are adding restrictions.

Before deciding to run a sweepstakes, seek legal guidance or contact one of the several full-service professional firms that administer sweepstakes. You can also consult the Promotion Marketing Association of America (New York City), which systematically tracks state requirements on sweepstakes and contests. The DMA has issued a set of guidelines on sweepstakes promotion by direct marketers. Request a copy from its Government Affairs Office, 1111 19th Street, NW, Washington, DC 20036-3603.

A Source of Legal Information

There is no substitute for the actual text of the rules and regulations that affect your business or for legal counsel's advice on your position and liabilities on many of these issues. But there is one informative monitor you may want to get your hands on each May. The DMA publishes the *Annual Compendium of Government Issues Affecting Direct Marketing* (1111 19th Street NW, Washington, DC 20036-3603). It is concise, yet encyclopedic in its coverage of many of the issues identified here as being of concern to catalogers. This DMA publication was the source for much of the background material used to illustrate this chapter's discussion of legalities.

❖ **CHECKLIST**

✔ Get copies of the USPS documents that state the physical-dimension requirements for third-class mail, as well as USPS prohibitions and definitions of mail fraud. Subscribe to postal publications so you'll be up to date regarding changes.

✔ Collect and remit sales and use taxes for the appropriate states according to the "sufficient nexus" theory. Keep your attorney informed regarding these procedures.

✔ Conform to the DMA's *Guidelines for Ethical Business Practice.*

✔ Be familiar with the FTC Mail or Telephone Order Merchandise Rule regarding delayed delivery. Make sure your option notices conform to the language requirements of the rule, that you are always within the time periods specified by the rule, and that your order fulfillment records are updated accordingly.

✔ If you offer direct or implied guarantee, you must be in compliance with the FTC "Guides Against Deceptive Advertising of Guarantees."

✔ If you sell any products covered under a written warranty, you must comply with FTC regulations regarding the presentation of such information.

✔ Establish an ongoing system whereby any item you offer that is covered under a written warranty is presented as such in your catalog copy.

✔ Make sure all testimonials and endorsements you run are acquired and presented in accordance with FTC requirements.

✔ Establish your pricing structures in compliance with the FTC "Guides Against Deceptive Pricing." Review these guides carefully.

✔ Carefully review all free offers.

✔ Be careful about how you use the word "new."

✔ If you ever dry test, stay within the FTC's suggested guidelines.

✔ If you use credit guides or prescreening techniques that fall under the Fair Credit Reporting Act, get a copy of the appropriate FTC guidelines.

✔ Check the practices of the agencies you retain for debt collection to be sure they are in agreement with the Fair Debt Collection Practices Act.

✔ Consider setting up your own internal system to initiate dunning for bad debts.

✔ Offer your customers the option of having their names removed from the lists you rent to other mail order marketers and from your own lists.

✔ See that your service bureau uses the DMA Mail and Telephone Preference Services quarterly "delete tapes" in any merge/purge operation you run with rented files.

✔ Have a copy of all FTC regulations affecting mail order practices on file within the company. Have all your key executives and your direct-marketing agency read these regulations.

CHAPTER SEVENTEEN
❖ ❖ ❖

Business-to-Business Catalogs

The business-to-business catalog sector has been given its own chapter for a reason. Virtually everything in the preceding chapters is translatable to business-to-business catalogers with some modifications. This chapter addresses those modifications and the most essential differences between consumer and business catalogs.

Even more explosive than the consumer catalog industry, business-to-business catalogs are experiencing both impressive growth and an evolution in marketing approach. Sales for the mail order industry as a whole were $237.19 billion in 1993; of that number, $67.73 billion was for business-to-business mail order.

Statistics indicate that only two or three of ten new consumer catalogs survive through the third year. New business-to-business catalog ventures, however, tend to be much less risky. The survival rate of these catalogs is seven to eight out of ten. This contrast is usually because business-to-business catalogs tend to be created for a new distribution channel as opposed to being a completely new venture.

The end user has become accustomed to and comfortable with the service that the mail order industry provides. This acceptance level originated from the buyer's need for product information supported by personal service and convenience. Catalogs offer end users a way to study visualized product information at their convenience and leisure. This has the added benefit of giving buyers the undivided attention of a company representative via a phone call.

Even such established marketers as Lands' End have answered the siren's song of business catalogs. Once of their newest entries is the Lands' End Corporate Sales Catalog, which offers customization of its merchandise with embroidered corporate logos or other symbols.

To help pinpoint the growth rate of this industry, you need only look at some statistics that highlight public catalog companies' sales gain: Viking Office Products' revenue for the quarter ending December 31, 1993, increased 25.2 percent to $133.1 million; the office supplies cataloger's net income rose nearly 180 percent to $6.2 million for the same quarter. Computer accessories cataloger Micro Warehouse posted a 70-percent increase in revenues to $140.7 million and net income rose 160 percent to $5.4 million for the same quarter.[1]

There is no reason to assume this growth trend will not continue for well-managed companies. One positive indicator is the influence women now have in the work force. Often already accustomed to the convenience of shopping by mail, they are receptive to this medium and help support it with their work-related purchases.

Telemarketing is providing a boost to this market, too. More sophisticated, well-trained operators have learned to use telemarketing in a logical and straightforward manner. Subterfuge doesn't work; showing the customers that you, as a direct marketer, offer a product they very well might need, then backing it up with superior customer service, gets the sale and the customer's loyalty.

The creation of informative databases means that the business mailer can now send customers more targeted promotions—promotions that are relevant to their past buying patterns. It's cost-efficient for the mailer and time-efficient for the buyer.

Who Are the Players?

Table 17-1 gives you an idea of the types of businesses involved and their sales volumes. It has been edited from *Catalog Age*'s second annual ranking of the top 100 U.S. catalogs (consumer catalogs have been eliminated from the listing). All sales figures are for calendar years 1993 and 1992; an asterisk denotes the figure is an estimate. Some catalogs listed have minor crossover into the consumer market.

Be aware that, as with consumer marketing, there are thousands of small catalogers with sales in the low millions who contentedly and professionally market to small niches.

Major Similarities to and Differences from Consumer Catalogs

Many marketers believe there are few differences between business-to-business and consumer cataloging, and, to a degree, this is true. Offer recipients are people, whether you reach them at the office or at their home. And catalogs have been created to target their specific needs, resulting in niche marketing very similar to that used in consumer catalogs. But there are also major differences. Because there is such diversity in the industries participating in business-to-business catalog marketing, it would be impossible to attempt to state exactly what is appropriate for each individual industry. However, there are distinct differences that tend to apply to almost all industries.

These differences are elaborated on throughout this chapter, but the following list gives you a quick overview:

- ◆ **Copy approach**—must be more detailed
- ◆ **Layout approach**—often by category rather than theme
- ◆ **Organization**—must reflect fact that the catalog is often used as ongoing reference tool, seldom for impulse sales
- ◆ **Back covers**—must address routing information
- ◆ **Catalog package**—often delivered with an envelope and a letter
- ◆ **Catalog size**—often larger, mailed less often than consumer books
- ◆ **Mailing plan/contact strategy**—sometimes less frequent mailings supplemented with interim mailings of offerings presented in other-than-catalog formats
- ◆ **Speed of delivery**—free or very inexpensive overnight or even same-day delivery becoming the norm for some industries
- ◆ **Finding buyers**—not as many lists to choose from and lists often in less-than-stellar condition
- ◆ **Alternate methods of acquisition**—more prevalent due to lack of good lists
- ◆ **Getting past the "gate keeper"**—catalogs sometimes intercepted or refused

❖ TABLE 17-1

Top Business-to-Business Catalogs

Rank	Company	1993 Sales ($ millions)	1992 Sales ($ millions)	Market Segment	*Catalog Age* Notes
2	Dell Computer	$2,299	$1,610	Computer hardware	
3	DEC Direct	$2,210	$1,800	Computer hardware	
4	Gateway 2000	$1,732	$1,102	Computer hardware	IPO in 1993
12	IBM Direct	$600*	$400*	Computer hardware	
16	Viking Office Products	$497	$393.9	Business supplies	
18	Premier Industrial	$462.5*	$436.5	Industrial electronics	Newark electronics
19	MicroWarehouse	$450.4	$269.6	Computer software	Five catalogs; int'l expansion
20	Henry Schein, Inc.	$425	$360	Medical and dental supplies	Looking to go public
22	Quill	$365	$341	Business supplies	
24	Inmac	$339.6	$315*	Computer products	Shut division in Italy
25	McMaster Carr	$308*	$308*	Industrial electronics	
26	Global	$277	$152	Business and computer supplies	Six catalogs; bought Misco
28	Computer Discount Warehouse	$271	$175	Computer products	IPO in 1993
30	New England Business Services	$244.9	$234.6	Business supplies and forms	New CEO last year
31	Compu-Add	$233.4	$262	Computer hardware	
36	Zeos International	$216.2	$206.1	Computer hardware	
38	PC Connection	$200+*	$150+*	Computer software	
42	Insight Distribution	$187	$139.8	Computer products	
44	Lab's Safety Supply	$180*	$150*	Industrial supplies	Owned by W. W. Grainger
45	Reliable Corp	$155	$180*	Business supplies	Bought by Boise Cascade in April
47	Day-Timers	$152*	$127*	Business planners and supplies	
48	Wear-Guard	$150	$135	Industrial apparel	Includes a separate catalog offering kingsize clothing
49	Northern Hydraulics	$141.4	$89.4	Hardware	
52	Black Box	$137	$121.6	Computer products	
56	Nasco International	$120*	$120*	Farm, educational supplies	Seven catalogs
63	Multiple Zones International	$95	$82	Computer software	Includes MacZone, PC Zone
70	Executive Greetings	$82	$77	Business supplies and greeting cards	Four catalogs
75	MidWest Micro	$80*	$77.5	Computer supplies	
76	Career Track	$79	$79	Educational aids	
78	Kaiser & Kraft	$78.2	$66.5	Industrial supplies	Includes C&H Distr.; BrownCor
85	Tiger Direct	$71.1	$62.2	Computer software	
86	Myron Manufacturing	$71*	$70*	Business supplies	
95	Northgate Computer	$63	$124.5	Computer hardware	
97	Elek-Tek	$60	$57	Computer products	IPO in 1993

* Estimated figure.

IPO = Initial public offering.

◆ **Database marketing**—more complicated due to need for more fields of information
◆ **Reactivation of inactive buyers**—retaining and reactivating buyers more critical because of higher average order
◆ **Purchasing options**—purchase orders often the main method of purchasing
◆ **Incentives**—not unusual for some type of businesses
◆ **Telemarketing**—a major marketing tool that often replaces the sales force
◆ **Order forms**—often not used due to customers' use of purchase orders
◆ **Seasonality**—fairly consistent selling throughout the year

Copy Approach

Unlike consumers, business recipients are seldom impulse purchasers. They are often responsible to someone else for their decisions. So you may face a multistep or layered buying process wherein an orderer must wait until his or her superiors have approved the recommended purchases. The immediate impact of this is a need for additional, highly explanatory copy. Business catalogs have to supply those interested in their products with enough valid information to make a decision and, if needed, back up their decisions with worthwhile facts.

Products offered are frequently more complicated than consumer products, meaning that copy needs to explain highly complicated technical information in an easy-to-understand manner that does not talk down to the reader. Because the catalog is going to someone in a particular industry, the recipient most likely has a comprehensive knowledge of the product area, so copy must concisely address the questions this knowledgeable person will have. Yet copy must not be so complex that it does not have a human appeal.

MacConnection shows how to incorporate traditional benefits-oriented copy with an understanding of the problems faced by its targeted market with boldface copy that leads into the paragraph (representative of the entire catalog) for a particular piece of software:

> No matter how complicated your business gets, your account software doesn't have to be. . . . Selected as a *Macworld* Editors' Choice, MultiLedger is an intuitive, integrated accounting program that includes general ledger, accounts receivable, accounts payable, inventory, job costing, and more. Best of all, MultiLedger gives you room to grow with an affordable Multi-User version that allows five people to access your books simultaneously.

Key points throughout the copy highlight the most important features and benefits.

Because of the copy-heavy nature of business catalogs, many techniques are employed to help readability. Call-outs, which highlight individual features, often appear in conjunction with the photography. Subheads are incorporated after headlines; captions appear in photos or next to them.

Although breaking out features for quick reading is important, it does put an additional strain on the layout, which must present all these different copy blocks in an orderly manner. Even though information must be conveyed, the point is to educate the reader, not fight for his or her attention with too many different elements. Business-to-business copy must always remember to be utterly *professional*. It must reflect the knowledge of the company and speak customers', not just the catalog's, language.

Collecting Copy Information.   As stated in Chapter 8, gathering the right information with which to write the copy is key. This is even more important for business catalogers, who absolutely must be the authority on the products they sell. Therefore, you may need to adapt the merchandise information form (MIF) used in Chapter 8.

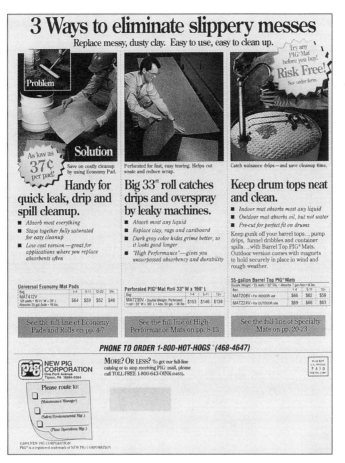

❖ **EXAMPLE 17-1**
Note New Pig's catalog message next to the name area. It reads, "Please route to: Maintenance Manager, Safety/ Environmental Plant Manager, Plant Operations Manager," and provides a check-off box as well as a line on which to write the manager's name.

❖ **EXAMPLE 17-2**
IBM Direct's RISC catalog uses call-outs to highlight features on its screen shots.

❖ **EXAMPLE 17-3**   The New Pig vendor information packet helps ensure the company compiles the information its writers and artists need.

NEW PIG CORPORATION
One Pork Avenue
Tipton, PA 16684-0304
(814) 684-0101

We Need Your Help
Part I: General Vendor Information

Here's your chance to tell us about yourself, your company and, most important of all, the product(s) you'd like to have featured in the New Pig Pigalog®. This form is the first step in developing a lasting, profitable relationship. So please be sure to provide all the information requested. Thank you! If you have questions, or need help with the form, please contact:

_____
_____
_____

Phone: ( )_____   Fax: ( )_____

I. Help us get to know you!
Company Name _____

Contacts
Outside Sales Rep. _____
Affiliation _____
Address _____
City, State, Zip _____
Telephone _____
Fax _____

PIG® is a registered trademark of NEW PIG CORPORATION

General Vendor Information

Inside Sales Rep _____
Address _____
City, State, Zip _____
Telephone _____
Fax _____

Technical Service Rep _____
Address _____
City, State, Zip _____
Telephone _____
Fax _____

Place Orders With _____
Address _____
City, State, Zip _____
Telephone _____
Fax _____

Remit To _____
Address _____
City, State, Zip _____
Telephone _____
Fax _____

-2-

General Vendor Information

Shipping Contact _____
Products Ship From _____
Address _____
City, State, Zip _____
Telephone _____
Fax _____

II. Help us get to know your company!
Are you a manufacturer or a master distributor?

Are you considered a small or large business by Federal Government standards?

Would your company be interested in co-op advertising or promotional programs? If so, please elaborate.
_____
_____

The New Pig Corporation name carries equity with our customers and has been shown to increase sales of products. Would your company be interested in entertaining a private label program on any of your products? _____

-3-

General Vendor Information

III. Help us learn your policies!
☐ Your Return Policy (3 copies)
☐ Your Terms of Sale (3 copies)
☐ A Full-Line Product Catalog with Distributor Pricing Information (3 copies)
☐ A Certificate of Product Liability Insurance Naming New Pig Corporation as Additional Insured (1 copy)

IV. Here's what we ask of you:
• To insure that we receive the correct product, we require a New Pig Purchase Order and New Pig Item Number on each incoming shipment.
• Due to catalog production and the nature of our business, we require at least a four-month prior notification of product specification or pricing changes and product cancellation in writing to the previously specified contact.

V. Is there anything else you need from us?
If so please use the spaces below to request it. Thank you!
_____
_____
_____
_____
_____
_____
_____
_____
_____

-4-

NEW PIG CORPORATION
One Pork Avenue
Tipton, PA 16684-0304
(814) 684-0101

We Need Your Help
Part II: Product Specific Information

I. Help us learn more about the product you supply us!
Product Number _____
Description _____

II. Help us get to know your purchasing and shipping policies! (This will allow us to predict our needs more accurately, as well as make doing business more cost effective for both of us.)

What is New Pig Corporation's cost per unit for this product? Please include quantity discounts.

What is the minimum order quantity for this product?

Can orders be split to different warehouses?

Do repeat orders less than the initial stocking order have the same price/quantity structure per unit? If not, please elaborate.

PIG® is a registered trademark of NEW PIG CORPORATION

Product Specific Information

How can the product be shipped from New Pig to our Customers? (Details: UPS, Class)

If we decide to drop ship this product, how can a New Pig Packaging Slip be included with the shipment?

NOTE: We request that Styrofoam and other non-environmentally friendly materials not be used for shipments destined for New Pig Corporation. Please call us with any questions or concerns.

III. Help us with marketing and technical assistance!
Would you be interested in private labeling this product? If so, please explain.

How long has this product been on the market?

When will an updated/modified version of this product be available?

Do you have samples of this product available for customers? If so, what is your sample program.

-3-

Product Specific Information

How long is this pricing valid?
_____

Who authorized this pricing?
_____

What is the normal lead time on this product?
_____

Is this product affected by seasonality or does it experience any other trends? If so, please elaborate. _____

How will you ship the product to us? (Please elaborate where necessary.)
☐ Weight of Unpackaged Product _____
☐ Size of Each Unit Box _____
☐ Contents of Each Unit Box _____
☐ Number of Unit Boxes/Master Box _____
☐ Weight of Unit Box _____ ☐ Weight of Master Box _____
☐ BOL Class _____ ☐ NMFC Class _____

Any additional packaging comments?
_____

-2-

Product Specific Information

Can you supply artwork or photographs of this product?

Please send us the following information of this product (If applicable/available)
☐ MSDS
☐ Chemical Compatibility Chart
☐ Product Data Sheets
☐ Parts List
☐ Assembly Instructions
☐ Technical Drawings
☐ Trouble Shooting Guidelines
☐ Parts Brochures
☐ List of Items Found in Product Package
☐ Test Data (Independent or Third Party)
☐ Approvals (UL Listed, FM Approved, USDA, etc.)
☐ Regulatory Compliance (i.e. Does your product help users comply with any regulations?)
☐ Target Audience/Market Studies

Please help us market your product by listing six or more features and benefits of this product (Use space provided below)

Feature 1 _____
Benefit 1 _____
Feature 2 _____
Benefit 2 _____

-4-

Product Specific Information

Feature 3 _____
Benefit 3 _____
Feature 4 _____
Benefit 4 _____
Feature 5 _____
Benefit 5 _____
Feature 6 _____
Benefit 6 _____

IV. Is there anything else you need from us ?
_____
_____
_____
_____
_____

-5-

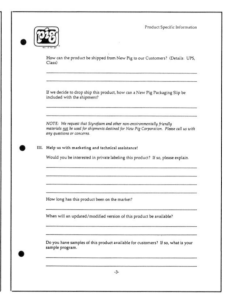

Layout Approach

Because of the need to be highly copy-oriented, business-to-business catalogers unfortunately have been noted for their less-than-glamorous approach to design. For the most part, individuality has been sacrificed, resulting in too many look-alike catalogs. Recently, business mailers have taken another look at their approach to graphics and have shown a tendency to incorporate more consumer ideas. (It should be noted that consumer catalogers are stealing ideas from business mailers, too. For instance, you'll find more and more consumer catalogs carrying product indexes on their inside front covers, a marketing technique that most business catalogers shouldn't be without.)

For a business catalog, the key to a layout that works is organization. Feature photos, insert photos, copy points, promotional blurbs, charts, line drawings, swatches, and all the other essential-to-the-market elements must be shown in a manner that is appealingly organized. The similarity between consumer and business needs is strong here; both are being sent to audiences with serious time constraints, so information must be interesting, quickly digested, and compelling. If the presentation is too confusing, you'll lose the audience and the sale.

As you would expect, there are a variety of ways to deal with layout density and organization. Two distinctly different styles, each effective in its own way, are employed by MacWarehouse and Lotus. MacWarehouse uses high density and bold prices to convey value and selection, whereas Lotus employs minimal density, but lots of sales facilitators, such as

- ◆ Crossed-out prices
- ◆ Captions
- ◆ Call-outs
- ◆ Price charts
- ◆ Bold type lead-ins of benefit points
- ◆ "What You Need" specifications in tinted boxes completed with an eye-catching icon
- ◆ A money-back guarantee
- ◆ A toll-free number for ordering and product information
- ◆ Screen captures
- ◆ Product reviews

MacWarehouse jams a lot of valuable information into a little space without being offensive or intimidatingly complicated. Subheads above the product name point up the benefit in minimal space. Neither treatment is better than the other, but both convey their company's positioning, incorporate hard-hitting marketing techniques, and are well-organized, using versions of four-column grids.

In another instance, 20th Century Plastics' upscale graphics combine the aesthetics usually associated with a consumer catalog with the nitty-gritty information necessary to a business catalog. Rather than simply photographing the many variations of photo pages they offer, the company employs line drawings in combination with a dramatic center photo. The line drawings make it easier to accurately identify the correct photo pages and encourage multiple sales. The photography (in conjunction with the headline) helps to immediately clarify the purpose of a page, while pulling the two pages together as a spread.

Two layout elements are key for almost all types of business catalogs:

1. Develop an index to make product categories easy to find. Put this important feature on the inside front cover, inside back cover, back cover, order form, or even the front cover, but choose a location that immediately catches the prospect's eye and becomes a useful tool.

2. Color-code individual sections within the catalog or use a code design that instantly identifies the section it represents. Do not use codes that are so clever they are not functional (more on this important point later in this chapter).

❖ **EXAMPLE 17-4**
MacWarehouse puts a lot of
sell into this high-density
spread. Notice the personal
touch of a name and photo
attached to the toll-free
number.

❖ **EXAMPLE 17-5**   Lotus does more than just show packages; the screen shots
come alive with call-outs and up-close presentations.

❖ **EXAMPLE 17-6** A large crossover photo pulls these two pages into one tidy spread for 20th Century Plastics.

❖ **EXAMPLE 17-7** IBM's AS/400 catalog makes a bold statement with the color it uses in its index and throughout the rest of the catalog.

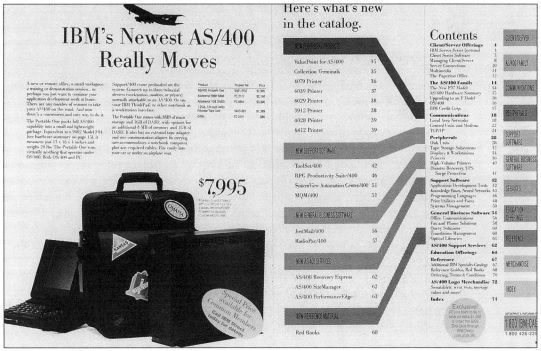

Graphic Techniques. Graphics presentation of important sales points helps the reader instantly understand why one product may be better or special. Icons take important differences and state them in a noticeable way. Graphic treatments can also be employed for customer endorsements, magazine reviews, and other forms of endorsements. Speed of delivery has become truly critical to the business-to-business marketer, and this information also should be shown in a way that makes it stand out.

❖ **EXAMPLE 17-8**   Lotus features symbols that clearly show its unique offers.

The Front Cover

Is the cover as important to business marketers as it is to consumer catalogers? Probably more so. Think about it. In a private home, if the cover is intriguing, the catalog is not only opened but, often, retained. In some ways, it can be a status symbol, kept out for its attractiveness and prestige, as well as for future ordering. A business catalog, on the other hand, needs to grab the recipient's attention immediately or it will end up in one of two places: the wastebasket or filed out of the way for future reference or oblivion.

One item you will most often find on a business cover but not on a consumer cover is the toll-free number. Always remember that a business catalog is most often a reference source and keeping the toll-free number immediately evident is important; hence, its cover position. Business covers should also almost always carry a date. Because they can be retained longer than consumer catalogs, the customer needs to know if the catalog they are using is current.

Even more than with consumer catalogs, business marketers tend to want to pack their entire product line on the cover. In some ways, this makes sense, as the breadth of line is important to convey. But too much of a good thing can also create a poorly designed cover that is unappealing to the potential user.

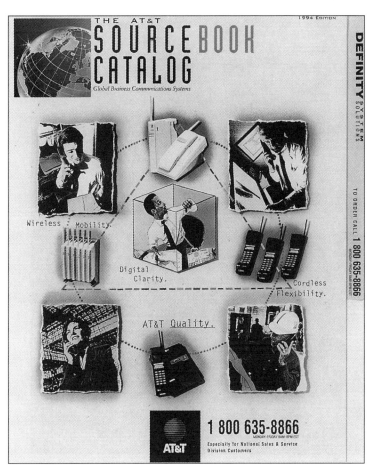

❖ **EXAMPLE 17-9**
''The AT&T Sourcebook''
catalog uses a contemporary art
approach for its grid showing
products in use. Notice the
die-cut tab.

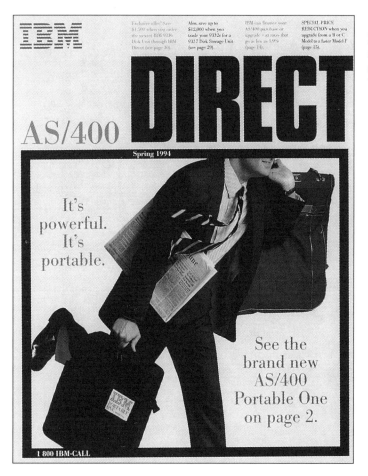

❖ **EXAMPLE 17-10**
IBM's AS/400 catalog features
a ''product as hero,'' putting
action and timeliness behind its
''new and portable'' message.

❖ **EXAMPLE 17-11**
Carrot-Top Industries promotes its extensive product line through an attractive collage and an insert specifying that this is a ''new, expanded edition.'' Notice the tag line that makes the catalog's positioning absolutely clear.

❖ **EXAMPLE 17-12**
MacConnection makes its catalog stand out by ignoring the traditional product approach. This cover promotes just one of the values of shopping from the office.

❖ EXAMPLE 17-13
New Pig makes a strong ''risk-free'' statement and ensures that it is noticed by using clever computer graphics.

The Back Cover

Back covers also are important; some statistics say they are viewed first as often as front covers. Back covers, as in consumer marketing, are prime space, so they are best used for product sales. If the catalog's products are too complicated for an effective presentation in this limited space, another viable option is to use the back cover as a pictorial index. In any case, be sure to reinforce your company's positioning and ask for the order in the form of an 800 number or other order-gathering device.

If a product is offered on the back cover, one question is whether it should also be offered inside. This question is more relevant in business-to-business catalogs because merchandise is so often categorized, and pulling one product out of the category to put it on the back cover could actually hurt the sales of that product. Therefore, consider repeating it, but showing it somewhat smaller on the inside page. The exception here, of course, is if the product can stand on its own and does not really fit well into a category. Always make sure the item is timely and its price is reflective of your overall offering.

Another key item on the back cover is the key code and the graphics used to draw attention to it. Since code collection is harder in business marketing than consumer marketing (largely due to the number of purchase-order orders), this is essential.

Many firms have learned how to combine all of these elements effectively. For example, Viking boasts a back cover that sells, sells, sells! Multicolor graphics, big bursts filled with the magical word ''free;'' highlighted savings, store locations, and a personalized ink-jetted message makes the cover work hard. MacConnection takes a more refined approach, but still conveys excitement with its featured price and framed product. The code collection area is tinted slightly to help phone representatives tell customers where to find the code when they call. And Carrot-Top Industries, maker of customer flags and banners, uses its back cover to promote its custom work. A table of contents and a list where you can find the items pictured on the front cover are included.

❖ **EXAMPLE 17-14**

Viking sells two products with strong prices and cross-reference. It also restates its customer-friendly policies dramatically on its back cover.

❖ **EXAMPLE 17-15**

MacConnection shows one way to highlight a code for superior code collection.

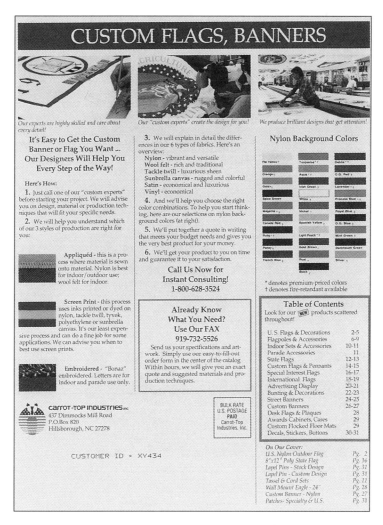

❖ **EXAMPLE 17-16**
Carrot-Top Industries promotes its customer service, providing a lot of information in a highly organized design.

Size

The most common size for a business catalog is the traditional $8\frac{1}{2}'' \times 11''$ (or $8\frac{3}{8}'' \times 10\frac{7}{8}''$ or close press variance). The reasoning here is that this size is the easiest to file, thus keeping it handy for immediate and future reference.

But there is an opportunity to use a different format, especially in cases where the catalog is mailed frequently and wants to have a very different look for certain issues. Additionally, business marketers tend to make greater use of wraps and poly bags. In the case of the paper wraps, this is one way they can use the same basic vehicle (the catalog) and make it look different. Hence, they get extra mileage out of an expensive catalog, yet grab the prospect's attention with what, at first, appears to be a new mailing. In-line polywrapping, by which catalogs can be wrapped in polyethylene film as they come off the bindery, is another alternative for catalogers.

Whether using on-line polywrapping, paper, or plastic envelopes, some mailers feel these carriers provide an invaluable opportunity to include a letter, coupons, extra (or only) order forms, almost any promotional piece, and even some product samples.

When contacting customers with a variety of different mailings, it is wise to be sure they understand just how you intend them to use the catalog. Some marketers clearly state "Master Catalog," "Full Line Catalog," or some other title that indicates this is the catalog customers should keep all year. Subsequent catalogs must also convey their purpose.

And don't forget the potential value of presenting your catalog in an envelope with a letter. Tests have frequently shown that an envelope, especially in appealing to prospects, will more than pay for its additional cost. This varies depending on the type of business, so make sure it is one of the first techniques you test.

❖ **EXAMPLE 17-17**
NEBS employs a smaller, digest-size catalog to promote its line of labels.

❖ **EXAMPLE 17-18**
Carrot-Top Industries uses a simple black-and-green wrap, designed with strong, attention-getting graphics, for its annual catalog, giving a new look to a requester mailing.

❖ **EXAMPLE 17-19**   NEBS's catalog is stitched on the shorter side of $8\frac{1}{2}'' \times 11''$ paper and comes wrapped in plastic.

❖ **EXAMPLE 17-20**
Drawing Board uses a simple but direct message on its envelope to welcome new customers.

Number of Pages

The same rule applies here as for the consumer market: Never just add pages to add pages. The temptation is stronger for business marketers who often mail only one time per year and want this edition to be the definitive one. There is also another reason—the desire to have a spine on the catalog.

A perfect-bound catalog (one that is glued together, not stapled) requires a spine on which you can print the name of the company, the toll-free number and, perhaps, the issue date, your tag line, or whatever sales information you can fit in this limited space. This is a big draw for some catalogers who believe a spine will imply that the catalog should be kept close by on a shelf, not in a file drawer.

Certainly, if your catalog warrants the number of pages needed to create a spine (usually over 100 pages, but highly dependent on the weight of the paper used), look into this option. Any technique that helps give your catalog added shelf life is worth knowing about, but weigh any additional costs and determine if this technique will produce the necessary sales to cover and exceed them.

Organization and Consistency

Keep the pagination of the product, most often in categories, clear. The layout and copy must be designed and written to walk the reader through what can be an extensive information process. Always consider the use of easy-to-spot information, such as category headings, a table of contents, and/or an index.

Most people do not like change, so think consistency in your approach, graphic design, and written message. This means category heads, or tabs, should remain in the area in

❖ **EXAMPLE 17-21**   New Pig uses bold, simple type in strong colors to display the category in the top banner and ordering information in the bottom banner.

which customers are used to finding them. Toll-free numbers and important company policy information should also be constant in placement. Many catalogers put a condensed version of service and ordering information along the bottom of each page; most also reinforce and elaborate on this information on the order form. Changes are necessary to keep new issues fresh, but evolve to them carefully.

Use of Four Color

Although some newcomers have "broken their rules," this is where business catalogers are traditionally different from consumer catalogers. Frequently viewed as a nuts-and-bolts business by both marketers and recipients alike, business catalogs once tended to show their products in one or two colors on low-grade paper. A few innovators, aware of the strides their associates were making in the more glamorous field of consumer cataloging, wondered how offering their products in four color would work. Because of the cost difference between four color and black and white, this idea was riskier and more innovative than it sounds. But those who took the risk were rewarded. Almost without exception, four-color catalogs more than paid for their investment. But the edge that four color once gave business marketers is disappearing as more and more use it. Therefore, it makes good bottom-line sense to look at other options, such as a change in format, if not in the base catalog, then in subsequent interim mailings.

Desktop Publishing

Everything stated about desktop publishing (computerized layouts) in Chapter 8 is emphasized for business marketers. Because most business catalogers repeat more items from book to book than consumer catalogers, it makes sense to keep a computerized database of photos and copy that can simply be adapted from issue to issue.

Another reason for computerization is that, unlike their consumer counterparts, business catalogs tend to have fairly consistent selling seasons, with no major ebbs and flows. This means they can safely internalize their computer operation, because workers are virtually guaranteed to be kept busy all year long.

Electronic Printing Options. Business mailers are also looking into the benefits of signatures gathered together in predetermined configurations (see Chapter 7). Using this technique, each catalog grouping of signatures can have two of its covers designed for a specific market and the others designed as a generic adaptation of the original. For instance, an office-supplies catalog could produce profession-specific signatures that would be mailed only to the particular profession for which the products were meant (for example, veterinarians or lawyers).

Many catalogers use the latest ink jet techniques in much the same way as consumer catalogers to encourage customer to take advantage of bonuses, direct them to particular savings pages, announce new merchandise, and so on.

The Mailing Plan

Traditionally, business catalogers mail less frequently than do consumer marketers. The main reason for this is that their product lines simply do not change as often as consumer lines do. As in all things, there are exceptions to this, but for our purposes, let's look at what a standard mailing schedule might be.

A lot of business mailers mail one large, often perfect bound, catalog a year. It contains their entire line and is meant to be retained for the year. Subsequent mailings can take the form of line-specific catalogs, solo mailings of new products and/or best-sellers, or reminders of some sort that encourage the customer to pick up the catalog and order (see Figure 17-1). Remember, this is most often not an impulse business, so there can be less opportunity to push the customer into ordering.

Other business marketers mail catalogs of varying page lengths (say from 32 to less than 100) several times a year—but, again, not usually with monthly frequency (see Figure 17-2).

❖ FIGURE 17-1   Mailing Plan: One Main Catalog

Year 1—Total Quantity, 600,000

	Jan.	Feb.	Mar.	Apr.	May	June	July	Aug.	Sept.	Oct.	Nov.	Dec.
In-mail	12/27	—	—	4/10	—	—	—	7/29	—	10/15	—	—
In-office	1/2–1/10	—	—	4/14–4/23	—	—	—	8/3–8/12	—	10/18–10/25	—	—
Quantity (thousands)	250	—	—	100	—	—	—	150	—	100	—	—
Type	Big book	—	—	Special issue	—	—	—	Special issue	—	Solo mailing	—	—
No. of pages	Several hundred	—	—	32	—	—	—	32	—	—	—	—
% new	20%–40%	—	—	10%	—	—	—	10%	—	Best-sellers only	—	—
Segments	House, all	—	—	House, segments	—	—	—	House, segments	—	House, segments	—	—
	Requesters	—	—	Requesters	—	—	—	Requesters	—	—	—	—
	—	—	—	Multis	—	—	—	Multis	—	—	—	—
	Rented	—	—	—	—	—	—	Rented	—	—	—	—

* This plan assumes that the cataloger issues a yearly catalog and targets a market which does not have particular seasonality.

❖ FIGURE 17-2   Mailing Plan: Smaller Catalog

Year 1—Total Quantity, 1 Million

	Jan.	Feb.	Mar.	Apr.	May	June	July	Aug.	Sept.	Oct.	Nov.	Dec.
In-mail	12/27	—	3/10	—	—	—	—	7/29	—	10/1	—	—
In-home	1/2–1/10	—	3/14–3/23	—	—	—	—	8/3–8/12	—	10/4–10/14	—	—
Quantity (thousands)	400	—	200	—	—	—	—	550	—	250	—	—
Type	New	—	Remail	—	—	—	—	New	—	Remail	—	—
No. of pages	32	—	32	—	—	—	—	48	—	48	—	—
% new	30%	—	Same	—	—	—	—	20%	—	10%	—	—
Segments	House, all	—	House, segments	—	—	—	—	House, segments	—	House, all	—	—
	Requesters	—	Requesters	—	—	—	—	Requesters	—	Requesters	—	—
	Rented	—	Rented	—	—	—	—	Rented	—	Rented	—	—
	—	—	Multi	—	—	—	—	—	—	—	—	—

* All versions have cover changes and/or wraps.

There is generally less seasonality in business-to-business than in consumer cataloging, as the consumer market is habitually very gift-oriented. Yet, the summer-month doldrums can affect even business marketers, so many mailers avoid them. Seasonality can be a big factor, too, if you are targeting an industry such as education. Understand the buying needs of your targeted businesses before constructing your mailing plan.

The secret to a successful mailing plan is learning, through trial and error, how many times you can profitably mail your particular audience. Only testing will tell you.

Contact Strategy

In addition to the catalog, you need to schedule regular contact with your customer. This can take many forms, but all should reinforce your brand in his or her mind, and almost all should inspire a decision to purchase.

Your plan should specify how you will handle customers who purchase from you regularly, those who are new to your list, and those who are inactive. These basic areas (shown in Figure 17-3) should receive different forms of contact; you may wish to expand the segments as your business grows and you see definite trends on which you can build a contact strategy.

Finding Buyers

The primary concern for all catalogers, whether business- or consumer-related, is getting customers. Higher returns generally result if you mail to an individual rather than a company, so collecting the individual's name is most important. Having accurate mailing lists is essential for business mailers, since their customers tend to be worth substantially more than those of a consumer cataloger. Business buyers quite often spend several thousand dollars a month (or even in one order!), which explains to a large extent why business mailers are willing to initially lose money on customer acquisition. Business mailers sometimes mail small quantities, often under 25,000—a number most consumer catalogers would consider too small even for a test. The reason for the difference is simple: Many business catalogers don't have the potential universe available to consumer mailers.

Finding Lists

Without a doubt, business mailers have a tougher job when it comes to finding mailing lists (the exceptions, of course, are those business mailers that are using an existing house list, previously marketed via a different medium). And even when they find lists, many mailers find they regularly have a waste factor of 25 percent or more. Some of the reasons for this include the following:

1. The lists are not clean. Updating can be a real problem, especially if your target moves (and people regularly change jobs).
2. There is a high duplication factor. Many companies operate under different names at the same address. And duplication of names within those companies cannot be caught by normal merge/purge methods, because the company names (which are the basis of the merge/purge) are different.
3. Deciding who to mail to within an organization is difficult. Should it be the purchasing agent, the head of the company, or just the company itself?
4. Getting through the secretary or administrative assistant is difficult. Even if you decide on the target that's right for your particular catalog, an estimated 50 percent of an executive's mail is intercepted by his or her secretary. Or, even more irritating, it's simply discarded in the mailroom.
5. People change jobs or move within an organization, especially in industries where the turnover rate is high.

Cleaning Lists.   Know your list broker/compiler! Work closely with the broker on all the lists you rent, making sure to clarify exactly who maintains the list and in what condition. Don't assume that just because you're renting from a compiler of good reputation, it has compiled the list you are renting. Compilers can, and often do, subcontract work. Also, it doesn't hurt to physically doublecheck a list for accuracy whenever possible. It's one way of reassuring yourself and of keeping list brokers/compilers on their toes.

❖ FIGURE 17-3   **Sample Contact Strategy**

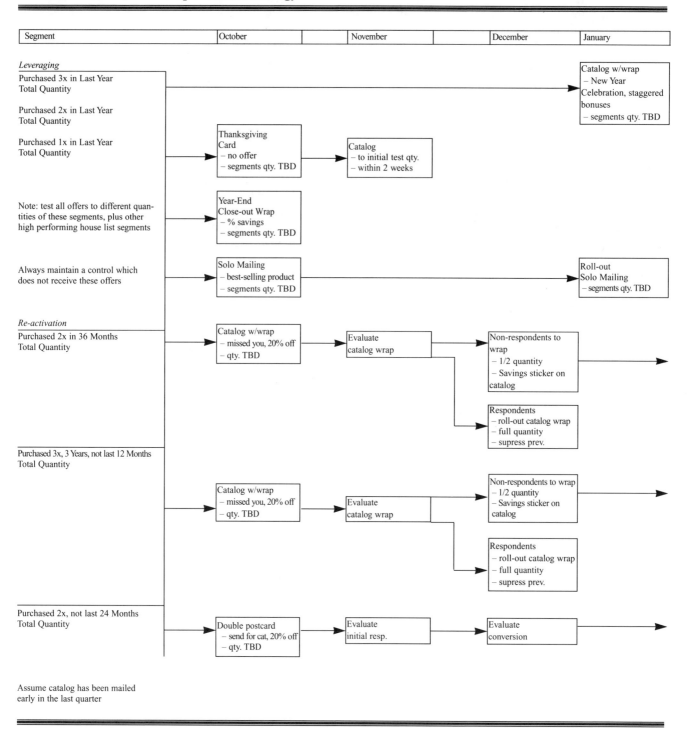

Assume catalog has been mailed
early in the last quarter

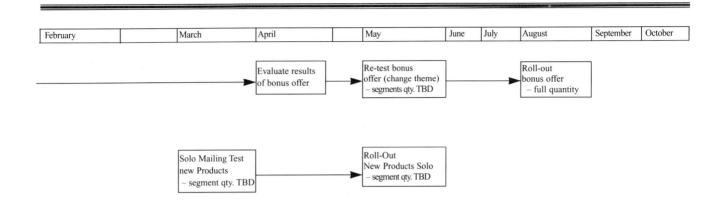

| February | | March | April | May | June | July | August | September | October |

Evaluate results of bonus offer

Re-test bonus offer (change theme) – segments qty. TBD

Roll-out bonus offer – full quantity

Solo Mailing Test new Products – segment qty. TBD

Roll-Out New Products Solo – segment qty. TBD

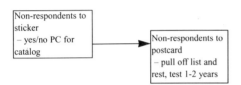

Non-respondents to sticker – yes/no PC for catalog

Non-respondents to postcard – pull off list and rest, test 1-2 years

Non-respondents to sticker – yes/no PC for catalog

Non-respondents to postcard – pull off list and rest, test 1-2 years

Roll-out remaining quantity

❖ **EXAMPLE 17-22**
New Pig, a catalog that "solves leak and spill problems," uses a visual call-out that pulls key points out of the main photo.

❖ **EXAMPLE 17-23**
IBM has a bind-in reader card to be filled out, supplying important information for future mailings.

Free Wrist Rest!

Enjoy Safer Computing with an IBM Wrist Rest

This comfortable, durable Wrist Rest helps maintain your wrists in the ideal position to relieve stress, boost productivity, and protect you against keyboard-related injuries. And it's yours FREE, simply by filling out the attached Reader Card in its entirety and dropping it in your nearest mailbox.

1 800 IBM-CALL.

Complete, fold, tape and send this card to receive your FREE IBM Wrist Rest.

Name
Your Title/Department
Your Company Name
Company Address
City   State   Zip   Telephone No.
My company currently owns or leases an IBM AS/400   ☐ No   ☐ Yes
Contact Name/Title

Total number of employees at this location:
Total number of employees in the
Data Processing Department at this location

I found the Spring '94 AS/400 Catalog:
☐ Very useful   ☐ Useful   ☐ Somewhat useful   ☐ Not useful

I will most likely use this catalog to:
☐ Place an order   ☐ Learn about products
☐ Comparison shop   ☐ Develop a recommendation

I plan to order from this catalog within:
☐ 0-3 months   ☐ 3-6 months   ☐ More than 6 months
☐ I am not responsible for ordering products

I currently use other catalogs for business purchases of:
☐ Less than $1,000   ☐ Less than $10,000
☐ More than $10,000   ☐ More than $100,000
☐ I do not purchase through catalogs

My AS/400 Model Number is:
Footprint - Check one: ☐ 9402   ☐ 9404   ☐ 9406
Series - Check one: ☐ B   ☐ C   ☐ D   ☐ E   ☐ F

In the last year I have bought AS/400 additions/enhancements from:
☐ IBM   ☐ An IBM Business Partner
☐ An IBM Used Equipment Broker   ☐ Other

In 1994, our organization expects to purchase AS/400 additions/enhancements:
☐ No   ☐ Yes   In the area of:
☐ Hardware   ☐ Software   ☐ Used Equipment

The president or senior official in my organization is:
Name
Title

The persons below are involved in decision-making regarding the purchase of enhancements or hardware/software additions for our company's AS/400(s).
Please send a catalog to those I have checked.
Name   Title
☐
☐
☐

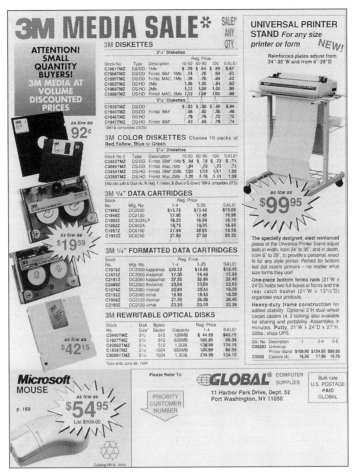

To help with this problem, consider including a facsimile of a routing slip on the back cover of your catalog. If you haven't gotten to the right person, this notation can invite the recipient to route your catalog to the correct person or department. For example, IBM gives the title of the person who should see its catalog. As previously mentioned, always make it easy for your customer to find the code you need to accurately track list results.

Some catalogers also bind-in postage-paid postcards that ask for qualifying information from the recipient and help ensure their list is up to date. Others keep their own rental corrections file and run it against all the lists they rent.

Getting Past the Gate Keeper.   This can be a difficult problem to solve. One reason catalogs are often mailed in an envelope is to let the mailer state specifically that the materials enclosed have been requested by the person whose name is on the envelope. If a company has a policy against processing third- and fourth-class mail (and some do), one way of getting your catalog to those who want it is to collect their home addresses. Also consider mailing to home addresses.

Database Marketing

Because of the generally smaller universe of available names and the need to maximize their performance, database marketing is often more important and, in some ways, more difficult for a business-to-business catalog than for a consumer catalog. Among the major differences between consumer and business-to-business catalog databases are:

1. In general, more data is kept for each customer on a business-to-business database. Not only the purchaser's name and address, but also the data regarding his or her organization is needed.

2. There are usually additional sources of data, such as a field sales force, data obtained at trade shows, and data obtained during outbound telemarketing, for businesses.

3. Because of the multiplicity of record changes beyond simple consumer changes of address, the need to frequently update the file is more urgent for a business-to-business database. For example a consumer database record might show the following:

    Account number
    Name
    Address
    City
    Zip code
    Transaction data

A similar business record might include:

    Account number
    Company name
    Location address, including city, state, and zip code
    Headquarters address, including city, state, and zip code
    Purchaser name
    Title
    Specifier name (if applicable)
    Title
    Influencer name (if applicable)
    Title
    Credit data
    Contact data (show attendance, field sales contact, literature fulfillment, dates for next contact, and so on)
    Transaction data

The increased number of data elements, data sources, and the need for a coherent contact strategy leads to a set of circumstances unique to business-to-business situations:

♦   A business catalog may have multiple names/buyers within one company at one or more addresses. This is usually accounted for by using a relational database format or possibly a hierarchical format with interrelated tables.

♦   The business-to-business purchaser may only be the purchasing agent. Others involved in the purchase may be the economic buyer (dollar commitment authority), the technical buyer (specifier), and the actual end user. There may also be identifiable influencers. All these can be delineated in the form of fields within the establishment record.

♦   Data freshness is a major problem. The relative frequency of change of data elements in the name, address, company, and title is much higher for business-to-business. A recent survey found over 70 percent of queried individuals had changes to one or more data elements. Every attempt must be made to ensure that information is updated periodically through such methods as field sales force queries, double postcards, conference and convention data input, and so on.

♦   There may be different pricing structures for the same individual. For example, the same person may be a purchaser as a government employee, a professor, an industrial consultant, or a part-time employee. In this case, the data structure is handled by using a relational or linked table structure, but take care that catalog staff place the purchaser in the proper context of order entry.

Reactivation

It's a truism that customers supply the necessary funds for prospecting. Therefore, it makes sense to be sure to allocate a sufficient budget to support a formal reactivation plan that concentrates on getting lapsed customers to buy again.

Think of how magazines treat their customers. They waste no time getting them to renew their subscriptions and do not let up when it comes to regenerating those who have not renewed. Use the same kind of approach with your customers. Most catalogers use a three-part plan:

1. An incentive, such as a percentage or dollars off, along with a "we missed you" approach
2. A reminder that if the customer does not order again he or she will be deleted from the mailing list
3. A postcard mailing that gives a clear choice of getting the catalog or not

An example of this is shown in the contact strategy in Figure 17-3.

Research, too, will give you insight into what is needed to bring customers back into the fold. Be sure not to stop at worrying about lost customers—do something about it with a definite plan.

Alternate Methods of Name Acquisition

Because of the inherent list-rental problems faced by business mailers, it's wise to investigate the many other means of attracting customers, including some variations on consumer techniques.

Tell-a-Colleague.   Business customers tend to be even more loyal than consumer customers; they can be your best source for new business. Besides allowing space for associates' names and titles on the order form, try postcard bind-ins or even incentives for the recommender.

Card Decks.   Although renting space in existing card decks is one approach, consider creating your own. Made up of best-sellers at promotional prices, it might be one way of distancing yourself from the competition.

Space Ads.   Use space ads to get leads and help build identity. Brand identity is as important to the business mailer as it is to the consumer mailer. Place space ads in highly targeted publications to sell your catalog and its services. Test bingo cards (postcards with promotional offerings inserted into magazines) very cautiously. It's an unfortunate fact that bingo cards seldom work for the majority of business mailers. Too often the person filling out the card is not really qualified to make a purchase decision. And the service house in charge of processing the names can take over a month to get the leads, too often misspelled and incorrectly addressed, to your fulfillment house.

Watch your fellow direct marketers in the consumer field and be one of the first to adopt their successful innovations.

Electronic Media.   This fast-changing field has proven a boon for some business marketers whose products appeal to computer-literate individuals employed by target companies (see Chapter 12). Because developments are happening all the time, be sure to stay up to date on the latest developments through subscriptions to industry publications and by attending industry trade shows.

Publicity.   Everything that was written about publicity in Chapter 12 holds true here. Magazines, in-house publications, newsletters, newspapers, and so on are all looking for interesting stories. And those stories can help you find the people who are interested in your particular product line.

Case history.   Think your product line may be too boring or too specialized to use publicity? Think again. New Pig has used publicity as one of its tools in building its business from a start-up venture in 1985 to estimated sales of over $50 million in 1994. Its growth rate has averaged 50 percent since its inception, and it has been able to expand to 30 foreign countries, including Japan, the United Kingdom, Germany, and Mexico.

What exciting product does the company offer? As its press release states: ''New Pig Corporation is the creator of the packaged absorbents industry and an innovator in providing solutions to industrial and hazardous materials leak and spill response problems.'' Hardly glamorous, but New Pig has created news through inventive marketing—and plenty of publicity. New Pig is ready with the ammunition it needs to get coverage; pig snout hats, pig tee-shirts, a nifty name (used because of its ''first crude, messy research lab''), clever copy and graphics (the number to call to place orders is 1-800-HOT-HOGS), and a professional-looking, inviting public relations kit.

Customers call for information and it arrives promptly in a bright blue folder with a hot pink ''Oink'' emblazoned on it. Open up the folder and nested in the pink interior (complete with little, three-dimensional pig ''tails'') are:

◆ An attractive brochure detailing New Pig's history, operation, and the people behind it
◆ Several copies of catalogs
◆ Reprints of articles about the company
◆ A list of awards it has received
◆ A press release

You don't need to invest as much in your first efforts, but be sure to put together a strategy for regular contact with the press, a powerful tool for customer acquisition and brand identity reinforcement.

A Few of the Key Marketing Areas

Many of the strategies used by business marketers have already been addressed, since consumer marketers do not differ greatly in their approaches. However, not only do some additional opportunities exist in business-to-business marketing, but there are also some interesting observations to be made.

Purchasing Options.   Although virtually every consumer catalog offers the standard Visa, MasterCard, and travel-and-leisure credit-card options, few provide their customers with house credit. Yet many business catalogs offer open accounts against company purchase orders. The reason is simple. Business catalogs are dealing with companies that are used to ordering merchandise and services with a purchase order; some, because of company policy, can place an order no other way.

Offering credit undoubtedly increases sales, but it also increases risk and calls for a careful monitoring program. One method of reducing bad debt seems to be universally accepted: get the invoice out immediately, and follow up on a regular basis (the recommended time is 15 days). One cataloger makes a policy of not sending statements, as it has been its experience that the purchaser will not want to pay until the statement is received, putting an unnecessary strain on your cash flow. Should the nonpayer continue to avoid fulfilling his or her financial obligation, don't hesitate to stop shipment. Also, know to whom you are offering credit. Some catalogers have found that hot-line names, especially those obtained through the use of a premium received before cash must be actually sent, are dangerous risks. Still, offering credit is something that all business mailers should consider.

Frequent Buyer Clubs.   Giving a person an incentive to select your product over someone else's is an idea that's as old as the hills. But it becomes a little more complicated when your target is usually someone who is responsible for purchasing merchandise and/or services for his or her employer. Does the incentive belong to the employee or the employer?

Most business marketers attempt to offer gifts that are appropriate for the office, thus acknowledging the potential moral dilemma. Hence, if the employee makes the purchase decision, the employee gets the benefits of the prize earned and, hopefully, will share the prize with others in his or her work environment. For example, the Drawing Board offers "free gifts" with each order totaling over a certain dollar amount. The value of the gift naturally increases proportionally to the amount of money spent.

Premiums. Although consumer catalogs offer their audience a comprehensive variety of premiums, they tend to offer only one premium for a set dollar amount ordered. Business catalogers, on the other hand, have a propensity for multipremiums earned at different levels of purchase amounts. In addition, some companies provide customers with product-specific bonuses. Probably one of the most popular is the free tape dispenser, given when a certain number of rolls of tape are purchased.

Telemarketing

It goes without saying that business marketers, by and large, offer toll-free numbers for customer orders. Most offer them for customer service, too, because they find that both services pay for themselves in initial orders and customer loyalty—and that the high average orders can support the additional cost.

Inbound. The product offerings in business catalogs are usually more complicated and/or technical than those offered in consumer catalogs. This means there is more to

❖ **EXAMPLE 17-25**   Drawing Board rewards its best customers with valuable gifts and features this information on its opening spread.

placing an order than simply picking up the phone and placing an order. Granted, a large percentage of orders come via purchase order and the mail, but even those often require phone contact before the order itself is written. This means your operators must be more than order takers. They have to understand the business and have the right answers ready at the time of the call.

In many cases, business catalogs have physically replaced the sales force. In others, they coexist with the sales force through a variety of different approaches. Either way, the telemarketer becomes the contact and in effect must replace that friendly salesperson who knew everything about the product line and even knew the names and birthdays of the best customers' children.

Rudy Oetting, a partner in Oetting and Co., says:

> In business-to-business marketing, the telephone has successfully evolved from supporting field sales with leads, to order-taking efforts integrated with field sales, to covering a field salesperson's small business accounts, to the present stand-alone account management with field specialists supporting the telephone reps who own the accounts.[2]

A well-trained, highly motivated, frequently monitored telemarketer can create the same bonds with his or her customers as the traveling salesperson of days gone by. Many catalogers create VIP phone centers, through which their best customers receive special attention, are alerted early to special offers, and have representatives who do actually know their children's birthdays!

Telephone account management is defined by Rudy Oetting this way: "Sales made through the telephone channel to customers who require frequent personal contact by *skilled* sales reps." These salespeople "own" a specific number of customer accounts and their basic goals are

- To keep accounts buying from the company, not from the competition
- To develop accounts through selling more of the same products, selling new products, and knocking out the competition.

Is the cost of a trained telephone representative worth it? Oetting put together two tables (see Tables 17-4 and 17-5) that illustrate both the number of contacts a telephone service rep (TSR) can effectively handle and the payback those reps are likely to generate.

❖ **TABLE 17-4**
Number of Accounts per Telephone Sales Rep

	Total Yearly DMCs per Rep	÷	Anticipated Contacts per Account	=	Number of Accounts per Rep
Routine Sale	7,500		5		1,500
Complex Sale	5,000		10		500

DMC = decision maker contact.
Reprinted with permission of *Sales & Marketing Management* and Oetting and Co.

❖ **TABLE 17-5**
The Cost of a Telephone Sales Rep

	Routine Sale	Complex Sale
Annual cost per rep	$37,500	$82,500
Number of rep phone days	235	220
Cost per day	$160	$375
DMCs per day	33	20
Cost per DMC	$4.85	$18.75
If expense to revenue (E/R) is targeted at	15%	10%
Then targeted revenue* per rep is	$250,000	$825,000

* For an agreed-to time period.
DMC = decision maker contact.
Used with permission of *Sales & Marketing Management* and Oetting and Co.

Outbound.   Some catalogers indicate that outbound telemarketing has worked well only as an upsell tool. In other words, it has been effectively used for follow-up sales of what may well be an already existing sale. As in all cases where there is cost to the cataloger, the amount of the sale must be high enough to warrant the outbound telemarketing cost. Liz Kislik, president of Liz Kislik Associates, says, "a typical upsell should cost no more than a third of the original purchase price."

In preparing to use outbound telemarketing, you must first prepare a script for all of the reps to use. Allow time to go over the script with the reps and integrate the system into your existing program. Things *will* go wrong, so allow time to monitor the system carefully and make the necessary changes. Give your people a chance to get used to the script and the whole idea of selling; with encouragement, they'll soon learn the ins and outs of how to make sales presentations that will both create sales and serve as customer-service calls.

Don't forget that if outbound telemarketing worked on a particular customer once, it may well work again. Be sure to follow up with other calls on subsequent orders and track the lifetime value of the customer. Many marketers are also successful in using telemarketing to reactivate customers who have stopped buying. Liz Kislik reminds all marketers:

> Telephone marketing reps conduct the only live contact many companies ever have with their customers. The personal interaction between customer and company can leave a lasting impression, positive or negative. Reps are unlikely to represent their employers to advantage if they hate their company, hate their boss, and hate what they do for a living. Motivating and training reps to represent well and sell well is, obviously, a management issue. . . . To be effective, reps need the flexibility to know when and how to make exceptions and adjustments, when to modify a deal, when to placate, when to stick to their guns. Management needs to sanction reps' exercise of discretion and give them the tools and feedback they need to constantly improve their judgment.[3]

Telephone Preference Service.   Telephone Preference Service (TPS) is a free consumer (and business) service provided by the Direct Marketing Association (DMA). Its purpose is to allow customers to have their names removed from calling lists. Calling lists should be matched against the list provided by service bureaus who maintain the DMA TPS file. There is generally no charge for this service. Business mailers should make every attempt to comply with this service and construct their own "do-not-call" list to suppress names and numbers of customers who do not wish to be called.

Voice Response Units.   Increasingly catalogers use automated forms of answering. There are many pluses and just as many minuses to this evolving technology. See Chapter 13 for more information.

Customer Service: The Heart of Business Catalogs

Customer service is of prime concern to business mailers, and almost without exception, the speed with which merchandise is delivered is noted throughout business catalogs. Understanding your customers and meeting their needs is paramount in this environment.

Often, when customers need something, it's because they've run out of it (or are about to), and they want it now. To make sure that the order processing goes smoothly and speedily, company managers spend quite a bit of time physically taking orders and personally monitoring both customer-service calls and quality control. For better control of shipping time, some catalogers have increased (or begun opening) regional warehouses.

Inmac, in an issue of *Direct Marketing* magazine, indicated that it believed its substantial growth was attributable to seven basic reasons:

1. Excellent customer service
2. Good-quality merchandise, much of it Inmac's own brand
3. A broad, innovative product line
4. Competitive prices
5. Local presence
6. A liberal return policy
7. Long warranties

In another example of customer-driven marketing, Paper Direct charges only $1 more than their standard delivery service for overnight delivery via Federal Express. Some catalogs with especially high-priced merchandise charge nothing at all for delivery.

Reliable Product's inside front cover showcases some of its many services; in other editions, Reliable condenses this information to one page, but still keeps it as the lead to the catalog. The company's major pints (from pages 2–3) include: free, next-day delivery; low, low prices; huge brand-name selection; custom shopping service; the best guarantee in the business; and toll-free ordering.

Customer service does not have to focus on information about your overall services. It can be specific to a product or product category and illustrate how you are the authority. For example, New Pig devotes a full page to smart information that addresses any questions its customers might have about the protective clothing offered. By answering your customers' questions before they ask them you have saved them time, frustration, and inconvenience.

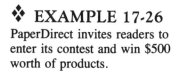

❖ **EXAMPLE** 17-26
PaperDirect invites readers to enter its contest and win $500 worth of products.

❖ **EXAMPLE 17-27**   This two-page spread shouts the benefits of buying from Reliable.

❖ **EXAMPLE 17-28**   An educational editorial, like this one from New Pig, is an excellent form of customer service.

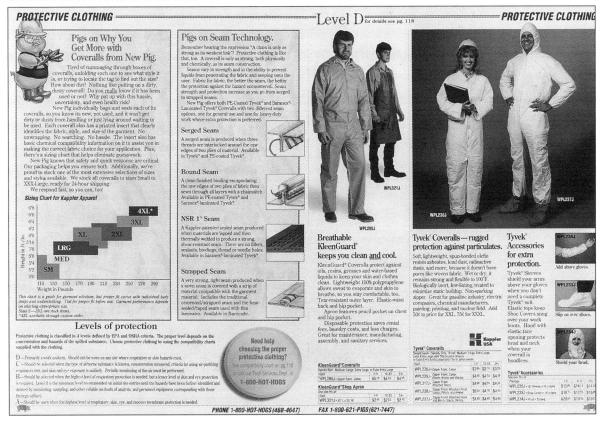

Understanding Your Customers' Needs

Every cataloger positions its catalog in a way that it feels is truly unique, and part of that positioning is the individualized services it can offer its customers. One excellent example of a company that saw an opportunity to learn from its customers and create a mechanism for bonding with those customers, is Paper Direct, whose front cover once read: "Win $500—enter our next 'Show Us Your Stuff' contest and win $500 worth of PaperDirect Paper." The company sprinkles stories from customers throughout the catalog. The benefit is that the stories help instruct readers in how to use the products PaperDirect sells while getting the customers to feel as though they are part of the PaperDirect family.

You can also address your customers' needs with the package you send them in answer to their request for a catalog. Quill has excelled in this area. Its outer envelope practically reached out and touched customers with a big, red, script "Thank you," but the best part was inside the package. And this was a package, not just an envelope with a catalog in it. Contents included:

◆ A personalized letter, complete with a pressure-sensitive label, that not only contains a brightly colored code but also gives the recipient a three-day extension on sales prices if he or she affixes the label to the order blank or tells the phone operator the code (easy to find because of its highlighting).

◆ A vivid yellow folder, just the right size for file drawers, made of such a bright yellow that it's bound to set itself apart from other catalogs that may be in the same file.

◆ A handwritten note from Jack Miller, the company president, that really looks handwritten and gives the customer access to Miller's direct phone line should they want to contact him about Quill's services.

❖ **EXAMPLE 17-29**
"Need anything else?" The Drawing Board asks just as you open your package. Brilliant!

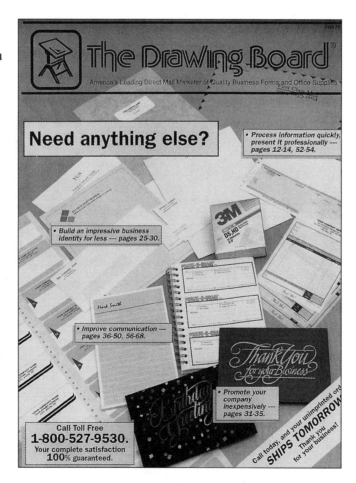

- A sensible little booklet filled with 48 pages of information on how to save money on office supplies.
- A four-color background piece on Quill's philosophy—a smart touch that gives Quill the opportunity to reinforce its credibility with photos of its headquarters, the company officers, its computer systems, its warehouse, and some of its personnel.
- Not one but two catalogs, all filled with savings.

All in all, it's a memorable package.

The Drawing Board, too, understands that you must tailor your message to the recipient's state of mind and purchase cycle. Not every business cataloger can use package inserts, because the person who opens the package may not be the person who does the ordering. But The Drawing Board seems to know this is not the case with its market and constructs a catalog cover that gets right to the point: It says, "Need anything else?" just as you open your package.

Order Forms

Because many business-catalog customers place their orders on company purchase orders, it is often said that the order form is not as important to business mailers as it is to consumer catalogers. This is true in its purest sense, but order forms have evolved, in many cases, to worksheets. The intent is to provide the user with an opportunity to compile information on what they want to order, then use the worksheet as a tool in the ordering process, which often includes getting approval from a superior. Alternatively, worksheets can often act as fax documents.

Order forms and worksheets have adopted many of the design elements more commonly found on consumer order forms, such as handwritten "examples" in the order-entry section, ink-jetted names and addresses, shipping and handling charts, and an overall "friendly" appearance not previously seen on business order forms. Although business mailers may adapt some consumerlike approaches, they will probably always need to include elements not found on consumer order forms, such as

- Quantity discounts
- House charge information
- An index
- Trade references
- A credit application
- Freight terms and unusual delivery information
- Information on foreign orders
- Company purchase order information
- Bid information
- Customer order information

Don't overlook the order form/worksheet as a selling tool, even if the majority of your current customers use company purchase orders. Keep the design simple, clean, and inviting, and encourage your customers to use it. If you do, your code tracking might be more accurate—and orders might increase, too.

The Business Plan

As stated in Chapter 15, the business plan is the single most important step you can take to ensure that your business has a solid foundation. It is the blueprint to building your house. Most of what was addressed in Chapter 15 holds true for business-to-business catalogers, but there are some differences. Therefore, new financial examples have been created to reflect the needs of business-to-business cataloging. The major differences are as follows:

1. **Catalog size.** The catalog is 64 pages rather than 32 for the consumer version. This is because business mailers generally use catalogs with larger page counts.

2. **Mailing plan.** The mailing plan calls for lower quantities to be mailed. This is typical of business cataloging, where universes tend to be smaller. The plan also reflects the fact that many business catalogs see added sales at the beginning of a calendar year and during the July period, which is often the beginning of a fiscal year. However, July is still mailed cautiously, as the summer quarter has some of the same negative effects as it does in consumer cataloging.

3. **Buyer file attrition.** The buyer file attrition rate is set at 30 percent rather than 33 percent as in the consumer model. In both cases, these are estimates and will, of course, depend on customer satisfaction and loyalty.

4. **Pre-press cost.** The pre-press cost is set lower for this case, reflecting the expected higher degree of pickup and product retention from book to book.

5. **Postage.** Postage is higher, reflecting the weight of the catalog (above the 3.306-ounce-per-piece maximum)

6. **Order split.** It is assumed that only 10 percent of the orders will be paid by credit card as opposed to 80 percent in the consumer case. Business-to-business assumes that 90 percent of orders will be open invoices paid by check.

7. **Fulfillment cost per order.** The fulfillment cost is based on internal fulfillment rather than the outside service costed for the consumer model. However, the cost is higher rather than lower because the facility will not reach expected efficiency until a greater throughput of orders is achieved.

8. **Cost of goods.** Cost of goods is lower, reflecting combinations of manufacturing and overseas sourcing more prevalent in business cataloging.

9. **Other merchandise costs.** Promotion and liquidation costs are included because promotions of various kinds seem to be a fact of life in this market.

10. **Staff.** The business model provides for a somewhat earlier and higher level of staffing than the consumer model. In part, this is due to internal fulfillment that requires an even higher level of trained service personnel than consumer catalogs, but it is also because business catalogers are generally less entrepreneurial and more corporate-oriented than consumer catalogers.

11. **Cash flow.** For this example, 90 percent of the revenue is offset an additional 30 days from time of sale. This is a result of open invoice sales. The remaining 10 percent is taken as revenue at the time of sale (credit-card sales). Costs associated with sales, such as fulfillment costs, are taken at the time of the sale rather than at the receipt of revenue. These differences have the effect of increasing the negative cash flow.

Financial Examples

The numbers contained in this section do not represent actual figures. Although they are consistent, they are only examples to show the new cataloger what formats and methods are used and illustrate how to set up his or her own projections.

Mail Plan.   The catalog is 64 pages, approximately $8^{1}/_{2}" \times 10^{7}/_{8}"$. The initial test quantity is 200,000. This would likely be divided among approximately 30 lists to obtain data on the performance of both individual lists and list categories. Consider the sample size in Table 11.1 (page 267) and a list that has a 1.75-percent response on a mailing of 6,250 names. This will be reproducible with 95-percent confidence in a future mailing as $1.75\% \pm 0.325\%$.

The mail plan in Figure 17-4 is based on two mailings of catalogs with completely new (full) creative with two remails where four pages have new creative. In reality, there would be some pickup and the "all new" issues would show some savings from the figures given.

Plan Parameters.   The plan parameters in Figure 17-5 give two columns of response data. The initial data are for the first mailing of each segment. The annual increments show the effect of learning which lists and merchandise perform best, as well as what creative approaches are most effective. The increases are added in equal increments over the year.

Year	Date	Quantity	Type	# of Pages
Year 1	January	200,000	Full	64
	March	100,000	Remail	64
	May	100,000	Remail	64
	July	150,000	Full	64
	September	150,000	Remail	64
	November	150,000	Remail	64

Two-Year Summary

	Orders	Sales	P/L	% of Sales
Year 1	17,583	$2,929,415	($208,717)	−7.12%
Year 2	22,705	$4,443,343	$498,049	11.21%

❖ FIGURE 17-4
Catalog Mail Plan and Summary

Revenue

	Initial	Annual Increments
Buyer response rate	5.00%	25.00%
Buyer average order	$210.00	15.00%
Buyer response rate	3.00%	20.00%
Buyer average order	$175.00	10.00%
Rental name response rate	1.75%	15.00%
Rental name average order	$165.00	10.00%
Multibuyer (rental) response rate	2.00%	15.00%
Multibuyer (rental) average order	$175.00	10.00%
Buyer file attrition per year	30.00%	
Request names/catalog	3,000	
Shipping and handling revenue	$3.00	

Merchandise

Cost of goods (including freight in)	$38.00%
Freight in	3.80%
Promotional expenses	3.00%
Liquidations	4.00%
Replacements/refunds	3.00%
Cancellations—not available to ship	4.00%

Marketing

Pre-press cost/page	$2,700
Page change (remail)	4
Printing cost per thousand	$325
Postage	See calculation

Operations

Number of catalogs per year	Year 1	6
Administration	See calculation	
Fulfillment cost per order	$15.92	

	% of orders	Costs
Card charges	10.00%	1.90%
Bad debt/checks	90.00%	1.00%

❖ FIGURE 17-5
Plan Parameters

Attrition is taken at 30 percent per year for the buyer file, and names are dropped in equal amounts at each mailing. For the time period covered, this is a convervative approach. Its use over longer time periods requires analysis to determine which names should be dropped from the mailings. Prepress costs include:

◆ Design, layout, and copy through disc/cartridge
◆ Photography (no model costs)
◆ Separations

Printing is based on 64 pages with a self-cover, on 60# (#3 grade) paper with a bound-in order form.

It is assumed that 10 percent of the orders will be paid by credit card and 90 percent by check and/or open invoicing. For the average order and reasonable chargebacks, the discount rate should be below 2 percent for credit cards. The bad debt from checks and/ or open invoices is estimated at 1 percent of the 90-percent check usage.

The fulfillment cost of $15.92 per order is based on internal fulfillment (see Figure 17-6). The $15.92 figure is high and represents investment in a fulfillment set-up that will not be fully used for a few years. The cost of goods is 38 percent, including freight in. This is commensurate with either large-scale overseas sourcing or manufacturing.

Postage Calculation.   The calculation assumes that the catalog is in the per-pound-plus-per-piece range and weighs 5.19 ounces. Presort ratios are approximate.

Rates are based on current (1995) rates.

Administrative Costs.   Costs for staff hired three months prior to mailing are included in the cash flow as start-up costs. All other costs are included in the Year-One profit/loss calculations. Furniture and equipment are expensed at the time of purchase, and office space (rent/utilities) is expensed at the time of need.

Profit/Loss Calculation.   The number of rental names needed for each mailing is the anticipated mailing quantity less inquiries, buyers, and rental multis from the last mailing that are being remailed. The multis are calculated as 20 percent of the prior mailing's rental file. The list cost calculation is based on a 25-percent overbuy factor (if 100,000 names are needed, 125,000 are rented).

Net sales are shown as revenues less returns and cancellations (not available to ship). Additional margin reductions include liquidations and promotional costs. Royalties are not included. Shipping and handling revenue is taken at an average of $3.00 per order.

Cash Flow Calculations.   Cash flow is based on the following:

◆ Sales are taken over three months as 60 percent in the month of mailing, 30 percent in the next month, and 10 percent in the third month. This is a slightly shorter cycle than that used for the consumer catalog. Revenues, however, are taken as 10 percent occurring in the month of the sale and 90 percent offset by

❖ **FIGURE 17-6**
Internal Fulfillment Costs

Labor and telephone line costs	$ 9.80
Packaging	$ 0.65
Shipping	$ 3.50
Insurance	$ 0.81
Building/equipment/depreciation	$ 0.30
Computer/software/phones depreciation	$ 0.85
	$15.92

30 days for those orders on open invoice. Shipping and handling revenue follows the same pattern.

♦ Goods are 100 percent in stock at the time of mailing and are paid for 30 days later.

♦ Pre-press is paid for 30 days after mailing.

♦ Printing and mailing are paid for 60 days after mailing.

♦ Lists are paid for 30 days after mailing.

♦ Fulfillment costs, credit-card discount and processing costs, and bad debt are charged as a percentage of net sales at the time the sale is recognized.

♦ Administrative costs are recognized as they occur.

♦ Consulting costs are a monthly average.

♦ Start-up costs are estimated at $100,000 and include three-month staff costs.

All terms vary with the nature of the catalog. A new mailer should expect to pay for most of the costs prior to mailing. As the catalog achieves some degree of success, or if the cataloger has independent credit, better terms may be obtained.

Amortization, capital costs, interest, and taxes are not considered. Depreciation is only used in the calculation of fulfillment cost.

❖ **FIGURE 17-7**
Approximate Postage*

Quantity		Percent	Additional Cost/piece	
100,000	Carrier Route	0.00%	$0.020	$0.079 Average piece cost
	five/three-digit	86.00%	$0.072	$0.223 Pound rate
	Basic	14.00%	$0.124	$0.303 Total per piece
150,000	Carrier Route	2.00%	$0.020	$0.076 Average piece cost
	five/three-digit	89.00%	$0.072	$0.223 Pound rate
	Basic	9.00%	$0.124	$0.299 Total per piece
200,000	Carrier Route	17.00%	$0.020	$0.066 Average piece cost
	five/three-digit	78.00%	$0.072	$0.223 Pound rate
	Basic	5.00%	$0.124	$0.289 Total per piece

* Based on 64 pages, 60# self-cover, 5.19 oz., not bar coded, 1995 rates. Approximate presort is based on Alden Press.
Pound rate = $.687   Rate for 5.19 oz. = $0.223

❖ **FIGURE 17-8**
Approximate Administrative Costs

Staff Needs	Starts Month	Base Salary	Fringe Benefits @ 27%	Total Salary	Actual Year-1 Cost
Manager	−3	$60,000	$16,200	$76,200	$76,200
Secretary/Assistant	−3	$20,000	$ 5,400	$25,400	$25,400
Merchandiser	−3	$35,000	$ 9,450	$44,450	$44,450
Fulfillment Manager	−3	$35,000	$ 9,450	$44,450	$44,450
Credit Manager	−3	$35,000	$ 9,450	$44,450	$44,450
Rebuyer/Inventory	11	$25,000	$ 6,750	$31,750	$ 2,646
Production Manager	11	$25,000	$ 6,750	$31,750	$ 2,646
Analyst	11	$30,000	$ 8,150	$38,100	$ 3,175
Controller	11	$45,000	$12,150	$57,150	$ 4,763
Legal and accounting					$10,000
Furniture; computers at $6,000 per person					$54,000
Space @ 300 square feet per person and $1.5 per square feet per month		Initial Group $27,000	Month-11 Hires $1,800		$28,800
			First-Year Total Administration		**$340,979**

❖ FIGURE 17-9   First-Year Profit/Loss Calculation

	January	February	March	April	May
Type of Mailing	Full		Remail		Remail
Number of pages	64		64		64
Quantity Mailed	200,000		100,000		100,000
File Sizes					
Buyers			3,125		4,827
Inquirers	3,000		3,000		3,000
Prospects/rentals	197,000		54,475		81,278
Multis			39,400		10,895
Total File	200,000		100,000		100,000
Response Rates					
Buyers			5.00%		5.21%
Inquirers	3.00%		3.10%		3.20%
Prospects/rentals	1.75%		1.79%		1.84%
Multis			2.00%		2.05%
Average Rate	1.77%		2.01%		2.07%
Number of Orders					
Buyers			156		251
Inquirers	90		93		96
Prospects/rentals	3,348		977		1,494
Multis	0		788		223
Total Orders	3,538		2,014		2,065
Average Order					
Buyers			$210.00		$215.25
Inquirers	$175.00		$177.92		$180.88
Prospects/rentals	$165.00		$167.75		$170.55
Multis			$175.00		$177.92
Overall AO	$165.25		$174.33		$177.27
Revenues					
Buyers	$0		$32,810		$54,112
Inquirers	$15,750		$16,546		$17,383
Prospects/rentals	$568,838		$163,917		$254,860
Multis	$0		$137,900		$39,737
Total Revenues	$584,588		$351,173		$366,092
Returns @ 3%	$17,538		$10,535		$10,983
Cancellations @ 4%	$23,384		$14,047		$14,644
Net Sales	$543,666		$326,591		$340,465
Cost of goods @ 38.00%	$206,593		$124,105		$129,377
Freight in @ 3.80%	$20,659		$12,410		$12,938
Promotional expenses @ 3.00%	$16,310		$9,798		$10,214
Liquidations @ 4.00%	$21,747		$13,064		$13,619
Gross Margin	$278,357		$167,215		$174,318
Marketing Costs					
Pre-press (creative seps)	$172,800		$10,800		$10,800
Lists	$36,938		$10,214		$15,240
Printing/mailing	$65,000		$32,500		$32,500
Postage	$57,824		$30,264		$30,264
Total Marketing Cost	$332,561		$83,778		$88,803
Contribution	($54,204)		$83,437		$85,515
Operating Costs					
Administration	$56,830		$56,830		$56,830
Consulting	$10,000		$10,000		$10,000
Fulfillment Cost $15.92	$56,315		$32,068		$32,877
Credit Card Charges	$1,111		$667		$696
Bad Debt/Checks	$5,261		$3,161		$3,295
Total Operating Cost	$129,517		$102,726		$103,697
Ship/handl. revenue $3.00	$10,613		$6,043		$6,196
Net Profit/Loss	($173,108)		($13,246)		($11,987)
Cumulative P/L	($173,108)		($186,354)		($198,341)

June	July	August	September	October	November	December
	Full		Remail		Remail	
	64		64		64	
	150,000		150,000		150,000	
	6,399		8,863		11,246	
	3,000		3,000		3,000	
	124,345		113,268		113,100	
	16,256		24,869		22,654	
	150,000		150,000		150,000	
	5.43%		5.65%		5.89%	
	3.31%		3.42%		3.53%	
	1.88%		1.93%		1.98%	
	2.10%		2.15%		2.21%	
	2.09%		2.22%		2.34%	
	347		501		662	
	99		103		106	
	2,343		2,188		2,239	
	342		536		500	
	3,131		3,327		3,508	
	$220.63		$226.15		$231.80	
	$183.90		$186.96		$190.08	
	$173.39		$176.28		$179.22	
	$180.88		$183.90		$186.96	
	$179.78		$185.34		$190.57	
	$76,598		$113,279		$153,468	
	$18,262		$19,185		$20,155	
	$406,311		$385,689		$401,326	
	$61,784		$98,500		$93,500	
	$562,955		$616,653		$668,448	
	$16,889		$18,500		$20,053	
	$22,518		$24,666		$26,738	
	$523,548		$573,487		$621,657	
	$198,948		$217,925		$236,230	
	$19,895		$21,793		$23,623	
	$15,706		$17,205		$18,650	
	$20,942		$22,939		$24,866	
	$268,057		$293,625		$318,288	
	$172,800		$10,800		$10,800	
	$23,315		$21,238		$21,206	
	$48,750		$48,750		$48,750	
	$44,850		$44,850		$44,850	
	$289,714		$125,637		$125,606	
	($21,658)		$167,988		$192,682	
	$56,830		$56,830		$56,830	
	$10,000		$10,000		$10,000	
	$49,850		$52,966		$55,838	
	$1,070		$1,172		$1,270	
	$5,067		$5,550		$6,016	
	$122,816		$126,517		$129,954	
	$9,394		$9,981		$10,523	
	($135,080)		$51,452		$73,251	
	($333,421)		($281,968)		($208,717)	

❖ FIGURE 17-10 Cash Flow

	Credit Terms	Start-up	January	February	March	April	May	June	July	August	September	October	November	December	January
Cash at Start		___	($100,000)	($199,647)	($397,027)	($364,408)	($335,548)	($329,551)	($324,731)	($329,785)	($482,678)	($452,923)	($421,654)	($377,262)	___
Revenues															
From net sales	30 days		$32,620	$309,890	$171,822	$235,087	$111,873	$223,458	$126,743	$329,064	$181,003	$374,007	$197,876	$405,958	
Shipping revenue			$6381	$6,049	$3,334	$4,400	$2,064	$4,075	$2,298	$5,912	$3,229	$6,535	$3,426	$6,896	
Total Revenues			$33,258	$315,939	$175,156	$239,487	$113,937	$227,534	$129,042	$334,977	$184,232	$380,542	$201,302	$412,854	
Expenses															
(all terms from mail date)															
COG's 100% in stock at mail date—includes freight in, promotions, etc.	30 days		$0	$265,309	$0	$159,376	$0	$166,147	$0	$255,491	$0	$279,862	$0	$303,369	
Creative/separations	30 days		$0	$172,800	$0	$10,800	$0	$10,800	$0	$172,800	$0	$10,800	$0	$10,800	
Printing and mailing	60 days		$0	$0	$65,000	$0	$32,500	$0	$32,500	$0	$48,750	$0	$48,750	$0	
Lists, including computer	30 days		$0	$36,938	$0	$10,214	$0	$15,240	$0	$23,315	$0	$21,238	$0	$21,206	
Postage	At time of sale		$57,824	$0	$30,264	$0	$30,264	$0	$44,850	$0	$44,850	$0	$44,850	$0	
Fulfillment costs	At time of sale		$33,791	$16,894	$24,872	$9,620	$22,933	$9,863	$33,198	$14,955	$36,764	$15,890	$38,799	$16,751	
Credit-card costs	At time of sale		$666	$333	$511	$200	$484	$209	$711	$321	$810	$351	$879	$381	
Bad debt			$3,157	$1,578	$2,422	$948	$2,293	$988	$3,369	$1,520	$3,837	$1,665	$4,165	$1,805	
Administration			$32,467	$14,467	$14,467	$14,467	$14,467	$14,467	$14,467	$14,467	$14,467	$14,467	$14,467	$40,934	
Consulting			$5,000	$5,000	$5,000	$5,000	$5,000	$5,000	$5,000	$5,000	$5,000	$5,000	$5,000	$5,000	
Total Expenses		$100,000	$132,904	$513,320	$142,537	$210,626	$107,941	$222,714	$134,095	$487,869	$154,478	$349,272	$156,910	$400,246	
Cash at End		($100,000)	($199,647)	($397,027)	($364,408)	($335,548)	($329,551)	($324,731)	($329,785)	($482,678)	($452,923)	($421,654)	($377,262)	($364,654)	

✔ There are many similarities between business-to-business catalogs and consumer books. Business marketers should investigate and adapt consumer techniques to their needs.

✔ Copy needs to address a multistep or layered buying process and must be absolutely complete in its information, yet still friendly.

✔ Use call-outs and subheads often.

✔ Use a merchandise information form to collect valuable product information.

✔ The key to a successful layout is organization; consider using an index and color-coded category headers.

✔ Icons can explain benefits in one quick glance.

✔ The cover must gain attention in a crowded mail-box; keep it timely.

✔ Back-covers are also a ''door'' to the catalog.

✔ Key codes are critical and should be designed to stand out so users can spot and use them easily.

✔ Back cover products should also be offered within the catalog in their appropriate category.

✔ Format is usually the standard 8½" × 11" (or 8⅜" × 10⅞") size for functional filing.

✔ Most business marketers have one large catalog per year, with smaller versions mailed intermittently.

✔ If using a perfect-bound catalog, be sure to imprint the company name and phone number on the spine.

✔ Keep the organization of the catalog consistent, even as you update the offering and approach.

✔ Desktop publishing is ideal for business catalogs, due to large percentage of pickup.

✔ Know the electronic options constantly becoming available from printers.

✔ Construct a mailing plan for at least one year.

✔ Prepare a contact strategy for the different segments of your list and prospecting efforts.

✔ Work closely with your broker to find clean lists.

✔ Use a routing slip on the back of your catalog to help it get to the right person(s).

✔ Consider sending prequalifying postcards to prospect lists prior to mailing the catalog.

✔ Test an envelope that indicates the enclosed catalog was requested as one method of getting past the mailroom.

✔ Database marketers usually need to have multiple fields in a relational database format.

✔ Data must be kept fresh through a host of methods to help ensure the target is reached.

✔ Design and use a formal, well-planned reactivation strategy.

✔ Be aware of and test methods of acquiring names other than through the use of lists.

✔ Consider testing the value of premiums.

✔ Experienced, knowledgeable telemarketing representatives are critical to success.

✔ Use the Telephone Preference Service provided by the Direct Marketing Association.

✔ Customer service must be of the highest caliber.

✔ Overnight delivery has become the standard for many business marketers.

✔ Order forms are evolving to worksheets, because many readers use purchase orders to place their orders.

✔ The business plan is paramount to success.

❖ **CHECKLIST**

End Notes

1. *Catalog Age,* March 1994.
2. *Sales & Marketing Management,* June 1991.
3. *Directions,* Winter 1991.

Resources

Chapter 2

Brass Tacks Entrepreneur by Jim Shell (Henry Holt & Co.) is "a no-nonsense guide to being an entrepreneur."

Response TV. Published monthly by Advanstar Communications, 201 East Sandpointe Avenue, Suite 600, Santa Ana, CA 92707-5761.

Chapter 5

Merchandising

Major Shows.

The National China, Glass and Collectibles Show/Washington Gift Show.
George Little Management, Inc., 10 Bank Street, White Plains, NY 10606-1933.

Boston Gift Show, March and September at Bayside Convention Center.
George Little Management, Inc., 10 Bank Street, White Plains, NY 10606-1933.

New York International Gift Show.
George Little Management, Inc., 10 Bank Street, White Plains, NY 10606-1933.

New York Home Textiles Show.
George Little Management, Inc., 10 Bank Street, White Plains, NY 10606-1933.

Consumer Electronics Show.
2001 Pennsylvania Avenue, NW, 10th Floor, Washington, DC 20006.

Mega Show.
Miller-Freeman, Inc., 1515 Broadway, 34th Floor, New York, NY 10035; or P.O. Box 939, New York, NY 10108-0939.

International Jewelry Trade Show.
Blenheim Fashion Shows, One Executive Drive, Fort Lee, NJ 07024.

Major Merchandise Marts.

The Chicago Merchandise Mart.
World Trade Center Chicago, 470 The Merchandise Mart, Chicago, IL 60654.

Dallas Market Center.
2100 Stemmons Freeway, Dallas, TX 75207

L.A. Mart
1933 S. Broadway, Los Angeles, CA 90007
Atlanta Merchandise Mart
240 Peachtree Street, Atlanta, GA 30303

Publications.

Clothing directories

Buyers Guide to the New York Market. Earnshaw Publications, 225 West 34th Street, New York, NY 10122.

Earnshaw's Infants, Girls, Boys Wear Review—Children's Wear Directory Issue. Earnshaw Publications, 225 West 34th Street, 12th Floor, New York, NY 10122.

WWD Buyers' Guide (retail) and *WWD Suppliers' Guide* (wholesale). Fairchild Publications, 7 West 34th Street, New York, NY 10001.

Clothing periodicals

Daily News Record (men's fashion). Fairchild Publications, 7 West 34th Street, New York, NY 10001.

Women's Wear Daily (women's fashion). Fairchild Publications, 7 West 34th Street, New York, NY 10001.

Kids Fashion Magazine (Children's fashion). Larkin Publications, 100 Wells Avenue, Newton, MA 02159.

Gifts

Gifts and Decorative Accessories. Geyer-McAllister Publications, Inc., 51 Madison Avenue, New York, NY 10010.

Gift & Stationery Business. Miller-Freeman, Inc., 1515 Broadway, 32nd Floor, New York, NY 10036.

Giftware News. Talcott Publishing Co., 20 N. Wacker Drive, Suite 3230, Chicago, IL 60606.

Greetings Magazine. Mackay Publishing Corp., 309 5th Avenue, New York, NY 10016.

Home

HFD—The Weekly Home Furnishing Newspaper. Fairchild Publications, Attn: Edmond Peterson, 7 West 34th Street, New York, NY 10001.

Electronics

Dealer Scope Merchandising. North American Publishing Co., 401 N. Broad Street, Philadelphia, PA 19108.

Electronic Business Buyer. 275 Washington Street, Newton, MS 02158.

Toys

Playthings. Geyer-McAllister Publications Inc., 51 Madison Avenue, New York, NY 10010.

Jewelry

Jewelers Circular-Keystone. Chilton Co., Radnor, PA 19089.

National Jeweler. Miller-Freeman, Inc., 1515 Broadway, New York, NY 10036.

Financial Sources.

National Federation of Business and Professional Women's Clubs. Offers personal loans up to $10,000 and home-equity loans up to $100,000.

Office of Women's Business Ownership. Provides information on loan programs for female entrepreneurs.

Women's World Banking. Locates financial and technical help for female business owners.

NAFE (National Association of Female Executives). Functions to support women in business and to help them succeed in achieving their career goals and financial independence. Has more than 250,000 members and 250 "networks" or local chapters.

AWED (American Woman's Economic Development Corporation). Holds an annual conference.

Marlene Sholod, director of events marketing and promotion for *Sales & Marketing Management* magazine, suggests some additional organizations and publications:

Organizations

♦ **Local chambers of commerce.** These provide the chance to network, work on committees, and meet other businesspeople as peers. Check your local telephone directory.

♦ **Small Business Administration.** Local offices are listed under "Federal Government" in the telephone directory.

♦ **State or city departments of economic development.** Names may vary, but many states have a separate small business division. Check city and state listings.

Centers and Institutes

♦ **Small Business Development Centers.** These government-sponsored centers are located within universities. Check with universities near you, the *Business Yellow Pages,* or the National Association of Small Business Development Centers.

Publications

♦ *Crain's Business.* This periodical publishes a small business edition in New York and Chicago. An annual section called "Business Survival Kit" is a comprehensive list of resources for small business owners.

♦ *Business Yellow Pages.* A reference book for businesses published annually by Yellow Pages of America containing lists of conventions, trade shows, state and U.S. government offices, information on business and travel abroad, and national listings via computer. For sale by Yellow Pages of America, P.O. Box 178, Niagara Falls, NY 14302-1708.

♦ **The Association of Area Business Publications.** This will give you the titles of local business publications in any part of the United States.

Chapter 7

Advertising Photographers of America, Los Angeles, CA.

American Society of Media Photographers, 14 Washington Road, Suite 502, Princeton Junction, NJ 08550.

Creative Black Book. Hunt Stehli, Black Book Marketing Group, 866 Third Avenue, New York, NY. Use to find location scouts.

CREF. Computer Ready Electronic Files, Scitex Graphic Arts Users Association, Inc. (SGAUA), 305 Plus Park Boulevard, Nashville, TN 3717.

Domestic Mail Manual and Postal Bulletin. U.S. Postal Service, Superintendent of Documents, U.S. Printing Office, Washington, DC 20402.

Chapter 9

Encyclopedia of Telemarketing by Richard Bencin (Prentice-Hall).

Successful Telemarketing by Bob Stone and John Wyman (NTC Business Books).

Chapter 11

The Complete Database Marketer by Arthur M. Hughes (Probus, 1991).

Strategic Database Marketing by Rob Jackson and Paul Wang (NTC Business Books, 1994).

Handbook of Relational Database Designs by Candace C. Fleming and Barbara vonHalle (Addison Wesley, 1989).

Standard Rate and Data Service, Inc., 3004 Glenview Road, Wilmette, IL 60091.

Privacy: The Key Issue of the 80's. Direct Marketing Association, 1120 Avenue of the Americas, New York, NY 10036.

Opening the Door. Direct Marketing Association, 1120 Avenue of the Americas, New York, NY 10036.

The Direct Marketing Association's Guidelines for List Practices. Available from the Ethics Department, Direct Marketing Association, 1101 17th Street, NW, Suite 705, Washington, DC 20035-4704.

Mailing List Strategies; A Guide to Direct Mail Success by C. Rose Harper (McGraw Hill).

NTC's Dictionary of Direct Mail and Mailing List Terminology and Techniques by Nat G. Bodian.

Chapter 12

"Executive Guide/Fraud Detection & Loss Prevention in Credit Card Transactions" (by Litle & Company) (DMA). Brochure.

Chapter 14

The New Direct Marketing by David Shepard Associates (Homewood, IL: Business One Irwin).

Multivariate Analysis by William R. Dillon and Matthew Goldstein (New York: John Wiley & Sons, Inc., 1984).

Chapter 16

Memo to Mailers. Public & Employee Communications Department, U.S. Postal Service, Washington, DC 20260-3100. Monthly. Free to firms generating large quantities of mail.

Postal World. JPL Publications, 128 C Street, NW, Washington, DC 20001. Biweekly.

A Direct Marketer's Self-Regulatory Guide to the Use of Information. Direct Marketing Association, 1120 Avenue of the Americas, New York, NY 10036.

Trade Regulation Rules. Federal Trade Commission, Office of Public Information, 6th and Pennsylvania Avenues, NW, Washington, DC 20580.

FTC regulations, U.S. Code of Federal Regulations, Title 16, Commercial Practices, Chapters 1 and 2 (January 1993). Office of the Federal Register, National Archives and Records Services, General Services Administration (U.S. Government Printing Office, Washington, DC 20036).

"Do's and Don'ts in Advertising Copy." Council of Better Business Bureaus, 1150 17th Street, NW, Washington, DC 20036.

"Business Guide to the 30-Day Mail Order Rule." FTC Office of Public Information or the DMA (Washington, DC office).

"Five Guides Against Deceptive Pricing." Federal Trade Commission, Office of Public Information, 6th and Pennsylvania Avenues, NW, Washington, DC 20580

"Credit Practices TRR." FTC Office of Public Information, 6th and Pennsylvania Avenues, NW, Washington, DC 20580.

"Internal Credit and Collection Procedures for Direct Marketers," *Direct Marketing Manual.* DMA, 1120 Avenue of the Americas, New York, NY 10036.

Promotion Marketing Association of America, 257 Park Avenue South, New York, NY 10010.

"Guidelines on Sweepstakes Promotion," Direct Marketing Association, 1120 Avenue of the Americas, New York, NY 10036.

Annual Compendium of Government Issues Affecting Direct Marketing. 1101 17th Street, NW, Suite 900, Washington, DC 20036. Published every May.

Useful Publications for Catalogers

Advertising Age. Published by Crain Communications, 740 North Rush Street, Chicago, IL 60611. Weekly.

Adweek. Published by ASM Communications, 49 East 21st Street, New York, NY 10010. Published weekly in five regional editions: East, Southeast, Midwest, Southwest, and West.

Catalog Age. Published by Catalog Age Publication Corporation, Six River Bend, Box 4949, Stamford, CT 06907-0949. Monthly.

Catalog Age Sourcebook. Published by Catalog Publication Corporation, Six River Bend, Box 4949, Stamford, CT 06907-0949.

Direct. Published by Catalog Age, Six River Bend, Box 4949, Stamford, CT 06907-0949.

Direct Marketing (magazine). Published by Hoke Communications, Inc., 224 Seventh Avenue, Garden City, NY 11530. Monthly.

DM News. Published by Mill Hollow Corp., 19 West 21st Street, New York, NY 10010. Weekly.

DMA Fact Book on Direct Marketing. Published by Direct Marketing Association, 1120 Avenue of the Americas, New York, NY 10036. Annual.

Domestic Mail Manual. Published by the U.S. Postal Service. Available from Superintendent of Documents, U.S. Government Printing Office, Washington, DC 20402.

Friday Report. Published by Hoke Communications, Inc., 224 Seventh Avenue, Garden City, NY 11530. Weekly.

Operations & Fulfillment, P.O. Box 16, Winchester, MA 01890-0016.

Target Marketing. Published by North American Publishing Co., 401 N. Broad Street, Philadelphia, PA 19108. Monthly.

GLOSSARY

The direct marketing industry is no different from others in that it has its own lingo, much of which has been used and explained in this book. Here we've compiled a list of those terms, and others, that you will most often hear and use.

action devices   Techniques used to encourage customer participation. For example, a sweepstakes offer may require recipients to remove and affix a *stamp*, rub off a *mystery number*, and so on.

actives   Respondents on a particular list who have taken action through purchase of a product, subscription to a magazine, and so forth, in a recent time period.

address correction requested   Printed in the upper left-hand corner of the mailing-address area of a catalog, this message alerts the post office that the mailer wishes, for a fee, to receive an updated address for persons who have moved.

alternate delivery   Any system that delivers mail to households via a means other than the postal system.

assigned mailing date   The date on which a rented list must be mailed, according to a prior agreement between the list owner and the user.

backbone   The back or spine of a book where the pages are connected.

back end   A term often used for the later part of a catalog operation, most often from order receipt and entry through fulfillment and customer service.

bangtail envelope   A preformed envelope with a perforated flap designed for use as an order form; most often used for promotional purposes. Often provided as the payment vehicle for oil companies, department stores, and so forth.

bar code   A coding structure printed in the mailing area; used for sortation by the U.S. Postal Service.

batch   A grouping of data records, such as orders.

BC   Acronym for back cover.

bill enclosure   Promotions for products or services that are inserted into bills received from companies. Product offerings may or may not be related to the companies issuing the bills.

bindery   An area where the final trimming, stitching/stapling, order-form (or other type printed material) insertion, and any necessary off-press folding is done.

binding   The fastenings of a catalog. *Perfect-bound*: Usually used only for thick catalogs or books. The bindery trims and glues the catalog together to form a stiff backbone. *Saddle-stitched:* The bind-ery gathers the sheets and staples them at the spine, creating a backbone. *Side-wire-stitched:* The bindery gathers and staples sheets on the left-hand side to form a backbone.

bingo card   A reply card, inserted into a publication, listing sales literature, catalogs, and so forth, that consumers may request simply by checking the appropriate box and mailing the card. Information requested may have a charge associated with it. Products/catalogs are generally covered in greater detail by advertisements or editorial copy within the publication or adjacent to the postcard.

block   A census term for the smallest area for which census data are tabulated. Each block is defined by a street, road, railroad track, stream, or other ground feature.

blow-up   An enlargement of a photograph.

blue line   Another name for blueprint.

blueprint   A prior-to-printing proof made from negative or positive film, used for checking type/photo position. Sometimes called "blues" or "bluelines."

BMC   Acronym for bulk-mail center (of the post office). One of the 21 locations at which bulk mail is sorted and routed to various parts of the country.

body type   The type or copy used for the main descriptive copy, as opposed to the headline.

boldface type   Type that is heavier than standard text type; often used for headings or paragraph lead-ins.

book   *See* catalog.

booklet   Usually a small flyer-type promotional piece.

bounceback   Promotional materials inserted in packages being sent to customers.

BRC   Acronym for business reply card.

bringing up the color   Correcting color; intensifying color on press or in separations.

BRM   Acronym for business reply mail.

broadside   A single sheet of paper used for promotional purposes in a variety of ways, such as newspaper insertion, bouncebacks, and so forth.

brochure   Loosely used term; often refers to a promotional piece larger than a broadside but smaller than a catalog.

broker   *See* list broker.

bulk　The thickness of paper.

bulk-rate mail　A category of third-rate mail that requires outgoing mail to be specially formatted prior to receipt at the post office so the sender is entitled to postal discounts.

bundling　Putting compatible items together at a discount.

buyer　The person responsible for sourcing merchandise for a catalog. Also, the person on a list who has responded to solicitations offering mail order merchandise.

carrier route　A geographical area consisting of 350 households as walked by an individual mail carrier.

carrier route presort　Mail that is sorted into a bundle and sent to the individual mail carrier level; receives a significant discount over unsorted mail.

cash buyer　A person who has responded to a mail order solicitation and has enclosed a check or money order with the order.

cash-with-order　A requirement made by some list owners for full payment at the time the list rental order is placed.

catalog　A promotional book offering a variety of merchandise; contains descriptive copy and prices.

catalog buyer　Someone who has purchased merchandise from a catalog.

catalog requester　A prospective catalog buyer who has requested a copy of a catalog, for which there may have been a charge.

CD-ROM　High-capacity, read-only memory in the form of an optically read compact disk.

census tract　A subdivision of a metropolitan statistical area; has an average population of 4,000.

CHADs　Acronym for change of address. Also called COA.

chargeback　A credit card transaction disputed by either the card holder or issuer.

charge buyer　A person who has charged merchandise ordered by mail. Some use this term for persons who have paid for merchandise only after it has been delivered.

Cheshire label　Label printed on specially prepared paper. List names are reproduced on the labels, then mechanically affixed to mailings.

chromalins　One method of proofing a color separation. Four separate, extremely thin plastic sheets (one for each color) are overlaid, producing a color reproduction of the separations.

chromes　An often-misused term that actually refers to color transparencies. Also used as a shortened form of ''chromalins.''

circulars　General term for printed promotion materials.

cleaning　The updating of mailing lists through removal of inaccurate or unusable data.

cluster　A group of names in a series, selected on an nth name basis.

COA　Acronym for change of address. Also called CHADs.

coding　Identifying alpha and/or numerical key used on reply devices, such as order forms, coupons, labels, and so forth. Codes are used to track rented-list performance, publication results, and other results.

collation　The orderly assembly of sheets or signatures during the bindery process.

color print　A printed reproduction of a transparency or negative; inexpensive, but not top quality. Also called a ''C'' print.

co-mailing　A process by which two catalogs can be mailed together for postal savings.

commission　The percentage a broker, list manager, or advertising agency receives on lists ordered or work done. Agreed to before the list is ordered or the agency work is done.

compiler　A company that gathers and records names and addresses of consumers with common characteristics. These names, which are made available for rental, are compiled from directories, registrations, and so forth.

comprehensive layout　A finely detailed layout showing a close facsimile of how the final printed piece will look. Also called a comp.

computerized layout　Layout designed on a computer, most commonly a Macintosh, which incorporates all components (copy, scanned photography, and design elements) into art for viewing before handoff to the separator.

computer personalization　Computer-generated, personalized printing used to tailor a particular message to a specific mailing or to code mailing segments.

computer service bureau　A data-processing facility that performs such functions as merge/purge, list maintenance, analysis, and so forth.

consumer list　At-home names and addresses of persons with similar buying interests or activities.

continuity programs　Products offered in a continuous series of mailings; usually consisting of a common theme (such as a book series) and shipped at regular intervals.

contributor list　A list of persons who have financially contributed, via the mails, to a particular fund-raising activity.

controlled circulation　Distribution of a publication at no charge.

conversion　Reformatting a number of computer types into a common format.

conversion rate　The percentage of potential customers who become buyers through a direct-mail solicitation.

co-op catalog　A combination of ''mini catalogs'' from a variety of companies, most often catalogers that already have existing independent catalog operations.

co-op mailing　A shared mailing in which different offers, often from different companies, are presented to the consumer in one envelope. Postage costs are divided among the participants, and a rental fee may be charged by the co-op organizer.

cost per inquiry (CPI)　The cost of a mailing or advertisement divided by the number of inquiries received from it.

cost per order (CPO)　Similar to cost per inquiry, but based on all costs associated with the acquisition of a customer or order.

cost per thousand (CPM)　Total ''in-the-mail'' cost on a per-thousand basis.

counts　Quantities (exact number) of records necessary to verify the accuracy of a computer run.

creative　Used as a noun in the catalog business; the preprinting aspect of catalog preparation, including design, layout, copy writing, and photography.

CREF　Acronym for computer ready electronic file. A set of guidelines, coined by CREF (an organization) that attempt to define some commonality of terms and practices within the computer industry.

crop　To trim part of a photo or copy.

cross section　A group of names and addresses segmented from a list in such a manner as to be as representative as possible of the entire list.

data appending   Attaching demographic or other data to individual records, usually in a house file.

database   A file of accessible and retrievable information input from a variety of sources to one central source and segmentable by particular groups of information.

data capture/entry   Any method of collecting and recording information.

deadbeat   Customer who orders merchandise but doesn't pay for it.

decoys   Uniquely identifiable names (often intentional misspellings of a preselected group of names) that are inserted into ordinary list-rental names. Decoys serve two main purposes: to alert catalogers to the arrival of mailings and to prevent list renters from unauthorized list usage.

delivery date   The date on which the list user or a designated representative is to receive a specific list order from the list owner.

demographics   Social and economic characteristics of individuals and/or households within particular geographic boundaries.

direct mail   The use of the post office for delivery of promotional materials soliciting some form of action on the part of the recipient.

direct marketing   Any method of promotion that prompts the consumer to respond in a way that results in sales from that specific promotion.

direct response   *See* direct marketing.

DMA   Acronym for Direct Marketing Association. The industry's major association.

DMA Mail Order Action Line   *See* Mail Order Action Line.

DMA Mail Preference Service   *See* Mail Preference Service.

donor list   List of persons who have given money to one or more charitable organizations.

DPI   Acronym for dots per inch. The number of dots per inch in scanned art indicates the quality of the resolution for reproduction.

drop date   The date(s) mailings actually go into the mail stream.

drop out   To delete type from all four colors of film, resulting in ''white'' type.

drop-ship   A fulfillment function whereby the manufacturer of the product ships the item to the customer.

dummy   A mock-up showing the position of photos and type and the folding format; shows the size, shape, and general ''feeling'' of promotional piece prior to printing.

duplicate   Two or more name-and-address records that are found to be equal under the list user's method of comparison. Often referred to as a dupe.

duplication elimination   Most often shortened to dupe elimination or de-duping. Refers to the removal of various names, determined to be the same by a variety of methods, from different lists.

dye transfer   A high-quality four-color print made from a transparency; most often used when noncomputerized retouching is needed.

enamel   Coated paper that has a glossy finish.

enhancement   Adding names from one or more lists to a main list; selected specifically to add some positive dimension or value to the main list.

envelope stuffer   Promotion material inserted into an envelope along with such other items as statements, invoices, and so forth.

EPS   Acronym for Encapsulated Post Script, a file format that describes a document using the PostScript programming language.

The file description contains a preview of the image and all the information needed to print the file.

exchange   *See* list exchange.

expire   A segment of a subscriber list that has allowed subscriptions to expire.

eyeball a list   To physically check the content of a list.

field   A specified record of data.

file   A named set of records stored or processed as a unit.

file maintenance   *See* list maintenance.

FIM   Acronym for facing identification mark.

FIM-e   Pre-bar coded business reply mail.

first-time buyer   A person who has purchased a product or service from a particular company for the first time.

f.o.b.   free on board. Without charge to the buyer for goods placed on board a carrier at the point of shipment.

folio   The page number as it appears on a printed page.

former buyer   A person who has purchased a product or service from a particular company but has now ceased to purchase.

FPO   Acronym for For Position Only. A graphics term meaning that art in place is not of reproducible quality and is for position approval only.

freelance   An independent artist, writer, or photographer who is not on staff but works on a per-project or hourly rate as the need arises.

frequency   How often a buyer has purchased during a certain period or in total.

free sheet   Paper without mechanical wood pulp.

free standing insert (FSI)   A promotional piece loosely inserted in a magazine or newspaper.

friend-of-a-friend   *See* tell-a-friend.

front end   Usually refers to the part of a catalog operation that occurs prior to actual receipt of orders; includes areas such as merchandising, creative, and catalog production.

fulfillment   The process of taking order information and selecting, packing, and sending the order. Also called the back end.

gathering   The assembly of folded signatures into the correct sequence.

GEO   Abbreviation for geographics. The segmentation of a list by particular areas of geography (for example, zip codes).

gift-giver   Someone who has purchased a product for another person.

gimmick   A promotional device, such as a sticker or rub-off area, designed to get consumers' attention and urge them to act.

groundwood   Paper that contains wood pulp.

guarantee   The promise made to the buyer of merchandise or services stating the terms by which the seller stands by that product or service.

high res   Shortened form of high resolution. High number of dots per inch, making material suitable for reproduction.

hit   A name showing up on two or more lists.

hot-line list   The most recent buyer segment of a particular list. The actual period within which these buyers have purchased may vary from list to list.

house list   The customer base of names owned by a particular company. Acquired through any number of methods, the list is used to sell that company's products or services.

IBC   Acronym for inside back cover of a catalog.

IFC   Acronym for inside front cover of a catalog.

IVR   Acronym for interactive voice response, an interactive method of electronically routing calls.

imposition   The way in which pages are positioned in order to print and fold them correctly on a press.

inactives   Someone who once purchased regularly but now has ceased to purchase.

indicia   Preprinted "stamp" issued by the post office; goes in upper right-hand corner of mailing area and indicates that postage has been paid.

infomercial   Most often taking the form of a talk show, this form of commercial usually has a "natural" setting where participants "discuss" the product in an interview-type format.

ink jetting   Computer-controlled printing process that applies ink jets through small orifices to form characters; often used for personalization.

inquiry   A person who has requested information about a particular product or service but has not purchased. There may be a charge for the information received.

interlist duplicate   Duplication of name/address between two or more lists. This does not mean duplication with the house-list names.

intralist duplicate   Duplication of name/address with the same list (frequently the house list).

Julian date   A serial number showing the number of days that have elapsed since the beginning of the calendar year; that is, January 31 would be 31, February 6 would be 37.

key coding   *See* coding.

keyline   *See* mechanical.

label   The paper on which the recipient's name and address are printed. *See also* Cheshire label and pressure-sensitive label.

layout   A drawing that indicates position of copy and artwork as they will appear in the printed promotion.

letterpress   A printing method based on relief printing; the inked or image area is raised.

lettershop   The area or service that sees that printed material is properly collated, addressed, prepared for mailing discounts, and mailed. Also called bindery.

lifetime value (LTV)   The true value of a customer over time.

list broker   The person who makes list recommendations and coordinates the necessary details between the list owner/manager and the list renter.

list cleaning   The removal of undesirable names and addresses from a house list.

list compiler   A company that assembles data, develops them into specific list categories (such as professions), and offers the resulting lists for rent.

list exchange   An agreement between two list owners to exchange portions of their lists, without a rental fee.

list maintenance   The updating of names and addresses in a house list.

list manager   The person responsible for encouraging others to rent a specific mailing list or lists; can be an employee of the list owner or a company specializing in list promotion.

list owner   One who, by promotional activity or compilation, has developed a list of names having something in common. Or one who has purchased (as opposed to rented, reproduced, or used on a one-time basis) such a list from the developer.

list rental   An arrangement by which a list owner furnishes names on his or her list to a mailer, together with the privilege of using the list on a one-time basis (unless otherwise specified in advance). For this privilege, the mailer pays the list owner a rental fee.

list sample   A segment of a list used for testing the profitability of that list.

list selection   The subsegments within a list which generally rent for an additional fee and can enhance results.

list sequence   Lists are generally arranged in zip code sequence from 00601 to 99950, but may be in some other order, such as alphabetical.

low res   Shortened form of low resolution. Minimal number of dots per inch, making material suitable for position only, not reproduction quality.

magnetic tape   A storage device for electronically recording and reproducing defined bits of data through the use of a computer.

mail date   The in-the-mail date agreed to between the list user and list owner. Only this date may be used, unless prior approval is obtained.

mail order   A method of business that, through the use of the U.S. Postal Service, solicits sales of products or services.

Mail Order Action Line (MOAL)   A service the DMA offers to help consumers with any problems they might have regarding mail order purchases.

mail order buyer   A person who has purchased a product or service in response to an offer received through the mail.

mail order mailer   The advertiser behind a mailing piece; the outer, protective container for a promotional piece; or a printed direct-mail advertising piece.

Mail Preference Service (MPS)   A DMA service designed to allow consumers to have their names deleted from mailing lists.

make-ready   The time it takes for a printing press to prepare plates, as well as properly adjust inks and registration.

manifest   A system which allows companies to ship products without a label showing the actual cost of shipping.

margin   The difference between the cost of goods and the retail price.

mark-up   The percentage an item is increased from its cost.

marriage mail   A cooperative mailing in which one advertiser pays the costs for all participants; different from a standard co-op, where costs are shared by the participants.

massage/manipulate   Refers to the transformation of data to make analysis simpler or more meaningful.

match code   An abbreviation of data extracted from name-and-address records attempting to simplify the sequencing of records in a list and/or the identification of duplicate records.

matte finish   A dull paper finish that has no gloss.

mechanical   The final assembly of positioned art and typeset copy. Also called paste-ups, boards, or finished art.

merge/purge   The combination of two or more lists and the elimination of duplicate names and addresses.

metropolitan statistical area (MSA) Used by the Census Bureau for standard metropolitan statistical area (SMSA). A county or group of counties may be part of an MSA if they are considered integrated with the city.

MIF Acronym for Merchandise Information Form, a form used to collect important data about products from vendors. Also used for copy information for copywriters.

monetary One of the mail order quality-designation triumvirate (recency/frequency/monetary) that relates to the amount of money spent by a customer, either in a specific period or in total.

multibuyer A person who has purchased two or more times from the same company, not someone who has bought more than one item from the same company. This term is frequently misused to denote both types of buyers.

multiple regression Mathematical techniques used to determine the relationship between a dependent variable, such as profitability of ordering and two or more independent variables such as income, prior orders, and the like.

name acquisition Any method of obtaining names and addresses for a mailing list.

negative Photographic image on film showing the reverse of what is seen by the naked eye; dark colors are light, light colors are dark.

negative option A buying plan in which the customer or club member agrees to accept and pay for products or services announced in advance at regular intervals, unless the individual notifies the company within a reasonable time after each announcement not to ship.

nesting The placement of one enclosure within another prior to inserting them into a mailing envelope.

net-name arrangement An agreement between a list owner and list user, at the time of ordering or before, in which the list owner agrees to accept adjusted payment for less than the total names shipped. The adjustment depends on the number of duplicate names, and the agreement may provide for a computer running charge.

net-net name An agreement between a list owner and list user, at the time of ordering or before, in which the user pays only for the names actually used after screening, including income, credit, house list duplicates, etc.

nine-digit zip code A postal system that provides an automated means of using extended zip codes to sort mail; goes down to continuous areas within a carrier route.

nixie A mailing returned to the sender by the post office because of undeliverability.

nonbuyers Those who have been solicited but have chosen not to purchase.

nth-name selection A fractional unit used in selecting a portion of a mailing list (for example, a 10,000 test from a universe or select of 200,000 would give an nth of every twentieth name).

OCR Acronym for optical character recognition. The reading of printed characters by a machine using light-sensitive technology.

OF Acronym for order form.

offset A printing method that transfers ink from a plate to a rubber surface and then to paper.

ok'd sheet The printed sheet supplied by the printer while both client and advertiser oversee a printing job. The cataloger's signature is required before the press can begin printing at top speed.

This sheet is retained by the pressman as a control check for the rest of the print run.

one-time buyer A person who has ordered only once from a particular company.

optical scanner An input device that optically "sees" a line of printed characters and converts each character into its electronic equivalent for processing.

"or current resident" A line sometimes added to the back of the catalog in the mailing area; designated that the catalog should be delivered to the address noted even if the addressee has moved.

overlay A transparent sheet, positioned over artwork, that indicates specifications about the art underneath (such as crop marks); over layouts, it might indicate props for photography; over paste-ups, it shows color breaks.

overlays Demographic data added to an existing file, allowing selections that can enhance response.

overwrap An extra four-page cover of coarser paper, attached to a catalog.

package insert A promotion designed for inclusion in outgoing mail order–generated packages.

packer A person who physically packs merchandise that has been picked from warehouse shelves.

pagination The final selection of products and determination of exactly what products go on what pages and in roughly what space allocation.

pallet A platform, often made of wood, on which goods are stored or transported.

peel-off label *See* pressure-sensitive label.

pencil sketches Simple drawings of planned layouts in pencil, often smaller than full size. Also called pencils.

penetration Proportion of the number of individuals (or families) on a particular list to the total number possible for a particular universe (in total, by state, by zip code, and so forth).

perfecting press A press that prints on two sides of the paper at once.

personalization Unique, printed message directed to an individual; often used on catalog order forms and back covers.

phone list Compiled names and numbers.

picker Someone who selects merchandise from warehouse shelves and takes it to the packing station(s).

piggyback An offer that is free with another offer.

poly bag A printed, clear plastic bag used instead of a paper envelope.

pop-up A three-dimensional paper construction that "pops up" as the mailing piece (of which it is a part) opens.

positive A photographic image on film that looks like the original; the opposite of a negative.

positive option A method of distributing products and services, incorporating the same advance notice techniques as negative option but requiring a specific order each time on the part of the member or subscriber.

postcard Single or double, card-stock self-mailers.

PostScript A page description language that helped launch desktop publishing.

premium A "bonus" product offered at no charge or at minimal cost to consumers as an incentive to purchase a product or service, or as an inducement to place an order totaling a set dollar amount.

press proof   A printed proof pulled on the paper to be used for actual printing, submitted prior to ''on press'' for color ok.

pressure-sensitive label   A peel-off label, initially attached to a backing sheet, that is used as an address label. The self-adhesive label, usually complete with list code, is peeled off by the customer and attached to the order form.

progressive proofs   A print proofing method that separates colors by sequence, showing each color density and, when combined, how color should look when actually printed on press. Also called progs.

propping   The items that are placed with a product during photography to convey an image or size relationship.

prospect   A name on a mailing list; considered a probable buyer for a product never before purchased by this person.

psychographics   Characteristics or qualities used to denote the life-style or attitudes of customers and prospective customers.

pull   Another word for response rate to a particular mailing.

purge   The process of eliminating duplicates and/or unwanted names and addresses from one or more lists.

random separations   Color separation of each individual chrome within a catalog prior to total page composition.

raster   Image processing. *See* RIP.

recency   The last purchase or other activity recorded for an individual or company on a specific customer list.

reformatting   Changing a magnetic tape format from one arrangement to another that is more usable. Also referred to as a list or tape conversion.

register   The alignment of color images in printing.

regression   A mathematical technique used to determine the relationship between two variables or among many variables.

repeat buyer   *See* multibuyer.

response rate   Percentage of orders received from a particular mailing.

retouching   A process that corrects or improves artwork.

return postage guaranteed   A line appearing on third-class bulk mail that tells the post office to return the mail to the sender, at his or her cost, if it is undeliverable.

RFM   Acronym for recency, frequency, monetary value scoring assigned to lists, segments, and customers.

RIP   Acronym for raster image processing. Processing that outputs a series of digital zeroes and ones in a format that permits reproduction.

ROI   Acronym for return on investment.

rollout   A larger continuation of a test mailing that initially consisted of a smaller quantity of a certain list.

rotogravure (gravure)   A method of printing that uses etched copper cylinders for printing; generally used for runs of one million units or more.

rough   The first phase of a layout; sketchy in nature; often done in pencil.

running charge   The price charged by a list owner for names run (or passed), but not used by a specific mailer.

S&H   Shipping and handling.

salting   Deliberate placing of decoy or dummy names in a list to trace list usage and delivery.

scanner   A device that uses a computerized method of color separating.

scanning   A computerized method of turning images into digital data.

SCF   Acronym for sectional center facility. A mechanized USPS mail-handling facility used for processing incoming and outgoing mail for a number of peripheral local post offices within a designated service area. Generally, an SCF is a postal service distribution unit consisting of different post offices whose zip codes contain the same first three digits.

scitex   A brand of color separations that has evolved to a somewhat generic term, as Kleenex has for tissues.

selects   Specific segments of a mailing list.

self-cover   A cover that is printed on the same paper as that used for the interior of the catalog.

separations (color)   Film, either negative or positive, made from photographs and supplied art, and used to create the printing plates for color printing.

sequence   The order of items according to specific instructions.

set-up charge   A one-time charge, usually imposed by a service bureau, for fulfillment, list rental, printing, and so forth.

sheetfed   A printing method in which each sheet of paper is fed into the printer individually; prints only one side of paper at a time.

shipping media   A term used when a computer disk is in transit from one place to another; refers to the disk on which the computerized art is stored as well as its container.

signature   The sheets that are automatically cut and folded as they come off a press; most often in forms of 16 pages.

SKU number   Acronym for stockkeeping unit number. The number assigned to a product that is used for data entry, order fulfillment, analysis, and so forth.

slimjim   A nickname for a tall, skinny catalog measuring $6'' \times 10^{7}/_{8}''$ that realizes postage discounts.

source code   Alpha or numerical characters used to distinguish media.

sourcing   Locating manufacturers or distributors of merchandise through a buyer or merchant.

space buyer   A person who has purchased a product via an advertisement that has appeared in a publication.

split test   Two or more samples from the same list, each considered to be representative of the entire list, used to test variations of a particular promotion.

spread   Two facing pages in a catalog.

spread record sheets   A form that details exactly what goes on every page of a catalog and includes directions for how the creative approach should be handled. Also, documents that list individual products and their relevant information per spread in the catalog.

standard metropolitan statistical area (SMSA)   *See* metropolitan statistical area.

state count   The number of names and addresses in a given list for each state.

statement stuffer   A promotion piece specifically designed for insertion in an envelope that contains a bill or statement of a customer's account.

stripping   The positioning of film (negative or positive) for platemaking prior to printing.

style guide   A uniform guide for copy and layout; indicates specifically how elements in the catalog should be handled.

suppression   The use of data on a file to eliminate particular segments from a mailing.

swatching   The enclosure of actual fabric samples in a mailing piece. Also, the photographic reproduction of fabric swatches representing color alternatives or pattern details.

syndicated catalog   Allows a well-known company to lend its prestigious name to a catalog to promote response, while another company (the syndicator) actually runs the catalog business.

Syquest   One brand of a portable storage device in cartridge form; holds many megabytes of data.

Telephone Preference Service (TPS)   A DMA service that allows consumers to have their names deleted from calling lists.

tell-a-friend   A customer or name acquired through the recommendation of a friend of that person. Also called friend-of-a-friend.

test panel   A term used to identify each of the parts or samples in a split test. Also, a preset test segment of a particular list.

test quantity   The number of names used to test the validity of responsiveness to particular lists; must be a statistically valid number and is usually a random sample of the universe.

three-digit zip   The first three digits of a five-digit zip code; represents a particular U.S. postal facility (sectional center facility).

token   A gimmick designed to be removed by the customer from one place and attached to another.

traffic generator   A sales promotion designed to induce prospects to go to a particular place of business.

transparency   A transparent photographic reproduction, such as a 35mm slide.

twofers   Two of the same item offered as a pair at a lower price than that charged per piece.

undeliverables   Mailing pieces that are returned because they are not deliverable as addressed. Also called a nixie.

unit of sale (UOS)   The average dollar amount spent by a customer.

universe   The total number of names contained on a particular list.

UPC   Acronym for Universal Product Code. A standard bar code that can be read and interpreted by a computer.

UPS   Acronym for United Parcel Service.

upsell   Add-on sales to an already existing purchase; often done through telemarketing.

USPS   Acronym for U.S. Postal Service.

vector   Electronically describes art in terms of mathematical outline.

WATS   Acronym for Wide Area Telephone Service. A service providing a special line allowing direct-dial calls within a certain zone for a flat monthly charge.

web   A web printing press that prints from continuous rolls, or webs, of paper.

white mail   Untrackable mail; orders that have been received but, for a variety of reasons, cannot be allocated to a specific source. Also refers to mail that does not include orders or payment.

widow   In typesetting, a word or short sentence on a line by itself at the end of a paragraph, especially at the top of a page.

zip code   A group of five digits used by the U.S. Postal Service to designate specific post offices, stations, or branches. Some large companies and buildings have their own zip codes.

zip code sequence   The arrangement of names and addresses in a list according to the numeric progression of the zip code in each record.

INDEX
❖ ❖ ❖